THEATER, CULTURE, AND COMMUNITY
IN REFORMATION BERN, 1523-1555

STUDIES IN MEDIEVAL AND REFORMATION THOUGHT

FOUNDED BY HEIKO A. OBERMAN †

EDITED BY

ANDREW COLIN GOW, Edmonton, Alberta

IN COOPERATION WITH

THOMAS A. BRADY, Jr., Berkeley, California
SUSAN C. KARANT-NUNN, Tucson, Arizona
JÜRGEN MIETHKE, Heidelberg
M. E. H. NICOLETTE MOUT, Leiden
HEIKO A. OBERMAN †, Tucson, Arizona
ANDREW PETTEGREE, St. Andrews
MANFRED SCHULZE, Wuppertal

VOLUME LXXXV

GLENN EHRSTINE

THEATER, CULTURE, AND COMMUNITY
IN REFORMATION BERN, 1523-1555

THEATER, CULTURE, AND COMMUNITY IN REFORMATION BERN, 1523-1555

BY

GLENN EHRSTINE

BRILL
LEIDEN · BOSTON · KÖLN
2002

This book is printed on acid-free paper.

Library of Congress Cataloging-in-Publication Data

Ehrstine, Glenn:
Theatre, culture, and community in Reformation Bern, 1523-1555
    p. cm. — (Studies in medieval and Reformation thought, ISSN 0585-6914 ; v. 85)
    ISBN 9004123539 (alk. paper)
    1. Swiss drama (German)—Switzerland—Bern (Canton)—History and criticism. 2. Swiss drama (German)—Early modern, 1500-1700—
—History and criticism. 3. Christian drama, German—Switzerland—Bern (Canton)—History and criticism. 4. Theater—Switzerland—Bern (Canton)-
—History—16th century. 5. Protestantism and literature. 6. Reformation-
—Switzerland—Bern (Canon) 7. Bern (Switzerland : Canton)—Church history—16th century. 8. Arts, Swiss—Switzerland—Bern (Canton)

PT3877.B39 T44 2001
792'.09494'5409031—dc21
                                                       2001043292

Die Deutsche Bibliothek - CIP-Einheitsaufnahme

Ehrstine, Glenn:
Theater, culture, and community in reformation Bern, 1523 - 1555 / by Glenn Ehrstine. – Leiden ; Boston ; Köln : Brill, 2001
  (Studies in medieval and reformation thought ; Vol. 85)
  ISBN 90–04–12353–9

ISSN 0585-6914
ISBN 90 04 12353 9

© *Copyright 2002 by Koninklijke Brill NV, Leiden, The Netherlands*

All rights reserved. No part of this publication may be reproduced, translated, stored in a retrieval system, or transmitted in any form or by any means, electronic, mechanical, photocopying, recording or otherwise, without prior written permission from the publisher.

*Authorization to photocopy items for internal or personal use is granted by Brill provided that the appropriate fees are paid directly to The Copyright Clearance Center, 222 Rosewood Drive, Suite 910 Danvers MA 01923, USA.
Fees are subject to change.*

PRINTED IN THE NETHERLANDS

In memoriam

ELLIS DUANE EHRSTINE
(1924–2001)

CONTENTS

Preface and Acknowledgements	ix
Illustrations	xiii
Abbreviations	xvii

Chapter One: Performing the Protestant Reformation 1
  a. Theater and Reformation in Bern 6
  b. The Stage as Pulpit: Reformers on Theater 15
  c. Enacting Community 31

Chapter Two: Bern at the Crossroads of Reform 42
  a. Bern, Swiss Protestantism, and the Helvetian
    Confederacy 44
  b. Literature and the Arts 58
  c. Plays and Playwrights 67

Chapter Three: Protestant Carnival: A Contradiction in Terms? 79
  a. Transgression, Politics, and Religion 84
  b. Niklaus Manuel and Bernese Carnival before 1528 90
  c. Reformation Theology and Carnival 113
  d. Post-Reformation Carnival in Bern (1530–1534) 117

Chapter Four: Theocracy and Theater 135
  a. Piety and Patriarchy 140
  b. The Armor of Faith: *Goliath* (1535, 1545, 1555) 148
  c. "Pious on account of good works": Potiphar's Wife
    in *Joseph* (1538) 157
  d. Revolt, Order, and Iconoclasm in *Gedeon* (1540) 166
  e. "That it be told every instant": Bearing Witness in
    Noe (1546) 176
  f. "Un-Luther Characters": Confessionalism in
    Osterspiel (1552) 186

Chapter Five: Protestant Visual Culture and the Stage 201
   a. Niklaus Manuel: From Painter to Playwright 205
   b. Protestant Theater as Visual Medium 214
   c. Theater as Broadsheet 222
   d. Theater as *Merkbild* 237

Chapter Six: Music, Play, and Worship 247
   a. Zwingli, Bern, and the Music of Swiss Protestantism 250
   b. The Choral Interludes of Renaissance Theater 262
   c. The Music of Bernese Reformation Drama 266

Chapter Seven: Mediating Change 289

Appendix: Song Texts 297
Bibliography 307
Index of Persons 333
Index of Places 339
Index of Subjects 342
Index of Biblical Citations 347

PREFACE AND ACKNOWLEDGEMENTS

With the publication of *Theater, Culture, and Community in Reformation Bern*, I take leave of a project that has accompanied me, with interruptions, for over ten years. Wolfgang F. Michael first directed my attention to the lack of research on Bernese playwright Hans von Rüte during my doctoral studies at the University of Texas at Austin, and David Price soon persuaded me that any study of Rüte's oeuvre would be incomplete without considering his better-known predecessor, Niklaus Manuel. After completing my dissertation on both authors under Prof. Price's supervision, however, I initially turned my attention to other research projects. There matters remained until two years ago, when I undertook a complete revision of my earlier theses upon learning of the pending publication of two editions fundamental for Bernese Reformation theater: *Niklaus Manuel. Werke und Briefe*, edited by Paul Zinsli and Thomas Hengartner (Bern: Stämpfli, 1999), and *Hans von Rüte. Sämtliche Dramen*, edited by Friederike Christ-Kutter, Klaus Jaeger, and Hellmut Thomke (Bern: Paul Haupt, 2000).

Whereas my previous study focused primarily on the local context of Bern's ten surviving Reformation plays, *Theater, Culture, and Community* situates them within the larger debate on the role of theater and the arts in early Protestantism. In particular, the book joins recent studies on the English Reformation stage in making a case for reformers' conscious exploitation of theater as a means of creating cultural identity among an urban populace estranged from Catholic tradition. In Bern, this included the cultivation of new visual and musical sensibilities, since the local adoption of Zwinglian reform categorically rejected the use of images and song for religious worship. Lastly, *Theater, Culture, and Community* complements the above mentioned editions by offering a unified interpretive framework for both Manuel's and Rüte's works.

I have shaped individual chapters around the plays' sociopolitical contexts (Chapters Three and Four), performative aspects (Chapter Five), and musical elements (Chapter Six). Each work is thus discussed in three different locations. While this requires the reader interested in one specific play to move around somewhat, I believe it allows for a more focused treatment of the cultural issues confronted by Protestant playwrights in their adaptation of late-medieval Catholic dramaturgy. By separating the discussion of the plays' staging and music from that of their politics, however, I by no means imply that song and sight were secondary in fostering a new socioreligious identity among audience members.

Very little English-language research exists on the Bernese Reformation. For this reason, I have designed the study to serve simultaneously as a source book on Bern during the first half of the sixteenth century. Chapter Two thus offers an historical and cultural overview of the city during this period. Moreover, the unique historical situation of the Helvetian Confederacy required certain choices regarding terminology. The adjective "German" in political contexts refers to the German-speaking regions of the Holy Roman Empire (excluding Switzerland, although Bern and other Swiss city-states were nominally still part of the empire at this time); "German" in a linguistic context denotes all German-speaking regions of Europe (including Switzerland). The use of the adjective "German-language" to include Swiss literature written in German proved too unwieldy. My choice of "canton" for members of the Helvetian Confederacy is somewhat anachronistic; they referred to themselves at this time as *Orte* (places, regions).

I am indebted to the editors of the new Manuel and Rüte editions and have in all instances followed their emendations when citing the original plays. In rendering quotes, I have regularized diacritical marks as follows: umlaut replaces a raised diacritic *e* above *a*, *o*, and *u*; *uo* replaces *u* with a raised diacritic *o*; nasal markers (*Nasalstriche*) are rendered as *-n*, *-m*, etc. as appropriate. The abbreviations *dz* and *wz* for *das* and *was* have been preserved. All translations from original sources are my own unless otherwise noted. Quotations from Scripture are based upon the *Oxford Annotated Bible*.

I owe special thanks to Hellmut Thomke and Klaus Jaeger for their collegial comments and critique at all stages of my project. Although my manuscript was largely complete upon the appearance of their edition, I have integrated their findings in my analysis where they present evidence previously unavailable to me. This applies especially to Jaeger's discussion of the plays' music and Friederike Christ-Kutter's biographical research on Rüte and his family. Otherwise, I have retained my original arguments. While our interpretations seldom diverge substantially, the reader should consult the commentaries by Jaeger (*Fasznachtspil* [= *Abgötterei*], *Gedeon, Osterspiel*), Christ-Kutter (*Noe, Goliath*), and Thomke (*Joseph*) for a complete picture of Rüte's plays.

A shortened version of Chapter Three has appeared as "Of Peasants, Women, and Bears: Political Agency and the Demise of Carnival Transgression in Bernese Reformation Drama," *The Sixteenth Century Journal* 31 (2000): 675–97. I would like to thank the journal's editors for their permission to reprint my findings here.

The assistance of numerous colleagues and institutions was crucial for the completion of my study. The Deutscher Akademischer Austauschdienst (DAAD) provided me with funding for my initial doctoral research, allowing me to spend time in Bern as well as in Berlin, where I benefitted from the advice of Hans-Gert Roloff. Margaret Eschler and Claudia Engler of the Stadt- und Universitätsbibliothek Bern and Anna Maria Reber of the Burgerbibliothek Bern assisted me with materials, while Judy Aikin and Shirley Harden read my manuscript in its entirety and offered insightful editorial advice. A generous subsidy from the University of Iowa allowed me to illustrate the text with forty-two images, and I am grateful to the following institutions for permission to reproduce material from their collections: Kunstmuseum Basel, Kunstmuseum Bern, Stadt- und Universitätsbibliothek Bern, Zentralbibliothek Zürich, Bernisches Historisches Museum, Burgerbibliothek Bern, Bayerische Staatsbibliothek Munich, Ashmolean Museum (Oxford), Harry Ransom Center (Austin, Texas), Korporation Luzern, Zentral- und Hochschulbibliothek Luzern, Kupferstichkabinett Dresden, Národní Galerie (Prague), Herzogin Anna Amalia Bibliothek (Weimar).

My most important acknowledgements come last. David Price has offered me inestimable advice since the project's inception; for his comments on my initial chapters, as well as for his continuing professional support, I owe him my profound thanks. Two equally important individuals will not see the book's publication. It was with great sadness that I learned of the passing of Heiko A. Oberman just before submitting my final manuscript. Prof. Oberman encouraged the completion of my project, and I am indebted to him for its inclusion in Brill's Studies in Medieval and Reformation Thought. His death was all the more poignant, as it came less than a month after the passing of my father, Ellis Duane Ehrstine. For his lifetime of love and support, I dedicate this book to him.

Glenn Ehrstine
Iowa City, Iowa
May 2001

ILLUSTRATIONS

1) Hans Rudolf Manuel, portrait of Bertold Haller (1562)
   Courtesy of Zentralbibliothek Zürich, Berchtold Haller I,13

2) Title page, *Handlung oder Acta gehaltener Disputation zuo Bernn in üchtland* (1528)
   Courtesy of Zentralbibliothek Zürich, Z ZW 209/6

3) Anonymous, portrait of Kaspar Megander (18th century)
   Courtesy of Burgerbibliothek Bern, Neg. Nr. 2883

4) Title page, *Berner Synodus* (1532)
   Courtesy of Zentralbibliothek Zürich, Z XVIII 273/3

5) Portrait of Simon Sulzer (1587)
   Courtesy of Bayerische Staatsbibliothek, Biogr. C.272

6) Portrait of Johannes Haller (1540)
   Courtesy of Staats- und Stadtbibliothek Augsburg, Graph 20/188

7) Portrait of Wolfgang Musculus (1587)
   Courtesy of Bayerische Staatsbibliothek, Biogr. C.272

8) Niklaus Manuel, *Self-Portrait* (1520)
   Courtesy of Kunstmuseum Bern, Inv. Nr. G 0326

9) Title page, *Vom Papst und seiner Priesterschaft* and *Von Papsts und Christi Gegensatz* (first edition, 1524)
   Courtesy of Stiftung Weimarer Klassik, Herzogin Anna Amalia Bibliothek, 0,9: 117
   Photographer: Sigrid Geske

10) Lucas Cranach the Elder and Philipp Melanchthon, *Passional Christi und Antichristi* (1521)
    Courtesy of Harry Ransom Humanities Research Center, The University of Texas at Austin, NE 1150.5 C7 1521 B

ILLUSTRATIONS

11) Niklaus Manuel, Der Ablaßkrämer (1525)
    Courtesy of Burgerbibliothek Bern, Mss. Hist. Helv. XVI 159

12) Diebold Schilling the Younger, *Lucerne Chronicle* (1513)
    Courtesy of Zentral- und Hochschulbibliothek Luzern (Property of Korporation Luzern)

13) Title page, *Elsli Tragdenknaben* (1530)
    Courtesy of Zentral- und Hochschulbibliothek Luzern, Handschriften und alte Drucke, H 15 137, 8°

14) Title page, Hans von Rüte, *Abgötterei* (printed 1532)
    Courtesy of Stadt- und Universitätsbibliothek Bern, Rar 105

15) Hans Holbein the Younger, Apocalypse 17 (1523)
    Courtesy of Zentralbibliothek Zürich, Gal Ch 87/1

16) Hans von Rüte, ink drawing for *Abgötterei* (1531)
    Courtesy of Stadt- und Universitätsbibliothek Bern, Rar 105

17) Title page, Hans von Rüte, *Goliath* (printed 1555)
    Courtesy of Stadt- und Universitätsbibliothek Bern, Rar 106

18) Title page, Hans von Rüte, *Joseph* (1538)
    Courtesy of Stadt- und Universitätsbibliothek Bern, Rar 121

19) Title page, Hans von Rüte, *Gedeon* (1540)
    Courtesy of Stadt- und Universitätsbibliothek Bern, Rar 102 (4)

20) Title page, Hans von Rüte, *Noe* (1546)
    Courtesy of Stadt- und Universitätsbibliothek Bern, Rar 102 (3)

21) Title page, Hans von Rüte, *Ein kurtzes Osterspil* (1552)
    Courtesy of Zentralbibliothek Zürich, Z 25.29/1

22) Niklaus Manuel, *Christ and the Adulteress* (1527)
    Courtesy of the Ashmolean Museum, Oxford, Parker I.330

23) Niklaus Manuel, *King Josiah Orders the Idols Destroyed* (1527)
    Courtesy of Kunstmuseum Basel, Kupferstichkabinett, Inv. U.I.77
    Photographer: Martin Bühler

24) Niklaus Manuel, Early Monogram (*The Flute Player*, ca. 1514–15)
    Courtesy of Kunstmuseum Basel, Kupferstichkabinett, Inv. U.X.5
    Photographer: Martin Bühler

25) Niklaus Manuel, Monogram with Ribbon (*Lucretia*, ca. 1518)
    Courtesy of Kunstmuseum Basel, Kupferstichkabinett, Inv. U.X.10a
    Photographer: Martin Bühler

26) Niklaus Manuel, Late Monogram (*Landsknecht*, 1529)
    Courtesy of Kunstmuseum Basel, Kupferstichkabinett, Inv. 1927. 115
    Photographer: Martin Bühler

27) Niklaus Manuel, *Girl with Impaled Heart* (ca. 1510)
    Courtesy of Kunstmuseum Basel, Kupferstichkabinett, Inv. U.XVI.46
    Photographer: Martin Bühler

28) Niklaus Manuel, *Half-Portrait of a Girl* (ca. 1510)
    Courtesy of Kupferstichkabinett Dresden, Inv. Nr. C 2206

29) Niklaus Manuel, *Two Grave Watchers* (ca. 1515)
    Courtesy of Kunstmuseum Basel, Kupferstichkabinett, Inv. U.X.1
    Photographer: Martin Bühler

30) Niklaus Manuel, *The Martyrdom of St. Ursula* (ca. 1513–14)
    Courtesy of Kunstmuseum Bern, Inv. Nr. G 0325

31) Detail from Niklaus Manuel, *The Martyrdom of St. Ursula*
    Courtesy of Kunstmuseum Bern, Inv. Nr. G 0325

32) Niklaus Manuel, *St. Eligius in His Workshop* (1515)
    Courtesy of Kunstmuseum Bern, Inv. Nr. G 2020b

33) Detail from Niklaus Manuel, *St. Eligius in His Workshop*
    Courtesy of Kunstmuseum Bern, Inv. Nr. G 2020b

34) Detail from Niklaus Manuel, *St. Eligius in His Workshop*
    Courtesy of Kunstmuseum Bern, Inv. Nr. G 2020b

35) Niklaus Manuel, Selected Figures from the *Schreibbüchlein* (ca. 1517)
Courtesy of Kunstmuseum Basel, Kupferstichkabinett, Inv. 1662.73, Koegler 55–56
Photographer: Martin Bühler

36) Niklaus Manuel, Selected *Schauspielfiguren* (ca. 1519–20)
Courtesy of Kunstmuseum Basel, Kupferstichkabinett, Inv. U.IX.36, U.X.27
Photographer: Martin Bühler

37) Niklaus Manuel, *The Judgment of Paris* (ca. 1517–18)
Courtesy of Kunstmuseum Basel, Inv. 422
Photographer: Martin Bühler

38) Johann Victor Manuel, copy (1735) of Niklaus Manuel, *Solomon's Idolatry* (1518)
Courtesy of Kunstmuseum Bern, Inv. Nr. A 1188

39) Albert Kauw, copy (1649) from Niklaus Manuel, *Dance of Death* (ca. 1516–19)
Courtesy of Bernisches Historisches Museum, Inv. Nr. 822.3

40) Albert Kauw, copy (1649) from Niklaus Manuel, *Dance of Death* (ca. 1516–19)
Courtesy of Bernisches Historisches Museum, Inv. Nr. 822.23

41) Lucas Cranach the Elder, *The Law and the Gospel* (1530)
Courtesy of the Národní Galerie (National Gallery), Prague, Inv. Nr. O 10732

42) Anonymous, *The Contrast Between the Pope and Christ* (1524)
Courtesy of Universitätsbibliothek Erlangen, Inv. Nr. B 1009

Figure 1. Hans Rudolf Manuel, portrait of Bertold Haller (1562). Courtesy of Zentralbibliothek Zürich, Berchtold Haller I,13

Figure 2. Title page, *Handlung oder Acta gehaltener Disputation zuo Bernn in üchtland* (1528). Courtesy of Zentralbibliothek Zürich, Z ZW 209/6

Figure 3. Anonymous, portrait of Kaspar Megander (18th century).
Courtesy of Burgerbibliothek Bern, Neg. Nr. 2883

BERNER SYNODVS

Ordnung wie sich pfarrer
vnd prediger zů Statt vnd Land Bern/in leer vnd
leben/halten söllen/mit wyterem bericht von
Christo/ vnnd den Sacramenten/be=
schlossen im Synodo da selbst
versamlet/am.ix.tag
Januarii.

AN. M. D. XXXII.

Ob wir ouch Christum nach dem fleysch ha=
bend/so kennend wir jn doch der massen
nit meer.ij.Corinth.v.

Figure 4. Title page, *Berner Synodus* (1532).
Courtesy of Zentralbibliothek Zürich, Z XVIII 273/3

Figure 5. Portrait of Simon Sulzer (1587).
Courtesy of Bayerische Staatsbibliothek, Biogr. C.272

Figure 6. Portrait of Johannes Haller (1540).
Courtesy of Staats- und Stadtbibliothek Augsburg, Graph 20/188

Figure 7. Portrait of Wolfgang Musculus (1587).
Courtesy of Bayerische Staatsbibliothek, Biogr. C.272

Figure 8. Niklaus Manuel, *Self-Portrait* (1520).
Courtesy of Kunstmuseum Bern, Inv. Nr. G 0326

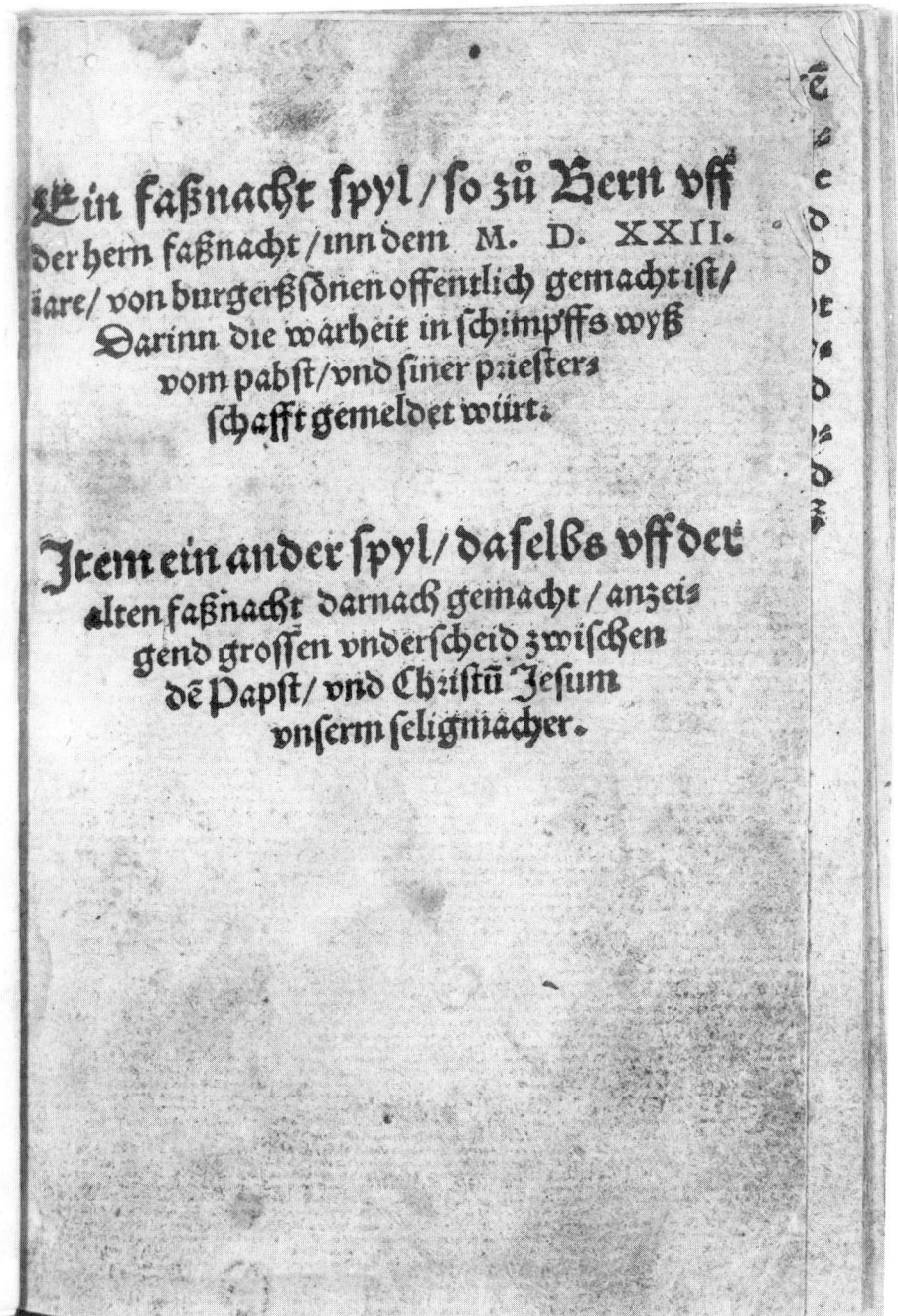

Figure 9. Title page, *Vom Papst und seiner Priesterschaft* and *Von Papsts und Christi Gegensatz* (first edition, 1524). Courtesy of Stiftung Weimarer Klassik, Herzogin Anna Amalia Bibliothek, 0,9: 117. Photographer: Sigrid Geske

Figure 10. Lucas Cranach the Elder and Philipp Melanchthon, *Passional Christi und Antichristi* (1521). Courtesy of Harry Ransom Humanities Research Center, The University of Texas at Austin, NE 1150.5 C7 1521 B

Figure 11. Niklaus Manuel, Der Ablaßkrämer (1525).
Courtesy of Burgerbibliothek Bern, Mss. Hist. Helv. XVI 159

Figure 12. Diebold Schilling the Younger, *Lucerne Chronicle* (1513).
Courtesy of Zentral- und Hochschulbibliothek Luzern
(Property of Korporation Luzern)

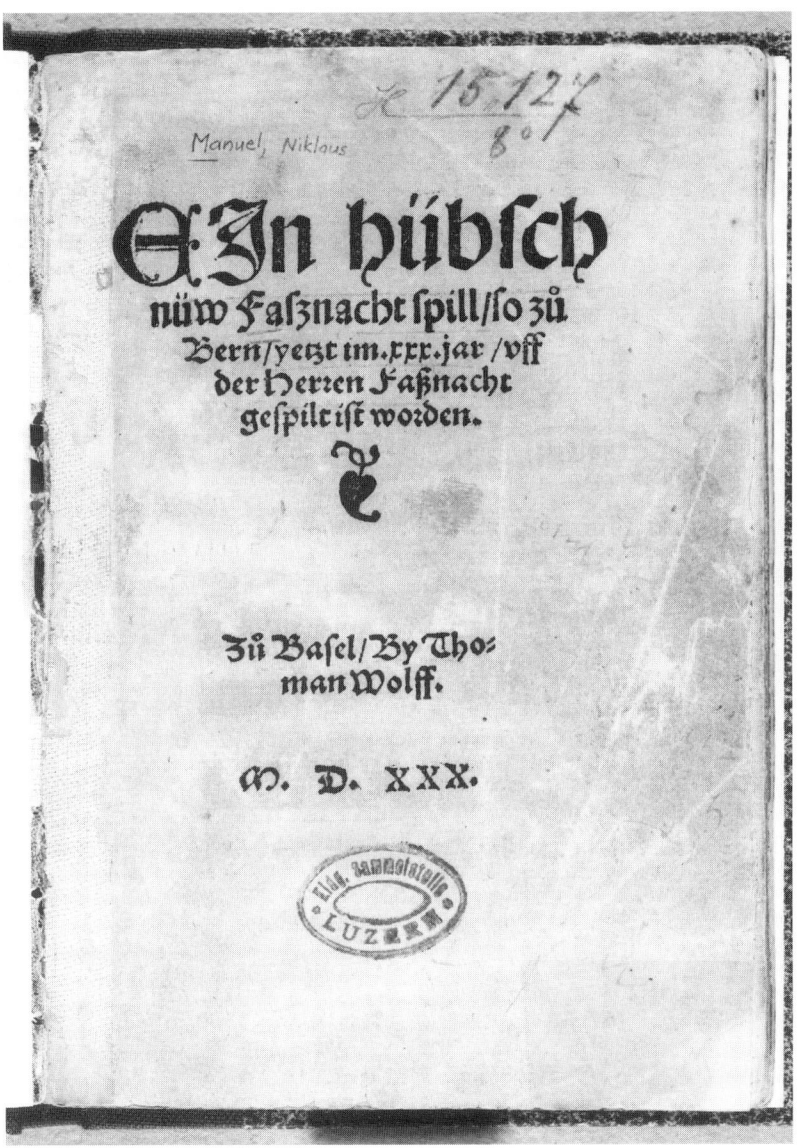

Figure 13. Title page, *Elsli Tragdenknaben* (1530).
Courtesy of Zentral- und Hochschulbibliothek Luzern, Handschriften und alte Drucke, H 15 137, 8°

Ein Faßnachtspil den vr
sprung/haltung/vnd das End beyder/
Heydnischer/vnd Bäpstlicher Abgötteryen allent-
klich verglychende/zů Bern inn öchtland
durch die jungen Burger
gehallten.

Hans von Rüte.

Gedruckt zů Basel/By Thoman Wolff.

Anno. M. CCCCC. XXXII.

Figure 14. Title page, Hans von Rüte, *Abgötterei* (printed 1532).
Courtesy of Stadt- und Universitätsbibliothek Bern, Rar 105

Figure 15. Hans Holbein the Younger, *Apocalypse 17* (1523).
Courtesy of Zentralbibliothek Zürich, Gal Ch 87/1

Figure 16. Hans von Rüte, ink drawing for *Abgötterei* (1531). Courtesy of Stadt- und Universitätsbibliothek Bern, Rar 105

Figure 17. Title page, Hans von Rüte, *Goliath* (printed 1555).
Courtesy of Stadt- und Universitätsbibliothek Bern, Rar 106

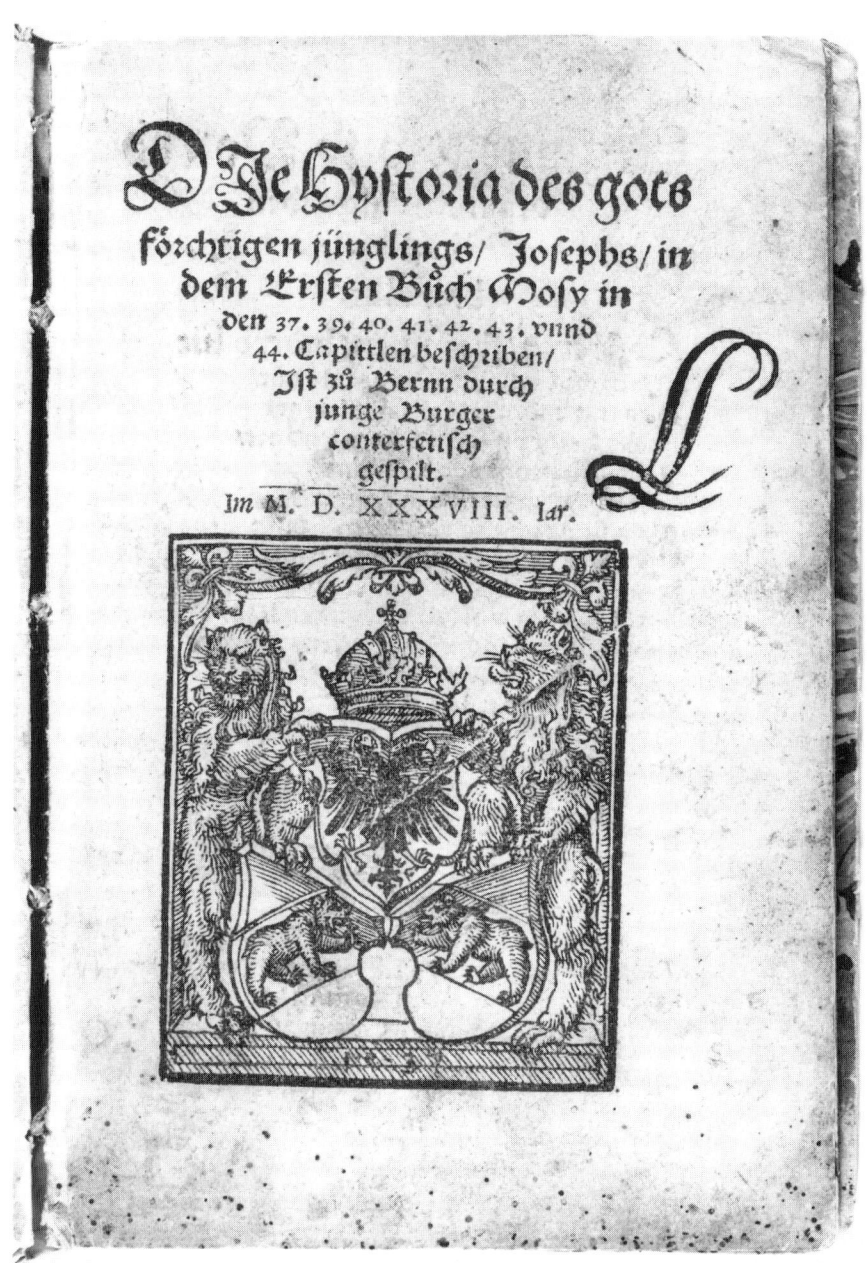

Figure 18. Title page, Hans von Rüte, *Joseph* (1538).
Courtesy of Stadt- und Universitätsbibliothek Bern, Rar 121

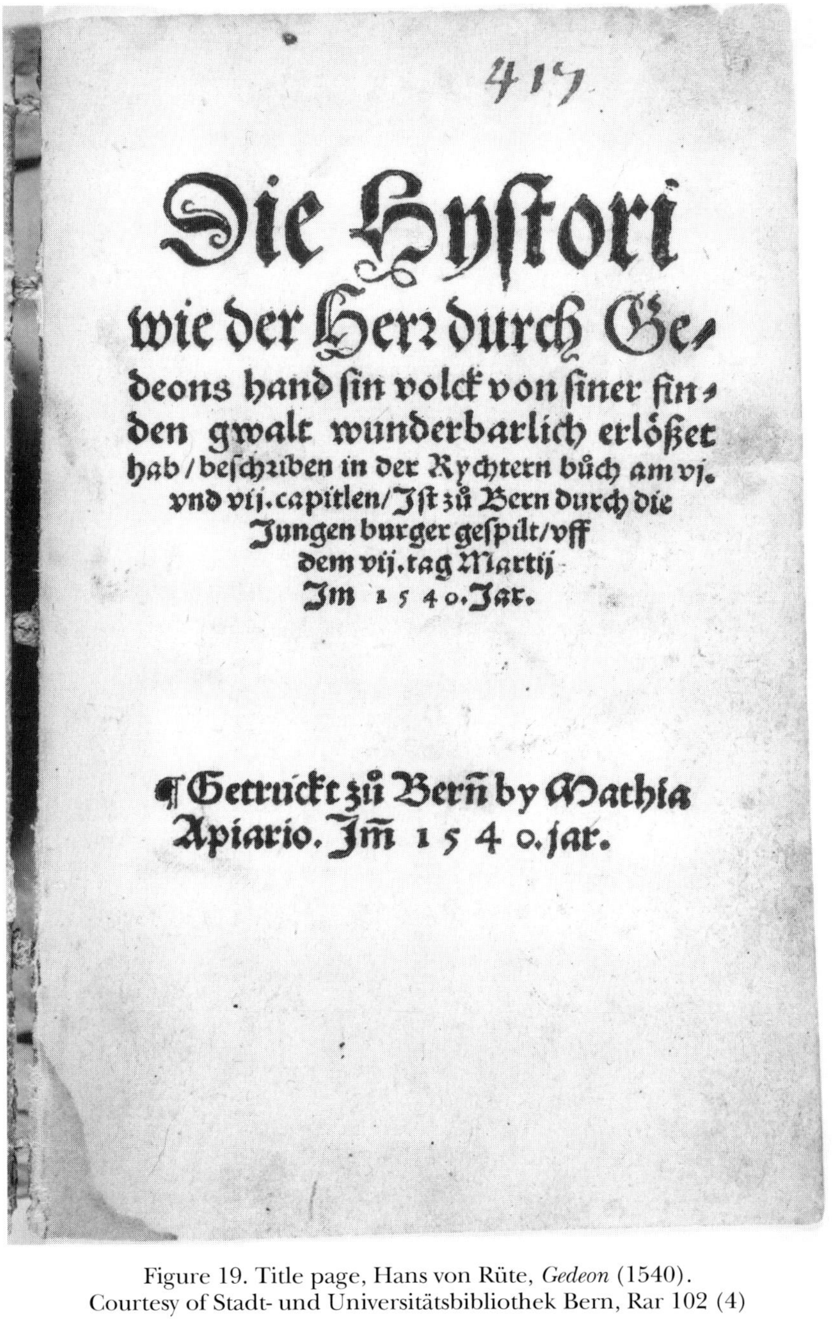

Die Hystori wie der Herr durch Gedeons hand sin volck von siner finden gwalt wunderbarlich erlöset hab / beschriben in der Rychtern bůch am vj. vnd vij. capitlen / Ist zů Bern durch die Jungen burger gespilt / vff dem vij. tag Martij Im 1540. Jar.

¶ Getruckt zů Bern by Mathia Apiario. Im 1540. jar.

Figure 19. Title page, Hans von Rüte, *Gedeon* (1540). Courtesy of Stadt- und Universitätsbibliothek Bern, Rar 102 (4)

Wie Noe vom

win vberwunden durch
sin jüngsten Sun Cham ge=
schmächt/aber die eltern beid/Sem
vnnd Japhet geehret/den sägen
vnnd flůch jnen eroffnet hatt/Ist zů
Bernn in Vchtland/durch junge
Burger gspilt vff 4.Aprilis
Anno 1546.

Mit K. K. Ma. fryheyt/vff Siben Jar.

Figure 20. Title page, Hans von Rüte, *Noe* (1546).
Courtesy of Stadt- und Universitätsbibliothek Bern, Rar 102 (3)

Ein kurtzes
Osterspil zů Bern durch
Jung gsellen ghandlet / vff dem
Sontag Quasimodo nach Ostern /
Im 1 5 5 2. Jar.

Figure 21. Title page, Hans von Rüte, *Ein kurtzes Osterspil* (1552).
Courtesy of Zentralbibliothek Zürich, Z 25.29/1

Figure 22. Niklaus Manuel, *Christ and the Adulteress* (1527).
Courtesy of the Ashmolean Museum, Oxford, Parker I.330

Figure 23. Niklaus Manuel, *King Josiah Orders the Idols Destroyed* (1527). Courtesy of Kunstmuseum Basel, Kupferstichkabinett, Inv. U.I.77. Photographer: Martin Bühler

Figure 24. Niklaus Manuel, Early Monogram (*The Flute Player*, ca. 1514-15). Courtesy of Kunstmuseum Basel, Kupferstichkabinett, Inv. U.X.5. Photographer: Martin Bühler

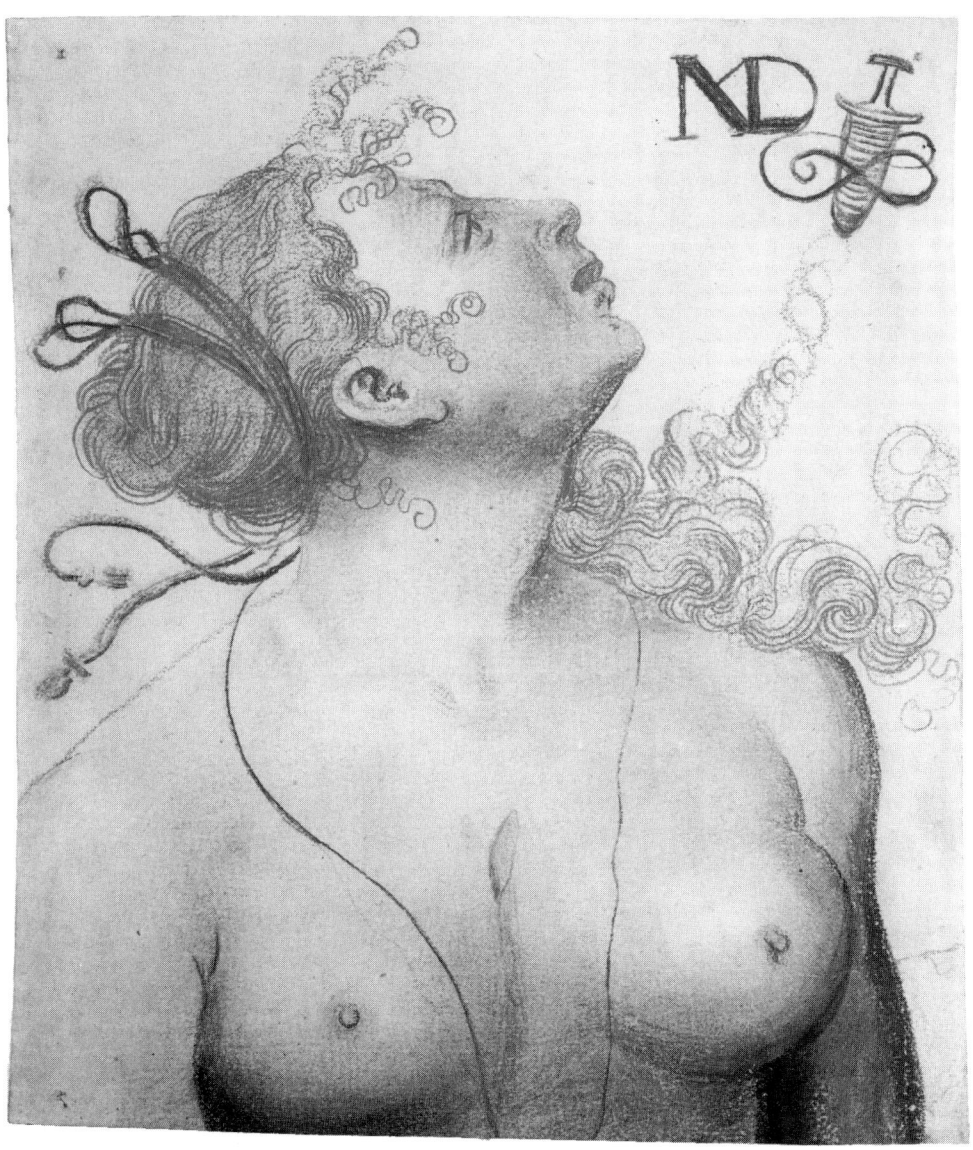

Figure 25. Niklaus Manuel, Monogram with Ribbon (*Lucretia*, ca. 1518).
Courtesy of Kunstmuseum Basel, Kupferstichkabinett, Inv. U.X.10a.
Photographer: Martin Bühler

Figure 26. Niklaus Manuel, Late Monogram (*Landsknecht*, 1529).
Courtesy of Kunstmuseum Basel, Kupferstichkabinett, Inv. 1927.115.
Photographer: Martin Bühler

Figure 27. Niklaus Manuel, *Girl with Impaled Heart* (ca. 1510). Courtesy of Kunstmuseum Basel, Kupferstichkabinett, Inv. U.XVI.46. Photographer: Martin Bühler

Figure 28. Niklaus Manuel, *Half-Portrait of a Girl* (ca. 1510).
Courtesy of Kupferstichkabinett Dresden, Inv. Nr. C 2206

Figure 29. Niklaus Manuel, *Two Grave Watchers* (ca. 1515).
Courtesy of Kunstmuseum Basel, Kupferstichkabinett, Inv. U.X.1. Photographer: Martin Bühler

Figure 30. Niklaus Manuel, *The Martyrdom of St. Ursula* (ca. 1513-14).
Courtesy of Kunstmuseum Bern, Inv. Nr. G 0325

Figure 31. Detail from Niklaus Manuel, *The Martyrdom of St. Ursula*.
Courtesy of Kunstmuseum Bern, Inv. Nr. G 0325

Figure 32. Niklaus Manuel, *St. Eligius in His Workshop* (1515).
Courtesy of Kunstmuseum Bern, Inv. Nr. G 2020b

Figure 33. Detail from Niklaus Manuel, *St. Eligius in His Workshop*. Courtesy of Kunstmuseum Bern, Inv. Nr. G 2020b

Figure 34. Detail from Niklaus Manuel, *St. Eligius in His Workshop*.
Courtesy of Kunstmuseum Bern, Inv. Nr. G 2020b

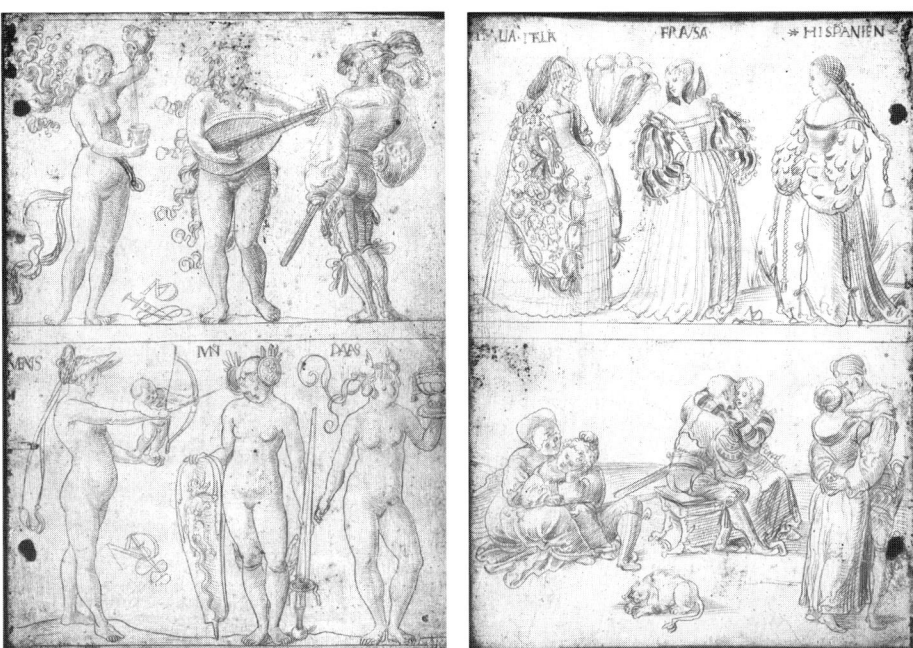

Figure 35. Niklaus Manuel, Selected Figures from the *Schreibbüchlein* (ca. 1517).
Courtesy of Kunstmuseum Basel, Kupferstichkabinett, Inv. 1662.73, Koegler 55-56.
Photographer: Martin Bühler

Figure 36. Niklaus Manuel, Selected *Schauspielfiguren* (ca. 1519-20).
Courtesy of Kunstmuseum Basel, Kupferstichkabinett, Inv. U.IX.36, U.X.27.
Photographer: Martin Bühler

Figure 37. Niklaus Manuel, *The Judgment of Paris* (ca. 1517-18).
Courtesy of Kunstmuseum Basel, Inv. 422. Photographer: Martin Bühler

Figure 38. Johann Victor Manuel, copy (1735) of Niklaus Manuel, *Solomon's Idolatry* (1518). Courtesy of Kunstmuseum Bern, Inv. Nr. A 1188

Figure 39. Albert Kauw, copy (1649) from Niklaus Manuel, *Dance of Death* (ca. 1516-19). Courtesy of Bernisches Historisches Museum, Inv. Nr. 822.3

Figure 40. Albert Kauw, copy (1649) from Niklaus Manuel, *Dance of Death* (ca. 1516-19). Courtesy of Bernisches Historisches Museum, Inv. Nr. 822.23

Figure 41. Lucas Cranach the Elder, *The Law and the Gospel* (1530). Courtesy of the Národní Galerie (National Gallery), Prague, Inv. Nr. O 10732

Figure 42. Anonymous, *The Contrast Between the Pope and Christ* (1524). Courtesy of Universitätsbibliothek Erlangen, Inv. Nr. B 1009

ABBREVIATIONS

ABäG	*Amsterdamer Beiträge zur älteren Germanistik*
Anshelm	*Die Berner Chronik des Valerius Anshelm*, ed. Historischer Verein des Kantons Bern, 6 vols. (Bern: K.J. Wyss, 1884–1901)
Beerli	Conrad-André Beerli, *Le peintre poète Nicolas Manuel et l'evolution sociale de son temps* (Geneva: Librairie Droz, 1953)
BGZ	*Berns grosse Zeit. Das 15. Jahrhundert neu entdeckt*, ed. Ellen J. Beer et al. (Bern: Berner Lehrmittel- und Medienverlag, 1999)
BZGH	*Berner Zeitschrift für Geschichte und Heimatkunde*
Feller	Richard Feller, *Geschichte Berns*, 2nd ed., 4 vols. (Bern: Herbert Lang, 1974)
Fluri	Adolf Fluri, "Dramatische Aufführungen in Bern im 16. Jahrhundert," in *Neues Berner Taschenbuch auf das Jahr 1909* (Bern: K.J. Wyss, 1908), 133–59
Garside	Charles Garside, *Zwingli and the Arts*, Yale Historical Publications, Miscellany 83 (New Haven: Yale University Press, 1966)
Guggisberg	Kurt Guggisberg, *Bernische Kirchengeschichte* (Bern: Paul Haupt, 1958)
JEGP	*Journal of English and Germanic Philology*
Kleinschmidt	Erich Kleinschmidt, *Stadt und Literatur in der Frühen Neuzeit. Voraussetzungen und Entfaltung im südwestdeutschen, elsässischen und schweizerischen Städteraum*, Literatur und Leben, Neue Folge 22, (Cologne/Vienna: Böhlau, 1982)
MGG	*Die Musik in Geschichte und Gegenwart*, ed. Ludwig Finscher, 2nd ed. (Kassel: Bärenreiter; Stuttgart: Metzler, 1994 ff.)
NBT	*Neues Berner Taschenbuch auf das Jahr...* (Bern: K.J. Wyss, 1896–1927)
NMD	*Niklaus Manuel Deutsch. Maler, Dichter, Staatsmann*, ed. Cäsar Menz und Hugo Wagner (Bern: Kunstmuseum Bern, 1979)

OER	*The Oxford Encyclopedia of the Reformation*, ed. Hans J. Hillerbrand, 4 vols. (New York/Oxford: Oxford University Press, 1996)
PBB	*Beiträge zur Geschichte der deutschen Sprache und Literatur*
Sämtliche Dramen	Hans von Rüte, *Sämtliche Dramen*, ed. Friederike Christ-Kutter, Klaus Jaeger, and Hellmut Thomke, 3 vols., Schweizer Texte, Neue Folge 14 (Bern: Paul Haupt, 2000)
Steck/Tobler	*Aktensammlung zur Geschichte der Berner Reformation*, ed. Rudolf Steck und Gustav Tobler, 2 vols. (Bern: K.J. Wyss Erben, 1923)
WA	*D. Martin Luthers Werke*, 89 vols. (Weimar: Hermann Böhlau, 1883 ff.)
Werke und Briefe	Niklaus Manuel, *Werke und Briefe*, ed. Paul Zinsli and Thomas Hengartner (Bern: Stämpfli, 1999)
ZfdPh	*Zeitschrift für deutsche Philologie*
ZfSAK	*Zeitschrift für Schweizerische Archäologie und Kunstgeschichte*
ZfSK	*Zeitschrift für schweizerische Kirchengeschichte/Revue d'Histoire Ecclésiastique Suisse*
ZW	*Huldreich Zwinglis sämtliche Werke*, ed. Emil Egli et al., 14 vols., Corpus Reformatorum 88–101 (Berlin: C.A. Schwetschke und Sohn; Zurich: Berichthaus; Zurich: Theologischer Verlag, 1905–1991)
450 Jahre	*450 Jahre Berner Reformation: Beiträge zur Geschichte der Berner Reformation und zu Niklaus Manuel* (Bern: Historischer Verein des Kantons Bern, 1980)

CHAPTER ONE

PERFORMING THE PROTESTANT REFORMATION

> I would not at all be displeased to see the acts of Christ performed in boys' schools as plays or rather comedies, in Latin and German, written in a chaste and fitting manner, for their remembrance and for a greater impression upon the more uncultivated.
>
> —Martin Luther, letter to Niklaus Hausmann, 2 April 1530

Sometime in 1538, the Dessau schoolmaster and occasional playwright Joachim Greff conceived the idea of presenting Christ's passion and resurrection as a "public action" in German verse.[1] Greff was certainly not the first to envision dramatizing the deeds of Christ, but his resulting *Geistliches schönes newes spil/ auff das heilige Osterfest gestellet* ("A Fine New Spiritual Play, Written for the Holy Feast of Easter"; 1542) was nonetheless a literary novum. In the two decades following the posting of Martin Luther's ninety-five theses in Wittenberg in 1517, no Protestant playwright had directly adapted late medieval Catholic drama to the needs and expectations of the new faith. Of course, biblical plays such as Paul Rebhun's *Susanna* (1535; first edition 1536) had begun to appear in abundance following Luther's praise of "comedies blessed to God" in his 1534 commentaries on the apocryphal books of Tobit and Judith.[2] Greff himself arguably initiated the vernacular tradition of Lutheran biblical drama with *Ein lieblich vnd nützbarlich spiel von dem Patriarchen Jacob vnd seinen zwelff Sönen* ("A Pleasing and Profitable Play on the Patriarch Jacob and his Twelve Sons"; 1534).[3] Yet these works dealt with Old Testament

---

[1] Joachim Greff, *Ein Geistliches schönes newes spil/ auff das heilige Osterfest gestellet/ Darinnen werden gehandelt die geschicht von der Aufferstehung Christi zu sampt der historien Thome* (Zwickau, 1542), Aij^r ff. See also Barbara Könneker, "'Wold ihrs den nicht schir gleuben do?' Joachim Greffs protestantisches Osterspiel," *Daphnis* 23 (1994): 309–44.

[2] Paul Rebhun, *Susanna*, ed. Hans-Gert Roloff (Stuttgart: Reclam, 1980). Luther's commentaries on both Tobit and the Book of Judith appear later in this chapter.

[3] Greff's play was the first biblical drama to appear in Lutheran central Germany. Vernacular Protestant plays had nonetheless already begun to appear on the periphery of the empire: Burkard Waldis's *De parabell vam verlorn Szohn* (Riga, 1527), an anonymous *Rich Man and Lazarus* (Zurich, 1529), and Sixtus Birck's *Susanna* (Klein-Basel,

figures, such as Joseph, or with New Testament parables, such as that of the Prodigal Son. Any portrayal of the savior himself necessarily evoked the passion plays of Catholicism, which theologians of the new faith soundly denounced. Even Greff realized that his initiative might not meet with unanimous approval. He first consulted the Dessau reformer Niklaus Hausmann, who advised against the undertaking.[4] Following Hausmann's fatal stroke of 1538, Greff sought advice in 1541 from Luther himself, who responded that such a play could only result in a fiasco (*lecherey*).[5]

Luther, however, was an ardent supporter of religious theater and had himself earlier recommended dramatizing the deeds of Christ to Hausmann.[6] This book, through close analysis of a specific regional tradition, seeks to resolve such apparent contradictions surrounding German Protestantism's adaptation of Catholic dramatic tradition. As the title *Theater, Culture, and Community in Reformation Bern, 1523–1555* makes apparent, the following pages concern themselves predominantly with the drama of reformed Switzerland, not with the Saxon context of Greff's play. Yet whereas the theology of Zurich reformer Ulrich Zwingli remained distinct from that of Luther, particularly in his opposing interpretation of the Eucharist, Lutheran and Zwinglian theater were virtually indistinguishable when compared with that of the old church. *Ein Geistliches schönes newes spil* provides a fitting point of departure for the study of Bernese drama, as the controversy surrounding the play ultimately produced the nearest approximation to

---

1532). On Greff and his oeuvre, see Wolfgang F. Michael, *Das deutsche Drama der Reformationszeit* (Bern: Lang, 1984), 51–60; Reinhard Buchwald, *Joachim Greff. Untersuchungen über die Anfänge des Renaissancedramas in Sachsen*, Probefahrten 11 (Leipzig: Voigtländer, 1907).

[4] Greff, Aij'. See also Könneker, "Greffs protestantisches Osterspiel," 316–20. On Hausmann, see Helmar Junghans, "Hausmann, Nikolaus," in *OER*, 2:214–5.

[5] Greff, Aiij'; Könneker, "Greffs protestantisches Osterspiel," 313.

[6] "[. . .] ego non illibenter viderem gesta Christi in scholis puerorum ludis seu comediis latine et germanice, rite et pure compositis, repraesentari propter rei memoriam, et affectum rüdioribus augendum." Martin Luther, WA, *Briefwechsel* 5, 271–2. A translation of this passage provides this chapter's epigraph; unless otherwise noted, all translations are my own. This and several other statements by Luther on drama are reproduced in Bernd Neumann, *Geistliches Schauspiel im Zeugnis der Zeit. Zur Aufführung mittelalterlicher religiöser Dramen im deutschen Sprachgebiet*, Münchener Texte und Untersuchungen zur deutschen Literatur des Mittelalters 84/85 (Munich: Artemis, 1987), 2:900–2, nos. 3738–44. See also Könneker, "Greffs protestantisches Osterspiel," 313; Thomas Ivey Bacon, *Martin Luther and the Drama* (Amsterdam: Rodopi, 1976), 29; Hugo Holstein, *Die Reformation im Spiegelbilde der dramatischen Literatur des sechzehnten Jahrhunderts* (Halle: Verein für Reformationsgeschichte, 1886), 18.

a theory of Protestant theater found in contemporaneous documents. After Greff modified and published his work in 1542, focusing now on the resurrection as opposed to the passion, Dessau pastors vociferously objected to the play's planned performance. Greff brought the matter before his territorial ruler, Prince George of Anhalt, who required him to seek out theological opinions on the dramatization of Scripture from Luther, Philipp Melanchthon, and three other Wittenberg theologians. Without exception, their replies supported Greff and demonstrate that Protestants did not censure the staging of the passion per se, but rather the manner of its portrayal.[7]

In general, three themes recur in the Wittenberg letters: 1) in and of itself, the dramatization of Scripture is adiaphorous, i.e. theologically neutral; 2) a play, decorously performed, is an effective means of disseminating God's word, surpassing sermons in its ability to move an audience, and ideal for instructing youth in tenets of faith; 3) the didactic efficacy of drama is rooted in a sign-like visuality. Luther and Melanchthon deal predominantly with the first of these aspects, addressing doctrinal issues and emphasizing the neutrality of religious theater. Both appear particularly irked that the Dessau pastors have found fault in so trifling a matter at a time when the "enemies of God" continue to oppose the spread of the Gospel.[8] Melanchthon rejects portrayals of Christ's passion, but allows for the dramatization of the resurrection, since "the people should be taught to gaze upon the resurrected Christ as he hears and saves those who call on him."[9] Echoing Luther's comments to Hausmann, he further

---

[7] Könneker provides a detailed account of the dispute: Könneker, "Greffs protestantisches Osterspiel," 316–20. See also Holstein, pp. 23–5. For Luther's response, see WA, *Briefwechsel* 10, 284–6. All other responses are edited in Neumann, vol. 2, nos. 3718, 3745, 3747, 3754.

[8] "Solchs hore ich nicht gern, Vnd sorge, Es kücke ein geistlin heraus, der raüm [sic] sucht, ettwas sonderlichs zu machen. Solche neutralia, weil sie ynn vnschedlichen brauch und nicht ergerlich, Solt man lassen gehen. [. . .] Weil nu E[ure] f[ürstlichen] g[naden] nicht allein oberherr, sondern auch Archidiaconus sind, sollen sie nicht leiden, das ein toller kopff [. . .] die Neutralia damnabilia schelte." WA, *Briefwechsel* 10, 286. Melanchthon writes: "Dolendum est, in tanta publica moestitia, cum Germania civilibus bellis dilaceratur, et hostis Dei adducit copias ingentes sicut de Gog et Magog praedictum est, ita adhuc otiosis animis aliquos rixari de rebus non necessariis. [. . .] Sentio [. . .] compescendos esse eos, qui hoc exercitium vituperant, qui rectius facerent, si hoc tristi tempore sua modestia tuerentur tranquilitatem ecclesiae." As quoted in Neumann, 2:903–4, no. 3747.

[9] "Doceantur homines intueri Christum resuscitatum et exaudientem ac salvantem eos, qui ipsum invocant." Ibid., 2:904.

recommends that adolescents perform the resurrection and similar true (biblical) events.[10] Implicit in his advice is the belief that students should perform in Latin to improve their skills in the language: Melanchthon actively endorsed school productions of the Roman playwright Terence and had already published an edition of Terence's six plays in 1516, which subsequently went through several reprints.[11]

The replies of Hieronymus Nopus and Georg Major go beyond those of Luther and Melanchthon in addressing the concept of drama as practiced by Protestant playwrights. Both begin by invoking the necessity of spreading God's word in any and all manners possible. "I respond," Nopus writes, "that Christ should be made known by any means, [...] as long as he is made known. Christ wished to infix the Gospel of our salvation upon our minds, not only by the Word, but even more so by spectacles of the sacraments."[12] Major's response bears perhaps the greater significance for Protestant stage theory, since, as rector of the Magdeburg Latin school (1529–1536), he had directed several school plays, had close ties to Lutheran dramatists, and was at one time considered the co-author of Greff's *Spiel von dem Patriarchen Jacob*.[13] The central passage of his reply reads as follows:

> Mandatum est omnibus hominibus, ut verbum Dei Patris provehant et propagent, quibuscunque id fieri potest rationibus, non tantum voce, sed scriptis, pictura, sculptura, psalmis, contionibus, instrumentis musicis, sicuti inquit Psalmus: "Laudate eum in tympano et choro, laudate eum chordis et organo." Et Moses ait: "Ligabis ea quasi signum in manu tua, eruntque et movebuntur inter oculos tuos, scribesque ea in limine et ostiis domus tuae." Vult cogitari et moveri inter oculos verbum Dei Moses, quod qua ratione possit fieri commodius et illustrius, quam talibus actionibus, gravibus tamen et moderatis, non histrionicis, ut olim erant in papatu. Incurrunt enim talia spectacula in oculos vulgi, ac interdum plus movent, quam conciones publicae. Scio, in

---

[10] "De recitatione historiae resurrectionis et similium verarum historiarum sentio utiliter exerceri ea recitatione adolescentiam." Ibid., 2:904.

[11] Concerning Melanchthon's views on classical drama, see James A. Parente, Jr., *Religious Drama and the Humanist Tradition: Christian Theater in Germany and the Netherlands 1500–1680*, Studies in the History of Christian Thought 39 (Leiden: E.J. Brill, 1987), 20 ff.

[12] "Respondeo, gaudere Paulum, ut quovis modo sive per occasionem sive per veritatem Christus annuncietur, dum modo annuncietur. Christus Evangelium salutis nostrae non verbo tantum, sed et sacramentorum quasi spectaculis quibusdam altius infigere mentibus nostris voluit." Neumann, 2:910, no. 3754.

[13] Könneker, "Greffs protestantisches Osterspiel," 318, note 20. Cf. Holstein, 39, 49, 85–6.

> inferiore Germania, ubi publica professio Evangelii prohibita est, ex actionibus de lege et evangelio multos conversos et amplexos sinceriorem doctrinam.[14]

> It has been mandated for all men to spread and propagate the Word of God our Father by whichever means possible, not only orally, but also through writings, painting, sculpture, psalms, songs, musical instruments, just as the Psalm says: "Praise him with timbrel and dance, praise him with strings and pipes." And Moses says: "You shall bind them as a sign upon your hand, and they shall be and move between your eyes, and you shall write them on the doorposts of your house and on your gates." Moses wishes the Word of God to be considered and pondered through the eyes; for this reason, earnest and moderate plays (not histrionic performances as earlier under the papacy) can render the Word more apt and distinct. For such spectacles strike the eyes of the masses and at times move more than public sermons. I know that in Lower Germany, where it is forbidden to preach the Gospel in public, many have been converted and have embraced the true faith through performances of the "Law and Gospel."[15]

Like Nopus, Major considers it proper to bear witness to the Gospel in any fitting manner. In citing the Vulgate text of Psalm 150 and Deuteronomy 6:8–9, he has chosen central scriptural passages to underscore his argument. Psalm 150 is the final, crowning hymn of the psalter, the culmination of all previous songs of praise. The passage from Deuteronomy is an elaboration on the great commandment "You shall love the Lord your God with all your heart, and with all your soul, and with all your might," which Christ cites as the first commandment when questioned by the Pharisees (Mark 12:29–30). Both are cardinal admonishments to consider God's commandments and deeds through any manner possible.

Perhaps the most striking aspect of Nopus's and Major's comments is that they include drama among visual means of contemplating Scripture. Nopus groups plays with painting as visual media, contrasting them with oral means of spreading God's word, such as sermons and singing. He declares, "What else are these plays than talking ceremonies and speaking depictions of past deeds, which customarily impress matters on the hearts of youths more than simple

---

[14] Neumann, 2:903, no. 3745. Holstein omits the scriptural quotations in his paraphrase of Major's comments: Holstein, 23–4. See also Könneker, "Greffs protestantisches Osterspiel," 319–20.

[15] The phrase "they shall [...] move" is a translation of the Vulgate text's "et movebuntur" as quoted by Major. This passage is faulty and is now rendered in translation with "as frontlets."

narration?"[16] Major similarly emphasizes this commemorative aspect and argues that the visuality of biblical plays makes them more effective than sermons. Following his citation of Deuteronomy, he restates the importance of visual contemplation in his own words ("Moses wants the word of God to be considered and pondered through the eyes") and attributes to drama the greatest efficacy in this undertaking.

Theater and Reformation in Bern

In his translation of the Old Testament, Luther had rendered *inter oculos*—the link between Deuteronomy 6,8–9 and Major's paraphrase—as *fur deynen augen* (before your eyes). This phrase reappears throughout countless remarks on stage theory by contemporary Protestant playwrights, not only in Greff's Easter Play (*leiblich fur ewren augen*), but also in works by Paul Rebhun, Sixtus Birck, Bartholomäus Krüger, and, above all, Bern's court secretary Hans von Rüte (?–1558).[17] Indeed, Nopus's characterization of Protestant theater as "talking ceremonies and speaking depictions of past deeds"—with its broad implications for plays' conception, staging, and reception—is especially apt for the works of Rüte and his better-known predecessor, the painter-poet Niklaus Manuel (ca. 1484–1530). Between 1523 and 1555, these authors produced nine plays that fostered and consolidated Protestant religious reform in Bern and its surrounding territories, aided by a tenth stage work, the anonymous *Elsli Tragdenknaben* ("Little Liz Buck-the-Boy"; 1530).[18] Five were carnival plays, performed or

---

[16] "Item memorabilium rerum Veteris Testamenti non ita multum referre existimo [. . .] concionando vel canendo, pictura vel actione Comica. [. . .] Et actiones istae comicae quid aliud sunt quam loquentes Ceremoniae et vocalis rerum gestarum repraesentatio, quae altius etiam puerorum pectoribus res consuevit infigere quam simplex narratio." Neumann, 2:910, no. 3754.

[17] See Glenn Ehrstine, "Seeing is Believing: Valten Voith's *Ein schön Lieblich Spiel von dem herlichen vrsprung* (1538), Protestant 'Law and Gospel' Panels, and German Reformation Dramaturgy," *Daphnis* 27 (1998): 532; Almut Agnes Meyer, *Heilsgewißheit und Endzeiterwartung im deutschen Drama des 16. Jahrhunderts. Untersuchungen über die Beziehungen zwischen geistlichem Spiel, bildender Kunst und den Wandlungen des Zeitgeistes im lutherischen Raum* (Heidelberg: Winter, 1976), 235–6. In Rüte's plays, the phrase and related variants appear in *Joseph* (v. 8, 30), *Gedeon* (v. 1769, 3961), *Noe* (v. 1692), *Osterspiel* (v. 712), and *Goliath* (v. 34).

[18] Manuel's three plays can be found in a new edition, together with *Elsli Tragdenknaben*, which has been attributed to the author: Niklaus Manuel, *Werke und Briefe*, ed. Paul Zinsli and Thomas Hengartner (Bern: Stämpfli, 1999). The full titles

written between 1523 and 1531, while the remaining five presented biblical themes. Yet whether rooted in secular or religious tradition, all ten plays treated the question of proper faith. No other texts survive from this period of the Bernese stage, nor is there any indication that non-religious performances took place publicly for forty-five years following the local Reformation of 1528.[19]

This singularity of focus distinguishes sixteenth-century Bernese drama from that of other Protestant communities within contemporary German-speaking Europe. In nearby Zurich, the birthplace of the Zwinglian reforms adopted by Bern, a comparable tradition of biblical dramaturgy developed under Jacob Rueff and Jos Murer, yet both playwrights also produced secular works, such as Murer's *Der Jungen Mannen Spiegel* (1560), or Rueff's *Etter Heini* (ca. 1538–9) and his William Tell play of 1545.[20] In addition, Hans Rudolf Manuel's

---

of Rüte's plays are as follows: *Ein Fasznachtspil den vrsprung/haltung/vnd das End beyder/Heydnischer/vnd Bäpstlicher Abgötteryen allenklich verglychende/zuo Bern inn öchtland durch die jungen Burger gehallten* (Basel: Thomas Wolff, 1532); *Dje Hystoria des gots förchtigen jünglings/Josephs/in dem Ersten Buoch Mosy in den 37. 39. 40. 41. 42. 43. vnnd 44. Capitteln beschriben/Jst zuo Bernn durch junge Burger conterfetisch gespilt* (Bern: Mathias Apiarius, 1538); *Die Hystori wie der Herr durch Gedeons hand sin volck von siner finden gwalt wunderbarlich erlößet hab/beschriben in der Rychtern buoch am vj. vnd vij. capiteln/Jst zuo Bern durch die Jungen burger gespilt/vff dem vij. tag Martij Jm 1540. Jar* (Bern: Mathias Apiarius, 1540); *Wie Noe vom win vberwunden durch sin jüngsten Sun Cham geschmächt/aber die eltern beid/Sem vnnd Japhet geehret/den sägen vnd fluoch jnen eroffnet hatt/Jst zuo Bernn in Vchtland/durch junge Burger gspilt vff 4. Aprilis Anno 1546* (Bern: Mathias Apiarius, 1546); *Ein kurtzes Osterspil zuo Bern durch Jung gsellen ghandlet/vff dem Sontag Quasimodo nach Ostern/Jm 1552. Jar* (Bern: Mathias Apiarius, 1552); *Goliath. Die Histori/Wie David der Jüngling den Risen Goliath vmbbracht vnd erlegt hat. Jst zuo Bern durch ein gemeyne Burgerschafft gespilt* (Bern: Samuel Apiarius, 1555). See figs. 9, 13–14, and 17–21 for the plays' original title pages. Rüte's six plays are also available in a new edition; see note 32.

[19] The first recorded public performance of a non-religious (or, more specifically, non-Protestant) play following the Bernese Disputation of 1528 is *Ein schön Christlich new Spil von der Kinderzucht* ("A Fine New Christian Play on the Discipline of Children"; performed 1573, printed 1574), written by Johann Rasser, the Catholic pastor in Ensisheim (Alsace). Only one sixteenth-century Bernese biblical play survives that was not written by Rüte, namely an anonymous Esther play of 1567 performed for the wedding of Magdalena Nägeli, daughter of former mayor Hans Franz Nägeli. In 1549, the students of Bern's theological academy (*Hohe Schule*) privately performed an apparently polemic play in which devils celebrated mass, but as indicated by the town council's response to the bishop of Constance, the play was not of local provenance, but rather from Strasbourg. Later, in 1554, the students staged Aristophanes's *Ploutos*, likely in Latin. Moreover, some form of carnival entertainment seems to have been performed in early 1552 and 1553, although the content of these plays is unknown. Like Rüte's carnival play of 1531, they could have treated religious matters. See Fluri, 139–41, 144. On Rasser and his play, see Michael, 233–5; Kleinschmidt, 100, note 128; 197, note 424.

[20] Jos Murer, "Der jungen Mannen Spiegel," in *Sämtliche Dramen*, ed. Hans-Joachim Adomatis et al. (Berlin: de Gruyter, 1974), 1:289–346; *Jakob Ruffs Etter Heini uss dem*

carnival play *Das Weinspiel* was performed in Zurich in 1548,[21] long after the suppression of carnival in Bern. Leonhard Culmann and Hans Sachs similarly cultivated a tradition of biblical theater in post-Reformation Nuremberg, but the city is much better known for the latter author's humoresque carnival sketches.[22] Nor did Bern's Reformation plays share much more than subject matter with humanist-oriented *Schuldrama*, which flourished predominantly in Lutheran territories to the north and is quintessentially represented by Rebhun's *Susanna*. Since humanist dramaturgy, both neo-Latin and vernacular, has long dominated the research on sixteenth-century religious theater,[23] Rüte's oeuvre in particular has been sorely neglected.[24]

Schwizerland, ed. Hermann Marcus Kottinger, Bibliothek der gesammten deutschen National-Literatur 14 (Quedlinburg/Leipzig: Gottfried Basse, 1847); "Das neue Tellenspiel von Jakob Ruf," in *Schweizerische Schauspiele des sechszehnten Jahrhunderts*, ed. Jakob Baechtold (Zurich: J. Huber, 1893), 3:49–136. On the authors, see Michael, 149–72. On Rueff's Tell play, see Randolph Head, "William Tell and His Comrades: Association and Fraternity in the Propaganda of Fifteenth- and Sixteenth-Century Switzerland," *Journal of Modern History* 67 (1995): 527–57.

[21] Hans Rudolf Manuel, "Das Weinspiel," ed. Walter Haas, in *Fünf Komödien des sechzehnten Jahrhunderts*, Schweizer Texte 10 (Bern/Stuttgart: Paul Haupt, 1989), 211–421.

[22] On Culmann, see Matthias Wilhelm Senger, *Leonhard Culmann: A Literary Biography and an Edition of Five Plays. As a Contribution to the Study of Drama in the Age of the Reformation* (Nieuwkoop: B. de Graaf, 1982). On Sachs, see among others Eckhard Bernstein, *Hans Sachs: Mit Selbstzeugnissen und Bilddokumenten* (Reinbek: Rowohlt, 1993).

[23] Significant studies of sixteenth-century drama in German-speaking Europe include: Otto Francke, *Terenz und die lateinische Schulcomoedie in Deutschland* (Weimar: Böhlau, 1877); Holstein, *Die Reformation im Spiegelbilde der dramatischen Literatur*; Alexander von Weilen, *Der ägyptische Joseph im Drama des XVI. Jahrhunderts: Ein Beitrag zur vergleichenden Literaturgeschichte* (Vienna: Alfred Hölder, 1887); P. Expeditius Schmidt, *Die Bühnenverhältnisse des deutschen Schuldramas und seiner volkstümlichen Ableger im sechzehnten Jahrhundert* (Berlin: Alexander Duncker, 1903); Jean Lebeau, *Salvator Mundi: L'"Exemple" de Joseph dans le Théâtre Allemand au XVIe Siècle*, 2 vols., Bibliotheca Humanistica et Reformatica 20 (Nieuwkoop: B. de Graaf, 1977); Michael, *Das Drama der Reformationszeit*; Parente, *Religious Drama and the Humanist Tradition*; David Price, *The Political Dramaturgy of Nicodemus Frischlin*, University of North Carolina Studies in Germanic Languages and Literatures 111 (Chapel Hill: University of North Carolina Press, 1990); Stephen L. Wailes, *The Rich Man and Lazarus on the Reformation Stage. A Contribution to the Social History of German Drama* (Selinsgrove: Susquehana University Press; London: Associated University Presses, 1997). Of those studies that include non-humanist works in their analysis, namely Holstein, von Weilen, Lebeau, Michael, and Wailes, only Lebeau and Wailes move beyond brief descriptions to a more serious treatment of these plays' sociopolitical aspects.

[24] Until recently, only two authors had studied Rüte's oeuvre in any detail: W. Crecelius, "Die Heiligenverehrung in der Schweiz im 16. Jahrhundert," *Alemannia: Zeitschrift für Sprache, Literatur und Volkskunde des Elsasses und Oberrheins* 3 (1875): 56–61; Crecelius, "Hans Rüte in Bern und sein Spiel von der heidnischen und päbstlichen

My study seeks to understand Bern's ten Reformation plays in the cultural context of local religious reform, which encompassed the distinct particulars of Swiss politics, Swiss dramaturgy, and Swiss Protestantism in both its Zwinglian and Calvinist forms. Although Manuel and Rüte clearly shared many theological and poetic concerns with contemporary Lutheran playwrights, they wrote for a Swiss audience accustomed to politically charged carnival entertainment as well as to extravagant two-day passion play performances in nearby Lucerne.[25] The aesthetic tastes and expectations of these theater-goers took precedence over the dictates of humanist poetics in determining the form of Bernese drama. While nine plays found their way into print,[26] only Manuel's two works of 1523, *Vom Papst und seiner Priesterschaft* ("On the Pope and His Priests") and *Von Papsts und Christi Gegensatz* ("On the Distinction between the Pope and Christ") went through more than one edition and reached a larger audience outside canton borders.[27] Even within the closer confines of the Swiss Confederacy, Bern's western geographical location and resulting francophilia often set it apart from eastern cantons. The city was a cultural microcosm unto itself, and nowhere is Bernese Reformation culture more manifest than in its theater, which united language, art, and music in a devotional *Gesamtkunstwerk*.

Most importantly, perhaps, Manuel and Rüte wrote for a patron concerned with political rather than poetic conformity. Following the local Reformation, the Bernese town council exercised authority over theological as well as political affairs in its surrounding territories,

---

Abgötterei," *Alemannia: Zeitschrift für Sprache, Litteratur und Volkskunde des Elsasses und Oberrheins* 3 (1875): 120–8; Kenneth Fisher, "Hans von Rüte: A Dramatist of the Swiss Reformation" (Ph.D. diss., University of Texas at Austin, 1975). These studies are now inadequate in methodology and scope.

[25] Swiss carnival plays were arguably more often political than those of Nuremberg, which are often considered the quintessential examples of the genre in Germany. See Heidy Greco-Kaufmann, *"Vor rechten lütten ist guot schimpfen": Der Luzerner Marcolfus und das Schweizer Fastnachtspiel des 16. Jahrhunderts*, Deutsche Literatur von den Anfängen bis 1700, vol. 19 (Bern: Peter Lang, 1994), 9–11, 253 ff. On the Lucerne tradition, see M. Blakemore Evans, *The Passion Play of Lucerne. An Historical and Critical Introduction*, MLA Monograph Series 14 (New York: Modern Language Association of America, 1943).

[26] Manuel's third carnival play, *Der Ablaßkrämer* of 1525, survives only in manuscript: Niklaus Manuel, *Der Ablaßkrämer*, ed. Paul Zinsli, Altdeutsche Übungstexte 17 (Bern: Francke, 1960); Niklaus Manuel, "Der Ablaßkrämer," in *Werke und Briefe*, 255–83.

[27] Zinsli and Hengartner list some twelve editions of the plays: *Werke und Briefe*, 116–24.

which together constituted the largest city-state north of the Alps. A dispute such as that surrounding the planned performance of Greff's *Osterspiel* could not have occurred in Bern for the simple fact that the city council, possessing both theological and political jurisdiction, would not have sanctioned a play's performance if not convinced of its conformity to Zwinglian theology and morals. This is particularly true of Rüte's plays, at which city magistrates were honored guests. Local councilors also charged the playwright with the censorship of other locally produced plays. The resulting symbiosis between theocracy and theater is most apparent in Rüte's *Ein kurtzes Osterspil* ("A Brief Easter Play") of 1552, which was performed on the occasion of council elections and lauded Bern's reformed church over that of Wittenberg, Geneva, and even Zurich. In their public presentation of Scripture, Rüte's five biblical plays reflect Bernese council policy and are indispensable sources for assessing Helvetian politics following the Second War of Kappel of 1531, which consolidated the confessional divisions between Swiss cantons for the remainder of the century and beyond.

In arguing that post-Reformation biblical drama continues the religious rhetoric of the carnival play through other means, I consciously place the lesser-known works of Hans von Rüte, in terms of their socio-historical significance, on a par with the oeuvre of Niklaus Manuel. Manuel, a true Renaissance figure in his triple capacity as painter, poet, and politician, is admittedly the more colorful of Bern's two Reformation playwrights and has been the subject of numerous monographs, exhibitions, and conferences.[28] His collected writings were among the first literary works of the sixteenth century to appear in modern edition,[29] and his best-known play, *Vom Papst und seiner Priesterschaft*, has been edited on five occasions, most recently in a new critical edition of Manuel's works and letters by Paul Zinsli and

---

[28] Exhibition catalogues and conference proceedings exist as follows: Hans Koegler, *Beschreibendes Verzeichnis der Basler Handzeichnungen des Niklaus Manuel Deutsch. Nebst einem Katalog der Basler Niklaus Manuel-Ausstellung im Kupferstichkabinett Mitte Februar bis Ende April 1930* (Basel: B. Schwabe, 1930); *Niklaus Manuel Deutsch: Maler—Dichter—Staatsmann*, ed. Cäsar Menz and Hugo Wagner (Bern: Kunstmuseum Bern, 1979); *450 Jahre Berner Reformation: Beiträge zur Geschichte der Berner Reformation und zu Niklaus Manuel*, Archiv des Historischen Vereins des Kantons Bern 64–5 (Bern: Historischer Verein, 1980).

[29] *Niklaus Manuel*, ed. Jakob Baechtold, Bibliothek älterer Schriftwerke der deutschen Schweiz und ihres Grenzgebietes 2 (Frauenfeld: J. Huber, 1878).

Thomas Hengartner.³⁰ Indeed, the scrutiny of *Vom Papst und seiner Priesterschaft* (performed 15 February 1523) and its sister play *Von Papsts und Christi Gegensatz* (performed 22 February 1523) has produced a detailed monograph by Peter Pfrunder on the plays' mix of carnival, theater, and religious reform as viewed in cross-section during a single week of Bernese history.³¹ Through its longitudinal approach, my study supplements and at times emends Pfrunder's theses from the perspective of over three decades of local dramatic tradition. It is Rüte who commands the local stage for two-thirds of this period, and it is he who consummates the marriage of theater and Reformation initiated by Manuel. *Theater, Culture, and Community* thus joins the new critical edition of Rüte's works by Friederike Christ-Kutter, Klaus Jaeger, and Hellmut Thomke in reflecting an increased awareness of Rüte's significance for the Reformation stage, both in Bern and beyond.³²

My analysis proceeds chronologically, with the examination of Bernese material situated at all times in the larger contexts of sixteenth-century literature and theology. In the remaining sections of Chapter One, I establish a theoretical framework for the study of Protestant theater as an agent of change and consolidation. Following

---

³⁰ After the publication of Baechtold's edition of Manuel's collected works, an earlier manuscript redaction of Manuel's two plays of 1523 was discovered in Hamburg: Fritz Burg, "Dichtungen des Niklaus Manuel. Aus einer Handschrift der Hamburger Stadtbibliothek," in *NBT 1897*, 1–136. Ferdinand Vetter based his later edition on the altered sequence of scenes in the Hamburg manuscript: *Niklaus Manuels Spiel evangelischer Freiheit "Die Totenfresser"*, ed. Ferdinand Vetter, Die Schweiz im deutschen Geistesleben 16 (Leipzig: H. Haessel, 1923). Arnold Berger similarly based his 1935 edition on the Hamburg manuscript: Niklaus Manuel, "Ein Fastnachtsspiel von Papst und seiner Priesterschaft," in *Die Schaubühne im Dienste der Reformation I*, ed. Arnold E. Berger, Deutsche Literatur in Entwicklungsreihen, Reihe Reformation 5 (Leipzig: Reclam, 1935), 45–113. The recent edition by Hellmut Thomke takes the play's first imprint of 1524 as its guiding text: "Vom Papst und seiner Priesterschaft," in *Deutsche Dramen des 15. und 16. Jahrhunderts*, ed. Hellmut Thomke, Bibliothek deutscher Klassiker 136 (Frankfurt: Deutscher Klassiker Verlag, 1996), 139–209. Zinsli and Hengartner also base their text on imprint "A" of 1524, but also include a transcription of the Hamburg manuscript for comparison: "Fasnachtsspiel," in *Werke und Briefe*, 101–253.

³¹ Peter Pfrunder, *Pfaffen, Ketzer, Totenfresser: Fastnachtskultur der Reformationszeit—Die Berner Spiele von Niklaus Manuel* (Zurich: Chronos, 1989).

³² Hans von Rüte, *Sämtliche Dramen*, ed. Friederike Christ-Kutter, Klaus Jaeger, and Hellmut Thomke, 3 vols., Schweizer Texte, Neue Folge 14 (Bern: Paul Haupt, 2000). See also Klaus Jaeger, "Zur Edition der Spiele Hans von Rütes," in *Editionsdesiderate zur Frühen Neuzeit. Beiträge zur Tagung der Kommission für die Edition von Texten der Frühen Neuzeit*, ed. Hans-Gert Roloff, Chloe 24/25 (Amsterdam/Atlanta: Rodopi, 1997), 2:1005–11.

a comparison of Protestant and Catholic stage practice, I argue for a conception of Reformation drama as community theater, i.e. as lay performances that brought together a broad cross-section of the local populace to address civic concerns.[33] In Bern, burghers observed their sons, brothers, and neighbors acting out the social, moral, and political issues left unresolved in the aftermath of the local Reformation. The plays offered orientation during a period of cultural transition, albeit in accordance with the policies of the local town council. To better understand those policies in their historical context, Chapter Two, "Bern at the Crossroads of Reform," offers a political and cultural overview of the city from roughly 1500 to 1560, closing with Manuel's and Rüte's ties to local government. Coupled with Chapter One's theoretical discussion of community theater, Chapter Two's review of Bernese politics and culture subsequently allows the plays themselves to become voices within the sociopolitical discourse of the local Reformation.

Chapters Three and Four examine the plays' treatment of specific issues of interest to the Bernese polity. Together, these chapters chart the transition of Reformation dramaturgy from the ribaldry of antipapal carnival plays to the solemnity of biblical theater. In both instances, a brief theoretical introduction precedes an analysis of these respective genres in light of the changing political circumstances of Bernese Zwinglianism, both locally and abroad. The city's five carnival plays—Manuel's *Vom Papst und seiner Priesterschaft* (1523), *Von Papsts und Christi Gegensatz* (1523), and *Der Ablaßkrämer* ("The Indulgence Peddler"; 1525); *Elsli Tragdenknaben* (1530); and Rüte's *Abgötterei* ("Idolatry"; 1531)—are the focus of Chapter Three, "Protestant Carnival: A Contradiction in Terms?" In its analysis of their transgressive elements, the chapter expands upon the recent research of Pfrunder and Heidy Greco-Kaufmann, whose studies of sixteenth-century Swiss carnival in Bern and Lucerne have amply demonstrated the political significance of the *Fastnachtspiel* for Protestants and Catholics alike.[34] Chapter Four, "Theater and Theocracy," examines Rüte's five biblical dramas—*Joseph* (1538), *Gedeon* (1540), *Noe* (1546),

---

[33] See the definition of theatrical community offered by Alan Hindley in *Drama and Community: People and Plays in Medieval Europe*, ed. Alan Hindley, Medieval Texts and Cultures of Northern Europe 1 (Turnhout: Brepols, 1999), ii.

[34] Pfrunder, *Pfaffen, Ketzer, Totenfresser*; Greco-Kaufmann, *"Vor rechten lütten ist guot schimpfen"*.

Osterspiel (1552), and *Goliath* (1555)—in their post-reform context. As recent studies on the English Reformation stage have demonstrated,[35] Protestants, even Puritans, actively cultivated drama as an especially effective vehicle for the dissemination of religious reform, creating a public forum in which the changes brought on by religious upheaval might be acted out. The political rhetoric of Rüte's plays similarly addressed the concerns of the Bernese community and town council, but did so in a much more direct manner than the touring performances of John Bale and his *felowes* or other itinerant English troupes could for any particular locality.[36]

Chapter Five, "Protestant Visual Culture and the Stage," deals with the plays' imagery. As illustrated by Major and Nopus's comments on Greff's Easter Play, the Reformation debate on the suitability of images for religious instruction directly impacted the Protestant reshaping of theatrical tradition. In staging their plays, Manuel and Rüte borrowed directly from contemporary Protestant visual media, namely the woodcuts of broadsheets and Bible editions, which Robert Scribner and others have shown to have been instrumental in disseminating the new theology.[37] Manuel's *Von Papsts und Christi Gegensatz* originated in one of the Reformation's most successful pamphlets, the *Passional Christi und Antichristi* of 1521 by Lucas Cranach the Elder and Philipp Melanchthon. Rüte later founded his *Osterspiel* directly

---

[35] Margot Heinemann, *Puritanism and Theatre: Thomas Middleton and Opposition Drama under the Early Stuarts* (Cambridge: Cambridge University Press, 1980); Patrick Collinson, *Birthpangs of Protestant England* (London: Macmillan, 1988); Paul Whitfield White, *Theater and Reformation: Protestantism, Patronage, and Playing in Tudor England* (Cambridge: Cambridge University Press, 1992); Bryan Crockett, *The Play of Paradox: Stage and Sermon in Renaissance England* (Philadelphia: University of Pennsylvania Press, 1995); Huston Diehl, *Staging Reform—Reforming the Stage: Protestantism and Popular Theater in Early Modern England* (Ithaca: Cornell University Press, 1997).

[36] On Bale, see White, 12–41.

[37] R.W. Scribner, *For the Sake of Simple Folk: Popular Propaganda for the German Reformation*, 2nd edition (Oxford: Clarendon Press, 1994); Scribner, ed., *Bilder und Bildersturm im Spätmittelalter und in der frühen Neuzeit*, Wolfenbütteler Forschungen 46 (Wiesbaden: Otto Harrassowitz, 1990); Kristin Eldyss Sorensen Zapalac, *In His Image and Likeness: Political Iconography and Religious Change in Regensburg, 1500–1600* (Ithaca: Cornell University Press, 1990); Zapalac, "'Item Perspective ist ein lateinisch Wort, bedeutt ein Durchsehung': A Reformation Re-Vision of the Relationship between Idea and Image," in *Meaning in the Visual Arts: Views from the Outside. A Centennial Commemoration of Erwin Panofsky (1892–1968)*, ed. Irving Lang (Princeton: Center for Advanced Study, 1995), 131–49. On the Protestant image debate in general, see Sergiusz Michalski, *The Reformation and the Visual Arts: The Protestant Image Question in Western and Eastern Europe*, Christianity and Society in the Modern World (London: Routledge, 1993).

upon the *majestas Domini* depictions of Revelation 4–5, in which twenty-four elders and four apostolic creatures pay homage to the Lamb of God. The authors further employed specific staging techniques throughout their plays to aid in audience interpretation, such as an antithetical division of the stage into opposing areas reserved respectively for Protestant and Catholic characters, or the employment of a herald or other exegetic figures in a deictic role, in which an actor literally pointed to the scenes and characters significant for the plays' comprehension. The plays' striking imagery, I argue, enabled them to assume a modified task of visual religious instruction following the iconoclastic destruction of local devotional art.

Chapter Six addresses the plays' music. Unlike Luther and Calvin, who actively encouraged singing as a means of fostering piety and solidarity among congregations and who were composers in their own right, Zwingli opposed church music on the grounds that it affected the senses and distracted the believer from true contemplation of God.[38] Religious worship in Bern thus relied on the word alone from 1528 until 1558, when the town council relented and allowed pupils of the local Latin school to sing one psalm in church before the weekly sermon. Not until 1574 did the congregation itself join in the singing.[39] Nonetheless, beginning at the latest in 1538 with the performance of *Joseph*, Rüte regularly incorporated musical works by local composers into his plays. The most accomplished of these musicians was Cosmas Alder, director of the *Kantorei* at the local St. Vincent convent from 1524 until the institution's secularization in 1528. His motet *Da Jacob nun das Klaidt ansach* ("When Jacob saw the coat"), written for the performance of *Joseph*, has often passed as the work of Ludwig Senfl.[40] "Music, Play, and Worship" explores this and other compositions found in Rüte's dramas, postulating that, as with the singing of hymns by Lutheran congregations, the musical interludes of Bernese theater helped solidify the religious community through the common experience of song.

---

[38] Garside, 27–75.

[39] Arnold Geering, *Die Vokalmusik in der Schweiz zur Zeit der Reformation. Leben und Werke von Bartholomäus Frank, Johannes Wannenmacher und Cosmas Alder*, Schweizerisches Jahrbuch für Musikwissenschaft 6 (Aarau, 1933; Amsterdam: Swets & Zeitlinger N.V., 1969), 41; Gerhard Aeschbacher, "Die Reformation und das kirchenmusikalische Leben im alten Bern," in *450 Jahre*, 234.

[40] See John Kmetz, "*Da Jacob nun das Kleid ansah* and Zurich Zentralbibliothek T 410–413: A Well-Known Motet in a Little Known 16th-century Manuscript," *Schweizer Jahrbuch für Musikwissenschaft* Neue Folge 4/5 (1984/85): 63–79.

Unifying the results of the book, "Mediating Change" argues that the re-creation of a common cultural community was just as critical to the success of the new religion as the establishment of a reformed theology. Bernese theater assumed the leading role in this endeavor by allowing local burghers to participate in the creation of religious symbolism. Although Zwinglianism permitted the laity to take communion in both bread and wine, religious worship otherwise remained a passive endeavor for the congregation. Participation in a play production offered a more tangible sign of faith, becoming in essence a physical *opus operantis* for actors as well as spectators, whose presence at a performance bore visible witness to their membership in the invisible church. Augmented by imagery and music, Protestant theater surpassed sermons in its ability to instruct and, above all, to instill faith in its audience. In establishing the new religion, the theatricality of the Bernese Reformation stage was the sole concession to the power of the senses in a theocracy otherwise committed to founding a society in direct communication with God and Christ, undistracted by the physical world.

The Stage as Pulpit: Reformers on Theater

In his *Actes and Monuments* of 1563, the Protestant martyrologist John Foxe explicitly included actors among the Reformation propagandists attacked by Stephen Gardiner, bishop of Winchester:

> He thwarteth, also, and wrangleth much against players, printers, preachers. And no marvel why: for he seeth these three things to be set up of God as a triple bulwark against the triple crown of the Pope, to bring him down; as, God be praised, they have done meetly well already.[41]

As Foxe was a playwright himself, producing *Titus et Gesippus* (1544) and *Christus Triumphans* (1556) for the Protestant stage,[42] it should perhaps come as no surprise that he placed stage plays on a par with sermons and pamphlets in disseminating Reformation theology. Given the centrality of Foxe's *Actes and Monuments* for English Protestantism,

---

[41] *The Acts and Monuments of John Foxe*, ed. Rev. Josiah Pratt, 4th ed. (London: Religious Tract Society, 1877), 6:57. See also White, 2.
[42] *Two Latin Comedies by John Foxe the Martyrologist. Titus et Gesippus—Christus Triumphans*, ed. and trans. John Hazel Smith (Ithaca/London: Cornell University Press, 1973).

it has lately served to refute the long-standing authority of Harold Gardiner's *Mysteries' End* (1946) and its assertion of an inherent antitheatricalism among English Puritans.[43]

Across the channel, cultural critics have accused German Protestants of much,[44] but the charge of antitheatricalism has never surfaced. This marked contrast to the research on early English drama is in no small part due to the authority of Luther himself, who on several occasions explicitly lent his support to a new Protestant theater, as we have seen above. Yet Luther is but one voice in the German Reformation discourse on drama. In addition to the Wittenberg reformer's oft-cited views on religious plays, the sentiments of other prominent continental theologians parallel—indeed, presage by some thirty years—Foxe's assessment of the affinity between playwrights, printers, and preachers in the Protestant cause.

Religious theater would not have warranted the attention of reformers had it not been traditionally linked with Christian worship. Medieval religious drama grew out of Catholic liturgy and was originally performed as part of the Mass.[45] While it did not give real presence to the body and blood of Christ, its reenactments of the crucifixion and resurrection nonetheless made Christ's sacrifice tangible in ways that the Eucharist could not. Indeed, the development of medieval theater reflects in part an on-going search for Christ's physical as well as spiritual body. The earliest Easter plays originated in the singing of the *Quem queritis* trope, which recorded the exchange between the angel at the tomb of Jesus and the three Marys who have come to annoint him (*Quem queritis* = Whom do

---

[43] Heinemann, 26; Collinson, 103, 114; White, 2; Crockett, 7. Diehl documents her introductory discussions of the rhetoric of reform with extensive material from *Actes and Monuments*: Diehl, 22–52. Cf. Harold C. Gardiner, *Mysteries' End: An Investigation of the Last Days of the Medieval Religious Stage* (New Haven: Yale University Press, 1946).

[44] The views of Friedrich Nietzsche, for example, reflect a common belief in the incompatability of Protestantism and high culture: "Verhältnissmässig war nämlich kein Volk jemals christlicher, als die Deutschen zur Zeit Luther's: ihre christliche Cultur war eben bereit, zu einer hundertfältigen Pracht der Blüthe auszuschlagen,— es fehlte nur noch Eine Nacht; aber diese brachte den Sturm, der Allem ein Ende machte." Nietzsche, "Die fröhliche Wissenschaft," in *Werke. Kritische Gesamtausgabe*, ed. Giorgio Colli and Mazzino Montinari (Berlin/New York: de Gruyter, 1973), 5,2:170–1.

[45] See, among others, Ursula Schulze, "Formen der *Repraesentatio* im Geistlichen Spiel," in *Mittelalter und frühe Neuzeit. Übergänge, Umbrüche und Neuansätze*, ed. Walter Haug, Fortuna Vitrea 16 (Tübingen: Niemeyer, 1999), 312–56.

you seek?). Even as the plays became more elaborate, moving from church interiors to public squares and replacing Latin with the vernacular, they retained their liturgical ties.[46]

By the late Middle Ages, passion and Corpus Christi plays had emerged as the most popular forms of religious theater. Both reenacted the passion, not just the resurrection, and Corpus Christi plays further incoporated the host itself in elaborate processions. The two genres reflected a now even greater desire among the laity to experience the savior's sacrifice physically, indeed vicariously. Drastic scenes of Christ's torture figured prominently in many of these works, and ingenious devices existed to provide the requisite realism. In Lucerne, for example, the lance used to pierce Christ's side squirted blood through a hidden nozzle.[47] In Freiburg im Breisgau, over a gallon of blood flowed through a system of tubes concealed within the cross during the Corpus Christi play of 1588.[48] The stark representation of physical punishment possessed a variety of cultural and political overtones,[49] but all plays emphasized that the spilling of Christ's blood was a necessary step in the process of salvation, as announced by the *Proclammator* at the close of the Lucerne Passion Play of 1545:

---

[46] See "Liturgical and feast-day drama" in Lynette R. Muir, *The Biblical Drama of Medieval Europe* (Cambridge: Cambridge University Press, 1995), 13–27; Johan Nowé, "Kult oder Drama? Zur Struktur einiger Osterspiele des deutschen Mittelalters," in *The Theatre in the Middle Ages*, ed. Herman Braet, Johan Nowé, and Gilbert Tournoy, Mediaevalia Lovaniensia I:13 (Leuven: Leuven University Press, 1985), 269–313.

[47] Evans, 211.

[48] Werner Mezger, "'Quem quaeritis—wen suchen ihr hie?' Zur Dynamik der Volkskultur im Mittelalter am Beispiel des liturgischen Dramas," in *Modernes Mittelalter. Neue Bilder einer populären Epoche*, ed. Joachim Heinzle (Frankfurt/Leipzig: Insel, 1994), 222–3. See also Neumann, 1:354, no. 1658.

[49] See, among others, Jody Enders, *The Medieval Theater of Cruelty: Rhetoric, Memory, Violence* (Ithaca/London: Cornell University Press, 1999); Véronique Plesch, "Killed by Words: Grotesque Verbal Violence and Tragic Atonement in French Passion Plays," *Comparative Drama* 33 (1999): 22–55; Claire Sponsler, *Drama and Resistance: Bodies, Goods, and Theatricality in Late Medieval England*, Medieval Cultures 10 (Minneapolis: University of Minnesota Press, 1997), 136–60; Seth Lerer, "'Representyd now in yower syght': The Culture of Spectatorship in Late-Fifteenth-Century England," in *"Aufführung" und "Schrift" in Mittelalter und Früher Neuzeit*, ed. Jan-Dirk Müller (Stuttgart/Weimar: Metzler, 1996), 356–80; Peter W. Travis, "The Semiotics of Christ's Body in the English Cycles," in *Approaches to Teaching Medieval English Drama*, ed. Richard K. Emmerson (New York: Modern Language Association, 1990), 72.

> Erwürdig, strenng, edel, vest vnnd fromen,
> ir hand verstanden, gsen vnnd ghört,
> wie Cristus hatt syn bluott vereert,
> für vnns gross angst vnnd not erlitten,
> am Crütz vnns ewigs heyl erstritten,
> ouch vff gsetzt das heilig sacrament,
> dohar wir all vnser seligkeyt hendt.[50]

> My honorable, stern, noble, steadfast, and pious lords, you have now seen and heard how Christ dignified his blood and suffered great fear and anguish for our sake. He won us eternal salvation on the cross and instituted the holy sacrament, from which we receive all our blessings.

By reenacting the passion, players, sponsors, and spectators hoped to participate in Christ's saving grace. Far from being morbid, the late medieval fascination with the savior's body, both on stage and elsewhere, grew out of a very real desire for spiritual sustenance.[51]

Indulgences were granted for play attendance or participation, further evidence that the portrayal of Christ's passion was believed to offer an audience real salvation. Bernd Neumann's collection of medieval German play records indicates that playgoers received remission of their sins in Lucerne, Mainz, Strasbourg, Vienna, and several other cities.[52] A forty-day remission was most common, but this amount appears niggardly compared to the 240 years granted the burghers of Calw by papal legate Raimund Peraudi for their performance of a Corpus Christi play in 1502.[53] Plays or processions were also performed in connection with the sale of indulgences by members of the clergy. The infamous performance of the Wise and Foolish Virgins in Eisenach on 4 May 1321, which left Landgrave Friedrich der Freidige so melancholic that he suffered a stroke and eventually died, coincided with a sale of indulgences by local Dominicans.[54] In Bern, members of the St. Vincent collegiate con-

---

[50] *Das Luzerner Osterspiel*, ed. Heinz Wyss (Bern: Francke, 1967), 2:293, vv. 10868–74.

[51] Indeed, as Caroline Walker Bynum has noted, the image of Christ as nourisher allowed him to take on both male and female characteristics. Caroline Walker Bynum, "The Body of Christ in the Later Middle Ages: A Reply to Leo Steinberg," in *Fragmentation and Redemption. Essays on Gender and the Human Body in Medieval Religion* (New York: Zone Books, 1992), 79–117; Travis, 71.

[52] Neumann, nos. 2106, 2258, 2660, 3024.

[53] "Tragoedia bene peracta, Lagatus [sic] benedicebat omni praesenti populo: dans indulgentias 240. annorum, de impositis poenitentiis." Neumann, 1:259, no. 1055.

[54] Ibid., 1:306–8, nos. 1481–3.

vent (*Chorherrenstift*) likely conducted a procession of the cross during the sale of the so-called Great Indulgence in 1516.[55] Judging from Neumann's records, most indulgences were granted for processions with *figurae*, tableaux vivants or portable statuary that depicted central typological moments in the Old and New Testaments. Many of these processions took place without spoken text, so that the audience received grace through an act of vision, not of hearing, and several letters granting indulgences specifically mention the importance of viewing in meditating on the passion.[56] Even in plays with dialogue, the audience perceived the actors foremost through sight: crowds frequently prevented the comprehension of players' speech, and Latin passages were comprehensible only for the educated.

The pre-Reformation stage was not alone in cultivating a devotional spectatorship. Late medieval piety was on the whole exceedingly visual, and in the course of the fifteenth century new forms of imagery emerged that fostered a personal and often highly emotional interaction between viewer and viewed. The printing press contributed to the process, creating inexpensive, portable graphic images that could be regarded at length in the privacy of one's home.[57] Artists also increasingly depicted figures that engaged the viewer directly through gestures and eye contact, creating the illusion of direct communication.[58] These developments combined to produce a "sacramental gaze," in which the viewer lingered over an image, seeking to experience the divine mystery behind it.[59] Even the Eucharist was consumed through the eyes: many parishioners believed that the elevation of the host, not its consecration, was the efficacious moment

---

[55] Kathrin Tremp-Utz, "Gottesdienst, Ablaßwesen und Predigt am Vinzenzstift in Bern (1484/85–1528)," *ZfSK* 80 (1986): 57.

[56] In his letter permitting the burghers of Kamenz to perform a figural procession on the Feast of the Invention of the Cross, bishop Johann von Meißen grants the participants an indulgence of forty days, since *figurae* representing Christ's passion are suitable "ad commovendum simplicium animos ad meditationem passionis dominice" and "ad excitandas mentes Christi fidelium in memoriam ejusdem dominice passionis." Neumann, 1:415, no. 1969.

[57] Hans Belting, *Bild und Kult. Eine Geschichte des Bildes vor dem Zeitalter der Kunst* (Munich: C.H. Beck, 1991), 457–509.

[58] Bob Scribner, "Ways of Seeing in the Age of Dürer," in *Dürer and His Culture*, ed. Dagmar Eichberger and Charles Zika (Cambridge: Cambridge University Press, 1998), 107–9.

[59] Robert Scribner, "Popular Piety and Modes of Visual Perception in Late-Medieval and Reformation Germany," *Journal of Religious History* 15 (1989): 456–61; Scribner, "Ways of Seeing," 109.

of the Mass, so that they left the church after witnessing this act.[60] Whether in church, on stage, or on canvas, a religious image was assumed to be a direct conduit to God; one could "look through" it to apprehend Christ directly.

In practice, however, the eyes did not always penetrate the surface of such portrayals, but lingered on their increasingly realistic details. In such cases, plays became spectacles performed for spectacle's sake,[61] as made clear by Joachim Greff in the foreword to his Easter play:

> So sag ich also/das man viel dings [...] hin vnd widder gespielet/welches doch vngeacht ist gewest bey yderman/dan niemandt hat gewust/was es sey odder war zu es diene/nur allein das es die augen gespeiset vnd gefüllet [...] Vnd dis ist ein mal wahr/das [...] fur der grossen vnd vbrigen pracht/auch fur der menge der personen wurden die werck vnd Mirackel Christi als seine geburt/leyden/vnd Aufferstehung etc. [...] Ja die gantze Action selbs/mus allein vertunckelt vnd verhindert Quia vbi multitudo ibi confusio/Sintemal ich weis/das der hunderste mensch/nicht die helfft sehen/geschweig dann hören oder etwas draus behalten kunde.[62]

> I say, then, that one [...] on occasion portrayed many things that were ignored by everyone, since no one knew what it was or what it was good for, only that it fed and filled the eyes. [...] And this also is true, that, [...] because of the great and sundry pomp and because of the mass of people, the works and miracles of Christ, such as his birth, passion, and resurrection, etc., [...] indeed, the whole play itself could not fail to be obscured and diminished, since *ubi multitudo, ibi confusio* (where there's a crowd, there's confusion). I'm certain that not one in a hundred could see half of it, much less hear or retain something.

The attention to visual realism thus often distracted an audience from the original intention of religious theater, which was to represent Christ's redemption of humanity. Instead of portraying Christ as savior, the vivid portrayal of the passion more often invoked spectators' compassion for Christ as sufferer.[63]

---

[60] Scribner, "Popular Piety," 459.
[61] Mezger, 222, 225; Schulze, 353.
[62] Greff, *Ein Geistliches schönes newes spil*, Avj^v–Avij^r. See also Neumann, 328, no. 1554; 891–2, no. 3730.
[63] On the role of *compassio* in late medieval theater, see Schulze, 340–5.

Luther's recommendations for a new Protestant theater explicity rejected the affective aspects of such realism, but retained the act of viewing as the central moment of audience reception. In addition to scattered comments in his letters and table talks, Luther discussed his views on drama in two prime documents: his commentaries on the apocryphal books of Judith and Tobit, and his 1519 *Sermon von der Betrachtung des heyligen leydens Christi* ("Sermon on Contemplating the Holy Passion of Christ").[64] The commentaries, written for the first complete High German edition of Luther's Bible (1534), are concerned with establishing a scriptural basis for the performance of religious plays. Here, Luther postulates that Greek tragedies and comedies originated in a (conjectural) Jewish religious theater,[65] and his description of biblical plays as *gottselig* (blessed to God) apparently removed any lingering doubts regarding the suitability of the stage for Protestant instruction. As evidenced by Paul Rebhun's reprinting of Luther's comments as an afterword to his *Susanna*, a host of Protestant schoolmasters, doctors, pastors, and civil servants took the reformer's comments to heart in composing plays for their communities. The passages cited by Rebhun are brief enough to be quoted here in full:

> Vnd mag sein, das sie solch geticht gespielet haben, wie man bey vns die Passio spielet, vnd ander heiligen geschicht, Damit sie jr volck vnd die jugent lereten, als jnn einem gemeinen bilde odder spiel, Gott vertrawen, from sein, vnd alle hülff vnd trost von Gott hoffen, jnn allen nöten widder alle feinde etc. Darumb ists ein fein, gut, heilig, nützlich Buch, vns Christen wol zu lesen, Denn die wort so die personen hie reden, sol man verstehen, als rede sie ein geistlicher heiliger Poet odder Prophet, aus dem Heiligen geist, der solche personen fur stellet jnn seinem spiel, vnd durch sie vns predigt. [...] WAs von dem Buch Judith gesagt ist, das mag man auch von diesem Buch Tobia sagen, Jsts ein geschicht, so ists ein fein heilig geschicht, Jsts aber ein geticht, so ists warlich auch ein recht schön, heilsam, nützlich geticht vnd spiel, eins geistreichen Poeten, Vnd ist zuvermuten, das solcher schöner geticht vnd spiel, bey den Jüden viel gewest sind, darinn sie sich auff

---

[64] For a general introduction on Luther's views concerning the theater, see Bacon, *Martin Luther and the Drama*. For a more specific analysis of Luther's influence on contemporary theatrical representation, see Barbara Könneker, "Luthers Bedeutung für das protestantische Drama des 16. Jahrhunderts. Geschichte und Heilsgeschichte in Bartholomäus Krügers *Newer Action von dem Anfang und Ende der Welt*," *Daphnis* 12 (1983): 545–73; Schulze, 345–53.

[65] Parente, 26–7; 77 ff.

jre Feste vnd Sabbath geübt, vnd der jugent also mit lust, Gottes wort vnd werck eingebildet haben, sonderlich da sie jnn gutem friede vnd regiment gesessen sind, Denn sie haben gar treffliche leute gehabt, als Propheten, senger, tichter vnd der gleichen, die Gottes wort vleissig, vnd allerley weise getrieben haben, Vnd Gott gebe, das die Griechen jre weise, Comedien vnd Tragedien zu spielen, von den Jüden genomen haben, Wie auch viel ander Weisheit vnd Gottes dienst etc. Denn Judith gibt eine gute, ernste, dapffere Tragedien, So gibt Tobias ein feine liebliche, Gottselige Comedien.[66]

It may well be that they [the Jews] performed such poetic works, as some among us perform the passion, as well as other [factual] holy stories so that they might, as in a public image or play, teach their people and youth to trust in God, to be pious, and to place all hope in God for help and consolation in all trials and against all enemies. Thus it [Judith] is a fine, good, holy, and useful book for us Christians to read, for one should take the words that the people speak here as if a spiritual, holy poet or prophet spoke them inspired by the Holy Ghost. He portrays these people in his play and preaches to us through them. [. . .] What has been said of the Book of Judith can also be said of the Book of Tobit. If it's a factual story, then it's a fine and holy story. But if it's a fictional work, then it's truly a quite lovely, healing, useful fiction and play by an ingenious poet. One may assume that the Jews had many such poems and plays, by which they prepared for their feasts and Sabbaths and impressed God's words and deeds with enthusiasm upon their youth, especially when they were at peace and well-governed. For they had talented people such as prophets, singers, poets, and the like, who vigorously and in all ways practiced God's word. And it may be that the Greeks took their manner of performing comedies and tragedies from the Jews just as they took other wisdom and forms of worship. For Judith makes a good, earnest, valiant tragedy, just as Tobit makes a fine, sweet comedy blessed to God.

Throughout his comments, Luther focuses on the didactic utility of drama for the teaching of Scripture. Like Foxe, he directly equates playwrights to preachers. He goes farther, however, attributing the effectiveness of their "sermons" to their augmentation of spoken language. In performance, they present an image (*bilde*) that vividly impresses God's word and works (*wort vnd werck*) upon the mind of the audience.[67]

---

[66] Quoted according to the 1534 Apocrypha edition in WA, *Deutsche Bibel* 12:8, 108. See also *Susanna*, 83.
[67] Luther expressed himself similarly in an Easter sermon of 1533. See Schulze, 348–9.

Fifteen years earlier, in the *Sermon von der Betrachtung des heyligen leydens Christi*, Luther had discussed how the visual interaction between spectator and scenic image should occur, delineating a "theological gaze" not unlike that encouraged by Protestant works of art.[68] In the reformer's assessment, the affective aspects of Catholic dramaturgy encountered above produced passive spectators who merely took pity on Christ. To impart salvation, religious plays required active participants who shared in the creation of meaning and, ultimately, redemption. The following excerpt demonstrates the relationship between (im)proper spectatorship and (im)proper worship from Luther's perspective:

> Zcum dritten haben sie eyn mit leyden mit Christo, yhn zu clagen und zu beweynen alß eynen unschuldigen menschen, gleych wie die weyber, die Christo von Jerusalem nach folgeten, und von yhm gestrafft wurden, sie solten sich selb beweynen und yhre kinder. Der art seynd, die mitten yn der passion weyt auß reyßen und von dem abschied Christi zu Bethanien und von der Junckfrawen Marien schmertzen viel eyntragen und kummen auch nit weyter. Da kumpt es, das man die passion ßo vill stund vorzeugt, weyß gott, ab es mehr zum schlaffen ader zum wachen erdacht ist. Jn dieße rote gehörenn auch die, die erlernet, wie große fruchte die heylige meße habe, und yhrer eynfeltigkeyt nach achten sie es gnug, wie sie die messe hören, da hyn man uns furet durch etlicher lerer spruch, das die messe opere operati, non opere operantis, von yhr selber, auch an unßer vordienst und wirde angenhem sey, gerad als were das gnug, so doch die messe nit umb yhr selbs wirdickeyt, sondernn unß zuwirdigen ist eyn gesetzt, ßonderlich umb des leydens Christi willen zu bedencken. Dan wo das nit geschicht, ßo macht man auß der messe eyn leyplich, unfruchtbar werck, es sey an yhmselb wie gut es mag, dan was hilfft dichs, das gott got ist, wan er dier nit eyn got ist?[69]

> Thirdly, they take pity on Christ, lamenting and crying over him as an innocent man, just like the women who followed Christ from Jerusalem und were scolded by him that they should rather weep for themselves and their children. Of this type are those who break down

---

[68] On the term "theological gaze" for the Protestant "reading" of images, see Scribner, "Popular Piety," 464. See also Joseph Leo Koerner's discussion of Protestant *Merkbilder* in *The Moment of Self-Portraiture in German Renaissance Art* (Chicago/London: University of Chicago Press, 1993), 363–410. For an expanded discussion of Luther's opinions on the passion play and the necessity to evoke faith, not pity, in the viewer, see Könneker, "Greffs protestantisches Osterspiel," 313–6; Schulze, 346–9.

[69] Martin Luther, "Eyn Sermon von der Betrachtung des heyligen leydens Christi," in WA 2:136–7.

[?] in the middle of the passion, make much of Christ's ascension at Bethany and of the lamentations of the Virgin Mary, but make no further progress. Hence the hour-long performances of the passion; only God knows whether they're performed more for sleeping or for waking. In this group also belong those who have learned what great profit the holy Mass bears, and in their naiveté they consider it enough to have heard the Mass, as one would have us believe through the teachings of certain theologians that the Mass is an *opus operatum*, not an *opus operantis*, i.e. that it is valid on its own, independent of our own merit and worth, as if that were enough, since the Mass on the contrary was instituted not for its own worth, but rather to enworthy us, and in particular for the contemplation of the suffering of Christ. For if that does not occur, then one makes of the Mass an earthly, inefficacious work, and be it in its own right the best it can be. For of what use is it to you that God is God, if he is not a God for you?

Given that late medieval plays were considered conduits of grace, Luther's equation of Catholic theater and the Mass is not surprising. However, he musters additional rhetorical ammunition for his argument by invoking the debate on the effectiveness of the Mass when performed by an unworthy priest. The interpretation of the Mass as an *opus operatum* (work performed), as opposed to an *opus operantis* (work of the performer), emerged in response to certain abuses of the office, in which a celebrant might be unordained or even drunk. By declaring the Mass effective *ex opere operato*, theologians argued that the rite itself conferred grace regardless of the subjective disposition of the participants. For Luther, of course, salvation was impossible without the subjective experience of faith, and both the consecration of the host and the portrayal of Christ's passion were empty theatrical acts if they did not encourage participation, indeed, spiritual completion by the viewer.[70] Both the Mass and a stage play were ineffective without a believing audience.[71]

The *Sermon von der Betrachtung* thus further implies that the Protestant interaction between viewer and viewed must ultimately emanate from the spectator. A playwright or artist, as creators of images both living and static, could only facilitate the reformed act of viewing. The

---

[70] For Protestant opinions on the theatricality of the mass, see Crockett, 3–7.

[71] Beyond their theological applications, Luther's arguments suggest a modern sensibility for theatrical representation. As Erika Fischer-Lichte notes, theater without an audience is not theater. Erika Fischer-Lichte, *Semiotik des Theaters: eine Einführung* (Tübingen: Narr, 1983), 1:16.

following passage, found later in the *Sermon*, demonstrates the necessity of active participation by the viewer in obtaining salvation through faith:

> Magst dich aber da zu reitzen [...] nit das leyden Christi mehr an zusehen (dan das hatt nu seyn werck gethan und dich erschreckt), sundern durch hyn dringen und ansehen seyn fruntlich hertz, wie voller lieb das gegen dir ist, die yhn da zu zwingt, das er deyn gewissen und deyn sund ßo schwerlich tregt. Alßo wirt dir das hertz gegen yhm susße und die zuvorsicht des glaubens gestercket.[72]

> If you can rouse yourself [...] not to view Christ's suffering (since that has accomplished its purpose and frightened you), but rather to look further and behold his friendly heart, which is full of love for you and forces him to bear your conscience and your sins so ponderously, then your heart will grow fond of him and the confidence of your faith become strengthened.

In the specific context of the passion, Luther clearly acknowledges that Christ's suffering has an emotional impact on the viewer, namely fright. Throughout the *Sermon*, he repeatedly emphasizes the necessity of a quasi-existential despair (*Erschrecken*) in preparing one for faith: "They consider the passion of Christ properly who gaze upon him such that they are terrified in their hearts and their conscience immediately sinks to despair. [...] One must become well-rehearsed in this point, for the profit of Christ's suffering is wholly dependent thereon, that one come to the recognition of oneself and despair of oneself and break down."[73] Only through such despair, caused by the recognition of one's sins and the ultimate inability to attain salvation by human means, can one then open one's heart and take a metaphorical leap of faith.

These comments are generally consonant with Luther's interpretation of the relationship between the Law of the Old Testament, which humanity is incapable of fulfilling, and the Gospel of the New Testament, which offers redemption. His discussion nonetheless has

---

[72] "Eyn Sermon von der Betrachtung des heyligen leydens Christi," 140.

[73] "Die bedenckenn das leyden Christi recht, die yhn alßo ansehn, das sie hertzlich darfur erschrecken und yhr gewissen gleych sincket yn eyn vorzagen. [...] Yn dießem punct muß man sich gar wol ubenn, dan fast der nutz des leydens Christi gar daran gelegen ist, das der mensch zu seyns selb erkentniß kumme und fur yhm selbs erschrecke und zurschlagenn werde." "Eyn Sermon von der Betrachtung des heyligen leydens Christi," 137, 138.

direct theatrical implications. The *Sermon*'s metanoia-like *Erschrecken* bears remarkable resemblance to Aristotelian catharsis, but it is a fundamentally religious catharsis, not an affective one.[74] Pity must play no role, and the emotion of fear or despair is useful only to break down a spectator's confidence in worldly works, which are ineffectual in divine matters. The act of viewing itself remains largely intellectual. Luther would otherwise not have given detailed instructions on contemplating the passion, nor would he have emphasized the necessity of practice for achieving proper contemplation.

Luther's instructions on promoting faith through the contemplation of the passion should not imply that he endorsed, even with modifications, the continuation of German *Passionsspiele*. This is apparent in Luther's initial response to Greff's plan for dramatizing the passion. The *Passio* of Nuremberg playwright Hans Sachs, printed in 1558, appeared well after the reformer's death in 1546 and seems to have been the only Protestant adaptation of this tradition (as opposed to the Easter play tradition adapted by Greff) in central Germany.[75] Even when Reformation plays treated the same eschatological material as their Catholic predecessors, as was the case in Bartholomäus Krüger's *Newe Action von dem Anfang und Ende der Welt* (New Play Concerning the Beginning and End of the World; 1580),[76] Luther's expectations for a new type of interaction between audiences and representations of divine truth led to a fundamental shift in the plays' structure and rhetoric.[77] Whereas medieval passion plays celebrated Christ's resurrection as a transcendent mystery occurring outside the normal course of human activity, Protestant stage works consistently emphasized the historicity of the events they portrayed, whether these were New Testament parables or the polemic framing of papal history as the thousand-year rule of the Antichrist.

Luther's influence was not absolute, however. Swiss Protestant playwrights apparently enjoyed greater freedom in adapting Catholic theater, which survived with vigor in Lucerne and other Swiss can-

---

[74] Cf. Kleinschmidt, 215 ff.

[75] Hans Sachs, "Der gantz Passio," in *Das Admonter Passionsspiel*, ed. Karl Konrad Polheim (Paderborn: Schöningh, 1980), 3:279–430.

[76] Bartholomäus Krüger, "Eine schöne vnd lustige newe Action, Von dem Anfang vnd Ende der Welt," in *Schauspiele aus dem sechzehnten Jahrhundert*, ed. Julius Tittmann (Leipzig: Brockhaus, 1868), 2:1–120.

[77] Könneker, "Luthers Bedeutung," 572–3.

tons throughout the sixteenth century.[78] Jacob Rueff composed a passion play in 1545, while his Zurich colleague Jos Murer produced a resurrection play in 1566.[79] In Biel (Bienne), Jakob Funkelin wrote both a Christmas play (1553) and a resurrection play (1562).[80] Taken together, the works of Rueff, Murer, and Funkelin demonstrate that reformed Switzerland had a higher tolerance for plays reminiscent of Catholic practice than the Lutheran North, although they also were composed in accordance with Protestant stage aesthetics.

As Ulrich Zwingli died in 1531 before the development of Protestant biblical dramaturgy, it is unknown whether he might have explicitly lent his support to the dramatization of Scripture. His comments on the education of youths suggest that he did not censure annual dramatic performances, although the exact nature of the plays in question is obscure.[81] We do know, however, that Zwingli thought enough of humanist dramaturgy to compose choral music for the performance of Aristophanes's *Ploutos* ("Wealth") in Zurich on New Year's Day of 1531.[82] Other Swiss reformers show clear support for humanist theater and were at times dramatists themselves. Heinrich Bullinger, Zwingli's successor in Zurich, composed a *Lucretia* drama in 1526.[83]

---

[78] See Evans, *The Passion Play of Lucerne*, as well as Oskar Eberle, *Theatergeschichte der inneren Schweiz: Das Theater in Luzern, Uri, Schwyz, Unterwalden und Zug im Mittelalter und zur Zeit des Barock 1200–1800*, Königsberger deutsche Forschungen 5 (Königsberg: Gräfe und Unzer, 1929).

[79] *Das Züricher Passionsspiel: Jacob Rueff, Das lyden vnsers Herren Jesu Christi das man nempt den Passion*, ed. Barbara Thoran (Bochum: Studienverlag Dr. N. Brockmeyer, 1984); Murer, "Ufferstäntnus," in *Sämtliche Dramen*, 1:457–534. See also Emil Ermatinger, *Dichtung und Geistesleben der deutschen Schweiz* (Munich: Beck, 1933), 178; Michael, 156–8, 166–8.

[80] Jacob Funckelin, *Ein Geistlich Spyl von der Empfengknuss vnd Geburt Jesu Christi* (Zurich: Froschauer, 1553); [Funkelin], "A Swiss Resurrection Play of the Sixteenth Century," ed. Newton Stephen Arnold (Ph.D. diss., Columbia University, 1949). Michael, 177–9.

[81] "Nit bin ich daran, das man dem jüngling verbüte zimliche fröud, als da ein volck, wyb und man, gemeynlich gewon ist, zuosamen ze kummen: als da sind hochzyt der verwandten, järliche spil, kurtzwyl und fäst; dann ich sich, das ouch Christus die hochzyt nit verachtet hat." *Spil* had a large semantic field in Early New High German; Zwingli may have possibly referred to annual competitions here, such as the popular Swiss marksmanship contests. "Wie man die Jugend in guten Sitten und christlicher Zucht erziehen und lehren soll," in *ZW*, 5:443.

[82] Garside, 71–3; Markus Jenny, "Die Lieder Zwinglis," *Jahrbuch für Liturgik und Hymnologie* 14 (1969): 73–5. *Ploutos* is frequently referred to by its Latinized title, *Plutus*.

[83] "Heinrich Bullingers 'Lucretia,'" in *Lucretia-Dramen*, ed. Horst Hartmann (Leipzig: VEB Bibliographisches Institut, 1973), 39–97.

While it treats a classical rather than a biblical motif, and while Bullinger dismissed it as a youthful experiment when it was published without his knowledge in 1533, it addresses contemporary confessional politics by focusing on the installation of reformed government following political insurrection, indicating that Bullinger recognized the utility of the stage in addressing current political and religious concerns of the community.[84] Even Calvin, the least theater-friendly reformer of all, sanctioned the performance of a play of the acts of the apostles,[85] and his successor Théodore de Bèze wrote *Abraham Sacrifiant* in 1550 while professor of Greek at the Lausanne Academy.[86]

Of all continental reformers, Martin Bucer perhaps best represents the general consensus among Protestant theologians on the utility of "honest plays" in fostering faith. Bucer was the leading reformer of Strasbourg and, for roughly two years prior to his death on 28 February 1551, Regius Professor of Divinity at the University of Cambridge. As theologian, he possessed a unique combination of Lutheran and Erasmian learning coupled with a basic pragmatism, which often enabled him to bridge doctrinal differences between Lutherans, Zwinglians, and Calvinists. He became an early practitioner of shuttle diplomacy, travelling widely between Switzerland, Southern Germany, and Saxony in his efforts to reach concord among the various Protestant camps. His treatise *De Regno Christi*, presented to King Edward VI in 1550, outlines Bucer's vision for the ideal Christian state and represents the culmination of his religious and political thought. The work's fifty-fourth chapter, entitled

---

[84] See Hans Stricker, *Die Selbstdarstellung der Schweizers im Drama des 16. Jahrhunderts*, Sprache und Dichtung, Neue Folge 7 (Bern: Paul Haupt, 1961), 128–31; Peter Ukena, "Flugschriften und verwandte Medien im Kommunikationsprozeß zwischen Reformation und Frühaufklärung," in *Flugschriften als Massenmedium der Reformationszeit*, ed. Hans-Joachim Köhler, Spätmittelalter und Frühe Neuzeit 13 (Stuttgart: Klett-Cotta, 1981), 163–6; Kleinschmidt, 213.

[85] Marguerite Soulié, "Le théâtre et la Bible au XVIe siècle," in *Le temps des Réformes et la Bible*, vol. 5 of *Bible de tous les temps*, ed. Guy Bedouelle and Bernard Roussel (Paris: Éditions Beauchesne, 1989), 649; Heinemann, 26, note 19.

[86] Théodore de Bèze, *Abraham Sacrifiant*, ed. Keith Cameron, Kathleen M. Hall, and Francis Higman (Geneva: Droz, 1967). For a facsimile edition, see *Abraham Sacrifiant*, ed. C.R. Frankish (New York: Johnson Reprint, 1969). On the play, see Béatrice Perregaux, "Théodore de Bèze, *Abraham sacrifiant* 1550: Rupture et innovation," in *Sondierungen zum Theater—Enquêtes sur le théâtre*, ed. Andreas Kotte, Theatrum Helveticum 1 (Basel: Editions Theaterkultur Verlag, 1995), 13–49; J.S. Street, *French Sacred Drama from Bèze to Corneille* (Cambridge: Cambridge University Press, 1983), 21–9.

De honestis ludis (On Honest Diversions), sets forth a complete Christian entertainment and recreation program, including singing, dancing, play acting, wrestling, gymnastics, hunting (for the nobility), and equestrian sports, all conducted in a decorous and pious manner. Approximately half of the chapter is given over to a discussion of Christian comedies and tragedies, which in Bucer's assessment teach religion by compensating for human nature's "weakness by which it cannot always concentrate on grave and serious matters."[87] Like Luther, Bucer took pains to guard against a type of theater that would be overly affective, which necessitated the subordination of poetic autonomy to didacticism:

> Adhibendae autem sunt in utroque genere poematum, comico et tragico, ut, cum hominum uitia et peccata describuntur et actione quasi oculis conspicienda exhibentur, id fiat ea ratione, ut, quamuis perditorum hominum referantur scelera, tamen terror quidam in his diuini iudicii et horror appareat peccati, non exprimatur exultans in scelere oblectatio atque confidens audacia. Praestat hic detrahere aliquid decoro poetico, quam curae aedificandi pietate spectatores, quae poscit, ut in omni peccati repraesentatione sentiatur conscientiae propriae condemnatio et a iudicio Dei horrenda trepidatio.[88]

> It must be observed, however, that when in both kinds of poetic material, comic and tragic, the activities and sins of men are described and actively presented to be seen with the eyes, it should be done in such a way that although the crimes of reprobate men are related, yet a certain terror of divine judgment and horror of sin should appear in these things, and a shameless daring and an exultant delight in crimes should not be expressed. It is better here to take something away from poetic fitness rather than from the concern for edifying the piety of the spectators, which demands that in every representation of sin there be felt the condemnation of one's conscience and the horrible fear of God's judgment.[89]

---

[87] Martin Bucer, "De Regno Christi," in *Melanchthon and Bucer*, ed. and trans. Wilhelm Pauck, Library of Christian Classics 19 (Philadelphia: Westminster, 1969), 346.

[88] Martin Bucer, *De Regno Christi*, ed. François Wendel, vol. 15 of *Martini Buceri Opera Latina* (Paris: Presses Universitaires de France; Gütersloh: Bertelsmann, 1955), 257.

[89] "De Regno Christi," trans. Pauck, 351. An abridged English translation of the section of "De Regno Christi" dealing with plays can be found in Glynne Wickham, *Early English Stages, 1300–1660* (London: Routledge and Kegan Paul, 1963), 2,1:329–31.

While Bucer does not specifically treat the contemplation of Christ's passion as Luther does in the *Sermon von der Betrachtung*, he is equally concerned that the viewing of biblical events promote the recognition of sin and a fear (≈ *Erschrecken*) of divine judgment rather than (merely) an aesthetic experience in the viewer. His proposed plays function by engaging the audience's conscience, guiding it to proper faith by their presentation of positive and negative Christian characters.

It is no accident that Luther's and Bucer's theater shares common goals with sixteenth-century Protestant homiletics. Bryan Crockett has recently devoted a whole monograph to the related rhetoric of English Reformation sermons and Renaissance stage plays, noting for example similarities between Bucer's proposal for a round amphitheatrical church and the "wooden O" of Shakespeare's Globe Theater.[90] The conviction of Nopus, Major and others that stage plays were akin to sermons, even surpassing them in terms of effectiveness due to their ability to engage an audience visually, appears to have universally shared by German Protestant playwrights.[91] Paul Rebhun, in his preface to Thomas Naogeorgus's *Pammachius* of 1538, recommends performing the play "for the simple layman and youth as visual instruction, which is more effective with them than oral efforts."[92] Sixtus Birck, playwright in both Klein-Basel and Augsburg, humorously summarizes the matter in his preface to *Beel* of 1539:

> Man sieht dich in der Kirchen nitt
> verachten das ist nur dein sitt
> Der Pfarrer schreyt sich haiser gar
> der leer nimbstu gar wenig war
> Du sprichst ich kan es nit verston

---

[90] Crockett, 1–6.

[91] The belief in plays' ability to surpass sermons was not limited to Protestant reformers. See Carla van Dauven-Knippenberg, "Ein Anfang ohne Ende: Einführendes zur Frage nach dem Verhältnis zwischen Predigt und geistlichem Schauspiel des Mittelalters," in *Mittelalterliches Schauspiel: Festschrift für Hansjürgen Linke zum 65. Geburtstag*, ed. Ulrich Mehler and Anton H. Touber, Amsterdamer Beiträge zur älteren Germanistik 38/39 (Amsterdam: Rodopi, 1994), 143–160; idem, "Wege der Christenlehre. Über den Zusammenhang zweier mittelalterlicher Gattungen," *ZfdPh* 113 (1994): 370–84.

[92] "Dem einfeltigem Leyen und Jugent zu sichtigem unterricht (welcher mehr bey ihnen thut den sunst der mündliche)." Thomas Naogeorg, "Tragoedia Nova Pammachius," in *Sämtliche Werke*, ed. Hans-Gert Roloff (Berlin/New York: de Gruyter, 1975), 1:459. See also Ukena, 167.

> was soll ich in der Kirchen thon
> Dieweil du dann bist also toll
> das du den handel nit fast wol
> Verfassen kannst/was doch diß sey
> das man nennet Abgötterey
> So wend wir dir das zaigen an
> das duß muost freylich wol verstan
> Mit deinen augen muostus sehen
> ja greyffen/mercken/gantz erspehen[93]

> One never sees you in church. Disdain is your only custom. The pastor yells himself hoarse, but you take little note of the lesson. You say, "I can't understand a thing; why should I be in church?" Since you're so mad that you can't comprehend what it is that one calls idolatry, we will present it to you in such a manner that you will understand. You must see it with your eyes; indeed, grasp, take note of, and regard it completely.

Above all, the concern for presenting Scripture in the most effective manner possible was not merely an academic issue for sixteenth-century theologians and playwrights. Preaching and playing were quite literally a matter of saving souls. In those instances where the performance of religious plays generated controversy among German Protestants, it did not stem from an inherent antitheatricalism, but rather from the concern that the dramatization of Christ's passion or resurrection might be an unconsidered continuation of Catholic tradition. When this concern was allayed, reformers such as Luther and Bucer were strongly pro-theater and actively endorsed religious drama as a means of spreading the new faith. The 1530s and -40s thus saw an upsurge in play production in those central European cities that embraced religious reform.

Enacting Community

Despite their cultivation of a new aesthetic, Protestant plays remained largely identical to their Catholic predecessors in terms of their social and political functions. Town inhabitants welcomed performances as festive occasions, a colorful caesura in the civic calendar when all

---

[93] Sixt Birck, "Beel," in *Sämtliche Dramen*, ed. Manfred Brauneck (Berlin: de Gruyter, 1969), 1:168–9.

classes convened to partake of a common experience.[94] Not all Protestant plays took the form of large public events, of course. Some were performed in schools, although these might also attract a larger audience, such as in Strasbourg.[95] Nonetheless, just as many towns regularly sponsored passion plays throughout the latter Middle Ages, reformed city governments in Bern and elsewhere staged elaborate productions in an ostentatious display of Protestant prosperity, with no expense spared for costumes, scenery, and the regalement of out-of-town guests.[96] Inwardly and outwardly, civic plays were symbols of the populace that performed them and served a variety of functions beyond their status as literary products. Indeed, as has been noted for the recent community theater movement,[97] the process of putting on a play in the sixteenth century was often just as significant as the resulting product, if not more so.

To explain the attraction of theater for urban communities of the period, recent research has drawn on cultural anthropology, analyzing performances as rituals through which a community defined itself and acted out certain conflicts. Indeed, plays constructed community along varying lines according to sponsors and audience.[98] When actors and spectators constituted a small, homogeneous group interested in maintaining a distinct identity, religious drama often reinforced social divisions, emphasizing kinship among those in attendance while excluding outsiders. For the large and complex audiences of English cycle plays, on the other hand, performances projected unity in diversity or, conversely, diversity in unity. Here, active participation by local guilds ensured that various economic and social

---

[94] Heinz Kindermann, *Das Theaterpublikum des Mittelalters* (Salzburg: Otto Müller, 1980), 43; Pfrunder, 150.

[95] James A. Parente, Jr., "Tragoedia Politica: Strasbourg School Drama and the Early Modern State, 1583–1621," *Colloquia Germanica* 29 (1996): 1–11.

[96] Kleinschmidt, 191–2, 199–200. See also C. Clifford Flanigan's discussion of the Künzelsau Corpus Christi play: C. Clifford Flanigan, "Liminality, Carnival, and Social Structure: The Case of Late Medieval Biblical Drama," in *Victor Turner and the Construction of Cultural Criticism. Between Literature and Anthropology*, ed. Kathleen Ashley (Bloomington: Indiana University Press, 1990), 51.

[97] Peter Reynolds, "Community Theatre: Carnival or Camp?" in *The Politics of Theatre and Drama*, ed. Graham Holderness (Houndmills/London: Macmillan, 1992), 89. On community theater in general, see Ann Jellicoe, *Community Plays: How to Put Them On* (London/New York: Methuen, 1987).

[98] On the following, see Kathleen M. Ashley, "Cultural Approaches to Medieval Drama," in *Approaches to Teaching Medieval English Drama*, 57–66.

interests were represented during a performance, while the playful portral of comic or unorthodox characters often laid bare the hierarchies and structures underlying civic life, challenging an audience to reexamine the ties that held their community together. Indeed, the willingness to contemplate alternative social norms and structures, even if ultimately to return to the status quo, is now considered a constitutive aspect of urban festivity and performance in general. Cultural anthropologists have referred to this festive mode of experimentation outside the course of quotidian affairs as reflexivity or subjunctivity, attributing a fundamental "what if" character to any type of human play.[99] Early theatrical performances thus extended a mirror to their audience, with the reflection tempered alternately by didacticism or satire. This bivalence is perhaps best summed up by Victor Turner: "As a 'model for' ritual can anticipate, even generate change; as a 'model of,' it may inscribe order in the minds, hearts, and wills of participants."[100]

Turner's theories of social drama have become an oft-cited touchstone for studies of English Renaissance drama.[101] Nonetheless, others have noted the limits of Turner's model of breach and schism for early European society.[102] Above all, Peter Pfrunder's exclusively Turnerian interpretation of Manuel's two carnival plays of 1523, while offering valuable cultural insights, does not acknowledge the multiplicity of social, economic, and religious concerns among Bernese playgoers.[103] By treating the performances of 1523 as council-sponsored communal efforts to enact reform, Pfrunder conflates the often competing interests of author, actors, audience, and the local authorities.[104] Not until 1528, when Protestant government was installed in Bern,

---

[99] Don Handelman, "Reflexivity in Festival and Other Cultural Events," in *Essays in the Sociology of Perception*, ed. Mary Douglas (London: Routledge & Kegan Paul, 1982), 162–90; Victor Turner, *From Ritual to Theatre. The Human Seriousness of Play* (New York: Performing Arts Journal, 1982), 82–84.

[100] Turner, *From Ritual to Theatre*, 82.

[101] Crockett, 32–5; Diehl, 1, note 1; Flanigan, passim. On Turner's theory of "social drama," see Turner, *Dramas, Fields, and Metaphors. Symbolic Action in Human Society* (Ithaca: Cornell, 1974), 23–59; idem, *From Ritual to Theatre*, 61–88.

[102] Robert L.A. Clark, "Community versus Subject in Late Medieval French Confraternity Drama and Ritual," in *Drama and Community*, 34–56; Caroline Walker Bynum, "Women's Stories, Women's Symbols: A Critique of Victor Turner's Theory of Liminality," in *Fragmentation and Redemption. Essays on Gender and the Human Body in Medieval Religion* (New York: Zone Books, 1992), 28 ff.; Flanigan, 52.

[103] See the critique of Pfrunder in Greco-Kaufmann, 113–4. Cf. Pfrunder, 249–60.

[104] Pfrunder clearly recognizes that the plays function "im Interesse einer Partei"

did the local stage begin to function as a direct or indirect forum for council policy. This makes Manuel's documented success in agitating for the new faith all the more remarkable, as his plays faced the formidable task of building consensus for religious change from a minority position. They could not shape majority opinion without addressing a variety of interpretational horizons that varied according to class, gender, political allegiance, and confessional sympathies. After 1528, the large-scale productions of Rüte's plays faced a similar task, addressing a broad spectrum of newly converted Protestants, but also Catholic and crypto-Catholic spectators from neighboring cantons as well as from conservative rural regions under Bernese jurisdiction. To create religious consensus, the plays constructed social and political commonalities among audience members more frequently than they engaged in divisive polemics.

The following section seeks to understand the mechanisms of sixteenth-century civic theater that allowed Manuel's and Rüte's plays to operate as overarching cultural vehicles capable of uniting a large cross-section of the community, even initially against the views of local authorities. By adapting long-standing stage traditions, Bernese Reformation drama united actors and audience in a community of performance encompassing both the political community of the sponsoring town and the community of believers as posited by Protestant reformers.[105] Above all, by embracing religious plays in a post-reform context, councils and consistories alike fostered a collective experience of faith and fealty towards molding a theologically unified polity. In general, civic plays built community through two principal means: 1) participation or sponsorship by prominent civic institutions, often town councils themselves or the local school, and 2) the fostering of a sense of common identity (*Identitätsstiftung*) among audience and participants.

Both mechanisms were already constitutive elements in the European tradition of public theater. In the course of the later Middle Ages, the responsibility for staging religious drama gradually passed from ecclesiastical to secular institutions. Trade guilds and confraternities

---

(p. 259), but his analysis unquestioningly identifies Manuel as a member of the political elite. See Chapter Three.

[105] On the essential unity of church congregation and civic community in the Zwinglian Reformation, see Gottfried W. Locher, *Die Zwinglische Reformation im Rahmen der europäischen Kirchengeschichte* (Göttingen/Zurich: Vandenhoeck & Ruprecht, 1979), 615–20.

frequently sought out the privilege of performing plays for the greater honor of their organizations.[106] Even a single annual public performance could generate elaborate preparations requiring substantial commitments of time and money, as documented by the records of the Merchants' Company (*Kaufleutekompanie*) the Confraternity of the Circle (*Zirkelbrüder*), and the Greverade Company (*Greveradenkompanie*) in Lübeck, which vied to produce the most elaborate carnival entertainment for local spectators.[107] In Corpus Christi plays, specific guilds often assumed responsibility for a particular section or scene that bore some significance for their trade; blacksmiths for example frequently portrayed Christ in chains before Pilate.[108] Actors were often expected to furnish costumes at their own expense, but municipal governments customarily shouldered the more costly burden of constructing scenery and scaffolds for actors and audience.[109]

Following the Reformation, Protestant town councils took a more active role in sponsoring religious theater, so that confraternities and trade guilds receded as play sponsors. They were replaced on occasion by municipal schools or Meistersinger guilds, whose performances nonetheless required the approval of local authorities.[110] In most instances, town councils assumed direct or indirect control over theatrical activity within their cities. The supervision of local performances, which at times encompassed the authoring of new plays,

---

[106] On the sponsors and actors of late medieval religious drama in Germany, see Linke, 748–9. On the larger European context, see Lynette Muir, "European Communities and Medieval Drama," in *Drama and Community*, 1–17.

[107] See Eckehard Simon, "Das Schauspiel der Lübecker Fastnacht," *ZfdPh* 116 (1997; Sonderheft), 208–223; Simon, "Organizing and Staging Carnival Plays in Late Medieval Lübeck: A New Look at the Archival Record," *JEGP* 92 (1993): 57–72.

[108] See Mezger, 228. The sparse play records in Bern before 1523 provide at least one instance of a local guild performance, in this case by the Weavers, though the source does not indicate whether the play was religious or secular in nature. See Neumann, 1:127, no. 56.

[109] Linke, 749. In 1550, Jacob Rueff specifically thanked the Zurich council for its *gross kosten* in constructing *die brüge* [stage] *und anders g'büw*: *Jacob Ruffs Adam und Heva*, ed. Hermann Marcus Kottinger, Bibliothek der deutschen National-Literatur 26 (Quedlinburg/Leipzig: Gottfried Basse, 1848), 189, vv. 6371–4. On this and other expenditures for Rueff's plays, see Robert Wildhaber, *Jakob Ruf. Ein Zürcher Dramatiker des 16. Jahrhunderts* (St. Gall: Gebr. Wildhaber, 1929), 125–6.

[110] Even the plays of Hans Sachs had to pass muster with the Nuremberg town council, which in 1551 forbade the performance of *Der Abt im Wildbad*. See also Kleinschmidt, 201–11. This is not to say that the performances of late medieval confraternities did not also occur under the watchful eye of local government: Simon, "Carnival Plays in Late Medieval Lübeck," 64.

customarily fell to a local schoolmaster, city secretary, or other educated municipal official. Actors were recruited among school pupils or from the sons of prominent families.

The Reformation plays of Bern are typical in this regard. During their periods as playwrights, both Manuel and Rüte were members of Bern's Great Council. Although this body was not the city's highest governing institution—that privilege belonged to the Small Council with its 27 members—election to the Great Council nonetheless required ownership of a house in the city, so that its members represented a broad cross-section of the city's social and financial elite. As representatives of this group, the views expressed by Rüte and Manuel in their works automatically gained credibility for a local audience. Furthermore, Rüte became *Gerichtschreiber* (court secretary) in the spring of 1531 soon after the performance of his first play and remained in this position, with a brief interruption, for the duration of his career as city playwright. He was thus directly involved in city administration and jurisdiction. Manuel did not enter city administration until after the performance of his plays, however. As we shall see later in more detail, the stage afforded him a middle position between citizenry and civic authority.[111] The circumstances of Rüte's administrative post place him much closer to that authority, although he did not directly wield it.

The actors of Manuel's and Rüte's plays were similarly linked to the local elite. In all instances, they were "sons of burghers," i.e. members of families with local citizenship.[112] Unlike in Lübeck or Lucerne,[113] Bernese performers were usually not directly affiliated with a particular confraternity or guild, although the Blacksmith Society, of which Rüte was a member, staged the author's *Osterspiel* in 1552.[114] Nor should the frequent reference in local documents to

---

[111] "Vielmehr erscheint er [Manuel] in einer ambivalenten Position zwischen 'Volk' und Obrigkeit," as Pfrunder states in affirming the results of Conrad-André Beerli's study. Pfrunder, 44–5.

[112] As was customary for medieval and early modern theater, men played women's roles as well. On exceptions to this practice, see Barbara Thoran, "Frauenrolle und Rolle der Frauen in der Geschichte der deutschsprachigen Passionsspiele," in *"Hört, sehet, weint und liebt." Passionsspiele im alpenländischen Raum*, ed. Michael Henker, Eberhard Dünninger, and Evamaria Brockhoff, Veröffentlichungen zur Bayerischen Geschichte und Kultur 20/90 (Munich: Süddeutscher Verlag, 1990), 113–9; John Tailby, "Drama and Community in South Tyrol," in *Drama and Community*, 151–2.

[113] Simon, "Carnival Plays in Late Medieval Lübeck," 59 ff.; Renward Brandstetter, *Die Regenz bei den Luzerner Osterspielen* (Lucerne: Gebrüder Räber, 1886).

[114] "Den 24ten April spielten die zum Schmieden das 4te und 5te Kapitel der

gsellen lead to the mistaken assumption, as it has for Nuremberg, that journeymen were primarily responsible for the plays' production.[115] The term instead refers to the young age of the performers.[116] While citizenship could be purchased for an apparently nominal fee and was open, from 1490 on, to anyone who belonged to a *Gesellschaft*,[117] the playwrights would have likely recruited their players from among the sons of fellow councilors. Participation in a production, as common elsewhere,[118] was thus most likely a privilege of the social elite. As has been suggested, the actors may have belonged to the *Äußerer Stand*, an organization of young prominent citizens,[119] but its participation in public festivals is documented only for the seventeenth and eighteenth centuries.[120]

The plays were further linked to civic authority through the location of their stage. Records indicate that the carnival plays of 1514, 1515, and 1523 took place on the *Kreuzgasse* (Cross Lane). Although there is no mention of location for *Elsli Tragdenknaben* and Rüte's plays, it has been suggested that Cross Lane was by this time the customary stage site, eliminating the need for specific identification.[121] This street lay at the center of the city, connecting the town hall

---

Offenbarung Johannis zu Barfußen, zu Ehren dem Schultheiß Nägeli, auch Venner Zülli, und Jkr. Beat Ludw. von Mülinen, so neulich erwählt waren." *Chronik aus den hinterlassenen Handschriften des Joh. Haller und Abraham Müslin von 1550 bis 1580*, ed. Samuel Gränicher (Zofingen: D. Sutermeister, 1829), 10. See also Fluri, 138–9.

[115] Fluri's documentation refers to *gesellen, gemeine spilß gesellen, spilknaben, spilgnossen*, and *spillüt*. Fluri, 134–46. On the mistaken interpretation of this term in Nuremberg records, see Thomas Cramer, *Geschichte der deutschen Literatur im späten Mittelalter* (Munich: Deutscher Taschenbuchverlag, 1990), 343.

[116] Klaus Stephan Jaeger, "Hans von Rütes Osterspiel. Edition und Untersuchung" (M.A. Thesis, Freie Universität Berlin, 1993), 32. See also Kleinschmidt, 187.

[117] Franz Bächtiger, "Bern zur Zeit von Niklaus Manuel," in *NMD*, 2.

[118] Council members of Fribourg, Solothurn, Lucerne and Lübeck performed in plays: Johannes Wagner, *Solothurner St. Mauritius- und St. Ursenspiel*, ed. Heinrich Biermann, Schweizer Texte 5 (Bern: Paul Haupt, 1980), 251; Eberle, 35; Simon, "Carnival Plays in Late Medieval Lübeck," 59; Kleinschmidt, 187.

[119] Cf. Jaeger, "Osterspiel," 32.

[120] See Richard Wolfram, *Studien zur älteren Schweizer Volkskultur. Mythos, Sozialordnung, Brauchbewußtsein*, Österreichische Akademie der Wissenschaften, Philosophisch-historische Klasse 362 (Vienna: Verlag der österreichischen Akademie der Wissenschaften, 1980), 167–228; Basilius Hidber, "Der ehemalige sog. äußere Stand der Stadt und Republik Bern," *Neujahrsblatt für die bernische Jugend 1858* (Bern: Huber und Comp., 1858), 3–34.

[121] Jaeger, 34. Rüte's *Osterspiel* was performed in the former Franciscan monastery of the city, which housed both the city Latin school and the *Hohe Schule* after the Reformation and was most likely the location for student performances as well. The *Kreuzgasse*, however, remained the site for the large civic dramas which drew the largest audience. For the locations of other Bernese performances, see Fluri, 148.

with the cathedral and bisecting the main street into two halves. Most importantly, court was held in this intersection, during which the mayor pronounced sentence while seated upon the Throne of Judgment (*Gerichtsstuhl*), flanked by the court secretary on one hand and the sergeant of arms on the other. The association of the site with the city's legal administration doubtless added a note of earnestness to the plays performed there, whether they were carnivalesque or biblical.[122]

Yet despite their ties to local authority, Bernese performances were so elaborate that their preparation required the active assistance of a substantial percentage of the city's approximately 5,000 residents. With extras, a cast might number well over one hundred: Rüte's *Goliath* for example required actors for 56 speaking parts, plus two large contingents to portray the Philistine and Israeli camps.[123] Scholars have frequently lamented the plays' tendency to include even the most minor characters from their sources, but local youths likely clamored for the chance to appear on stage, forcing the director to accommodate as many as possible.[124] Bernese players were also reimbursed for their efforts by the civic authorities. Indeed, no record of several plays would exist if the council had not recorded its expenditures in its treasury books (*Seckelmeisterrechnungen*). The council further loaned out costumes and props from the spoils of the Burgundian Wars or the possessions of secularized monasteries.[125]

Moreover, large-scale productions attracted great crowds and held the promise of additional income for several segments of the community. Innkeepers and merchants benefitted from the influx of outside guests, who for Rüte's plays would have had to seek lodging for at least one night to take in the two-day performances. Carpenters were required to build both seating and a *brügi* (stage/podium), and bailiffs were given extra pay as well as new deputies to keep order among the visiting spectators.[126] It is impossible to say precisely how

---

[122] For a description of the broader connotations of the location, see Pfrunder, 162.
[123] Fluri suggests that the opposing camps were portrayed by guild members: Fluri, 149.
[124] For Lucerne, Evans records that "many more wished to take part than could be accommodated." Evans, 112.
[125] Fluri, 149.
[126] Compare the security measures required for the Lucerne Passion Play or for a procession on the feast of St. John in Dresden: Evans, 106–9; Neumann, 1:281, no. 1234.

many visitors the plays attracted, but news of Bernese performances must have travelled wide, crossing confessional boundaries in the process. Hans Salat, who had been court secretary and playwright in Lucerne from 1531 to 1540, recorded the performance of Rüte's *Noe* in 1546 after having moved to neighboring Catholic Fribourg.[127] Similarly, in 1549 the report of Milan envoy Angelo Rizio noted that many Swiss Protestants travelled to Lucerne to see the performance of a Last Judgment play under the direction of Zacharias Bletz.[128] At least two Bernese musicians helped out with the Lucerne Passion Play of 1571, and in 1597 Renward Cysat remarked on the presence of *vnCatholischen* during performances.[129]

Most importantly, the plays crossed social boundaries, attracting peasants from the countryside as well as residents of nearby smaller towns. Bernese plays had not always portrayed rustics in the most flattering light, as indicated by the grievances lodged by rebellious peasants during the Köniz uprising of 1513, in which they complained to Bernese authorities of the ridicule suffered by their estate during the carnival celebration of the preceding spring.[130] However, the valorization of the "common man" by Protestant reformers led Manuel to portray them extremely positively. Similarly, Rüte's *Joseph* and *Goliath* assured their audience that no one would take umbrage at the play's content, although these remarks could also have referred to Catholic spectators.[131] Even though the performances lay in the hands of the political elite, the absence of social polemics was a crucial component in the plays' efforts to construct the broadest religious community possible.

The artlessness of local play texts is the final indication that participation took precedence over poetics in Bernese play productions.[132]

---

[127] "Suntag letare hands z'Bern gspilt." "Salats Tagebuch," in *Hans Salat: Ein schweizerischer Chronist und Dichter aus der ersten Hälfte des XVI. Jahrhunderts. Sein Leben und seine Schriften*, ed. Jacob Baechtold (Basel: Bahnmaiers Verlag, 1876), 66.

[128] On Rizio, see Greco-Kaufmann, 263–4. Rizio's original report is reproduced in Leonhard Haas, "Über geistliche Spiele in der Innerschweiz," *ZJSK* 47 (1953): 118–20; Haas's German translation of the letter can be found in Neumann, 1:486–90, no. 2099.

[129] Evans, 110–11, 230.

[130] "[. . .] dass purengspöt und äschensäk an vergangner fasnacht ze vil verachtlich wider si gebrucht. Verachtung und spot vergessen kum on vergelten." Anshelm, 3:446.

[131] "Zum andern/Bringen wir nit sachen / Dardurch yemand werd gschmützt old gschmächt / Dasselb vns wenig willens brächt": *Goliath*, vv. 18–20. "Hie wirt niemans in sonders brürt": *Joseph*, v. 21.

Rüte's works are admittedly more modest in this regard than those by Manuel, whose lively language and caustic satire have lost little of their bite even today. Yet not even an unabashed Manuel promoter such as Derek van Abbé would have claimed a timeless universality for the author's plays,[133] which were clearly intended for local consumption only, either published after their performance, as with the two 1523 plays, or circulating in manuscript, as was the case with *Der Ablaßkrämer*.[134] Both Manuel and Rüte created their works for the requirements of a living audience, not for the aesthetic tastes of elite and remote readers. To indulge in a modern comparison, Bern's Reformation plays were not unlike contemporary church Christmas pageants, only on a much larger scale. Weeks of rehearsal precede these events, during which parents discuss costumes and roles, while the "youth"—the audience commended by reformers for all sixteenth-century Protestant plays—learn Scripture through the memorization of dialogue. On the date of performance, the congregation watches as its children reenact biblical events, most often followed by a reception in which all participants come together for socialization. The purpose of such an undertaking is not the production of high art, but the reaffirmation of group identity and vitality, especially that of the coming generation.

Nonetheless, despite the collaborative nature of civic theater, it remains crucial not to view the plays solely as a group effort. Their content was at all times selected, defined, and interpreted for the

---

[132] "Die Bevorzugung glanzvoller Aufführungen betont den funktionalen Charakter des Theaterspiels für die Stadtgesellschaft im Sinne einer Rechtfertigung von Anlaß und Aufwand. Was inhaltlich gespielt wurde, war dabei allem Anschein nach eher gleichgültig. Diesem Sachverhalt muß die literaturgeschichtliche Bewertung der städtischen Spielkultur im 16. und 17. Jahrhundert Rechnung tragen, um das wenig anspruchsvolle Erscheinungsbild der Texte selbst zu verstehen und angemessen bewerten zu können." Kleinschmidt, 195.

[133] Derek van Abbé, "Change and Tradition in the Work of Niklaus Manuel of Berne," *Modern Language Review* 47 (1952): 181–98; idem, "Niklaus Manuel of Bern and His Interest in the Reformation," *Journal of Modern History* 24 (1952): 287–300; idem, *Drama in Renaissance Germany and Switzerland* (Melbourne: Melbourne University Press, 1961).

[134] Zwingli himself borrowed a copy of *Der Ablaßkrämer* together with other writings, as a letter by Manuel to the reformer indicates: "Wußend Daß ich ein badenfartt hab mitt guotwilliger cristenlicher gesellschafft, [...] darumm Jch gernn wett by mir habenn Etliche schimpfschriften Jn rymen verfaßt/So ich vch vor/ettlichr zyt vber anttwurt vnnd zuo Besechen gebenn hab/namlich/ein gougler vomm aplaß sprechend Ein aplaß kremmer/ein troumm/fier man vnd fier wyb/in einer zech/ein kor gericht." *Werke und Briefe*, 730, no. XXXVI.

community by their creators, whether those were Manuel, Rüte, or their supporters. Moreover, the plays might at times manipulate local political power, but they did not wield it. As will become apparent in Chapter Two, the final institution of religious reform came from above, not below.

CHAPTER TWO

BERN AT THE CROSSROADS OF REFORM

> What, o citizens of Bern, would be in any way more fortunate, what more proper, and what more decorous among mortals of any era, than, lest you pass through life silently, to leave behind in some manner after your passing the fame of your name and your illustrious deeds as a noble monument of a life lived to the fullest (by which you would be more like the immortal gods)? It seems to me more proper for you, to whom men of strong body are given abundantly enough, to seek earnestly the glory of the mind and the fine arts and, since this life we enjoy is short, to make your remembrance the longest possible.
>
> —Heinrich von Gundelfingen, *Topographia urbis Bernensis* (1486)

By 1515, Bern had become the largest and most powerful city-state in the Swiss confederacy. With roughly 5,000 inhabitants, the town itself was of a moderate size, but it controlled an area that stretched north from the alpine Upper Simme valley (*Obersimmental*) to Brugg in the present canton of Aargau and whose total population numbered near 70,000.[1] The city government consisted of two bodies, the Great and Small Councils (*Großer und Kleiner Rat*). The Great Council, also called the Council of the Two Hundred (despite a membership of up to 300), was open to all residents of the city who possessed citizenship, belonged to a local guild-like society (*Gesellschaft*),[2] and were over 14 years of age. It met once a week. The Small Council consisted of 27 members and met daily to conduct the day-to-day business of governing. It customarily determined city policy, which the Great Council then ratified. Among these 27 individuals

---

[1] Information on pre-Reformation Bern stems from the recently published catalogue *Berns grosse Zeit* (*BGZ*) as well as from the following older works: Franz Bächtiger, "Bern zur Zeit von Niklaus Manuel," in *NMD*, 1–16; François de Capitani, *Adel, Bürger und Zünfte im alten Bern des 15. Jahrhunderts*, Schriften der Berner Burgerbibliothek 16 (Bern: Berner Burgerbibliothek, 1982); Feller, esp. 2:16–24.

[2] Guilds were officially forbidden in Bern. In their stead, there existed "societies" (*Gesellschaften*), which in the course of time assumed many guild-like characteristics and protected the interests of a certain trade. See Roland Gerber, "Zünfte und Gesellschaften," in *BGZ*, 227–43; Capitani, *Adel, Bürger und Zünfte*, 53 ff.

were not one, but two mayors (*Schultheißen*). Upon the completion of a two-year term, the "old" mayor attended to matters of defense, while the new, officiating mayor chaired the sessions of both councils. In addition, four *Venner* sat upon the Small Council, each elected from one of the city's four leading societies: the Butchers (*Metzger*), the Blacksmiths (*Schmiede*), the Bakers and Millers (*Pfister*) and the Tanners (*Gerber*). The *Venner* were responsible for the administration of one of the city's four quarters, and together with the two mayors and the treasurer (*Seckelmeister*), they held the highest political power in the city.[3]

At a distance to major overland routes, Bern's geographical location was somewhat disadvantageous for trade. Craftsmen far outweighed merchants among the city's burghers.[4] This led to a chronic shortage of money, which in turn explains the great attraction, both for city and citizens, of *Reislaufen*, the Swiss term for mercenary service for a foreign power. Following their overwhelming victories over Charles the Bold of Burgundy in 1476–77, Swiss *Reisläufer* were in high demand throughout the continent.[5] During the course of the Italian Wars at the beginning of the sixteenth century, Bern formed shifting alliances with the Duke of Milan, the French king, and the pope, all of whom paid handsomely. Several members of the local elite received yearly French pensions that allowed them to live comfortably, and the city soon found that its military prowess could be parlayed into a substantial source of income.

According to contemporary accounts, Bern's vigor in battle was but one characteristic it shared with its heraldic device, the bear. On the positive side, these traits included a cautious circumspection and a practicality in political affairs; on the negative, a reputation for dim-wittedness, lethargy, and lack of refinement.[6] Bertold Haller

---

[3] Gerber, "Zünfte und Gesellschaften," 230–3.

[4] See Roland Gerber, "Die Berufsstruktur," in *BGZ*, 205–9.

[5] Michael E. Mallett, "The Art of War," in *Structures and Assertions*, vol. 1 of *Handbook of European History, 1400–1600: Late Middle Ages, Renaissance, and Reformation*, ed. Thomas A. Brady, Jr., Heiko A. Oberman, and James D. Tracy (Leiden: E.J. Brill, 1994), 543–4; Bruno Koch, "Reislauf und Pensionen," in *BGZ*, 277–85.

[6] As seen in this chapter's epigraph, Heinrich von Gundelfingen felt obliged to recommend the pursuit of learning over that of military glory for Bern's inhabitants: "Quid (o cives Bernenses) usquam felicius, quid decencius, quidque decorum magis aput mortales umquam fuerit, quam, ne vitam silencio transirent, famam nominis aut preclari facinoris aliquid peracte vite nobile monumentum (quo Diis

(fig. 1),⁷ Bern's lay priest and Reformation counterpart to Zurich's Ulrich Zwingli, invoked the bear as a symbol of strength,⁸ while Zwingli himself employed it in reference to the guilelessness of burghers who required the discipline of the Gospel.⁹ However clichéd these comments might be, they contain at least a grain of truth concerning the historical context of the Bernese Reformation. The ultimate success of the Swiss Reformation was in a large part due to Bern's initial moderate policy of reform, which sought to reconcile Protestant and Catholic camps within the city,¹⁰ as well as to its later course of fostering the new religion while preserving the alliances of the Helvetian Confederacy. Moreover, without Bern's military conquest of the Savoy territories surrounding Geneva in 1536, John Calvin might never have articulated his own Reformation theology, which was soon to spread far beyond the Alps.

Bern, Swiss Protestantism, and the Helvetian Confederacy

The first stirrings of the Reformation in Bern had a decidedly Lutheran character.¹¹ Zwingli's militant opposition to the mercenary trade of

---

immortalibus similiores essent) post decessum relinquere? Quo mihi rectius esse videtur, vos, quibus corporis virium satis abunde est, ingenii atque artis bone magnopere gloriam querere, et, quoniam vita ipsa qua fruimur brevis est, memoriam vestri quam maxime longam efficere." Heinrich von Gundelfingen, "Topographia urbis Bernensis," ed. Emil Blösch, *Archiv des Historischen Vereins des Kantons Bern* 10 (1880): 177–90.

⁷ On this and other representations of Haller, including the sole surviving contemporary portrait on a Zurich medallion of 1535, see Leo Caflisch, "Zur Ikonographie Berchtold Hallers," *Zwingliana* 4 (1928): 455–70.

⁸ Feller, 2:64.

⁹ Haller should preach the gospel "damit die wilden Bären durch Anhören der Lehre Christi anfangen zahm zu werden." As quoted in Bächtiger, "Bern zur Zeit von Niklaus Manuel," 6.

¹⁰ In general, the older studies of Feller and Guggisberg perpetuate the myth of the wise Bernese Bear by attributing Bern's moderate course to the sagacity of the city's Reformation founding fathers, while the more recent studies of Ernst Walder and Heinrich Richard Schmidt forego such stereotypes and point to the interplay and compromise between the city's Protestant and Catholic factions and thus the political expediency of early reforms. Guggisberg, 55–242; Ernst Walder, "Reformation und moderner Staat," in *450 Jahre*, 441–583; Heinrich Richard Schmidt, "Stadtreformation in Bern und Nürnberg—ein Vergleich," in *Nürnberg und Bern: Zwei Reichsstädte und ihre Landgebiete*, ed. Rudolf Endres, Erlanger Forschungen A46 (Erlangen: Universitätsbibliothek, 1990), 81–119.

¹¹ The following comments on the course of the Bernese Reformation are gar-

Reislaufen and to Swiss alliances with the French, which Bern favored due to its shared borders with francophone regions to the west, initially garnered him little sympathy with council or citizenry. As might be expected, the first recorded appearance of Luther's teachings in Bern concerned the matter of indulgences. In 1518, the Franciscan friar Bernhardin Samson arrived in Bern to sell papal indulgences for the construction of St. Peter's in Rome. Apparently, Samson's mercantile zeal was more becoming of a market huckster than a man of the cloth, and his appearance left a negative impression, enabling Manuel to assail him later in *Vom Papst und seiner Priesterschaft* (1523) and *Der Ablaßkrämer* (1525). During Samson's visit, however, it was the wealthy merchant Bartholomew May who criticized the sale of indulgences in Lutheran terms.[12] When the news of his unflattering comments reached Samson, May was forced to beg the council for mercy on his knees and state that Luther was a heretic. Despite such Draconian measures, Lutheran writings continued to circulate.[13] By 1522, many inhabitants were sympathetic to the new religion, and the Franciscan preacher Sebastian Meyer could afford to defend the Wittenberg theologian openly during a meal with other clerics on the feast of St. Anne.[14] Finally, if suggestions are true that Doctor Lütpold Schüchnit in Manuel's *Vom Papst und seiner Priesterschaft* is based on Luther,[15] this would also indicate the reformer's early influence in the city.

On 29 August 1522, shortly after Meyer's unreserved defense of Luther, a second incident forced local authorities to take a stand on the new religion. Jörg Brunner, pastor of Kleinhöchstetten to the

---

nered from the above studies, as well as from Rudolf Dellsperger, "Zehn Jahre Bernischer Reformationsgeschichte (1522–1532). Eine Einführung," in *450 Jahre*, 25–59. For a broader introduction to the Swiss Reformation as a whole, see Bruce Gordon, "Switzerland," in *The Early Reformation in Europe*, ed. Andrew Pettegree (Cambridge: Cambridge University Press, 1992), 70–93; Steven Ozment, *The Age of Reform 1250–1550. An Intellectual and Religious History of Late Medieval and Reformation Europe* (New Haven: Yale University Press, 1980), 318–39.

[12] Anshelm, 4:259.

[13] A large shipment of Luther's writings from Basel to Bern is recorded for the fall of 1518. See Hans von Greyerz, *Studien zur Kulturgeschichte der Stadt Bern am Ende des Mittelalters* (Bern: Gustav Grunau, 1940), 396.

[14] Steck/Tobler, 1:56–7, no. 212. For a short biography of Meyer, see Petra Roettig, *Reformation als Apokalypse. Die Holzschnittfolge von Matthias Gerung im Codex germanicus 6592 der Bayerischen Staatsbibliothek in München*, Vestigia Bibliae 11/12 (Bern: Peter Lang, 1991), 28–30.

[15] Max Huggler, "Niklaus Manuel und die Reformatoren," in *NMD*, 101.

southeast of Bern, had begun to attack the pope openly, bringing upon himself the ire of the dean of Münsingen, who requested that the council strip Brunner of his benefice. Rather than refer the matter to the bishop of Basel, under whose jurisdiction the case would normally fall, the council formed its own commission to judge the pastor. Bern had already gradually assumed control of several church institutions within its territory and had founded its own St. Vincent collegiate convent (*Chorherrenstift*) in 1484–85.[16] Despite episcopal protests against such usurpation, Bern could generally be assured of the support of the pope, who did not wish to cross the power that helped protect him. It was also to Bern's advantage that its territory fell under the jurisdiction of four dioceses: Constance, Lausanne, Basel, and Sitten, all of which were situated at a convenient distance so that episcopal influence, in comparison with cities such as Naumburg and Cologne, remained limited. In Brunner's case, the Bernese commission decided in his favor, since he could document all claims with Scripture. Although the council itself did not claim ecclesiastical authority, it hand-picked the theologians who examined the issue.[17] In this manner, the council began to exercise direct authority over the question of proper religion.

Soon, much more was at stake for Bern than episcopal displeasure. With the developments in Zurich and the reactionary attitude of the five so-called "inner" or "forest" cantons—Uri, Schwyz, Unterwalden, Zug und Lucerne—religious reform threatened to shatter the alliances that formed the heart of the Helvetian Confederacy. This Bern wished to avoid at all costs. Nor did it care to reject the new faith completely and isolate Zurich. Even before the unambiguous condemnation of Luther and Zwingli by the five inner cantons, which occurred at Beckenried in 1524, Bern chose a middle path that sought to appease the opposing camps, not only in the confederacy, but also within its own borders. It did so, whether consciously or unconsciously, by formulating its mandates in ambi-

---

[16] See Jürg Leuzinger, "Berns Griff nach den Klöstern," in *BGZ*, 361–5; Kathrin Tremp-Utz, *Das Kollegiatstift St. Vinzenz in Bern, von der Gründung 1484/5 bis zur Aufhebung 1528*, Archiv des historischen Vereins Bern 69 (Bern: Historischer Verein, 1985).

[17] Against Feller's and Guggisberg's assertion that the council itself determined matters of bible exegesis in Brunner's case, Walder points out that the council did not consider itself capable of such a decision, but rather left the matter to clergy—clergy, however, of its own choosing. Walder, 499 ff.

guous language, which both parties could agree upon, but interpret differently.[18] Indeed, the dispute over the correct interpretation of Bern's first religious mandate, the so-called *Mandat Viti et Modesti*, continues to this day.[19] Here, the council attempted to quell the growing conflict by requiring all preachers to base their sermons on the Gospel. Whereas this step was elsewhere often tantamount to an open declaration of Protestant reform, the Bernese councilors apparently regarded preaching from Scripture as a neutral compromise between both camps, as subsequent mandates made it quite clear that the city was not about to abandon the old faith. In the following months, the council enforced the mandate among both parties and adopted a wait-and-see approach. While the magistrates declined to circulate the imperial mandate against Luther, they equally refused to call the legitimacy of religious orders into question. Furthermore, when Sebastian Meyer and Jörg Brunner continued to agitate for the Reformation, the council expelled them from the city.

Several factors contributed to Bern's circumspection. Above all, the peasant uprisings of 1525 threatened to radicalize any attempts at religious reform. Although the Bernese territories did not experience unrest of the magnitude that raged in Germany, the situation was tense, and the council did its best to address the peasants' economic concerns and keep them separate from religious issues.[20] To ensure security, it formed additional alliances with the inner cantons. Moreover, Bern was still desirous of Savoy territories to the west, which it had captured in the Burgundian Wars, but had had to forfeit in the following peace. The city could not expand westward without the support of its confederates to the east.[21] Although a large portion of the urban populace favored the new religion, the outlying areas clung to the old, as became apparent when the council polled its territories on religious reform (*Ämterbefragung*).[22] Most

---

[18] Walder, 489.

[19] Dellsperger, "Zehn Jahre Bernischer Reformationsgeschichte," 30–1.

[20] See Peter Bierbrauer, *Freiheit und Gemeinde im Berner Oberland 1300–1700*, Archiv des Historischen Vereins des Kantons Bern 74 (Bern: Historischer Verein des Kantons Bern, 1991), 250–5; Edgar Bonjour, *Die Bauernbewegungen des Jahres 1525 im Staate Bern* (Bern: Paul Haupt, 1923), 13.

[21] See especially Leo von Muralt, "Berns Westpolitik von 1525–1531," *Zwingliana* 4 (1928): 470–76.

[22] On the Bernese practice of *Ämterbefragung* in general, see Catherine De Kegel-Schorer, "Die Ämterbefragungen—zur Untertanenrepräsentation im bernischen Territorialstaat," in *BGZ*, 356–60.

importantly, several members of the Small Council were staunchly Catholic and had no intention of changing parties. Preserving the status quo apparently seemed the safest policy. In the so-called *Pfinstmontagseid* of Whitmonday, 21 May 1526, Bern renewed its oath of alliance with the inner Swiss cantons, joined by Solothurn and Fribourg, promising never to abandon the old faith.

However, events following the Baden Disputation, held from 21 May to 9 June 1526, continually estranged Bern from its Catholic confederates. Representatives of the old faith assembled in Baden such luminary speakers as Johannes Eck, Luther's opponent at the Leipzig Debate of 1519, and Thomas Murner, who had recently been installed as Lucerne's lay priest following his flight from Strasbourg. But their claim of victory over Zwingli, who had refused to attend, did not prevent Bern's Protestants from gaining in numbers and influence. Proponents of the new faith scored a modest success on 26 June 1526, when they forced the Small Council to retain Bertold Haller as lay priest despite his refusal to celebrate mass. Senior councilors, such as Ludwig von Diesbach and Anton von Erlach, were so upset by this decision that they quit their office. Most decisive, however, was the resolution of the inner cantons to withhold the proceedings of the Baden disputation from Bern. When the council repeated its desire to review the materials, the seven Catholic cantons demurred and threatened to agitate against the Reformation within Bern's own territories. Bern rejected this as interference in its own affairs and gravitated more and more towards Zurich.

The tide finally turned with the Easter elections of 1527. Protestants now held the majority of seats in the Great Council. By altering existing statutes, they gained the right to select members of the Small Council, and by reissuing a forgotten law allowing only those born in the city to hold office, they effectively silenced Kaspar von Mülinen, one of the leading council members of the old faith. The *Mandat Viti et Modesti* was reinstated, now with a clear tendency towards the Reformation. On 17 November, Bern announced its own disputation to settle the matter once and for all. Bertold Haller and his new colleague Franz Kolb formulated ten reformed theses (*Schlußreden*) for debate. Invitations to the four local bishops threatened them with the loss of their rights in Bernese territories if they did not attend. In response to Emperor Charles V, who advised the council to wait, it replied that his missive had arrived too late.

The Bernese Disputation lasted three weeks: 6–26 January 1528.[23] The bishops did not appear, nor did Eck or Murner, who had also been invited. The inner cantons similarly declined to attend, arguing that a second disputation was superfluous following that of Baden. Swiss Protestants, however, turned out in force. Zwingli came from Zurich, accompanied by 69 burghers, pastors, and councilmen. Johannes Oecolampadius, Martin Bucer, Wolfgang Capito, and other prominent reformers were in attendance as well. Bernese clerics from both city and countryside were required to attend regardless of their disposition towards the new faith, and Niklaus Manuel served as moderator. At the close of the event, 235 of 281 priests supported the reformed theses. Local inhabitants were then invited to bring forward objections. There were none.

The council commissioned the Zurich printer Christoph Froschauer with the publication of the proceedings (fig. 2)[24] and immediately set about putting the new theology into practice. On 27 January, it allotted seven days for the removal of altars, statues, and paintings from the town's St. Vincent minster. Eager iconoclasts accomplished this task in two, so that the minster was already stripped of its ornamentation by the time Zwingli preached there on 30 January.[25] On

---

[23] For a discussion of the course and consequences of the Bernese Disputation, see Irena Backus, *The Disputations of Baden, 1526 and Berne, 1528: Neutralizing the Early Church*, Studies in Reformed Theology and History 1 (Princeton: Princeton Theological Seminary, 1993); Gottfried W. Locher, "Die Berner Disputation 1528," in *450 Jahre*, 138–55. An image from a 1605–06 transcription of Heinrich Bullinger's Reformation chronicle offers a rough depiction of the disputation, including the podium erected for the occasion in the city's Franciscan church. See Franz-Josef Sladeczek, "'Da ligend die altär und götzen im tempel'. Zwingli und der Bildersturm in Bern," in *BGZ*, 590, fig. 480.

[24] Concerning the title page of the published preceedings, see Locher, "Die Berner Disputation 1528," 142–3.

[25] The discovery of broken statuary underneath Bern's cathedral platform in 1986 has led to a reevaluation of the supposed orderly removal of images following the disputation. Franz-Josef Sladeczek has published a series of articles on the find, culminating in his recent monograph *Der Berner Skulpturenfund. Die Ergebnisse der kunsthistorischen Auswertung* (Bern: Benteli, 1999). See also Sladeczek, "Da ligend die altär und götzen im tempel," 588–604; idem, "Der Skulpturenfund der Münsterplattform in Bern (1986). Werkstattfrische Zeugen des Bildersturms der Berner Reformation," in *Les iconoclasmes*, ed. Sergiusz Michalski, vol. 4 of *L'Art et les révolutions* (Strasbourg: Société Alsacienne pour le Développement de l'Histoire de l'Art, 1992), 71–94; idem, "'Die götze in miner herren chilchen sind gerumpt!' Von der Bilderfrage der Berner Reformation und ihren Folgen für das Münster und sein Hauptportal. Ein Beitrag zur Berner Reformationsgeschichte," *Theologische Zeitschrift* 44 (1988): 289–311. For a general overview, see Carlos M.N. Eire, *War against the Idols. The Reformation*

2 February, the citizenry swore to follow the councilors in religious and worldly matters. Six days later, the council sent out its Reformation mandate, which proclaimed its obligation to provide instruction in religious matters and presented a list of reforms: the abolishment of the Mass, the establishment of a scriptural basis for all sermons, the release of all Bernese citizens from feudal obligations to the local bishops, and the permission for pastors to marry, to name but a few. Monasteries were dissolved and donations were returned to their patrons. The council apparently exercised little pressure and took pains to encourage a peaceful transition from the old to the new faith. When the inhabitants of the Oberland region coupled their preference for Catholic tradition with political insurrection in the fall of 1528, however, Bern vigorously quelled the uprising and underscored its willingness to support reform with military might, even against its confederate Unterwalden, which had indiscreetly sent troops to support the Catholic stirrings.[26] Prior to the Oberland riots, Bern had entered into a new alliance with Zurich, the *Christliches Burgrecht*, which firmly established Protestantism in the Helvetian Confederacy and eventually encouraged Basel, Schaffhausen, and Glarus to join the Reformation camp.

However, disputation and decree alone were insufficient to alter the religious habits of a populace reared on Catholicism. On 29 May 1528, the council created an initial institution to oversee the observation of the new religion: the *Chorgericht*, or marriage court. This board, composed of four members including, for a time, Niklaus Manuel, assumed the function of the now deposed episcopal courts and watched over local mores.[27] The court had no punitive power itself, but notified local authorities when its initial warnings did not put an end to the transgression in question. To provide the populace with reformed guidelines concerning every-day affairs, the coun-

---

of Worship from Erasmus to Calvin (Cambridge: Cambridge University Press, 1986), 108–12. Unfortunately, Eire exaggerates Manuel's role in these events; other comments are inaccurate or out-dated. In particular, he asserts that two of Manuel's pamphlets, *Krankheit der Messe* and *Testament der Messe*, are one play and that the anonymous *Klagred der armen Götzen* is also by Manuel.

[26] Bierbrauer, 257–85.

[27] On Bern's marriage court, see Hans Rudolf Lavater, "Die 'Verbesserung der Reformation' zu Bern," in *Der Berner Synodus*, 2:51–3; Guggisberg, 176–84; Theodor de Quervain, *Kirchliche und soziale Zustände in Bern unmittelbar nach der Einführung der Reformation (1528–1536)* (Bern: Gustav Grunau, 1906), 24–37.

cil introduced a package of sumptuary laws (*Sittenmandat*) before the month was out. The laws not only stipulated a new modesty in clothing,[28] but also abolished continuing Catholic practices such as the veneration of saints. Many burghers had retained religious images for themselves at home, so that the council advised the *Venner* in 1534 to examine all dwellings in their quarters to ensure that the images were indeed destroyed. Countless infractions of other ordinances demonstrated that centuries of religious habit died hard.

Bern largely followed Zurich's example in articulating a policy of reform. This was not without consequences, however. Emboldened by Bern's entrance into the Reformation camp, Zwingli became increasingly confrontational towards the Catholic inner cantons. He first exploited Unterwalden's still unredressed actions in the Oberland uprisings to coerce the inner cantons into allowing reformed pastors to preach in their territories. Then, in June 1529, it was Unterwalden's turn to supply the rotating steward for the mandated territory (*Gemeine Herrschaft*) of Baden, which it shared with Zurich. The latter resolved to prevent this at all costs. The Bernese council was less enthusiastic, sending Niklaus Manuel to convince its ally of the foolhardiness of military conflict. However, when the Unterwaldeners prepared to invest their steward by force, both Bern and Zurich mustered their troops on 4 June. Suddenly, Unterwalden chose to wait. Zwingli, determined to cross swords with Swiss Catholics, declared war on the five inner cantons on 8 June, the so-called First War of Kappel. This left Bern furious. It sent its troops eastwards towards Zug, but kept them separate from the Zurich camp in Kappel; furthermore, it informed Zurich of its intent to call a conference of all Swiss cantons to decide the matter. On 26 June 1529, this conference agreed upon the First Peace of Kappel, which favored the Protestants: the Catholic cities had to dissolve their alliance with King Ferdinand, the *Christliche Vereinigung*, and open preaching was allowed in the mandated territories administered by two cantons of opposing faiths.

Nonetheless, Zwingli's thirst for a unified, reformed Switzerland was not stilled, and continued infractions and incriminations on both sides eventually led to a grain embargo by Bern and Zurich against

---

[28] For a general description of pre-Reformation clothing, see John Martin Vincent, *Costume and Conduct in the Laws of Basel, Bern, and Zürich 1370–1800* (New York: Greenwood Press, 1935), 47–51. Vincent's survey is quite general and does not address Reformation reforms in detail.

the five inner cantons. This was the prelude to the Second War of Kappel of October 1531. On this occasion, Swiss Catholics turned the tables on their Protestant compatriots and attacked first. Zurich and Bern, who had assumed that their opponents would avoid a military conflict despite an encroaching winter with no food stores, were caught off guard. Zwingli, together with 51 other leading religious and political reformers of Zurich, fell in the initial battle on 11 October 1531. Although the inner cantons declared that their argument was with Zurich alone, Bern and its reformed confederates soon gathered their troops. Numbers were now on their side, but a carelessly led night assault was itself unexpectedly set upon and repulsed. The resulting morale in the Protestant camp was catastrophically low, and Bern immediately accepted offers of negotiation. In the peace treaty that followed, the Swiss reformed cities lost much of what they had gained through military conflict two years earlier. Each confederate was free to decide over its own religion, but most mandated territories eventually chose the old faith. The Protestant alliance, the *Christliches Burgrecht*, was dissolved. Solothurn returned to the Catholic fold after the victory at Kappel stifled earlier Protestant successes there. The confessional divisions in the Helvetian Confederacy grew static, and Bern was afterwards surrounded by Catholic neighbors. This, again, necessitated a great degree of prudence in religious matters during the following years.

The loss at Kappel left the council and citizenry confused and insecure. Many felt that the Protestant pastors were the true warmongers and thus demanded that their influence over matters of state cease.[29] Conversely, Kaspar Megander (fig. 3), a staunch Zwinglian who had been appointed as professor of theology to Bern's new Academy (*Hohe Schule*) in 1528, publicly blamed the Kappel defeat on Bern's reluctance to wage war.[30] It had additionally become apparent that many pastors of the Bernese countryside only superficially grasped the central tenets of the new faith. To address these concerns, the Bernese council turned to the urgent consolidation of its new church, convening local clergy and select members of the Small and Great Councils at the Bernese Synod, held from 9 to 14 January 1532. When the Strasbourg reformer Wolfgang Capito unexpectedly

---

[29] De Quervain, 57–8.
[30] See Lavater, "Die 'Verbesserung der Reformation,'" 2:61–4.

appeared in Bern while travelling through Switzerland, Bertold Haller entrusted him with the formulation of the synod's ordinances for the clergy. In the assessment of both contemporaries and current scholars, he fulfilled his task masterfully.[31] His *Synodus* (fig. 4) delineated the intertwined tasks of secular and religious government that subsequently determined the Bernese state church (*Staatskirchentum*).[32] The synod adopted Capito's text with apparently few changes,[33] and with the blessings of the council it became the binding document for the local Reformation.

The council also kept a watchful eye on the press, both inside and outside its territories. In 1528, Lucerne's Thomas Murner composed two pamphlets against the Bernese Disputation, *Des alten christlichen Bären Testament* ("The Last Will and Testament of the Old Christian Bear") and *Des jungen Bären Zahnweh* ("The Young Bear's Toothache").[34] These openly fanned the flames of revolt in the Oberland territories, so that Bern sought redress.[35] Following the Protestant victory in the First War of Kappel, Bern and other Protestant cantons insisted that Lucerne banish or punish the Franciscan. Rather than suffer an uncertain fate, Murner took flight, returning to his hometown of Oberehnheim near Strasbourg. After the Second Peace of Kappel officially forbade religious polemics by either party, Bern similarly forced Lucerne to imprison its city secretary Hans Salat,

---

[31] Gottfried W. Locher, "Der Berner Synodus als reformierte Bekenntnisschrift," in *Der Berner Synodus*, 2:17; Dellsperger, "Zehn Jahre Bernischer Reformationsgeschichte," 52. See also Ernst Saxer, who treats Anabaptist aspects of Capito's synod text: "Capito und der Berner Synodus," in *Der Berner Synodus von 1532*, 150–66.

[32] The magesterial administration of Bern's church was but one form of Zwinglian theocracy. See Gottfried W. Locher, *Die Zwinglische Reformation im Rahmen der europäischen Kirchengeschichte* (Göttingen/Zurich: Vandenhoeck & Ruprecht, 1979), 616, note 5. The text of the *Synodus* in its German, Latin, and French versions can be found in the first volume of *Der Berner Synodus*.

[33] Dellsperger, "Zehn Jahre Bernischer Reformationsgeschichte," 52.

[34] Thomas Murner, "Des alten christlichen Bären Testament," ed. Max Scherrer, *Anzeiger für schweizerische Geschichte* 50 [= Neue Folge 17] (1919): 6–38; Murner, "Des jungen Bären Zahnweh. Eine verschollene Streitschrift Thomas Murners," ed. Josef Lefftz, *Archiv für elsässische Kirchengeschichte* 1 (1926): 141–67.

[35] On Bern's dispute with Murner, see Paul Zinsli, "Manuel und Murner. Die Begegnung zweier doppelt begabter Glaubensstreiter in der Reformationszeit," *BZGH* 50 (1988): 165–96; Basilius Hidber, "Dr. Thomas Murners Streithandel mit den Eidgenossen von Bern und Zürich, mit Urkunden" *Archiv für schweizerische Geschichte* 10 (1855): 272–304; Theodor von Liebenau, *Der Franziskaner Dr. Thomas Murner*, Erläuterungen und Ergänzungen zu Janssens Geschichte des deutschen Volkes 9:4–5 (Freiburg: Herder, 1913), 241–50.

whose *Tanngrotz* had accused the Bernese troops of murder and pillage during the war.[36] Given the council's further efforts to suppress carnival play performances, an unspoken censorship was apparently firmly in place by the mid-1530s, but the city did not draft an explicit censorship ordinance until 1539, when Unterwalden protested against the "Interlaken Song," possibly composed by Cosmas Alder.[37] This polemic ditty once again accused the neighboring canton of having fomented unrest within the Oberland region in 1528. The text had been printed anonymously, but the inner cantons gave no peace until Bern determined Alder's involvement and punished him. To avoid similar occurrences in the future, the council established a commission of four censors who were to examine all writings before they were printed in the recently established press of Mathias Apiarius.[38] No derision of the confederates was allowed, and even foreign book sellers were required to present their books to the commission before selling them at market.

The revitalization of the inner cantons following their victory at Kappel did not curtail Bern's preeminent position in the western part of the confederacy. The Catholic cantons lay largely to the east; only Fribourg guarded the old faith to the west. Once before, during the Wars of Burgundy, Bern had conquered the Vaud territories surrounding the city of Geneva, but had been forced to return them in the Peace of Fribourg in 1476. Even after its embrace of Zwinglianism, it remained allied with many of its western neighbors, which subsequently provided a convenient handhold to introduce the new religion in these territories. After the Wars of Burgundy, Bern

---

[36] Karl Müller, *Die Geschichte der Zensur im alten Bern* (Bern: K.J. Wyss, 1904), 77; Hans Salat, "Tanngrotz," in *Hans Salat: Ein Schweizer Chronist aus der ersten Hälfte des XVI. Jahrhunderts. Sein Leben und seine Schriften*, ed. Jacob Baechtold (Basel: Bahnmaier, 1876), 89–109.

[37] For a summary of the affair, see Müller, 78 ff. The text is reprinted in Rochus von Liliencron, ed., *Die historischen Volkslieder der Deutschen vom 13. bis 16. Jahrhundert* (Leipzig: F.C.W. Vogel, 1867), 3:572–6, no. 407. Though it had long been assumed that Alder actually wrote the song, Arnold Geering suggests that Alder merely assisted the printer, Matthias Apiarius, in its composition and that Niklaus Manuel had written the lyrics following his suppression of the Oberland uprising. Arnold Geering, *Die Vokalmusik der Schweiz zur Zeit der Reformation. Leben und Werke von Bartholomäus Frank, Johannes Wannenmacher, Cosmas Alder*, Schweizerisches Jahrbuch für Musikwissenschaft 6 (Aarau, 1933; reprint Amsterdam: Swets and Zeitlinger, 1969), 162–4. See also Adolf Fluri, "Das Interlachnerlied," in *NBT 1904*, 263–5.

[38] Adolf Fluri, "Matthias Apiarius, der erste Buchdrucker Berns," in *NBT 1897*, 209–30.

had retained Aigle near Montreux; it was here that Guillaume Farel began preaching the Reformation with Bern's blessing in 1527. Although unsuccessful in Lausanne, Farel soon converted Murten and Neuchâtel. When Bern came to the aid of Geneva to protect it against the machinations of the Duke of Savoy in 1530, miscommunication between the council at home and its representatives abroad defeated the chance to anchor the Reformation in the resulting peace treaty. Nonetheless, Farel travelled to the city in 1532 and planted the first seeds of Protestantism. When the Duke of Savoy, in supposed defense of the old faith, renewed his attacks on the city, Bern declared war in January 1536. The duke was unprepared, and Bern easily occupied the Vaud territories. Although religious reform did not take place throughout the new territories immediately, Farel's efforts had already born fruit in Geneva, which officially introduced its own Reformation on 21 May 1536.

With the conquest of the Pays de Vaud, however, another major reformer soon made his presence felt in Bern. At the Lausanne Disputation of October 1536, which officially introduced the Reformation in Bern's new possessions, a young man by the name of John Calvin spoke together with Farel. While traveling through Geneva the previous summer, Calvin had been approached by Farel to aid in the Reformation of the local church. Struck by the earnestness of Farel's plea, he stayed and quickly began restructuring the church, which Farel had created according to the Zwinglian model.[39] When both reformers, in their zeal for adherence to Scripture, eliminated traditional celebrations such as Christmas, pressure mounted from within and without to pursue a more moderate course of reform. When Calvin and Farel resisted, the Genevan council dismissed them in 1538 with Bern's less-than-tacit approval. To the latter's chagrin, however, the Genevan elections of 1539 and 1540 brought an anti-Bernese faction to power, which invited Calvin to return to his former position. His acceptance and subsequent success were afterwards constant reminders to Bernese councilors that their authority had its limits, particularly in religious matters.

Nonetheless, that authority remained absolute in Bern itself, where magistrates kept a watchful eye on local theologians. In Calvin's view, the power of Bern's theologically unschooled council to decide

---

[39] For more detail see Ozment, 360 ff.

religious affairs amounted to tyranny, and there is certainly some truth to the charge that confessional politics often dictated the council's religious policy.[40] This is most apparent in the fortunes of the city's crypto-Lutheran theologians. While Luther's influence in Bern had been strong from the first stirrings of local reform sentiment, it grew even more so during Strasbourg reformer Martin Bucer's efforts in the 1530s and 1540s to unite the Swiss reformed church with Wittenberg.[41] As long as religious concord seemed attainable, the council lent a sympathetic ear to Bucer while turning a blind eye to the Lutheran interpretation of the Eucharist held by prominent pastors and theologians such as Sebastian Meyer, Peter Kunz, and Simon Sulzer. Indeed, Sulzer (fig. 5) replaced Kaspar Megander as professor of theology at the Bernese Academy in 1538 after the latter was removed from office for protesting against Bucer's "ecumenical" altering of the eucharistic passages of Megander's own catechism. Once the prospect of concord faded, however, Lutherans fell into disfavor in Bern. Meyer had left the city as early as 1541, while Sulzer was forced to join local clergy in swearing in 1545 to uphold the *Synodus* and the ten *Schlußreden* of the Bernese Disputation. Nonetheless, Sulzer continued to voice Lutheran views, and when he later lent his support to the 99 theses of Calvin's disciple Pierre Viret, which were adopted in 1548 by the Synod of Lausanne, the council summarily dismissed him. Moving to Basel, he subsequently made a name for himself from 1552 to 1587 as Oswald Myconius's successor as head of the local church (*Antistes*).[42] His successors in Bern, Johannes Haller (fig. 6) and Wolfgang Musculus (fig. 7), reestablished the theological stability of the Bernese church and ensured the lasting success of the reforms begun in 1528.[43]

---

[40] Guggisberg, 200–1, 208.

[41] See the sections on "Unionsversuche" and "Die Auseinandersetzung mit der lutheranisierenden Richtung" in Guggisberg, 198 ff. See also C.B. Hundeshagen, *Die Conflikte des Zwinglianismus, Lutherthums und Calvinismus in der Bernischen Landeskirche von 1532–1558* (Bern: C.A. Jenni, 1842).

[42] See Gottlieb Linder, *Simon Sulzer und sein Antheil an der Reformation im Lande Baden, sowie an den Unionsbestrebungen* (Heidelberg: Carl Winter, 1890).

[43] On Haller, see Guggisberg, 210 ff.; Eduard Bähler, "Dekan Johann Haller und die Berner Kirche von 1548 bis 1575," in: *NBT 1923* (Bern: E.J. Wyss, 1922), 1–52; *NBT 1924*, 1–62; *NBT 1925*, 1–58; and *NBT 1926*, 1–61. On Musculus, see most recently Craig Farmer, *The Gospel of John in the Sixteenth Century. The Johannine Exegesis of Wolfgang Musculus*, Oxford Studies in Historical Theology (New York/Oxford:

Nevertheless, the competing demands of politics and theology led at times to Bern's estrangement from Zurich. Although Zwingli had paid for his beliefs with his life, the Bernese long blamed the Protestant defeat in the Second War of Kappel on his bellicosity and afterwards insisted on their independence in religious as well as secular matters. When Zurich and Basel formulated a common statement on the Zwinglian interpretation of the Eucharist in 1535, Bernese theologians refused to sign, claiming the document was created solely to appease Luther.[44] Fourteen years later, Zwingli's successor Heinrich Bullinger joined with Calvin to create the *Consensus Tigurinus*, which effectively bridged the theological differences between the Zurich and Genevan churches. Despite Haller's and Musculus's approval, the Bernese council again refused—or ostensibly declined—to sign the document, stating that it was already in accord with Geneva and that this needed no public recognition.[45]

In one way or another, all ten Bernese Reformation plays took an active stand on these issues affecting the community. This has long been apparent for Manuel's plays, but it applies equally to those by Rüte. As we shall see, *Abgötterei* responded to the threat of an alliance between Swiss Catholic cantons and Emperor Charles V, discussed by the parties at the Diet of Augsburg in 1530. Similarly, *Osterspiel* championed the Bernese church on the occasion of council elections, reflecting the continuing theological disputes between Zwinglianism, Lutheranism, and Calvinism following the *Consensus Tigurinus*. While no literature is completely free of the political and cultural biases of its time, the Reformation drama of sixteenth-century Bern wore its politics on its sleeve as in perhaps no other period of literary history.

Oxford University Press, 1997); *Wolfgang Musculus (1497–1563) und die oberdeutsche Reformation*, ed. Rudolf Dellsperger, Rudolf Freudenberger, and Wolfgang Weber, Colloquia Augustana 6 (Berlin: Akademie Verlag, 1997); Rudolf Dellsperger, "Wolfgang Musculus (1497–1563)," in *Die Augsburger Kirchenordnung von 1537 und ihr Umfeld*, ed. Reinhard Schwarz (Gütersloh: Gerd Mohn, 1988), 91–110.

[44] Guggisberg, 201.
[45] Otto Erich Strasser, "Der Consensus Tigurinus," *Zwingliana* 9 (1949): 14–5; Guggisberg, 203–4.

Literature and the Arts

According to Thomas Murner's account of the Jetzer affair (1507–09)—in which a Dominican lay brother in Bern by the name of Hans Jetzer faked a series of miracles involving the Virgin Mary, all the while denouncing the then rival Franciscan tenet of Mary's immaculate conception—the Dominicans ostensibly agreed to stage their deception in Bern on the grounds that the population was uneducated and simple-minded.[46] As Murner spent much of 1509 as *Lesemeister* in the Bernese Franciscan monastery and was present during the public execution of four Dominicans monks for their role in the affair, there is perhaps some truth to his assessment of sixteenth-century Bernese artlessness, with both its positive and negative connotations. Valerius Anshelm echoes Murner's comments in his Bernese chronicle,[47] and the Bernese reformer Bertold Haller himself complained that the saying *Die Gelehrten, die Verkehrten* (roughly translated: "The Lettered, the Fettered") circulated so frequently in Bern that he himself began to believe it.[48] It would of course be a grave error to portray sixteenth-century Bern as devoid of culture, as music and the local stained-glass industry flourished during this time.[49] Rather,

---

[46] "Darumb gib ich ein andren ratt,/Das wirs zuo Bern wol in der statt/Zünden an/im Schweizer landt./Do ist nit vil der künst bekandt./Sye seind einfeltig/guot zuo btriegen/Vnd mercken nit eins yeden liegen." Thomas Murner, *Von den fier ketzeren*, ed. Eduard Fuchs, Thomas Murners Deutsche Schriften mit den Holzschnitten der Erstdrucke I,1 (Berlin: Walter de Gruyter, 1929), 21. As Guggisberg notes, this claim is not verifiable, "bezeichnend ist aber schon, daß man sie überhaupt aufstellen konnte." Guggisberg, 38.

[47] "... dass semlichs zuo Bern angericht wurde, da wenig gelerter und ein schlecht [i.e. schlicht] volk wär, aber, so das beredt wurd, mächtig und hantvest, die sach zeschirmen und zuo erhalten." Anshelm, 3:51.

[48] Feller, 2:58. Heiko Oberman, who renders *die Gelehrten, die Verkehrten* as "those dangerous deviant doctors—they stray and 'stroy,'" utilizes the phrase to illustrate the dialectics between learned and popular culture in the Devotio Moderna: Heiko A. Oberman, "*Die Gelehrten die Verkehrten*: Popular Response to Learned Culture in the Renaissance and Reformation," in *Religion and Culture in the Renaissance and Reformation*, ed. Steven E. Ozment, Sixteenth Century Essays and Studies 11 (Kirksville, Missouri: Sixteenth Century Journal Publishers, 1989), 43–63.

[49] See François de Capitani, *Musik in Bern. Musik, Musiker, Musikerinnen und Publikum in der Stadt Bern vom Mittelalter bis heute*, Historischer Verein des Kantons Bern 76 (Bern: Historischer Verein, 1993), 17–33; Geering, 8–29; Hans Lehmann, "Die Glasmalerei in Bern am Ende des 15. und Anfang des 16. Jahrhunderts," *Anzeiger für schweizerische Altertumskunde* Neue Folge 14 (1912): 287–309; NF 15 (1913): 45–52, 100–16, 205–26, 321–46; NF 16 (1914): 41–57, 124–50, 207–33, 304–24; NF 17 (1915): 45–65, 136–59, 217–40, 305–29; NF 18 (1916): 54–74, 135–53, 225–43.

that culture reflected the interests of the surrounding community. Devout piety, francophilia, the absence of a university and a printing press, and the aristocratic pretensions of a council still largely composed of landed lesser nobility: all were contributing factors to Bern's cultural life in the early sixteenth century.

Literary activity, where it existed, was predominantly a privilege of the elite and promoted the ideals and interests of this group.[50] The simple wish to record events and experiences for later generations produced traditional chronicles, such as those by Benedict Tschachtlan and Ludwig Schwinkhart,[51] or the memoirs of Ludwig von Diesbach, one of Europe's first autobiographers.[52] When personal experiences bore witness to special devotion and honor, the eagerness to record them was doubly great. Thus the councilmen Niklaus von Diesbach and Kaspar von Mülinen, together with the humanist Heinrich Wölflin (Lupulus), all recorded their pilgrimages to the Holy Land.[53]

---

[50] While Urs Martin Zahnd remarks that literary activity by members of the Small Council was rare, it is important to note that most local literary works were produced by or at least oriented to this group. Ludwig Schwinkhart and Wilhelm Ziely, whom Zahnd does not consider members of the "politische Führungsschicht," were nonetheless members of the Great Council. Urs Martin Zahnd, *Die Bildungverhältnisse in den bernischen Ratsgeschlechtern im ausgehenden Mittelalter. Verbreitung, Charakter und Funktion der Bildung in der politischen Führungsschicht einer spätmittelalterlichen Stadt*, Schriften der Berner Burgerbibliothek 14 (Bern: Berner Burgerbibliothek, 1979), 152.

[51] "Bendicht Tschachtlans Berner Chronik nebst den Zusätzen des Diebold Schillings," *Quellen zur Schweizer Geschichte* I, ed. Gottlieb Studer (Basel: Felix Schneider, 1877), 199–298; Ludwig Schwinkhart, *Chronik 1506–1521*, ed. Hans von Greyerz, Archiv des historischen Vereins des Kantons Bern 36, 1. Heft (Bern: Feuz, 1941).

[52] Urs Martin Zahnd, ed., *Die autobiographischen Aufzeichnungen Ludwig von Diesbachs. Studien zur spätmittelalterlichen Selbstdarstellung im oberdeutschen und schweizerischen Raume*, Schriften der Berner Burgerbibliothek 17 (Bern: Berner Burgerbibliothek, 1986). See also the recent study by Christoph Lumme, *Höllenfleisch und Heiligtum: Der menschliche Körper im Spiegel autobiographischer Texte des 16. Jahrhunderts*, Münchener Studien zur neueren und neuesten Geschichte 13 (Frankfurt/Bern: Peter Lang, 1996), 115, 138.

[53] "Die Pilgerreise der Ritters Caspar von Mülinen ins heilige Land," ed. R. Röhricht, *Zeitschrift des deutschen Palästinavereins* 11 (1888): 184–97; *Heinrich Wölflis Reise nach Jerusalem 1520/21*, ed. Hans Bloesch (Bern: Schweizer Bibliophilengesellschaft, 1929). The original record of Niklaus von Diesbach's pilgrimage is lost; however, a vassal of the house of Diesbach recorded the travels of his lords: *Hans von der Grubens Reise- und Pilgerbuch*, ed. Max von Diesbach, Archiv des Historischen Vereins des Kantons Bern XIV (Bern: Historischer Verein, 1894). On these and other sixteenth-century Swiss journeys to the Holy Land, see Arnold Esch, *Alltag der Entscheidung. Beiträge zur Geschichte der Schweiz an der Wende vom Mittelalter zur Neuzeit* (Bern: Paul Haupt, 1998), 335–7, 355–99.

Early prose novels found particular favor in Bern. Through its contact with the francophone areas to the west, the city offered fertile soil for German translations of French models, which simultaneously adapted the adventures of their courtly protagonists to the moral and aesthetic tastes of an aristocratic civic audience.[54] Perhaps the best-known early modern literary work from Bern is *Melusine* by Thüring von Ringoltingen,[55] one of the city's leading citizens and later mayor. Based on the French epic poem of the same name by an otherwise unknown Couldrette, it was one of the most popular works of its time, appearing in at least sixteen fifteenth-century manuscripts and approximately twenty-eight printings before its 1587 redaction in Siegmund Feyerabend's *Buch der Liebe*.[56] The success of Ringoltingen's work places it on a par with the early modern German translations of the Swabian humanists Niklas von Wyle, Albrecht von Eyb, and Heinrich Steinhöwel.[57] Over fifty years later, two translations by Wilhelm Ziely, an official at the municipal *Kaufhaus*, revealed a continued interest in the genre: his renderings of *Olivier und Artus* and *Valentin und Orsus* appeared in 1521 in Basel.[58] All three novels follow a young nobleman who must prove himself—or fail, as in *Melusine*—through a series of often marvelous adventures. The orientation of the Bernese elite towards French cultural models is most evident in these local translations.[59]

The humanist movement, although not completely absent, had only modest influence in Bern. The local representatives of the *studia*

---

[54] Both Jan-Dirk Müller and Thomas Cramer distinguish the largely aristocratic tastes of the Bernese audience from the bourgeois readers of the *frühbürgerlicher Roman*. Jan-Dirk Müller, "Melusine in Bern: Zum Problem der 'Verbürgerlichung' höfischer Epik im 15. Jahrhundert," in *Literatur—Publikum—historischer Kontext*, ed. Gert Kaiser, Beiträge zur Älteren Deutschen Literaturgeschichte 1 (Bern: Peter Lang, 1977), 29–77; Thomas Cramer, *Geschichte der deutschen Literatur im späten Mittelalter* (Munich: Deutscher Taschenbuchverlag, 1990), 79.

[55] Thüring von Ringoltingen, *Melusine*, ed. Karin Schneider, Texte des späten Mittelalters 9 (Berlin: Erich Schmidt, 1959). See also André Schnyder, "Weltliteratur in Bern: die 'Melusine' des Thüring von Ringoltingen," in *BGZ*, 534–42.

[56] Hans-Gert Roloff, afterword to *Melusine* (Stuttgart: Reclam, 1969), 175.

[57] Schneider, foreword to *Melusine*, 35.

[58] These works are presently unedited. See, however, Hans Frölicher, *Thüring von Ringoltingens "Melusine", Wilhelm Zielys "Olivier vnd Artus" und "Valentin vnd Orsus" und das Berner Cleomades-Fragment mit ihren französischen Quellen verglichen* (Solothurn: Vereinsbuchdruckerei, 1889).

[59] See also Jacob Baechtold, "Zwei Berner Romanschriftsteller des XV. und XVI. Jahrhunderts," in *Berner Taschenbuch auf das Jahr 1878* (Bern: B.F. Haller, 1877), 43–52.

humanitatis are quickly enumerated: schoolmasters Melchior Volmar, Jakob Fullonius (Walker), doctor and chronicler Valerius Anshelm, canon Michael Rubellus (Röttli), theologian Thomas Wyttenbach, and Niklaus Manuel's grandfather, the city secretary Thüring Fricker.[60] Volmar and Fullonius, the latter a friend of Beatus Rhenanus, lingered but briefly in the city, while the others placed their talents predominantly in civic service. Even after the Reformation, the professors of Bern's newly founded *Hohe Schule* occupied themselves with theological as opposed to poetic matters.[61] The school's literary production did not extend beyond Johannes Rhellican's Latin translation of Plutarch's *Life of Homer* and two poetic encomia on the Alpine mountain Stockhorn, one by Rhellican and the other by a later professor, Benedikt Marti.[62]

Only one local humanist gained a reputation that extended beyond the city walls: Heinrich Wölflin, who, in humanist manner, latinized his name to Lupulus. Both Heinrich Bullinger, Zwingli's successor in Zurich, and the Basel scholar Oswald Myconius praised Wölflin as a leader among Swiss humanists,[63] and his fame as director of the city Latin school from 1494 to 1498 drew not only the Rottweilers Bertold Haller and Valerius Anshelm to Bern, but also, briefly, Zwingli.[64] Yet even Wölflin's writings retained a certain provincial character: he composed odes to St. Vincent, the patron of the Bernese

---

[60] Von Greyerz, 433. On Fricker, see also Christine Göttler and Peter Jezler, "Doktor Thüring Frickers 'Geistermesse': Die Seelgerätskomposition eines spätmittelalterlichen Juristen," in *Materielle Kultur und religiöse Stiftung im Spätmittelalter*, ed. Gerhard Jaritz, Veröffentlichungen des Instituts für mittelalterliche Realienkunde Österreichs 12 (Vienna: Österreichische Akademie der Wissenschaften, 1990), 187–231.

[61] On the *Hohe Schule*, modeled after Zurich's *Prophezey* but also serving as Bern's first institute of higher learning, see Ulrich im Hof, "Die reformierte Hohe Schule zu Bern. Vom Gründungsjahr 1528 bis in die zweite Hälfte des 16. Jahrhunderts," in *450 Jahre*, 194–224.

[62] Both Rhellican's and Marti's poems, with French translations, can be found in W.A.B. Coolidge, *Josias Simler et les origines de l'alpinisme jusqu'en 1600* (Grenoble: Allier Frères, 1904), Pièces Annexes, 186–95, 222–47.

[63] "[Zwingli wurde] darnach gan Bern zuo M. Heinrychen Wölfflin (Lupulo) gesandt, alls zuo einem verrümpten gelerten man, derglychen damalen in der Eydgnoschafft nitt was." Heinrich Bullinger, *Reformationsgeschichte*, ed. J.J. Hottinger and H.H. Vögeli (Frauenfeld: Ch. Beyel, 1838; Zurich: Theologische Buchhandlung, 1985), 1:6. Oswald Myconius, *Vom Leben und Sterben Huldrych Zwinglis*, ed. and trans. Ernst Gerhard Rüsch, Mitteilungen zur vaterländischen Geschichte 50 (St. Gallen: Fehr'sche Buchhandlung, 1979), 38.

[64] Ulrich Gäbler, *Huldrych Zwingli. Eine Einführung in sein Leben und sein Werk* (Munich: C.H. Beck, 1983), 29.

cathedral, as well as an officium dedicated to the martyrdom of the Ten Thousand, whose feast of 22 June also commemorated the Bernese victories of Laupen (1339) and Murten (1476).[65] Moreover, despite Lupulus and his Latin school, the otherwise ubiquitous language of learning led a meager existence in Bern. The city composed its official documents and chronicles in the local German dialect, and if the affluent aspired to learn a second language, it was French.[66]

The culprits in this dearth of high literary products are easily found: the absence of a university and the astonishingly late appearance of a printing press. Young minds were forced to leave the city for their education, many of them supported by French scholarships to Paris and elsewhere. In 1475, a press was established in Burgdorf to the northeast of the city, but it survived only briefly.[67] Even during the fledgling years of the Reformation, if the city wished to publish official documents, it turned to the printers of Basel, Zurich, or Geneva. At times, politics found their way into the choice of one press over another: According to Bertold Haller, the council entrusted the proceedings of the 1532 Synod to Froben in Basel, and not Froschauer in Zurich, because the bears on the title woodcut of the Disputation proceedings lacked claws.[68] Finally, in 1537, printer Mathias Apiarius arrived in Bern from Strasbourg to continue his press's activities on the Aare.[69] Born Mathias Biener in Bavarian Berchingen, Apiarius had also lived for a time in Basel, traveling from there to Bern in 1528 to attend the disputation.[70] In Strasbourg since the early 1530s, he worked closely with the reformers Capito

---

[65] Feller, 2:60. Regarding the development of this cult in Bern and the related window of the Bernese cathedral, see Brigitte Kurmann-Schwarz, "Das 10.000–Ritter-Fenster im Berner Münster und seine Auftraggeber. Überlegungen zu den Schrift- und Bildquellen sowie zum Kult der Heiligen in Bern." *ZfSAK* 49 (1992): 39–54.

[66] Feller, 2:57.

[67] Von Greyerz considers a possible connection between the press and the Toggenburg monastery. Von Greyerz, 336.

[68] "Quod autem acta non mittuntur ad Christophorum excudenda, hinc est: quidam, ut sunt apud omnes, habend imm das wort thon, es syend bären truckt, die habind keini kräwel an den tapen, et nescio quae alia." As quoted in Hans Rudolf Lavater, "Der 'Synodus' in der Berner Kirche bis zum Ausgang des 18. Jahrhunderts," in *Der Berner Synodus*, 2:304. See also Locher, "Die Berner Disputation 1528," 142.

[69] See Fluri, "Mathias Apiarius," 203 ff.

[70] Hans Bloesch, ed., *Dreißig Volkslieder aus den ersten Pressen der Apiarius* (Bern: Schweizer Bibliophilengesellschaft, 1937), 10.

and Bucer, but also published several musical works together with Peter Schöffer, the son of Johannes Gutenberg's one-time partner.[71] He continued specializing in songs while in Bern, but did not limit himself to music. Various works by well-known contemporary authors such as Johannes Pauli, Thomas Naogeorgus, Jakob Funkelin, Burkard Waldis and, of course, both Niklaus Manuel and Hans von Rüte appeared at his press.[72] Upon his death in 1554, his sons Samuel and Sigfrid assumed the family business, with Sigfrid concerning himself solely with book-binding and Samuel attending to the actual press.[73] Following a dispute in 1559, likely involving debts, Samuel was required to leave the city. After a brief period in Solothurn (1565–1566), he settled in Basel, where he died in 1590.[74] Sigfrid, who was also a piper in the city music corps, died in 1565.

Music played a prominent role in the city's cultural life. Musical talent was so valued in Bern prior to the Reformation that the local Dominican monastery supposedly courted Zwingli, an excellent singer, to join their order during his time in the city.[75] The St. Vincent convent fostered this muse through its own singing school,[76] whose six positions for choir boys were highly coveted and largely reserved for sons of local burghers.[77] The school's cantors, including Bartholomäus Frank, Heinrich Wölflin, Johannes Wannenmacher, Melchior Volmar and Cosmas Alder,[78] were responsible for the education of the choir boys as well as for the choir music in the St. Vincent cathedral. Musical works by Frank, Wannenmacher, and Alder survive.[79] Despite the demise of the convent choir in 1528 and Zwingli's opposition to liturgical music,[80] musical activity in Bern retained its

---

[71] Adolf Thürlings, "Der Musikdruck mit beweglichen Metalltypen im 16. Jahrhundert und die Musikdrucke des Mathias Apiarius in Straßburg und Bern," *Vierteljahrsschrift für Musikwissenschaft* 8 (1892): 389–418.

[72] For a list of Apiarius's imprints, see Bloesch, ed., *Dreißig Volkslieder*, 19–47.

[73] Adolf Fluri, "Die Brüder Samuel und Sigfrid Apiarius, Buchdrucker in Bern (1554–1565)," in *NBT 1898*, 168–213.

[74] Adolf Fluri, "Samuel Apiarius, der erste Buchdrucker Solothurns (1565–1566)," in *NBT 1898*, 214–6; Fluri, "Samuel Apiarius, Buchdrucker in Basel (1566–1590)," in *NBT 1898*, 217–28.

[75] See Garside, 9.

[76] See Geering, 8 ff.; for a general introduction on the canon convent, see Tremp-Utz, *Das Kollegiatstift St. Vinzenz in Bern*.

[77] Geering, 19.

[78] Ibid., 13–4.

[79] For the extant manuscripts and imprints, see Geering, XVII–XVIII.

[80] Garside, 27 ff.

vigor. Alder wrote a number of songs for Rüte's plays,[81] and in 1553, Wolfgang Musculus edited Alder's earlier hymns for a Protestant audience.[82]

Although circumstances of patronage and the absence of a printing press prevented Bern from becoming a center for the arts, these were nonetheless well-represented in the city in the early 1500s. Even following the iconoclastic destruction of local religious art,[83] a handful of artisans continued to pursue their trade for a now largely secular demand. According to Paul Leonhard Ganz, over fifteen painters were active in Bern between 1434 and 1586.[84] In addition, several painters from Southern Germany temporarily sought out the city, but it is difficult to determine their exact number.[85] Except for Manuel's oeuvre, extant Bernese works from the sixteenth century are rare. Paintings survive by Hans Fries (ca. 1460–ca. 1518), Jakob Boden (mentioned in city documents from 1502 to 1534), Master HF (dates unknown), and the so-called Masters of the Carnation (*Nelkenmeister*; dates unknown).[86] After Manuel, Fries was perhaps the most prominent local painter of this period. Born in Fribourg, he initially worked there before moving to Bern around 1510;[87] he gained particular notoriety by testifying that the tears of blood wept by a local image of Mary during the Jetzer swindle were genuine. As their cognomina suggest, little is known about Master HF or the Master(s) of the Carnation. The *Nelke* signature was apparently quite common in Switzerland and Southern Germany, and at least two workshops used this signature in Bern alone.[88] Even less is known about the activity

---

[81] Geering, 170–5.

[82] Andreas Marti, "Gottesdienst und Kirchenlied bei Wolfgang Musculus," in *Wolfgang Musculus (1497–1563) und die oberdeutsche Reformation*, 218–23; Geering, 159.

[83] The loss of late medieval art works as a result of iconoclasm makes it extremely difficult to reconstruct the artistic life of the city, although the discovery of broken statuary beneath the cathedral platform has allowed for fresh insights. See Charlotte Gutscher-Schmid and Franz-Josef Sladeczek, "'bi unns und in unnser statt beliben'. Künstler in Bern—Berner Künstler? Zum künstlerischen Austausch im spätmittelalterlichen Bern," in *BGZ*, 410–21; Sladeczek, *Der Berner Skulpturenfund*.

[84] Paul Leonhard Ganz, *Die Malerei des Mittelalters und des 16. Jahrhunderts in der Schweiz* (Basel: Birkhäuser, 1950), 165 ff.

[85] Hugo Wagner, "Kunst in Bern vor und neben Niklaus Manuel," in *NMD*, 207.

[86] On the *Nelkenmeister*, see Charlotte Gutscher-Schmid, "'Diss alles würd er herlich und erberlich, köstlich und guot machen'. Kirchliche Auftragskunst im Zeichen der Nelke," in *BGZ*, 516–23.

[87] See Anna Kelterborn-Haemmerli, *Die Kunst des Hans Fries*, Studien zur deutschen Kunstgeschichte 245 (Strasbourg: J.H. Ed. Heitz, 1927), 1–22.

[88] Gutscher-Schmid, "Im Zeichen der Nelke," 517. A project of the Schweizerischer

of Sigmund Holbein, the brother of Hans Holbein the Elder. In 1540, he composed his will in Bern, although no records exist concerning his activity there.[89] Of the existing works attested for Bern, only Master HF and Manuel adopted Renaissance techniques; all others remained firmly in the late medieval tradition of religious painting.

Several painters also had close ties to the flourishing local stained-glass industry.[90] Its roots extended well into the fifteenth century, and civic governments and affluent individuals had developed the custom of donating glass windows for churches and secular buildings, embellished with the donor's coat of arms.[91] The chronicler Valerius Anshelm complained in 1501 of vain burghers who felt they now needed colorful stained glass in their homes.[92] As the glass industry produced not only devotional panels for churches and monasteries, but also secular panels for cities, villages, and private individuals, it became perhaps the most important artisan trade following the local eschewal of religious images. Whereas Ganz lists only six painters who were active in sixteenth-century Bern following the Reformation,[93] Paul Boesch counts nineteen glass painters for the same period.[94] Thus Hans Lehmann can report that the local stained-glass industry suffered no serious setbacks after 1528.[95] Designs for stained-glass windows (*Scheibenrisse*) survive for Manuel as well as for Jakob Kallenberg (ca. 1510–1565).[96]

Little documentary evidence survives from Niklaus Manuel's early years as artist, but it is likely that he apprenticed in one of the city's

---

Nationalfonds under the direction of Hans Lüthy has been reevaluating the work of the Swiss Masters of the Carnation. Charlotte Gutscher-Schmid, "Fotografische Wiederentdeckung einer Nelkenmeistertafel im Archiv des Bodemuseums Berlin," *ZfSAK* 50 (1993): 180; 185, note 2.

[89] Wagner, "Niklaus Manuel—Leben und künstlerisches Werk," 20.
[90] Heinz Matile, "Zum Thema 'Niklaus Manuel und die Glasmalerei,'" in *NMD*, 67.
[91] Brigitte Kurmann-Schwarz, "'... die Fenster in der kilchen allhier, die meine Herren zu machen und in Ehr zu halten schuldig ...' Andenken—ewiges Seelenheil—irdische Ziele und Verpflichtungen gezeigt an Beispielen von Glasmalerei-Stiftungen für das Münster," in *BGZ*, 457–65; Paul Boesch, *Die Schweizer Glasmalerei*, Schweizer Kunst 6 (Basel: Birkhäuser, 1955), 27–31.
[92] Anshelm, 2:345.
[93] Ganz, 165 ff.
[94] Boesch, 35–6.
[95] Lehmann, "Die Glasmalerei in Bern," *Anzeiger für schweizerische Altertumskunde* Neue Folge 17 (1915): 139–40.
[96] See Franz Bächtiger, "Scheibenriss mit Berner Pannerträger," in *NMD*, 163–5, no. 16; Wagner, "Kunst in Bern vor und neben Niklaus Manuel," 202–9, nos. 41–50.

stained-glass workshops.[97] Although he remains unmentioned in local treasury records until 1513, and although none of his surviving paintings carries a date from before 1515, two stained-glass windows in the church of Kirchberg, completed 1507/1508, are based on surviving designs by Manuel.[98] Because many of his drawings are undated, the development of Manuel's trademark signature, a Swiss dagger, has proved a useful tool for dating his works.[99] The artist's early daggers are slim, pointed, and unadorned, while the later ones are more rounded, accompanied by a decorative ribbon. Based on this evidence, approximately forty *Scheibenrisse* originated prior to 1515.[100] In all, some ninety drawings by Manuel survive. They reveal the influence of Hans Holbein the Younger, Hans Baldung Grien, and Albrecht Dürer,[101] and together with Lucas Cranach the Elder, these contemporaries exercise a similar influence on some thirty extant paintings by the artists. Despite the enormous popularity of woodcuts at this time, Manuel apparently produced only one series of six images of the Wise and Foolish Virgins, although he may have provided designs for other cuts.[102] His last graphic works, two 1529 drawings of a Swiss and German mercenary (*Reisläufer—Landsknecht*), are his final artistic products altogether. His graphic work shows affinity to that of Urs Graf, and like Graf, Manuel based his portrayal of Swiss mercenaries on personal experience, having engaged

---

[97] Reasonable suggestions, that Manuel trained with Hans Fries or a Master of the Carnation, vie with unlikelier claims that Manuel spent his years as journeyman in Augsburg with Hans Burgkmair or in Nuremberg with Dürer. Wagner, after reviewing the evidence from Manuel's earliest known works, comes to the conclusion that Manuel most likely learned his trade in the workshop of a glass painter. Wagner, "Niklaus Manuel—Leben und künstlerisches Werk," 20–2.

[98] Hans Christoph von Tavel, "Notizen zu den Zeichnungen und Holzschnitten Manuels," in *NMD*, 44.

[99] First noticed by Max Grütter, "Der Dolch als Datum, zur Datierung der Werke Niclaus Manuels," *Der kleine Bund*, 15 April 1949.

[100] Wagner, "Niklaus Manuel—Leben und künstlerisches Werk," 22. This largely verifies the chronological order originally established by Lucie Stumm, which the influential Basel scholar Hans Koegler had subsequently rejected. See Lucie Stumm, *Niklaus Manuel Deutsch von Bern als bildender Künstler* (Bern: Stämpfli, 1925), 87–97; Hans Koegler, *Beschreibendes Verzeichnis der Basler Handzeichnungen des Niklaus Manuel Deutsch. Nebst einem Katalog der Basler Niklaus Manuel-Ausstellung im Kupferstichkabinett Mitte Februar bis Ende April 1930* (Basel: B. Schwabe, 1930).

[101] Hans Christoph von Tavel provides a detailed discussion of the connections: von Tavel, "Notizen zu den Zeichnungen und Holzschnitten Manuels," 47 ff.

[102] See Hans Koegler, "Die Holzschnitte des Niklaus Manuel Deutsch," *Jahresbericht der öffentlichen Kunstsammlung Basel 1924* Neue Folge 21 (1925): 43–75.

in the Italian campaigns of 1516 and 1522, if not others. The horrors of war likely encountered by Manuel at the Swiss defeat in the Battle of Bicocca in 1522 subsequently led him to compose the biting "Song of Bicocca," which ridiculed the German *Landsknechte* who boasted of their victory over the supposedly invincible Swiss. His artistic production lags following this date, so that the year 1522 has often been interpreted as a turning point in Manuel's life, leading to his Protestant conversion and subsequent literary production.[103] Chapter Five will examine this assumption more closely.

Plays and Playwrights

Long before Rüte or Manuel were active in Bern, public play performances were apparently a regular occurrence on the Aare. Records, sparse at first, become more frequent by the early sixteenth century. Prior scholarship has documented pre-Reformation performances for the years 1437, 1448, 1461, 1486, 1506, 1513, 1514, 1515, 1516, and 1521.[104] Unfortunately, it is unclear for the earliest of these dramas whether they were religious or secular in content. The assumption that biblical drama of some type was staged in the city during the later Middle Ages is, of course, reasonable, but documentation is lacking.[105] Even for the two dates included in Bernd Neumann's

---

[103] Jean-Paul Tardent, *Niklaus Manuel als Staatsmann*, Archiv des Historischen Vereins des Kantons Bern 51 (Bern: Historischer Verein, 1967), 74 ff.

[104] In his nineteenth-century assessment of the history of the Bernese stage, Armand Streit notes only the performance of several carnival plays before those of Manuel: 1461, 1486, 1513 and 1520. Judging, moreover, from his description of the 1461 and 1486 "performances," he has wrongfully attributed a dramatic nature to festive occasions, also referred to as *spil*. Bernd Neumann's more recent work lists only two plays in Bern, performed in 1437 and 1448. Basilius Hidber simply begins with Niklaus Manuel. All other dates are taken from Adolf Fluri. Streit, 95 ff.; Bernd Neumann, *Geistliches Schauspiel im Zeugnis der Zeit. Zur Aufführung mittelalterlicher religiöser Dramen im deutschen Sprachgebiet*, Münchener Texte und Untersuchungen zur deutschen Literatur des Mittelalters 84/85 (Munich: Artemis Verlag, 1987), 1:127; Basilius Hidber, "Das Theater der alten Berner. Proben aus den drei letzten Jahrhunderten," *Archiv des Historischen Vereins des Kantons Bern* 5 (1863): 611–23; Fluri, 133–59.

[105] Though both Hidber and Streit begin their histories of the Bernese stage with religious drama, neither discusses any documented plays, referring instead to the tradition of medieval drama practiced elsewhere in Switzerland. Cf. Hidber, 612; Streit, 1–2, 95. Pfrunder assumes only a carnival tradition in the city: Pfrunder, 142. Peter Schibler begins with the Reformation, but he completely omits Rüte's plays: Peter Schibler, *Vom Kultspiel zum Kleintheater. Aus der Geschichte des bernischen*

Geistliches Schauspiel im Zeugnis der Zeit, the actual records are inconclusive and could point to secular performances as well.[106] Similarly, Franz-Josef Sladeczek's suggestion that the rosette of the main portal of the Bernese minster was at one time a hinged opening used for play performances on the cathedral square is based in part on inaccurate documents.[107] It also seems unlikely, as Richard Feller suggests, that a recorded 1448 performance was part of a tradition of Latin plays performed by pupils of the city school,[108] as neo-Latin drama did not emerge in German-speaking lands until Jakob Wimpfeling's *Stylpho* of 1480. Judging from the attested Bernese performances after 1500, all of which take place during the carnival season, no long-term tradition of religious drama existed in Bern.

Bernese carnival plays began no later than the 1506 performance of the non-extant *Spiel der zwölf Planeten* ("Play of the Twelve Planets"). This was well before the 1515 Basel performance of Pamphilus

---

Theaterwesens, Berner Jahrbuch 1983 (Bern: Verbandsdruckerei/Betadruck, 1982), 3, 5. Lastly, Barbara Könneker incorrectly suggests that Cross Lane had long been the site of religious performances prior to Manuel's plays: Könneker, *Satire im 16. Jahrhundert: Epoche—Werk—Wirkung* (Munich: Beck, 1991), 171–2.

[106] Neumann has the following entries: "1437: Den webren, als die ein spil gemacht hattend, hiessen min herren zu stur gen 1 lb.; 1448: Denne den schuolern hiessen min herren schencken ze stur an ir spil 2 lb." Neumann, 1:127. While Franz-Josef Sladeczek questions whether these records reflect religious plays, Hellmut Thomke argues that the performances cannot have been secular, since the carnival play as genre was not yet developed in the first half of the fifteenth century. However, Thomke does not consider the evidence of early Swiss secular plays such as the *Basler Fastnachtspielszenen* (ca. 1434) or *Des Entkrist Vasnacht* (original play likely written in Zurich ca. 1350). See Franz-Josef Sladeczek, *Erhart Küng. Bildhauer und Baumeister am Münster zu Bern (um 1420–1507)* (Bern/Stuttgart: Paul Haupt, 1990), 67 and 159, note 574; Hellmut Thomke, "Niklaus Manuel und die Anfänge des Theaterspiels in Bern," in *BGZ*, 542; *Frühe Schweizerspiele*, ed. Friederike Christ-Kutter, Altdeutsche Übungstexte 19 (Bern: Francke, 1963).

[107] See Sladeczek, *Erhart Küng*, 67–8, and especially Sladeczek, "Weltgerichtsthematik im geistlichen Schauspiel und der bildenden Kunst des Mittelalters. Gedanken zur Frage der gegenseitigen Beeinflussung von Drama und Bildkunst," *Unsere Kunstdenkmäler* 44 (1993): 367–8. The "Comödie vom Jüngsten Gericht" of 1535, which Sladeczek refers to as evidence for religious plays in Bern, cannot have existed, at least not as cited by his source Raoul Nicolas, who provides the following quote, allegedly from the Bernese *Ratsmanual* entry for 21 March 1535: "Simon Marti dem Comödianten erlaubt allhier eine Comödie vom jüngsten Gericht und Auferstehung von den Todten aufzuführen und von jedem Zuschauer einen Kreuzer zu nehmen." Unfortunately, 21 March 1535 was a Sunday, when no council meetings took place. Cf. Berner Staatsarchiv, Signatur A II 122 (vol. 251) and Raoul Nicolas, *Die Hauptvorhalle des Berner Münsters und ihr bildnerischer Schmuck: Eine kunstgeschichtliche Studie*, Neujahrsblatt der Literarischen Gesellschaft Bern auf das Jahr 1921 (Bern: K.J. Wyss Erben, 1921), 97.

[108] Feller, 2:57.

Gengenbach's *Die Zehn Alter der Welt*, which, despite the clear evidence for a thriving Swiss carnival play tradition prior to 1500,[109] is often considered the link between Nuremberg and Swiss carnival plays.[110] Although the play *Die Totenfresser* from Gengenbach's press assumedly served as Manuel's inspiration for *Vom Papst und seiner Priesterschaft*,[111] Bern had already produced polemical plays biting enough to earn the scorn of Matthäus Schiner, Cardinal of Sitten.[112] Local tradition thus influenced Manuel's first play just as much as Gengenbach's play did, if not more so.[113]

Given the lack of texts from these earlier performances, the picture of theatrical life in Bern becomes much clearer with the survival of Manuel's and Rüte's plays. Their biographies are also relatively well-documented, allowing for additional conclusions about the cultural status of plays and their makers. Painting and playwriting were, for example, but two of Manuel's varied occupations during a colorful, but comparatively short life.[114] His date of birth is not recorded, but several later sources give his age at death as 46, so that he was likely born in 1484.[115] His mother was Margaretha Fricker, the daughter

---

[109] Eckehard Simon, "Shrovetide Plays in Late-Medieval Switzerland: An Appraisal," *Modern Language Notes* 85 (1970): 323–31.

[110] Wolfgang F. Michael, *Das deutsche Drama der Reformationszeit* (Bern: Peter Lang, 1984), 34; Barbara Könneker, *Die deutsche Literatur der Reformationszeit. Kommentar zu einer Epoche* (Munich: Winkler, 1975), 126.

[111] Zinsli, "Niklaus Manuel, der Schriftsteller," in *NMD*, 81.

[112] In 1521, Cardinal Schiner taunted Bernese mercenaries, held prisoner in Milan after a French defeat. Schiner's words are recorded in Anshelm, 4:450, and quoted in Chapter 3. See also Heinrich Dübi, "Miscellen zur bernischen Geschichte: 1) Ein anonymes Fastnachtspiel vom Jahre 1521," *Blätter für bernische Geschichte, Kunst und Altertumskunde* 23 (1927): 161–6. The play itself does not survive.

[113] Pfrunder, 143; cf. Herbert Walz, *Deutsche Literatur der Reformationszeit: Eine Einführung* (Darmstadt: Wissenschaftliche Buchgesellschaft, 1988), 121.

[114] In addition to the two recent compendia *450 Jahre Berner Reformation. Beiträge zur Geschichte der Berner Reformation und zu Niklaus Manuel* and especially *Niklaus Manuel Deutsch. Maler—Dichter—Staatsmann*, the past biographies of Baechtold and Grüneisen are still useful: Jacob Baechtold, ed., *Niklaus Manuel*, Bibliothek älterer Schriftwerke der deutschen Schweiz und ihres Grenzgebietes 2 (Frauenfeld: J. Huber, 1878), XI–LVIII; Carl von Grüneisen, *Niclaus Manuel: Leben und Werke eines Malers und Dichters, Kriegers, Staatsmannes und Reformators im sechszehnten Jahrhundert* (Stuttgart: J.G. Cotta, 1837). For Manuel's political activities, see especially Tardent, *Niklaus Manuel als Staatsmann*. The best treatment of Manuel's pamphlets is found in Beerli, 253–303. For a discussion of Manuel's life in English, see Glenn Ehrstine, "Niklaus Manuel (Niklaus Manuel Deutsch)," in *German Writers of the Renaissance and Reformation, 1280–1580*, ed. James Hardin and Max Reinhart, vol. 179 of *Dictionary of Literary Biography* (Detroit: Gale Research, 1997), 152–65.

[115] See Hugo Wagner, "Niklaus Manuel—Leben und künstlerisches Werk," 17.

of city secretary Thüring Fricker, whose ties to humanist circles once led to the likely mistaken assumption that Manuel had enjoyed a humanist education and attended school with Ulrich Zwingli during the latter's time in Bern.[116] His father was in all likelihood Emanuel Alleman, a druggist whose own father had emigrated to Bern from Chieri in Italy. As later records list Margaretha Fricker's husband as Hans Vogt, it is assumed that Manuel was an illegitimate child. This did not seem to have stigmatized the young painter, however, who boldly signed his works *NMD* for Niklaus Manuel Deutsch, adopting the latter cognomen in an apparent Germanized reference to his father's name. In 1509, he married Katharina Frisching, the daughter of city councilor Hans Frisching. Together, they had five children before Manuel's death on 28 April 1530: Margaretha (1516), Hieronymus (1520), Hans Rudolf (1525), Niclaus (1528) and daughter Magdalena (1524), who died young.[117] His self-portrait of 1520 preserves his appearance around the time of his first son's birth (fig. 8).[118]

Manuel had been involved in civic affairs as early as 1510, when he became a member of the Great Council. In 1522, citing the dwindling returns of his trade in a letter from the Italian campaign, he sought the position of *Großweibel* (sergeant-at-arms) with the city. His application failed, but in the following year the council appointed him steward of Erlach, a small Bernese possession near Neuchâtel, which his father-in-law had also administered. Here he served until 1528. His administrative experience, coupled with his continued support of the Reformation, eventually led him into the highest ranks of local government. Upon the opening of the Bernese Disputation, it was decided that Manuel would moderate the event. Following the success of Zwingli and the other Protestants in attendance, it was merely a matter of time before Manuel was elected to the Small Council at Easter in 1528. In May, he became a member of the newly created *Chorgericht*, and in October he advanced to *Venner*,

---

[116] Existing documents suggest that Manuel had no knowledge of Latin, so that a humanist education is improbable. Wagner, "Niklaus Manuel—Leben und künstlerisches Werk," 18.

[117] In his letter to the council of 1522 requesting the position of "Großweibel," Manuel states that he has "vil klÿner kinder," which would imply that he had more than two at this date. However, no other records of children exist. The letter is reproduced in *Werke und Briefe*, 649–50, no. III.

[118] *NMD*, 250–1, no. 93, fig. 24. The image erroneously reproduced by the press as a self-portrait in Ehrstine, "Niklaus Manuel (Niklaus Manuel Deutsch)," 152 likely represents a Bernese goldsmith: *NMD*, 220, no. 67, fig. 34.

assuming one of the highest civic offices next to that of mayor. As a member of the Small Council, he spent much of his remaining time as envoy in an effort to preserve the integrity of the Helvetian Confederacy.[119] Manuel's role as diplomat climaxed in his speech of 3 June 1529 in Zurich, which pleaded against civil war with the Catholic inner cantons.[120] Although this appeal was ultimately unsuccessful, Manuel helped negotiate a bloodless peace that respected the sovereignty of the Catholic confederates. Unfortunately, the atmosphere in the confederacy remained tense, and Manuel continued to mediate where needed. Most scholars assume that his untimely death on 28 April 1530 was due to overexhaustion in the service of the Reformation.[121]

Manuel's two carnival plays of 1523 were the first public indication of his lasting commitment to the Protestant cause.[122] Yet although Manuel is best known for these works and *Der Ablaßkrämer* of 1525, his plays comprise less than half of his writings. The rhymed quatrains accompanying his "Dance of Death" mural (1516–19), formerly located on the inner courtyard wall of the Dominican monastery in Bern,[123] represent his first (surviving) verse. His participation in the Battle of Bicocca led to the "Song of Bicocca" (1522),[124] mentioned earlier, and possibly to *Der Traum* ("The Dream"; 1522), a fragmentary work contained in a Hamburg manuscript, which also preserves the earliest redactions of *Vom Papst und seiner Priesterschaft* and *Von Papsts und Christi Gegensatz*.[125] Portraying the early events of the Reformation in a dream as viewed from heaven, the work has a clear Protestant tendency, but lacks the biting satire of Manuel's other works, so that his authorship has been called into question.[126] As if to avoid this

---

[119] Tardent provides a day by day record of Manuel's activities as councilor: Tardent, 23 ff.
[120] See the detailed analysis by im Hof, "Niklaus Manuel als Politiker und Förderer der Reformation," 97 ff.
[121] Im Hof, "Niklaus Manuel als Politiker und Förderer der Reformation," 99.
[122] *Der Traum*, which may be Manuel's work, apparently circulated only in manuscript.
[123] "Totentanz," in *Werke und Briefe*, 23–72. See also Paul Zinsli, *Der Berner Totentanz des Niklaus Manuel*, 2nd ed., Berner Heimatbücher 54/55 (Bern: Paul Haupt, 1979).
[124] "Bicoccalied," in *Werke und Briefe*, 73–99.
[125] "Der Traum," in *Werke und Briefe*, 585–623; "Fasnachtsspiel, Variantenapparat II: Integraler Abdruck der Hamburger Handschrift," in *Werke und Briefe*, 213–50. See also Fritz Burg, "Dichtungen des Niklaus Manuel. Aus einer Handschrift der Hamburger Stadtbibliothek," in *NBT 1897*, 1–136.
[126] See Paul Zinsli, "Der 'Seltsame wunderschöne Traum'—ein Werk Niklaus Manuels?" in *450 Jahre*, 350–79.

problem, Manuel "signed" his next works with his trademark Swiss dagger, which appears in the last line of his plays as well as of *Barbeli* (1526), a rhymed dialogue in which a young daughter, bound for the convent, quotes Scripture to convince her mother and attendant clerics of the fruitlessness of monastic life.[127] In the same year, he composed *Ecks und Fabers Badenfahrt* ("Eck's and Faber's Trip to Baden"), a song lampooning the Catholic disputation held in Baden.[128] When the Bernese disputation convened to abolish the mass, Manuel greeted the occasion with a final polemic salvo, composing both *Die Krankheit der Messe* ("The Affliction of the Mass") and *Das Testament der Messe* ("The Last Will and Testament of the Mass") in 1528.[129] Two further works once associated with Manuel, *Die Klagred der armen Götzen* ("The Plaint of the Poor Idols"; 1529) and *Elsli Tragdenknaben* (1530), are no longer attributed to him.[130]

In contrast, the canon of works by Hans von Rüte has not changed in over a hundred years.[131] Whereas Manuel published anonymously, necessitating speculative attributions, Rüte proudly appended his name to each of his six plays. Unfortunately, historical sources on Rüte are much sparser, leaving the details of his life sketchy. Moreover, the author was not born in Bern, and as the name "von Rüte" is common throughout German-speaking Switzerland, it is difficult to connect him to one particular family or region. Prior to the recent publication of the author's *Sämtliche Dramen*, what was known about his life was largely the product of haphazard discovery. Friederike Christ-Kutter has now presented the first exhaustive biography of Rüte as part of this critical edition.[132] Her research lays to rest some speculation, while opening up other, seemingly resolved issues, in particular the question of the author's background before his first

---

[127] "Barbeli," in *Werke und Briefe*, 285–404.
[128] "Ecks und Fabers Badenfahrt," in *Werke und Briefe*, 405–28.
[129] "Krankheit und Testament der Messe" in *Werke und Briefe*, 429–517.
[130] Both are edited under "Manuel zugeschriebene Werke" in the Zinsli/Hengartner edition: *Werke und Briefe*, 521–84, 631–8.
[131] There have been occasional misattributions of works to Rüte, but none has met with consensus. Emil Weller's original bibliography of Rüte's six dramas thus remains accurate. See Klaus Jaeger, "Rechenschaftsbericht," in *Sämtliche Dramen*, 3:10; Emil Weller, *Das alte Volkstheater der Schweiz* (Frauenfeld: J. Huber, 1863), 58–97.
[132] Friederike Christ-Kutter, "Zur Biographie Hans von Rütes," in *Sämtliche Dramen*, 3:15–60.

appearance in Bernese sources in 1528.[133] Christ-Kutter questions the most recent thesis that Rüte hailed from Aarau, a city along the river Aare to Bern's northeast.[134] Noting the economic and religious ties linking Aarau to Solothurn and the Emme Valley (*Emmental*), where the name "von Rüte" is also documented, she postulates that the author had familial connections to all three regions. Returning to an earlier assumption, based on eighteenth-century sources, that Rüte came to Bern from Solothurn, Christ-Kutter then reconciles the data by arguing that Rüte was born in Burgdorf, the largest city of the Emme Valley, and afterwards completed his professional training in Solothurn before moving to Bern.[135] The date of Rüte's arrival in the city remains unresolved, however. His election to the Great Council in 1531 suggests that he arrived in Bern in 1526 or earlier, as membership in this body was open only to those who possessed a house and had been residing in the city for five years.[136] In light of the seemingly contradictory evidence, the most reasonable conclusion is that the facts of Rüte's birth, youth, and education as a civil servant are irretrievably lost.

The details of the author's biography become more concrete in Bern. Once in the city, Rüte quickly advanced and soon founded a

---

[133] Rüte became a member of the city's pro-Reformation Blacksmith Society in 1528: "Diß nägst hie obgesagten Hans ward zuo einem stubengesellen [...] vf vnd angenomen." As quoted by Christ-Kutter in *Sämtliche Dramen*, 3:33, note 108.

[134] In 1978, Anna Dorothea Noser-Hasler pointed to a document in Aarau that names Hans von Rüte and a brother Werner as the next-of-kin of the recently deceased Anna von Rüthi. As the name von Rüti existed in the fifteenth century among clerics in Aarau, Noser-Hasler concluded that these were possibly Rüte's forebears. See Anna Dorothea Noser-Hasler, "Einheimische Volksschauspiele des 16. Jahrhunderts," *Lenzburger Neujahrsblätter* 49 (1978): 14; *Aargauer Urkunden—Neunter Teil: Die Urkunden des Stadtarchivs Aarau*, ed. Georg Boner (Aarau: H.R. Sauerländer, 1942), 296, no. 801.

[135] "Eine Abstammung aus Burgdorf, dem Hauptort des Emmentals, Besuch der Schulen dort, in Bern oder Solothurn, Hochschulbesuch in Basel, Freiburg im Breisgau, wenn nicht doch in Italien oder Frankreich, vereinzelte Teilnahme an Kriegszügen, Schreiberlehre in Solothurn und provosorische Beamtung dort, Kontakt mit der Reformation auch in Solothurn und schließlich im Jahre 1527, als fertiger Schreiber die Entscheidung zum Umzug nach Bern, das scheint mir als supponierter Lebenslauf eine vertretbare, in vielen Teilen sogar belegbare These." Christ-Kutter in *Sämtliche Dramen*, 3:22.

[136] Klaus Stephan Jaeger, "Hans von Rütes Osterspiel. Edition und Untersuchung" (M.A. Thesis, Freie Universität Berlin, 1993), 17. The *Wappenbuch der burgerlichen Geschlechter der Stadt Bern* gives either 1525 or 1528 as the date of Rüte's arrival: *Wappenbuch der burgerlichen Geschlechter der Stadt Bern* (Bern: Burgergemeinde, 1932), T.63.

large family with Cathrin Hetzel, a former nun.[137] In 1530, he appeared as under-secretary (*Unterschreiber*). Following his election to the Great Council in 1531, he became the city's court secretary (*Gerichtsschreiber*) and remained in this office—disregarding a temporary dismissal from the fall of 1545 to summer 1546 for adultery[138]—until his appointment in 1555 as *Stiftsschaffner* in Zofingen, where he was responsible for the administration of the secularized convent and its Latin school.[139] As Bernese baptismal records do not begin until 1530, the birthdates of Rüte's first sons, David and Georg, are not recorded. His eldest daughter, Cathrin, was born in 1531, and at least nine more children issued from his marriage.[140] However, as Christ-Kutter has demonstrated, Rüte did not marry a second time. Margareta Bodmer, mistakenly believed to have been Rüte's second spouse, was wed to the author's youngest son, also named Hans.[141] Rüte died in Zofingen on 23 March 1558 and was buried in the convent church. Cathrin, previously thought to have passed away sometime before 1552, lived until at least 1568.

Through his juristic duties as court secretary, Rüte had close ties to civic government. The office of *Gerichtsschreiber* was the highest secretarial position in Bern after the city secretary (*Stadtschreiber*). In this position, Rüte was solely responsible for the local judicial system. Indeed, he was one of the few residents of the city with legal expertise and training. Together with the mayor and the sergeant-at-arms (*Großweibel*), he oversaw local trials at the city's central *Kreuzgasse*

---

[137] The date of Rüte's marriage is uncertain, but must have occurred before 8 April 1529, when Cathrin Hetzel signed a document as Rüte's wife. One of the most important contributions of Christ-Kutter's biography is her detailed information on Hetzel, who belonged to an eminent Bernese family: *Sämtliche Dramen*, 3:47–52.

[138] Rüte was discovered with one of his household servants and had to appear before the marriage court: "Ist min her grichtschriber hanns vom Rhüte bekhantlich wordenn vor minen gnädigen herren des Eegrichts, das Er sich mit siner Einen Junckfrouwen vergangen habe und gehuret;—hatt aber min g.[nädigen] herren betten umb gnad und verziehung des ampts halb." As quoted by Christ-Kutter in *Sämtliche Dramen*, 3:43. See also Mathias Sulser, *Der Stadtschreiber Peter Cyro und die bernische Kanzlei zur Zeit der Reformation* (Bern: Carl Fromme, 1922), 112.

[139] On the convent, see Christian Hesse, *St. Mauritius in Zofingen: Verfassungs- und sozialgeschichtliche Aspekte eines mittelalterlichen Chorherrenstiftes*, Veröffentlichungen zur Zofinger Geschichte 2 (Aarau: Sauerländer, 1992).

[140] Bernese baptismal records give contradictory evidence for Rüte's children. See Appendix 1 of Christ-Kutter's biography in *Sämtliche Dramen*, 3:53–4.

[141] Christ-Kutter in *Sämtliche Dramen*, 3:51–2.

(Cross Lane), during which he combined the duties of district attorney, bailiff, notary public, and legal secretary. He not only kept minutes of all trials and legal proceedings, such as a 1538 disputation with local anabaptists,[142] but also brought charges and was required by oath to pursue all infractions of the law and collect fines. On occasion, he joined Bernese delegations representing the city in legal matters abroad. Thus, in 1551, he sojourned in Basel to settle a dispute with the Teutonic Order, whose monasteries Bern had secularized following the Reformation. A similar dispute with the monastery of St. Peter in the Black Forest led him to Herzogenbuchsee in 1556; beforehand, he had helped to resolve a border dispute with Lucerne in 1555.

A more concrete link between Rüte's legal duties and his literary career are his activities as censor, in which Rüte inspected plays and other writings for their conformity with council politics and theology. In 1556, Rüte is referred to as a member of a censorship commission, the *zum Druck Verordneten*,[143] perhaps the same institution that the council had created in 1539 following the unpleasantries surrounding the "Interlaken Song." How long and in what capacity Rüte served on this committee is unclear. Nevertheless, surviving records establish that Rüte was required to examine local plays on two specific occasions: In 1553, he inspected a play performed by residents of Langental; later, in 1556, both he and his successor as court secretary examined a text to be performed in Burgdorf.[144] In the second instance, the council vested him with the broad authority to censor anything that might be disadvantageous for its reputation, suggesting that Rüte regularly interpreted council policy for the stage. Moreover, Rüte joined Johannes Haller and others in examining three pastors suspected of Lutheran tendencies in 1549,[145] indicating that city leaders trusted his judgment in matters of faith as well as literature.

---

[142] The 1538 *Täufergespräch* was the last of three disputations between the city's theologians and local anabaptists: "Gespräch der Berner Prädikanten mit den Täufern, gehalten vom 11. bis 17. März 1538 zu Bern," *Quellen zur Geschichte der Täufer in der Schweiz*, ed. Martin Haas (Zurich: Theologischer Verlag, 1974), 4:257–467.

[143] Eduard Bähler, "Dekan Johann Haller und die Berner Kirche von 1548 bis 1575," in *NBT 1926*, 6.

[144] Fluri, 139–40.

[145] Eduard Bähler, "Dekan Johann Haller und die Berner Kirche von 1548 bis 1575," in *NBT 1925*, 9; see also Haller, *Tagebuch*, 309, note 28.

The frequent coincidence between the dates of Rüte's plays and his professional advancement further suggests that he was at times rewarded if a performance found the approval of the council. The decision to entrust Rüte with the redaction of existing city law, which resulted in his *Stadtsatzung* of 1539,[146] fell on 18 April 1538, less than three weeks after the performance of *Joseph*. In December of the same year, the council generously subsidized his new house with 150 pounds.[147] While *Gedeon* did not seem to bring any direct rewards from his superiors, *Noe* may have been instrumental in restoring him to their good graces following his removal from the office of court secretary in 1545 for adultery. The play was performed in the spring of 1546; by the summer, Rüte had regained his old position. Finally, whereas the performance of *Goliath* did not necessarily take place in 1555, its publication alone, which the council supported by remunerating Samuel Apiarius for his introductory dedication on 16 May,[148] certainly provided Rüte with a strong recommendation for his promotion as administrator of the Zofingen convent on 28 July, where he spent the last three years of his life. It would thus appear that Rüte's activities as playwright were in many ways extensions of his work as a civil servant.

Lastly, Rüte's prosperity and personal relations demonstrate close connections to the city's political and social elite. As Jaeger notes, Bernese tax records indicate that Rüte's wealth in 1556 totaled 5000 pounds, while that of other prominent citizens was substantially less, such as 1600 pounds for Wolfgang Musculus or 600 pounds for Benedikt Marti, at the time professor of Greek and Hebrew at the *Hohe Schule*.[149] Moreover, the godparents of Rüte's children were all

---

[146] "Die Stadtsatzung von 1539," in *Die Rechtsquellen des Kantons Bern. Erster Teil: Stadtrechte*, ed. Friedrich Emil Welti, Sammlung Schweizerischer Rechtsquellen, 2. Abteilung (Aarau: Sauerländer, 1971), 585–683. In contrast to the introduction of Roman law in many imperial cities during this period, Rüte's redaction remained in the tradition of medieval legal practice, yet still represents a successful systematization of contemporary law: Eugen Huber, "Die Satzungsbücher der Stadt Bern," *Zeitschrift des Bernischen Juristen-Vereins* 10 (1874): 97–134. Richard Feller emphasizes the elimination of legal privileges for the nobility in the "Stadtsatzung" and the bourgeois pride in Rüte's foreword: Richard Feller, "Die bernische Reformation und der Staat," in *Feier zum 400jährigen Gedächtnis der Berner Reformation* (Bern: Gustav Grunau, 1928), 39.

[147] Jaeger, "Hans von Rütes Osterspiel," 25.

[148] Fluri, 139.

[149] Jaeger, "Hans von Rütes Osterspiel," 24.

leading members of the city administration or their wives, further demonstrating his ties to the Small Council. Even mayors Hans Jakob von Wattenwyl and Hans Franz Nägeli, the hero of the Vaud campaign of 1536, are among them.[150]

In closing, it should be noted that not all Bernese plays in the first half of the sixteenth century stemmed from Manuel's or Rüte's pen, although, with the exception of *Elsli Tragdenknaben*, only their plays have survived. Indeed, that the anonymous *Elsli* was long considered to be Manuel's product may have contributed to the survival of the original edition of 1530.[151] In a few instances, we also know the names or subjects of non-extant plays. Pupils of the city German school performed a prodigal son play, the first of the city's biblical dramas, in 1534.[152] The 1535 and 1545 performances of a *Goliath* have been equated with Rüte's *Goliath* of 1555, merely performed at an earlier date.[153] Subsequent performances at the *Hohe Schule* occurred in 1540, 1549, and 1554, when the students enacted Aristophanes's *Ploutos*. Whether this took place in Latin or Greek is unclear,[154] but the few recorded performances suggest that, as at so many schools of the era, a tradition of school play productions existed, intended to improve the students' linguistic and rhetorical skills. Additional performances took place during Rüte's active period in 1537, 1552, and 1553. Performances in other parts of the Bernese territories, as well as performances following the publication of Rüte's *Goliath* in 1555, remain outside the scope of this investigation.[155] The remaining Bernese dramas of the sixteenth century—an anonymous

---

[150] *Sämtliche Dramen*, 3:53; Sulser, 115.

[151] The sole exemplar of the 1530 edition by Thomas Wolff has the following entry on the penultimate page: "Diß Spil sol gestelt haben Niclaus ma/nuel ein guotter maaler vnd burger zuo/Bern." As quoted in *Werke und Briefe*, 522.

[152] The council record speaks solely of *ler knaben*; Fluri later states that these were pupils of the city's German school. However, the term *spilknaben* is later used for students at the *Hohe Schule*, so that the 1534 entry could refer to them as well. Cf. Fluri, 144, 154.

[153] Fluri, 156–7; *Sämtliche Dramen*, 3:300.

[154] The play was performed in Greek in Zurich in 1531. See Garside, 71–3.

[155] Streit lists a 1540 performance of *Wie man alte Weiber jung schmiedet* in Utzistorf: Streit, 102–3. *Appius und Virginia*, long considered a likely Bernese play, was performed in Burgdorf in 1591, as Edmund Stadler has demonstrated: Edmund Stadler, "Das Volksschauspiel Burgdorfs im 16. Jahrhundert," *Burgdorfer Jahrbuch* 39 (1972), 22–42; cf. Michael, 148. An edition of the play exists in Fr. von Fischer-Manuel, ed., "'Appius und Virginia.' Ein bernisches Schauspiel aus dem 16. Jahrhundert," in *Berner Taschenbuch auf das Jahr 1886* (Bern: B.F. Haller, 1885), 73–149.

Esther play in an eighteenth-century copy, Johann Rasser's *Kinderzucht* (1573; printed 1574), and Johannes Haller's *Glückwünschung zu der ernüwerten Alter Eydgenoßischer trüw vnd fründtschafft beyder stett Zürich vnd Bern* ("A Congratulatory Play on the Renewal of Old Helvetian Loyalty and Friendship between the Cities of Zurich and Bern," 1584)—belong to an altered tradition, in which performances are no longer strictly biblical, but now promote Swiss patriotism or pay homage to local personalities.[156]

---

[156] The Esther play was performed for the wedding of Johannes Steiger and Magdalena Nägeli. See Fluri, 140. On *Kinderzucht*, see Michael, 233–5. On Haller's play, see Katrin Gut, "Johannes Hallers *Glückwunschung* von 1584: ein vaterländisches Spiel," in *Sondierungen zum Theater—Enquêtes sur le théâtre*, ed. Andreas Kotte, Theatrum Helveticum 1 (Basel: Editions Theaterkultur Verlag, 1995), 51–95.

CHAPTER THREE

PROTESTANT CARNIVAL:
A CONTRADICTION IN TERMS?

> This year, to the great advancement of evangelical freedom, two well-informed and widely circulated plays, predominantly by the skillful painter Niklaus Manuel, were composed and performed publicly on Cross Lane. One, namely the "Corpse Eaters" [*Vom Papst und seiner Priesterschaft*], treating all abuses of the whole papacy, was performed on the "Pfaffenfastnacht" [Sunday, 15 February], the other [*Von Papsts und Christi Gegensatz*], concerning the opposition of the nature of Jesus Christ and that of his so-called vicar, the Roman pope, on the "Alte Fastnacht" [22 February]. In between, on Ash Wednesday, the Roman indulgence, to the accompaniment of the "Bean Song," was carried through all streets and ridiculed. Through these wondrous exhibitions, heretofore uncontemplated (since they were thought blasphemous), a great mass of people were moved to consider and distinguish Christian freedom and papal servitude. In the Protestant cause, there has hardly been a booklet which has been printed so often and distributed so widely as these plays.
>
> —Valerius Anshelm, *Berner Chronik*

As a genre, the German *Fastnachtspiel* (carnival or Shrovetide play) is distinguished not so much by internal characteristics as by external circumstances, namely by its staging during the pre-Lenten season, usually in the week preceding Ash Wednesday. Most carnival plays, especially early texts from the fifteenth century, were transgressive in nature and frequently contained graphic depictions of violence and unabashed discussions of bodily functions such as fornication and defecation. Nonetheless, there also existed a substantial subsection of *Fastnachtspiele* with moral or didactic content. This was apparently true for the century-long tradition of Lübeck carnival performances, whose titles, preserved in the records of the local *Zirkelbrüderschaft* (Confraternity of the Circle) and the *Kaufleutekompanie* (Merchants' Company), recall morality plays.[1] Unfortunately, the play texts of

---

[1] Eckehard Simon, "Organizing and Staging Carnival Plays in Late Medieval

this tradition are lost, with one solitary exception.² Of those cities from which carnival play texts survive for the fifteenth century, only the Nuremberg tradition is well-represented, comprising 108 of the total 144 extant texts from this period.³ Correspondingly, research on German-language carnival plays has focused on Nuremberg.⁴

This state of affairs has unfortunately skewed observations on other centers of carnival play production, not only Lübeck, but also Sterzing in South Tirol or the "Alemannic" plays of Switzerland and Alsace, which form the context for the five carnival plays of the Bernese

---

Lübeck: A New Look at the Archival Record," *JEGP* 92 (1993): 57–72; Dieter Wuttke, afterword to *Fastnachtspiele des 15. und 16. Jahrhunderts*, 4th ed. (Stuttgart: Reclam, 1989), 449–51. Simon has more recently uncovered the records of a third company, the *Greveradenkompanie*, which also performed carnival plays, but apparently not on wagons as was the practice of the Merchants and Circle Brothers: Simon, "Das Schauspiel der Lübecker Fastnacht," *ZfdPh* 116 (1997; Sonderheft), 208–23.

² Christoph Walter, ed., "Das Fastnachtspiel Henselin oder von der Rechtfertigkeit," *Jahrbuch des Vereins für niederdeutsche Sprachforschung* 3 (1877): 9–36.

³ Wuttke, *Fastnachtspiele*, 441.

⁴ The following are some of the more recent studies to focus on the Nuremberg carnival tradition: Konrad Schoell, "Individual and Social Affiliation in the Nuremberg Shrovetide Plays," in *Drama and Community: People and Plays in Medieval Europe*, ed. Alan Hindley, Medieval Texts and Cultures of Northern Europe 1 (Turnhout: Brepols, 1999), 161–78; James R. Erb, "Fictions, Realities and the Fifteenth-Century Nuremberg *Fastnachtspiel*," in *Carnival and the Carnivalesque. The Fool, the Reformer, the Wildman, and Others in Early Modern Theatre*, ed. Konrad Eisenbichler and Wim Hüsken, Ludus 4 (Amsterdam/Atlanta: Rodopi, 1999), 89–116; Edelgard E. DuBruck, *Aspects of Fifteenth-Century Society in the German Carnival Comedies. 'Speculum Hominis'*, Studies in German Language and Literature 13 (Lewiston, Queenston, Lampeter: Edwin Mellen Press, 1993); Elisabeth Keller, *Die Darstellung der Frau in Fastnachtspiel und Spruchdichtung von Hans Rosenplüt und Hans Folz* (Frankfurt/Berlin/Bern: Peter Lang, 1992); Hedda Ragotzky, "'Pulschafft und nachthunger': Zur Funktion von Liebe und Ehe im frühen Nürnberger Fastnachtspiel," in *Ordnung und Lust: Bilder von Liebe, Ehe und Sexualität in Spätmittelalter und Früher Neuzeit*, ed. Hans-Jürgen Bachorski, Literatur-Imagination-Realität 1 (Trier: Wissenschaftlicher Verlag Trier, 1991), 427–46; Johannes Müller, *Schwert und Scheide: Der sexuelle und skatologische Wortschatz im Nürnberger Fastnachtspiel des 15. Jahrhunderts*, Deutsche Literatur von den Anfängen bis 1700 2 (Bern: Peter Lang, 1988); John E. Tailby, "The Origins and Beginning of the Nuremberg Shrovetide Plays," in *Le Théâtre au Moyen Age. Actes du 2e colloque de la Societé Internationale pour l'Etude du Théâtre Médiéval, Alençon, 11–14 juillet 1977*, edited by Gari R. Muller (Quebec: Aurore-Université, 1981), 187–91; idem, "Peasants in Fifteenth-Century 'Fastnachtspiele' of Nuremberg. The Problems of Their Identification and the Significance of Their Presentation," *Daphnis* 4 (1975): 172–8; Rüdiger Krohn, *Der unanständige Bürger. Untersuchungen zum Obszönen in den Nürnberger Fastnachtsspielen des 15. Jahrhunderts* (Kronberg/Taunus: Scriptor, 1974); Johannes Merkel, *Form und Funktion der Komik im Nürnberger Fastnachtspiel* (Freiburg/Br.: Schwarz, 1971); Gerd Simon, *Die erste deutsche Fastnachtsspieltradition. Zur Überlieferung, Textkritik und Chronologie der Nürnberger Fastnachtsspiele des 15. Jahrhunderts*, Germanische Studien 240 (Lübeck/Hamburg: Matthiesen, 1970).

Reformation. In particular, two myths continue to circulate regarding the Alemannic tradition as propagated by Eckehard Catholy: 1) Swiss Shrovetide texts are unusually didactic or political, while the Nuremberg plays treat largely quotidian issues of sex, greed, and other human foibles; 2) the Swiss tradition did not exist until the early sixteenth century, when Basel author Pamphilus Gengenbach imported northern carnival custom following his apprenticeship as a printer in Nuremberg.[5] Despite the clear evidence for fifteenth-century carnival play performances in Switzerland,[6] Catholy's assertions on the nature and origin of the Swiss carnival play tradition found their way into several subsequent studies of sixteenth-century theater.[7] As a result, Swiss Shrovetide texts were long considered derivative and deviant from the "standard" plays of Nuremberg.

Recent research, however, has turned this paradigm on its head by arguing that the innhouse Shrovetide performances of Nuremberg, when compared to the open-air performances of Lübeck, Tirol, and Switzerland, were in reality the exception.[8] This is not to say that Swiss carnival plays were any less political than previously considered. On the contrary, Heidy Greco-Kaufmann's analysis of the

---

[5] Eckehard Catholy, *Fastnachtspiel*, Sammlung Metzler 56 (Stuttgart: Metzler, 1966), 75–7. Catholy nonetheless was among the first researchers to approach the carnival on its own terms, and his theses rightfully displaced the antiquated efforts of Maximilian Rudwin and the German nationalist Robert Stumpfl to link carnival plays to Germanic ritual: Maximilian Rudwin, *The Origin of German Carnival Comedy* (New York: G.E. Stechert, 1920); Robert Stumpfl, *Kultspiele der Germanen als Urpsrung des mittelalterlichen Dramas* (Berlin: Junker und Dünnhaupt, 1936).

[6] Eckehard Simon, "Shrovetide Plays in Late-Medieval Switzerland: An Appraisal," *Modern Language Notes* 85 (1970): 323–31; *Frühe Schweizerspiele*, ed. Friederike Christ-Kutter, Altdeutsche Übungstexte 19 (Bern: Francke, 1963). For a thorough assessment of Catholy's initial theses on carnival plays, see Dieter Wuttke, "Zum Fastnachtspiel des Spätmittelalters. Eine Auseinandersetzung mit Catholys Buch," *ZfdPh* 84 (1965): 247–67. Cf. Catholy, *Das Fastnachtspiel des Spätmittelalters. Gestalt und Funktion*, Hermaea NF 8 (Tübingen: Niemeyer, 1961).

[7] See for example Barbara Könneker, *Die deutsche Literatur der Reformationszeit: Kommentar zu einer Epoche* (Munich: Winkler Verlag, 1975), 126; David Brett-Evans, *Von Hrotsvith bis Folz und Gengenbach. Eine Geschichte des mittelalterlichen deutschen Dramas*, Grundlagen der Germanistik 15/18 (Berlin: Schmidt, 1975), 2:174; Erika Kartschoke, "Fastnachtspiel," in *Einführung in die deutsche Literatur des 12.–16. Jahrhunderts*, ed. Winfried Frey et al. (Opladen: Westdeutscher Verlag, 1981), 3:120; Wolfgang F. Michael, *Das deutsche Drama der Reformationszeit* (Bern: Peter Lang, 1984), 34.

[8] Heidy Greco-Kaufmann, *"vor rechten lütten ist guot schimpfen": Der Luzerner Marcolfus und das Schweizer Fastnachtspiel des 16. Jahrhunderts*, Deutsche Literatur von den Anfängen bis 1700 19 (Bern: Lang, 1994), 9 ff., 289–91. James Erb also acknowledges the exceptionality of Nuremberg carnival in his recent research: Erb, 89 ff.

ostensibly unpolemical *Marcolfus* play by Lucerne municipal secretary Zacharias Bletz confirms that even this reworking of the popular *Salomon und Markolf* chapbook had a decidedly political component designed to legitimate the secular authority of the Lucerne town council.[9] Rather, it has become apparent that Nuremberg plays themselves were often highly political, either subtly endorsing prevailing hierarchies and habits or loudly agitating for or against a particular cause. Indeed, Nuremberg performances often actively supported council policies, as evidenced by Hans Folz's three anti-Semitic plays, which bolstered the city's efforts to expel local Jews in opposition to imperial reluctance.[10]

The study of Bern's five Reformation *Fastnachtspiele* allows a longitudinal approach to the carnivalesque rhetoric of transgression and is thus particularly relevant within the larger discussion of the genre's political tendencies. In their respective analyses, both Peter Pfrunder and Greco-Kaufmann focus on a single moment in the history of Swiss carnival, the former on Bern in 1523,[11] and the latter on Lucerne in 1546. Lying between these two dates, among other events, is the victory of Swiss Catholics in the Second War of Kappel of 1531, which proved to be a major watershed in confessional politics within the Helvetian Confederacy. The subsequent peace negotiations forbade religious polemic by either party. Performed prior to 1531, the text of *Marcolfus* or any other post-Kappel Catholic play would have likely borne greater resemblance to the militant diatribe of *Vom Papst und seiner Priesterschaft*.[12] Indeed, while Manuel's players lambasted the pope during the carnival of 1523, Shrovetide celebrants in Lucerne were occupied with burning Ulrich Zwingli in effigy.[13]

---

[9] Greco-Kaufmann, 253–64.

[10] David Price, "Hans Folz's Anti-Jewish Carnival Plays," *Fifteenth Century Studies* 19 (1992): 209–28. Cf. Samuel Kinser, "Presentation and Representation: Carnival at Nuremberg, 1450–1550," *Representations* 13 (1986): 1–41. A more recent study has appeared that confirms Price's results, but is unaware of his prior research: Guy Borgnet, "Jeu de Carnaval et Antisémitisme: Pureté Théologique et Pureté Ethnique chez Hans Folz," in *Carnival and the Carnivalesque. The Fool, the Reformer, the Wildman, and Others in Early Modern Theatre*, ed. Konrad Eisenbichler and Wim Hüsken, Ludus 4 (Amsterdam/Atlanta: Rodopi, 1999), 129–45.

[11] Peter Pfrunder, *Pfaffen, Ketzer, Totenfresser: Fastnachtskultur der Reformationszeit—Die Berner Spiele von Niklaus Manuel* (Zurich: Chronos, 1989).

[12] Greco-Kaufmann acknowledges this in her study: 256–60, 263–4.

[13] Gottfried W. Locher, *Die Zwinglische Reformation im Rahmen der europäischen Kirchengeschichte* (Göttingen: Vandenhoeck & Ruprecht, 1979), 426.

A diachronic analysis of Bernese performances between 1523 and 1531 can thus better focus on the development of confessional polemics leading up to the Second War of Kappel.

The substantial body of research on Manuel's plays alone demonstrates the difficulty of assigning a priori any political tendency to carnival plays in general. Depending on which interpretation one reads, the Bernese council either employed Manuel's *Vom Papst und seiner Priesterschaft* and *Von Papsts und Christi Gegensatz* to test the receptivity of the citizenry to the Reformation,[14] or silenced his assumed insurrection by afterwards shipping him off as steward to Erlach on the south shore of Lake Bienne, which he administered for the city until 1528.[15] Similar controversy surrounds *Der Ablaßkrämer*: For some, the play is an open manifesto for peasant revolt;[16] for others, it contains a base portrayal of popular insurrection that reveals Manuel's abhorrence of the 1525 Peasant Wars.[17] And whereas Pfrunder's analysis is highly successful in exposing the mechanisms of carnivalesque rhetoric, even his conclusions must be revised in light of more recent research, which indicates that Bern's governing Small Council was in 1523 still intent on a Catholic reform policy intended to preserve the old faith against the will of the citizenry.[18]

After situating the particularities of Bernese carnival plays within the current theoretical discussion on carnival transgression, the following pages analyze the plays' development within the specific context of the Swiss Reformation. In general, I argue for a four-stage progression in the Bernese interaction between carnival poetics and Protestant polemics: 1) The years 1523 to 1525 represent an initial period of anti-papal sentiment—although not necessarily anti-Catholic—during which the political implications of religious reform are not fully apparent, allowing Manuel to agitate for change without appearing to foment insurrection; 2) following the Peasant Wars, which left

---

[14] Könneker, *Die deutsche Literatur der Reformationszeit*, 125; idem, *Satire im 16. Jahrhundert: Epoche—Werk—Wirkung* (Munich: C.H. Beck, 1991), 170.

[15] Feller, 2:139.

[16] Beerli, 243.

[17] Jean-Paul Tardent, *Niklaus Manuel als Staatsmann*, Archiv des Historischen Vereins des Kantons Bern 51 (Bern: Archiv des Historischen Vereins des Kantons Bern, 1967), 98–9; Hans Christoph von Tavel, "Rychardus Hinderlist," in *NMD*, 506.

[18] Heinrich Richard Schmidt, "Stadtreformation in Bern und Nürnberg—ein Vergleich," in *Nürnberg und Bern: Zwei Reichsstädte und ihre Landgebiete*, ed. Rudolf Endres, Erlanger Forschungen A46 (Erlangen: Universitätsbibliothek, 1990), 109 ff.

the Bernese territories largely unscathed, but instilled a fear of revolt in local authorities, confessional tensions prohibited the performance of religious polemics; 3) after the local Reformation of 1528, Protestants were again at liberty to perform carnival plays, albeit in a modified form that responded, consciously or unconsciously, to the growing suppression of all remnants of Catholicism; 4) following the performance of Rüte's *Abgötterei* in 1531, theological and political pressures merged to stifle carnival polemics in Bern once and for all, the result of determined efforts to eradicate the last vestiges of the former liturgical calendar as well as of the delicate truce observed by both religious parties following the Protestant defeat in the Second War of Kappel. In addressing these changes, my guiding question will be how the genre of *Fastnachtspiel* could continue to function in a post-Reformation context as a vehicle for Protestant polemics while Protestant theologians were engaged in eradicating the carnival celebration at the root of such invectives. The answer lies in the plays' altered representation of political agency. While Manuel ascribes the power of change to unruly (Protestant) peasants, Rüte's rustics are pious, but disenfranchised, replaced by a less imitable agent, the allegorical Bernese Bear. Transgressive behavior continues in the later plays, but its locus shifts, becoming the sole domain of Catholic characters.

Transgression, Politics, and Religion

Over the last two decades, the theories of Soviet scholar Mikhail Bakhtin have attained canonical status within the field of carnival studies. *Rabelais and His World*,[19] the author's dissertation of 1940, interpreted François Rabelais's *Gargantua* and *Pantagruel* as expressions of the sixteenth century's "culture of folk humor." For Bakhtin, this humor could take several forms, such as ritual spectacles (carnival pageants, market plays), comic verbal compositions (Latin and vernacular parodies), and various forms of billingsgate (oaths and curses).[20] Bakhtin placed these manifestations of comic laughter in opposition to ecclesiastical and feudal institutions. During carnival as a time of license, popular laughter could assert itself and invert traditional hier-

---

[19] Mikhail Bakhtin, *Rabelais and His World*, trans. Hélène Iswolsky (Bloomington: Indiana University Press, 1984).
[20] Ibid., 4–5.

archies between "high" and "low" cultures. This celebration of low culture occurred in what Bakhtin termed "grotesque realism," an unabashed indulgence in images of bodily functions, such as fornication, flatulence, and gluttony.[21] In Bakhtin's interpretation, society's lower classes received their own autonomous voice during carnival, so that the festival ultimately celebrated their otherness from sanctioned culture.

Much of Bakhtin's terminology has become common coinage for studies of the carnivalesque, even when the term has little to do with carnival per se but rather denotes the seemingly ubiquitous inversion of sociocultural hierarchies across time and place. Nonetheless, the limitations of the author's Shrovetide populism have become equally apparent. To give an in-depth discussion of Bakthin's theories, their reception, and their subsequent modifications would require a book of its own; the following comments are limited to representative studies whose critique of Bakhtin bears particular relevance for late medieval and Renaissance drama. In their consensus, one cannot reduce the complexities of carnival and transgression to a simple monologic system.[22]

Opposing Bakhtin's theory of carnival are anthropological models of ritual such as those of Max Gluckmann, who believed that "rites of rebellion" function as a type of safety valve, releasing pressure from the social system to preserve the status quo.[23] Indeed, Gluckmann's model would seem more consonant with the majority of carnival celebrations in Bern and elsewhere, as the arrival of Ash Wednesday customarily put an end to all pretended subversion and ushered in a time of introspection. Similarly, Dietz-Rüdiger Moser has argued that carnival by no means stood in opposition to the church, as

---

[21] See especially the chapter "The Grotesque Image of the Body and Its Sources": Bakhtin, 303–67.

[22] See the introduction to Katerina Clark and Michael Holquist, *Mikhail Bakhtin* (Cambridge, Mass./London: The Belknap Press of Harvard University Press, 1984), 1–15. Clifford Flanigan notes with irony that Bakhtin, who is otherwise so preoccupied with plurality, polyphony, and dialogism, succumbs to the monologic in *Rabelais and His World*: C. Clifford Flanigan, "Liminality, Carnival, and Social Structure: The Case of Late Medieval Biblical Drama," in *Victor Turner and the Construction of Cultural Criticism. Between Literature and Anthropology*, ed. Kathleen Ashley (Bloomington: Indiana University Press, 1990), 55. As Clark and Holquist discuss, Bakhtin's valorization of popular culture was largely a veiled critique of Stalinism: Clark/Holquist, 305 ff. See also Greco-Kaufmann, 62–3.

[23] Max Gluckman, *Custom and Conflict in Africa* (Oxford: Blackwell, 1965), 109; see also the section "Revolte oder Ventil?" in Pfrunder, 54–5.

Bakhtin claims, but rather prepared the faithful for the Lenten season by providing first-hand experience of the depravity of worldly pursuits, which then subsequently contrasted with the Lenten community of God.[24] Yet as the strongly critical responses to Moser's theories within the German anthropological community have demonstrated, an interpretation of the carnival festival solely as an expression of ecclesiastical, i.e. sanctioned, culture is equally monologic and problematic.[25]

Clearly, any effort to assign carnival an inherently reactionary or revolutionary tendency is futile in light of historical evidence indicating that the festival could alternately foment insurrection or avert it. Emmanuel Le Roy Ladurie's *Carnival in Romans*, for example, describes in detail how the city's reactionary patriciate and insurgent craftsmen vied to exploit the carnival of 1580 to their own ends, ending in the craftsmen's tragic slaughter.[26] In Switzerland as well, carnival could be both conservative and progressive. The city-states of the Swiss Confederacy often chose the festival to host and entertain delegations from other cantons, conducting business while at the same time indulging in costly self-aggrandizing entertainment.[27] The celebration also traditionally encompassed martial activities, such as parades and marksmanship contests, a reflection of widespread pride in contemporary Swiss military prowess. However, the risk inherent in quasi-military gatherings outside of sanctioned government was real and posed a danger for local authorities.[28] The peasant revolt of 1489 against Zurich mayor Hans Waldmann, which resulted in his execution at the hands of patrician enemies, began with a carnival celebration in Meilen on Lake Zurich.[29] The Köniz uprising

---

[24] Dietz-Rüdiger Moser, "Lachkultur des Mittelalters? Michael Bachtin und die Folgen seiner Theorie," *Euphorion* 84 (1990): 98–108; idem, *Fastnacht—Fasching—Karneval. Das Fest der "Verkehrten Welt"* (Graz: Verlag Styria, 1986), 29–48.

[25] See above all Hans Moser, "Zu Problematik und Methodik neuester Fastnachtsforschung," *Zeitschrift für Volkskunde* 80 (1984): 2–22; Hans Moser, "Kritisches zu neuen Hypothesen der Fastnachtforschung," *Jahrbuch für Volkskunde* Neue Folge 5 (1982): 9–50. For a review of the reception of D.R. Moser's theories, see Greco-Kaufmann, 54–60; Pfrunder, 58–61.

[26] Emmanuel Le Roy Ladurie, *Carnival in Romans*, trans. Mary Feeney (New York: George Braziller, 1979).

[27] Pfrunder, 72–8; Greco-Kaufmann, 22–4, 27–30.

[28] Pfrunder, 82–4; Greco-Kaufmann, 36–41.

[29] Greco-Kaufmann, 36; Moritz von Stürler, ed., "Beschreibung des Waldmannischen Auflaufs zu Zürich von einem Zeitgenossen," *Archiv für schweizerische Geschichte* 9 (1853): 279–329.

against the feudal authority of Bern similarly had its origins in the bourgeois ridicule of peasants during the city's carnival of 1513, although the Köniz parish fair (*Kirchweih*) on 26 June provided the actual impetus for the revolt.[30]

Early modern carnival thus possessed a protean element, allowing transgressive symbols to be exploited by different factions to different ends.[31] Again, Le Roy Ladurie's *Carnival in Romans* illustrates the complex interplay of economic, religious, and social factors that determined the actions of sixteenth-century carnival celebrants. Based on tax records and other surviving documents, the author identified not only four social ranks within the city—landowners and nobles, merchants, craftsmen, and peasants—but also additional divisions resulting from disparate taxation, religious beliefs, and even personal animosity.[32] The Romans carnival of 1579 triggered the insurrection of an initially broad alliance of craftsmen, peasants, and even select bourgeois, substantially a victory of the "low" in Bakhtinian terms, but with clear participation by higher elements who had their own reasons for supporting revolt. Conversely, the ultimate patriciate victory during the following year's carnival would not have been possible without the participation of a substantial faction of moderate craftsmen. Perhaps most instructive for the study of Reformation carnival,[33] Le Roy Ladurie makes clear that members of differing confessions often allied themselves politically according to common social and financial interests. Many Catholic craftsmen and peasants sided with the elected leader of the revolt, Jean Serve alias Paumier, although he was said to be in league with Dauphiné Huguenots. Meanwhile, select Protestant patricians supported the Catholic faction around judge Antoine Guérin after an initial flirtation with rebellion.[34]

---

[30] The perpetrators stated "dass purengspöt und äschensäk an vergangner fasnacht ze vil verachtlich wider si gebrucht. Verachtung und spot vergessen kum on vergelten." Anshelm, 3:446. On the uprising itself, see Feller, 1:531–8.

[31] Peter Stallybrass and Allon White, *The Politics and Poetics of Transgression* (Ithaca: Cornell University Press, 1986), 14–6; Hermann Bausinger, "Für eine komplexere Fastnachtstheorie," *Jahrbuch für Volkskunde* Neue Folge 6 (1983): 101–6.

[32] Le Roy Ladurie, 1–34, passim.

[33] On Reformation and carnival in general, see Robert Scribner, "Reformation, Carnival and the World turned Upside-Down," in *Städtische Gesellschaft und Reformation*, ed. Ingrid Bátori, Spätmittelalter und Frühe Neuzeit 12 (Stuttgart: Klett-Cotta, 1980), 222–52.

[34] Le Roy Ladurie, 145, 184 ff.

Unfortunately, Bernese records do not allow for the same detailed historic reconstruction of staged revolt as in Romans. Based on existing documents, such as the testimony of Valerius Anshelm found in this chapter's epigraph,[35] one could not possibly expect a more minute examination of Bernese carnival than Pfrunder's *Pfaffen—Ketzer—Totenfresser*. Nonetheless, as others before him,[36] Pfrunder presumes that the silent majority of Bern's councilors and burghers were pro-reform by 1523, so that the carnival performances of young bourgeois actors allowed proponents of the new faith to agitate with full support at home while distancing themselves from the plays in the Confederacy, since the carnival actions of young men could not be taken as an official expression of city policy.[37] As evidenced by the

---

[35] Anshelm's original text is as follows: "Es sind ouch dis jars zuo grosser fürdrung evangelischer friheit hie zuo Bern zwei wolgelerte und in wite land nuzlich ussgespreite spil, fürnemlich durch den künstlichen malermeister Niclausen Manuel, gedichtet und offenlich an der krüzgassen gespilet worden, eins, namlich der totenfrässer, berüerend alle misbrüch des ganzen babstuoms, uf der Pfaffen-Vassnacht, das ander von dem gegensaz des wesens Kristi Jhesu und sines genämten stathalters, des Römschen babsts, uf der alten Vassnacht. Hiezwischen uf der Aeschen mitwochen ward der Römsch ablas mit dem bonenlied durch alle gassen getragen und verspotet. Durch dis wunderliche und vor nie, als gotslästerliche, gedachte anschowungen ward ein gross volk bewegt, kristliche friheit und bäbstliche knechtschaft zuo bedenken und ze underscheiden. Es ist ouch in dem evangelischen handel kum ein büechle so dik getrukt und so wit gebracht worden, als diser spilen." Anshelm, 4:475. There is some dispute as to whether "fürnemlich" implies that Manuel had assistance in preparing the performances. See Zinsli, "Niklaus Manuel, der Schriftsteller," 89, note 17. Furthermore, Anshelm records his entry under the year 1522, yet internal evidence from the plays themselves, together with Manuel's presence in Italy during early 1522, makes it highly likely that the plays were not performed until 1523. See Ferdinand Vetter, "Über die zwei angeblich 1522 aufgeführten Fastnachtsspiele Niklaus Manuels," *PBB* 29 (1904): 80–117.

[36] Könneker, *Die deutsche Literatur der Reformationszeit*, 125; Könneker, *Satire im 16. Jahrhundert*, 170.

[37] "Offiziell ist die Stadt immer noch katholisch. Aber wenn auch von seiten der konservativen Grundbesitzer, des Klerus oder der katholischen Orte in der Eidgenossenschaft antireformatorischer Druck ausgeübt wird, so dürfte doch der Einfluss dominieren, den die reformatorisch gesinnten, bürgerlichen Ober- und Mittelschichten und die zu Reichtum gelangten Aufsteiger in ihren Gesellschaften besitzen. Was könnte in dieser Situation willkommener sein als die propagandistisch-symbolische Aktion einer Vereinigung von Bürgersöhnen, die diesen Kreisen mit ihrer Kritik an der alten Kirche und ihrer Sympathie für die Reformation nahestehen? Dabei nimmt die Aktion offiziösen Charakter an, indem sie gleichzeitig die Gesinnung einer Mehrheit von einflussreichen und regierenden Bürgern kundtut—ohne dass diese direkt dafür verantwortlich gemacht werden können. Eine Gruppe von ledigen jungen Männern übernimmt also an ihrer Stelle und mit ihrer Zustimmung die Aufgabe, das—vorderhand noch diffuse—reformatorische "Gewissen der Stadt" zu artikulieren und zu inszenieren. Den Jungen ist erlaubt, was sich etablierte Kreise und vor allem

so-called Whitmonday Oath, however, the Bernese Small Council was hopeful of preserving the old faith as late as 1526, with or without the support of the citizenry. Indeed, recent research by Heinrich Richard Schmidt has demonstrated that Bernese authorities pursued a Catholic "reform" policy until the elections of 1527 ushered in a Protestant majority in the Small Council.[38] Moreover, it is doubtful that the members of the elite Small Council, who were descended from the region's lower nobility or emulated them in manners and dress,[39] unilaterally shared the reform interests of the burghers whose sons performed the plays of 1523 under Manuel's direction. Similarly, Manuel, at this time a member of the less influential Great Council, did not yet represent the concerns of the political aristocracy. Even if one assumes the complicity of reform-minded councilors such as Bartholomew May and Niklaus von Wattenwyl,[40] their staunchly Catholic colleagues would not have remunerated the performers of *Vom Papst und seiner Priesterschaft* (as noted in the *Seckelmeisterrechnungen*, or municipal treasury books)[41] if they had perceived the work as truly subversive. Stated simply, the historical record does not support Pfrunder's thesis. It is thus necessary to examine Manuel's 1523 plays for elements that permitted their call for religious change without apparently arousing the overt displeasure of the Catholic majority within the Small Council.

Two main factors allowed Manuel to cast his anti-Catholic diatribe as pro-Bernese satire: the linking of Protestant polemics to already strong anti-papal sentiments in Bern following the Swiss defeat at the Battle of Bicocca in 1522, and the assurance that religious revolt did not encompass political insurrection. Scholars have long noted the especially militant portrayal of the pope in *Vom Papst und seiner Priesterschaft*.[42] The image of Christ's vicar as warmonger

---

die Obrigkeit noch nicht gestatten dürfen: nämlich ein klares Bekenntnis zur Reformation." Pfrunder, 174–5.

[38] Schmidt, 109 ff.
[39] See for example François de Capitani, *Adel, Bürger und Zünfte im Bern des 15. Jahrhunderts*, Schriften der Berner Burgerbibliothek 16 (Bern: Berner Burgerbibliothek, 1982); Urs Martin Zahnd, *Die Bildungsverhältnisse in den bernischen Ratsgeschlechtern im ausgehenden Mittelalter. Verbreitung, Charakter und Funktion der Bildung in der politischen Führungsschicht einer spätmittelalterlichen Stadt*, Schriften der Berner Burgerbibliothek 14 (Bern: Berner Burgerbibliothek, 1979), 222 ff.
[40] Beerli, 193.
[41] Fluri, 135.
[42] Beerli, 202–4; Pfrunder, 192; Zinsli, 81–2.

was particularly resonant in a city that still mourned its losses of ten months earlier, when *Landsknechte* (imperial mercenaries) in papal service had cut down over fifty prominent Bernese burghers allied with French forces battling for control of Northern Italy. Even if Pope Adrian VI was merely defending his Lombard possessions against French incursion in April of 1522, the memory of Leo X's aggressive military policy continued to fester, uniting the city beyond class and, above all, confessional boundaries.[43] As we shall see, the carnivalesque derision of high church officials was nothing new in Bern, allowing the anti-papal polemics of Manuel's first plays to appear as part of local tradition. Nonetheless, to ensure that his call for change did not threaten local authorities, Manuel placed explicit support for secular government in the mouths of select play characters. Just as Martin Luther urged political obedience while preaching religious change, the carnival plays of Manuel and his two Bernese successors distinguished between secular and ecclesiastical rule, assuring their audience of the necessity of divinely ordained government while advocating Protestant reform.

Niklaus Manuel and Bernese Carnival before 1528

Of Bern's pre-Reformation carnival play performances, only one play's content is known in more detail. We owe this information to the enmity existing in 1521 between the citizens of Bern and their former ally Cardinal Matthäus Schiner, Charles V's most vigorous supporter within the Swiss Confederacy.[44] Following Charles's election as Holy Roman Emperor in 1519, the Swiss were justifiably concerned that the emperor might renew Habsburg claims to Swiss territories. To Schiner's dismay, Helvetian representatives, supported

---

[43] Beerli, 184.
[44] The family records of Manuel's father-in-law Hans Frisching, whose fourteen-year old son Ludwig was killed in the battle of Marignano in 1515, give an idea of the hate felt locally for Schiner: "Uff fritag, waß deß heiligen Crütz tag im herbsch, ist ummkomen unn erschossen durch beid schenckell unnser obgenanter sun Ludwig an der schantlich schlacht in Meyland, durch stiftung deß mörderschen und vererterschen, schantlichen böszwichtz, deß bischoff von Wallisz [Kardinal Matthäus Schiner] und siner anhengern. Dz inen sölichß gott niemer mer welle vergeben." As quoted in Arnold Esch, *Alltag der Entscheidung. Beiträge zur Geschichte der Schweiz an der Wende vom Mittelalter zur Neuzeit* (Bern: Paul Haupt, 1998), 304.

by Bern, entered into negotiations with Francis I of France, which resulted in May of 1521 in a mutual defense alliance.[45] According to Anshelm, Schiner avenged himself the following November upon the emperor's conquest of French-occupied Milan, when he derisively reminded captured Bernese mercenaries of the ridicule he and the emperor had suffered during the Bernese carnival of the preceding spring:

> Wie stats nun um uwerer gemaleten gilgenknaben Eschenmitwochenspotspil, darin unser her, der Römsch keiser, mit kutzen und hutzlen, und ich, uwer puntgnos, uf einem stecken mit lärer däschen postende, hond müessen offentlich durch alle stat verachtet und verspotet werden?[46]

> How do you feel now about your ornamented [?] lily-boy [i.e. francophile] Ash Wednesday play of mockery, in which the [Holy] Roman emperor, with owls and goats, and I, your confederate, propped on a pole in effigy with an empty pocket, were publicly scorned and ridiculed throughout the whole city?

Charles's tattered clothing and Schiner's empty pocket likely referred to the emperor's assumed inability to pay his mercenaries as handsomely as Francis, even though Bern had to loan the French king money following the treaty's signing to help him meet his financial obligations.[47] Yet this did not substantially sour Bernese-French relations, and in early 1521 Francis's generosity seemed genuine, so that the play likely found favor with local authorities, if not their active patronage. In the mockery of Schiner, Northern Italy's volatile mixture of Swiss, French, imperial, and papal interests was already the subject of anti-Roman carnival ridicule in Bern prior to 1523.

In the events that followed, Bern's most serious miscalculation was its belief that Pope Leo X was Charles's enemy. When the pope suddenly announced his alliance with the emperor in June of 1521 and declared war on France, shock overtook the city's councilors,[48] likely turning to anger following the combined imperial-papal conquest of Milan in the fall. The Habsburgs were familiar adversaries, but the pope had been united with the Swiss in a protective alliance.

---

[45] Feller, 2:73–5.
[46] Anshelm, 4:450. See also Heinrich Dübi, "Miscellen zur bernischen Geschichte: 1) Ein anonymes Fastnachtspiel vom Jahre 1521," *Blätter für bernische Geschichte, Kunst und Altertumskunde* 23 (1927): 161–6.
[47] Feller, 2:74.
[48] Ibid., 2:75.

Although Anshelm's post-Reformation record of events has a clear confessional tinge, the bitterness of his comments arguably exceeds the expected level of Protestant diatribe:

> Als dan vil nach die schweristen und schädlichsten krieg, so in Tütschen und Wälschen landen indert und ob 500 jar har gewüetet haben, wie das der Römschen bäbsten und keiseren geschicht bezügen, fürnemlich angericht oder selbs gefüert sind durch die Römschen bäbst, die sich Gots und Kristi stathalter und der kristen väter und hirten rüemen und nemmen; warlich irem rüemen und nemmen so ganz unglich, dass iemand nit on ursach glowen möchte, si wärid nit des barmherzigen Gots und des fridsamen Kristi, sunder des grimmen, todschlächtigen sattans stathalter, und pluotsichtige tyrannen und wölf der tür erkouften herd Kristi. Dem glich zuo diser zit, da der babst Leo sich berüempt, einen fünfjarigen friden in aller kristenheit ufgericht haben, aber im zuo lang wolt wären, [...] do ward geraten, dass er vom Franzesischen küng sölte abston, als von dem, so im sine unghorsamen an sich zuge und starkte, den herzogen von Ferrer und ander, und bi dem in Italia kein frid, noch vereinung bestüende, und mit hilf des mächtigen keisers helfen uss Italia vertriben, und den elichen erben, herzog Franzen Sfortia, gon Meyland insetzen, der dem Römschen babst und keiser schuldige ghorsame tuon, und mit den Italischen ständen als ein glichmässiger friden halten müsste.[49]

> As attested by imperial and papal chronicles, the fiercest and most harmful wars to have wreaked havoc in German and Romance lands over the last 500 years and beyond were for the most part either caused or waged by the Roman popes, who boast and call themselves God's and Christ's vicars and the fathers and shepherds of Christians. Truly, they are so wholly unlike their boast and title that one might with good reason believe that they are vicars not of merciful God and peaceloving Christ, but of fearful, manslaughtering Satan and that they are bloody tyrants and wolves of Christ's dearly bought flock. Correspondingly, at this time, during which Pope Leo boasted that he had established a five-year peace in all Christendom, but which then lasted too long for him [...] it was advised that he should forsake the French king—who had taken in and nourished traitors to the pope, such as the Duke of Ferrara and others, and with whom no peace or union would exist in Italy—and drive him out of Italy with the aid of the mighty emperor and to install the rightful heir, Duke Francis Sforza, in Milan, who would be compelled to do dutiful obeisance to the Roman pope and emperor and to keep peace with the Italian estates.

---

[49] Anshelm, 4:419–20.

The unexpected imperial-papal alliance, renewed by Leo's successor Adrian, made Bern's situation seem all the more precarious in the months leading up to Manuel's plays of 1523. With Habsburg possessions to the east (Tirol), to the west (Franche-Comté), and to the north (*Vorderösterreich*, i.e. Breisgau and parts of Alsace), the Swiss feared that Charles would completely surround them if Milan remained in imperial hands. The council thus did all it could to aid Francis in regaining Lombardy in order to break the emperor's stranglehold. It mustered 2100 men and, against prior custom, allowed French officers to choose personally among the recruits. Local *Kronenfresser* (crown-eaters) were so accustomed to the king's freely dispensed money that, when the French commanders turned away eager, but unfit volunteers, the council had to pacify those rejected with gifts from its own treasury.[50] After joining other Swiss troops and, slightly later, French forces in February 1522, the Bernese mercenaries fatefully began to distrust the French general Lautrec, who led them through Lombardy for two months without a battle. Finally, the Swiss captain Albrecht vom Stein, fooled by a ruse into believing the enemy at a disadvantage, demanded with a haughty "We want at them!" that Lautrec engage the opponent.[51] Charles's and Adrian's forces had been buying for time and had set up well-fortified entrenchments, but the Swiss gave Lautrec no choice. On 27 April 1522, the combined French and Swiss army attacked. Swiss battle fever was so great that the troops under Stein and his co-captain Arnold von Winkelried disregarded Lautrec's commands and charged before French artillery could breach the enemy's fortifications. They paid dearly for their zeal: within minutes, the papal/imperial cannons left 3000 Swiss dead or dying on the battlefield.[52] In addition to some 50 representatives of the Great Council, several members of the Small Council were among the casualities, including Hans Rudolf

---

[50] Feller, 2:78; Anshelm, 4:510.
[51] "Und als ein züg reisiger und fuosknecht einen guoten weg vorm läger haruss in ebnem veld hielt, ein gereiz zemachen, do karten die genempten hoptlüt um, sagten dem hern [Lautrec] und den knechten, dass d'viend lägid in ebnem veld und wärid guot zeschlahen, man sölte illen. Daruf sagt der her, er hätte sin gwisse kuntschaft und späh, dass d'viend dergstalt lägid, dass si nit on merklichen schaden zegwinnen; so wäre der züg, den si gesehen, nun ein luoder; man sölte nit gahen, noch den listigen viend verachten. Do fieng der vom Stein an zetoben und schrien: 'Ir wöllend, wie in vergangnem jar zuo Pontuick [Pontevico], uns die viend uss unsern händen lassen entrinnen; wir wöllend dran!'" Anshelm, 4:516.
[52] Esch, 112; Feller, 2:79.

Nägeli, Anton von Diesbach, Hans Rudolf Mülinen, and Bat Wilhelm von Bonstetten, as well as Albrecht vom Stein and his own son Brandolf.

This ignominy was not to be forgotten the following February. For Manuel, or for anyone in Bern who wished to argue for the necessity of religious reform at this time, papal militancy offered a convenient propagandistic handhold and ensured a sympathetic audience, even among the most fervent Catholics. Besides, Manuel had already vented his anger on imperial *Landsknechte*, the other culprit in the Swiss defeat, in his "Song of Bicocca."[53] And although he would make an appearance in *Vom Papst und seiner Priesterschaft*, Cardinal Schiner could no longer serve as the play's main scapegoat, having passed away in September 1522. This time, the pope himself suffered the brunt of Bernese ridicule.

Thus, after an initial scene in which two professional mourners carry in a coffin and praise its occupant for having willed much money for masses to be said in his name, *Vom Papst und seiner Priesterschaft* (fig. 9) begins its portrayal with the pope, who leads a parade of ecclesiastical officials from cardinals to beguines and hermits. All sing the merits of death and the profits it brings the church, but as the revue progresses down the church hierarchy, the monologues become more plaintive. Whereas deacons and abbots complain that the laity has begun to read the Gospel for themselves and no longer takes their word for truth, the lower echelons of priests, monks, and nuns lament their growing impoverishment. Subsequently, other "victims" of the church speak: a beggar who lacks alms, an invalid, and an impoverished nobleman who now regrets the money he has wasted on good works. The play then returns to the theme of profitable death and dying, with members of the Swiss papal guard praising the financial rewards of papal mercenary service. Suddenly, a Knight of Rhodes appears, who asks the pope for aid in battling the Turkish siege of the island. After he departs unsuccessful, a Turk comments on the sad state of Christendom before the Protestant preacher Dr. Lütpolt Schüchnit (Leopold Fear-Nothing) steps forward and asks several peasants for their opinions on the pope. These they express in vivid bodily terms. Further papal mercenaries arrive in preparation for a campaign, followed by the appearance of the apostles Peter

---

[53] "Biccocalied," in *Werke und Briefe*, 73–99.

and Paul, who closely examine the pope and find him to be the exact opposite of Peter, Rome's first bishop.[54] The pope then makes a final, militant speech, followed by Schüchnit's supplications for the end of papal rule.

The pope's initial appearance at the pinnacle of the church hierarchy establishes the play's general theme of ecclesiastical corruption with its topics of indulgences, purgatory, canon law, excommunication, and general financial and moral excesses. His second appearance, however, forms the central scene of the play and speaks to Bern's wounded military pride. The speech of the Knight of Rhodes directly reflects the historical situation of 1522, in which the Knights of the Order of St. John valiantly, but ultimately unsuccessfully, defended Rhodes from late July until Christmas Day against the overwhelming forces of Sultan Suleiman II.[55] In describing the defenders' hardships suffered for the sake of Christ, the knight embodies a military code of honor and bravery meant to appeal to the Bernese mercenaries in Manuel's audience. His speech and manners contrast directly with the sadistic hedonism of the Swiss papal guards who appear earlier in the scene, as illustrated by the monologue of Heine Anckennapff (Butter Pot), whose given name marks him as a stereotypical Swiss mercenary:[56]

> Der pabst ist mir ein grechter got
> Er fügt wol für die armen rott
> Er weißt wol was eim kriegßman gbrist
> So er selbs ouch ein krie[g]ßman ist
> Er hat mir dry guot pfründen geben
> Die sol ich nützen diewil ich leben
> Die verdienen ich mit hallapartten
> Der kilchen darffe ich nit vast wartten

---

[54] The Hamburg manuscript of *Vom Papst und seiner Priesterschaft* places the apostles' appearance before the mercenaries' mustering and the pope's final militant speech, so that Ferdinand Vetter and others believe this to be Manuel's original sequence of scenes, later altered by his Zurich printer. See Fritz Burg, "Dichtungen des Niklaus Manuel. Aus einer Handschrift der Hamburger Stadtbibliothek," in *NBT 1897* (Bern: K.J. Wyss, 1896), 1–136; *Niklaus Manuels Spiel evangelischer Freiheit "Die Totenfresser"*, ed. Ferdinand Vetter, Die Schweiz im deutschen Geistesleben 16 (Leipzig: H. Haessel, 1923), *16.

[55] That the siege of Rhodes had not yet begun in early 1522 is, considering the central position of the Knight of Rhodes scene in Manuel's play, Vetter's main reason for redating it from 1522 to 1523: Vetter, "Über die zwei angeblich 1522 aufgeführten Fastnachtsspiele Manuels," 87, 92–3, 108.

[56] Zinsli/Hengartner, foreword to "Fastnachtspiel," in *Werke und Briefe*, 107.

> Jch sing die syben zyt by dem wyn
> Jch kan ein gewaltiger korher sin
> Vnd hab ein hürli an dem barren
> Die puren sind groß toppel narren
> Das sie mir gebend zinß vnd gült
> Da wirt huoren vnd buoben gefült
> Sag an du huor wie gefalt es dir.[57]

> As far as I'm concerned, the pope is a just god. He takes care of the poor crowd. He knows what a soldier lacks, since he's a soldier himself. He's given me three nice benefices, from which I shall profit for the rest of my life. I earn them with the halberd; I needn't concern myself with a church. I sing the seven canonical hours over wine. I can be a mighty canon and have a concubine at my bidding. The peasants are big stupid fools to give me interest and money; it fills the bellies of whores and bums. Speak up, you whore, how do you like it?

The guards' cynicism makes the knight's appeal all the more poignant and the pope's refusal to help Rhodes's Christian warriors all the more cold-hearted. As an excuse, the pope refers to the on-going hostilities between Francis I, Charles V, and himself, in which Manuel paints the pope as aggressor:

> Zuo diser zyt so denck nur nit
> Das ich Rodis ietzund entschüt
> Jch hab ietz wol anders zuoschaffen
> Jch vnd ouch noch vil miner pfaffen
> Zuo kriegen ietz mit minen Christen
> Da dörfft ich sorg vnd aller listen
> Wie ich dem künig vß Franckrich
> Den venedigern ouch des glich
> Möchte gewinnen ab ir land [...]
> Do hab ich gemacht gar vyl der armen
> Wytwen/weyßen/edel/burger/puren
> Wen mich das Christen bluot möcht beduren
> So het ichs wol vnderwegen gelan
> Vnd dem turgken ein widerstand gethan
> Das er in vngren nit gewunnen het
> So vil Christen land vnd ouch bürg vnd stet
> Der keiser Carolus vnd ich sind ietz gsellen. (vv. 942–66)

---

[57] This and following quotes are taken from Niklaus Manuel, "Fasnachtsspiel," in *Werke und Briefe*, ed. Zinsli/Hengartner, 125–80, here vv. 781–96. As an alternative edition, see also Niklaus Manuel, "Vom Papst und seiner Priesterschaft," in *Deutsche Dramen des 15. und 16. Jahrhunderts*, ed. Hellmut Thomke, Bibliothek deutscher Klassiker 136 (Frankfurt: Deutscher Klassiker Verlag, 1996), 175, vv. 942–63.

Don't think that I'll dig out Rhodes just yet. I've got other things to do, I and many of my clerics, waging war with my Christians. In that matter, I have need of care and deceit concerning how I might capture territory from the King of France as well as from the Venetians.... There I've made many wretched: widows, orphans, noblepersons, burghers, peasants. If I took pity on Christian blood, I might have let that all be and put up resistance to the Turk, so that he would not have captured so many Christian territories, fortresses, and cities in Hungary. Emperor Charles and I are now partners.

The knight, who has already stated that the pope has spilt much Christian blood (v. 937), now indirectly blames the pope and emperor for the loss of Christian life at the hand of the Turks:

> Du pabst vnd keiser Carolus ir bed
> Sind nit vnschuldig an dem bluot
> Deß ietz der türck vergiessen thuot
> O pabst pabst furchtestu nit gott
> Dine roten hütt/vnd beschorne rott
> Hand bluotig vnd raubwölffen zen
> Jr hetten guot würstmacher gen
> So ir so gern im bluot vmbgand
> Ein lust die lüt zuo metzgen hand
> Das bluot das ir vergossen hend
> Leg es ietz frisch an einem end
> Jr möchtend all darinn ertrincken
> Ja schier garnach gantz Rhom versincken
> Meynstu drum das dich gott hie nit wel straffen [...]
> Fürwar fürwar es kompt die stund
> Das dich das schwert vß sinem mund
> Wirt zuo boden richten gar [...]
> Wie das vom endtcrist gschriben stat. (vv. 1041–60)

You, pope, and emperor Charles, you both are not innocent of the blood that the Turk now spills. O pope, pope, do you not fear God? Your red hats [i.e. cardinals] and your tonsured folk have the bloody teeth of predatory wolves. You would have been good sausage makers, since you like to wade in blood so much. What a shine your people have taken to butchering! The blood that you've spilled, if you were to collect it together, you would all drown in it, indeed, you'd submerge all of Rome! Do you thus believe that God will not punish you in this world? [...] Truly, truly, the time will come when the sword of his mouth will strike you down [...], as it is written of the Antichrist.

The knight's willingness to sacrifice his own life in the name of Christianity—before the above quote, he has just noted that he will return with the pope's response to Rhodes, where he hopes to die as a good Christian (vv. 1017–9)—lends moral authority to his condemnation of pope and emperor. Most importantly, although the play's readers have already encountered the pope as "Entcristelo" in the text's rubrics, the knight is the first to utter this association aloud.

At other points in the play, and throughout all of *Von Papsts und Christi Gegensatz*, the pope's arrogant militancy contrasts with Christ's humble pacificism. However, the appearance of Peter and Paul places greater emphasis on the antithesis between the present papacy and Peter's service as Rome's first bishop. While the knight represents military honor, Peter represents a higher authority. It is thus all the more significant that he, and not the knight, condemns the pope's killing of "many thousand men" on a single day in an apparent reference to the Swiss casualities at Bicocca:

> So lat der bluotz wolff vil tusend töten
> Jn schlachten/stürmen vnd scharmützen
> Die er söt schirmen vnd beschützen
> Das hat er than on alle zal
> Vff einen tag zuom dickern mal
> Er tödtet menig thusend man
> Das er groß richtumb möchte han (vv. 1745–51)

> Thus the bloodthirsty wolf, in battles, assaults, and skirmishes, has many thousand killed whom he is supposed to guard and protect. He's done this countless times, often on a single day. He kills many thousand men so that he might have great wealth.

This passage is transmitted in a slightly different form in the fragmentary Hamburg manuscript which contains *Der Traum*, frequently attributed to Manuel, and sections of *Vom Papst und seiner Priesterschaft* and *Von Papsts und Christi Gegensatz*, which represent the earliest surviving redactions of these plays. While the priority of the Hamburg manuscript over the first Zurich imprint of 1524 is open to debate,[58] it is important to note that the linking of many thousand dead to one specific day is even stronger in the former and may represent Manuel's original text:

---

[58] Though Vetter has attempted to reconstruct Manuel's "original" text by combining sections of the Hamburg manuscript with those taken from the 1524 imprint, it is difficult to ascertain what passages are truly authentic, so that the recent editions of Thomke and Zinsli/Hengartner are based on the Zurich copy. See Thomke, ed., 1000.

Die lat er töden zum dickermal
Das hat er thon lang on alle zal
Vff ainen tag vil tusent man
Das er grosse herschafft mug han.[59]

He often has them killed; he's long done this in countless numbers—
many thousand men on one day—so that he might rule far and wide.

The constant mention of papal bellicosity and his alliance with the emperor amply demonstrate that the stinging defeat of Bicocca still resonated for Manuel and his audience, but Peter's above enumeration of the pope's victims is the clearest evidence that the loss of Bernese life ten months prior formed the wellspring of the author's anti-papal diatribe. It is quite possible that, prior to the performances, both council and citizenry expected Manuel to avenge Stein, Nägeli, and others by lampooning Schiner, as had been done in 1521, and lambasting the *Landsknechte* in a continuation of his "Song of Bicocca." The inclusion of Reformation propaganda was then his surprise. Still, the critique of papal military policy was prominent enough so that the council could sanction the play. Any extraneous disagreements regarding theological matters could be excused as carnival license.

Indeed, Schiner assumed a posthumous place in Manuel's revue, linking *Vom Papst und seiner Priesterschaft* to the Bernese carnival play of 1521, which had apparently lambasted Leo's protegé without confessional polemics. There is widespread agreement that the character of Anshelm von Hochmuot (Anshelm of Hubris) is a parody of the cardinal:[60]

Wan mir nit wer mit todten wol
So läg nit mencher acker vol
So durch mich vnd myn gesellen
Die stätz nach kriegen stellen
Sind erschlagen vnd erschossen
Des hab ich mechtig wol genossen
Das ich so gern sahe Christen pluot

---

[59] "Fasnachtsspiel, Variantenapparat II: Integraler Text der Hamburger Handschrift," in *Werke und Briefe*, vv. 1008–11. Vetter opts for the Zurich variant in his edition: Vetter, ed., *Die Totenfresser*, vv. 1529–34.

[60] See Thomke, commentary on "Vom Papst und seiner Priesterschaft," in *Deutsche Spiele des 15. und 16. Jahrhunderts*, 1015; "Vom Papst und seiner Priesterschaft," in *Niklaus Manuel*, ed. Jakob Baechtold, Bibliothek älterer Schriftwerke der deutschen Schweiz und ihres Grenzgebietes 2 (Frauenfeld: J. Huber, 1878), 35; *"Die Totenfresser"*, ed. Vetter, 9; Feller, 2:120.

> Darumb trag ich ein roten huot
> Vnd hab daruon groß nutz vnd auch eren
> Järlich zwentzig tusend florin zuouerzeren. (vv. 111–20)

If I weren't fond of the dead, many a field wouldn't be full with those who have been struck and shot down by me and my cronies, who constantly seek out war. I've profited quite well from my enjoyment of seeing Christian blood. That's why I wear a red cap and have the great privilege and honor of consuming twenty thousand florins a year.

Later, in an apparent reference to Schiner's humble origins in Oberwallis, a member of the papal Swiss guard states that it is a pleasure to serve a master who can take a boy from a cattle stall and make him cardinal—provided that he "splits the heads of a few Christians."[61]

To secure the pivotal support of Catholic councilors, Manuel further depicted the lesser nobility, who in Bern had taken up residence in the city and assumed leading roles in municipal affairs, as victims of papal corruption on a par with peasants.[62] Just as the knight's portrayal is strikingly positive, so too is that of *edelman* Hans Ulrich von Hanenkron. The nobleman's forebears, hoodwinked in their pious naiveté into donating the majority of their possessions to the church, have now left him bereft of any means to support his family while the "tonsured fellows" (*bschorne gsellen*) live a life of leisure.[63] At the close of his speech, he makes an appeal to deprive clerics of "princely possessions" which, in its inclusive *wir*, could include the then staunchly Catholic Bernese families von Erlach, von Diesbach, and von Mülinen:

> Jr hend die lüt mit dem fegfür erschreckt
> Das hat üch fürsten guot zuo bracht
> Jr hantz vß üwerm gyt erdacht [...]
> Welcher ist so frisch vnd frum
> Vnd zeigt mir heilig schrifft drumb

---

[61] "Dem papst dem ist gar guot zuo dienen / Sins glichen ist vff ertrich nienen / Er nimpt ein buoben vß dem stal / Vnd macht vß im ein kardinal / Wen er sich wol in kriegen helt / Vnd vyl cristen die köpf zerspelt" (vv. 834–9). See also Thomke, ed., 1026.

[62] Beerli, 196. Stephan Schmidlin sees in Manuel's negative portrayal of the Swiss papal guard a critique of the nobility. I would agree that the depiction is critical of Swiss mercenaries, but I do not see any specific ties to the nobility in their portrayal. Cf. Stephan Schmidlin, *"Frumm byderb lüt." Ästhetische Form und politische Perspektive im Schweizer Schauspiel der Reformationszeit*, Europäische Hochschulschriften I, 747 (Bern: Peter Lang, 1983), 136.

[63] "Fasnachtsspiel [i.e. 'Vom Papst und seiner Priesterschaft']," vv. 679–752.

Den wil ichs glouben vnd sunst gantz nütt
Also beschyßend ir land vnd lüt
Wir edlen mögentz nit mee erlyden
Wir mößend üch den kabis bschniden (vv. 738-52)

You've terrified people with purgatory; that has brought you princely possessions. You conceived of it through your greed. [...] If one of you is bold and pious enough to show me its basis in Holy Writ, then I'll believe it, but otherwise not. We noblemen can bear it no longer: We must circumcise your cabbage-heads!

Elsewhere as well, there is an overriding concern with the church's sources of income, such as with the episcopal tax on priestly concubines and helpmates, a common practice at the time despite the priests' vow of chastity, or with alms, which in Manuel's typically Protestant argument should be administered by secular government rather than entrusted to corrupt clerics. By including the lesser nobility among those who have squandered their resources in a vain attempt to help others or attain their own salvation, Manuel implies that the need for religious reform transcends matters of class.

The carnivalesque locus of *Vom Papst und seiner Priesterschaft* is nonetheless situated at the lower end of the social spectrum, namely in the portrayal of seven male peasants who appear on stage with the Protestant preacher Schüchnit. Although the Catholic characters from the play's opening sequence confess to numerous bawdy acts, their unruliness simply illustrates their depravity, while the peasants' later boorish behavior clearly has the approval of Schüchnit, who solicits their comments on papal corruption: "Dise schindery kompt vom pabst vß Rhom / Jr frommen landlüt wüssen ir nit daruon?" ("This exploitation comes from the pope in Rome. You pious farmers, do you know nothing of this?"; vv. 1108-09). The men subsequently give full expression to their contempt for indulgences, canon law, and other aspects of Catholic theology. Just as Cardinal Schiner served as a lightning rod for Manuel's critique of papal military policy, the Franciscan friar Bernhardin Samson, who as the Swiss counterpart of Johann Tetzel had hawked indulgences in Bern in 1518 and would be the inspiration for the title character of Manuel's *Ablaßkrämer*,[64] triggers here a critique of indulgences and papal theology by Nickli

---

[64] On Samson (also spelled "Sanson"), see Guggisberg, 56; Kathrin Tremp-Utz, "Gottesdienst, Ablaßwesen und Predigt am Vinzenzstift in Bern (1484/85–1528)," *ZfSK* 80 (1986): 57-8.

Zettmist (Nicholas Dung-Spreader) and Ruofli Pflegel (Ruofli Flail) (vv. 1110–223). Both express their sentiments bodily, as exhibited by Zettmist, who learns that the indulgence he has purchased with his last money from the *ablaß kremer* Samson is worthless:

> Gar trüwlich ich den ablaß kremer bat
> Das er mir wette ablaß geben
> Vber min armes sündiges leben
> Vnd wot ich han darumb ein brieff
> So muost ich gryffen in seckel tieff
> Vnd muost im gen ein guldin rot
> Jch het sin baß törffen umb brot [...]
> Do mir min hußfraw entgegen lieff
> Knüweten wir bede für den brieff
> Bettend bede mit nassen trehen
> Jch wand ich het got selber gesehen
> Biß das ich vernam es sötte nüt
> Deß ward ich bericht durch witzig lüt
> Do ward ich gantz von zorn entrüst
> Vnd han den arß an brieff gewüst. (vv. 1143–61)

I asked the indulgence peddler quite sincerely that he might give me remission for my poor sinful life. For a corresponding indulgence, I had to reach deep into my purse and give him a crown of red gold, which I needed more dearly for bread. [...] When my wife ran to greet me, we both knelt before the letter and prayed with moist tears. I thought I had seen God himself, until I discovered that it was worthless. This was told to me by knowledgeable people. I was then overcome by anger and wiped my ass with the indulgence.

Pflegel is perhaps less crude, merely passing gas when given the opportunity to purchase his own indulgence (v. 1195). Later, Heini Filzhuot (Henry Felt Hat), in reference to the legendary Pope Joan, repeatedly calls the pope a whore (v. 1283 ff.).

Although the peasants' gestures and curses are crass, their transgressions discredit the play's papists, not themselves. Manuel portrays them as innocent victims who naturally resort to the only means of defense at their disposal. As seen above, Schüchnit deems them *fromm* (pious); they alone among the play's numerous Protestant figures quote Scripture to support their anti-papal arguments. Moreover, their boorishness is more a carnival device than a reflection of Manuel's sociology of reform; their crudities do not imply that Manuel considered the peasant estate inherently uncultured or that their disobedience was in any way a call for emulation among members of Manuel's audience. Rather, they represent orderliness of a higher level. Through their alliance with the preacher, they suggest that popular support for religious change has reached a critical mass and can no longer be ignored if order is to be maintained. It is thus a peasant who argues for the necessity of secular rule above and beyond religious reform. After Heini Filzhuot has demonstrated that the church has no right to tithes because they are not called for in the Bible, the Amman von Maraschwil soothes any concerns about peasant disobedience, such as the refusal to pay worldly taxes, by pointing to the support for secular authority found in Scripture:

> Aber weltliche herschafft die muoß man han
> Das zeigt vns Christus an menchen orten an
> Weltliche oberkeit kompt von gott herab
> Als Christus Pilato zuo antwurt gab
> Du hettest kein gewalt über min leben
> Er wer dir denn von oben herab geben
> So hat er ouch geben zins vnd zol
> Das hör ich im euangelio wol
> Do Christus Petrum selber hieß
> Das er sin züg in das wasser ließ
> Vnd bracht ein fisch an das landt
> Do er das gelt inen fand
> Vnd gab der herschafft zol guotwillig
> Jch mag nit wissen wie vil schillig
> Jch kan aber noch nienen vernen
> Das er den pfaffen gelt hab gen. (vv. 1320–34)

> But secular rule, that one must have. Christ points to this in several passages. Secular authority comes down from God, as Christ answered Pilate: "You would have no power over my life if it were not given you from above." Thus he gave tolls and tribute: I hear that indeed in the Gospel, where Christ commanded Peter to cast his net in the water. When he brought a fish on land and found money inside, he gave tribute willingly to the authorities; I don't know how many shillings. Yet I can't discover anywhere that he gave money to clerics.

It has been suggested that these lines were added to the Zurich imprint by an official censor,[65] but there is no reason to assume that the author did not originally compose them himself.[66] Manuel echoes

---

[65] Beerli, 193.
[66] It is unfortunately impossible to determine whether these lines were in the original version of the play, as they are part of the pages missing from the Hamburg manuscript. However, the passage reveals none of the characteristics of other added sections, such as impure rhyme, and has not been identified as spurious by any of

here standard scriptural arguments for the necessity of secular rule. The oblique reference to Christ's demand of Peter to render unto Caesar what is Caesar's would certainly mollify the concerns of community leaders that the abolition of church tithes could endanger their sources of income as well.[67] It is, moreover, hardly coincidental that the author placed this appeal in the mouth of an *amman* (*Amtmann*, here a type of village mayor). As a representative of village authority, he commanded respect from both his fellow peasants and from his civic superiors.[68] It is this pledge of political obedience, coupled with the drastic portrayal of the city's maltreatment at the hands of allegedly diabolical Catholics, that allows the call for religious change to appeal to as broad an audience as possible.

If the assurances of these peasants guarantee the peaceful nature of Manuel's proposed revolution, the figure of Doctor Lütpolt Schüchnit provides the required theological authority. Whether he is modeled after Martin Luther, Bern's Bertold Haller, or neither,[69] he is both God-fearing and audacious in challenging the pope's power. Although he first associates himself with peasants, he is equally concerned with Bern's political elite at the close of the play, where his prayer to Christ subtly appeals to the council's conscience towards soliciting its assistance in the success of the new faith:

> Ach süßer Jesus Christ ich bitten dich
> Erlücht vns alle durch dinen geist
> Die oberkeiten ouch aller meist
> Das sie die schäfli füren recht
> Und sich erkennend dine knecht
> Und nit selb wellend herren syn
> Ir eigen gedicht müschlend yn
> Vnd dinen schäflin schüttend für (vv. 1931–8)

---

the play's editors. See Thomke, commentary on "Vom Papst und seiner Priesterschaft," 999, 1032.

[67] Schmidlin, 150. In certain Bernese territories, the spread of Protestantism led some peasants to refuse the payment of their tithes as early as mid-1523. It is possible, however, that this issue had already become a concern earlier in the year. See Edgar Bonjour, *Die Bauernbewegungen des Jahres 1525 im Staate Bern* (Bern: Paul Haupt, 1923), 36 ff.

[68] Schmidlin, 144.

[69] Opinions vary as to whether the name "Lupolt Schüchnit" contains a hidden reference to an actual reformer. While the interpretation "Lup[priester Bercht]olt" suggests Bertold Haller, the variant ("Luth[er]-bold") would point to Luther himself. See Thomke, commentary on "Vom Papst und seiner Priesterschaft," 1029–30; Max Huggler, "Niklaus Manuel und die Reformatoren," in *NMD*, 101–2.

> Oh sweet Jesus Christ, I ask of you: Illuminate us all with your spirit, and the authorities especially, so that they shepherd their sheep properly and recognize that they are your servants and do not wish to be lords themselves, mixing in their own compositions and dumping them before your sheep.

The entreaty is a rhetorical stratagem: Without denying the council's authority, it portrays any refusal to accept the biblically based legitimacy of Protestant theology as ungodly. If the peasants recognize and accept the biblical foundation of secular authority, Schüchnit implies, then the council must fulfill its own obligations and institute reform. Through the contrast with the papal hordes who had just appeared on the stage, Schüchnit's solitary presence again underscores the peaceable, obedient disposition of the adherents of the new faith. Coupled with its articulation as prayer, the plea appears as a humble reminder of divine obligation, not a demand.[70]

Manuel thus employs varied rhetorical strategies in *Vom Papst und seiner Priesterschaft* to convince his audience of the necessity of religious change. The play's carnival context allows for the clergy's demasking, both through the opening revue's mimetic satire, in which decreasing ranks of church officials own up to financial or sexual excesses, and through their association with grotesque bodily realism, such as the peasants' scatalogical gestures, which discredit the supposedly "higher" clerics. Set against this general stigmatization, the play addresses real concerns of the community, with Manuel justifying religious reform through financial, moral, and political arguments. Financially, the diversion of money from the ostensibly inept church administration promises to improve the finances of all members of Bernese society: gullible peasants will now shun costly indulgences, well-to-do burghers forego ineffectual requiems, and local nobility dispense with the establishment of altars. Morally, the city would abolish hypocrisy, lust, and war-mongering. And the reassurance that religious reform would preserve the city's political structures would have appealed not only to the councilors, but likely to a majority of citizenry and peasants. Indeed, Manuel seems to make few distinctions based on social standing, addressing the community as a whole while acknowledging specific interest groups and adapting his arguments to win their support. Above all, following the tragedy of

---

[70] Schmidlin, 150.

Bicocca, the desire for redress on all fronts—financial, moral, and political—galvanized the community against papal authority.

As related by Anshelm, one week after the performance of *Vom Papst und seiner Priesterschaft* and four days following the satirical Ash Wednesday indulgence procession through Bern to the satirical tune of the "Bean Song,"[71] Manuel's second play was staged on Cross Lane. *Von Papsts und Christi Gegensatz* ("On the Distinction between the Pope and Christ"; see also fig. 9) features two peasants, who comment on the discrepancies between passing processions of Christ and the pope. It is substantially shorter than its sister play—215 verses compared to 1945—but the contrast drawn between present-day Rome and Christ is nearly identical to that between the pope and Peter in the previous work, so that in terms of content it can be considered an extension of *Vom Papst und seiner Priesterschaft*. For this reason, and due to the play's striking visuality based on the *Passional Christi und Antichristi* by Lucas Cranach the Elder and Philipp Melanchthon (1521; fig. 10), its main analysis will occur in Chapter Five. In the present discussion of the carnivalesque, however, it should be noted that the play's two peasants, Cleywe Pfluog (Clyde Plow) and Rüde Vogelnest (Rudi Bird Nest), repeat the theme of papal militancy presented the previous week, describing the pope, who appears in armor in the midst of his mercenaries, as "bellicose, seditious, and wild" (*kriegsch/rümorisch vnd wildt*; v. 106). The peasants, moreover, engage in the same Christian disobedience as those of *Vom Papst und seiner Priesterschaft*. On the one hand, they are pious and praise Christ's humility, care for the weak, and ultimate sacrifice for humanity's salvation. They nonetheless also partake of carnival license, physically expressing their contempt for indulgences and other aspects of traditional theology. At the close of the play, signed by Manuel with his customary Swiss dagger, Rüede Vogelnest discusses how he will "vent" his anger should his Protestant faith earn him the stigma of excommunication:

> Gott geb, sie tügend mich in ban oder ach
> Da fragen ich denn gantz vnd gar nüt me nach
> So ich denn ablaß in Jesu Christo wol mag han
> Jch schiß in ablaß vnd wüste den ars an ban
> Der allein vmb gelt wirt erdacht

---

[71] On the "Bohnenlied" procession and the likely text of the song, see Pfrunder, 176–88.

Von Rhom vff einer hundßhut bracht
Wenn sie mich nuon me beschissen
So sönd sie miers ouch verwyssen
Des hab ich mich ganz eigentlich verwegen
Vnd sött es mich kosten min schwitzer tegen.[72]

If ever they should pronounce the ban or excommunication over me, I'll think nothing more of it, as I have remission of sins through Jesus Christ. I'll crap on the indulgence and wipe my ass with the ban, which is conceived for the sake of money alone and brought from Rome on bad parchment. If they deceive me again, then they'll be sorry for it. That is what I've resolved, even if it should cost me my Swiss dagger.

The modification of church documents from instruments of salvation to implements of defecation, already encountered a week earlier, is Manuel's most common carnivalesque motif.

If such scatology appears compatible with peasant piety, the open violence of Manuel's next play, *Der Ablaßkrämer*, in which a village crowd hangs the indulgence peddler Richardus Hinderlist (Richard Trickery) by his hands (fig. 11), shocks most scholars into reassessing the author's attitude towards the peasant class. For Jean-Paul Tardent, Manuel's disposition towards the *Volk* changed from esteem to disappointment upon the realization that the peasants clung conservatively to the old faith.[73] Beerli also feels that the peasants no longer represent the ideal rustic of earlier Protestant pamphlets, such as Karsthans, but he maintains that Manuel still considered them an indispensable force for the success of the movement.[74] In Tardent's view, *Der Ablaßkrämer* implicitly rejects the violence of the Peasant Wars; for Beerli, the play's depicted upheaval is necessary if the Reformation is to succeed. Both scholars thus maintain that the peasant violence of *Der Ablaßkrämer* is fundamentally distinct from that of *Vom Papst und seiner Priesterschaft*.[75]

This distinction is not borne out by the plays. The difference is rather one of degree: the latter peasants merely enact what Nickly Zettmist and his cohorts had wished upon the clergy. Just as the rustics of *Vom Papst und seiner Priesterschaft* remain *fromm* despite their carnivalesque behavior, so, too, do those of *Der Ablaßkrämer*. Their

---

[72] "Fasnachtsspiel ['Von Papsts und Christi Gegensatz']," 187–8, vv. 205–14.
[73] Tardent, 98. Gordon largely seconds Tardent's views: Gordon, 136–8.
[74] Beerli, 244–7. Beerli is seconded by Schmidlin, 141.
[75] Cf. Tardent, 98; Beerli, 244.

devout naiveté, once abused by the indulgence peddler (alias Bernhardin Samson), triggers their outraged reaction. The peasants are, for example, well versed in Scripture: Anne Suwrüßell (Pig Snout) makes reference to St. Peter, and Manuel notes the corresponding biblical passage in the margin.[76] In particular, Manuel reveals their Christian charity in an act of kindness towards the lame beggar Stefan Gygenstern, the play's ideal Christian.[77] In elaborating Hinderlist's sins, Gygenstern bemoans the clergy's lack of Christ's compassion:

> Wie beschißend jer die armen lüt
> wider alles dz das got verbüt
> got wirt nitt am jungsten tag erfragen
> wer hab zuo santt petters münster tragenn
> aber nach den wercken der barmmhertzickeitt
> dar von hat vns cristus selber geseitt
> da wirt er fragen öb man sy hab gethan
> Demm armen nitt turst noch mangel gelan
> die nackenden bekleitt die gefangnen tröst
> jn summa brüderlich liebe ist dz gröst. (vv. 140–9)

> How you delude the poor people, against everything that God forbade. At the Last Judgment, God will not ask who donated to the construction of St. Peter's Cathedral, but for works of compassion, about which Christ himself has instructed us. He will ask whether one has done these: Allowed the poor to suffer neither thirst nor want, clothed the naked, and comforted the imprisoned. Summed up, brotherly love is the most important thing.

Although Gygenstern articulates a ubiquitous complaint among Protestants, his remarks on true Christian compassion assume greater authority due to his disability. Proper charity is measured against the criterion of helping others. Once the peasants have regained their money, they fulfill the requirement of brotherly love splendidly:

> *Zilia Nasentutter*:
> Nun loßend Es schickt sich eben fyn
> wier hend nun jeder man grad daß syn
> so ist der aplaß bößwicht vertribenn
> vnd ist noch ein gellt hie über blibenn

---

[76] "actum [v] am viij ca." Manuel, "Ablasskrämer," in *Werke und Briefe*, 258–80, here v. 90, note 90. All subsequent quotes are taken from this edition. See also Manuel, *Der Ablaßkrämer*, ed. Paul Zinsli, Altdeutsche Übungstexte 17 (Bern: Francke, 1960), v. 91.

[77] Tardent, 99; Schmidlin, 141; Beerli, 246.

> jch rat das mans recht dem pettler geb
> das er sich mitt bekleyd vnd wol leb.
> *Bertschi schüch den brunnen*:
> Billich wemm söt mans sunst gen (vv. 562–8)

Zilia Snot Nose:
Now listen, as luck would have it we each have now regained our losses. The indulgence scoundrel has been driven off and some money is left over. I advise that we rightly give it to the beggar that he might clothe himself and live comfortably.
Bert Bathless:
Certainly, whom else should we give it.

By taking no more than their due, the peasants demonstrate that they have not accosted Hinderlist for their own gain. Their rebellion is selfless and just: they do not disregard authority so much as obey the higher authority of Scripture. Moreover, Manuel reiterates the necessity of secular obedience, appealing once again for a revolution confined to the religious sphere:

> Fröw dich bößwicht das man dich nitt
> noch wyter straft an lyb und lebenn
> doch wirtt dir noch der lon drumm gebenn
> ein oberkeitt wirt dier drumm lonenn
> man sol din ouch nun gar nütt schonenn (vv. 514–9)

> Be happy, scoundrel, that we don't further exact our punishment on your life and limb. But you'll still get your proper reward: the authorities will give you your recompense. They should show no mercy towards you.

No mention occurs of tithes or other issues surrounding peasant unrest in the Bernese territories, which, unlike Southern Germany in 1525, did not see open revolt.[78] Manuel's portrayal thus does not mirror real events, but rather depicts an ideal uprising that would institute religious change while leaving local government intact.

The author did, however, make one substantial modification in the portrayal of peasant rebellion from that found in *Vom Papst und seiner Priesterschaft*. Religious change is now squarely in the hands of

---

[78] For a description of peasant demands in Bernese territories, where rural inhabitants were apparently unaware of the twelve articles of Memmingen, see Bonjour, 74 ff. See also Peter Bierbrauer, *Freiheit und Gemeinde im Berner Oberland 1300–1700*, Archiv des Historischen Vereins des Kantons Bern 74 (Bern: Historischer Verein des Kantons Bern, 1991).

women. Zilia Nasentutter and Anne Suwrüssel are the first to take the indulgence peddler Richardus Hinderlist to task for the worthless paper he has sold them (v. 53 ff.). As illustrated by Manuel's ink drawing for the play, Zilia is armed with the traditional tool of the Swiss mercenary trade, the halberd (after v. 52), while Anne transforms an innocuous kitchen utensil, the ladle, into a cudgel (v. 239). Thus equipped, the women lead the attack on Hinderlist, bind him, and hang him by his hands until he confesses to the worthlessness of indulgences. Manuel describes the attack as follows:

> Sy namend jn gemeinlich vnd schluogend jn zuo der erdenn/mitt kellen kuncklen schytrenn vnd Ein allt böß wyb lüff darzuo mitt einer rostigen alltenn Hallenbarttenn/vnd bundend imm hend vnnd füß zugend jn an einem seyl hoch vff in aller wyß form vnd gestallt wie man ein mörder streckt Biß er sprach er wett vergechenn. (vv. 285–91)

> They took him together and knocked him to the ground with ladles, distaffs and split-logs, and a nasty old woman ran up with a rusty old halberd, and they tied his hands and feet and strung him up with a rope, just as one does with a murderer, until he promised to confess.

Although Bertschi Schüchdenbrunnen and the beggar Gygenstern appear among the female villagers, Manuel places special emphasis on the fact that women have unseated the peddler, especially at the end of the play, when Hinderlist laments that "the devil has placed me among these women. [. . .] If they were to arrive [in hell], they'd beat the devil himself."[79]

The women triumph over Hinderlist through brute force, but their victory has strong sexual overtones. Many of Hinderlist's ill-gotten gains stem from fines he has imposed on peasants for allegedly sinful sexual acts between married individuals.[80] Schüchdenbrunnen must pay a gulden for having slept with his wife during a forty-day period following childbirth (v. 98), while Trine Filtzbengel (Crude Rascal) must render two gold crowns for having engaged in intercourse with her husband on a day of fasting (vv. 202–3). Moreover,

---

[79] "Der tüfel hätt mich vnder die wyber tragenn / [. . .] jst in der hellen sölich pin / Sind die thüfel all bös alls dißse wiber gegen mier / So ist es pyn vnd grußemm gnuog das Bedunck mich schier / jch gloub kemend die wyber an / sy törftend den tüfel selber schlann" (vv. 530–7).

[80] Schmidlin, 152–3.

as the beggar Gygenstern reveals, Hinderlist has misappropriated funds collected to ward off the Turks for his own sexual escapades:

> Du hast von einemm türgken geseitt
> vnd wie das geltt werde an geleitt
> wider den selben türgen zuo strytenn
> jch sach in hüt in din herberg rytenn [...]
> er hatt for hin ein große wundenn
> er hatt dins strytens dick empfundenn
> du magst in noch krutzlich aber zwingen
> hinacht am bett vnder dich bringenn
> sin brüst gend milch sin har ist lang
> o wolf das dich der todt an gang.[81]

> You spoke of a Turk and how the money would be spent to fight him. I saw him riding today to your quarters. [...] He has a large wound in front; he has often felt your fighting. You can still compel him a second time during confession and throw him down under you in bed tonight. His breasts give milk, his hair is long. Oh wolf, may death befall you.

Hinderlist's sexual abuses form a substantial component of the peasants' grievances. When the peddler fails to grasp that his tormentors demand a confession not only of his embezzlements, but also of his exploitation of women, the peasants string him up a second time (vv. 383–94). Only then does he admit to dispensing indulgences for women's sexual favors:

> Jch han pürinen dick überrett
> jn der bicht mitt glatten wortenn
> daß werlich jer man nitt hortten
> jch geb ablaß vnd hette deß guot brief
> wellche frow ein nacht früntlich by mier schlief
> die hette abplaß für schuld vnd pyn
> doch sött es treffenlich heimlich sin
> jch han wol ein hüpsche pürin über rett
> daß sy die buoß von stund an jn der kilchenn tett. (vv. 395–403)

---

[81] "Ablasskrämer," vv. 156–66. Zinsli and Hengartner suggest that "krutzlich" is misspelled and should read "kurtzlich." However, the word could possibly refer to "Chrutz": "abgeschlossener Bet- oder Kirchenstuhl für 1–2 Personen." See *Schweizerisches Idiotikon: Wörterbuch der schweizerdeutschen Sprache*, ed. Friedrich Staub, Ludwig Tobler, et al. (Frauenfeld: J. Huber, 1895), 3:937.

> I often persuaded peasant women in the confessional with smooth words, so that their husbands would not hear, that I could dispense indulgences and had documents stating that whichever woman willingly slept with me for a night, she would receive remission for her sins and their punishment, yet it must occur secretly. Indeed, I convinced a pretty peasant woman to perform her penance immediately in church.

In a turnabout of the hierarchy of the confessional, the women now hear Hinderlist's admissions of sin and impose their own penance. Moreover, in hanging him by his arms, they render him "impotent" in every sense of the word. When at their mercy, Hinderlist is "mied" (v. 293; "dull"/"limp"), deprived of vigor and no longer able to abuse them sexually.[82]

By depicting women, not men, as the agents of change in *Der Ablaßkrämer*, Manuel effectively adds the element of gender inversion to the topsy-turvy social hierarchy that previously made allies of peasants and Protestants in *Vom Papst und seiner Priesterschaft*. As Natalie Zemon Davis has noted, women often enjoyed a certain impunity in agitating for reform, as they were not always held responsible for their actions.[83] Indeed, men occasionally donned feminine attire to demonstrate for tax reforms or other change.[84] If any one factor allowed for Manuel's vivid depiction of peasant revolt against the backdrop of the 1525 Peasant Wars, it is that women enact it. This is not to suggest that female agency weakened Manuel's call for change. Rather, the coupling of feminine intransigence and religious reform rendered *Der Ablaßkrämer* all the more effective as Protestant propaganda. The indulgence peddler's humiliation at the hands of the "weaker sex" severely undermined any authority possessed by the clergy. At the same time, the element of female agency renders the stark depiction of violence less real and threatening to its audience. Most importantly, in the larger context of the Bernese Reformation, the gap between the carnival representation of revolt and real revolt had, by 1525, narrowed to the point where additional rhetorical strategies were necessary for the carnival play's continued function as a locus for political debate.

Indeed, this gap had apparently grown too narrow for Manuel's work to be shared with a larger audience. The play circulated in

---

[82] Schmidlin, 153.
[83] Natalie Zemon Davis, "Women on Top," in *Society and Culture in Early Modern France* (Stanford: Stanford University Press, 1975), 124–51.
[84] Ibid., 147–50.

manuscript among the author's acquaintances, including Ulrich Zwingli,[85] but it was never published. Despite the women's claim to respect secular government, their extraction of Hinderlist's confession nonetheless emulated the sanctioned interrogation methods of Swiss authorities, as seen in an illustration from the 1513 Lucerne Chronicle of Diebold Schilling the Younger (fig. 12).[86] If Manuel created the play's drawing as a design for a title woodcut, as has been suggested,[87] this image alone, with its seditious overtones, may have been sufficient to prevent the play's publication.

Reformation Theology and Carnival

The Bernese alliance of carnival and Reformation had already become problematical before Manuel's composition of Der Ablaßkrämer. Council records contain repeated prohibitions of überlouffen (a type of carnival "trick-or-treat" that involved begging for food) in the years 1522, 1523, and 1524. The evident increase in carnival aggression during these years likely reflected tension between the proponents of the old and new faith.[88] The situation in 1523 was apparently not yet so acute as to prohibit the expression of reform wishes within the privileged space of council-supported plays, at least not if it were combined with a healthy portion of polemic against papal militarism. However, no record of local carnival performances exists for the remainder of the decade, suggesting that the situation grew so volatile as to allow no public articulation of Reformation theology whatsoever. On 29 January 1524, for example, the council prohibited all forms of carnival mummery during the pre-Lenten season.[89] The

---

[85] A letter by Manuel to Zwingli asks for the return of "ein aplaß kremmer." See Werke und Briefe, 730, no. XXXVI.

[86] The image represents the interrogation of a certain Hans Spiess. Die Luzerner Chronik des Diebold Schilling 1513, facsimile edition (Luzern: Kunstkreis Faksimile-Verlag, 1977), 437, Folio 216ʳ. Reprinted in Dietrich Schwarz, "Innerschweizer Alltag im 15. Jahrhundert," in 500 Jahre Stanser Verkommnis: Beiträge zu einem Zeitbild, ed. Ferdinand Elsener (Stans: Historischer Verein Nidwalden, 1981), 98, illustration 32.

[87] Zinsli suggests that Manuel's meticulous manuscript was a final copy intended for a publisher. Zinsli, foreword to Der Ablaßkrämer, 6. See also Max Herrmann, Forschungen zur deutschen Theatergeschichte des Mittelalters und der Renaissance (Berlin: Weidmannsche Buchhandlung, 1914), 454.

[88] Pfrunder, 90–2; Steck/Tobler, 14, 52, 91; nos. 68, 191, 344.

[89] "Am cantzel das butzenwerk abzuostellen by einem monat leistung." Steck/Tobler, 92, no. 349.

Bernese mandate provides little detail, but Zurich had also promulgated a similar ordinance, which explicitly censured the ridicule of the pope, emperor, and others. The list enumerates a cast of characters not unlike those of *Vom Papst und seiner Priesterschaft*:

> Unser Herren BM [Bürgermeister] und RR [Räten] der stadt Zürich ist angelangt, wie dass etlich arden söllint vorhanden sin und jetz dise dry fasnachten wöllen umbgon, die mer zuo schmach, reizung und widerwillen dienen und kommen mügint, dann zuo kurzwil oder guotem. Uf das gebietend die gemeldten unser Herren, dass uf anzöigt fasnachten niemas sölle in arden umbgon, so bäpstlich Heligkeit, keiserliche Majestät, die Cardinal, unser Eidgnossen, die landsknecht, münch, pfaffen, klosterfrowen, noch ander fürsten, herren, gmein noch sonder personen, frömbd noch heimsch, geistlich noch weltlich, mügent berüeren, bedüten, schmähen, reizen oder widerwillig machen.[90]

> Our lords the mayor and councilors of the city of Zurich have discovered that certain costumes are said to exist and will be paraded during carnival, which serve and foster shame, provocation, and anger more than enjoyment or benefit. Thus our lords command that during the mentioned carnival no one shall parade in costumes that might touch upon, indicate, ridicule, upset or rile his Holiness the Pope, his Majesty the Emperor, the cardinals, our confederates, the *Landsknechte*, monks, clergy, nuns, or other princes, lords, or persons in common or individually, strangers or locals, clergy or laymen.

Although it was already openly pursuing a Reformation policy at the time, the Zurich council enacted the ban in an effort to quell iconoclastic rumblings that might have exploited the festival.[91] Bern

---

[90] *Actensammlung zur Geschichte der Zürcher Reformation in den Jahren 1519–1533*, ed. Emil Egli (Zürich: J. Schabelitz, 1879), 191, no. 467. Creizenach, who notes the above prohibition, wrongly suggests that circumstances were different in Bern at this time: Wilhelm Creizenach, *Geschichte des neueren Dramas*, 2nd ed. (Halle: Max Niemeyer, 1923), 3:167. Egli includes another prohibition of carnival mummery among the "Mandate ohne Datum" that close his work: "Verbot des 'Böggenwerchs'... Besonders wird einmal das Umziehen mit dem Trottbaum, dem Pflug und der Egge auf den Hirsmontag als ein neues Fastnachtspiel verboten." Egli does not indicate whether this ban belonged to the *Verbotbuch*, whose prohibitions were valid year in, year out throughout the 1520s and 1530s, but this prohibition likely belonged to similar post-Reformation efforts to curb carnival activity. *Actensammlung*, 896, no. 2005.

[91] Peter Jezler, Elke Jezler, and Christine Göttler, "Warum ein Bilderstreit? Der Kampf gegen die 'Götzen' in Zürich als Beispiel," in *Bilderstreit. Kulturwandel in Zwinglis Reformation*, ed. Hans-Dietrich Altendorf and Peter Jezler (Zürich: Theologischer Verlag, 1984), 99.

likely followed a similar policy as it suppressed carnival mummery. Both councils apparently tolerated carnival only so long as they were confident that its celebration would not threaten the stability of their theologically torn communities. Moreover, as long as the Bernese council remained largely Catholic, it would have been loathe to support any further plays that openly agitated for religious reform.

The official introduction of the Reformation in 1528 initially reopened an avenue for carnival expression of Protestant theology in Bern. *Elsli Tragdenknaben* was performed in 1530, followed by Rüte's *Abgötterei* in 1531. Nevertheless, the revival of the carnival play was short-lived. Only 11 years after Manuel's first plays, town authorities found it advisable to censure carnival performers in Seftigen, a region to the south of Bern, as indicated by the following entry from council records of 1534:

> Dem friweibel Gurtner [von Seftigen], min hern verstanden das Faßnacht spill, so etlich angefangen, und wie wol min hern doran wenig gefallens, so aber sollichs im besten ungesinnot beschechen, lassens min hern also beliben. Doch hinfür söllicher sach sich müssigent, dan gar bald ein geschrey und unwillen gegen den anstößern doruß ervolgen möchte.[92]

> To Sergeant Gurtner [of Seftigen]: My Lords have noted the carnival play that some have begun rehearsing. Although this does not please My Lords, it occurred unwittingly in the best of intents, and thus My Lords shall let it pass. In the future, however, you must avoid all such matters, since it may quickly result in clamour and indignation against the initiators.

This council entry is the only direct indication that the carnival celebration had, within six years of the Bernese Disputation, become anathema. However, whereas the pre-Reformation prohibition of carnival in Bern was likely due to the danger of civic unrest and meant to silence religious dissent, the newly installed Protestant council had no political reasons to object to pro-reform carnival plays. The censure now came from Protestant theologians, who objected to the festival on moral grounds. Catholic authorities had also occasionally banned carnival festivities, but their prohibitions were temporary; they censured excesses, not the institution itself.[93] Luther, Zwingli,

---

[92] As quoted in Fluri, 136–7.
[93] Dietz-Rüdiger Moser, "Die Fastnachtsfeier als konfessionelles Problem," in *Das*

and other Protestant leaders assailed the festival for its perceived wickedness and, most importantly, its inherently Catholic character.[94] Luther for example condemned the Nuremberg *Schembartlauf*, which, following its suppression by local authorities in 1524, was restaged by opponents of the local Protestant pastor Andreas Osiander in 1539:[95]

> Norimbergensium malitiam indicabat, qui in despectum evangelii et odium praedicatorum in proximis carnispriviis iterum impiissimum spectaculum, Schonpara, erexerunt, das sie ihn 15 jaren nicht gethan haben.[96]

> Luther spoke of the spite of the Nurembergers, who during the last carnival, in contempt of the Gospel and out of hate for the pastors, had again instigated that most impious spectacle, the "Schembart," which they hadn't done in 15 years.

While the attack against Osiander likely raised Luther's ire more than the festival itself,[97] several Protestant church statutes (*Kirchenord-*

Reich und die Eidgenossenschaft 1580–1650. Kulturelle Wechselwirkungen im konfessionellen Zeitalter, ed. Ulrich im Hof and Suzanne Stehelin (Fribourg: Universitätsverlag Freiburg Schweiz, 1986), 131.

[94] For Protestant opposition to carnival in Early Modern Switzerland, see D.-R. Moser, "Die Fastnachtsfeier als konfessionelles Problem," 129–78. For an analysis of modern Protestant admonitions against the celebration, see Fritz Mack, "Evangelische Stimmen zu Fasnacht," in *Masken zwischen Spiel und Ernst. Beiträge des Tübinger Arbeitskreises für Fasnachtsforschung*, ed. Hermann Bausinger et al. (Tübingen: Tübinger Vereinigung für Volkskunde, 1967), 35–49.

[95] Dietz-Rüdiger Moser, "Bemerkungen zum gegenwärtigen Stand volkskundlicher und literarhistorischer Fastnachtsforschung," in *Fastnachtspiel—Commedia dell'arte. Gemeinsamkeiten—Gegensätze*, Akten des 1. Symposiums der Sterzinger Osterspiele, ed. Max Siller (Innsbruck: Universitätsverlag Wagner, 1992), 132; Moser, "Lachkultur des Mittelalters?" 99.

[96] As quoted in the Latin and German mix of Luther's table talks: WA, 61:297, no. 4406.

[97] In discussing Luther's occasional condemnation of carnival plays, Thomas Bacon notes the reformer's approval of Terentian immodesties, which Luther believed could instruct through their negative example. To explain this discrepancy, Bacon postulates, by his own admission, the "far-fetched" theory that Luther could approve of the antics of Terentian characters as they led to matrimony, while carnival plays abounded with adultery. This, however, does not account for Luther's commendation of carnival masks as one possible manner of clothing moral didacticism in more appealing garments within the introduction to his translation of Aesop's Fables, itself later quoted by Bacon, nor for Luther's enjoyment of other carnival performances. The more plausible explanation is that Luther did not object to the crudity of carnival plays any more than he objected to the lasciviousness of Terence, but that he did object to the plays and other carnival activities when he felt them to be inherently Catholic, as was the case with the Nuremberg *Schembartlauf*. Thomas Ivey Bacon, *Luther and the Drama* (Amsterdam: Rodopi, 1976), 62–3. For a discussion of

nungen) condemn *Fastnacht* as the work of the devil and of heathens.[98] The "heathens," of course, were Catholics.[99]

Carnival was equally frowned on by Zwingli and Calvin. As early as 1524, Guillaume Farel warned against the *bacchanales* of carnival, as they were products of men, not of the Holy Spirit.[100] In his Reformation chronicle, Heinrich Bullinger cites a Zurich mandate condemning all manner of carnival activities, "as these were the depraved and impure entertainments of the papacy."[101] When the burghers of Basel attempted to perform a Dance of Death in 1531, they were arrested; the city prohibited all carnival activities in 1546 with the explanation that, since the Reformation had done away with the 40-day fasting season, the preceding revelry was now equally superfluous.[102] While Zwingli apparently tolerated weddings and other festivals,[103] he most certainly would have joined Bullinger in condemning carnival as a reminder of Catholic custom.[104]

Post-Reformation Carnival in Bern (1530–34)

Given the lack of explicit statements on carnival from Bertold Haller, Wolfgang Capito, or other theologians contributing to the consolidation of the Bernese Reformation during this period,[105] one must

---

Luther's visits to student and carnival plays, see Erika Kohler, *Martin Luther und der Festbrauch*, Mitteldeutsche Forschungen 17 (Cologne: Böhlau, 1959), 40, 95.

[98] See *Die evangelischen Kirchenordnungen des 16. Jahrhunderts*, ed. Emil Sehling et al. (volumes 1–5: Leipzig: O.R. Reisland, 1902–13; volumes 6–15: Tübingen: J.C.B. Mohr, 1955–1977), 2:349; 3:478; 4:315, 473, 474, 537; 5:270, 289, 505; 8/1:384; 13:200, 311; 14:66, 471; 15:144–5, 157, 544, 580, 587.

[99] Moser, "Die Fastnachtsfeier als konfessionelles Problem," 131.

[100] Ibid., 130.

[101] "Dann das alles warend die wüsten vnreynen kurtzwylen, die man vom Bapsthumm har hatt." Heinrich Bullinger, *Reformationsgeschichte*, ed. J.J. Hottinger and H.H. Vögeli (Frauenfeld: Ch. Beyel, 1838–40; Zurich: Theologische Buchhandlung, 1985), 2:45. See also Leo Zehnder, *Volkskundliches in der älteren schweizerischen Chronistik*, Schriften der Schweizerischen Gesellschaft für Volkskunde 60 (Basel: G. Krebs, 1976), 301–2.

[102] Moser, "Die Fastnachtsfeier als konfessionelles Problem," 131. See also *Aktensammlung zur Geschichte der Basler Reformation in den Jahren 1519 bis Anfang 1534*, ed. Emil Dürr and Paul Roth (Basel: Verlag der historischen und antiquarischen Gesellschaft Universitätsbibliothek Basel, 1945), 5:118–9, no. 134.

[103] Huldreich Zwingli, "Wie man die Jugend in guten Sitten und christlicher Zucht erziehen und lehren soll," in *ZW*, 5:443.

[104] On Swiss Protestant censure of carnival in general, see Kaspar von Greyerz, "Switzerland," in *The Reformation in National Context*, ed. Robert Scribner, Roy Porter, and Mikuláš Teich (Cambridge: Cambridge University Press, 1994), 40.

[105] Capito was the main architect of the Bern Synod of 1532; Martin Bucer

rely on the plays themselves, as well as on archival records of their performances, to draw conclusions as to the status of carnival in the city after 1528. All told, Bernese council manuals from 1530 to 1534 preserve records for four plays that deserve, in one sense or another, the name carnival play: *Elsli Tragdenknaben* (performed 27 February 1530), Hans von Rüte's *Abgötterei* (performed 19 March 1531), a February 1534 performance of a non-extant Prodigal Son play by the pupils of the Bernese German school, and the Seftigen play of 1534.[106] As the council remunerated the pupils on 24 February 1534,[107] it is reasonable to assume the play took place on the *Alte Fastnacht*, or 22 February, as most payments occurred a day or two after a performance.

Of these four works, *Elsli Tragdenknaben* is the only play that remained firmly in the older tradition and raised no protest among council members. Rüte and the pupils, on the other hand, altered tradition in one of two ways. The pupils retained the carnival date, but presented a biblical work, just as Burkard Waldis had done for his Prodigal Son play performed in Riga in 1527.[108] Their performance took place without apparent censure less than a month after the council had reprimanded the Seftigen players. Three years prior, Rüte had chosen a second option: *Abgötterei* retained the carnival license of its genre, but was performed on Laetare Sunday, four weeks into the Lenten season.[109] Lenten performances of carnival plays were not unheard of, but they had apparently never before taken place in Bern. The new date represented a significant break with tradition and was retained for the performances of *Joseph* (1538), *Gedeon* (1540), and *Noe* (1546).[110]

---

attended the Bernese Disputation and occasionally visited the city in his efforts towards religious concord between the Protestant camps. See Guggisberg, 101–15, 147–54, 198–212.

[106] Fluri, 136–7, 144.

[107] "Der seckelmeister alles das usrichten, so die ler knaben mit dem verlorn sun verzert und darüber gangen." As quoted in Fluri, 144.

[108] Burkard Waldis, "De parabell vam verlorn Szohn," in *Die Schaubühne im Dienste der Reformation I*, ed. Arnold E. Berger, Deutsche Literatur in Entwicklungsreihen, Reihe Reformation 5 (Leipzig: Reclam, 1935), 143–220. On Waldis's play, see Könneker, *Die deutsche Literatur der Reformationszeit*, 157–65.

[109] Anna Dorothea Noser-Hasler, "Einheimische Volksschauspiele des 16. Jahrhunderts," *Lenzburger Neujahrsblätter* 49 (1978): 14.

[110] Glenn Ehrstine, "From Iconoclasm to Iconography: Reformation Drama in Sixteenth-Century Bern," (Ph.D. diss., University of Texas at Austin, 1995), 223–5.

Elsli Tragdenknaben ("Little Liz Buck-the-Boy"; fig. 13),[111] Bern's first post-Reformation carnival play, seems at first glance more a continuation of earlier tradition than a fresh beginning. Nineteenth-century scholars identified the play as the *korgricht*, a *schimpfschrift* that Manuel had lent to Zwingli before asking for its return in 1529.[112] Indeed, the play's courtroom setting, in which the young girl Elsli demands that the peasant Uli Rechenzan (Ulrich "Rake-Tooth") marry her after he has deflowered her, seemed to represent the newly created Bernese *Chorgericht* (marriage court). Manuel himself was briefly a member of this institution, so that his first biographer, Carl von Grüneisen, had no qualms in identifying him as the author.[113] Manuel's 19th-century editor Jakob Baechtold agreed, all the more so as the surviving 1530 Basel imprint of the play, on which Baechtold based his edition, contains a note in a later hand attributing the play to Manuel.[114] At the turn of the century, however, Adolf Kaiser demonstrated that *Elsli Tragdenknaben* was a redaction of earlier "Rumpolt and Mareth" plays from Tirol.[115] His investigation revealed several obvious misreadings of an older source, making the play a hodgepodge of traditional courtroom farce and Reformation diatribe; he then wished to do Manuel a "favor" by denying him authorship of such an "inferior" work.[116] Despite a recent effort to reclaim the work for Manuel,[117] most literary scholars have since concurred that Manuel is not the play's author.[118]

---

[111] "Elsli Tragdenknaben," in *Werke und Briefe*, 536–71. All subsequent quotes are taken from this edition.

[112] *Werke und Briefe*, 730–1, no. XXXVI.

[113] Carl von Grüneisen, *Niclaus Manuel. Leben und Werke eines Malers und Dichters, Kriegers, Staatsmannes und Reformators im sechzehnten Jahrhundert* (Stuttgart: J.G. Cotta, 1837), 232.

[114] "Diß spil sol gestelt haben Niclaus Manuel ein guotter Maaler vnd burger zuo Bern." As quoted in Baechtold, foreword to *Niklaus Manuel*, CCV.

[115] Adolf Kaiser, *Die Fastnachtspiele von der Actio de sponsu. Ein Beitrag zur Geschichte des deutschen Fastnachtspieles* (Göttingen: Vandenhoeck und Ruprecht, 1899), 51–120.

[116] "Ich glaube, wir [...] leisten dem trefflichen Niklaus Manuel einen Dienst, wenn wir ihn von dem Verdachte reinigen, der Verfasser dieses in seiner Doppelnatur geringwertigen Spieles zu sein." Kaiser, 104–5.

[117] Bernd Moeller, "Niklaus Manuel Deutsch—ein Maler als Bilderstürmer," *Zwingliana* 23 (1996): 92–4. Moeller provides little more than the weight of his own authority in reascribing the work to Manuel. Greco-Kaufmann also tentatively identifies Manuel as the author, though she errs in the play's date of composition: Greco-Kaufmann, 139.

[118] Ferdinand Vetter, "Schwert und Feder: Niklaus Manuel als Kriegsmann und Dichter, 1522–1528." *Die Persönlichkeit* 1 (1914): 113; Emil Ermatinger, *Dichtung und*

Far more interesting than the question of authorship is the clearly hybrid nature of the play, which reflects a unique Reformation adaptation of the older "Rumpolt and Mareth" tradition.[119] Kaiser demonstrated that the Bernese redactor-author added eight figures to his pre-Reformation source, namely a grey friar,[120] a devil, Pauli Scharmütz, the reformed peasant Küni Süwtrog (Pig Trough), and four judges from the play's closing courtroom scene: Arnold Spitzdenwind (Hear-the-Wind), Sigwart Hübentütsch (Cap [Sophistic?] German), Herr Seltenrouch (Strange Fog), and Otman Zünfuoss (Fence Post [?]).[121] Each addition betrays the author's Protestant reworking of his source. The grey friar represents a parody of the ubiquitous Bernhardin Samson, while the four judges constitute a critique of episcopal courts.[122] Above all, Küni Süwtrog's conversion of Elsli and Uli from shameless sinners to pious, wedded Protestants constitutes the play's central adaptation of carnival culture to the ideals of the new faith.[123]

The parallels between the grey friar's transgressions and those of Manuel's indulgence peddler once again conjure up the figure of Bernhardin Samson on the Bernese stage. Given that Samson's hawking of papal grace in 1518 was so notorious that Manuel could

---

Geistesleben der deutschen Schweiz (Munich: Beck, 1933), 160; Zinsli, "Niklaus Manuel der Schriftsteller," 86; Edmund Stadler, "Einmal Duldung und einmal Verbot des Fasnachttreibens," *Der kleine Bund. Beilage für Literatur und Kunst* 138, no. 55, 7 March 1987: 1–2. Derek van Abbé, in questioning Ermatinger's rejection of Manuel's authorship, was apparently unaware of Kaiser's work: Derek van Abbé, "Change and Tradition in the Work of Niklaus Manuel of Berne 1485–1530," *Modern Language Review* 47 (1952): 196–7.

[119] On other "Rumpolt and Mareth" plays, see Dieter Trauden, "'... daz man dier die recht nit prech...' Die Bearbeitungen des Fastnachtspiels von Rumpold und Mareth," in *Mittelalterliches Schauspiel: Festschrift für Hansjürgen Linke zum 65. Geburtstag*, ed. Ulrich Mehler and Anton H. Touber, ABäG 38/39 (Amsterdam: Rodopi, 1994), 349–75.

[120] The monk does not belong to the Rumpolt/Mareth plays. However, his association with distant towns and the misreading of his stage direction ("ietzt sol sich der münch hinweg schleiken") as part of Uli's spoken text suggests that this figure already existed in *Elsli Tragdenknaben*'s immediate source. Kaiser, however, demonstrated that the second half of Uli's tirade against the monk contains longer verses characteristic of other additions. Kaiser, 79; 99–100.

[121] Kaiser, 77. Unfortunately, Kaiser points to these additions merely to demonstrate the play's ostensible inferiority, rather than to analyze the clearly Protestant alterations.

[122] Moeller correctly identifies episcopal jurisdiction as the target of the play's courtroom satire: Moeller, 93, note 66. Unfortunately, the Reformation redaction concerning the judges is quite complex, so that space constraints prohibit their discussion here. See Ehrstine, "From Iconoclasm to Iconography," 150–5.

[123] Greco-Kaufmann, 141, 281.

exploit it for his plays of 1523 and 1525, the monk's ill repute obviously survived until 1530, taking on legendary proportions as he became a stock figure in local Reformation diatribe. In *Vom Papst und seiner Priesterschaft*, Ruofli Pflegel refers to Samson as *der graw münch* (v. 1166); in *Elsli Tragdenknaben*, Uli accuses his *graw münch* of trading in false, filthy indulgences (v. 315). Like Richardus Hinderlist (*Der Ablaßkrämer*, vv. 398–406), the grey friar abuses his authority by seducing women in the confessional (v. 340). Furthermore, both clerics collect body parts from under the gallows and sell them as relics.[124] This was an especially grave crime in Bern, where fragments of the skull of St. Anne, which Albrecht vom Stein had so proudly acquired in Lyon in 1518 and brought to town in a triumphal procession, had turned out to be a mere *hirnschalenscherble*, a piece of skull sold by a monk for profit.[125] Lastly, where the indulgence peddler had to endure "stretching," the grey monk is put in chains and driven from town with canes (vv. 324–30). The friar's exemplification of ecclesiastical corruption is the main link between earlier Bernese plays and *Elsli*'s resurrection of carnival diatribe.

Otherwise, the play inverts carnival tradition, altering a conventional farce so that it becomes a Protestant celebration of marriage. The whole array of licentious elements from the play's traditional first half—Elsli's stint in a brothel, Uli's sexual escapades, their parents' excesses as well as numerous vulgar and scatological references—does not merely vanish in the second section.[126] Rather, their very absence emphasizes the compassion and tolerance both parties exercise in subsequently accepting each other. Küni Süwtrog wins Uli over by appealing to Christ's acceptance of sinners, referring to the popular Protestant parable of the Prodigal Son (vv. 774–849). Uli then accepts the marriage on the basis of the equally popular exemplum of Christ and the adulteress:

> Küni süwtrog ich bin bekert [. . .]
> Das gots wort dringt durchs herz hynyn
> Jch bin des willens gar nüt gsyn
> Das ich das Elßly nemen wett
> Des hett mich niemand über rett
> Dann so ich hör die heylsam ler

---

[124] "Ablasskrämer," vv. 410–8; "Elsli Tragdenknaben," vv. 317–24.
[125] Anshelm, 4:263.
[126] Cf. Kaiser, 76–7; 85–6.

> So dunkt mich glych ich hab syn ein ehr
> So ich bedenck das Jesus Christ
> Ein künig hymmel vnd erden ist
> Ja vnd hat sich doch nie verschemmt
> Die sünder syne brüder genempt
> Jch denk auch vnd falt mir yn
> Es was ein eebrecherin gsyn
> Die jm die Juden hend bracht
> Die was biß zuo dem tod verschmacht
> Das man sie versteyngen sott
> Aber der barmhertzig gott
> Wolt sy nit versteynget han
> Und hat sy fry ledig glan [. . .]
> Und sprach zuo ir/sünd nümmen mee
> Darumb yrrt mich nit ann der ee
> Das Ellßly ein grosse sünderin ist
> Jch hab ein exempel by Jesu Christ (vv. 876–903)

> Küni Pigtrough, I'm converted! [. . .] The word of God has taken hold of my heart. I was not willing to take Elsli: No one could have convinced me. Now, when I hear the healing word, it at once seems as if it were an honor to have her, especially when I consider that Jesus Christ is king of heaven and earth and was never ashamed to call the sinners his brothers. It also occurs to me: It was an adulteress whom the Jews brought to him; she was sentenced to death by stoning. But compassionate God did not wish to see her stoned and let her go free [. . .] and spoke to her: sin no more! Thus it does not trouble me that Elsli is a great sinner. I have an example in Jesus Christ.

Elsli invokes Christ as well when accepting Uli:

> Uly myn eelicher gmahel vnd fröud
> Behüt vns gott vor ewigem leyd
> Und verlich vns durch syn lieben sun
> Herr Jesum Christum das wir vns nun
> Hinfür in synem willen halten
> Und das wir mit ein andren alten
> Und lebend in sym göttlichen bott (vv. 926–32)

> Uli, my spouse and joy, may God protect us from eternal sorrow and grant us in the name of his son, Lord Jesus Christ, that we may from now on observe his will and that we may grow old with each other and live in his divine commandment!

Finally, Elsli's mother and Uli's father determine that it is God's will that they also marry (v. 975 ff., 983 ff.). All vulgarity ceases, and both pairs are transformed into model Christian couples. There is no doubt that all will now lead a productive life of work and prayer in accordance with Protestant ideals. What the corrupt lawyers of the episcopal court can't resolve, the power of Scripture can and does.

This sudden turnabout of carnival licentiousness in the service of piety represents the first step in the carnival play's adaptation to Protestant decorum. Although the characters initially function in a carnivalesque context, conversion leads them to Protestant ideals. And while the redactor-author retains much of his original source, he simultaneously distances himself from it. To ensure that the audience not mistake the pre-conversion antics of both parties as worthy of emulation, he introduces a devil, who claims the disputants as his own:

> Das völkly hab ich zämmen gelesen
> Dann mir gliebt vnd gfalt ir weßen [...]
> Myn sprach spürtman [sic] an jnen wol
> Die ist fluochens vnd scheltens vol
> Kein früntlich wort noch Christlich berd
> Jst by jnen lieblich noch werd
> Alle buobery/laster vnd sünd vnd schand
> Wie sy es von mir glert hand
> Zeygt ye einer dem andern an (vv. 395–407)

> I rounded up this crowd, because I like their nature. [...] One recognizes my language well with them, it's full of cussing and curses; no friendly word or Christian gesture is dear or valuable to them. Each accuses the other of all the antics, evils, sins, and disgraces that they have learned from me.

Judge Seltenrouch echoes this assessment at the end of the play: "It's the devil's crowd and servants!"[127] As the characters' frivolity is rooted in pre-Reformation carnival, these comments condemn the transgression inherent in the Shrovetide celebration. By adapting a carnival motif, the play paradoxically enjoins the audience to shun carnivalesque immoderation. Above all, the double nature of *Elsli Tragdenknaben*—the bawdiness of the first half, followed by the civility of the second—is wholly befitting of the first Bernese play to straddle two religious epochs. Unlike Manuel's plays, there is no depiction of disobedience, no call for rebellion. Even the diatribe

---

[127] "Es ist des tüffels völkly vnd gsynd." "Elsli Tragdenknaben," v. 1098.

against the pope is slight.[128] Political rhetoric recedes in favor of moral and theological elements.

Given *Elsli*'s relative lack of polemics, it is all the more surprising that religious invective resurges in Rüte's *Abgötterei* ("Idolatry"; fig. 14).[129] Once again, steadfast Protestants ridicule the pope and his followers on stage, condemning the mass, indulgences, and the profits they bring. Yet as with *Elsli*, the play is much more than an epigonal restaging of Manuelian satire. Unlike his predecessor, Rüte strikes not so much at ecclesiastical abuses, but at central issues of Catholic theology, including the cult of saints. The play's structure centers around a revue of luckless petitioners in need of aid: barren women yearning for healthy children; a merchant concerned with the safety of his goods; two young prostitutes hoping to attract new clients; and two peasants eager for a bountiful harvest. Heathen and Catholic priests alternately advise them as to what deity or saint to call upon in their need. Interspersed among these petitions, Frouw Wirrwärr (Dame Confusion), a thinly veiled Babylonian Harlot, counsels Pope Starrblind (Determinedly Blind) regarding his on-going accumulation of power and riches.

The return of drastic polemics becomes understandable when one considers the tenacity of the old faith in the Bernese territories. The disputation of 1528 had been successful in abolishing Catholicism as an institution, but it could not erase overnight the customs and rituals rooted in centuries of tradition.[130] While a brief outburst of iconoclasm had quickly purged Bernese churches of devotional art, the removal of images in the surrounding countryside proceeded slowly.[131] As late as 1534, five years after the council had officially forbidden the veneration of saints, municipal officials had to check the houses in their districts to ensure that the inhabitants had removed all images.[132] Efforts to circumvent the prohibition were often ingenious, as in 1532, when Bernese customs officers discovered devotional images en route to Bremgarten in a keg filled with dried cod.[133] Even

---

[128] Baechtold, foreword to *Niklaus Manuel*, CCIV–CCV.
[129] The play is edited under the title *Fasznachtspil* in *Sämtliche Dramen*, 1:9–105.
[130] Cf. Carlos M.N. Eire, *War Against the Idols. The Reformation of Worship from Erasmus to Calvin* (Cambridge: Cambridge University Press, 1986), 101, note 196.
[131] Theodor de Quervain, *Kirchliche und soziale Zustände in Bern unmittelbar nach der Einführung der Reformation (1528–1536)* (Bern: Gustav Grunau, 1906), 96–101.
[132] Ibid., 99.
[133] Ibid., 99.

after the council had the entrance to the cave of Swiss patron St. Beatus on Lake Thun sealed off in 1530 to prevent pilgrimages, devout worshippers, many from Catholic inner cantons, repeatedly broke through the mortar work.[134] In 1531, Rüte combatted tradition with tradition, aiming to eradicate lingering Catholic ritual through the biting satire of the *Fastnachtspiel*. As the council officially sanctioned the participation of young burghers,[135] concerns regarding the performance apparently existed, but were perhaps superceded by the necessity to use strong medicine in support of the fledgling faith.

The clearest evidence of the play's frontal assault on Catholic tradition lies in its date. As discussed earlier, its performance did not occur before Ash Wednesday, but rather on Laetare Sunday in the midst of Lent. The sale of indulgences in Bern had occurred on Laetare Sunday since 1479, so that this was no arbitrary date in the Lenten season.[136] It was originally the occasion of a *Jubiläumsablaß* (jubilee indulgence): Anyone who visited the St. Vincent minster during Laetare Sunday or the following week and who donated an amount equivalent to his expense for eight days of nourishment received remission for the same amount of sins as if he had visited Rome during a jubilee year. The sale of the jubilee indulgence recurred on this date during the 1480s, except for 1481 and 1486.[137] Although this indulgence was renewed only once more in 1496, the council received papal permission in late 1510 and again in early 1513 to transfer an episcopal indulgence, which had hitherto been sold on Palm Sunday, to Laetare Sunday. The indulgence was then sold yearly on this date through 1522. It was apparently very popular, and many individuals came to the city from the surrounding countryside to purchase it. Its sale likely ceased following the public derision of indulgences in the "Bean Song" of Ash Wednesday 1523. Finally, in April 1525, the council forbade the sale of indulgences in its third *Glaubensmandat*.

Although nine years had passed since Laetare Sunday had served such traffic, the date's significance no doubt lingered in the memory of most Berners. By transferring his play to the midst of Lent, Rüte openly snubbed the Catholic trade in indulgences. Simultaneously,

---

[134] Guggisberg, 128–9.
[135] "Den burger sünen ist die brüge erloubt." As quoted in Fluri, 136.
[136] Tremp-Utz, 52–8.
[137] Ibid., 53–4.

the accustomed solemnity of the season contributed to the earnestness of the play's performance. There may have even been a precedent for spectacles on this occasion. If Tremp-Utz's linking of *die große Indulgenz* to Laetare Sunday is correct, then, in 1516 and perhaps later as well, the members of the St. Vincent convent formed a procession of the cross to the Zytglogge Tower on this day.[138] In doing so, they likely passed through the *Kreuzgasse* (Cross Lane), the most probable location for the performance of *Abgötterei*,[139] on their way to or from the convent near the minster. While there are no processional elements in Rüte's play, he may have chosen Laetare Sunday as the only date in the Lenten season with a tradition of public spectacle.

The play lampoons local cults and practices that were dear to Berners and their Swiss confederates.[140] The Ten Thousand Martyrs, whose feast was celebrated on 22 June, had enjoyed immense popularity since the Bernese victory over Austrian forces at the Battle of Laupen (21 June 1339)[141] and especially since the Battle of Murten (22 June 1476), the decisive Swiss victory over Charles the Bold during the Wars of Burgundy. So significant was their feast day that the council, on 29 May 1528, had initially retained it as a holiday, albeit only in commemoration of these battles.[142] *Abgötterei* now ridicules their cult and its popularity among Swiss mercenaries through its commendation by the papist Adrian Küßdenpfennig (Kiss-the-Penny).[143] Rüte devotes even more attention to the cult of Mary as practiced at the chapel of Oberbüren near Biel (Bienne), where the Virgin

---

[138] "Es ist möglich, daß die beiden Ablässe—an Letare und an Judica—als 'große' und 'zweite' Indulgenz unterschieden wurden; jedenfalls beschloß das Stiftskapital am Ende des Jahres 1515, 'uff die grossen indulgentz mit crützen (zu) gan zuo der Zytglocken und in secundis indulgentiis umb die kilchen zu gan cum penitentibus.'" Tremp-Utz, 57.

[139] Unlike Manuel's plays, council records do not mention the location of Rüte's stage. However, it is reasonable to assume that it was performed on Cross Lane as were earlier carnival plays. On the significance of Cross Lane as the locus for municipal jurisdiction, see Pfrunder, 162–7.

[140] On the following, see Ehrstine, "From Iconoclasm to Iconography," 162–79.

[141] This victory alone earned the saints their own stained glass window in the Bernese minster. See Brigitte Kurmann-Schwarz, "Das 10.000–Ritter-Fenster im Berner Münster und seine Auftraggeber. Überlegungen zu den Schrift- und Bildquellen sowie zum Kult der Heiligen in Bern," *ZSAK* 49 (1992): 39–54.

[142] Quervain, 32.

[143] "Man mag ouch anrüffen S. Barblen vnd S. Vrß / Ouch die zächen tusent ritter/inn gmeiner burß / Wenn jr jren pfaffen guote opffer gäben / So werdint jr gwüß vil krieg überläben." *Abgötterei*, vv. 1691–4.

was believed to revive stillborn infants long enough to be baptized.[144] Soon, the Oberbüren Marian cult reached such notoriety that Bern itself assumed the right of collation, and several prominent burghers and noblemen of the region became members of the Confraternity of Oberbüren, among them Duke Sigmund of Austria, Adrian von Bubenberg, Wilhelm von Diesbach, Rudolf von Erlach, and Thüring Fricker. Following the Bernese Disputation, one of the first measures of the city's new Protestant council was the destruction of the Oberbüren altar; councilor Anton Noll accomplished the task, while a large crowd waited in vain for divine punishment to descend on the desecrator. In *Abgötterei*, Rüte resurrects the image: Instructed by papal priests, Dichtli Schnabelräß (Sharp-Beaked) kneels before the altar in supplication, praying (vainly) for liberation from the curse of stillbirth (vv. 698–709). As the most recent archeological excavations in Oberbüren demonstrate, the baptism and burial of stillborn children continued at the site even after the destruction of the chapel in 1530,[145] indicating that Schnabelräß's concerns reflected those of many mothers in the community even after local reform.

Indeed, following the First War of Kappel in 1529, the veneration of saints became a political issue that threatened to divide the Swiss Confederacy. Rüte directly addresses Swiss religious discord and its implications for imperial politics in his comments on St. Ursus, the patron saint of neighboring Solothurn. The political isolation of Bern, Zurich, and other Protestant cantons was especially precarious following the Diet of Augsburg (1530), in which Charles V rejected the *Confessio Augustana* and gave Protestants until 15 April 1531 to return to the old faith. Although Zwingli had also composed a confessional treatise for the diet, the *Fidei ratio*,[146] Swiss Protestants had not sent representatives, largely due to their increasing estrangement from

---

[144] See Glenn Ehrstine, "Motherhood and Protestant Polemics: Stillbirth in Hans von Rüte's *Abgötterei* (1531)," in *Maternal Measures: Figuring Caregiving in the Early Modern Period*, ed. Naomi J. Miller and Naomi Yavneh (Aldershot, Engl./Brookfield, Vt.: Ashgate, 2000), 121–34; Guggisberg, 35, 128; Paul Hofer, "Die Wahlfahrtskapelle zu Oberbüren," in *NBT 1904* (Bern: K.J. Wyss, 1903), 102–22.

[145] Daniel Gutscher, Susi Ulrich-Bochsler, and Kathrin Utz Tremp, "'Hie findt man gesundtheit des libes und der sele'—Die Wallfahrt im 15. Jahrhundert am Beispiel der wundertätigen Maria von Oberbüren," in *BGZ*, 391.

[146] "Fidei ratio," in *ZW*, 6,2:753–817. Though Johannes Eck responded in Augsburg to the *Fidei ratio* in his *Repulsio articulorum Zuinglii Caesareae maiestati oblatorum*, it is not known whether the treatise ever reached the emperor: Ulrich Gäbler, *Huldrych Zwingli. Eine Einführung in sein Leben und sein Werk* (Munich: Beck, 1983), 130.

northern Lutherans following the Marburg Colloquies of 1529. Swiss Catholics had taken advantage of their absence, traveling to Augsburg to gain imperial support. When Bern afterwards expressed interest in joining the anti-imperial Schmalkaldic League in February 1531, Lutherans insisted that the Swiss abandon their interpretation of the Eucharist, which the city rejected.[147] Thus, in March 1531, Bern and other reformed Swiss cantons were spurned by Lutherans, threatened by a possible alliance of Swiss Catholics with the emperor, and hampered by religious unrest in their own territories, such as in the Bernese Oberland.[148]

Rüte's ridicule of St. Ursus, who had become an unwitting pawn in Swiss confessional politics, was a unmistakable signal that Bern stood fast in its Zwinglian path. In 1530, Solothurn Catholics had profited enormously from a purported miracle: when local Protestants stated metaphorically that the preaching of Bern's Bertold Haller, in town to support the Reformation, would make St. Ursus sweat, droplets of liquid appeared on the saint's altar image in the city's main church.[149] Loyal Catholics, as well as those still undecided as to religious reform, interpreted this as a divine sign that the city must not waver in its faith, which ensured the demise of the local Reformation. From here, the event found its way to the Diet of Augsburg, where Solothurn mayor Hebolt recounted it to Charles to illustrate the divine necessity of imperial intervention in Switzerland.[150] Word of Hebolt's appearance before the emperor leaked out, and when he unsuccessfully sued in Zurich for libel, his conversation with Charles was recorded for posterity.[151] At the time of *Abgötterei*'s performance, then, the appropriation of St. Ursus's "sweat" as a divine appeal for Hapsburg assistance was a hotly debated topic. The par-

---

[147] Feller, 2:212–3.
[148] Bierbrauer, 250.
[149] Anshelm, 6:21–3.
[150] Rudolf Steck, "Berchtold Hallers Reformationsversuch in Solothurn (1530), nach seinen eigenen und Niklaus Manuels Briefen dargestellt," *Blätter für bernische Geschichte, Kunst und Altertumskunde* 3 (1907): 261.
[151] The speech, reported by a third party, greatly exaggerates the few drops which originally appeared: "Wie er, schultheiß Hebolt, Sant Ursen Bild zuo Solothurn herfür tragen oder tragen lassen, und je wöllen sechen, ob dasselb schwitzen wölte ald nit, und in disen dingen hett sölich bild so heftig geschwitzt, dass das tuoch, darin es gelegen oder umgeben gsin, ganz und gar nass, also dass der schweiß durch das tuoch ushin getrungen sye; dessglich [. . .], eb sy sich vom alten glouben zuo Solothurn lassen tringen, ee wöltind sy sich wider an ein hus Österrych ergeben und undertänig machen." *Actensammlung zur schweizerischen Reformationsgeschichte*, ed. Johannes Strickler (Zurich: Meyer & Zeller, 1880), 3:49, no. 125. See also Steck, 261.

allels to Hebolt, the emperor, and Swiss politics are unmistakable in the following passage, where the papal priest Eusebius Buchsorg (Belly Minder) advises the young emperor Melissus Alsmär (All-Powerful) to worship saints according to their chosen cities:

> Deßglichen darff ich nit vast erzellen
> Wie yede Stat mag ein eygnen heylgen erwellen
> Jr dörffent üch das nit vast erkhunnen
> Es lyt am tag/wie der pur an der sunnen
> Wie groß acht sy vff die Stet hand
> Man mag es spüren inn allem land
> Vnd bsonders in der Stat/do S. Vrß sitzt
> Des biltnus hat ein mal merckclich gschwitzt
> Als man der heylgen hilff wot verachten
> S. Ludigarj/Martj/Oßwalt sich ouch vffmachten
> Zerechen/dz S. Felix vnd Vincentz waren vertriben. (vv. 1238–48)

> Similarly, I don't need to elaborate on how every city can choose a saint. You don't need to inquire about it, the protection they offer these cities is as obvious as the nose on your face. You can notice it everywhere, but especially in the city where St. Ursus resides. His image once sweated noticeably when residents disdained the help of the saints. St. Leodegar, St. Martin and St. Oswald also arose to avenge the expulsion of St. Felix and St. Vincent.

The closing lines deride the patron saints of other Catholic cantons and their opposition to Bern and Zurich during the First War of Kappel. St. Leodegar is patron saint of Lucerne, while St. Oswald represents Zug. St. Martin, moreover, was the patron of Schwyz and likely symbolized, *pars pro toto*, the two other original Swiss cantons as well, Uri and Unterwalden. St. Felix and St. Vincent, meanwhile, stand for Zurich and Bern.[152] In alluding to the first military exchange between the parties, as well as to the emperor's deferment to Catholic theologians, Rüte implied that Bern was confident of its ability to defend its new faith, if need be by arms. Although this defense would end tragically just seven months later in the Second War of Kappel, *Abgötterei* demonstrated, in the calm before the storm, Bern's allegiance to the Zwinglian Reformation to Lutherans, Swiss Catholics, and the emperor alike.

---

[152] On the fate of St. Felix during the Zurich Reformation, see Peter Jezler, "Die Desakralisierung der Zürcher Stadttheiligen Felix, Regula und Exuperantius in der Reformation," in *Heiligenverehrung in Geschichte und Gegenwart*, ed. Peter Dinzelbacher and Dieter R. Bauer (Ostfildern: Schwabenverlag, 1990), 296–319.

Yet what of the peasants who had led the anti-papal charge in *Vom Papst und seiner Priesterschaft* and *Der Ablaßkrämer*? The decorum that suddenly befell the peasants of *Elsli Tragdenknaben* upon their conversion to Protestantism remained in effect for Rüte's play as well. Only the peasants Heiny Khühorn (Cow Horn) and Nicly Märenzan (Mare's Tooth), the last of the petitioners who approach the play's priests for aid, harken to the words of the preacher Theodorus Gottlieb (Theophilus) as he debates the veneration of images with Buchsorg and Jeronymus Seltenlär (Jerome Strange-Doctrine). Their reaction, however, is one of piety rather than anger. Khühorn, who had originally foreseen his son Christan for the priesthood (v. 2169), now has him come forward to read from the Bible:

> Das büchly heißt das nüw Testament
> Darin wirt rechter Gotsdienst erkent
> Wie jnn die heylgen Apostel hand triben
> Hör vatter/was sy hand von Gotsdienst gschriben
> Gott [...] spricht/Wär inn mich wirt hoffen
> Der darff niemant pitten/jhm hilff zgäben
> Jch bin der wäg/dwarheit/vnd läben. (vv. 2427–36)

> The book is called the New Testament. Here one can find proper worship as the holy apostles practiced it. Listen, father, what they wrote about worship. God [...] says: Whosoever places his hope in me, he may ask no one else to assist him. I am the way, the truth, and life.

Khühorn and Märenzan do articulate their distress at the priests' deceit, but feebly at best.[153] At no time do they enact their protest physically. In short, all transgressive behavior vanishes among *Abgötterei*'s Protestant characters.

Rüte wholly reserves that transgression for Frouw Wirrwärr as the Babylonian Harlot. As opposed to the women of *Der Ablaßkrämer*, feminine unruliness is accorded no license here, but remains decidedly negative. Wirrwärr's very name, "Dame Confusion," symbolizes disorder. She first appears on stage after Pope Starrblind expresses his desire to foster the veneration of saints for his personal gain; there, she reveals her power to grant his wishes:

---

[153] Heiny Kuohorn: "Jch wött ee/das jhn (Buchsorg) der Tüfel nem" (v. 2424); Nicly Märenzan: "Huß/ußhin/mit den schantlichen pfaffen" (v. 2464).

> Starblind/ich mag üch üwers wünschens gwären
> Die lüt volgen mir/wie ich des begären
> Dann ich bin die betriegerin dißer wellt
> Jch würt nit vnder die menschen zellt
> Sonders gott hat mich gschaffen ein vnsichbar ding
> Das ich dmenschen in blintcheit vnd jrthumb bring
> Jch bin des menschen vernunfft/begire vnd waan
> Das ich aber des glyssenden dings so vil an mir han
> Bedütet myn anmütige leer vnd Rhadt
> Dem der mensch darumb flyssig nach gadt
> Das er domit überkhöm vil Eer vnd guot
> Vnd alles/was dem lyb wol thuot (vv. 279–90)

> Starrblind, I can grant you your desire. People follow me as I wish, for I am the deceiver of the world. I am not of humankind. Rather, God created me as an invisible force, so that I might lead people into blindness and error. I am humanity's reason, desire, and opinion. That I have so many dazzling attributes signifies my pleasing doctrine and advice, which people industriously pursue in order to obtain great honor and possessions and all that is pleasing to the body.

In Frouw Wirrwärr, Rüte creates an allegorical archetype for the assumed failings of Catholicism. In analogy to *frouwe werlt* of medieval German literature, she is outwardly beautiful, but inwardly corrupt. Her domain is the body; all who seek earthly pleasures subject themselves to her sway. Theologically, she subsumes all that opposes God's divinity, including humanity's reason (*vernunft*) and opinion (*waan*), which Protestant reformers considered inadequate to fathom the mysteries of God's will. She thus symbolizes humanity's erroneous belief in the infallibility of its own intellect, as expressed by the herald at the close of the play:

> Das duncken ist einr reitzigen huoren verglycht
> Die dman mit hürschen worten und wysen hinderschlycht
> Wie dise huor/dz sibenhöuptig thier hat beritten
> Also hat das guotduncken/alle rych überschritten (vv. 2679–82)

> Opinion has been compared to a comely harlot, who seduces men with whorish words and wiles. Just as this harlot has ridden the seven-headed beast, so opinion has conquered all kingdoms.

By viewing Frouw Wirrwärr allegorically as a force in church history, the audience can grasp the ostensible source for all extra-biblical aspects of the Catholic cult. She convinces the pope to establish *vil Ceremonien* and *usserlichen Gottsdienst* (vv. 313–4) and later advises him in one long passage to create indulgences, confession, taxes on benefices and clerical concubines, and finally many monastic orders—with their houses preferably situated in areas of plentiful grain and wine (vv. 1376–429). Her influence then extends to the pope's alliances with secular rulers, especially with the emperor (vv. 2144–8). Finally, she convinces the emperor that the adherents of the new faith are more harmful to the pope than the Turks, at least in terms of income (vv. 2491–546).

The resultant mingling of church history (*Kirchengeschichte*) with the history of salvation (*Heilsgeschichte*) has long been considered one of the original aspects of Thomas Naogeorgus's *Pammachius* of 1538.[154] Rüte, of course, cannot claim originality for Frouw Wirrwärr, whose apocalyptic embodiment of the papacy is based on Protestant woodcut illustrations for the Book of Revelation. This is apparent in two illustrations accompanying copies of the play: the Zurich exemplar of *Abgötterei* contains, tipped in, Hans Holbein the Younger's woodcut illustration of Apocalypse 17 (fig. 15), and Rüte himself pictures the harlot on the seven-headed beast in the top center of his own sketch for his play's title vignette (fig. 16).[155] Nonetheless, through Frouw Wirrwärr, Rüte can claim precedence in bringing apocalyptic imagery to the Protestant stage seven years before the appearance of *Pammachius*.

In *Abgötterei*'s post-Reformation context, the banishment of carnival transgression to the realm of allegory was apparently a necessary condition if the local carnival play tradition was to continue at all. This seems to have been equally true for the representation of political agency. The play's peasants, as has been noted, are too pious to challenge the reign of Frouw Wirrwärr. The instigation to revolt, with its obligatory billingsgate, now comes from the burly Bernese Bear brandishing Manuel's trademark *schwytzer dägen* (v. 476):

---

[154] See Hans-Gert Roloff, "Heilsgeschichte, Weltgeschichte und aktuelle Polemik: Thomas Naogeorgs *Tragoedia Nova Pammachius*," *Daphnis* 9 (1980): 743–67.

[155] Holbein created the woodcut in the Zurich exemplar (Züricher Zentralbibliothek Gal Ch 87) for the 1523 edition of *Das gantz New Testament* published by Thomas Wolff in Basel. The original is housed in the Basel *Kupferstichkabinett*. Emil Weller offers a brief description of the Zurich illustration which has gone unnoticed: Emil Weller, *Das alte Volkstheater der Schweiz* (Frauenfeld: J. Huber, 1863), 59. The Holbein woodcut also appears in two other exemplars, one in the British Museum and a second in the Züricher Zentralbibliothek: Klaus Jaeger, commentary on "Fasznachtspil," in *Sämtliche Dramen*, 3:92. Rüte's drawing is preserved in the Bernese exemplar of *Abgötterei* (Berner Stadt- und Universitätsbibliothek Rar 105).

Jr verflüchten pfaffen/jr nütsöllenden läcker
Jr Tüfelsüchtigen/lasterlichen dellerschläcker
Jr lüt trieger/gots verköuffer/jr fulen kunden
Mich lust/ich schlüg üch kouffmans wunden
Jch wond/ich hett üch all verryben
Der Tüfel hat üch vmbher tryben
Mir ist yetz ernst/es darff nit lachen
Dem schimpff wurd sunst den boden krachen
Rumend wir dise reine Stat
Die Gott mynen vordern gäben hat
Das gricht vnd grechtigkeit khäme druß
Nit das sy wär ein pfaffen huß
Vast vß jr buoben mit üwerm gyt
Machent üch hinnen ferr vnd wyt
Jr gotslestrigen fulen khat büch
Myn zorn der gat sunst über üch (vv. 2587–602)

You cursed priests, you good-for-nothing sycophants, you devil-addicted, blasphemous panhandlers, you swindlers, god-peddlers, you foul customers. I've half a mind to knock you silly. I thought I had eradicated you all. The devil has brought you back here. I'm serious now, this is no laughing matter; the joke would otherwise shatter the earth. Let us clean out this pure city, which God gave to my forebears so that law and justice might dwell in it, not that it become a den of clerics. Clear out, you rogues, with your greed. Take to the hills far and wide, you blasphemous, stinking dung bellies, otherwise you will feel my wrath.

The Bear, symbol of the city's proud independence and military might,[156] could unite disparate elements among the play's audience beyond issues of class or gender. Ultimately, of course, the beast embodied the council and its religious authority, appealing to the necessity for cohesion in the face of political and religious adversity. The Bear's expulsion of the play's papists thus celebrates the new Bernese church and reiterates the case for religious change.

While it is possible that following *Abgötterei* additional carnival plays were performed in Bern of which no records survive, it is highly

---

[156] The Bernese Bear, represented by an actor clothed in bear hide, continued to symbolize city government in the seventeenth- and eighteenth-century Easter processions of the *Äußerer Stand*, the organization of the city's young patricians. See Richard Wolfram, *Studien zur älteren Schweizer Volkskultur. Mythos, Sozialordnung, Brauchbewußtsein*, Österreichische Akademie der Wissenschaften, Philosophisch-historische Klasse 362 (Vienna: Verlag der österreichischen Akademie der Wissenschaften, 1980), 176.

unlikely. In the double bind of Protestant theology and Swiss politics, the local tradition of *Fastnachtspiele* imploded. Objections to carnivalesque transgression had already excised impious behavior from Protestant characters and assigned that behavior to the demonized depiction of religious foe. Without any further refuge for the constitutive licentiousness of the carnival play, continued censure necessarily led to the death of the genre. To paraphrase Rüte's Bernese Bear, questions of salvation were no longer "a laughing matter." Even if the performance of *Abgötterei* proved effective in suppressing surviving aspects of the Catholic cult, the confessional tensions within the Swiss Confederacy following the Second War of Kappel soon dictated an end to all religious polemics. If Rüte's *Goliath* was indeed performed in 1535, then the following comments by the play's herald provide a fitting epilogue, if not epitaph, for the carnival play's demise as Protestantism's preferred dramatic vehicle for religious instruction:

> Zum ersten sol ich vßher sagen/
> Das wir nit werdind üch fürtragen/
> Wie üwer möchtend warten vil/
> Ein args/lychtfertigs Faßnachtspil/
> Daruß kein grösser frucht/nutz/lon/
> Leer/guots/noch bessrung möchte kon [. . .]
> Darumb yeder betracht vnd fassz
> Das gmeynen Spilßgsellen hat gfallen [. . .]
> Ein Spil zhalten/das Göttlich sy
> Das alle welt ersech darby
> Wie Gott ye handlet mit der welt (vv. 9–27)

To begin with, I should state that we will not perform, as many of you might expect, a raucous, frivolous carnival play, from which no greater profit, advantage, reward, instruction, goodness nor betterment might come. [. . .] Therefore, may you each consider that it has pleased the players [. . .] to perform a divine play, so that the whole world might see how God deals with the world.

CHAPTER FOUR

THEOCRACY AND THEATER

> But since we've observed that many other cities, large and small, allow plays to be performed before the community, we've taken heart and chosen an honest play. [...] We've striven to teach, so that we might please and honor you, our benevolent Lords, councilors of the laudable city of Bern.
>
> —Hans von Rüte, *Noe*

With the demise of the carnival play, Rüte and other like-minded playwrights were forced to seek an alternative form of Protestant theater. The direct adaptation of Easter, passion, or Corpus Christi plays was out of the question; like carnival entertainments, they were closely associated with the old church. Greff and Swiss playwrights such as Jacob Rueff did eventually attempt to reconcile late medieval dramatic tradition with the new theology, but they did so only after 1542, by which time they were firmly established as upstanding Protestant authors. In the early 1530s, there was only one dramatic tradition that was not immediately reminiscent of Catholicism: that of humanist dramaturgy.

Originally a strictly secular imitation of classical theater, humanist drama had at this time just produced its first widely successful biblical adaptation in Gulielmus Gnapheus's *Acolastus*, a Latin Prodigal Son play of 1529. Prior to this, humanists promoting the study and imitation of ancient drama had been more concerned with advancing rhetorical eloquence than religious piety.[1] Beginning in the final decade of the fifteenth century, the works of Plautus, Terence, Seneca, and others were recited or publicly performed by school boys and university students as part of their Latin studies. Terence, whose plays were considered models of conversational Latin, proved especially popular. However, as the *studia humanitatis* gained adherents,

---

[1] On humanist playwrights' concern with classical rhetoric and Renaissance imitation, see David Price, *The Political Dramaturgy of Nicodemus Frischlin*, University of North Carolina Studies in the Germanic Languages and Literatures 111 (Chapel Hill/London: University of North Carolina Press, 1990), 10 ff., 22–7.

humanists increasingly had to defend the study of pagan authors against scholastic charges of immorality and even heresy. In response, they adopted patristic arguments for the utility of classical literature, emphasizing the plays' sententious wisdom, the pedagogical value of negative exempla, and the necessity of rhetorical training to fully understand the tropes of Scripture.[2] Not until the late 1520s, however, did humanist playwrights begin infusing neo-classical poetics with Christian ideals in works of their own. Suddenly, all aspired to become a *Terentius Christianus*, the title of a popular 1592 play collection by Haarlem school rector Cornelius Schonaeus. Although the authors were often staunchly Catholic or Protestant, the resulting tradition of *dramata sacra* (sacred dramas) was surprisingly free of overt confessional polemics. While Gnapheus may have intended *Acolastus* as a crypto-Lutheran work, for example, this did not prevent Jesuits from embracing it for Counter-Reformation purposes.[3]

Philipp Melanchthon proved to be a pivotal figure in placing humanist dramaturgy in the service of the new faith. His great-uncle, Johannes Reuchlin, had authored the first successful neo-Terentian comedy north of the Alps in 1497,[4] and in 1516, at the precocious age of 19, Melanchthon published his own edition of Terence, the first to restore the plays' meter.[5] After moving to Wittenberg in 1519 to assume the university professorship of Greek, Melanchthon founded a private school, in which students performed works by Terence,

---

[2] Ibid., 14 ff.; James A. Parente, Jr., *Religious Drama and the Humanist Tradition. Christian Theater in Germany and in the Netherlands 1500–1680*, Studies in the History of Christian Thought 39 (Leiden: E.J. Brill, 1987), 13 ff.

[3] Parente, 62, note 2; 76. On the interpretation of *Acolastus* as a Lutheran parable, see W.E.D. Atkinson, introduction to Gulielmus Gnapheus, *Acolastus: A Latin Play of the Sixteenth Century* (London, Ontario: Hunter Printing, 1964), 47–72.

[4] In 1497, Reuchlin wrote *Scenica Progymnasmata*, more commonly known as *Henno*, which was hailed by contemporaries: Johannes Reuchlin, *Henno*, ed. and trans. Harry C. Schnur (Stuttgart: Reclam, 1970). On the author, see Stefan Rhein, "Johannes Reuchlin," in *Deutsche Dichter der Frühen Neuzeit (1450–1600). Ihr Leben und Werk*, ed. Stephan Füssel (Berlin: Erich Schmidt, 1993), 138–55; David Price, "Johannes Reuchlin," in *German Writers of the Renaissance and Reformation, 1280–1580*, ed. James Hardin and Max Reinhart, vol. 179 of *Dictionary of Literary Biography* (Detroit: Gale Research, 1997), 231–40. On the play, see Otto Brunken, "Johannes Reuchlin (1455–1522): Scenica Progymnasmata: Hoc est: Ludicra Preexercitamenta. Basel 1498," in *Handbuch zur Kinder- und Jugendliteratur. Vom Beginn des Buchdrucks bis 1570*, ed. Theodor Brüggeman (Stuttgart: Metzler, 1987), 331–44, 1163–7.

[5] "Enarratio comoedarum Terentii," in *Philippi Melanchthoni Opera quae supersunt omnia*, ed. Heinrich Ernst Bindseil, Corpus Reformatorum 19 (Braunschweig: C.A. Schwetske et filius, 1853), columns 655–784.

Plautus, Seneca, and Euripides.[6] His advocation of classical theater proceeded to influence Luther's views on drama, especially as regarded its pedagogical applications. Following Melanchthon's example, Luther hosted the performance of a classical drama by Wittenberg students in his home during the carnival of 1525.[7] He further supported the performance of Terence "for the sake of school boys" on numerous occasions, noting that if one were to censure the author's plays because they portrayed adultery and other lascivious behavior, then one would also have to reject the Bible, as it contained similar stories.[8] Following Melanchthon's recommendation in the School Ordinance of Saxony (1528) of performing Latin plays as a rhetorical exercise, numerous Protestant *Schulordnungen* mandated the regular performance or recitation of works by Plautus or Terence.[9] The Strasbourg Academy under the direction of Johannes Sturm soon became the leading center of this new *Schuldrama*, with performances eventually moving from the classroom to the school's courtyard to accommodate a larger public audience.[10]

Of course, the ancients' much vaunted eloquence and moral instruction were of little use to those without knowledge of Latin. Vernacular translations offered one means of acquainting the general public with the benefits of classical literature. German renditions of Terence had begun to appear soon after the first incunable Latin editions,[11] and none other than Joachim Greff translated Plautus's *Aulularia* in 1535.[12]

---

[6] On Melanchthon's private school, see Thomas Ivey Bacon, *Martin Luther and the Drama* (Amsterdam: Rodopi, 1976), 51–7; Ludwig Koch, *Philipp Melanchthons Schola Privata* (Gotha: Perthes, 1859).

[7] Bacon, 49–50.

[8] "Und Christen sollen Comödien nicht ganz und gar fliehen, drum, daß bisweilen grobe Zoten und Bühlerey darinnen seyen, da man doch um derselben willen auch die Bibel nicht dürfte lesen." WA 58 (*Tischreden I*), 432, no. 867.

[9] Reviewed by Bacon, 23–31. See also P. Expeditius Schmidt, *Die Bühnenverhältnisse des deutschen Schuldramas und seiner volkstümlichen Ableger im sechzehnten Jahrhundert*, Forschungen zur neueren Literaturgeschichte 24 (Berlin: Alexander Duncker, 1903), 5–20; Johannes Maassen, *Drama und Theater der Humanistenschulen in Deutschland* (Augsburg: Benno Filser, 1929), 39.

[10] See James A. Parente, Jr., "Tragoedia Politica: Strasbourg School Drama and the Early Modern State, 1583–1621," *Colloquia Germanica* 29 (1996): 1–11; Wolfgang F. Michael, *Das deutsche Drama der Reformationszeit* (Bern: Lang, 1984), 236–44; Günter Skopnik, *Das Straßburger Schultheater: Sein Spielplan und seine Bühne* (Frankfurt: Selbstverlag des Elsaß-Lothringen-Instituts, 1935).

[11] See for example *Der Eunuchus des Terenz. Übersetzt von Hans Neidhart 1486*, ed. Hermann Fischer, Bibliothek des Litterarischen Vereins in Stuttgart 265 (Tübingen: Laupp, 1915).

[12] Derek van Abbé, *Drama in Renaissance Germany and Switzerland* (Melbourne:

Popular neo-Latin plays also appeared in German. These included, among others, Gnapheus's *Acolastus* (translated ca. 1530 by Georg Binder),[13] the anti-papal *Pammachius* by Thomas Naogeorgus (1538; translated 1540 by Hans Tirolf),[14] and two adaptations by Hans Sachs: those of Reuchlin's *Henno* (original 1497, translation 1531) and, later, *Hecastus*, an Everyman play by the Dutch humanist Georg Macropedius (original 1538, translation 1549).[15]

Himself a translator, Luther recognized the need to engage audiences in a language they could comprehend, so that he wholeheartedly endorsed play performances in German.[16] The instruction of playgoers in tenets of the new faith, however, required vernacular works based on Scripture, not pagan authors. Without abandoning humanist models, Protestant authors began to create a vernacular theater around the motto of *sola scriptura*. The resultant German-language biblical dramas began appearing sporadically in the late 1520s and early 1530s, such as Burkard Waldis's Prodigal Son play of 1527,[17] the anonymous Zurich *Rich Man and Lazarus* of 1529,[18] and Sixtus

---

Melbourne University Press, 1961), 78, 92. Van Abbé incorrectly claims that Greff was the first to translate Plautus into German. That honor belongs to Albrecht von Eyb, whose translations of *Menaechmi* and *Bacchides* were published posthumously in 1511. See Otto Francke, *Terenz und die lateinische Schulcomoedie in Deutschland* (Weimar: Böhlau, 1877), 42–4; John L. Flood, "Albrecht von Eyb," in *German Writers of the Renaissance and Reformation, 1280–1580*, ed. James Hardin and Max Reinhart, vol. 179 of *Dictionary of Literary Biography* (Detroit: Gale Research, 1997), 51–3.

[13] Binder's translation did not appear in print until 1535: Georg Binder, "Acolastus," in *Schweizerische Schauspiele des sechzehnten Jahrhunderts*, ed. Jacob Baechtold (Zurich: J. Huber, 1890), 1:171–271.

[14] Naogeorgus's Latin text and Tirolf's translation are edited in the first volume of Thomas Naogeorg, *Sämtliche Dramen*, ed. Hans-Gert Roloff (Berlin/New York: de Gruyter, 1975). Two less successful translations of *Pammachius* by Justus Meni and Thomas Kirchbauer appeared in 1539.

[15] "Ein comedi, mit 10 personen zu recidiern, doctor Reuchlins im Latein gemacht, der Henno," in *Hans Sachs*, ed. Adelbert von Keller, Bibliothek des Litterarischen Vereins in Stuttgart 115 (Tübingen: H. Laupp, 1873), 7:124–53; "Ein comedi von dem reichen sterbenden menschen, der Hecastus genannt, hat neunzehen personen und 5 actus zu spielen," in *Hans Sachs*, ed. Keller, 6:137–87.

[16] Luther recorded his thoughts on translation in "Ein Sendbrief vom Dolmetschen," in WA 30,2: 632–46. For Luther's recommendations on performing the deeds of Christ in Latin and German, see Chapter One's epigraph.

[17] Burkard Waldis, "De parabell vam verlorn Szohn," in *Die Schaubühne im Dienste der Reformation I*, ed. Arnold E. Berger, Deutsche Literatur in Entwicklungsreihen, Reihe Reformation 5 (Leipzig: Reclam, 1935), 143–220.

[18] "Eine waarhafftige History vß dem heyligen Euangelio Luce am XVI. Capitel von dem Rychen mann vnnd armen Lazaro," in *Das Zürcher Spiel vom reichen Mann und vom armen Lazarus—Pamphilus Gengenbach, Die Totenfresser*, ed. Josef Schmidt (Stuttgart: Reclam, 1969), 7–38.

Birck's first *Susanna* of 1532.[19] However, Luther's 1534 commentaries on Judith and Tobit opened the flood gates. Protestant playwrights subsequently mined the Bible for edifying tales and characters suitable for portrayal upon the stage. Susanna and the Prodigal Son continued as highly popular subjects, vying with Joseph as the most frequently dramatized figures of the sixteenth century. Works based on Job, David, and the Rich Man and Lazarus, while somewhat less ubiquitous than those above, were also widespread.[20]

A broad heterogeneity nevertheless distinguishes these plays as regards their imitation of humanist models. This is perhaps most readily apparent in the seemingly capricious adoption or omission of the five-act schema of Roman New Comedy, but is also evident in a continuing admixture of late medieval elements taken from both the carnival and passion play traditions. A comparison of three or four dramas alone makes apparent that sixteenth-century German-language playwrights did not imitate ancient theater so much as borrow from it ad hoc, creating an idiosyncratic combination of classical and indigenous elements with each new drama. When audience expectations took precedence over an author's humanist leanings, the resulting plays might bear little resemblance to contemporary neo-Latin works.[21]

This latter scenario applies particularly to the biblical dramas produced by Swiss Protestant playwrights, such as Rüte, Jacob Rueff, or Jakob Funkelin. Rüte is, for example, particularly oblivious to act divisions; his scenes are separated, if at all, by occasional musical

---

[19] Sixt Birck, "Susanna," in *Sämtliche Dramen*, ed. Manfred Brauneck (Berlin: de Gruyter, 1976), 2:1–53.

[20] Michael offers a comprehensive bibliography of sixteenth-century German-language plays: Michael, 401–10. On select traditions, see Alexander von Weilen, *Der ägyptische Joseph im Drama des XVI. Jahrhunderts: Ein Beitrag zur vergleichenden Literaturgeschichte* (Vienna: Alfred Hölder, 1887); Paul F. Casey, *The Susanna Theme in German Literature: Variations of the Biblical Drama* (Bonn: Bouvier, 1976); Jean Lebeau, *Salvator Mundi: L'"Exemple" de Joseph dans le Théâtre Allemand au XVIe Siècle*, Bibliotheca Humanistica et Reformatica 20 (Nieuwkoop: B. de Graaf, 1977); Stephen L. Wailes, *The Rich Man and Lazarus on the Reformation Stage. A Contribution to the Social History of German Drama* (Selinsgrove: Susquehana University Press; London: Associated University Presses, 1997).

[21] We know, for example, from Johannes Sturm's comments that the general Strasbourg audience desired something other than the Academy's classical performances. Although Sturm does not state why his plays did not fulfill audience expectations, it is likely that they wanted something with more pomp and spectacle along the lines of late medieval dramaturgy. See Schmidt, 11–2.

interludes. The sheer length of his plays, at times exceeding 6000 lines, is also typically medieval, producing characterizations ranging from "expansive" to "unbearably broad."[22] Yet Rüte was clearly familiar with contemporary humanist dramaturgy, as his *Joseph* is based in part on the Latin drama of the same name by the Dutch playwright Cornelius Crocus.[23] His expansion of Crocus's work into a two-day performance has been considered paradigmatic for the diverging poetics of Swiss biblical plays and their northern cousins.[24]

Given the pronounced typology and exegetical herald of *Joseph*, both common features of late medieval Catholic plays, a more indigenous model for certain elements of Rüte's dramas immediately suggests itself: the passion plays of Lucerne, which had been performed in this nearby city intermittently since the fifteenth century. The Lucerne plays were similarly performed over two days, were introduced by a heraldic proclamator, and emphasized the Old Testament's prefiguration of Christ. Additional Catholic plays from Lucerne, such as Hans Salat's *Verlorener Sohn* ("Prodigal Son," 1538) likewise bear a striking outer resemblance to Rüte's dramas.

Piety and Patriarchy

The dramaturgical parallels between Protestant and Catholic plays of this period, both in Switzerland and southern German areas, point to the common cultural and political exchange among these regions. The economic and political ties between southern regions of the Holy Roman Empire were much greater than those to the north,[25] especially in towns partial to Zwinglian theology such as Augsburg or Strasbourg, Lindau, Constance, and Memmingen, the signers of the Tetrapolitan Confession. The likelihood that Rüte or members of his audience chanced to attend play performances in Lucerne, Zurich, or even Augsburg was much greater than the probability

---

[22] "Ausladend": Michael, 138; "unerträglich breit": Emil Ermatinger, *Dichtung und Geistesleben der deutschen Schweiz* (Munich: Beck, 1933), 199.

[23] Otto W. Tetzlaff, "Neulateinische Dramen der Niederlande in ihrer Einwirkung auf die deutsche Literatur des 16. Jahrhunderts," *ABäG* 1 (1972): 162 ff.

[24] Michael, 139.

[25] See in general Thomas A. Brady, Jr., *Turning Swiss: Cities and Empire, 1450–1550*, Cambridge Studies in Early Modern History (Cambridge: Cambridge University Press, 1985).

that they might have traveled to Zwickau, Magdeburg, or Wittenberg. In this common cultural context, community plays continued as political vehicles, representing their sponsoring towns to visitors and residents alike.

In the Swiss Confederacy proper, the performance of biblical plays functioned much as pre-Reformation carnival celebrations had, providing divertissement for visiting delegations among the various confederates, but now additionally reaching across confessional divides. Evidence exists that Swiss playgoers regularly attended plays in neighboring "heretic" cantons, such as the Protestant spectators who travelled to Lucerne in 1549 to attend the performance of a Last Judgment play by Zacharias Bletz.[26] Moreover, according to treasury records of 1549/50, the Zurich council invested nine pounds and ten shillings in the regalement of representatives "from all cantons" immediately prior to a play performance, most likely that of Rueff's *Adam und Eva* (1550).[27] No such treasury records exist for Rüte's plays, but the reference to "guests" in *Gedeon*, in which Rüte assures that the play will not offend, likely alludes to Catholic visitors.[28] The prologues of *Goliath* and *Joseph* equally promise that no particular group will take umbrage at the plays' content. Moreover, Swiss Protestant plays were often performed in Catholic towns and vice versa. In 1543, Johannes Wagner performed Binder's Zurich translation of Gnapheus's *Acolastus* in Catholic Solothurn, followed by a performance of Rueff's *Job* in 1549.[29] The Bernese council supported the printing of Johannes Aal's John the Baptist drama, performed in Solothurn in 1549, and most likely allowed the same play to be performed in the city in 1591.[30]

---

[26] As reported by Milan envoy Angelo Rizio. See Leonhard Haas, "Über geistliche Spiele in der Innerschweiz," *ZSK* 47 (1953): 118–20. Haas's German translation of the letter can be found in Bernd Neumann, *Geistliches Schauspiel im Zeugnis der Zeit. Zur Aufführung mittelalterlicher religiöser Dramen im deutschen Sprachgebiet*, Münchener Texte und Untersuchungen zur deutschen Literatur des Mittelalters 84/85 (Munich: Artemis, 1987), 1:486–90, no. 2099.

[27] Ermatinger, 184; *Jacob Ruffs Adam und Heva*, ed. Hermann Marcus Kottinger, Bibliothek der deutschen National-Literatur 26 (Quedlinburg/Leipzig: Gottfried Basse, 1848).

[28] "Niemand wirt gmeint noch angetast// Wäder nachpur/burger noch gast." *Gedeon*, vv. 11–12.

[29] Eugen Müller, *Schweizer Theatergeschichte: Ein Beitrag zur Schweizer Kulturgeschichte*, Schriftenreihe des Schauspielhauses Zürich 2 (Zurich: Oprecht, 1944), 120–2.

[30] Regarding the performance, municipal documents record only a play of "John's decapitation." Eugen Müller considers this to be Aal's work. See Müller, *Schweizer Theatergeschichte*, 117; Fluri, 142.

This cross-confessional cultural exchange, while obviously competitive at times, nonetheless helped to preserve the social and political bonds that held the confederacy together. Despite their theological differences, Protestant and Catholic cantons were well aware that their continued cooperation was essential to maintain Swiss independence from the empire, just as it was necessary, beginning with the Diet of Regensburg in 1532, for Charles V and German Protestant princes to set aside their differences in the common defense of the empire against Turkish encroachment.[31]

Protestant town councils of the period took an especially active role in determining the theatrical repertory of their cities, so that the local stage at times became an extension of council policy.[32] After moving to Augsburg from Klein-Basel, Sixtus Birck chastised the council there in his Latin-language *Susanna* of 1537 for having required him to compose religious drama as opposed to the political play he would have preferred.[33] Greff, too, states that the Magdeburg council commanded him to compose *Jacob* in 1534:

> Dis unser itzt vergangen spiel
> Furwar es vns von hertzen gefiel/
> Es ist furwar am allermeist
> Von wegen der itzigen frembden gest/
> Vnd zu gefallen eim erbarn Rat
> Der solchs befolhen vnd geboten hat/
> Geschehen [. . .][34]

> This play of ours, just performed, truly pleased us from the bottom of our hearts. It was performed mainly for the sake of our foreign guests and for the pleasure of the honest council, which ordered and commanded it.

In Zurich, Rueff commended his *Joseph* of 1540 to the civic authorities,[35] although it is unclear how much influence they exercised over the play.

---

[31] On the "Nuremberg Standstill" of 1532 and the long-term threat of Turkish invasion, see Hajo Holborn, *A History of Modern Germany. The Reformation* (Princeton: Princeton University Press, 1959), 217–9.

[32] Ermatinger, 184.

[33] Birck, "Susanna," 2:170–6.

[34] Joachim Greff, *Ein lieblich vnd nützbarlich spiel von dem Patriarchen jacob vnd seinen zwelff Sönen/Aus dem ersten buch Mosi gezogen/vnd zu Magdeburg auff dem Schützenhoff/im 1535. iar gehalten* (Nuremberg: n.p., 1535), Ev^v.

[35] *Ein hüpsch nüwes Spil von Josephen dem frommen Jüngling/vß etlichen Capitlen deß buochs*

Rüte's prominent dedications to the Bernese council indicate that it, too, took an active interest in the local stage. Rüte specifically refers to the dramatic practice of other cities while commending *Noe* to the local councilors:

> Aber d'wyl wir g'send/vnd hand acht/
> Das vil ander Stett/groß vnd klein
> Die Spil land handlen vor jr gmein/[...]
> So hand wir ein hertz vberkhon
> Vnd ein eerlich Spil für vns gnon [...]
> Das hand wir vns gflissen zeleeren
> Zuo wolgfallen vnd grossen eeren
> Vch vnseren gnädigen Herren
> Loblicher Statt Bern Oberkeit.[36]

It is uncertain whether the Bernese council actually determined the content of performances, but Rüte's constant deference to its judgment suggests that it at least decided the success or failure of his efforts:

> Wir bittent üch zuohörer all
> Jnsonders vnser gnädig Heren
> Denen diß spil ist gmachet zeeren
> Jr wöllents im besten verstan
> Für die kunst vnsern willen han.[37]

> We ask all those listening, especially our benevolent Lords, to whom this play is dedicated, to judge the play kindly and take our good will in art's stead.

No specific mention of the council is made in *Joseph* or *Goliath*, but it is likely that the magistrates attended and were honored at these performances as well. The council in turn rewarded Rüte's players handsomely, providing as much as 200 pounds for the actors in *Gedeon*, plus another 100 pounds for the musicians.[38]

---

der Gschöpfften gezogen/in sonders lustig vnd nutzlich zeläsen. (Zurich: Augustin Frieß, 1540), Miij^v. Barbara Thoran has recently questioned Rueff's authorship of the play, which appeared anonymously: Thoran, "Untersuchungen zu den Dramen Jacob Rueffs, des Züricher Zeitgenossen von Hans Sachs," in *Dialog. Festschrift für Siegfried Grosse*, ed. Gert Rickheit and Sigurd Wichter (Tübingen: Niemeyer, 1990), 75–89.

[36] *Noe*, vv. 84–126. For a translation of this passage, see the epigraph at the beginning of the chapter.

[37] *Gedeon*, vv. 4045–9.

[38] The *Seckelmeisterrechnungen* record further disbursements of 100 pounds for the Goliath play of 1535, 166 pounds for *Joseph*, fifty crowns for *Noe*, twelve crowns

In contrast to Protestant carnival plays, the absence of topical polemics in Rüte's and other Swiss biblical dramas makes it difficult to discern any specific confessional issues they might have addressed. Yet this should not suggest that the plays lacked a confessional or sociopolitical agenda. In Bern, one such social aspect is immediately apparent in Rüte's choice of patriarchal protagonists. Whereas Lutheran dramaturgy often celebrated feminine virtue in figures such as Susanna, Esther, and Judith, the heroes of Bernese plays—David, Joseph, Gideon, and Noah—are exclusively male.[39] Considered individually, the choice of David and Joseph would not be conspicuous, as both stories enjoyed widespread popularity.[40] As dramatic characters, however, Gideon and Noah were unique in sixteenth-century literature,[41] suggesting that Rüte pursued a specific program in bringing them to the stage. Upon comparing these four plays, it becomes evident that their champions share one thing in common: each upholds his faith, if need be by arms, against a competing religion that threatens assault from without, corruption from within, or both. David conquers Goliath, Gideon destroys Baal's altar, Noah punishes a demonized Ham, and Joseph must withstand the seductions of Potiphar's wife, who in Rüte's portrayal places good works over chaste behavior. The protagonists' frequent references to opponents' "idolatry," a common Protestant metaphor for the veneration of saints, indicate that Rüte equated the confessional and political isolation of Swiss Protestants with the trials of Old Testament Judaism. By attributing its victories over seemingly overwhelming odds to its unwavering faith in God, Rüte's biblical plays admonished their Bernese audience to remain steadfast in the chosen path of religious reform.

---

for *Osterspiel*, and 3 bushels of dinkel for Samuel Apiarius following his printing of *Goliath* in 1555. Fluri, 138.

[39] This is not to suggest that the playwrights of central and northern Germany shunned male protagonists; there as well, they likely appeared more often than their female counterparts. Rüte's plays are nevertheless almost exclusively male, with women characters appearing only when dictated by Scripture. As far as I can determine, only one woman appears in Rüte's plays without a direct biblical precedent: David's mother in *Goliath* (v. 4115 ff.).

[40] Michael notes David and Goliath plays by Hans Tirolf (*Ein Gottseligs/Tröstlichs/vnd fast lustigs Teutsch Gerheimts Spil [. . .]*; 1541), Wolfgang Schmeltzl (*Ein schöne tröstliche Hystoria von dem Jungling Dauid*; 1545), Jakob Schöpper (*Monomachia Davidis et Goliae*; 1550), and Valentin Boltz (*Ölung Davidis des Jünglings*; 1554), including sections of Mathias Holtzwart's *Saul* (1571). Michael, 74, 230, 231, 249, 266.

[41] Only one other sixteenth-century Gideon play exists, composed by Hans Sachs in 1556. See Klaus Jaeger, *Sämtliche Dramen*, 3:175.

In at least two dramas, that faith coincides with military prowess. Both *Goliath* and *Gedeon* indulge in detailed descriptions of wartime strategy and morale. The interest in armed conflict is not surprising in a city that had until recently profited enormously from the mercenary trade. Among Rüte's spectators, there were doubtlessly many veterans of recent battles, not only at Bicocca, but also at Marignano (1515), Novara (1513), and perhaps Dornach (1499), where the Swiss cantons repelled the last serious attempt by the emperor to reclaim their territories for the Holy Roman Empire.[42] Although the city had taken final steps to forbid mercenary service (*Reislaufen*) in 1530, the lure of French ducats remained great, all the more so as young Bernese correctly suspected that several prominent burghers secretly continued to receive French pensions.[43] This younger generation comprised Rüte's players, so that a work such as *Goliath* offered them the opportunity to engage in military action, if only vicariously. Indeed, staged military skirmishes were not at all uncommon in Bern. We know from the chronicle of Johannes Haller and Abraham Müslin (son of Wolfgang Musculus) that young locals held mock sieges in 1551 and 1552.[44] Nor was Bernese military glory merely a thing of the past following the local Protestant disputation. In 1536, one year following the first local performance of a Goliath play, Bernese troops could take David's example to heart, demonstrating the power of their God by routing the forces of the Duke of Savoy much as the Israelites had done to the Philistines.

The portrayal of Old Testament militancy is but one way in which Rüte tailored his source to the tastes of his audience. This was not

---

[42] On these battles, see Feller, 1:486–8, 524–31, 545–60.

[43] On Bern's efforts to control the mercenary service of its subjects after the Reformation, see Theodor de Quervain, *Kirchliche und soziale Zustände in Bern unmittelbar nach Einführung der Reformation* (Bern: Grunau, 1906), 158–69.

[44] 1551: "Am 13ten April macht man ein papierenes Schloß auf dem Kilchenfeld, und zogen die jungen Gesellen aus mit Spießen und stürmten es." 1552: "Den 6ten März war die alte Faßnacht, zog eine gemeine Burgerschaft aus in Harnisch auf's Breitfeld, da ein Schloß von Laden vor dem Kirchhof über gemacht, das ward belageret, beschossen mit 12 Stucken, darinn lag ein Fähndliknecht, geschahen auch viel Scharmützel, Sturm u. Schlachten, und viel Schimpfs, auch waren bey 50 oder 60 Reuter zu beyden Seiten, deren einer genannt Hans Wyß, Schaffner auf der Stift, eine Hand gar nach in einem Scharmutz abgehauen wäre; sonsten zergieng der Schimpf ohne sondern Schaden, und war das Schloß gewonnen und verbrannt, kam viel fremdes Volk zuzusehen." *Chronik aus den hinterlassenen Handschriften des Joh. Haller und Abraham Müslin von 1550 bis 1580*, ed. Samuel Gränicher (Zofingen: D. Sutermeister, 1829), 5, 9–10.

merely a concession to plebian palates. For the community to profit from the performances, it had to recognize itself in them, and military concerns had permeated daily life during the Italian Wars from 1500 to 1525. Rüte similarly transported the setting of his plays to the Bernese countryside. In *Goliath*, David is an "Alpknecht" (Alpine sheep herder; v. 4050), *Gedeon* makes mention of the city's new *Zytglogge* (Clock Tower; v. 888) and *Noe*, as we shall see, makes frequent references to mountain pastures and dairy farming, so that it would seem the Ark has come to rest in Bern's alpine Oberland. Moreover, as was common for the theater of the period, actors wore contemporary clothing without attempting to historicize the play through costumes or scenery.[45] In dress and manner, actors resembled the spectators around them, inviting them to see themselves in the events unfolding on stage.

In fact, Rüte asked his audience to draw parallels from the plays' protagonists in two directions: to itself, and to the typological fulfillment of these figures in Christ. Rüte is not alone in this regard among Protestant playwrights: Joachim Greff, Jacob Rueff, and Thiebold Gart all explicitly point to the prefiguration of Christ's salvation in their Joseph plays,[46] as Rüte himself does in introducing the second day's performance of *Joseph*:

> Der Joseph hat vnß Christum düt
> Der ist verkhoufft in glycher gstalt
> Durch siner brüdern list vnd gwalt
> Vnd dardurch khon vß eigner krafft
> Vber all welt in sin herschafft
> Vnd den frömden worden erkhant
> Jn maß er gnempt ist jr heilland (vv. 2088–94)

> Joseph signifies Christ for us. He was sold in the same manner through his brothers' treachery and force. By his own power, he rose above this to dominion over all the world and was made known to foreign nations; thus he is called their saviour.

---

[45] Adolf Fluri suggests that the players costumed themselves from the council's wardrobe, which contained precious cloths and fashions from secularized monasteries and the plunder of the Burgundian Wars. Fluri, 149.

[46] Greff, *Spiel von dem Patriarchen Jacob*, Ev; Rueff, *Joseph*, Miij; Thiebold Gart, "Joseph," in *Die Schaubühne im Dienste der Reformation II*, ed. Arnold E. Berger, Deutsche Literatur in Entwicklungsreihen, Reihe Reformation 6 (Leipzig: Reclam, 1936), 48, vv. 27–34.

Such typological exegesis was but one mode of the four-fold method of biblical hermeneutics, which attributed to Scripture four layers of meaning: literal (or historical), allegorical (or typological), tropological (or moral), and anagogical (or mystical). Humanist and Protestant scholars were apt to dismiss the allegorical and anagogical levels as speculative, and there has been a long-standing assumption that Reformation drama similarly dispensed with typology, emphasizing instead the moral character of its protagonists.[47] More recent studies have however noted that the rejection of the four-fold method largely occurred in the context of anti-scholastic polemics and that figures such as Erasmus and Luther were not averse to employing typological exegesis in their own writings.[48] Indeed, playwrights of both faiths freely assigned moral and allegorical interpretations to their works.

Nonetheless, the focus of most biblical plays on a single protagonist lent itself to tropological explication, allowing audience members to follow a character through a series of moral trials and to consider their own behavior under similar circumstances. Hence the focus of most Protestant dramas was on the individual and her path towards salvation, whether that concerned morals or, on a typological level, Christ's redemption of the believer. In Bern, however, this had a decidedly political component. The salvation of the individual was intimately connected to the community of all believers, which in their totality constituted God's church.[49] In the Lutheran north, the congregation as a religious body was considered distinct from the citizenry. In Bern's Zwinglian context, this was not the case: the

---

[47] "Gewiß sind es die exemplarischen Gestalten und Vorgänge der biblischen Überlieferung, die den Dramen den Stoff geben. Aber sie dienen nicht mehr als Präfigurationen der Heilsgeschichte, sondern vermögen von sich aus die moralisch-religiösen Spannungen des menschlichen Verhaltens zu erhellen." Paul Böckmann, *Formgeschichte der deutschen Dichtung* (Hamburg: Hoffmann und Campe, 1949), 298.

[48] Parente, 67, 70–1. Lebeau discusses the general relationship in typological portrayal between passion plays and Protestant drama: Lebeau, 1:208. On Joseph, Luther for example states: "Ynn Josephs person hat Gott auffs aller feinest Christum und sein gantzes reich geistlich abgemalet." Martin Luther, "Predigten über das 1. Buch Mose," WA 24:615.

[49] "Die Soteriologie ist von vornherein weniger auf das Individuum als auf die Gemeinschaft bezogen, daher die Tendenz zu einer prophetisch-pneumatologischen Theokratie, zu erstreben durch Obrigkeit und Volk." Gottfried W. Locher, *Die Zwinglische Reformation im Rahmen der europäischen Kirchengeschichte* (Göttingen/Zurich: Vandenhoeck & Ruprecht, 1979), 225.

visible church of Christ subsumed and encompassed the polity.[50] Even when addressing matters of salvation, Rüte's biblical plays were implicitly political, establishing divine will as the source of earthly power, whether wielded by patriarch or prophet. Due to the essential unity of Zwinglian religion and politics in Bern following the local Reformation, the separation of religious and secular government as postulated by Manuel in his carnival plays is no longer present.

To preserve the success of local reform, Rüte's plays no longer agitate, but rather maintain and consolidate. Transgression still serves to discredit confessional opponents, but now expresses itself in a simple lack of faith rather than carnivalesque disorderliness. In some plays, such as *Goliath*, this failing alone is sufficient to demask any would-be usurper of divine authority. In *Joseph* and *Gedeon*, however, the discreditation of a religious opponent is more complex, incorporating strategies that Rüte had employed earlier in *Abgötterei*. In 1538, the unruly woman, now in the guise of Potiphar's wife, once again subsumes the alleged perversions of Catholicism. In 1540, religious disorderliness distinguishes two separate groups: Baal's priests on the one hand, and overly zealous iconoclasts on the other, reflecting the two-front religious struggle now waged in Bern against Catholics and Anabaptists. All five biblical plays thus focus on a challenge to religious authority, followed by the restoration of that authority. The following pages will examine each play's maintenance of theocratic rule, both on stage and within the larger context of the Bernese Reformation. In all instances, as we shall see, proper government requires proper faith.

The Armor of Faith: Goliath *(1535, 1545, 1555)*

Depending on one's point of reference, *Goliath* is either Bern's first biblical drama following the local disputation or its last biblical drama prior to the Religious Peace of Augsburg. As indicated by local records, the story of David and the Philistine was performed in public in 1535, Bern's first biblical performance whose subject is known.[51]

---

[50] Ibid., 615–20. See also Bruce Gordon, "Switzerland," in *The Early Reformation in Europe*, ed. Andrew Pettegree (Cambridge: Cambridge University Press, 1992), 76.

[51] As discussed in Chapters Two and Three, local pupils had performed a Prodigal

At the same time, *Goliath* is the last of Rüte's six plays to be published, appearing in 1555 with a foreword by local printer Samuel Apiarius (fig. 17). No further records exist to indicate if the text performed in 1535 was Rüte's, nor is there any indication that the published text was performed in 1555. Prior to 1537, however, Bern lacked its own printing press, so that *Abgötterei* had been published by Thomas Wolff in Basel. Perhaps Rüte, writing in 1535, found no outside press for his second manuscript. It would have then remained filed away for twenty years until Samuel Apiarius, having assumed ownership of the local press from his father Mathias, requested material from Rüte and added his own foreword.[52] This scenario would place *Goliath* at the beginning of Rüte's biblical play production. Offsetting this view is the fact that the 1535 Goliath's performance on Sunday Trinitatis does not fit the established pattern of performance dates for Rüte's plays: With the exception of *Osterspiel*, which was tied to council elections at Easter, all other plays by Rüte were performed on Laetare Sunday during Lent.[53] Rüte's *Goliath* must have been performed at some time—the title page of the 1555 imprint tell us so without revealing when—but there is no conclusive proof that this occurred as early as 1535.

Goliath nonetheless leads off the discussion of Rüte's biblical plays for the simple fact that the story of David and the Philistine giant was by far the most popular subject matter to appear on the Bernese stage during this period. One decade after the 1535 performance, an anonymous Goliath play was again performed in Bern.[54] Whether or not this second work belonged to Rüte's oeuvre, the material's repeated performance indicates that this particular Old Testament tale resonated with the local population. Several factors may have

---

Son play as early as February 1534, though most likely before a private audience. In addition, both the *Ratsmanuale* and *Seckelmeisterrechnungen* record expenditures for an otherwise unknown play performed in April of 1534. Given the expenditure of one hundred pounds, this was probably a public performance, most likely of a biblical play. See Fluri, 137.

[52] Klaus Stephan Jaeger, "Hans von Rütes Osterspiel. Edition und Untersuchung" (M.A. thesis, Freie Universität Berlin, 1993), 40.

[53] Dates are known for the performance of *Abgötterei* (19 March 1531), *Gedeon* (7 March 1540), *Noe* (4 April 1546), and *Osterspiel* (25 April 1552). Furthermore, council records indicate that the performance of *Joseph* occured between 21 March and 2 April in 1538. As Laetare Sunday fell on 31 March in this year, it is reasonable to assume that *Joseph*, too, was performed on this date.

[54] Fluri, 138.

contributed to its popularity. In addition to the audience's likely fondness for battle scenes, the Bernese had long had a penchance for heroes. The Ten Thousand Martyrs, whose cult had been ridiculed in *Abgötterei*, had become popular following Bernese military victories at Laupen and Murten on or around June 22, the saints' feast day. Sometime before 1517, Niklaus Manuel created an altarpiece based on the saints' legend, and a stained-glass window in the Bernese minster also testifies to their popularity.[55] Christopher (*Christophorus*), who according to legend had carried the Christ child across a raging river, was also held in great esteem in Bern. The city's westernmost gate bore a giant wooden carving of the saint, so that when travelers left the city on a journey, their last sight was that of Christopher, whose image was believed to protect from sudden death. Nonetheless, Christopher's legendary strength did not save his carving from an ignominious fate following the local Reformation. Unlike most other religious images, it was not destroyed, but rather altered to become a gigantic Goliath.[56] Whether the reverence earlier accorded Christopher turned to scorn for the desanctified carving is of course impossible to say, but its very presence must have daily reminded local residents of the religious changes that had swept through their city. Physically and symbolically, Christopher continued to inhabit Goliath's image. Considering that French Huguenots also framed their religious struggle as a battle between David and Goliath,[57] the saint-turned-Philistine signified to passers-by that Bern, like David, had conquered a supposedly invincible opponent through its unquestioning faith in God's Word.[58]

---

[55] Brigitte Kurmann-Schwarz, "Das 10.000–Ritter-Fenster im Berner Münster und seine Auftraggeber. Überlegungen zu den Schrift- und Bildquellen sowie zum Kult der Heiligen in Bern," *ZSAK* 49 (1992): 39–54.

[56] The alteration likely occurred in 1534: Franz Bächtiger, "Zur Revision des Berner Christoffel," *Jahrbuch des Bernischen Historischen Museums* 59/60 (1979/80): 118. See also Guggisberg, 123.

[57] Marguerite Soulié, "Le théâtre et la Bible au XVIe siècle," in *Le temps des Réformes et la Bible*, vol. 5 of *Bible de tous les temps*, ed. Guy Bedouelle and Bernard Roussel (Paris: Éditions Beauchesne, 1989), 643 ff.

[58] Franz Bächtiger argues that the former Christopher statue was not associated with Goliath until ca. 1583, when a figure of David was placed on a fountain across from the gate, and thus that the three Bernese Goliath plays have no relation to the statue. However, the association with Goliath must have occurred earlier, providing the impetus to place David on the fountain, rather than another figure. Indeed, Birgit Hahn-Woernle speculates that the Christophorus figure originated in a Goliath statue created for Bern's carnival celebration in 1465. Her source is by

With the Goliath carving daily testifying to Bern's defiance of Rome, Rüte did not need to belabor the point in his text of 1555. *Goliath* arguably indulges in the fewest polemics, veiled or otherwise, of Rüte's five biblical plays. Still, the play clearly speaks to Bern's geopolitical situation as Europe's southwesternmost defender of the new faith, surrounded by Catholic cantons within the Swiss Confederacy and flanked by French and Habsburg territory without. In the opening *Argument*, Rüte's herald immediately equates Israel's faith with Bern's and states that hostile enemies surrounded Saul's people:

> Nun hörend zuo/so werdend jr
> Diß gschicht kurtzlich vernän von mir/
> Als dann vor etlich tusent jaren
> Vff erdtrich Jßrahel die waren
> So einig bekanten vnsern Gott
> Vnd hattindt syne heilgen Pott/
> Vnd deßhalb all Gottlosen lüt
> So von Gots sachen wißten nüt
> Sy haßtend vnd verfolgtend drumb
> Von allen landen vmb vnd vmb/
> Do waren sunderlich jr fynd
> Ein volck/Philister sy gnant sind/
> Z'nechst glegen an jr grentz vnd land/(vv. 37–49)

> Listen now, and you will hear from me the story in brief. Many thousand years ago, Israel was the only nation on earth to profess our God and keep His commandments. For this reason, all godless people, knowing nothing of God's workings, hated and persecuted them from all regions roundabout. Their particular enemies were the Philistines, their neighbors.

Israel's isolation figures in later passages as well (v. 2980; vv. 5303–12). While Rüte does not directly associate the five Philistine kingdoms of Ashdod, Ashkelon, Ekron, Gath, and Gaza (1 Samuel 6:17) with the five forest cantons, repeated emphasis is placed on the number five within the Philistine alliance. Each kingdom has its own "(Ge-)Biet" just as the cantons: "Wir fünff Küng im Philister land / Die fünff houptstatt z'regieren hand / Mit iren pieten vnd Landtschafft"

---

no means conclusive, however, and she herself states that there is likely no connection between this beginning and the statue's later transformation: Birgit Hahn-Woernle, *Christophorus in der Schweiz. Seine Verehrung in bildlichen und kultischen Zeugnissen*, Schriften der Schweizerischen Gesellschaft für Volkskunde 53 (Basel: G. Krebs, 1972), 34. Cf. Bächtiger, 118, 122.

(We five kings of Philistine rule over the five capitals with their regions and countryside; vv. 209–11). Among the Philistine army are also troops of *zuogwandten* (v. 151), i.e. *zugewandte Orte*, the term for the "Associated Members" allied with, although not part of, the Swiss Confederacy.[59] Finally, there is repeated emphasis that the Philistines wish to deny the Jews their "freedom of conscience" (*conscientz fryheit*: v. 2941, v. 3487), a common catchword for Protestants' cherished Christian liberty. Even if Rüte did not intend to equate the Philistines with Swiss Catholics, he describes the two camps in terms familiar to his audience. And although the text of the 1535 performance need not have been identical to the published text of 1555, the association of the forest cantons with Israel's armed enemies would have been nearly involuntary less than four years after the Second War of Kappel.

After having established the differences between the Israelites and Philistines, Rüte contrasts them to demonstrate good government and, above all, proper worship. As king, Saul makes very few unilateral decisions, but rather consults with the twelve tribes or their rulers. This is most obvious after Goliath has first approached the Israeli camp to issue his challenge. Advised by Jonathan, his son, and Abner, his general, Saul agrees to seek the advice of the tribes, referred to here as the *gmeind* (community), concerning the course of action to be taken:

> *Jonathas*:
> Der handel brürt all vnser lüt/
> Söltent dann wir yetz handlen üt
> On sy/das wurdens vngern han
> Drumb wölt ichs an dgmeind langen lan [. . .]
> *Abner*:
> Jch wölt jn ouch yetz wysen hein
> Vnd angends dsach vff gän der gmein
> *Saul*:
> Wiewol man mit der Gmeinden rhat
> Anschlachen sol kein krieglich that
> Dann einr wil diß der ander das
> Da darff ein meer werden etwas
> Das wol als bald schad ist/als guot [. . .]

---

[59] On the Associated Members, see Kaspar von Greyerz, "Switzerland," in *The Reformation in National Context*, ed. Robert Scribner, Roy Porter, and Mikuláš Teich (Cambridge: Cambridge University Press, 1994), 31.

Dwyl aber diß ist kein anschlag
Deßhalb ich üch wol volgen mag (vv. 1632–55)

Jonathan:
The matter concerns all our people. If we should do anything without them, they wouldn't approve. Therefore I'd like to consult the community. [. . .]
Abner:
I would also send him [Goliath] home and quickly refer the matter to the community.
Saul:
Although one shouldn't consider matters of war based on popular majority [lit. "on the advice of the community"], since one wants one thing, another something else, and a majority opinion can be as soon bad as good, [. . .] because this does not concern an attack, I will take your advice.

Although this plebiscite is not successful in producing a champion to challenge Goliath, the Bernese council regularly referred similarly earnest matters to the municipalities (*Ämter*) within its territories in a procedure known as *Ämterbefragung*. These referendums proved to be a crucial component of local religious reform: At least four *Ämterbefragungen* were conducted between 1524 and 1528 as the council weighed whether to follow Zurich in abolishing the mass.[60] In having Israel's king enact the same process, Rüte suggests that the Bernese councilors have acted according to biblical models in pursuing the best interests of their subjects, thereby legitimizing reformed government.[61]

On the whole, however, the play delegitimizes Saul's rule, offering Jonathan and David instead as models of Christian faith and fortitude. As is apparent in the discussion above, the suggestion to consult with the tribes comes from Jonathan, not his father. When David later approaches the king hoping to fight against Goliath, only Jonathan of all Saul's councilors recognizes that God's will is acting through the youth (vv. 5707–11), foreshadowing his later friendship with David as related in the Bible. According to Scripture, Saul's

---

[60] The referendums and their corresponding responses are reproduced in Steck/Tobler, nos. 382, 384, 813, 824, 882, 891, 1196, 1205. See also Rudolf Dellsperger, "Zehn Jahre Bernischer Reformationsgeschichte (1522–1532). Eine Einführung," in *450 Jahre*, 33–7.

[61] The continued propogation of such an image was all the more important since, as Kaspar von Greyerz has noted, the process of consulting the *Ämter* fell into disuse after 1531: K. von Greyerz, 41.

transgression is his failure to obey the Lord's command (1 Samuel 13:13–14; 1 Samuel 15:17–29), but Rüte attributes his failing to immorality and lack of faith. When David first appears on stage during the second day of performance, he reveals to his brother Jahel that the corruption of Saul's court has led him to return to his pastoral life:

> Man denckt am Hoff niemer an Gott
> Sunders bricht mengklich syne pott
> Mit allerley vngrechtigkeit/
> Gotsforcht daselbs ist zschlaffen gleit/
> Jr Regiment ist glyßnery/
> Jch gloub nit/das ein Rhatßherr sy/
> Der nach dem gsatz vrteyl vnd rhat (vv. 3899–905)

> The people at court no longer think of God. Many break His commandments with all types of injustice; the fear of God has been lulled to sleep. Their government is hypocrisy. I don't believe there is a single councilor who judges and advises according to the law.

In a departure from the biblical narrative found in 1 Samuel 17, Jonathan and Elisur meanwhile seek out Samuel for his advice on how to respond to Goliath's challenge. His subsequent rebuke of Saul, occurring as Israel seeks in vain for a hero, becomes the center point of the drama. Samuel explains to his visitors that Israel cannot conquer the Philistines through force of arms, but through faith alone. Saul, however, has become an idolater, precisely because he places hope in earthly rewards, promising for example his daughter in marriage, not the kingdom of heaven, to the man who will brave Goliath on the battlefield:

> Die sind vor Gott abgötler gschetzt/
> Als dick man trost vnd hoffnung setzt
> Jn ander ding/dann nun in Gott/
> Das thuot Küng Saul mit syner rott
> Er setzt syn trost in zytlich guot
> Vol gyt hangt jhm sinn/hertz vnd muot/[...]
> Ach Gott der sig dahinden blybt
> Vnd ist manheit vnd sig daruon/
> Das hertz muoß oben abher kon
> Das willig sich in tod ergit
> Myn Jonatha/Saul gloubt das nit (vv. 4589–646)

> Before God, idolaters are considered those who place their succor and hope in things other than God. King Saul and his minions do just this. He places his hope in earthly goods; greed fills his senses, heart,

and mind. [...] O Lord, victory remains distant, and manhood and triumph are nowhere to be found. The courage to resign oneself to death willingly must come down from above. My Jonathan, Saul does not believe that.

The Philistines, of course, are idolaters, too; Saul himself warns against their *götzendienst* (v. 593), echoed by Jonathan in a later speech (v. 3459). Rüte, however, defines the term broadly, ultimately placing Saul on a level with the enemies of Israel. Just as in *Abgötterei*, idolatry encompasses not just the worship of graven images, but all trust in human endeavor.

In Saul's case, however, this criticism pertains to a compatriot rather than a competing creed. The herald's closing comments suggest that Rüte modeled Saul after luke warm adherents of Bern's new faith, practitioners of Protestantism in name only:

> Got hat ouch gnommen allen rath
> Dem Saul/vnd synen wysen lüten/
> Jn glycher gstalt wirt Gott vernüten
> All die dem Saul damit sind glych/
> Myn lieben fründ ich meynen üch/
> Die jhr üch rümend selbs mit mund
> Gots wort vnd will sy üch wol kund
> Vnd fürend pärden halb ein schyn
> Vnd redend vil von Gott als fyn
> Als ob jhr syend heilig lüt
> Vnd ist im grund darhinder nüt (vv. 6665–75)

> God also deprived Saul and his wise retinue of all counsel. In the same manner, God will ruin all those who take after Saul. My dear friends, I mean you who boast with your own lips that God's word and will are known to you, creating an illusion through empty gestures and talking so fine of God as if you were holy. Yet there is no substance behind it all.

It is unclear whether Rüte targeted any particular group with these comments. They could have been intended for crypto-Catholics, cladestinely continuing to celebrate the mass, or perhaps for those whom Calvin labeled Nicodemites, after Nicodemus, a Jew who believed in Christ's divinity but could not grasp the significance of being born anew (John 3:4). The term applied in general to Protestants who simulated faith.[62] Like *Abgötterei*'s condemnation of lingering

---

[62] There is some dispute as to whether Calvin reserved this label for a particular group, perhaps French humanist reformers. I apply it here in a general sense. See

Catholic practices in 1531, Rüte's portrayal of Saul as a false believer implies that wholehearted acceptance of the new theology was far from universal in 1535 (or 1555).

The valorization of David parallels Saul's denigration. Even before David appears on stage, the herald informs the audience at the close of the first day that David "ein vorbild ist / Deß lieben Herren Jesu Christ" (is a prefiguration of the dear Lord Jesus Christ; vv. 2957–8). Rüte's spectators then encounter the future king as an obedient son, tending sheep in the fields and faithfully fulfilling his father's request to deliver proviant to his brothers in Saul's camp. This and other embellishments, such as David's criticism of the corruption at Saul's court, provide for the tale's moral content, while his final victory over a demonized Goliath rounds off the story typologically.

Saul's failing is also a crisis of government, however, so that Rüte does not limit himself solely to the moral and typological aspects of David's victory. By incorporating Samuel's rebuke, he legitimates David's ultimate replacement of Saul as king of Israel:

> Gott hat g'ordnet ein andern Hirt
> Vber syn lieb volck Jsrahel
> Der trüwet jhm von aller seel (vv. 4792–4)

> God has ordained another shepherd over his dear people of Israel. He believes in Him with his whole soul.

As the play ends with Goliath's death, i.e. before David's crowning, the emphasis on the legitimacy of government is even more conspicuous. The play thus sanctions the replacement of government when that government has abandoned God's commandments. Seen in this context, *Goliath* helped in retrospect to justify the political coup that allowed Protestants to gain control of Bernese government in 1527. Following the Easter elections of this year, the new Protestant majority of Bern's Great Council had altered traditional election procedure to gain control of the Small Council, which subsequently convened the local disputation. If any one individual would have fit the role of Saul during the transition of governments, it would have been Kaspar von Mülinen, one of the leading defenders of the old faith,

---

Steven Ozment, *The Age of Reform 1250–1550. An Intellectual and Religious History of Late Medieval and Reformation Europe* (New Haven/London: Yale University Press, 1980), 356–7.

who was disqualified from office after the supporters of reform reissued an old law denying office to those who were not born in the city.[63] Like Saul, Mülinen's lack of (Protestant) faith rendered him in the view of the Great Council unfit to rule, necessitating a change in government that would ensure the pious administration of the city in agreement with God's law.

"Pious on account of good works": Potiphar's Wife in Joseph *(1538)*

Given its vague polemics and uncertain date of origin, much concerning *Goliath* remains speculative. The opposite is true of Rüte's next play, *Joseph* (fig. 18). Council records indicate that the play was performed sometime between 21 March and 2 April 1538, most likely on 31 March, Laetare Sunday. Moreover, the text, published later the same year, is based in part on the Latin Joseph play of 1536 by the Dutch humanist Cornelius Crocus. With its connection to humanist dramaturgy, as well as the subject matter's overall popularity among contemporary dramatists, *Joseph* is relatively speaking Rüte's best researched play. Studies by Alexander von Weilen, Otto Tetzlaff, and Jean Lebeau have noted the general distinctions between Rüte's populist dramaturgy and the neo-classical ideals of his Dutch predecessor.[64] Unfortunately, their research does not address the singular purpose pursued by Rüte throughout his adaptations: the allegorization of female transgression in a confessional context much like that of *Abgötterei*. Whereas Crocus paints a tragic portrayal of Potiphar's wife, Rüte aims to shock, discrediting Joseph's would-be seductress by criminalizing her behavior. Like Dame Confusion, her shameless lust and worldliness become metaphors for the corruption of the Catholic church. Her punishment, however, now lies squarely in the hands of secular authority. Rüte has her convicted in an appended courtroom trial, ensuring that male hegemony, and with it religious order, is reestablished. With its portrayal of wantonness and its regulation, Rüte's *Joseph* illuminates the contemporary humanist debate on licentious poetics as well as the plays' on-going legitimation of post-Reformation government.

---

[63] Dellsperger, 37.
[64] Von Weilen, 30–9; Tetzlaff, 162 ff.; Lebeau, 93–4, 127, 146, 218, 371–4.

Crocus's play is firmly situated in the humanist tradition. Stock Terentian characters appear in the portrayal of several figures. Potiphar's wife, here named Sephirah, is cast as a courtesan, while Mago, Potiphar's servant, is the clever slave. Limiting his attention to the attempted seduction of Joseph, his subsequent incarceration, and his final miraculous release, the author rigorously prunes his source material and reduces plot and cast to the bare necessities.[65] The resulting emphasis is on Joseph's steadfastness in the face of adversity. This did not hinder Crocus from portraying Sephirah's passion for Joseph in realistic terms, however. Before her disrobing of Joseph, which decorously occurs off stage between Acts One and Two, she urgently pleads with the youth to do her bidding. Joseph, being chaste, successfully resists temptation and remains a model of moderation; no casual fornication occurs as in Roman New Comedy. Nonetheless, Crocus knew that the successful imitation of classical amatory poetics bore risks. In a lengthy dedicatory epistle attached to the beginning of his play, he defended his undertaking with patristic apologies regarding the moral neutrality of literary characters. Here, he proudly distinguished between his biblical source and the lascivious plays of Plautus and Terence:

> Apporto nanque, non Plauti aut Terentii,
> Quas esse fictas nostis omnes fabulas,
> Vanas, prophanas, ludicras ac lubricas:
> Verum veram, sacramque porto, et seriam,
> Castam, pudicam, sic ut ipsas virgines
> Dictasse Musas, ac Minervam deieres:
> Novamque; iam scriptam recens comoediam.[66]

> I bring you, moreover, not the counterfeit tales of Plautus and Terence, which you know to be vain, profane, playful, and slippery; instead, I bring a new, recently written, true comedy, sacred, serious, chaste, and modest, such that you would swear the virgin Muses or Minerva had dictated it.

Most of Crocus's contemporaries judged the play favorably, so that his *Joseph* followed Gnapheus's *Acolastus* as the second humanist play to successfully meld classical poetics with Christian ideals.

There were, however, dissenters who found Crocus's play too

---

[65] Lebeau, 301 ff.
[66] I cite the following edition: Cornelius Crocus, "Joseph," in *Dramata Sacra* (Basel: n.p., 1547), 157.

graphic in its depiction of Sephirah's attempted seduction.[67] Cornelius Schonaeus, who edited the work for his *Terentius Christianus* collection, expunged much of Sephirah's sensual language. Antonius Schottus, the seventeenth-century editor of Crocus's *Opera Omnia*, went still further, eliminating the entire seduction scene from his redaction. Uneasiness with the play was apparent even before Rüte's *Joseph* appeared: In the prologue to his Latin *Susanna* of 1537, Sixtus Birck cited both Crocus's work and the *Acolastus* of Gnapheus as dramas of ambiguous morality.[68]

Such objections obviously did not deter Rüte from adapting the play for his Bernese audience. Indeed, where Crocus is brief, Rüte is prolix. To portray Joseph as a "salvator mundi" with typological parallels to Christ, he treats the entirety of the Genesis narrative from Joseph's sale into slavery to his exaltification in Egypt at the right hand of pharaoh; the cast correspondingly swells from Crocus's eight actors to a total of forty-five. Moreover, the humanist five-act structure of the Dutch play disappears completely, replaced during *Joseph*'s first half by four musical interludes, each announcing a change of venue.[69] The play's subsequent half completely lacks an organizing principle except as provided by the herald, whose exegetical monologues bracket the second day of performance. All told, Rüte's borrowings from Crocus represent less than one-sixth of *Joseph*'s total length.[70]

Given the liberties taken with his source, as well as the post-Reformation decorum of the biblical stage in general, one might assume that Rüte would have had little use for Crocus's more daring passages in which Potiphar's wife declares her love for Joseph. However, the opposite proves true. The majority of Rüte's borrowings are drawn from Crocus's first act, in which the attempted seduction takes place.[71] Far from being troubled by the passion displayed by Potiphar's wife, Rüte retained and accentuated it where he could.

---

[67] On the following, see Parente, 34–8.
[68] Ibid., 91; Sixt Birck, "Susanna," in *Sämtliche Dramen*, 2:179–80.
[69] The action moves from Israel to Potiphar's house, from there to prison, onward to Pharaoh's court, and finally back to Potiphar's house for the trial scene. See Kenneth Fisher, "Hans von Rüte: A Dramatist of the Swiss Reformation," (Ph.D. Diss. University of Texas at Austin, 1975), 50.
[70] The borrowings begin at v. 667 and extend, with interruptions, to v. 1481 of Rüte's *Joseph*.
[71] Von Weilen tallies Rüte's borrowings in his study: von Weilen, 30–9.

He translates her impassioned monologue (vv. 709–88) and ensuing exchanges with Joseph (v. 793 ff.) almost verbatim. Unlike Crocus, he reveals Joseph's disrobing to the audience, the climax of the attempted seduction (v. 1088). Immediately prior to this, he had added several stichomythic lines of his own invention for dramatic effect:

> *Frow*: Du muost thuon/was ich an dich bringen/
> *Joseph*: Die liebe laßt sich nit erzwingen/
> *Frow*: Ich wil dich dim herren verclagen/
> *Joseph*: Ir sönd mich nit falschlich vertragen
> *Frow*: Joseph/wilt nit wenden min schmertz?
> Du hast doch gar ein steine hertz
> Hilfft doch kein weinen? lon? noch pit?
> *Joseph*: Min frow ir dörffent hoffen nit (vv. 1070–77)

> *Woman*: You must do as I ask of you.
> *Joseph*: Love cannot be coerced.
> *Woman*: I'll accuse you before your master.
> *Joseph*: You should not bear false witness.
> *Woman*: Joseph, will you not avert my pain?
> You have a heart of stone indeed.
> Shall no tears, reward, or entreaty help?
> *Joseph*: My lady, you must not hope.

These alterations accentuate the intemperance of Potiphar's wife's passion, graphically illustrating her immoderation. Equally telling are Rüte's omissions from his source. After the failed seduction, Crocus has Joseph meet Potiphar at the door upon the latter's return home.[72] He wishes to inform him of recent events, but cannot bring himself to incriminate his master's wife, allowing Sephirah's charges to go unchallenged. Later, Potiphar provides Joseph with an opportunity to mount a defense, yet again he remains silent.[73] Rüte, however, deprives Joseph of any chance to vindicate himself. Potiphar's wife greets her husband as soon as he arrives home and tells him her fabricated tale. Potiphar becomes enraged, and Joseph can only briefly appeal to his mercy before he is led away. By striking Joseph's interaction with Potiphar, Rüte exonerates him from all liability in his fate as portrayed by Crocus, shifting blame wholly to Potiphar's wife.

---

[72] Crocus, 181.
[73] Ibid., 191–3.

Rüte's single most significant change, however, is the alteration of Sephirah's accusation of rape into that of attempted homicide. When it becomes clear that Joseph will not yield to her advances, she begins to cry murder.[74] Later, she demands capital punishment for him: "den tod hat er verdienet wol" (he well deserves death; v. 1206). With this, her false accusations cease to be a mere crime of passion and approach manslaughter. As the audience is told at the close of the first day's performance, her desire to see Joseph put to death is her "greatest guilt" (*gröste schuld*; v. 2035).

In the Bible, Potiphar's wife goes unmentioned after Joseph's imprisonment, leaving her transgressions unpunished. To judge from the play's subsequent events, Rüte considered it imperative that justice be served. Alone among sixteenth-century authors of Joseph plays, he appends a courtroom trial to the biblical narrative that results in her imprisonment pending possible execution.[75] His reasons for this addition were likely varied, and indeed the legal proceedings serve to drive home several points regarding the wife's transgression. First among these was the essential unity of earthly and divine justice.[76] Following Joseph's incarceration, the subsequent events in Potiphar's household demonstrate that true justice is realizable only when all observe a mutual belief in divine retribution and God-ordained social order. Just as David scorns armor and weapons, Joseph refuses to seek revenge via earthly means, placing his trust wholly in God. Not coincidentally, this preserves the social hierarchy as well; as Joseph reveals, he did not repel Potiphar's wife with force out of respect for his master's reputation:

> Jch hätt gern gwalt mit gwalt vertriben
> Vnd ir mit fünsten die hut griben
> Jch wolts mim herren nit thuon zschmach
> Sonders hab Got beuolchen rach (vv. 1104–7)

> I would have gladly answered violence with violence and tanned her hide with my fists. I did not want to shame my lord; instead, I have asked God for vengeance.

---

[74] "Der mörder wolt mir nodt zwang thuo// Nun ylent flucks/ich bin im zschwach// Er wil mich mörden in mim gmach" (vv. 1089–91).

[75] Von Weilen, 38.

[76] Hans Stricker discusses the tendency of Swiss Reformation plays to equate human and divine justice in accordance with Zwinglian theology: Hans Stricker, *Die Selbstdarstellung der Schweizers im Drama des 16. Jahrhunderts*, Sprache und Dichtung, Neue Folge 7 (Bern: Paul Haupt, 1961), 131 ff.

Similarly, Potiphar, although not a Hebrew, refrains from corporal punishment of Joseph for fear of divine revenge (v. 1218). Later, after he learns of his former servant's innocence, his fear of God leads him to place his wife on trial:

> Jch weyß es niemerme zversprechen
> Er old Gott werdents an mir rechen/
> Jch muoß ouch des han schmach vnd schand/
> Wo es vß khumpt/in alem lannd
> Doch will ich Joseph pitten gnad
> Das mir vnwüssenheit nüt schad [...]
> Jch muoß aber min eewyb schelten
> Vnd straffen umb die bübery
> Daßs mengklichem ein warnung sy (vv. 1772–81)

> I don't know how to answer for it. He or God will exact vengeance on me. It will also bring me shame and disgrace when it is known throughout the land. But I will ask for Joseph's mercy, that my ignorance of the affair cause me no harm. [...] Yet I must take my wife to task and punish her for her treachery so that she might serve as an example.

Whereas Potiphar's wife had disturbed the social order by abusing her power over Joseph, Joseph and her husband each restore it by recognizing their proper place in the self-regulation of society. The former acknowledges the authority of his master, who in turn wields his authority justly, even when it harms his personal interests. Motivating both is their fear of God, implying that a God-less society can only be unjust.

The social contract of the religious community continues to function ideally once the wife is in legal custody. Similar to the lengthy legal proceedings in Sixtus Birck's *Susanna*, the trial afforded Rüte an opportunity to illustrate the workings of divine justice in the context of post-Reformation jurisdiction. Contrary to previous suggestions, however, it is unlikely that the proceedings directly represent a sitting of the *Chorgericht*, the morality court established in Bern following the Reformation to handle the domestic disputes that earlier fell under episcopal jurisdiction.[77] Cases that came before the *Chorgericht*

---

[77] Cf. Lebeau, 1:373–4. Lebeau is correct in noting the contrast in the portrayal of jurisdiction between *Elsli Tragdenknaben* and *Joseph*. At no point, however, does Rüte polemicize against the earlier episcopal courts, and it is highly doubtful that Rüte added the trial scene to pay homage to Manuel and his brief service to the *Chorgericht*. On the *Chorgericht* (marriage court), see Chapter Two.

were decided by a commission of clergy, council members, and citizens, whereas a single judge presides over Rüte's courtroom. Nonetheless, the proceedings are a model of fairness. After the judge allows both sides to present their arguments, Potiphar suddenly produces three witnesses: his servant, a matchmaker, and a former confidante of his wife. All three confirm that she sought to commit adultery with Joseph. The wife, exposed, appeals for mercy, and the judge recommends clemency to Potiphar:

> Her hoffmeister ir sönd sy bgnaden
> Man sol nit rechen alten schaden
> Joseph hat doch jr nüt engolten
> So wirts in keiner kuntschafft gscholten
> Das sy an vch eebruchig sy
> Lieber thuond ßbest vnd land sy fry (vv. 1991–6)

> Lord Master of the Household, you should pardon her. One should not open old wounds. Joseph did not suffer for her accusations. In no testimony is she accused of adultery. You should do what's best and let her go free.

Rather than overzealously pursuing the letter of the law, the judge mediates between the parties in search of a mutually agreeable solution. Nevertheless, Potiphar refuses to show mercy. The wife's spiteful desire to see Joseph dead, emphasized at several points during the proceedings, now returns to haunt her, and the judge reluctantly orders her placed in prison pending Pharaoh's decision of her fate.

The moral lesson to be drawn from the wife's punishment seems clear: You shall not commit adultery. Yet Rüte could have easily made this point without having expended so much effort to paint Potiphar's wife as especially wicked. Upon further investigation, it becomes evident that her depiction responds to a heightened typological portrayal of Joseph. Rüte took small, but significant steps to establish unmistakable parallels between Joseph and Christ. For example, he tacitly renamed the brother who originally suggests selling Joseph; called Judah in the Bible, he now received the telling name of Judas (before v. 191 ff.). Potiphar similarly pays thirty pounds for Joseph as a slave, reminiscent of Judas's thirty pieces of silver (v. 655). Lest these embellishments be lost on his audience, Rüte has the herald stress Joseph's christological aspects while introducing the second day of performance, as quoted earlier. The wife's treason then functions in this broader typological context. Stated drastically, she has betrayed Joseph as Christ to the prison of the tomb, so that she, too, becomes a Judas figure. Her accentuated criminalization, above all her willingness to bring about Joseph's death through a (thwarted) kiss, meshes with Joseph's reinforced prefiguration to set the stage for the trial's ultimately confessional verdict.

On an allegorical level, Rüte's punishment of Potiphar's wife for her attempted seduction harbors a veiled critique of works theology. In her plea for clemency, the wife notes that she did not actually lie with Joseph and thus has committed no "work" of adultery: "Vnd das hand für das aller gröst / Das ich kein werck mit jm han than" (And consider this most of all: I did no deed with him; vv. 1974–5). Potiphar responds by distinguishing between work and intent in a decidedly Protestant manner:

> Du bist vil böser dann ein dieb
> Das du der wercken halb bist frum (vv. 1984–5)

> You're much worse than a thief if you are pious on account of works.

Just as Reformation theology condemned good works and looked instead at inner faith, Potiphar condemns his wife's reliance on outer signs of fidelity when it is clear that she has been faithless at heart. The comparison is admittedly forced, as her works are by no means good. Nonetheless, it is clear that Rüte returns here to a proven technique of discrediting the old faith: the association of Catholic theology with feminine impropriety as found in Dame Confusion of *Abgötterei*. Like the figure of the harlot, she represents earthly desires, as revealed by the herald at the beginning of the next day's performance:

> Noch eins hand ir ouch gester gsechen
> Was durch die frowen ist beschechen
> Wie sy greitzt hat den fromen knaben
> Vnd als sy nit an jm mag haben
> Das er thuon wöll was jra gfelt
> Wie sy jm drum vffs läben stelt
> Darby sönd jr die welt verstan
> Die jr bgird nit verdrucken khan
> Sonders eigner nathur vnd art
> Jn allem muotwillen harfart
> Wer ir dar zuo nit helffen wil
> Sonders jr ist jm widerspil
> Der muoß hinweg/vnd lyden drum
> Das ist der kern in kurtzer sum
> Der handlung vff gestrigem tag (vv. 2105–19)

Yesterday, you observed yet another matter: what happened on the woman's account, how she enticed the pious youth and how, when he would not do her bidding, she plotted to have him killed. In this, you should perceive the world, which cannot suppress its desires, but maliciously roams about of its own nature. Whosoever will not help her in her pursuits, but rather opposes her, must be eliminated and suffer. That is, in short, the essence of yesterday's performance.

The herald, it should be noted, does not explicitly tie Potiphar's wife to Catholicism. That connection nonetheless remains implicit in her worldliness, which ignores the divine and places its faith in human matters. She is thus also guilty of Saul's idolatry, as revealed in her comments to Joseph at the very beginning of her appearance on stage: "Jn dich hab ich min hoffnung gleidt" (I've placed my hope in you; v. 796).[78] Yet the gulf of the Second War of Kappel separates her portrayal from that of Dame Confusion: Rüte no longer openly identifies the unruly woman with Catholicism, resorting instead to indirect, even cryptic means.

Lastly, Potiphar's wife is distinguished from Dame Confusion in that the latter is wholly allegorical, an abstract, timeless force, while the wife remains rooted in the every-day domestic environment of marriage and the household. In this context, she becomes an "anti-Susanna," allowing Rüte to draw conclusions from her trial for the social behavior of women in his audience. Two peasants deliver the resulting moral precepts; unlike the anonymous and aloof herald, they judge her transgressions as peers. Bur Hirßhut (Peasant Staghide) and Bur Ankenbock (Peasant Butter Dish) appear immediately after the trial and unabashedly advocate corporal punishment for similar cases of adultery:

> Ho/ich weiß noch gar vil frowen
> Die etwan ouch ein allso houwen
> Drum das jr mann sind hoch am gwalt
> Wer jnen nit thuot was ihn gfalt
> Den vachtents an leyden vnd schelten [. . .]
> Biß daßs jren lust mag biessen [. . .]
> Hetsluot/jr wyber luogent eben
> Jr dörfftent kürtzern vwer leben (vv. 2045–62)

---

[78] It should be noted that Rüte translated directly from Crocus at this point: "in quo uno spes opesque sunt sitae meae omnes." See von Weilen, 33.

> Ho, I know of many women who would fop one in a like manner, since their husbands are in a position of power. If you don't do what they want, they begin to persecute and slander you [...] until they can attain their desire. [...] So watch out, you girls, you might shorten your life.

The threat of corporal punishment for adulterous women graphically illustrates that feminine disorder was not merely a convenient metaphor for religious polemics, but had very real consequences for women who did not adhere to social norms. Although the debate as to the Reformation's ultimate impact on women's position in society still continues,[79] Rüte's extremely reactionary stance in this passage borders on the misogynistic and makes his portrayal of Potiphar's wife arguably one of the most repressive representations of women in Reformation literature. By 1538, the figure of the unruly woman had become the foil of confessional stability in Bern, an image upon which Rüte projected any and all socioreligious prohibitions.

Revolt, Order, and Iconoclasm in Gedeon *(1540)*

The decade prior to *Joseph*'s performance had meanwhile seen the emergence of a new and real transgressor of religious authority: the Anabaptist movement. In many ways, Anabaptists' insistence on the letter of Scripture and its absolute authority took Protestant principles of biblical exegesis to their logical conclusion. For Protestant magistrates, the rub lay in the movement's all too literal interpretation of passages such as Matthew 20:26—"whoever would be great among you must be your servant"—which did not exactly support secular rule. Conrad Grebel, the movement's likely founder, was an early ally of Zwingli in Zurich, but broke with the reformer following the Second Zurich Disputation of October 1523, whose reforms did not go far enough for him. Among other matters, the disputation failed to order the immediate removal of devotional images in Zurich churches, which Grebel and like-minded followers had already begun to desecrate in sporadic outbreaks of iconoclasm. Zwingli and

---

[79] For a recent survey on this subject, see Merry E. Wiesner, "Studies of Women, the Family, and Gender," in *Reformation Europe: A Guide to Research II*, ed. William S. Maltby, Reformation Guides to Research 3 (St. Louis: Center for Reformation Research, 1992), 159–87.

the Zurich council postponed the matter until June 1524, when all religious art was removed in an orderly fashion. This delay in a matter so clearly void of scriptural foundation was indefensible for Grebel, and Anabaptists came to reject all magisterial authority over their lives and their property. The movement quickly spread to Bern and gained a small, but tenacious following despite the increasingly Draconian efforts of local authorities to convert or suppress them. Despite persecution, the Bernese Anabaptist community survived intact into the seventeenth century; Jakob Amman, after whom the Amish order is named, is believed to have been born ca. 1656 in the Simme valley (*Simmental*) south of Bern.[80]

Prior to *Gedeon*'s performance (7 March 1540) and subsequent publication (fig. 19), Rüte had already confronted Anabaptism on at least one occasion. When the movement took root in the Emme valley (*Emmental*), the council held a *Täufergespräch* (Anabaptist Disputation) in Bern from 11–17 March 1538; Rüte attended and recorded the debate as court secretary.[81] The 1538 assembly was the last in a series of three disputations during the 1530s, in which the city's theologians debated prominent Anabaptists from Bern and abroad.[82] Embarassingly for the Zwinglian party, the Anabaptists discharged themselves quite well at the second and largest of these, the Zofingen Disputation of July 1532. Both sides claimed victory, and the Anabaptists continued to make substantial inroads in nearly all Bernese territories. When milder measures to stem the tide proved ineffective, the magistracy resorted to exile and, if the violator returned, to execution by drowning.[83] The period following the 1538 disputation proved to be the most repressive of all: at least twelve executions occurred in 1538 alone, and (coercively) converted Anabaptists were required to swear obedience to the council's mandates at the *Gerichtsstuhl*

---

[80] Ernst Müller, *Geschichte der Bernischen Täufer* (Frauenfeld: J. Huber, 1895).

[81] "Gespräch der Berner Prädikanten mit den Täufern, gehalten vom 11. bis 17. März 1538 zu Bern," in *Quellen zur Geschichte der Täufer in der Schweiz*, ed. Martin Haas (Zurich: Theologischer Verlag, 1974), 4:257–467. See also Ulrich J. Gerber, Hans Rudolf Lavater, and François de Capitani, eds., *Berner Täufertum und Reformation im Dialog. Eine Ausstellung zum 450–jährigen Jubiläum der Täuferdisputation in Bern 1538–1988* (Bern: Bernisches Historisches Museum, 1988).

[82] Guggisberg, 233–6.

[83] Council policy subsequently vacillated between harsh persecution and tolerance with the hope of conversion. As Anabaptists did not acknowledge the authority of the council, neither approach seemed to impact the movement substantially. Guggisberg, 233 ff.

at Cross Lane.[84] These harsh provisions garnered the movement's otherwise meek followers much sympathy among the local population, but persecution did not cease until 1541, when mayor Hans Franz Nägeli directed pastors Peter Kunz and Erasmus Ritter to locate the graves of deceased Anabaptists with those of the rest of the congregation.[85]

Occurring at the height of Anabaptist persecution, *Gedeon*'s militant destruction of Baal's altar as found in Judges 6 speaks directly to the issue of civil obedience, suggesting that it belonged at least in part to the council's orchestrated efforts to contain the movement. Indeed, the performance of *Joseph* occurred no more than three weeks after the *Täufergespräch* of 1538, and this coincidence may have suggested to Rüte the topic for his next play. At the very least, he set about writing soon after *Joseph*'s performance: the two-year interval between *Joseph* and *Gedeon* is the shortest among Rüte's dramas. As the play's text contains serious typographic errors,[86] this also suggests that someone—author, printer, and/or council—wished to publish and distribute it as soon as possible. Yet the portrayal of Baal's cult also provided a tempting opportunity to polemicize once again against the "idolatry" of the old faith—too tempting an opportunity for Rüte to pass up. Gideon's iconoclasm is thus bivalent: on the one hand it reestablishes unadulterated worship according to God's commandments, on the other it is narrowly defined to guard against illegitimate imitators who would challenge religious rule without right. Add to this the sudden civil unrest following the destruction of Baal's altar, and Rüte's *Gedeon* defends Zwinglian authority on three fronts: against Catholic clerics, populist insurgents, and radical Protestants.

The setting of *Gedeon* is largely familiar. As in *Goliath*, enemy forces advance on Israel, threatening to eradicate the Jewish faith. The mood among the Jews is desolate, for they have suffered devastating losses to the enemy over the last seven years and despair of their ability to mount an adequate defense. The cause of their infirmity,

---

[84] Ibid., 236.
[85] Ibid., 236.
[86] Unlike the errors in other plays, in *Gedeon* rhyme is affected: "Wie wol ich keins dings/hilff/notturfftig bin// Vnd kein mensch mir mag sin verlurst noch *gwi*" (vv. 443–4); "Verlan/hingworffen/geschmächt/*veracht*/vertutzt / Vch selbs ander götter vnd helffer gmacht" (vv. 469–70). Jaeger interprets the dot over the "i" of *gwi* as an abbreviated nasal and edits the word as *gwin*.

of course, is that they have abandoned God and fallen into idolatry. Thus Gideon is visited by an angel of the Lord and receives the task of destroying Baal's altar. Like David, he is young and lacks experience in war, so that both he and his soldiers doubt his ability as commander (vv. 1931–85; vv. 2436–47). Other concerns pertain to his lineage: the Abiezrite clan of the tribe of Manasseh is small and seemingly insignificant (v. 2479). His humble origins in the end allow God the greater glory of the victory: Gideon gives his skeptics leave to go, and with only 300 select Israelites he triumphs over the gathered host of Midianites and Amalekites.

Rüte again augmented this familiar framework by tailoring the material for his Swiss audience. In contending against the enemy, the alliance among the twelve tribes of Israel takes on characteristics of the Helvetian Confederacy's thirteen member cantons. Rüte frequently refers to the tribes not as *gschlecht* (families, clans), but as *ort*, the term used by Swiss confederates to refer to member city-states.[87] Furthermore, Gideon has recruited his soldiers solely from the four tribes of Manasseh, Asher, Zebulun, and Naphtali. This causes concern among the other eight tribes, who advise him to break off his campaign:

> Gmeinen knechten so von dem land
> Sich zuo kriegen versamlet hand
> Embiettend wir von den acht orten
> Gruoß/vnd zwüssen mit wening worten
> Das vns duret vnd wundret vast
> Das jr vff üch ladent ein last
> Der üch vnmüglich ist zetragen [...]
> Drumm vnser will vnd meinung ist
> Das jr diser sorglichen frist
> Jlentz wider kerint zuo huß (vv. 2686–96)

We, the eight *Orte*, extend greetings to our allies, who have gathered from the country to wage war, and council you in few words: We regret and are amazed that you have assumed a burden which is impossible for you to bear. [...] Our will and advice is thus that you should at this dire moment quickly head back home.

---

[87] The five inner cantons are *die fünf inneren Orte*, and the thirteen members of the confederacy from the sixteenth century are known as *die dreizehn alten Orte*. See K. von Greyerz, 31.

In the biblical narrative, this issue is not raised until after Gideon's victory, and then only by the tribe of Ephraim, who prevent the fleeing Midianites from crossing the Jordan and kill two of their kings, Oreb and Zeeb. Rüte, however, omits the Ephraimites' aid and portrays only Gideon's capture of the remaining Midianite kings Zebah and Zalmunna. Not only does the victory become wholly Gideon's, but the eight non-participating tribes are conspicuously adverse to protecting the true faith. Indeed, Gideon's general Aßriel suggests before the battle that a civil war could result if their forces act unilaterally (v. 2494). In the Swiss Confederacy, that war had occurred in 1531.

It is moreover striking that, for Bern, a military campaign against a confessional opponent had indeed just taken place without the support of its confederates, even that of the reformed cantons. The conquest of the Pays de Vaud was to keep Bern on its diplomatic and military guard until the Peace of Lausanne in 1564.[88] Already during the Wars of Burgundy, the eastern cantons had eyed Bern's ambitions in the west with suspicion, and the failure of the Reformation in the neighboring cantons of Freiburg and Solothurn left the city an isolated outpost of the new faith. To counter this, it began to promote the preaching of the Gospel in cities to the west such as Neuchâtel, which were often dependent on Bern for military protection.[89] When Francis I of France appeared poised to occupy Geneva, in which Bern had established regular Protestant services in 1534, the city mustered 6000 men to prevent the king from undoing its handiwork. The Catholic forest cantons, as well as Zurich, urgently advised against the campaign, and the other reformed cantons feared it would be Bern's ruin.[90] The "Bear," however, marched through the Pays de Vaud without resistance and occupied Geneva on 2 February 1536. Less than four months later, the Genevan council officially adopted the Reformation. By the performance of *Gedeon* in March 1540, it was clear that Bern's initiative against a seemingly overwhelming opponent, undertaken against the advice of allies, had secured the success of the Reformation in Geneva.[91]

---

[88] Feller, 2:412–5.
[89] Ibid., 2:354–61.
[90] Ibid., 2:372.
[91] Little did Berners suspect at the time that Calvin, whom Bernese opposition had driven from Geneva in 1538, would be invited in September 1540 to return to the city.

The portrayal of Baal's cult is perhaps the most blatant caricature of Catholicism in Bernese drama after *Abgötterei*. Rüte clearly identifies the cult of Baal with the veneration of images and the "old faith."[92] He further attributes the creation of images to the greed of Baal's priests, as acknowledged by a cleric on his way to Baal's altar, which, unbeknownst to him, has already been destroyed by Gideon and his helpers:

> Der mönsch was listig/vnd wolbdacht
> Der zersten vff die ban hat bracht
> Das bilder gschnitzt vnd gmalet sind/
> Dann dmönschen sind so kindsch vnd blind
> So bald sy bilder sähent an/
> So wend syß glich für heilig han/
> Buwent darzu kilchen vnd plätz
> Bringent jnen richtum vnd schätz/
> Damit man mög erhalten wol
> Den/so dem gotzdienst pflegen sol/
> Das ist vns Baals pfaffen guot/
> Mencher/der sunst nit het ein gluot
> Darby er sich warm machen könt/
> Der bsitzt groß guot/zinß/gült/vnd Rent (vv. 1136–49)

> The person who first initiated the practice of carving and painting images was clever and wise, for people are so childish and blind that they consider images holy as soon as they see them. They build churches and squares for them and bring them riches and treasures so that one might support those who attend to this idolatry. That's good for us priests of Baal: Many a priest, who wouldn't otherwise have a hearth to warm him, has great possessions, tithes, money, and benefices.

The similarities to clerics of the old faith become more pronounced after the altar's destruction. Upon seeing the rubble, a priest bemoans the loss of his benefice, not only for himself, but also for his concubine and children (v. 1202). At the end of the first day's performance, the herald warns the audience of "all those who support themselves through idolatry."[93]

---

[92] One of Baal's priests refers to the cult as "der durch alt vnzwyflich gloub" (v. 1249). In lamenting Gideon's destruction of Baal's altar, the *Schreyer* states "Sol er den alten glouben schenden?" (v. 1443).
[93] "Zuom fünfften zöugent dpfaffen an / Eb sy jr narung wöllent lan// Die sy on mü vnd arbeit gnommen / Ee müssint vmb kommen die frommen// [...] Also thuond alle die warlich / So durch abgöttery nerent sich" (vv. 1761-8).

In placing Gideon's destruction of the altar on stage, the play reenacts the Swiss iconoclasm of the late 1520s and early 1530s. Just as councilor Anton Noll's public desecration of the Oberbüren Marian altar in March 1528 had vividly demonstrated that divine retribution would not be visited on the perpetrator, the play highlights the lifelessness and inefficacy of Baal's image. Before he and his ten helpers set about their work, Gideon mocks the god and challenges it to avenge itself:

> Du götz/du block/ich sag dyr nüt/
> Du Baal/den disers bild düt/
> Bistuo ein Gott/ein ding/ein wäsen/
> Wie dyne pfaffen von dir läsen/
> Bist doch etwas/erzöug dich hie/
> Wer du doch syest/was/vnd wie
> Bist etwas anders dann ein block
> Ein blosser nam/ein stumm/ein stock
> So rich dich/straff mich/gryff mich an (vv. 909–17)

> You idol, you block of wood, I'll say nothing to you. But you, Baal, whom this image signifies, if you're a god, a thing, a being, as your clerics recite concerning you, if you're something, reveal yourself here, who you are, what, and how. If you are anything but a block, a mere name, a mute, a stump, then avenge yourself, punish me, strike me down.

Following a mock trial in which they condemn Baal to death by axe, the eleven speedily execute the sentence. Gideon's challenge goes unanswered: No avenger appears to smite him for his defilement of ostensibly holy ground, and he drops to the earth in prayer. The text does not indicate the altar's appearance, but if Baal's priests are so clearly identified with Catholic clerics, then there is reason to assume that it might have resembled the altar image of a particular saint. Staged and actual iconoclasm would have then merged, and the audience would have once again borne witness to the futility (and hence idolatry) of venerating anything or anyone other than God Himself. Even if the altar represented some fantastic anthropomorphism, the violent destruction of a human-like image could well have had a cathartic effect upon spectators, especially if Catholic viewers were among them.

Noll's iconoclasm differed from Gideon's in one respect, however: the Bernese council had sanctioned his act in advance. Gideon's authority comes from God, of course, but outside of a select few no one yet knows of his divine calling. Following the desecration of Baal's altar, the play reveals to the audience the destabilizing effects of (seemingly) usurped religious authority. The dismay at the altar's demise leads to open insurrection against Joash, Gideon's father, who in Rüte's portrayal is the leader of the Abiezrite clan of Manasseh. Incited by Baal's priests (vv. 1212–1303), the people march upon Joash's home to demand that he release Gideon. However, upon arrival they abandon all pretext of religion; the issue suddenly becomes one of wealth and revolt:

> Joas/gang fürhar mit dem Sun
> Wir sind jn der stat herren nun
> Wir hand gnuog glitten üweren pracht
> Wend vns fryen mit gantzer macht (vv. 1373–6)

> Joash, come out with your son. We are now the lords of the city. We've suffered enough of your pomp and will liberate ourselves with all possible force.

Joash must inquire twice before the rioters finally give Gideon's destruction of the altar as the reason for their insurgence. They justify their actions, moreover, with majority rule: In toppling Baal, Gideon has acted against the will of the community as a whole and thus deserves death. *Das volck* affirms this in unison before Joash's house:

> Wer handlet wider gmeinen stand
> Den sol man rütten von dem land
> Wer widers mer jm glouben thuot
> Der hat verlorn sin lyb vnd bluot
> Wer falt von Baal/vnd Eyd bricht
> Der sol vmbkon vnd werden gricht (vv. 1465–70)

> Whoever acts against the common class should be eliminated. Whoever goes against the majority in matters of faith has forfeited life and limb. Whoever falls from Baal and breaks oaths should perish and be executed.

While Bern's concilar government ensured the city a measure of representative democracy, the concept of majority rule was foreign to the magistrates, especially as concerned the countryside. Nor did Christ redeem humankind according to popular vote. The people's demand that their will be heard functions as a cautionary tale, especially since the rioters have shrouded their political motives in the cloak of religion. The *ander Landman*, a passing farmer who has observed the riot, thus draws a political lesson from their insurrection:

> Es ist ein grosse sach vff erden
> Das dmönschen als vnrüwig werden
> Wenn man sy wyßt von kinden ding
> Gott geb wie man jhn sag old sing/
> Das Gott volgen/sy recht allein [...]
> So wöllents doch selbs götter machen [...]
> Doch truren ich/wenn jch dran denck
> Das darumm dstül wend vff die benck
> Vnd dvnderthanen bringent waffen/
> Vnd wend jr fromme herschafft straffen/
> Drumm das jhn gnon ist/der hanff butz
> Der jhn doch mer schad/bringt dann nutz (vv. 1625–38)

> It is a great problem on earth that people become so restless when forced to abandon childish matters. Regardless of how one tells them that only faith in God is correct [...], they still want to make their own idols. [...] But it saddens me to think that those in the visitors gallery would deign to sit on the judge's bench and that subjects would arm themselves to punish their pious magistracy, just because a scarecrow [lit. "hempen visage"] that actually causes more harm than good has been taken from them.

That a *Landman* makes these remarks implies that even (sensible) members of the peasant estate recognize the God-given authority of the magistrate, and the herald repeats this lesson at the close of the first day's performance.[94]

To guard against unwanted imitators of Gideon's iconoclasm or the people's rebellion, Rüte painstakingly documents the divine authority behind Gideon's mission. This begins by locating the source of Israel's (and Bern's) secular rule in heaven. The prophet who chastises the Jews for their fall from God at the play's outset stresses that all their power emanates from Him:

> Vß nüt hab ich üch gmacht herscher der welt
> Jch hab üch vber alle völcker gstelt/
> Wer warent jr in Egyptischen landen [...]
> Hand jr üch selbs vß diserm zwang erlöst?

---

[94] "Zuom letsten ist für dougen gstelt// Wie glych vnrüwig wirt die welt// Wenn man sy wyßt von bösen sachen// Sgmein volck laßt sich vffrürisch machen / Doch ist sin zorn bald wider gleit / Wenn sich ein fromme oberkeit / Mit vnschulden versprechen kan/" (vv. 1769–75).

Nein/Jch Jch/verschupfft all menschen vff erden
Allein das jr möchtent zuo herren werden (vv. 453–60)

> Out of nothing, I have made you rulers of the world. I have placed you over all nations. Who were you in Egypt? [...] Did you deliver yourselves from that bondage? No! It was I, I created all people of the earth only so that you might become lords.

Once Gideon receives his charge, his ordination must be emphasized at every critical juncture, lest he appear rebellious. The first mention of the *oberkeit* (authorities) who protect Baal's altar requires Gideon to divulge his mission to his accomplices (v. 806). His frequent requests for heavenly signs, in the Bible seemingly a sign of hesitation, are motivated in the play by his father's admonition to do nothing without assurance that God wills it. This admonishment comes only after Joash takes Gideon to task for having destroyed Baal's altar, as he believes, without a divine mandate:

> Wie wol ich erkennen vnd weyß
> Was vffgricht ist wider Gots gheiß
> Wenn man das selb zerstört vnd bricht
> Das Gott daran ein gfallen bschicht
> Aber niemandt den nit sendt Gott/
> Noch ordnet durch ein bsonder pot/
> Sol eigens muots das vnderstan/
> Jnn wirt sunst niemer glück an gan
> Drumm soltest Baal nit han gschent
> Dwyl Gott dich nit gordnet noch gsent (vv. 1675–84)

> Although I recognize and know that God is pleased when one destroys and fractures that which has been set up against His commandment, no one who is not sent by Him or ordained by a special messenger shall endeavor to do so independently. Otherwise, he will never experience a happy outcome. Thus you should not have desecrated Baal, since God did not ordain or send you.

As the audience has earlier seen Gideon conversing with an angel, it of course knows that he is exempt from Joash's rebuke. In the absence of such divine messengers off stage, however, only the Bernese council could claim to be in possession of a divine mandate. It was moreover in a position to require any others claiming godly election to produce evidence, which would not be easily forthcoming. This was its deterrent against all religious dissenters, whether they be Catholics, Anabaptists, or a member of any of the numerous sects arising in the wake of the Reformation.

Judging from *Gedeon*, the Bernese authorities in 1540 had both the need and the ability to assert their authority, or were at least comfortable with Rüte doing so for them. Other than the general context of Anabaptist persecution during this time, there are no apparent reasons for the play's vigorous defense of local religious rule. Nor was the council at this time adverse to a more openly antagonistic stance towards the Catholic cantons. Just a year prior, the scandal surrounding the "Interlaken Song," which ridiculed Unterwalden's support of the 1528 Oberland uprising, had forced the council to institute a censorship commission to ensure that Mathias Apiarius printed nothing that derided Bern's Catholic confederates. Apparently, the commission took a relaxed approach to its assignment.[95] In 1540, *Gedeon* was not the only product of Apiarius's press to flaunt the provisions of the Peace of Kappel, which had prohibited the printing and distribution of religious polemics. Apiarius also printed the first local edition of Manuel's two carnival plays of 1523,[96] a much more flagrant violation of the Peace of Kappel than Rüte's play. These two imprints perhaps represented an inofficial response to the inner cantons' repression of the "Interlaken Song." At the very least, they indicated that the council was willing to circumvent the confessional cease-fire to consolidate its gains.

"That it be told every instant": Bearing Witness in Noe (1546)

Noe (fig. 20) is perhaps the most sophisticated drama performed in Reformation Bern. In past plays, Rüte had seldom allowed events to speak for themselves; instead, a herald had mediated between author and audience at the end of each day's performance, extracting pre-packaged lessons for ready consumption. In *Noe*, this figure recedes to little more than an announcer, welcoming spectators, requesting their silence, and bidding them farewell at the close of the performance. The play itself now assumes an exegetical role in a multi-layered self-explication. Select characters, such as the brothers of Nimrod, serve as the author's mouthpiece, observing and com-

---

[95] Karl Müller, *Die Geschichte der Zensur im alten Bern* (Bern: K.J. Wyss, 1904), 84.
[96] *Ein fast Kurtz wylig Fasznachtspil/ so zuo Bernn vff der Herrenfaßnacht in dem M.D.XXII. jar/von burgerßsönen offentlich gemacht ist [. . .]. Item ein ander spil/ daselbs vff der alten faßnacht darnach gemacht [. . .]. Erstlich/Getruckt zuo Bern by Matthia Apiario. im 1540. jar.*

menting on the events around them without participating in them. The survivors of the flood teach their grandchildren of the deluge and admonish them to tell the cautionary tale to their children. Most importantly, Noah's children perform a play for their father on the wickedness of the antedeluvian world. During this play-within-a-play, which comprises one-fifth of Rüte's total text, Noah's offspring contemplate the iniquity of Cain's descendents before the flood,[97] just as the Bernese new covenant audience observed Ham's treachery against his father. Both groups preserve the memory of past events by reenacting them. By dramaturgically constructing his own play around the re-presentation of Scripture on stage, Rüte thematizes the obligation of every Christian to contemplate God's word through any means possible. In content and form, *Noe* bears witness to the necessity of bearing witness.

This theme begins in the contrastive portrayal of the three clans descended from Noah: the families of Shem, Ham, and Japheth. In educating their children, Noela and Noegla, Japheth's and Shem's respective wives, insist on retelling the tale of the flood. They have seen God's wrath with their own eyes and feel compelled to hand their experience down to future generations, lest the world forget the wickedness of its ways:

> *Noela*:
> Schwöster es ist min flissig bit
> Wenn ich min döchtern schick zuo dir
> Du wöllest jnen bilden für
> Mit ernst offnen die grosse nodt
> Deß sündfluß vnd der menschen todt
> Die wir mit vnsern ougen gsechen
> Wann sy dann ghörent/was ist bschechen
> So werdent sy sich frombklich tragen
> Vnd das jren nachkommen sagen
> *Noegla*
> Man sols allen menschen verkünden
> Darmit sy schüchint ab den sünden [...]
> Es ist guot sag ich dir fürwar
> Das mans erzell all ougenblick (vv. 394–407)

---

[97] On the small play, see Fritz Hammes, *Das Zwischenspiel im deutschen Drama von seinen Anfängen bis auf Gottsched, vornehmlich der Jahre 1500–1660* (Berlin: Emil Felber, 1911), 17–8.

Noela:
Sister, it's my sincere wish that, when I send my daughters to you, you will describe and earnestly portray for them the great suffering of the flood and the demise of humanity which we have seen with our own eyes. When they hear what transpired, they'll carry themselves with piety and tell it to their descendents.
Noegla:
One should proclaim it to all humanity, so that they shun sin. [...] I tell you truly: it is fitting that it be told every instant.

Their comments equally apply for Rüte and his audience; the production of *Noe* continues a tradition of biblical renarration that extends back to the author of Genesis. Nevertheless, when Chia, Ham's daughter, returns from a visit with Noela and Noegla and tells her mother of the fascinating tales told by her aunts, the mother advises against dwelling on the subject. Rüte gives the wife the name Pandora, indicative of the troubles her simple suggestion will later create:

> Man sol nit zvil reden daruon/
> Eins möcht sunst in verzwyfflung kon [...]
> Got wil nit/das wir denckent dran
> Wir wurdent sunst niemer fröüd han/
> Die straff hat ghört der vordren welt
> Gott hat sich mit vns z'fryden gstelt
> Vnnd vns verheyssen eygentlich/
> Wie die menschen joch halten sich
> So wöll er d'welt nit mer ertrencken
> Hieran söllent wir alweg dencken (vv. 433–44)

> One shouldn't speak too much of it; it could otherwise drive one to despair. [...] God doesn't want us to think about it, since we would otherwise never be happy. His punishment belonged to the former world. God is satisfied with us and has promised that He will never again inundate the world no matter how we behave. That is what we should always consider.

Pandora further instructs the women in Ham's clan that a wife's "pretty clothes" will ensure her husband's fidelity (v. 479), leading daughters Omphale and Pamphila to praise the virtues of cotton and silk.[98] Ham has at this point in the play already indicated his displeasure with his father, but he has not yet come under the sway

---

[98] Omphale and Pamphila are further names from classical antiquity. The latter represents the prostitute in Terence's plays, while the former is the mythical Lydian queen who has Hercules do her bidding.

of "false spirits" who aid him in the creation of a new pantheistic religion. His clan's neglect of God's memory represents its first step in its fall from grace.

As might be expected, *Noe* condemns Ham's subsequent "idolatry" and commends solafideism, but religious polemics within the main play are muted. In the portrayal of Noah's offering of thanksgiving (Genesis 8:20), occurring here during a Sukkoth feast at which all his descendents are gathered, the audience perceives God speaking directly with Noah, establishing that their relationship needs no intermediaries. Shem and Japheth further praise their Christian liberty, which at all times allows them to eat meat or any food they wish (vv. 1831–3). Ham, however, grows annoyed with his father's belief that no human work can effect salvation, which he interprets as the naiveté of an increasingly senile man. Led astray by demons and his own desire for power, he preaches a new religion to his clan. Like the priests of *Abgötterei*, he teaches that God stands aloof from human affairs, so that humankind requires intermediaries to appeal to His benevolence (vv. 2033–45). The elaborate ceremonies he establishes contrast with the simplicity of Noah's faith. Still, Ham's doctrine is not explicitly linked to Catholicism.

The opposite is true of the portrayal of Lamech in the play-within-a-play performed for Noah at the Sukkoth feast. Here, Rüte depicts a despotic ruler who joins with "God's vicar" on earth to persecute all those who would challenge their religion. As Rüte distinguishes Lamech, the slayer of Cain (Genesis 4:23–24), from Lamech, son of Methuselah and father of Noah (Genesis 5:25–29), there are actually two Lamechs in the small play, one corrupt, and one pious. While the latter sends a young Noah out to proselytize, the former celebrates his rule with his children Jabal, Jubal, and Tubalcain. Their accomplishments in agriculture, music, and metallurgy lead Lamech to compare himself with God in heaven. A priest (*Pfaff*) appears to modify this slightly: Lamech is a God on earth, namely God's vicar (vv. 621–3), an office shared by the priest (v. 723). As if the worldly pomp and pleasures of Lamech's court were not enough to mark his rule as ungodly, Tubalcain suddenly expresses the desire to marry his sister Naamah; the *Pfaff* does not object, so long as they promise to uphold his religion (vv. 716–27).[99] Suddenly, "Enoch's

---

[99] The incestuous relationship between Tubalcain and Naamah is conspicuous

brother" and "Enoch's son" appear in quick succession, disrupting the wedding festivities with their admonishments to turn from idolatry. Encouraged by the *Pfaff*, Lamech slays both lest their preaching lead to revolt. He then dismisses as squeamishness the fears of his two wives, who have dreamt that a great flood will come to avenge such crimes. God reveals the pending deluge to Noah, and the play ends.

Situated as it is at the height of festivities in *Noe*, the *klein spil* (small play) essentially holds a mirror up to the Bernese audience so that its members might reflect on the act of play watching itself. In the play's foreword, Rüte had already primed his spectators to contemplate the variety of contemporary plays and the reasons for their performance (vv. 11–129). Echoing Luther's apocryphal commentaries on Judith and Tobit, he states that the Jews themselves practiced theater:

> Die Spil sind gsin in übung gar/
> Gwüß nit allein im Griechenland [. . .]
> Ouch nit allein zuo Rom darnach [. . .]
> Sonders ouch zuo Hierusalem [. . .]
> Wenn wir dann ouch trachtent daby
> Wie Spil üben so nutzlich sy/
> Notwendig/eerlich/vnd loblich/
> Deß yeder selbs erinner sich/
> Dann daruß nüt böß volgen mag/(vv. 88–101)

> Play performances were common not only in Greece [. . .], nor afterwards in Rome alone [. . .], but also in Jerusalem. [. . .] When we consider then how useful, essential, honest, and praiseworthy the performance of plays can be, that should be borne in mind by everyone, for nothing bad can come of it.

The audience is then asked to view the utility of a play for itself. Like *Noe*, the small play is performed by young males to honor the

---

enough to suggest that Rüte engaged here in topical polemics. Given *Osterspiel*'s openly anti-Lutheran stance, a potential target exists in Landgrave Philip of Hesse. In 1541, Philip secretly entered a second marriage. Beforehand, he had obtained Luther's approval, but not, unfortunately, a divorce from his first wife. Philip's bigamy soon became public knowledge, besmirching both his and Luther's reputation. While Tubalcain does not have two wives, Lamech does; meanwhile, the priest's unquestioning approval of Tubalcain's marriage is strongly reminiscent of Luther's willingness to compromise theological custom for political benefits. Rüte may have simply taken the circumstances of Philip's case and added the element of incest to accentuate his transgression.

leader(s) of the community. Rüte's spectators are separated from Noah's age by thousands of years, while the viewers of the small play are only one or two generations removed from antediluvian events. Yet as the Bernese audience discovers, even a brief passage of time is equally impassable for Noah's descendents without the play's re-presentation of their elders' first-hand experiences. The play thus forms a crucial link in a chain of remembrance, as Shem states following the performance:

> Jr hand ghört vnd vor ougen gsehen
> Was vor dem sündfluß ist bschehen
> Jn diserm kurtzen spil vnd dicht
> Von Lamechs handel/wyß vnd gschicht
> Mögent jr wyter bilden yn
> Wie es ein ding vff erdtrich gsin
> Denckent d'ran üwer leben lang
> Das es üch ouch nit vbel gang
> Jr sönd ouch von den vordern tagen
> Ewigklich üwern kindern sagen
> Das dessen nit vergessen werd
> Als lang wirt b'stan himel vnd erd. (vv. 1692–703)

> In this short play, you have heard and seen with your own eyes what transpired prior to the flood. Based on Lamech's actions, manner, and story, you can imagine how things must have been on earth. Consider this your whole life long so that you too do not fare so poorly. You should also constantly tell you children of the former days, so that they are not forgotten as long as heaven and earth exist.

Through the juxtaposition of the two plays, it becomes apparent that commemoration must assume the role of natural memory for all latter-day Christians. Rüte thus portrays the performance of biblical plays as imperative in preserving the remembrance of God's workings with the world. Some fifteen and a half centuries after Christ's nativity, they provided vivid testimony of original events, a remembrance and sign of faith not unlike Zwingli's symbolic understanding of the Eucharist.

Should the spectators have difficulty seeing themselves reflected in Noah's descendents, Rüte again makes the play's setting as familiar as possible. *Noe* is likely the most thoroughly Swiss play in Rüte's oeuvre. Although the action supposedly transpires in Armenia,[100]

---

[100] "Ghandlet im Armenier land" (v. 1893).

Noah and his children move about in what Emil Ermatinger has called a "Bern-ified" landscape of alpine meadows.[101] In accordance with Genesis 9:20, Noah is a "proper farmer" (*rechter bur*; v. 518) as well as a consummate vintner (vv. 600–6). Jabal, who in the Bible is the progenitor of tent-dwelling herders, here establishes dairy farming, grazing his cattle in alpine pastures, constructing sedentary cottages with stalls, and single-handedly inventing butter and cheese (vv. 429–48). It would moreover appear that Mount Ararat is part of the Alps or, conversely, that the latter have been relocated east of the Bosporus. Rüte first identifies Ararat as the resting place of the ark (v. 659), but the character Mannus later finds it in "high alps."[102]

The play's Swiss perspective is equally manifest in its rejection of overlordship. Nimrod, "the first on earth to be a mighty man" (Genesis 10:8), figures prominently in Rüte's account of Ham's insurrection. Ham first breaks with Noah theologically, ridiculing his father as he lies drunk with open robe. He and his offspring then elect Nimrod, Ham's grandson, to rule over them. He has curried their favor through flattery as well as through elaborate banquets and entertainments at which his guests seek their pleasures in dance, song, food, and drink. After plotting with Ham to deprive Shem of the Asian lands promised him by Noah (vv. 4473–502), Nimrod betrays the full magnitude of his hubris by announcing his plans to construct the future Tower of Babel. When it becomes clear that he will stop at nothing to consolidate his power, his brothers Sabus and Sabatius, figures of Rüte's own creation,[103] choose exile rather than suffer his tyranny. Sabatius's monologue becomes an impassioned plea for liberty:

---

[101] "Anmutig ist, wie der Verfasser die Berge und Weiden des biblischen Landes verbernert." Ermatinger, 200.

[102] "Jch bin vff hochen alpen gsin// [...] Da funden wir den höchsten schatz / Den gott vff erdtrich hat erschafft// [...] Es ist die Arch/das heilig huß" (vv. 690–708). Ermatinger unhesitatingly identifies these alps with the Alps (p. 200). The opposite could however also be true, namely that Rüte portrayed the near eastern mountain in Swiss terms.

[103] With Sabatius, Rüte may have again had a specific figure from classical antiquity in mind, now with positive associations befitting Sabatius's faith in God. Born of peasant origins, the Roman Sabbatius was brother-in-law to the Emperor Justin and father of Emperor Justinian. See *Der kleine Pauly. Lexikon der Antike* (Munich: Alfred Druckenmüller, 1972), 4:1480.

> Ein fry volck muoß es sin vnd blyben/
> Sich keins wegs lan von fryheit tryben
> Fryheit/fryheit/din Maiestat/
> Din dächtnus mir tieff zhertzen gat/
> Jch wil dich bhalten all min tag
> Niemands mich von dir scheiden mag/
> Min läben setz ich zur fryheit
> Min nachkommen in ewigkeit
> Werdent durch d'fryheit ß'erdtrichs gnoß
> Die fryheit wirt sy machen groß (vv. 4665–74)

A free people must be and remain free, not let itself by driven from freedom. Freedom, freedom, your majesty, your monument live deep in my heart. I shall preserve you my life long; no one can sunder me from you. I pledge my life for freedom. My descendents in all eternity shall by virtue of freedom be citizens of the whole world. Freedom shall make them great.

The play's combination of Christian and political liberty would be largely unthinkable in Lutheran territories, where authors such as Johann Eberlin von Günzburg recommended that a true Christian must tolerate the caprices of secular authority.[104] In Rüte's ideal Zwinglian union of heavenly and earthly dominion, however, tyranny is by definition non-existent. Noah embodies the play's ideal ruler as father, not lord. Uz, Shem's grandson, informs the audience that Noah is *keyser vber lyblich sachen* (emperor over earthly matters; v. 1181). Noah himself pleads for patriarchal government in his farewell address to his children before they depart to inhabit Asia, Africa, and Europe:

> Keinr soll sich lassen nennen Herr
> Keiner soll herrschen noch regieren
> Noch gwaltig das regiment füren
> Sonders wer ye der eltist sy
> Der halt vffrecht die policy
> Nit als ein Herr/das merckent wol
> Aber wie ein vatter thuon sol (vv. 3724–30)

No one should have himself called "lord." No one should reign or rule, nor govern by force. Rather, the eldest should uphold public policy, not as lord, understand this well, but as a father should do.

---

[104] Stricker, 131.

Noah's comments of course indirectly referred to the Small Council of Bern, whose members were in attendance.[105] The topos of fatherly benevolence surfaced frequently within the Swiss literature of the period, legitimating the Swiss concilar system of government against the autocratic rule of nobility within the Holy Roman Empire.[106] Outside of Bern, authors devoted whole plays to such patriotism, such as Jacob Rueff's *Etter Heini* in Zurich. In Bern, the valorization of Swiss independence took place only within an overarching religious sphere that validated secular authority.

Conversely, the conviction of faith could serve patriotic interests, as is apparent in the martyrdom of the small play's two preachers at the hands of the ruler Lamech. Their death rounds off Rüte's catalogue of the varieties of religious testimony. In his final words before Lamech strikes him down, Enoch's son announces that he and his uncle will continue to bear witness even in death:

> Wir beid/die dran gstreckt hand das leben
> Werdent/Herr Gott/dir zügknuß geben/
> Mit vnserm tod/vnd vnserm bluot/
> Das dem Lamech din straff vnd ruot
> Gar heitter vnd wol ist kund than
> Wenn er nit wöll von sünden stan
> Deß wirt er b'zügt vnd vnderricht
> Wenn du wider jn sitzest z'gricht ("Small Play," vv. 948–55)

> We two, who have sacrificed our lives, shall with our deaths and our blood bear witness for you, Lord God, that your staff and rod were made well known to Lamech in the event that he would not renounce sin. This testimony will serve against him when you sit in judgment of him.

Young Noah, too, missions to the world as a witness to God's judgment. An angel of the Lord assigns him the same task as Enoch's relatives, to preach against the corruption of the world:

> Noe züch vß in alle welt
> Gott hat dich zuo eim zügen gstelt
> Du muost die welt gotts willen leeren
> Will sy sich dann yetz zletst nit bekeeren

---

[105] See this chapter's epigraph.
[106] See for example Stricker, 126.

So muostu darumb kuntschafft tragen
Das kein mensch möge zuo mir sagen
Hättest mich vor dins willen b'richt
So hett ich mich ghüt vor dim gricht/("Small Play," vv. 287–94)

Noah, go forth into the whole world: God has appointed you as witness. You must teach the world God's will. If its inhabitants will not reform, then you must bear testimony that no one may say to me, "Had you informed me earlier of your will, I would have endeavored to escape your judgment."

The courage of all three missionaries demonstrates that true faith does not shirk from death. Moreover, eternal salvation justified the open defiance of powerful rulers such as Lamech and his clerical accomplice. The papal-imperial alliance suggested by these characters indeed loomed large at the time of *Noe*'s performance in April 1546: The Council of Trent, after much delay, had finally convened in March 1545, and the 1544 Peace of Crépy had committed the defeated French king to aid Charles V against Protestants and to restore the Duke of Savoy. Although the death of Francis's second son in 1545 ended the treaty's additionally planned marriage between the houses of Valois and Habsburg, Bern continued to face the prospect of a combined Catholic assault on its western border, and even Zurich remained unwilling to help it protect Geneva and the Pays de Vaud.[107] With little support in the confederacy, the council supported the Schmalkaldic League against the emperor, allowing Bernese mercenaries to join the Protestant troops following the outbreak of hostilities in June. In impassioned language much like that of Sabatius, it pleaded later that summer at the *Tagsatzung* for other reformed cantons to declare war on Charles.[108] Even if their death lacked the military glory of *Goliath*, the martyrdom of believers by Lamech exemplified the potential sacrifice of Berners willing to defend the reformed faith in the pending Schmalkaldic War. This spirit of defiance continued after the emperor's decisive victory over Protestant forces at the Battle of Mühlberg in April of 1547, so that *Noe* also anticipates Bern's anti-imperial stance during the Augsburg Interim, when the city accepted Johannes Haller, Wolfgang Musculus, and

---

[107] Feller, 2:391.
[108] Ibid., 2:392; Brady, 210–11.

other Zwinglian refugees from Augsburg in addition to mustering 7000 troops in a vain attempt to protect Constance against the emperor.[109]

"Un-Luther Characters": Confessionalism in Osterspiel (1552)

Despite its apparently familiar title, *Ein kurtzes Osterspil* (fig. 21) is unlike any of Rüte's previous plays or, for that matter, any other play of the sixteenth century. Beyond the Easter date of its performance, specifically in celebration of the Bernese council elections on 24 April 1552, it has little in common with late medieval dramatizations of Christ's resurrection.[110] Indeed, no one approach does justice to the work. Its divers choral interludes have led scholars to classify it as an oratorium or even as a *Singspiel*.[111] It further transposes the visionary imagery of Revelation 4–5 directly to the stage, resulting in a monumental living tableau that continues the tradition of Protestant Apocalypse illustrations begun by Luther's September Testament in 1522. The play's visuality and musicality far exceed that of Rüte's other works, so that their analysis forms a substantial component of Chapters Five and Six. As its affiliation with council elections suggests, however, *Osterspiel*'s political overtones were no less pronounced. Alone among Rüte's six plays, it was performed in the city's secularized Franciscan monastery for a select audience. Behind closed doors, actors and council members were among friends, so that the accolades showered by Rüte upon the magistrates were matched only by the scorn displayed for those who opposed them. In 1552, three years after Heinrich Bullinger and John Calvin established concord between the Zurich and Genevan churches in the *Consensus Tigurinus*, the council perceived opposition all around it. *Osterspiel* is unabashed in its defense of the Bernese church, not only against Catholicism, but also against Lutherans, Calvinists, the mediating theology of Martin Bucer, and even Zwingli's Zurich.

---

[109] Feller, 2:392–3; Rudolf Pfister, *Kirchengeschichte der Schweiz* (Zurich: Theologischer Verlag, 1974), 2:249.
[110] See the chapter "Zum Gattungsproblem" in Jaeger, 44–61.
[111] See, respectively, Ermatinger, 200; Baechtold, *Geschichte der deutschen Literatur in der Schweiz*, 316.

The apocalyptic visions of the Book of Revelation enjoyed extraordinary popularity in Reformation Bern. In Protestant polemics, of course, the equation of the papacy with the Antichrist or the Harlot of Babylon was widespread,[112] so that Rüte's adaptation of Revelation 17 for *Abgötterei* appears unremarkable. However, Bernese theologians demonstrated an earnest exegetical interest in the book. Sebastian Meyer, whose outspoken anti-Catholicism had led to his expulsion from the city during the mid-1520s, returned to Bern in 1536 to assume Bertold Haller's preaching duties upon the latter's passing. Soon afterwards, in 1539, he published a commentary on the Apocalypse with Froschauer in Zurich: *In Apocalypsim Iohannis Apostoli [. . .] Commentarius*.[113] His explication subsequently proved quite popular. The Zurich reformer Konrad Pellikan was so impressed with Meyer's work that he adopted it verbatim for his own biblical commentary, and Count Ottheinrich of Pfalz-Neuburg, patron of learning and later Elector of the Palatinate (1556–59), commissioned the artist Matthias Gerung in 1544 to complete a series of polemic woodcuts to accompany a German translation of Meyer's text.[114] In addition, Heinrich Bullinger dedicated his unpublished collection of sermons on Revelation to the Bernese council in 1556. Although the council eventually decided against the sermons' publication due to their polemical content,[115] the collection appeared later in Basel with a dedication to councilor Niklaus von Diesbach.[116] Lastly, Benedikt Marti (Aretius), who had become professor of theology at the *Hohe Schule* upon Wolfgang Musculus's death in 1563, composed a commentary on Paul's epistles and Revelation: *Commentarii in Omnes Epistolas*

---

[112] See among others Robert W. Scribner, *For the Sake of Simple Folk: Popular Propaganda for the German Reformation*, 2nd ed. (Oxford: Clarendon, 1994), 171 ff.; Barbara Sher Tinsley, "Pope Joan Polemic in Early Modern France: The Use and Disabuse of Myth," *Sixteenth Century Journal* 18 (1987): 381–98.

[113] *In Apocalypsim Johannis Apostoli D. Sebastiani Meyer Ecclesiastiae Bernen. Commentarius, nostro huic saeculo accommodus, natus, & aeditus* (Zurich: Froschauer, [1539]). See also Guggisberg, 174.

[114] Unfortunately, Gerung's series was never published. See Petra Roettig, *Reformation als Apokalypse. Die Holzschnittfolge von Matthias Gerung im Codex germanicus 6592 der Bayerischen Staatsbibliothek in München*, Vestigia Bibliae 11/12 (Bern: Peter Lang, 1991), 30, passim; Scribner, *Simple Folk*, 2nd ed., 256–8.

[115] Lest the council's reluctance to publish the sermons seem spiteful, it should be noted that their anti-papal tone had already led Froschauer in Zurich to shy away from publishing them himself. See Eduard Bähler, "Dekan Haller und die Berner Kirche," in *NBT 1926* (Bern: E.J. Wyss, 1925), 6–8.

[116] Guggisberg, 174.

D. Pavli, et Canonicas, itemqve in Apocalypsin D. Ioannis.[117] Dedicated to Johannes von Wattenwyl, the later Bernese mayor who lost his office after military defeat against Savoy in 1589,[118] it went through several editions. To judge from these tracts, the attraction of the Apocalypse cut across confessional boundaries in Bern: Marti was a moderate Zwinglian, while Meyer belonged to the local Lutheran camp and chose to leave the city again in 1541. Moreover, the dedications by Bullinger and Marti, even if intended to win patronage, indicate that local council members shared an interest for John's visions.

Rüte was thus not alone in dedicating an apocalyptic work to the Bernese council. As the opening speech by the first of the play's four heralds indicates, the author composed the work expressly to honor local magistrates on the occasion of their (re-)election to office:

> Wolglertenn/Edlen/wysen frommen
> Das jr sind willig zuo vns kommen/
> Diß kurtzwyl zhören vnd zesehen
> Drumm wir üch lob vnd danck verjähen
> Wend ouch allzyt mit embsigkeyt
> zThuon eüwern willen syn bereyt/
> Alls wir diß tagen hand betracht
> Das aber yetz nüw wurdint gmacht
> Jn eüwerm Regiment die stät
> Der Schultheiß der Venner/vnd die Rät
> Do hand wir die hie wöllen ehren
> Jr gnaden z'gfallen ettwas leeren
> Daran sy möchten han kurtzwyl
> Hand deßhalb gleert ein Osterspil (vv. 1–14)

Learned, noble, wise, and upstanding gentlemen! We praise and thank you that you have come to us willingly to hear and see this entertainment. We are at all times prepared to do your bidding eagerly. As we have observed these past days that in your government the offices of mayor and *Venner*, as well as the councilors, have been renewed, we wished to honor them here and, in order to please their grace, to teach something that would also provide entertainment. For this reason, we've chosen an Easter play.

---

[117] I have unfortunately been unable to locate the first edition of this work and its date of publication. I quote the title from the second edition of 1596. See also Guggisberg, 170–1.

[118] Feller, 2:452–4.

We can paint an even more detailed picture of *Osterspiel*'s patronage thanks to the chronicle of Johannes Haller, dean of the Bernese church since 1552. Whereas council records or the disbursement records of the city's treasury books offer extratextual documentation for Rüte's previous plays, Haller offer specific information on actors, location, and the play's honorees:

> Den 24ten April spielten die zum Schmieden das 4te und 5te Kapitel der Offenbarung Johannis zu Barfußen, zu Ehren dem Schultheiß Nägeli, auch Venner Zülli, und Jkr. Beat Ludw. von Mülinen, so neulich erwählt waren.[119]

> On 24 April, the members of the Blacksmith Society performed the fourth and fifth chapters of the Revelation of John in the former Franciscan monastery, honoring mayor Nägeli, *Venner* Zülli and squire Beatus Ludwig von Mülinen, who were recently elected.

The Blacksmith Society, one of the four guild-like *Gesellschaften* that shared in city government, had supported the Reformation in Bern since its early days, and Rüte was its long-term member, having joined in 1528 soon after his arrival in the city. Andreas Zülli and Beatus Ludwig von Mülinen were also members of the society, and the Easter elections had just secured them positions in the Small Council, with Zülli assuming the *Venner* position reserved for the Blacksmiths.[120]

The accomplishments of these men paled however in comparison with those of the third honoree, Hans Franz Nägeli, perhaps the most esteemed Berner of his generation. Nägeli had gained prominence as the commander of Bernese troops during the conquest of the Pays de Vaud and had subsequently served as mayor from 1540 until 1568, alternating for most of this period with Hans Jacob von Wattenwyl. Nägeli apparently did not belong to the Blacksmith Society, but its members likely wished to secure his good graces by performing in his honor. Rüte, moreover, had personal reasons for dedicating his play to the mayor: Nägeli was the godfather of his daughter Ursula, born in 1544.[121]

---

[119] *Chronik aus den hinterlassenen Handschriften des Joh. Haller und Abraham Müslin von 1550 bis 1580*, ed. Samuel Gränicher (Zofingen: D. Sutermeister, 1829), 10.

[120] Ibid., 10.

[121] Mathias Sulser, *Der Stadtschreiber Peter Cyro und die bernische Kanzlei zur Zeit der Reformation* (Bern: Carl Fromme, 1922), 115.

Together with the remaining audience, these three councilors were asked to view the allegory of God-ordained government found in the *majestas Domini* motif of Revelation 4–5, as seen in the play's title-page woodcut (fig. 21). Encircling the throne of God, twenty-four crowned elders do homage as they wait for one who is worthy to open the scroll of seven seals, soon found in the Lamb. Protestant commentaries on the Apocalypse customarily interpreted these elders as heavenly representatives of reformed civic government with its combined secular and religious authority. Bullinger, Meyer, and Aretius all interpret the Latin terms *seniores* or *senatus* as "magistrate" or "body of councilors."[122] Moreover, the "New Song" of Revelation 5:10—"For thou [. . .] hast made them a kingdom and priests to our God, and they shall reign on earth"—provided biblical support for the doctrine of universal priesthood as well as the religious authority of secular institutions. The third herald thus draws the audience's attention to the allegorical interpretation of the elders as representatives of the Christian church:

> Dann ß'Lämmli Gots in synem bluot
> Hat dwelt schon gwaltig vberwunden/
> Den synen gnad bym vatter funden/
> Sy gsetzt in sömlichs Regiment
> Wies ist in der figur erkennt/
> Wölch vns bedüt die Christlich gmein (vv. 671–6)

> For the Lamb of God, with his blood, has mightily conquered the world, found favor for his followers with his father and placed them in such rulership, as is apparent in the *figura*, which signifies the Christian church.

Together, the image of the twenty-four elders and the New Song were especially suited to honor the re-election of reformed government. With its emphasis on Christ's redemption of humanity as the Lamb, the image contrasts with representations of the Last Judgment, which had customarily hung in council chambers to signify civic authority prior to the Reformation.[123] Still, the image retained the Judgment's eschatological context, unlike the allegorical representations of good government that appeared in Regensburg and elsewhere.[124]

---

[122] Meyer, *In Apocalypsim Iohannis*, C3ᵛ; Marti, *In Apocalypsin D. Ioannis*, 569; for Bullinger, see Jaeger, 124.

[123] Craig Harbison, *The Last Judgment in Sixteenth Century Northern Europe: A Study of the Relation Between Art and the Reformation* (New York/London: Garland, 1976), 51–64.

[124] Cf. Kristin Eldyss Sorensen Zapalac, *"In His Image and Likeness": Political*

After introducing John's vision, the play portrays the search for one worthy to open the scroll of seven seals. Between the strong angel's challenge of "Who is worthy . . .?" and the appearance of the Lamb, the biblical text states only that "no one in heaven or on earth or under the earth was able to open the scroll or look into it" (Revelation 5:3). *Osterspiel*, however, repeats the angel's question twice; each recurrence heightens the christological aspects of the yet unpresent Lamb. The first repetition (vv. 188–209) enumerates the accomplishments necessary to open the scroll, such as the conquest of death, the harrowing of Hell, and the consolation of sinners. The second recurrence (vv. 218–97) anticipates Christ's fulfillment of God's first covenant. The angel calls upon numerous Old Testament patriarchs, prophets, and kings to come forward and break the seals.[125] None, of course, do, so that the angel then challenges figures from mythology and philosophy such as Hercules, Hermes, Socrates, and Pythagoras; their subsequent silence indicates the insufficiency of human reason for obtaining salvation. To drive the point home, the "first elder on the left side" pronounces that none of these individuals are worthy of the heavenly scroll. His comment implies that his peers among the Bernese councilors had both the authority and ability to discern between the true Christ and pretenders to his office.[126]

The play then turns to such pretenders in particular. In continuation of the search for one worthy to open the scroll, a second angel appears, now addressing contemporary matters on earth (v. 310 ff.). Here, he has witnessed several groups who all claim to have the authority to loosen the scroll's seals. At first, the angel's criticisms are vague, rendering identification of his targets difficult. Roughly speaking, Rüte first describes two groups as Epicureans and their opposites, virtuous pagans.[127] The comments may generally refer to all who lack morals versus those who are moral, but nevertheless trust in human endeavor. No specific confessional overtones are apparent in these characterizations.

Iconography and Religious Change in Regensburg, 1500–1600 (Ithaca: Cornell University Press, 1990), 26–54.

[125] The angel calls upon Enoch, Noah, Abraham, Isaac, Job, Moses, Joshua, Gideon, Samson, David, Salomon, Elijah, Elisha, Samuel, and Jonas (vv. 238–77).

[126] It is tempting to speculate that Rüte might have assigned his guests of honor the role of elders in his play, so that, for example, Venner Zülli himself could have expressed this judgment.

[127] "Nit jene [. . .] / Wie Epicurus mit sinr Rott / [. . .] Sunders der wysen nammen hand" (vv. 315–22).

In contrast, Rüte's further discussion of the "keys" to the scroll's seals reflects the full confessional spectrum of the Holy Roman Empire in the mid-sixteenth century and treats theological issues in a detail that exceeds even *Abgötterei*'s treatment of idolatry. The second angel continues with a thinly veiled description of the Catholic cult:

> Denn ist vff Erd ein grosser huff
> Die mit vil Ceremonien [. . .]
> Vber das heilig Buoch wend kon [. . .]
> Vnd vnder denen ist ein Fürst [. . .]
> Der gibt sich vß/jm syg erloubt/
> Das er diß Buoch mög wol vffthuo
> Die schlüssel hab er selbs darzuo/
> Fürt die im Sigel vnd im Fan
> Wil drumb den namen/Heilig/han/
> Dann er vff Erd halt Gottes statt.
> Wäm er verzych/kein sünd mer hat/
> Wän er da bind/syg hoben bunden (vv. 327–44)

> Then there is a large crowd on earth who wish [. . .] to fall upon the Holy Book with many ceremonies. [. . .] Among them is a prince [. . .] who claims authority to open the Book and that he himself has the keys to it, displaying them in his seal and banner. He thus wishes to have the name "Holy," since he is God's vicar on earth. Whomever he forgives has no more sins; whomever he binds, is bound above.

Rüte identifies the pope by the keys of the papal banner, symbols of his power to bind and loose according to Matthew 16. Here they become not only symbols for the forgiveness of sins, but also the capacity to unlock the heavenly scroll. The pope's inability to unseal the scroll points to Protestants' rejection of the papal forgiveness of sins or, in terms of early Reformation debate, his redemption of souls from purgatory through indulgences and masses for the dead. As becomes clear through the subsequent appearance of the Lamb, only Christ possesses the ability to include or exclude sinners from the community of the church.

Had *Osterspiel* been written twenty-five years earlier, Rüte's diatribe might very well have ended here. However, by 1552, the so-called "power of the keys" had become a hotly debated topic in the Bernese church as a metaphor for excommunication.[128] Since his

---

[128] For a history of the term, see G.H. Joyce, "Keys, Power of the," in *The Catholic Encyclopedia* (New York: Robert Appleton, 1910), 8:631–3.

arrival in Geneva in 1536, Calvin had sought the power of the keys as a means of regulating and disciplining his congregation. Bern was loathe to grant the clergy such sweeping authority,[129] and the issue of excommunication became one factor in Calvin's temporary dismissal from Geneva under Bernese pressure. The conflict inevitably flared again following Calvin's return, but was now fought out in Lausanne. As part of the Pays de Vaud, Lausanne was under Bernese lordship, but the director of the Lausanne Academy at the time, Pierre Viret, was an ardent Calvinist. During a disputation at the Lausanne spring synod of 1548, Viret and others debated the power of the keys, and Viret ultimately demanded a similar power for the church in the Pays de Vaud.[130] When Simon Sulzer, dean of the Bernese church and a crypto-Lutheran, supported the Lausanne theses, the council summarily dismissed him and began to suspect that Lutherans and Calvinists had united in opposition to Bern's Zwinglian theology.[131] Calvin brought about a partial reconciliation between himself and the Bernese magistrates through his participation in the anti-Lutheran synod of March 1549, which resulted in the rehabilitation of Viret and the appointment of Théodore de Bèze, Calvin's future successor in Geneva, to the Lausanne Academy. Nevertheless, tensions remained high for several years, exacerbated by further disputes over communion and Calvin's renewed abolishment of weekday religious holidays.[132]

The council's aversion to Lutheran or Calvinist theology stemmed largely from the belief that their deviations from Zwinglian practice often preserved questionable Catholic doctrine. Luther's view of Christ's real presence in the bread and wine of the Eucharist smacked, for Zwingli and his symbolic view of the sacraments, of Catholic transubstantiation. Likewise, Calvin's excommunication of "unbelievers," indeed, all Calvinist efforts to establish a church administration separate from civic authority, appeared redolent of canon law

---

[129] Guggisberg, 215.
[130] C.B. Hundeshagen, *Die Conflikte des Zwinglianismus, Lutherthums und Calvinismus in der Bernischen Landeskirche von 1532–1558* (Bern: C.A. Jenni, 1842), 207 ff.
[131] Guggisberg, 217.
[132] In describing Bern's reaction to the Genevan abolishment of weekday holidays in late 1550, Hundeshagen writes: "In Bern haftete nichts destoweniger das Gefühl erlittener Beleidigung gegen Genf überhaupt und man nahm von jetzt an, abgesehen vom Politischen, für's Erste in manchen kleinlichen Reckereien und Reibungen in Kirchensachen Rache, so oft sich ein Anlaß bot." Hundeshagen, 266.

as a haven for clerical tyranny and corruption. Bernese fears of reviving Catholic practice lay at the heart of the crisis surrounding the Lausanne synod of 1548: When Viret petitioned for greater independence for Vaud clergy, his opponents charged that he wished to introduce a new papacy that would be worse than the old.[133]

Considering the indiscriminate designation of both Lutherans and Calvinists as "papists," it is not surprising that *Osterspiel*'s anti-Catholic polemic segues into a critique of the two rival Protestant camps. Indeed, this assessment must have been so common place in Bern as to render any further identification of Rüte's targets unnecessary. He refers to them only as *vnLuter kunden*:

> Nach jm findt man vnLuter kunden/
> (Man sölts vß Butzen all mit hunden)
> Die disem Fürsten zöugend schmach/
> Vnd folgend doch synr art ouch nach/
> Sagend das Buoch syg jnen kund
> Sy heigind d'Schlüssel in jr mund (vv. 345–50)

> After him (the pope) one finds unsavory characters—one should drive them all out with dogs—who claim to revile this prince, yet follow him in his manners. They say the scroll is known to them and claim to hold the keys in their mouth.

If a reader of the play had any doubt as to the groups in question, certain orthographical clues provided guidance. While the term *vnLuter* literally means "unclean" or "impure," the conspicuously capitalized "L" indicates that Rüte intended the word to be read as "un-Luther," an obvious reference to the Wittenberg reformer. For a listening audience who did not have the text in front of them, an actor could have easily drawn attention to this word play through stilted pronunciation. The passage does not elaborate on how the "unsavory, un-Luther characters" followed the manner of the papacy, but the mere association of Luther and the pope undoubtedly referred to the Lutheran insistence on the real presence of Christ in the Eucharist. Four years after the expulsion of Simon Sulzer, Rüte trumpeted Bern's continued opposition to a non-symbolic interpretation of the sacrament.

---

[133] Ibid., 208; Guggisberg, 217.

Meanwhile, the passage's reference to *Schlüssel* (keys) is a direct attack on Calvinist desires for the power of excommunication and an independent church constitution in the Pays de Vaud.[134] Rüte had already foregrounded the question of the forgiveness of sins in his reference to the papal keys. Similar to his accusations against the pope, Rüte portrayed Calvin's demands for the ability to admit or exclude a purported sinner from communion, and thus the church itself, as the usurpation of a power reserved for Christ alone. At the same time, this allowed him to portray the Bernese council, in their denial of this power to the Pays de Vaud clergy, as the watchful defenders of God's true word.

As the debate over the power of the keys had played no role in the local conflict with Lutheran theology, it is clear that Rüte predominantly addressed Calvinists with his reprimand. Nonetheless, from a Bernese perspective, the two camps often represented one common enemy and were so intertwined that Rüte could not attack one without accosting the other. He thus not only subsumed Calvinists under the rubric *vnLuter*, but also Martin Bucer, whose good reputation in Bern during the 1530s had dissipated following his failure to reconcile the Swiss with Northern Protestants.[135] Eventually, his continuous attempts to formulate an expression of the Eucharist broad enough to accommodate both Lutherans and Zwinglians garnered him a local reputation as adulterator of God's word. After Rüte accused his *vnLuter kunden* of similar adulteration, he suggested that dogs should drive them out of town. The verb, *vß Butzen*, displays the same conspicuous capitalization as the veiled reference to the Wittenberg reformer. In addition to Bucer's collaboration with Luther, he regularly corresponded with Calvin and his associates, even during his final years in England during the Augsburg Interim. In 1549, Viret, knowing how sensitive the Bernese council might react to any theological exchange between Geneva and Bucer, prudently declined the latter's request for a theological critique of his English reforms, noting that Bern might intercept the correspondence, which would

---

[134] See Jaeger, 163 ff.
[135] Johannes Haller sums up Bernese opinion of Bucer around 1550. "Hie gilt er gar nüt. Ich hör ihn oft dermaß zwahen, daß mich selbs dunkt, es gang etwan grob gnug an." Bähler, "Dekan Haller und die Berner Kirche," in *NBT 1925*, 2–3.

not bode well for either party.[136] In a letter of 26 July 1557, Johannes Haller himself warned Bullinger of the Buceran tendencies of Calvin and his followers, and elsewhere he equates Bucer with Sulzer.[137] As Bucer had died on 28 February 1551, Rüte may have unkindly ridiculed the reformer after his recent passing or was at least less reluctant to add his name to Luther's, who had himself passed away in 1546.

Of course, Luther's, Bucer's, and Calvin's disputes with the Bernese church rendered them easy targets; Bern's quarrels with them were common knowledge. Moreover, each name possessed a certain representative function that allowed Rüte proudly to declare Bern's theological independence from Wittenberg, Strasbourg, and Geneva, all prominent centers of Reformation theology. Nevertheless, it comes as a surprise when Rüte suddenly includes Zwingli in this circle of reformers:

> Vil wunder Secten/örden vil/
> Erwachsen denn vß disem Spil/
> Ein yeder will syn meynung bharren/
> Vnd schetzt die andern all für Narren
> Ja Ketzer/syns ist einig guot/
> Da fachtß an kosten/lyb und bluot/
> Würgend einander drob/krag ab/
> Wer stercker syg/den vordrit hab/
> Wän sy nit b'redend mit einfalt/
> Den wend sy denn mit trutz vnd gwalt
> An sich Zwingen mit hilff der welt (vv. 351–61)

> Many wondrous sects and orders arise from this state of affairs. Each one insists on his opinion and considers the others all to be fools or even heretics; only his doctrine is good. The price is soon life and limb; they strangle each other on this account, off with the collar. Whoever is stronger has the advantage. If they cannot convince someone through humility, they want to force him with resistance and violence to join them with the aid of the world.

---

[136] Hundeshagen, 256.

[137] "Du weißt, daß ich unseren Welschen nicht ohne Ursache mißtraue. Sie sind unbeständig und haben mehr als zu viel vom Geiste Bucers eingesogen." As quoted in Bähler, "Dekan Haller und die Berner Kirche," in *NBT 1925*, 21. I have been unable to check Bähler's translation against the original Latin, as the excerpt of Haller's letter in the "Thesaurus Epistolicus Calvinianus" does not contain this passage: See *Ioannis Calvini opera quae supersunt omnia*, Corpus Reformatorum 44 (Braunschweig: C.A. Schwetschke et filius, 1877), 16:548, no. 2670. Bähler incorrectly gives

Like *vnLuter* and *vß Butzen*, *Zwingen*, with its majuscule "Z," invokes the name of a prominent reformer, namely Ulrich Zwingli.[138] More difficult, however, is the explanation of its negative context: The passage bemoans the fragmentation of Protestantism and eagerness of supposedly devout Christians to take up arms over theological hairsplitting. Why would Rüte associate Zwingli, upon whose theology the Bernese church was based, with militant religious intolerance?

In offering a tentative answer, it is necessary to examine Bernese foreign policy, both during the Revolt of Princes against Charles V in 1552 and during the two wars of Kappel earlier in the century. Although Bern had unsuccessfully pleaded for Swiss participation in the Schmalkaldic War—in part because it feared that the emperor, if victorious, would support Savoy demands for the return of the Pays de Vaud, in part because the emperor's siege of Constance might easily spread to the Confederacy—it assumed a neutral position in 1552. As long as events did not directly threaten its interests, Bern was reluctant to come to the aid of northern Protestants who continued to polemicize against the Reformed Church, leading Johannes Haller to complain of the council's "coldbloodedness" towards the "neighbors" in the empire.[139] Moreover, although Bern was customarily eager to weaken the emperor's position, with Henry II's recent occupation of Metz, Toul, and Verdun threatening its western borders, Bern was again dependent on the balance of power between the emperor and the French king and did not wish to alienate the former. While news of the Protestant liberation of Augsburg by Maurice of Saxony reached Bern on 11 April 1552, thirteen days before the performance of *Osterspiel*, the emperor's humiliating flight from Innsbruck did not transpire until a good month later. Thus Rüte's complaints concerning uncompromising violence among various religious factions, seen from the perspective of Bernese neutrality

---

Corpus Reformatorum, vol. 42 as his source and dates the letter to June 1557. The comparison of Sulzer and Bucer can be found in a letter of Haller's to Bullinger from 21 April 1557: *Calvini opera omnia*, Corpus Reformatorum 44, 16:454, no. 2619.

[138] While one could argue that "Z" does not occur in medial position and would thus be more subject to the whims of sixteenth-century German orthography, a close examination of *Osterspiel* reveals that no other verb is capitalized throughout the entire play, with the exception of "zThuon," which occurs at the beginning of a line: "Wend ouch allzyt mit embsigkeyt / zThuon eüwern willen syn bereyt" (vv. 5–6).

[139] Bähler, "Dekan Haller und die Berner Kirche," in *NBT 1926*, 53–4.

during the uprising of the German princes, likely referred to the renewed and still unresolved struggle for political supremacy among Protestants and Catholics in the empire.

While Zwingli was long since dead by 1552, in Bernese eyes he had also been guilty of overzealous religious coercion during the First War of Kappel in 1529. Following Zurich's refusal to allow Unterwalden's steward to assume office in the mandated territory of Baden, but before the actual begin of hostilities, Niklaus Manuel had made a last appeal against a religious war before the Zurich council, pleading that "one cannot sow faith with pike and halberd."[140] Nevertheless, Zurich opted for war, which despite initial success eventually led to Protestant defeat, and Zwingli's death, in the Second War of Kappel. There were many in Bern who believed that the new faith would have gained more converts on its own if Zwingli had not relied on force.[141] There is no reason to assume that this opinion, despite all respect for Zwingli as theologian and founder of the Swiss Reformed Church, did not still linger in Bern during the 1550s.[142] Indeed, the critique seems to be predominantly concerned with Zwingli's militantism and does not directly associate him with the specious theology of the *vnLuter kunden*, whose rejection had occurred several lines earlier.

Nonetheless, Rüte would likely not have risked criticism of the Swiss reformer had theological relations between Bern and Zurich been completely harmonious in 1552. In the aftermath of the Lausanne dispute on excommunication, Calvin and Bullinger had suddenly issued the *Consensus Tigurinus* of 1549, a first articulation of common Reformed theology leading to the *Confessio Helvetica posterior* of 1566.

---

[140] "Warlich man mag mit spies vnd halbarten den glouben nit ingeben." Manuel cautioned against war with reference to the territorial designs of the emperor and the Duke of Savoy, the two powers whose claims to Bernese territory made neutrality in 1552 seem equally wise. "Niklaus Manuels Rede vor dem Rat von Zürich, 3. Juni 1529," in *Werke und Briefe*, 766–8, Beigabe 1.

[141] Feller, 2:187. See also the testimony of Anshelm's chronicle: "Und also ward geglowt, dass, wo die von Zürich, so am pflug stift für sich zesehen vermeinten, sich an irer oberkeit kreis hetid lassen benüegen und ir anfengliche gedult und frintlikeit behalten, so doch der grösser und fürnemer teil einer loblichen Eidgnosschaft dem gotswort zuogefallen, dass in kurzem die ganz Eidgnosschaft im gotswort warlich und recht vereint wäre worden. Aber das füre schwert muost sin ampt behalten." Anshelm, 5:375.

[142] Bähler notes that "Volk und Regierung" were united in their rejection of a religious war during the 1530s. Bähler, "Dekan Haller und die Berner Kirche," in *NBT 1926*, 3.

Even the *Consensus* possessed political overtones: in anticipation of a possible alliance of German Protestant princes with the French king against the emperor, Calvin wished to articulate his doctrine of the Eucharist in a form more palatable to Lutherans. After receiving a copy of the confession, Johannes Haller responded to Bullinger that although the Bernese clergy was pleased that Geneva and Zurich had reached an agreement concerning the interpretation of the Eucharist, they dared not sign the confession; the council was opposed to any steps which might appear as a concession to Lutheran theology.[143] There was a tone of disapproval in Haller's letter, and the council let it be known that it considered a declaration of concord unnecessary, as it had no quarrel with Geneva. The confession remained unsigned, despite Calvin's and Bullinger's efforts to address Bernese concerns, which delayed the publication of the *Consensus* until 1551. Nor had the resulting mistrust of the Zurich church improved by 1552, as an incident between mayor Hans Franz Nägeli and Haller demonstrates. Haller supported the candidacy of Michael Schlatter, a former pastor in Biel (Bienne) who hailed from Zurich, for the open position of assistant at the former St. Vincent cathedral. Nägeli, however, suspected that Schlatter might oppose his policies and vehemently rejected Haller's suggestion:

> Die Zürcherpredikanten sind unrüwig, schribend viel hin und wieder, steckend sich in all Sachen. Und was gand uns die von Zürich an? Wir sind als wohl als sie. Machend sie, was sie wellend und lassend uns auch machen, was uns gut dunke![144]

> The preachers of Zurich are restless, write letters back and forth, and stick their noses in all matters. Why should we be concerned with the Zurichers? We're just as good as they are. They should do what they want and let us do what we think right!

Given Nägeli's presence in the audience as the guest of honor, he would have likely had few objections to the play's criticism of Zwingli's militant "restlessness." Indeed, *Osterspiel* on the whole extravagantly endorses Nägeli's religious policies on the occasion of his re-election as mayor and de facto leader of the Bernese church.

Rüte's act of homage was to have little lasting influence on the councilors in its audience, however, nor on their opposition to Calvin.

---

[143] Bähler, "Dekan Haller und die Berner Kirche," in *NBT 1925*, 10–8.
[144] As quoted in Bähler, "Dekan Haller und die Berner Kirche," in *NBT 1924*, 61.

The French reformer won the power of excommunication in 1555, following Genevan elections which brought his supporters to office.[145] Moreover, when its own religious authority was not threatened, the Bernese council was less reluctant to grant Calvin authority over life and limb. In 1553, it gave Calvin its blessings as he pursued the execution of the Antitrinitarian Michael Servetus, who was burned at the stake in Geneva on 27 October 1553 for his heretical views.[146] The lesson of religious tolerance drawn by Manuel during the wars of Kappel seems to have lived on only in Nikolaus Zurkinden, Bern's general commissioner of the Pays de Vaud. Zurkinden, whose erudition and theological interests led him to translate the Bernese Catechism into French and pursue an active correspondence with Calvin, admonished the Genevan reformer in words not unlike those of Manuel before the Zurich council twenty-four years earlier: "I am concerned, frankly, that the sword and the stake are not the most certain means to combat intellectual opposition and to preserve the reputation of established dogmas."[147]

---

[145] Ozment, 367.

[146] See Alister C. McGrath, *A Life of John Calvin: A Study in the Shaping of Western Culture* (Oxford: Basil Blackwell, 1990), 119–20.

[147] "Ich besorge, offen gestanden, daß Schwert und Scheiterhaufen nicht das sicherste Mittel sind, die Auflehnung der Geister zu bekämpfen und das Ansehen der aufgestellten Dogmen zu erhalten." As quoted in Guggisberg, 223.

CHAPTER FIVE

PROTESTANT VISUAL CULTURE AND THE STAGE

> The following play is created in such a way that it not only speaks of the lesson in words, but also, when performed, portrays and represents the matter in all actuality before the very eyes of the audience. I merely wish that we took the great grace to heart that the Almighty has demonstrated to us in recent times. For truly, God speaks to us now in many ways, extending to us his holy word not only in sermons, but also in books, in writings, in psalms and religious songs, and in elegant plays, through which the more prominent stories are taken from Holy Scripture, repeated, refreshed, and portrayed as if they were alive before people's eyes, so that we may well say that the wisdom of God shouts and cries in the street.
>
> —Bernese printer Samuel Apiarius, foreword to *Goliath*

Twenty-four years before Bern's Blacksmiths performed Rüte's apocalyptic *Osterspiel*, they had been the city's premiere iconoclasts. On 27 January 1528, upon the conclusion of the Bernese Disputation, the town council ordered the removal of all religious images within the city. The smiths immediately set to work in St. Vincent's minster, accomplishing in two days a task for which the council had allotted seven.[1] Not all were pleased with the destruction of the minster's twenty-five altars: Hans Zender, a conservative member of the guild, rode into the cathedral on a mule during the destruction, declaring: "Since you're making a stall here, my donkey belongs inside. I wish that the hands of all those involved in this would fall off."[2] His tart tongue cost him twenty guldens and his membership

---

[1] Anshelm, 5:245. See also Franz-Josef Sladeczek, "'Da ligend die altär und götzen im tempel'. Zwingli und der Bildersturm in Bern," in *BGZ*, 588–604.

[2] "So man hie ein rossstall machet, so muss min esel ouch drin. Ich wölte, dass allen, so rat und tat harzu getan, die händ abfielid." Anshelm, 5:245. The council manual for 1528 contains a slightly altered version of this encounter: "Hat Gilgian Tremp gezügt, wie Hans Zender mit dem esell in die kilchen geriten und geluogt, wie man die bilder hinssussgethan [sic], habe zuo dem zügen gesprochen: 'ist es nit ein gots erbermd, das man also husshalt und die bilder zerbricht?' Antwurt der züg: 'es ist gots will'. Zender: 'es ists des düffels will; bist du by got gsin und vernomen, das ess sin will sig? Ich wellt, das allen denen die hend abfielen, so darmit

in the Great Council. After the iconoclasts had completed their task, Zwingli praised their handiwork in a sermon delivered amid the destruction:

> Da ligend die älter und götzen im tempel. [. . .] Es sind gar schwache oder zenggische gemüt, die sich von abthuon der götzen klagend, so sy yetz offentlich sehend, das sy nützid heyligs habend, sonder tetschend und bochßlend wie ein ander holtz und steyn. Hie lyt einer, dem ist's houpt ab, dem andren ein arm, etc. Wenn nun die säligen, die by gott sind, damit verletzt wurdind unnd den gewalt hettind, als wir inen, nit sy selbs, zuogelegt habend, so hette sy nyeman mögen entwegen, ich gschwyg enthoupten oder lemmen.³

> There lie the altars and idols of the temple. [. . .] Those who complain about the removal of idols are weak or quarrelsome types, since they now plainly see that the idols have nothing holy about them, but rather splat and crack like all other wood or stone. Here lies one with its head off, another with its arm gone, and so on. If the blessed souls who are with God were now injured by this and had the power that we—not they—have attributed to them, then no one could have budged them, much less decapitated or lamed them.

Stripped of beauty and function, the city's broken statuary became landfill for construction work on the cemetery platform to the south of the minster. Surviving fragments, often torsos lacking arms and heads as described by Zwingli, were discovered during conservation work in 1986; they vividly illustrate the iconoclasts' ritualistic disfigurement of church images.⁴

There is a seeming contradiction in the Blacksmiths' iconoclasm of 1528 and their support of *Osterspiel*'s vivid religious imagery in 1552. Considering that the Bernese council of 1552 enforced a more doctrinal Zwinglianism than that of 1528, the intervening years did not necessarily bring about a greater tolerance for devotional images.

---

umbgangen und darzuo rhat und that gethan'. Zuber hat ouch gezüget wie Tremp, und siend noch ander mer darby gsin." Steck/Tobler, 1:612–3, no. 1490. See also Carlos M.N. Eire, *War against the Idols: The Reformation of Worship from Erasmus to Calvin* (Cambridge: Cambridge University Press, 1986), 111.

³ "Die beiden Predigten Zwinglis in Bern," in *ZW*, 6,1:497. See also Eire, 111–2; Sladeczek, "Zwingli und der Bildersturm," 599–601.

⁴ Franz-Josef Sladeczek, *Der Berner Skulpturenfund. Die Ergebnisse der kunsthistorischen Auswertung* (Bern: Benteli, 1999); idem, "Der Skulpturenfund der Münsterplattform in Bern (1986). Werkstattfrische Zeugen des Bildersturms der Berner Reformation," in *Les iconoclasmes*, ed. Sergiusz Michalski, vol. 4 of *L'Art et les révolutions* (Strasbourg: Société Alsacienne pour le Développement de l'Histoire de l'Art, 1992), 71–94.

Indeed, given the vibrant visuality of local carnival plays during the 1520s, when Swiss iconoclasts began to engage in the toppling of altars, theatrical iconophilia and theological iconophobia had existed side by side since the first decade of Zwingli's Reformation. While it would be erroneous to suggest that the dramatic tableaux of the late Middle Ages were venerated with the same fervor or in the same manner as saints' images, Catholic audiences nonetheless believed that reenactments of Christ's resurrection, performed as part of the liturgy, possessed similar powers of salvation.[5] The salvific aspects of images as well as those of dramatic performances were rooted, as Robert Scribner has argued, in a "sacramental gaze" that sought to look through physical appearances to the assumed transcendent reality behind them.[6]

As noted in Chapter One, Luther's critique of passion play performances in his *Sermon von der Betrachtung des heyligen leydens Christi* ("Sermon on Contemplating the Holy Passion of Christ") similarly located the plays' epistemics, specious or otherwise, in the act of viewing. To reform the sacramental gaze of playgoers, the Wittenberg reformer encouraged a fundamentally different type of interaction between audiences and the religious imagery of contemporary plays, one that fostered intellectual comprehension as opposed to an emotional response in the viewer. So long as playwrights shunned affect in favor of edification, Luther considered both religious drama and images adiaphorous, or theologically neutral.

Zwingli, however, did not share Luther's views on religious imagery. Given the Zurich reformer's belief that devotional images inherently promoted idolatry,[7] it is striking that he did not censure religious plays in a similar manner, especially when one considers that iconophobia and antitheatricalism often went hand in hand, as is later

---

[5] Bob Scribner, "Das Visuelle in der Volksfrömmigkeit," in *Bilder und Bildersturm im Spätmittelalter und in der frühen Neuzeit*, ed. Bob Scribner, Wolfenbütteler Forschungen 46 (Wiesbaden: Harrassowitz, 1990), 15.

[6] Bob Scribner, "Popular Piety and Modes of Visual Perception in Late-Medieval and Reformation Germany," *The Journal of Religious History* 15 (1988/9): 459.

[7] For Zwingli's views on religious images, see among others Garside, 76–178; Sergiusz Michalski, *The Reformation and the Visual Arts*, Christianity and Society in the Modern World (London/New York: Routledge, 1993), 51–9; Hans-Dietrich Altendorf, "Zwinglis Stellung zum Bild und die Tradition christlicher Bildfeindschaft," in *Bilderstreit. Kulturwandel in Zwinglis Reformation*, ed. Hans-Dietrich Altendorf and Peter Jezler (Zurich: Theologischer Verlag, 1984), 11–8.

evident in Zurich as well as England.[8] While Zwingli made no official pronouncements concerning drama prior to his untimely death in 1531, his comments on religious imagery nonetheless suggest that contemporary theater would have fallen into the one category of visual depictions that met with his approval, namely narrative and/or historical images (*in geschichteswyß*) located outside of church.[9] If a picture aided in the intellectual comprehension of a story or historical event and was clearly not intended for veneration, it was then acceptable. Zwingli, for example, distinguished between an image of Charlemagne in Zurich's Great Minster and a statue of the emperor located high on the city's Charles Tower; the latter did not promote idolatry in the reformer's eyes.[10] Similarly, biblical images in the home, including the portrayal of Christ, were unobjectionable.[11] Zwingli even excepted stained-glass windows from the purging suffered by Zurich's other "idols" on 15 June 1524.[12]

In the following, I argue that Bernese Reformation plays, in their staging, created living narrative images, fostering in their own way a reformed act of viewing as delineated by both Luther and Zwingli. My analysis begins with the most obvious link between drama and devotional art in Reformation Bern, namely Niklaus Manuel's transition from painter to playwright. Afterwards, the reconstruction of

---

[8] The Zurich theologian Breitinger condemned the stage in 1624, and Geneva prohibited all plays in 1617. See Eugen Müller, *Schweizer Theatergeschichte. Ein Beitrag zur Schweizer Kulturgeschichte*, Schriftenreihe des Schauspielhauses Zürich 2 (Zürich: Verlag Oprecht, 1944), 38; Thomas Brunnschweiler, *Johann Jakob Breitingers "Bedencken von Comoedien oder Spielen". Die Theaterfeindlichkeit im Alten Zürich. Edition—Kommentar—Monographie*, Zürcher Germanistische Studien 17 (Bern: Peter Lang, 1989). On England, see Michael O'Connell, *The Idolatrous Eye: Iconoclasm & Theater in Early-Modern England* (New York/Oxford: Oxford University Press, 2000); Clifford Davidson, "The Anti-Visual Prejudice," in *Iconoclasm vs. Art and Drama*, ed. Clifford Davidson and Ann Eljenholm Nichols, Early Drama, Art and Music Monograph Series 11 (Kalamazoo, Michigan: Medieval Institute Publications, 1989), 33–46.

[9] "Wo sy in geschichteswyß ieman hette one anleytung der eerenbietung usserthalb den templen, möchte geduldet werden." "Eine kurze christliche Einleitung," in *ZW*, 2:658. See also Garside, 149–50; Margarete Stirm, *Die Bilderfrage in der Reformation*, Quellen und Forschungen zur Reformationsgeschichte 45 (Gütersloh: Verlagshaus Mohn, 1977), 146.

[10] Garside and Michalski disagree as to whether the image of Charlemagne inside the church was a painting or statue: Garside, 150; Michalski, 56–7.

[11] Michalski, 56; Stirm, 146.

[12] Michalski, 54; Hans Lehmann, "Die Glasmalerei in Bern am Ende des 15. und Anfang des 16. Jahrhunderts," *Anzeiger für Schweizerische Altertumskunde* Neue Folge 17 (1915): 319.

Bernese staging practices—especially for the performances of *Vom Papst und seiner Priesterschaft, Von Papsts und Christi Gegensatz, Abgötterei*, and *Osterspiel*—illustrates Protestant theater's reform of late medieval spectatorship. Through deixis and spatial antithesis, the Bernese stage promoted contemplation, not commiseration, eventually producing in Rüte's plays "vocal depictions of past deeds" similar to those envisioned by Paul Nopus and Georg Major in their comments on Joachim Greff's Easter Play.

Niklaus Manuel: From Painter to Playwright

Following his election to the Small Council on 14 April 1528, Niklaus Manuel played a prominent role in the secularization of monasteries and churches within Bernese territory. Although there is no evidence that he took part in Bern's iconoclastic riots,[13] he oversaw with goldsmith Bernhard Tillmann the confiscation of liturgical objects, which were afterwards melted down at the local mint for their gold and silver.[14] Thus, by the end of the 1520s, the former image maker had become image destroyer. Many studies of Manuel as painter focus particularly on this irony of Reformation art history.[15] However, none considers Manuel's intermediate period as dramatist in its analysis. In the following section, I argue that Manuel's activities as Protestant playwright represent an integral stage in his artistic development, the final step in a long-term textualization of image. In the context of Reformation iconoclasm, Manuel's movement from canvas to stage is paradigmatic for the emergence of Protestant theater as an alternative medium of visual religious instruction.

---

[13] Cf. Hans Christoph von Tavel, "Kunstwerke Niklaus Manuels als Wegbereiter der Reformation," in *Von der Macht der Bilder. Beiträge des C.I.H.A.-Kolloquiums "Kunst und Reformation"*, ed. Ernst Ullmann (Leipzig: E.A. Seelmann, 1983), 223.

[14] See the "Säkularisationsrodel" in *NMD*, 524–5, nos. 377–8.

[15] Bernd Möller, "Niklaus Manuel Deutsch—ein Maler als Bilderstürmer," *Zwingliana* 23 (1996): 83–104; Michalski, 80; von Tavel, "Kunstwerke Niklaus Manuels als Wegbereiter der Reformation," 223–31; Ulrich im Hof, "Niklaus Manuel und die reformatorische Götzenzerstörung," *ZfSAK* 37 (1980): 297–300. There is some disagreement as to whether Manuel spared his own works while cleansing local churches of devotional art. Hugo Wagner thinks not, but Walter Hugelshofer explains the existence of certain altarpieces in Manuel's posthumous collection by assuming that the artist withdrew them following the Reformation and kept them for himself. Wagner, "Niklaus Manuel—Leben und künstlerisches Werk," in *NMD*, 40; Walter Hugelshofer, "Überlegungen zu Niklaus Manuel," in *NMD*, 52.

The year 1522 appears to have been a watershed in Manuel's life. Prior to this date, he was an active painter; afterwards, he became a civil servant, politician, and Protestant polemicist, rising to the position of *Venner* by the end of the decade. To explain this turnabout, several scholars have pointed to Manuel's participation in the tragic military campaign of Bicocca in the spring of 1522. These theorists speculate that the horrors of Swiss defeat triggered a cathartic Protestant conversion in the artist; afterwards, his new faith estranged him from the devotional images he had produced in abundance.[16] Manuel himself is silent on the issue with the exception of one letter, written to the Bernese council from Italy on 2 April. Here, he applies for the city's vacant position of sergeant-at-arms (*Großweibel*), explaining that his trade as painter is no longer able to support him and his family.[17] The cause of Manuel's declining income is uncertain. Some suggest that commissions may have grown sparse due to the encroachment of the Reformation,[18] but this explanation seems premature considering that Protestant theology was just beginning to make itself felt in the city at this time. Lacking further evidence, one must take Manuel at his word and assume that economic factors, not religious, led him to seek a career in civil administration, where his duties left him little time for the fine arts.

Above all, one must exercise caution when asserting that Manuel's sparse artistic output during the 1520s indicates that he radically renounced his earlier profession upon becoming Protestant.[19] The first iconoclastic excesses in Zurich did not take place until September 1523,[20] well after Manuel had taken up the pen to produce the

---

[16] See above all Jean-Paul Tardent, *Niklaus Manuel als Staatsmann*, Archiv des Historischen Vereins des Kantons Bern 51 (Bern: Historischer Verein, 1967), 74 ff. Zinsli questions Tardent's reading of *Der Traum* as an autobiographical work by Manuel: Paul Zinsli, "Der 'Seltsame wunderschöne Traum'—ein Werk Niklaus Manuels?" in *450 Jahre*, 371.

[17] "Ich bin ein junger xell [gesell] und hab vil klÿner kinder und ein frouwen, ob godt will noch lang fruchtbar, die ich mit Eeren gern wedt erziehen; und mÿn handwerch solichs nit wol ertragen mag; sunders dass ich fremden herren dienen muoss, und so ich dienen muss wett ich üch, minen natürlichen herren lieber dienen, denn jeman anders." *Werke und Briefe*, 649, no. III.

[18] Hugo Wagner, "Niklaus Manuel—Leben und künstlerisches Werk," in *NMD*, 37; Beerli, 211–2.

[19] Cf. Hans Christoph von Tavel, *Niklaus Manuel. Zur Kunst eines Eidgenossen der Dürerzeit* (Bern: K.J. Wyss Erben, 1979), 7: "In diesem singulären Schritt Manuels stellt sich die Frage nach dem Sinn künstlerischer Tätigkeit überhaupt."

[20] For a study of Zurich iconoclasm, see Lee Palmer Wandel, *Voracious Idols and*

"Song of Bicocca" and his first two carnival plays. It would be remarkable if the artist had been so theologically clairvoyant as to anticipate the coming demise of devotional imagery and cease his own production in advance. Similarly, Manuel's work on the choir stalls of the Bernese minster, occurring in late 1522, indicates that the Battle of Bicocca in the spring of that year may have shattered his faith in the pope, but not in his profession.[21] Most importantly, Manuel clearly retained ties to the local stained-glass industry throughout the 1520s.[22] Of his seven extant drawings dated after 1522, four are designs for windows; all resulted in completed panes.[23] Even following Manuel's death, the chronicler Valerius Anshelm refers to him as a painter.[24] Considering that artists such as Lucas Cranach the Elder or Hans Holbein the Younger continued to paint following their own Protestant conversions, Manuel's religious disposition can only partially account for his lagging production following 1522. Even in Zwingli's Zurich, artists went on with their work.[25] Given Manuel's combination of satiric wit and artistic talent, he would have been seemingly predestined to create woodcuts for polemic broadsheets such as those by Cranach, Erhard Schoen, and others.[26] Although there was no press in Bern at this time, his woodcut series

---

Violent Hands: Iconoclasm in Reformation Zurich, Strasbourg, and Basel (Cambridge: Cambridge University Press, 1995);—, "Iconoclasts in Zürich," in *Bilder und Bildersturm im Spätmittelalter und in der frühen Neuzeit*, 125–41.

[21] This applies even if Manuel contributed to the stalls in an advisory capacity only. See Cäsar Menz, "Niklaus Manuel und das Chorgestühl im Berner Münster," in *NMD*, 490.

[22] Beerli suggests that he may have even formed new contacts during this period. Beerli, 218.

[23] *NMD*, 453–69; nos. 288, 289, 292, 293, 295, 296, 298, 299. In addition, the Manuel catalogue includes a photograph of a window from the Pulsnitz [sic] palace near Dresden, now missing, which portrays Manuel's coat of arms, monogram, full name, and the date 1525. The photograph is unfortunately insufficient to identify the window as Manuel's work. *NMD*, 480, no. 305.

[24] Anshelm, writing in the 1530s, records Manuel's leadership in suppressing the Oberland riots of 1528 as follows: "Niclausen Manuel, einen jungen, aber wolberedten, tätigen man—malerhantwerks von der Gerberstuben [...]—gon Thun verordnet." Anshelm, 5:303.

[25] *Zürcher Kunst nach der Reformation: Hans Asper und seine Zeit* (Zurich: Kunstmuseum, 1979).

[26] Samuel Scheurer's *Bernisches Mausoleum* (1740–1744) further reports the existence of a non-extant window in Zollikofen near Bern with the portrayal of two priests in wolf's clothing, Manuel's coat of arms, and the comment "Deep down they are ravenous wolves." If this window was Manuel's work, it reveals an attempt on his part to adapt his art to Protestant polemics. [Samuel Scheurer], "Leben und

of the Wise and Foolish Virgins indicates that he had access to printers.[27] If he nonetheless turned to text over image in his support of the Reformation, other factors must have been at work, factors already present in his professional production prior to his adoption of the new faith.

Manuel produced two religious drawings after 1522: Christ's protection of the adulteress in the temple according to John 8 (1527; fig. 22), and the destruction of heathen idols at the command of King Josiah as recorded in 2 Kings 23 (1527; fig. 23). Manuel was apparently the first to portray King Josiah in Protestant art,[28] but he may have drawn inspiration from local clergy, who had already referred to Josiah's rediscovery of the Book of Law in their 1525 petition for the right to marry.[29] The depiction of Christ and the adulteress was, however, one of the most popular motifs among artists of the Reformation.[30] For this latter window design, Manuel could have drawn from either Cranach or Holbein. Two works do not constitute a program, of course, but these stained-glass window designs (*Scheibenrisse*) nonetheless demonstrate that Manuel was aware of the new directions of Protestant art and sought to give pictorial expres-

---

Wichtige Verrichtungen Niclaus Manuels.... Das V. Stück," in *Bernisches Mausoleum oder Vorderst GOTT Zur Ehr/Lob/und Danck: demnach Berühmten/und sonderlich um die Kirchen GOttes in diesem Land Hochverdienten Männeren zu ruhmlichem angedencken Aufgerichtetes Ehren-Maal . . .* (Bern: Joh. Bondeli seel. Wittib, 1743), 231. See also Lehmann, "Die Glasmalerei in Bern am Ende des 15. und Anfang des 16. Jahrhunderts," 138–9. Stained glass windows seem to have been a popular polemical outlet for confessional artists in Switzerland. See also Johann Rudolf Rahn, "Konfessionell-Polemisches auf Glasgemälden," *Zwingliana* 2 (1903): 355–61; Paul Boesch, "Eine antipapistische Zeichnung von 1607," *Zwingliana* 9 (1952): 486–9.

[27] *NMD*, 404–9, nos. 241–50.

[28] Von Tavel states that Manuel's drawing is unique; nevertheless, Josiah appeared in later Dutch engravings. Von Tavel, "Commentary on 'König Josia läßt die Götzen zerstören,'" *NMD*, 462. Cf. *Luther und die Folgen für die Kunst*, ed. Werner Hofmann (Munich: Prestel-Verlag, 1983), 148–9, nos. 21–3.

[29] "Es ist der gewaltig küng Josias hoch in der gschrift gerümpt, der nachdem Helchias der priester das buoch des gsatzis, das ist das buoch der tröwung, so lang verloren war, widerum fandt, nach inhalt desselbigen handlet. Nit minders lobs, sunder meres ü.g. ist, welche in diserm handel, nach dem das heilig evangelium, das ist das buoch des trosts und heils, lang zytt mit menschen lerungen verduncklet, widerumb an den hellen lichten tag ist komen, darnach handlent, hinweg ze thont alle menschen leren und allein anzehangen dem claren gotteswort, ouch alles das dem zewider ergernuss bringende usszerütten und hinweg ze thuont." Steck/Tobler, 1:203, no. 629.

[30] Carl C. Christensen, *Art and the Reformation in Germany* (Athens: Ohio University Press, 1979), 130.

sion to reform theology. A comparison with his earlier Catholic works thus promises insight into Manuel's altered artistic ideals.

The window designs indicate that Manuel's Reformation imagery, like most Protestant art, now required the mediation of text. *King Josiah Orders the Idols Destroyed* and *Christ and the Adulteress* distinguish themselves from Manuel's earlier works in their prominent inclusion of Scripture. The works' biblical references—one paraphrase, one quote—are written in a hand other than Manuel's,[31] but the artist himself planned for their addition by providing large plaques in the drawings' framing architecture, a position most often reserved for battle scenes in Manuel's earlier window designs. This places him among Protestant peers who integrated the written word in their works to guard against any possible ambiguity in their depiction of divine matters.[32]

Moreover, the drawings' lengthy inscriptions were not Manuel's first attempt to clarify his imagery by abandoning a strict illusionism. As Hans Christoph von Tavel has demonstrated, Manuel's art became increasingly sign-like during the latter half of his career.[33] In composition, individual figures grew detached from the perspectival portrayal of space, stepping towards the viewer through a strong contrast of foreground and background. The artist's device, a Swiss dagger, participated in this development, allowing for an accurate dating of Manuel's works.[34] Initially inscribed upon stones or otherwise integrated into an overall spatial composition (*The Flute Player*, fig. 24), the dagger originally subordinated itself to the artist's efforts to portray a scene illusionistically. Beginning in 1515, it sprouts a decorative ribbon, accentuating its ornamentive, non-realistic character. At the same time, the device emerges from its surroundings, taking on a life of its own. It is no longer a mere signature, but self-consciously involves the artist in the work's creation of meaning.

---

[31] The designs' captions read as follows: "Josia der küng zuo Jerusalem dett das dem herren wol gfiel, det ab die altar der abgötter verbrannt sy zerstört die höchinen veget vß alle Warsager, vnnd Zeichen dütter Billder vnnd götzen, mitt für, vnd druog den Staub in den Bach Kidron, am andren Buoch der künig am XXIII Cap"; "Wer under üch an sund ist, der werff den Ersten Stein vff sy [...] Johani amm viij Cap." *NMD*, 458, 461.

[32] Werner Hofmann, "Die Geburt der Moderne aus dem Geist der Religion," in *Luther und die Folgen für die Kunst*, 30 ff.

[33] Von Tavel, *Niklaus Manuel*, 27–8.

[34] Max Grütter, "Der Dolch als Datum, zur Datierung der Werke Niclaus Manuels," *Der kleine Bund* (15) 15 April 1949.

For example, in Manuel's drawing of a stabbed and dying woman, likely Lucretia (fig. 25), the dagger represents an instrument of death, but also, on some level, the artist's participation in that death.[35] However, following Manuel's adoption of Protestantism, the device loses all polysemy. As seen in one of the artist's final two drawings, the German *Landsknecht* of 1529 (fig. 26), the dagger is merely a cipher, lacking all spatial or interpretive relationship to the work. Von Tavel summarizes this progression as follows: "Manuel's artistic development can be generally characterized by the following catchwords: from perception to legibility, from perspective to sign, from image to word."[36]

Manuel's incorporation of language in his works parallels this trend towards clarity of statement. His earliest textual additions are of a cryptic nature; they complement an image, but require clarification themselves. The drawing *Girl with Impaled Heart* (ca. 1510) provides an especially vivid example (fig. 27).[37] Several inscrutable groups of letters appear in the banner above the girl: SNE, NRG, NISM, GGVG, NKAW, SASD, HDNM and GWS[P]. Rather than explicate the image, the abbreviations themselves beg interpretation. Even when two of these encrypted maxims appear in their complete form elsewhere—*Gott geb uns Glück* (GGVG; May God grant us good fortune) and *Niemann kann als wüssen* (NKAW; No one can know everything)—their meaning is still not readily apparent.[38] Only through their appearance in countless depictions of the piercing inconstancy of love, represented by the impaled heart in the drawing of the girl, does it become apparent that the sayings pertain to the uncertain outcome of amorous affairs. No one can know this outcome; only God can assure a fortuitous end. Even complete phrases, such as *Ich han begert, des bin ich gwert und hof, das es beser werd* (I have desired; it has been granted to me. I hope that it grows better) in the draw-

---

[35] Joseph Leo Koerner, *The Moment of Self-Portraiture in German Renaissance Art* (Chicago/London: University of Chicago Press, 1993), 143–5. Von Tavel suggests that Manuel may have been inspired to create the drawing by an affair: *NMD*, 369, no. 198.

[36] "Die künstlerische Entwicklung Manuels läßt sich verallgemeinernd mit den folgenden Schlagwörtern charakterisieren: Von der Anschauung zur Lesbarkeit, vom Raum zum Zeichen, vom Bild zum Wort." Von Tavel, *Niklaus Manuel*, 28.

[37] *NMD*, 316–7, no. 152.

[38] See "Studie zu einer 'Törichten Jungfrau'" and "Der Hahnrei," *NMD*, 331, 334–5, nos. 167, 172.

ing *Half-Portrait of a Girl* (fig. 28),[39] require their own elucidation and offer no immediate clarification of an image. Indeed, beyond the acronyms GGVG and NKAW, scholars have been unable to decipher the remaining abbreviations.[40]

These cryptic messages appear predominantly in Manuel's private drawings and sketches, suggesting that they were a type of personal code with significance for the artist alone. It has, in fact, been argued that the "nobody" of *Niemann kann als wüssen* is the artist himself.[41] Nonetheless, unintelligible inscriptions appear in commissioned pieces as well, such as on the sarcophagus of the fragmentary window design *Two Grave Watchers* (fig. 29),[42] across the horse's bridle of *The Martyrdom of St. Ursula* (figs. 30–31),[43] and upon the work table and columns of *St. Eligius in His Workshop*, an outer panel of Manuel's St. Anne altar (figs. 32–34).[44] It is unclear whether these inscriptions bore any significance for the works' commissioners.

Beginning around 1517, this textual obscurity gives way to a straightforward treatment, encompassing a direct labeling of individual figures and, in Manuel's murals, an explicit interpretation of the accompanying image. The naming of figures occurs as early as ca. 1513 in *Pyramus and Thisbe*,[45] but becomes common in the period surrounding Manuel's work on the *Dance of Death* mural in the courtyard of Bern's Dominican monastery. His model book (*Schreibbüchlein*, ca. 1517),[46] the so-called *Schauspielfiguren*,[47] and other individual drawings display allegorical, mythological, and quotidian figures by name or profession: Venus, Juno, Pallas Athena, Italia, Fransa, Hispanien, *Gerechtigkeit* (Justice), Rosendorn, *Richter* (Judge), *Töchterli* (Daughter), *Bettler* (Beggar), Lucretia Romana (figs. 35–36). The figures of *The Judgment of Paris* are similarly labeled, but display additional cognomina that provide the painting's underlying moral (fig. 37). Paris

---

[39] *NMD*, 312–3, no. 148.
[40] See the commentaries on "Edelmann und Fräulein im Gespräch," "Mädchen mit aufgespiesstem Herzen" and "Der verweigerte Liebesantrag" by von Tavel in *NMD*, 313–4, 316–8, nos. 149, 152–3.
[41] Koerner, 418–21.
[42] *NMD*, 344–5, no. 179.
[43] Ibid., 217–8, no. 65.
[44] Ibid., 223–5, nos. 69, 71.
[45] Ibid., 216–7, no. 64.
[46] Ibid., 349–66, nos. 184–95.
[47] Ibid., 372–77, nos. 202–11.

is *der Torecht* (the foolish one) and Juno, in the original inscription uncovered by radiograph, is *ein Götin der Uberwindung inn. Strits* (a goddess of overcoming inner [?] dispute).[48] Similarly, the inscription accompanying *Solomon's Idolatry* (1518; fig. 38) leaves no doubt as to the misogynistic overtones of the mural: "Oh Solomon, what are you doing here, the wisest man ever born of woman? If a woman has made a fool of you, then she shall surely do so of me."[49]

Last, but certainly not least, the verses accompanying the *Dance of Death* note the failings of each individual whom Death claims (figs. 39-40). That Manuel's use of text burgeons around 1517 lends credence to Paul Zinsli's suggestion that Manuel became attracted to the possibilities of the written word during his work on this mural.[50] At the same time, the artist may have experienced a dissatisfaction with the ambiguity of visual images, which led to the inscriptions in *The Judgment of Paris* and *Solomon's Idolatry*.[51] Nonetheless, as the above examples show, Manuel began experimenting with language prior to 1517. Indeed, if he himself composed the verses on the reverse of his drawing *Soldier Become a Beggar* (ca. 1514-15), this would be the earliest instance of textual explication of one of his drawings.[52] The coupling of text and image in the *Dance of Death* did not initiate his pre-occupation with language, then, but altered its use from cryptic to instructive.

Most importantly, Manuel apparently encountered the written or perhaps spoken word in another medium at this time. Evidence exists to suggest that he began to occupy himself with the stage around 1518. The above-mentioned *Schauspielfiguren* (ca. 1519-20), a series of thirteen figures including Justice, a judge, and two devils, seem to

---

[48] Ibid., 233-6, no. 80. For more recent discoveries through infrared analysis of Manuel's works, see Emil E. Bosshard, "Fortschritt in der naturwissenschaftlichen Gemäldeuntersuchung. Die Erforschung der Unterzeichnung mit dem Infrarot-Fernsehgerät," *ZfSAK* 39 (1982): 76-80.

[49] "O SALOMON W/AS DUOST DU HIE/DER WYSEST SO/VFF ERDEN IE/VON FROWEN/LIB WARD GEB/OREN. MACHT DICH EIN WYP ZV EIN/NEM TOREN SO/SOL MICH OVCH." *NMD*, 293-8, nos. 132-5.

[50] Zinsli, "Niklaus Manuel, der Schriftsteller," in *NMD*, 78.

[51] Hans Christoph von Tavel, "Niklaus Manuel Deutsch als Maler und Zeichner," in *450 Jahre*, 321.

[52] *NMD*, 338-40, no. 175. Though the writing is not Manuel's, he may have composed the text. See Paul Zinsli, "Zu den Versen auf der Rückseite der Zeichnung Niklaus Manuels vom 'Krieger, der zum Bettler wird,'" *ZfSAK* 37 (1980): 260-3.

be designs for woodcuts intended for a play edition (fig. 36).[53] In these drawings, a Swiss mercenary and a burgher by the name of Rosendorn both appear to offer money to Justice and the judge, so that von Tavel has suggested bribery as a possible topic for such a play.[54] In addition, Hans Koegler has attributed to Manuel a series of woodcuts from the press of Adam Petri in Basel; these could have originally illustrated a carnival play.[55] However, with the obvious exception of the drawing accompanying *Der Ablaßkrämer*, the most probable example of Manuel's artistic interest in the stage is the mural *Solomon's Idolatry* of 1518, originally located on the east exterior wall of Anton Noll's house in the northwest corner of Bern's minster square.[56] Destroyed in 1758, it is preserved in a watercolor copy of 1735 by Johann Victor Manuel (fig. 38). The biblical account of Solomon's submission to his wives' idolatry unfolds in the work's foreground, while a host of contemporary Swiss figures populates a raised platform that strikingly resembles a stage. A crowned woman, possibly Dame Venus,[57] leans lasciviously against the leg of a Swiss mercenary in the center. To the right, two elders eye prostitutes, while a man slumbers guilelessly in the lap of a seemingly coquettish woman on the left. The fool points down to Solomon, linking the failings of the couples above to Solomon's transgression below. Although the elaborate Renaissance columns and arch are likely a typical border ornament, the platform, theatrical gestures, and presence of cuckolded men and dominating women suggest that the mural imitates the performance of a carnival play along the lines of Pamphilus Gengenbach's *Gouchmatt*.[58]

Given the inherent relation of theater to Protestant visual culture, Manuel's activities as playwright constitute not an abandonment of the pictorial arts, but rather their application to a related medium. This transition appears to have occurred in two steps. The first is

---

[53] *NMD*, 372–7, nos. 202–11.
[54] Von Tavel, "Folge von Figuren zu einem Schauspiel," in *NMD*, 373.
[55] Hans Koegler, "Die Holzschnitte des Niklaus Manuel Deutsch," *Jahresbericht der öffentlichen Kunstsammlung Basel 1924*, Neue Folge 21 (1925): 55. Von Tavel doubts that all figures were designed by Manuel, but attributes to him the most theatrical ones, in which devils interact with burghers and judges: Hans Christoph von Tavel, "Die Stände der Menschen und Schauspielfiguren," in *NMD*, 412–3.
[56] Cäsar Menz, "Salomons Götzendienst," in *NMD*, 293–6.
[57] Ibid., 294.
[58] Ibid., 294–6.

found in Manuel's artistic products of the years 1517–1520, during which he began to adopt a sign-like legibility at the expense of Renaissance illusionism. Not that Manuel, in 1517, foresaw the reform of religious imagery under the new faith, but his adoption of a more readable compositional style nonetheless anticipated the Protestant eschewal of polysemous images. The increasing presence of text, in particular in his murals, also characterizes his work of this period. His apparent contact with theater, beginning ca. 1518 and reflected in the *Schauspielfiguren* and *Solomon's Idolatry*, forms the second half of this development. After 1520, his increasing pre-occupation with language and drama, as well as the apparent necessity to find additional sources of income, led to his neglect of painting. Upon his acquaintance with Cranach's *Passional Christi und Antichristi* sometime after its publication in 1521, his transition had progressed to the point that, rather than imitate Cranach pictorially, he chose to present the *Passional*'s images as a living play, resulting in 1523 in *Von Papsts und Christi Gegensatz*.

Protestant Theater as Visual Medium

Even if it does not portray an actual stage, *Solomon's Idolatry* suggests how a carnival performance might have incorporated contemporary iconic symbols. Visual cues connect several figures to the mural's overall theme of female sexual power.[59] The flute behind the couple on the lower left points to the sexual nature of their relationship and underscores the mural's admonishing inscription that the sign-bearer will soon follow in Solomon's footsteps. The owl, borne by the woman in the center, denotes her magical powers,[60] while her connection to the mercenary suggests that he, too, will suffer Solomon's fate. In both cases, these symbols could easily appear as props on the carnival stage; indeed, it is unlikely that the playwright Manuel would have done without the symbolism that the painter Manuel employed so liberally. Clothing, such as the prostitutes' feathered hats and daggers, identifies other figures. Most important, however, is the overall bipartite composition of the mural. The fool in the

---

[59] For the following, see Menz, 294; cf. von Tavel, "Kunstwerke Niklaus Manuels als Wegbereiter der Reformation," 229.
[60] Beerli, 70.

upper left, in his traditional role as moralizer,[61] functions as the juncture between the lower, biblical level of the painting and the upper section, whose figures belong to the present.[62] Assuming a deictic role, the fool literally points to Solomon's weakness and its typological significance. Gesture and the antithetical division of space guide the viewer through the mural's otherwise unstructured visual cues.

The proximity of painter and playwright was not at all unusual during this period. Wilhelm Creizenach was among the first to note that many painters, qualified through their experience in iconography, directed local plays or otherwise helped create a play's scenic design.[63] Following upon Creizenach's research, Leopold Schmidt in 1958 produced a list of "painter-directors" (*Maler-Regisseure*) from France, Germany, and the Netherlands.[64] Many of Schmidt's artists were actors or designers of scenery, but several actually directed local plays, such as Wilhelm Rollinger of Vienna, Painter Narziß of Bozen, and both Sebald Bockstorfer and Paul Dax of Innsbruck.[65] In Switzerland, the Zurich playwright Jos Murer was also a glass painter by profession, and his Schaffhausen colleague Hieronymus Lang directed a performance of "Daniel in the Lions' Den" and assisted Sebastian Grübel with the translation of Rudolf Gwalther's *Nabal*.[66] In 1522, Michael Schwarz, most likely a student of Albrecht Dürer, directed an anti-papal carnival play in Danzig, which portrayed Martin Luther's struggle against Rome until his disappearance following the Diet of Worms.[67] Lastly, the Sterzing painter-playwright Vigil Raber was perhaps Manuel's closest Catholic counterpart.

---

[61] See Heinz Wyss, *Der Narr im schweizerischen Drama des 16. Jahrhunderts*, Sprache und Dichtung, Neue Folge 4 (Bern: Paul Haupt, 1959), 86 ff.

[62] G.F. Rettig, "Über ein Wandgemälde von Niklaus Manuel und seine Krankheit der Messe. Ein Beitrag zur Reformationsgeschichte der Schweiz," in *Programm der Berner Kantonschule 1862* (Bern: C. Rätzer, 1862), 15.

[63] "Die Maler (wurden) sehr oft als Regisseure und sachkundige Berater bei den Aufführungen zugezogen [...], daß sie also in ihren Schöpfungen nicht bloß die szenischen Bilder wiederholten, sondern auch bei der Hervorbringung dieser Bilder selbstschöpferisch beteiligt waren; auch mag es vorgekommen sein, daß auf diese Art manche ikonographische Einzelheiten, die durch geistliche Vermittlung den Malern schon geläufig waren, sich auch auf der Bühne einbürgerten." Wilhelm Creizenach, *Geschichte des neueren Dramas* (Halle: Niemeyer, 1893), 1:219.

[64] Leopold Schmidt, "Maler-Regisseure des Mittelalters: Bildende Künstler des Mittelalters und der Renaissance als Mitgestalter des Schauspielwesens ihrer Zeit in West- und Mitteleuropa," *Maske und Kothurn* 4 (1958): 55–87.

[65] Ibid., 65–7, 68, 72–6.

[66] Müller, 55, 58–9.

[67] Schmidt, 76–7; Creizenach, 3:164.

As indicated by numerous illustrations preserved in early dramatic texts from Switzerland, the Swiss stage seems to have been especially linked to contemporary visual culture, leading theater historians Max Hermann and Eugen Müller to deem Switzerland the "earliest and most important soil for illustrations of German drama."[68] Several plays by the Basel author Pamphilus Gengenbach contain detailed woodcuts that portray their respective plots. Of these, Ambrosius Holbein's woodcuts for *Nollhart* as well as the anonymous cuts for *Die Zehn Alter* depict the plays' original stage; the detail of the latter illustrations most likely extends to actual props and costumes.[69] Zurich is also well-represented. Hans Asper illustrated the 1539 performance of Jacob Rueff's *Von des Herrn Weingarten*, in which he himself played a table servant and the printer Christoph Froschauer a German mercenary.[70] Gerold Edlibach, stepson of the ill-fated Zurich mayor Hans Waldmann, offers perhaps the most striking document of early Switzerland's visual reception of the stage. Known especially for his chronicle of the Zurich Reformation,[71] Edlibach as a young man also recorded his impressions of two local plays, a *Zehn Alter* work of 1484 and a carnival play by an otherwise unknown Brunner von Zofingen.[72] His drawings are simple, but nonetheless faithfully reproduce the plays' characters and their locations during a performance. The sketches indicate that, for Edlibach, the plays' image, not their dialogue, left a lasting impression on his mind.

The connection between the visual arts and theater was thus already well-established when the Reformation began to adapt the stage to its own ends. As seen in Chapter One, the conception of theater as a visual medium was widespread among Protestant reformers. In addition to his comments on viewing plays in the *Sermon von der Betrachtung des heyligen leydens Christi*, Luther regularly referred to plays as paintings (*Gemälde*), pictures (*Bild*) or even, in an oblique ref-

---

[68] "Der ursprünglichste und wichtigste Boden für die deutsche Dramenillustration." Max Herrmann, *Forschungen zur deutschen Theatergeschichte des Mittelalters und der Renaissance* (Berlin: Weidmannsche Buchhandlung, 1914), 412; Müller, 370.
[69] Müller even postulates that Gengenbach himself might have created the *Zehn Alter* illustrations. Müller, 27, 43.
[70] Ibid., 53–5.
[71] Peter Jezler, ed., "'Da beschachend vil grosser endrungen.' Gerold Edlibachs Aufzeichnungen über die Zürcher Reformation 1520–1526," in *Bilderstreit. Kulturwandel in Zwinglis Reformation*, 41–74.
[72] Müller, 25–6; Herrmann, 412–9.

erence to Cicero's conception of drama as *speculum vitae*, as a mirror.[73] In other recommendations for placing Scripture *vor Augen* (before the eyes) on stage, playwrights such as Sixtus Birck and Melchior Neukirch could point to the endorsements of classical authorities like Horace,[74] whose *Ars poetica* is cited by playwright Thomas Naogeorgus in his introduction to *Iudas Iscariotes* (1538):

> Si Theologiae officium est docere pietatem verumque Dei cultum, et vitam Deo placentem bonaque opera tradere, atque è regione reprehendere impietatem, falsosque cultus vitamque pravam, haec omnia quoque nostris insunt Tragoediis, et efficacius quodammodo docentur. Nam, Segnius irritant animos demissa per aurem. Quam quae sunt oculis subiecta fidelibus. Ut Flaccus ait.[75]

> If it is the duty of theology to teach piety and the true worship of God and to advocate a lifestyle that pleases God and works that are good, and consequently to rebuke impiety, incorrect worship of God and depraved behavior, all of these things are also in our tragedies, and in a certain way they are taught there more effectively; for, as Horace said, "things heard incite the mind much less than those things our trusting eyes see."[76]

In the preface to *Ein Geistliches schönes newes spil*, Joachim Greff similarly emphasized the superiority of plays' visual instruction:

> [...] weil jhr zu guter mas
> Heute seit vnderrichtet das
> Wie die histori ist geschen
> So sold ihrs nu auch itzund sehn
> Leiblich fur ewern augen hir
> Ein ding welches do sehen wir
> Pflegt vns tieffer ins hertz zu ghen
> Vnd darumb werden auch nur allein

---

[73] Hugo Holstein, *Die Reformation im Spiegelbilde der dramatischen Literatur des sechzehnten Jahrhunderts* (Halle: Verein für Reformationsgeschichte, 1886), 19, 20.

[74] James A. Parente, Jr., *Religious Drama and the Humanist Tradition: Christian Theater in Germany and in the Netherlands 1500–1680*, Studies in the History of Christian Thought 39 (Leiden: E.J. Brill, 1987), 69, note 30.

[75] Thomas Naogeorg, "Iudas Iscariotes," in *Sämtliche Werke*, 4,1:272. Horace's original passage reads as follows: "Aut agitur res in scaenis aut acta refertur. / segnius irritant animos demissa per aurem, / quam quae sunt oculis subiecta fidelibus et quae / ipse sibi tradit spectator [...]." "Ars Poetica," in *Q. Horati Flacci Opera*, ed. Edward Wickham and H.W. Garrod (Oxford: Clarendon Press, 1975), vv. 179–82.

[76] As translated by David Price, *The Political Dramaturgy of Nicodemus Frischlin*, University of North Carolina Studies in Germanic Languages and Literatures 111 (Chapel Hill: University of North Carolina Press, 1990), 19.

> Solche Historien agirt
> Was wir sehen besser moniert
> Dann was wir nie gesehen han
> Wie wol der glaub mus forn an stan.[77]

> Because you are today well instructed as to how the story took place, you should now see it physically before your very eyes. A thing we see tends to penetrate our heart more deeply, and this is the reason such stories are performed. What we see leaves a more lasting impression with us than that which we have never seen, although faith must always come first.

Even English opponents of theater such as Philip Stubbes might paraphrase Horace in excepting some plays as edifying.[78]

If the first generation of German and even Swiss Protestants embraced plays as visual representations of the divine, it was because they did not encourage veneration, but were content to recount biblical events in a straightforward manner. In this regard, they resembled *Merkbilder*, simple, schematic images that portrayed a biblical event or basic doctrine.[79] Cranach's *Law and Gospel* motif (1530; fig. 41) is considered the period's quintessential *Merkbild*.[80] In the image's two halves, Cranach contrasts the ultimately unfulfillable Law of the Old Testament with the redemptive theology of the New. Based upon the numerous sixteenth-century representations of this theme, Joseph Leo Koerner has demonstrated how Cranach and other Reformation artists employed antithesis as a type of exegetical corset, safeguarding against an image's veneration by restricting the inter-

---

[77] Greff, *Osterspiel*, B1ᵛ.

[78] "For such is our gross and dull nature, that what thing we see opposite before our eyes, do pierce further, and print deeper in our hearts and minds than that thing which is heard only with the ears." As cited in Margot Heinemann, *Puritanism and Theatre: Thomas Middleton and Opposition Drama under the Early Stuarts* (Cambridge: Cambridge University Press, 1980), 29.

[79] Luther defined *Merkbilder* as *grob* (coarse) and *anschaulich* (vivid, concrete): "Darum muß man einfältigen Menschen die göttlichen Tatsachen in recht groben und anschaulichen Bildern nahe bringen; recht anschaulich, damit sie es begreifen und verstehen; recht grob, damit sie auch merken, daß es nur ein Gleichnis ist." As quoted in Stirm, 91. Elsewhere Luther emphasizes their narrative element: "Aber die andern Bilder, da man allein sich drinne ersihet vergangener Geschicht und Sachen halben als in einem Spiegel, Das sind Spiegel Bilde, die verwerffen wir nicht, denn es sind nicht Bilder des Aberglaubens, [...] man setzet kein vertrawen drauff, sondern es sind Merkbilde." WA 28:677.

[80] "The most characteristic and complete expression of Lutheran theology in sixteenth-century art." Christensen, 124.

pretive freedom of the viewer.[81] Similarly, Kristin Zapalac has examined Protestants' eschewal of illusionistic images as transcendent conduits to a divine reality, tracing how Protestant painters distanced themselves from the technique of perspective and its assumed expression of the unity of physical and divine laws.[82] It is here that Scribner speaks of a "theological gaze," which, as an intellectual act designed to remind the viewer of a doctrine, contrasted with the affective sacramental gaze of late medieval piety.[83]

Protestant playwrights took an active interest in such *Merkbilder*, as demonstrated by Magdeburg playwright Valten Voith's direct adaptation of Cranach's *Law and Gospel* imagery to the stage in *Ein schön Lieblich Spiel von dem herlichen vrsprung* ("A Fair and Pleasant Play on the Glorious Origin"; 1538). Most importantly, however, they believed plays to be inherently superior to mere images, whose lifelessness did not allow them to capture human actions. After originally encountering a *Law and Gospel* panel in the Magdeburg town hall, for example, Voith wished to "embellish and clarify" (*ausstreichen und vorkleren*) the painting through the addition of the spoken word (*das Eusserliche wort*).[84] Only by enacting biblical images, Voith claims, do such images enter the heart of the viewer. Joachim Greff makes a similar argument in the preface to *Ein Geistliches schönes newes spil*. If the performance of plays were simply a matter of viewing, sculptures could take the place of actors; rather, one must contemplate the deeds of the play's protagonists and draw moral conclusions from them:

> Darumb wirds nicht gespilt allein
> Dan jhr nur söllet hier zu sehen
> Holtz vnd steine künnens aus wol
> Der mensch sichs aber bessern sol
> Auff das wenn das spil ist gar aus

---

[81] Koerner, 363–410.

[82] Kristin Eldyss Sorensen Zapalac, *"In His Image and Likeness": Political Iconography and Religious Change in Regensburg, 1500–1600* (Ithaca: Cornell University Press, 1990), 1–25; Zapalac, "'Item Perspective ist ein lateinsch Wort, bedeut ein Durchsehung': A Reformation Re-Vision of the Relationship between Idea and Image," in *Meaning in the Visual Arts: Views from the Outside. A Centennial Commemoration of Erwin Panofsky (1892–1968)*, ed. Irving Lang (Princeton: Center for Advanced Study, 1995), 131–49.

[83] Scribner, "Popular Piety," 464.

[84] Glenn Ehrstine, "Seeing is Believing: Valten Voith's *Ein schön Lieblich Spiel von dem herlichen vrsprung* (1538), Protestant 'Law and Gospel' Panels, and German Reformation Dramaturgy," *Daphnis* 27 (1998): 503–37.

> Das darnach yder was zu haus
> Künne mit sich heim tragen fein
> Und behaltn durchs gantz leben sein (Biij^r–Biij^v)

> The play is not performed only that you might look upon it. Wood and stone could do that, too. Rather, it should serve to better people, so that, when the play is over, everyone can take something home with them and retain it for the rest of their lives.

This same attitude extended to Bern, where Rüte contrasted inanimate images with living beings in *Abgötterei*'s critique of the veneration of saints. Although Theodorus Gottlieb makes no direct reference to religious plays in his debate with the papists Martius Stichfinster (Martius Pitch Black) and Jeronymus Seltenlär (Jerome Strange Doctrine), his comments nonetheless have applications for Protestant theater:

> Wolan/ich wil achten/man eére bilder nüt
> Sye allein anzöyg/wie dheylgen vnd göt warint lüt
> So muoß ich dennocht üwers götzenwerchs lachen
> Wie könd man jnen glycher bildnuß machen
> Dann säch einer den nechsten by jhm an
> Da gsicht er/wie sy hand gstalten khan
> Din nechster lept/wie sy hand glept
> Mit lyb vnd seel/er sich bewegt vnd strept
> So stadt stein vnd holtz/allweg an eym ort
> Sy vernämet/vnd gend dir nit ein wort
> Zuo frombkeit vnd guotthät/dies hand erzeigt
> Jst der mensch mee dann stein vnd holtz gneigt
> Jn Summa/so müßt jr lassen gschächen
> Das man jr nathur baß mag sächen
> Am läbendigen menschen dann ein stock. (vv. 2233–47)

> Very well, then, I'll assume that images are not venerated; they only indicate that the saints and gods were at one time people themselves. Nonetheless, I still must laugh at your idolatrous folly. How could one make an accurate image of them? For if you look at your neighbor, then you will see how they appeared. Your neighbor lives as they lived; he moves and strives with body and soul. Stone and wood are inanimate, they neither hear nor respond. People tend more than wood or stone to the piety and good deeds that the saints worked. In short, you must admit that one can see their nature better in a living person than in a piece of wood.

For all three playwrights, the issue seems to have been one of verisimilitude: to best represent the actions of exemplary Christians, they must be reenacted in time and space. Only in this manner can one capture the psychological dimension of their trials and moral dilemmas, from which audience members might then extrapolate to themselves. Just as solafideism emphasized one's inner disposition in the attainment of salvation, Protestant plays encouraged their audience to observe the inner faith of biblical characters faced with hardship and temptation.[85]

All above factors—the professional links between painters and playwrights, the evident visual reception of theater in Switzerland, and the Protestant emphasis on viewing actions over static images—allowed Manuel's and Rüte's plays to function, *mutatis mutandis*, like Reformation broadsheets or *Merkbilder*. On the most conspicuous level, the similarities between Bernese theater and Protestant visual culture lie in a shared iconography, such as the contrasting images of the pope and Christ in Manuel's *Von Papsts und Christi Gegensatz*, or the apocalyptic imagery of *Abgötterei* and *Osterspiel*.[86] At a deeper level, however, the plays were staged in accordance with the reformed visual culture of the new faith. Like much Reformation art,[87] the effectiveness of Bernese theater derived from the juxtaposition of antithetical tableaux,[88] contrasting either Catholics and Protestants, as

---

[85] Paul Böckmann, *Formgeschichte der deutschen Dichtung* (Hamburg: Hoffmann und Campe, 1949), 298.

[86] Unfortunately, the examination of iconographic similarities between drama and art often degenerates to an ultimately circular discussion of primacy and influence between the two media, as witnessed by the seemingly endless debate surrounding Emile Mâle's turn-of-the-century thesis that medieval painters modeled their depictions of Christ's crucifixion on contemporary passion play performances. Emile Mâle, *L'art religieux de la fin du moyen âge en France* (Paris: Librairie Armand Colin, 1908). Translated as Emile Mâle, *Religious Art in France—The Late Middle Ages: A Study of Medieval Iconography and Its Sources*, trans. Marthiel Mathews, Bollingen Series XC 3 (Princeton: Princeton University Press, 1986). For an assessment of the debate surrounding Mâle's theses, see Alois M. Nagler, *The Medieval Religious Stage: Shapes and Phantoms* (New Haven: Yale University Press, 1976), 89–105.

[87] Peter-Klaus Schuster, "Abstraktion, Agitation und Einfühlung. Formen protestantischer Kunst im 16. Jahrhundert," in *Luther und die Folgen für die Kunst*, 117–21.

[88] See Klaus Aichele, *Das Antichristdrama des Mittelalters, der Reformation und Gegenreformation* (Den Haag: Martinus Nijhoff, 1974), 58; Stefan Schmidlin, *"Frumm byderb lüt." Ästhetische Form und politische Perspektive im Schweizer Schauspiel der Reformationszeit*, Europäische Hochschulschriften I, 747 (Bern: Peter Lang, 1983), 131. On the general use of juxtaposition on the early stage, see Pamela Sheingorn, "The Visual Language of Drama: Principles of Composition," in *Contexts for Early English Drama*, ed. Marianne G. Briscoe and John C. Coldewey (Bloomington: Indiana University Press, 1989), 184.

found in the carnival plays, or Jews and Gentiles, such as in Rüte's *Goliath*. Similarly, the plays united exegesis and image through a variety of deictic figures who literally pointed to a particular scene while explicating its significance for the audience. These figures might be integrated into a play's larger plot, such as Peter and Paul in *Vom Papst und seiner Priesterschaft*, or may simply observe the action in order to comment on it later, such as Rüte's heralds or the two *Landman* of *Gedeon*. Through them, the playwrights invited the audience to read the stage much as they would have read a contemporary broadsheet or illustrated bible.[89]

Theater as Broadsheet

Broadsheets, also known as broadsides or *Flugschriften*, were one of Protestantism's most effective weapons in the Reformation's war of propaganda. Cheap and easily circulated, the standard broadsheet united a woodcut or series of woodcuts with a text of varying length. Beginning with the collaboration between Andreas Karlstadt and Lucas Cranach the Elder on the *Fuhrwagen* of 1519,[90] well-known authors and artists often joined forces to produce biting antipapal polemic. Partnerships existed between Hans Sachs and Hans Sebald Beham or also between Cranach and Philipp Melanchthon, creators of the *Passional Christi und Antichristi*, Manuel's inspiration for *Von Papsts und Christi Gegensatz*. Despite the medium's acknowledged role in disseminating Protestant doctrine, however, its less-than-decorous imagery often led earlier scholars to shy away from giving it serious scrutiny. Only in the last quarter-century have researchers begun to examine broadsheets as a mass medium whose rhetoric, while at times coarse, was anything but common.[91]

---

[89] For a study of how medieval audiences might "read" the stage, see Meg Twycross, "Beyond the Picture Theory: Image and Activity in Medieval Drama," *Word and Image* 4 (1988): 589–617.

[90] Peter-Klaus Schuster, "'Fuhrwagen' des Andreas Karlstadt," in *Luther und die Folgen für die Kunst*, 191–2, no. 65.

[91] Hans-Joachim Köhler, ed., *Flugschriften als Massenmedium der Reformationszeit: Beiträge zum Tübinger Symposion 1980*, Spätmittelalter und Frühe Neuzeit 13 (Stuttgart: Klett-Cotta, 1981); Robert Scribner, *For the Sake of Simple Folk. Popular Propaganda for the German Reformation*, Cambridge Studies in Oral and Literate Culture 2 (Cambridge: Cambridge University Press, 1981); Hofmann, ed., *Luther und die Folgen für die Kunst*.

Like broadsheets, theater was capable of reaching a large audience. What it lacked in portability, it made up for in spectacle. While news of an especially effective performance might circulate locally by word of mouth, the text could also appear in print and reach a larger audience, as demonstrated by the numerous editions of Manuel's plays. In terms of audience potential, Reformation theater was thus a close cousin of the *Flugschrift*.[92] However, the parallels between stage and broadsheet did not end there. All three carnival plays considered in this section—*Vom Papst und seiner Priesterschaft*, *Von Papsts und Christi Gegensatz*, and Rüte's *Abgötterei*—drew upon biblical imagery to vivify their anti-papal polemic. Just as text and image stood in a complex reciprocal relationship to one another in broadsides, a speaker's dialogue often referred to a specific tableau on stage, so that a play's visuals reemphasized the Protestant lessons of the text. In the words of Bernese chronicler Valerius Anshelm, the combination of spoken exegesis and image in Manuel's plays resulted in *wunderliche anschowungen* (wondrous sights) that were among the Reformation's most effective propaganda.[93]

In the absence of pictorial records or detailed descriptions, it is of course impossible to reconstruct Manuel's or Rüte's stage as it actually appeared on Cross Lane, the location of the 1523 plays and the likely venue for Rüte's dramas. However, stage directions do exist, and additional textual clues allow for a general reconstruction of the plays' mansion staging, in which all actors and scenes were visible at once. As indicated by such evidence, each play physically revolved around a central biblical figure or figures. By observing these characters' actions on stage, even when they were silent, the audience determined the proper response to a particular scene. In Manuel's works, these central characters are Christ and the apostles Peter and Paul. In Rüte's carnival play, however, the guiding figure is Frouw Wirrwärr as the Babylonian Harlot, who possessed decidedly negative associations. In each play, these characters are assigned

---

A second, more recent edition of Scribner's study was published in 1994 by Clarendon Press.

[92] Peter Ukena, "Flugschriften und verwandte Medien im Kommunikationsprozeß zwischen Reformation und Frühaufklärung," in *Flugschriften als Massenmedium der Reformationszeit*, 163–9; Robert W. Scribner, "Flugblatt und Analphabetentum. Wie kam der gemeine Mann zu reformatorischen Ideen?" in *Flugschriften als Massenmedium der Reformationszeit*, 73.

[93] Anshelm, 4:475. See also Chapter Three's epigraph.

a specific location on the stage; other figures take on positive or negative connotations in accordance with their proximity to this space.

In *Vom Papst und seiner Priesterschaft*, Manuel's first play of 1523, the characters Peter and Paul do not speak until verse 1466, nearly three-quarters through the work. Nonetheless, as the play's initial stage direction makes apparent, they have been active on stage since the opening scene. No directions exist in the original Hamburg manuscript, but the formulation of stage directions from the 1524 editio princeps in the past tense indicates that the author inserted them prior to publication to illustrate the plays' actual performance:[94]

> DEs ersten truog man ein todten in einem boum/in gestalt in zuouergraben/vnd saß der pabst da in großem geprächt mit allem hoffgesindt/pfaffen vnnd kriegslüten hoch und nider stands. Vnd stuond aber Petrus vnd Paulus wyt hindenn/sahendt zuo mit vil verwunderens/auch waren da edel leyen/betler vnnd ander. Vnnd aber es giengend zwen leytman nach der bar/die klagten den todten/vnd do die bar für die pfeffisch rott ward nider gestelt/do fingent die leytlüt an ir klag deß ersten also.[95]

> At first, a corpse in a coffin was carried in as if for burial. The pope sat there in great splendor with his courtiers, priests, and mercenaries of high and low rank. Peter and Paul stood at the far back and looked on with great amazement. Noblemen, laymen, beggars, and others were there as well. Two mourners went to the bier and lamented over the deceased. When the coffin was laid down before the priestly mob, the mourners began their plaint as follows.

---

[94] See Manuel's stage directions in "Fasnachtsspiel" before v. 1, v. 753, v. 864, v. 1026, v. 1388, v. 1486, v. 1834. The Hamburg manuscript introduces speakers with present verbs: "De Caplon Spricht"; "Die Nonn Clagt sich"; "Der Edelman Fart inher"; "Der Schryber Spricht"; "Petrus Antwurt Paulo"; "Paulus antwurtet Petro"; "Der Cardinal spricht": "Fasnachtsspiel, Variantenapparat II: Integraler Abdruck der Hamburger Handschrift," in *Werke und Briefe*, before v. 275, v. 419, v. 571, v. 717, v. 958, v. 980, v. 1042. There is thus a consistent distinction between the present tense of the Hamburg manuscript directions and the past tense of the 1524 Zurich imprint. As others have noted, the preterite stage directions of sixteenth-century play imprints can only be descriptions of past performances of the text: Otto Koischwitz, *Der Theaterherold im deutschen Schauspiel des Mittelalters und der Reformationszeit. Ein Beitrag zur deutschen Theatergeschichte*, Germanische Studien 46 (1926; Nendeln: Kraus, 1967), 56–7; Kleinschmidt, 196, note 421. Ferdinand Vetter and Arnold Berger similarly assume that the stage directions of the 1524 Zurich imprint correspond to the 1523 performances: Vetter, ed., *Die Totenfresser*, 3; Niklaus Manuel, "Ein Fastnachtspiel vom Papst und seiner Priesterschaft," in *Die Schaubühne im Dienste der Reformation I*, ed. Arnold E. Berger, Deutsche Literatur in Entwicklungsreihen, Reihe Reformation 5 (Leipzig: Reclam, 1935), 100.

[95] "Fasnachtsspiel," in *Werke und Briefe*, before v. 1.

Peter and Paul are the only figures assigned a specific location on the stage: *wyt hindenn* (at the far back). This location nonetheless remains somewhat vague, so that scholars disagree as to the apostles' exact position. Barbara Könneker suggests that they stood off stage among the audience,[96] but they would not have been widely visible here. Ferdinand Vetter, apparently construing the words *auch waren da* to refer specifically to *wyt hindenn*, places with Peter and Paul all characters who do not appear in the opening scene.[97] While the peasant figures and Doctor Lüpolt Schüchnit no doubt stood separately from the church hierarchy, it is unlikely that they mingled with the apostles; even after the peasants have spoken, Peter and Paul are still *hinden* (behind; before v. 1466). Thus Emil Ermatinger's assessment is likely more accurate, placing Peter and Paul alone at the far back of the stage, from which they could overlook and comment on the action before them.[98] Manuel, moreover, expends inordinate energy to ensure that the audience could readily identify the apostles. Other figures are identified aloud once at most, either through their own words or those of the following speaker,[99] but the courtier who informs Peter about the pope addresses the apostle by name a total of eight times.[100] If one considers the courtier's reference to *Sant Peters erbteil* (v. 1507) to be a direct address, then the courtier mentions Peter's name at least once every time he speaks. The repeated reference to Rome's first bishop invests these figures with special authority.

Thus identified, the apostles embodied Scripture not only when they spoke, but in all their actions on stage. From their privileged space, they could frown, gesticulate, and otherwise demonstrate the incompatibility of the Bible with papal decrees. Manuel specifically describes one such theatrical reaction, Peter's examination of the pope with eyeglasses once the apostles move upstage:

> Demnach so kam sant Peter vnd Paulus hinden herfür/vnd fand ein cortisanen/by dem stuond Petrus lang/vnd sahe den bapst an mit

---

[96] Könneker, *Satire im 16. Jahrhundert*, 173.
[97] Vetter, ed., *Die Totenfresser*, 3.
[98] Ermatinger, 155; Müller also postulates a three-tiered stage with the rear section reserved for the apostles: Müller, 48.
[99] For example: "Wir Bischoff hand ein guote sach" or "Her apt der thüffel ist im spil." "Fastnachtsspiel," v. 123, v. 379.
[100] "Das Fasnachtsspiel," v. 1472, v. 1514, v. 1530, v. 1552, v. 1575, v. 1578, v. 1610. See also Schmidlin, 139.

ougspieglen/vnd sunst/vnnd kund in nit verwundern wer der were der so mit grossem volck/richtum vnd bracht vff der menschen achßlen getragen ward. (before v. 1466)

Afterwards, St. Peter and St. Paul came out from behind and approached a courtier. Peter stood next to him for a long time and regarded the pope with spectacles and such. He did not cease to be amazed as to who this man might be, who was borne in such a manner on people's shoulders, with a great retinue, great wealth, and pomp.

The similar description of the opening scene, *sahendt zuo mit vil verwunderens* (looked on with much amazement), indicates that both apostles had been acting in a like manner throughout the performance. Earlier references to Peter and Paul likely provided the opportunity for other figures to direct their comments to the apostles' section of stage and have them respond through gesture.[101] The clerics refer only to Paul, as if unable to recall the original bishop of Rome; Peter is first mentioned by one of the papal guards. In all instances, however, the deeds and words of the apostles, as biblical representatives, contrast with the practices of the pope. As the apostles and papists are accorded their own areas on stage, the resulting antithesis between Christian humility and papal pomp assumes physical dimensions. Ermatinger directly equates this division of space with the heaven and hell of the medieval *Simultanbühne* (simultaneous stage, i.e. mansion staging),[102] but the absence of devils and of an overtly eschatological context suggests that the contrast was more between biblical and non-biblical zones, similar to the horizontal division of space in Manuel's *Solomon's Idolatry*. This contrastive use of space continues in *Abgötterei* and in Rüte's biblical plays.

The play's other figures function as points in a continuum between these biblical and anti-biblical poles. Pfrunder has noted that the characters of the play can be divided into three groups: papists, papal victims, and Protestants with Peter and Paul, with the play moving

---

[101] "Paulus thuot vns liden wee / Mitt sin tieff gegrünten episteln"; "Das ist ein selig mensch gesin / Der dich hat bracht zuo solchem stat / Den Petrus nie gesinnet hat"; "Was gat unß den Cristus an / Vnd Petrus mit dem glatzetten grind." "Fasnachtsspiel," vv. 282–3, vv. 772–4, vv. 861–2. See also v. 282, v. 319, v. 517, v. 1061, v. 1328. The Hamburg manuscript provides additional examples: "Wie wol sy och sind Paulus wort verkunder / so sind sy doch als offen sunder." "Fasnachtsspiel: Hamburger Handschrift," vv. 153–4.

[102] Ermatinger, 155.

from the former to the latter.[103] However, a further division among papists and victims is necessary. Before the introduction of Doctor Lüpolt and the peasants, Manuel's revue can be divided into three segments: 1) members of the ecclesiastical hierarchy, 2) non-clergy affiliated with the church in some regard, and 3) papal mercenaries. Within each of these groups, the figures progress from supporters of the pope to those who suffer under him. Within the church hierarchy, the further removed from the pope, the more wretched an individual is.[104] Beginning with the pastor and his concubine, the clerics' situation worsens until it reaches the misery of the monk and nun. Whereas the upper ecclesiastical ranks lament the spread of Protestant teachings, lower clergy, such as the monk, bemoan the condition of the church itself. In some instances the suffering of the lower ranks stems from the Protestant refusal to donate alms and provide tithes, but overall their lot illustrates the underlying corruption of the church. Subsequently, other victims appear who, while not direct members of the church hierarchy, are thought to benefit from their association with Rome. Again, the portrayal moves from those who are more satisfied with their lot, such as the beguine and the lay brother (*Nollbruder*), to the impoverished nobleman whose forebears squandered their estate as benefactors of the church. Lastly, the Swiss Guard appears. Here, rather than a gradual movement, there is an abrupt break between the mercenaries, who profit enormously through their service for the pope, and the Knight of Rhodes. In all three groups, increased distance from the pope renders an individual more receptive to, and worthier of, the Gospel. Furthest removed, and closest to the appearance of Peter and Paul, are Doctor Lüpolt and the peasants. Bridging both camps, and thus the turning point of the progression as a whole, is the knight.[105]

The tension between the play's antithetical poles is realized in its staging. According to a character's sympathies, either Protestant or

---

[103] Pfrunder, 191–2. See also Schmidlin, who notes Manuel's additions to Gengenbach: Schmidlin, 133 ff.

[104] Steven E. Ozment, *The Reformation in the Cities: The Appeal of Protestantism to Sixteenth-Century Germany and Switzerland* (New Haven: Yale University Press, 1975), 114. Pfrunder sees a similar movement from papists to papal victims: Pfrunder, 191–2.

[105] Though Vetter does not speak of a progression per se, he also views the knight's appearance as the center of the play. Vetter, "Über die zwei angeblich 1522 aufgeführten Fastnachtspiele Niklaus Manuels," 93. Cf. Schmidlin, 131 ff.

Catholic, he or she stood nearer to the biblical or papal section of the stage.[106] The knight faces the pope as long as he hopes for assistance; after failing to secure aid, he moves away before announcing that the Roman bishop is in reality the Antichrist (before v. 1026). Judging from the proximity of the peasants and Dr. Lüpolt Schüchnit to Peter and Paul in the text, it is likely that they stood in association with the biblical pole of the apostles. Whether the lower members of the church hierarchy also stood closer to the apostles than the pope is unclear, but even if this were not the case, the reactions of Peter and Paul to their appearance on stage would have indicated to the audience the compatibility of their views with Scripture.

Following Peter's and Paul's dialogue, the final scenes reprise the contradistinction of the play's two camps. The first comparison had advanced slowly from the pope to Peter and Paul; the second now occurs in the immediate juxtaposition of papal troops with the lone figure of Doctor Lüpolt Schüchnit. The discrepancy between the pope's legions and the humble prayer of the doctor again reveals the incompatibility of the two religions. Moreover, the sudden emptiness of the stage following the papists' departure effectively demonstrates the immediate relationship between Christ and the believer in Protestant theology. With no intermediaries, Schüchnit appeals directly to the savior in his plea for proper guidance, encouraging the audience to enter into a similarly direct relationship with God.

One week after the performance of *Vom Papst und seiner Priesterschaft*, Rome and the Bible again stood in opposition to each other on the streets of Bern. *Von Papsts und Christi Gegensatz* reduces their contrast to a strict binarism by eliminating all extraneous elements. Peter and Paul are replaced by Christ himself, so that the audience might directly compare the Savior and his self-proclaimed vicar side by side. In 1521, the same unmediated juxtaposition of a humble, peace-loving Christ and an allegedly vain, war-mongering pope had made the *Passional Christi und Antichristi* one of the Reformation's most suc-

---

[106] Both Michael and Edmund Stadler suggest that Manuel could have identified the papal section of the stage as Rome. Stadler even postulates a section identified as Bern for the peasants and pastors. Wolfgang F. Michael, *Frühformen der deutschen Bühne*, Schriften der Gesellschaft für Theatergeschichte 62 (Berlin: Selbstverlag der Gesellschaft für Theatergeschichte, 1963), 90; Edmund Stadler, "Mit Hohn und Spott gegen den Papst und seine Getreuen," *Der kleine Bund. Beilage für Literatur und Kunst* 138, no. 49, 28 February 1987: 1–2.

cessful pamphlets (fig. 10). Manuel most likely drew directly on the *Passional* for his second play,[107] yet the motif had become quite popular by 1523, so that he may have had secondary sources.[108] An anonymous Swiss drawing of the period (fig. 42), now housed in the university library at Erlangen, was considered Manuel's own illustration of the play until Lucie Stumm and Max Herrmann independently demonstrated some eighty-five years ago that the work neither belonged to Manuel's oeuvre nor actually illustrated the play.[109] However, many of Herrmann's objections to the Erlangen drawing, for example that its Christ has no crown of thorns as in Manuel's play,[110] apply to Cranach's work as well, so that a comparison of Cranach's imagery and that of the play is at best inconclusive. As before, an analysis of the play itself for clues as to its staging is more revealing.

The 1524 editio princeps again introduces new descriptions of the play that are absent in the earlier Hamburg manuscript.[111] The first occurs on the title page itself:

> Ein fasnacht schimpff/so zuo Bern vff der alten fasnacht gebrucht ist/im xxij. iare. Namlich wie vff einer siten der gassen der einig heiland der welt Jesus Christ/vnser lieber herr ist vff einem armen eßlin geritten/vff sinem houpt die dörnin kron/by im sine iünger/die armen blinden/lamen vnd mancher ley bresthafftig. Vff der andern siten reit

---

[107] Zinsli, "Niklaus Manuel, der Schriftsteller," 82.

[108] See Pfrunder, 196, and especially Beerli, 207, note 1. On the numerous imitators of Cranach, see Scribner, *For the Sake of Simple Folk*, 157.

[109] *NMD*, 504–5, no. 337. Lucie Stumm, "Deutsch, Niklaus Manuel," in *Allgemeines Lexikon der bildenden Künstler*, ed. Ulrich Thieme and Felix Becker (Leipzig: E.A. Seemann, 1913), 9:177; Herrmann, 446 ff.; Paul Zinsli, "Des Papstes und Christi Gegensatz," in *NMD*, 504–5. The thoroughness of Herrmann's comparison between play and drawing is unfortunately offset by his speculative dating and interpretation of Manuel's dramas. See Zinsli's critique of Herrmann's attempted reconstruction of the "original" *Ablaßkrämer*: Zinsli, foreword to *Der Ablaßkrämer*, 16 ff.

[110] Herrmann, 446.

[111] Unlike *Vom Papst und seiner Priesterschaft*, the version of *Von Papsts und Christi Gegensatz* in the Hamburg manuscript contains a fragmentary stage direction: "Fasnachtsspiel: Hamburger Handschrift," vv. 1212–8. The only finite verb, *erbidmet*, could be both present tense or a preterite form with loss of final -e through apocope. The text however continues with "Do sprach Cläwy Stromäyer." Though all other speeches are introduced with present tense (*antwurt*, *spricht*, and *redt*), it would appear that the manuscript contained at least one description of the action in the past tense. It is possible that Manuel had already inserted this description before the scribe copied the play, after which he or the scribe introduced Cläwy Stromäyer's next lines with *sprach*.

der bapst im harnisch/vnnd mit großem kriegszüg/als hernach verstanden wirt durch die sprüch so die zwen buren geret hand/Rüde fogelnest vnd Cleywe pfluog.[112]

A carnival amusement, performed on Old Carnival (22 February) in the 22nd year. Namely, how on one side of the lane the only savior of the world, Jesus Christ our dear lord, rode on a poor donkey, the crown of thorns on his head, with him his disciples, the poor blind, lame and other sickly souls. On the other side rode the pope in armor and with a great war arsenal, as can hereafter be understood through the speeches spoken by two peasants, Rudi Bird's Nest and Clyde Plow.

This passage confirms the play's simple, yet powerful antithetical imagery. As in *Vom Papst und seiner Priesterschaft*, biblical characters are assigned their own distinct, privileged space. No mingling occurs with the papists across the street. It is unclear, however, how the processions moved; as Herrmann has pointed out, they cannot have approached each other as in the Erlangen drawing, as there would have been no place for Rüde Fogelnest (Rudi Bird's Nest) and Cleywe Pfluog (Clyde Plow), the two peasant commentators, to stand.[113] His solution, that the peasants stood in the middle as both processions passed on either side, would seem possible in light of the above quote. However, a second description of the pope's entourage corrects this assumption slightly:

Hie zwischen kam der bapst geritten in großem tryumpf im harnisch mit grossem kriegß züg zuo roß vnd fuoß mit großen panern vnd fenlinen/von allerley nationen lüt. Sin Eidtgnossen Gwardi all in siner farb/trummeten/pausunen/trummen/pfyffen/karthonen/schlangen/huoren vnd buoben/vnd was zuom krieg gehört/richlich/hochprachtlich/als ob er der türckisch keiser wer (before v. 63)

Meanwhile, the pope came armored, riding in great triumph with a great military procession on horse and on foot with huge banners and little flags from all nations, his Swiss guard all in his color, horns,

---

[112] "Ein fasnacht schimpff," in *Werke und Briefe*, 181. The Zinsli/Hengartner edition unfortunately does not distinguish between *Vom Papst und seiner Priesterschaft* and *Von Papsts und Christi Gegensatz* in its titles, combining both under the heading "Fasnachtsspiel" while numbering the plays' verses separately. I thus refer to *Von Papsts und Christi Gegensatz* in the Zinsli/Hengartner edition as "Ein fasnacht schimpff," the title under which it appears in the 1524 Zurich imprint. The quote incorrectly gives 1522 as the date of the play's performance. See Vetter, "Über die zwei angeblich 1522 aufgeführten Fastnachtsspiele Niklaus Manuels," 82.

[113] Herrmann, 446–7.

trumpets, drums, pipes, light and heavy artillery, whores and their suitors and everything that belongs to war, rich, pompous, as if he were the Turkish sultan.

Hie zwischen ("meanwhile") indicates that the papal procession did not pass simultaneously, but rather somewhat after Christ's retinue.[114] Either the first train had completely passed on the other side of the street before the pope and his followers appeared, or the second group tarried just long enough for Rudi and Clyde to complete their comments on the Messiah and then turn their attention to the approaching group.[115] In either scenario, a slight delay was necessary, otherwise the pope, at the head of his procession, would have passed by the two peasants before they had concluded their remarks on the blind and lame followers of Christ.

Furthermore, by introducing lengthy descriptions of the processions to the first edition of 1524, Manuel compensated for a text now sundered from an actual performance.[116] The play's title page, quoted above, alerted the reader to the importance of the peasants' remarks on the papal entourage. In Cleywe Pfluog's case, his comments grow from four lines in the Hamburg manuscript to a total of twenty-six in the first edition:

> Vetter Rüde/vnd wer ist aber der groß keiser
> Der mit im bringt so vil kriegischer pfaffen vnd reyßer
> Mit so großen mechtigen hochen roßen
> So mencherley wilder seltzamer bossen
> So vil multhier mit gold/samet beziert
> Vnd zwen spycher schlüssel im baner fiert
> Das nimpt mich frembd/vnd mechtig wunder
> Werend nit so vil pfaffen dorunder
> So meinte ich doch es werend türcken vnd heyden
> Mit denen seltzamen kappen vnd wilden kleyden
> Der rot/der schwartz/der brun/der plaw
> Vnd etlich gantz schier eßel graw
> Der wyß vnd schwartz in agristen wyß
> Vnd hand darneben ouch großen flyß
> Das ieder ein besondere kappen hab
> Der ein in lougsacks wyß hinden ab

---

[114] Stadler also speaks of "aufeinanderfolgenden gegensätzlichen Gruppen." Stadler, "Mit Hohn und Spott gegen den Papst und seine Getreuen," 2.

[115] Pfrunder, who also assumes a delayed appearance of the pope, suggests that the two processions passed in opposite directions. Pfrunder, 24, 193.

[116] Beerli, 207, note 2.

Der ander wie ein pfannen stil
Der drit groß holtzschuoch tragen wil
Rot hüt/schwartz hüt/vnd die flach/breit
Der drit zwen spitz am huot vff treit
Das sind doch werlich wild faßnacht butzen
Die sich doch so gar seltzamlich mutzen
Wie große rychtumb schint an disen heren
Jch gloub es möcht all fürsten übermeren
Vnd warumb dreit er dry hüpscher guldner kronen
Das sag mir das dir got trüwlichen well lonen (vv. 63–88)[117]

Cousin Rudi, who is the great emperor, who brings with him so many militant clerics and mercenaries with such grand, powerful, tall horses, so many wild, strange antics, so many mules adorned with gold and velvet and who carries two keys in his banner? I find it most strange and amazing. If there weren't so many clergymen among them, I'd think they were Turks and heathens with their odd hats and eccentric clothes. That one blue, this one red, he brown, he blue, and several just plain mule-grey; he white and black like a magpie, and furthermore they all take great pains that each one have a special head covering; one hanging down the back like a sack of ashes, the second like a panhandle, the third wants to wear large wooden shoes; red hats, black hats, and some flat and broad, the third carries two points on his. Those are truly bizarre carnival masqueraders, who dress up so strangely. How much wealth is apparent upon these gentlemen! I believe it exceeds that of all princes. And why does he wear three lovely golden crowns? Tell me, so that God may reward you loyally.

Beerli notes that the printed play is nearly twice as long as the Hamburg manuscript—215 to 126 lines in the Zinsli/Hengartner edition—but these numbers are misleading. The beginning of the play, which makes up 62 lines of the 1524 imprint, is missing in the Hamburg redaction, leaving a ratio of 153 to 119 within the remaining comparable sections of text, discounting stage directions.[118] Twenty-two of these thirty-four added lines in the imprint form the description of the pope's entourage quoted above. Another addition explicates the pope's tiara.[119] Finally, two short supplements elaborate on non-

---

[117] The corresponding speech in the Hamburg manuscript consists of the first two and the last two lines above. See "Fasnachtsspiel: Hamburger Handschrift," vv. 1219–22.

[118] For the Hamburg manuscript, the Zinsli/Hengartner edition assigns line numbers to stage directions, but does not do so for the Zurich imprint.

[119] "Ein fasnacht schimpff," vv. 93–6 (replaces vv. 1227–8 in the Hamburg manuscript).

visual elements, namely indulgences and Christ's sacrifice.[120] Altogether, twenty-four lines are added to recreate the original impression of the pope's train, representing three-quarters of all new material and over ten percent of the play. Although the description of Christ's retinue is lost in the Hamburg manuscript, in the first edition it is nearly identical in length to the amplified portrayal of the pope. Thus Manuel likely lengthened it as well.[121] In the unperformed text, a thorough description of both processions is crucial so that their disparity becomes *ougenschyn*, or visible to the eye (v. 98).

Manuel also adds extra detail to clothing and attributes of wealth, which contrast with Christ's simplicity and humility. Particulars such as the double-peaked miter of a bishop or the flat, red cap of a cardinal identify specific members of the church hierarchy, much as in *Vom Papst und seiner Priesterschaft*. The introduction of the pope in the text occurs as it would have for a spectator: the reader first encounters his insignia, the crossed keys of his banner and the tiara, before learning his actual title several lines later (v. 106). Rüde Fogelnest elaborates upon the tiara, as if its mere mention, as occurs in the Hamburg manuscript, were insufficient. Once the distinction between the two processions has become clear, Rudi and Clyde draw conclusions about the current state of the church. Its wealth and haughtiness, contrasted with Christ's humility, indicate to the peasants that its concern for their salvation is self-serving and hypocritical.

Taking place just a week after *Vom Papst und seiner Priesterschaft*, *Von Papsts und Christi Gegensatz* derives a significant portion of its effectiveness through the reinforcement and adaptation of the earlier piece.[122] Both sets of personnel, especially the pope's retinue, are largely identical, so that the same actors may have appeared in the same roles. Nonetheless, there is an unfortunate tendency to treat Manuel's second play as a mere appendage of the first. I would argue instead

---

[120] Ibid., vv. 117–24 (replaces vv. 1249–50 in the Hamburg manuscript) and vv. 199–200.

[121] As each page in the Hamburg manuscript consists of 22–25 lines, Burg has demonstrated that the missing lines of the manuscript gap between the knight's appearance in the first play and the pope's procession in the second must have been fewer in number than in the later printings. He then uses this to argue that the figures of the vicar, inquisitor, and the captain of the guard did not exist in the original version of *Vom Papst und seiner Priesterschaft*. However, this could equally indicate that the description of Christ's procession in *Von Papsts und Christi Gegensatz* was originally shorter. Cf. Burg, "Dichtungen des Niclaus Manuel," 125 ff.

[122] Pfrunder, 194.

that it culminates the discreditation of the Roman church begun a week earlier. Viewed together, the plays' critics of the papacy progress from apostles to peasants. In *Vom Papst und seiner Priesterschaft*, the weight of biblical authority, represented by Peter and Paul, first tips the scales in favor of Protestantism. By the play's final tableau, however, Lüpolt Schüchnit has assumed the role of papal critic and mediator of the Gospel, giving Rome a vocal opponent on earth. The peasants of *Vom Papst und seiner Priesterschaft* criticize the pope as well, but they act under the aegis of Schüchnit. In *Gegensatz*, however, Rüde Fogelnest and Cleywe Pfluog exercise their own judgment without direction from above. The evidence of their own eyes is sufficient to convict the pope and his followers. Moreover, they are on a par with the audience, inviting them to see the papal procession as they see it. Whereas Peter and Paul had interacted with other characters in the first play, the peasants' function is wholly deictic, merely directing audience attention to the self-apparent signs of Roman corruption.

By giving physical form to Protestant propaganda, *Vom Papst und seiner Priesterschaft* and *Von Papsts und Christi Gegensatz* thus reified theological issues much as Protestant broadsheets did.[123] In both works, stage tableaux distill criticisms of the existing church down to one or more basic images: Peter and Paul looking askance at papal corpse-eaters, or the pope's pomp set against Christ's humble entry into Jerusalem. The plays' dialogue, meanwhile, replaced the textual commentary of a broadsheet. Of course, the interaction between text and image occured in ways unique to theater. The apostles responded to the utterances of Catholic figures through silent gestures, whereas Rüde Fogelnest and Cleywe Pfluog verbally commented upon the silent action they observe before them.

Eight years later, Rüte's *Abgötterei* continued the staging practices of Manuel's plays. Once again, all characters and scenes were present at once. Rüte reserved areas of the stage not only for traditional *loca* such as earth or the underworld as marked by the jaws of hell,[124] but also for places of local notoriety, such as the chapel

---

[123] On the reification of Protestant theology in broadsheets, see Scribner, *For the Sake of Simple Folk*, 242. Conversely, Scribner also notes elements of religious plays in Cranach's *Passional Christi und Antichristi* (p. 155).

[124] "Zuoletst/so württ der find der wellt / Den Bapst/die huoren/jr gold vnd gellt / Mit sampt beyder syd pfaffen inn dhelle grund / Dem Tüfel stossen inn

at Oberbüren. To further ensure that the audience correctly identified the play's three religious camps, the play's herald physically pointed in his introduction to the heathens, Catholics, and Protestants on stage.[125] This suggests that each group had a section of the stage set aside solely for its use, much like Manuel's plays of 1523. As no divine characters appear, it is uncertain whether heaven was depicted. Nonetheless, the text makes evident that the Protestant preacher Theodorus Gottlieb observed events throughout the play even when he himself was not speaking. Like Peter and Paul in *Vom Papst und seiner Priesterschaft*, he likely indicated his disapproval of the play's heathen and Catholic priests through gestures. While the latter advised a series of supplicants, waiting petitioners looked on in anticipation of their own counseling.[126] The distinct areas of the stage aided the audience in identifying the play's numerous characters and their respective affiliations.

Abgötterei also continues the earlier plays' reification of religious issues, but extends it to more abstract theological concepts through the allegorical figure of Frouw Wirrwärr (Dame Confusion). Wirrwärr's attributes are those of the Babylonian Harlot of Revelation 17. Both are dressed in scarlet, both wear costly jewels, and both bear a wine chalice from which men drink (vv. 165–71).[127] References to *die huore* (the whore) occur throughout the text (v. 132, v. 1445, v. 2409,

---

syn schlund." *Abgötterei*, vv. 131–4. See also Stadler, "Einmal Duldung und einmal Verbot des Fasnachttreibens," 1.

[125] "Die zugend diße dry heydischen pfaffen" (v. 113); "An dißen dry Bäpstlern/werdent jr mercken [...]" (v. 121); "Jr werdent ouch von dißen gottlieben vernän [...]" (v. 127).

[126] Several figures have obviously been observing events prior to their first appearance: Dichtli Schnabelräß: "So wil ich gon diße wysen lüt fragen" (v. 579); Lienhart Stolz: "Knecht heinnj/wir wend ouch zuo dißen heeren" (v. 1555); Heiny Khühorn: "Luog aber Etter Nicly märenzan/shouw/shouw / Was gsen ich do für Erwirdig priester" (vv. 1894–5).

[127] Compare the contemporary description of the Babylonian whore in the Zurich Bible of 1531: "Vnd es kam einer vonn den siben englen [...] redt mit mir/vnnd sprach zuo mir: Kumm/ich wil dir zeygen das vrteil der grossen huoren/die da auff vil wassern sitzt/mit welcher gehuoret habend die künig auff erden/vnnd truncken worden sind vonn dem weyn jrer huorey/die da wonend auff erden. Vnd er bracht mich im geyst in die wüste: Vnd ich sach das weyb sitzen auff einem rosenfarben thier/das was voll nammen der lesterung/vnd hatt zehen hörner/vnnd das weyb was bekleydet mit scharlachen vnd rosenfarb/vnnd übergült mit gold vnd edlen steynen/und pärlin/vnnd hatt ein guldinen kelch in der hand/voll grüwels vnd vnsauberkeyt jrer huorey." *Die Zürcher Bibel von 1531*, facsimile edition (Zurich: Theologischer Verlag, 1983), CCCXIX^v.

v. 2667, v. 2679, v. 2681), and she is specifically mentioned as riding a seven-headed beast (v. 2657, v. 2681). Three exemplars of the play contain a woodcut illustration of Revelation 17 by Hans Holbein the Younger (fig. 15), originally created for the 1523 edition of *Das gantz New Testament* published by Thomas Wolff in Basel.[128]

An ink drawing by the author (fig. 16), possibly created while preparing the play's manuscript for publication, further suggests how Frouw Wirrwärr appeared on stage. Given the widespread popularity of apocalyptic imagery in Protestant polemics,[129] the audience was likely able to identify Wirrwärr as the harlot based upon visual cues alone. If not, the preacher Gottlieb was bold enough to name names, possibly reinforced by a pointing gesture: "The devil's council will harm many souls thanks to the chaotic whore of Babel."[130]

As discussed in Chapter Three, the allegorized Frouw Wirrwärr embodies all that is worldly, including human reason. The play's staging renders her earthly presence among humankind physically tangible. While she is an instrument of Satan—Teufel Schür-den-Brand (Devil Fan-the-Flames) deems her *unser dochter* (v. 1471)—she interacts only with temporal beings and, although addressed once by Schür-den-Brand at the end of the play (v. 2645), has no direct traffic with any representative of hell on stage. Indeed, from the play's dialogue it becomes evident that all demons keep to their designated section of the stage except for the close of the play, when they "travel" to earth to carry all heathens and papists off to hell (after v. 2370, vv. 2617–22). Their speeches function solely as commentary upon the unfolding action of the play on earth, which they can influence only through Wirrwärr, their agent.

This strict division of the earthly and the divine, the creature and the creator, derives from a corresponding distinction in Zwingli's theology.[131] Indeed, the stage of *Abgötterei* is a physical model of the

---

[128] Klaus Jaeger, *Sämtliche Dramen*, 3:92.
[129] For more on Protestant adaptations of the Apocalypse, see Scribner, *For the Sake of Simple Folk*, 148–89; Hofmann, ed., *Luther und die Folgen für die Kunst*, 171–83; Peter Martin, *Martin Luther und die Bilder zur Apokalypse*, Vestigia Bibliae 5 (Hamburg: Wittig, 1983).
[130] "Der tüfels rath/wirt vil seelen gschenden / das thuot die verwirte huor von Babel" (vv. 1449–50). This is Gottlieb's second reference to the harlot; in the first, he uses a demonstrative pronoun, suggesting that he pointed to Frouw Wirrwärr across the stage as he spoke: "All menschen müssen an diser huoren rath erworgen" (v. 1445).
[131] W.P. Stephens, *The Theology of Huldrych Zwingli* (Oxford: Clarendon Press, 1986), 86.

Zwinglian universe, revealing to spectators the vanity, indeed blasphemy of all faith in earthly affairs. As an archetype of this misplaced faith in human reason, Frouw Wirrwärr embodies, for Zwingli, the ultimate idol:

> One zwyffel, das, so der mensch uß siner vernunfft etwas für guot bildet, und aber das recht und guot nit allein von gott und sinem wort lernet, einen abgott in im selbs uffricht, namlich sinen eygnen verstand und guotduncken. Welcher abgott schwarlich umbgestossen wirdt; dann er hebt sich glych ußwending ouch an mit zouberwerck, das ist: mit glychsnendem schin vor den menschen, für war und grecht verkouffen.[132]

> Without a doubt, when humanity creates something from its own reason, but does not found it solely in God and His word, then it erects an idol within, namely its own understanding and whim. This idol can hardly be toppled, for it immediately begins through deception—that is with false appearances before humankind—to present itself outwardly as true and just.

All figures who rely on Wirrwärr's guidance—the emperor, the pope, the play's petitioners—have thus not succumbed to an external force, but have rather unconsciously abandoned God's word out of confidence in their own inner ability to determine good from evil. This is most apparent in the figure of Pope Starrblind. Although Rüte identifies him with the Antichrist (vv. 1458–60; v. 2413; v. 2410), he remains at all times a puppet of Frouw Wirrwärr, rather than an active agent of evil such as the popes of Manuel's plays. He, too, has no direct contact with the play's demons. However, he is beholden to Satan through Wirrwärr, i.e. through his faith in his own capacity to fathom God's will.

Theater as Merkbild

Bern's subsequent biblical theater presented living examples of Christian conduct similar to those recommended by Theodorus Gottlieb in *Abgötterei*. In offering morally edifying role models, such as Joseph or David, the plays promoted the emulation of exemplary figures rather

---

[132] *ZW*, 3:29. See also Gottfried Locher's discussion of Zwingli's views on idolatry: Gottfried W. Locher, *Zwingli's Thought. New Perspectives*, Studies in the History of Christian Thought 25 (Leiden: E.J. Brill, 1981), 160.

than their veneration. The comments of *Goliath*'s herald echo Gottlieb's comments in their request that the audience not dwell on outer appearance, but rather inner behavior:

> Achtend nit z'vil/wie yeder bkleidt
> Angleit/verbutzet vnd zuogrist
> Diß Spil nit drumb angsehen ist/
> Sunders/das ouch durch narrenwerck
> Der welt kundt werd Gots gwalt vnd sterck
> So er mit guoten/bösen yebt/
> Ouch was Gott hasset/was er liebt/
> Hie wirt abgmalet/vnd dargeben
> Wyß/anfechtung/wort/werck vnd leben
> Beyder/der bösen vnd der frommen
> Vnd was eim yeden zlon wirt kommen/(vv. 84–94)

> Don't pay too much attention to the clothing, attire, costumes, and outfits of the actors. This play is not intended for that, but rather that, through a work of folly, the power and strength that God exercises upon the good and the bad be made known to the world, as well as what He hates and what He loves. Here, you will find depicted and portrayed the behavior, trials, words, works, and lives of both the evil and the pious and what they will receive as their reward.

By referring to the performance as "folly" (*narrenwerck*), Rüte cautions the audience on the one hand that plays cannot substitute for Scripture itself, much less for the actual events they portray. Nonetheless, *Goliath*'s herald assures viewers that the players' reenactment of David's victory conveys the essence of actual events:

> Die werdends nit nun üch erzellen/
> Sunders für üwer ougen stellen
> Als läbendig vnd wesenlich
> Wie'ß hat mögen begeben sich. (vv. 33–6)

> They won't narrate events for you, but rather place them before your eyes, as living and real as they likely took place.

Again, the issue is one of verisimilitude. In providing a living approximation of real events, Rüte implies, biblical theater assumes a documentary function, recreating scriptural evidence of God's covenant with humanity. The author further avails himself of painting metaphors to describe his handicraft, arguing that the superiority of religious theater lies in its ability to engage an audience visually. Not only does he join other Protestant playwrights in characterizing the task of theater as *vor Augen stellen* (to place before the eyes),[133] but he also speaks of the stage as if it were a canvas, as here in *Joseph*:

> Es ist ein bruch von alter har
> Ouch diser zyt in übung gar.
> Das man etwan ein bschächen ding
> Den mönschen für ir ougen bring/
> Recht conterfeit vnd gmalet ab
> Wie es sich warlich verlouffen hab/
> vnd bschicht das (mins dunckens) darum
> Das die welt in betrachtung kumm/
> Wie sy thuon oder lassen söll
> Das/so Got von ir haben wöll (vv. 5–14)

> Since time immemorial, and in our time as well, it has been a custom to present an event before people's eyes, reproduced and depicted as it truly transpired. This occurs (in my opinion) so that the world might consider how to accomplish or refrain from that which God wants of it.

The events portrayed on stage are painted from life, or *gmalet ab*. As such, they are *conterfeit* in the sense of a *contrafactum*, or copy. Similarly, *Joseph*'s title page boasts that the play was *conterfetisch gespilt* (played in a "counterfeit" manner). By suggesting that the actions viewed by the audience were indistinguishable from past events, the term *conterfeit* perhaps best captures Rüte's concern for creating living images of Scripture. The author's contemporaries in Bern saw the matter similarly. In his forward to *Goliath*, Samuel Apiarius states that the play portrays biblical events "as if they were alive before people's eyes,"[134] and the Bernese council apparently seconded that

---

[133] See Chapter One and *Joseph* (v. 8, v. 30), *Gedeon* (v. 1769, v. 3961), *Noe* (v. 1692), *Osterspiel* (v. 712), and *Goliath* (v. 34).

[134] A section of Apiarius's forward is translated as this chapter's epigraph. The full text is as follows: "Wje fürnem vnd wichtig dise Histori seye/in wölcher die H. schrifft vns in der kleinen person Dauids gegen den Goliat zuorechnen fürhelt/wie der allmächtig wz klein vnd vngeachtet vor der welt ist/mit besondern gaben zieret/vnd durch dz selbig zuo schanden machet vnd stürtzet/wz prächtig vnd groß ist/achte ich von vnnöten syn allhie zuomelden/diewyl diß nachfolgend spil dermassen gestaltet/dz es nit allein mit worten hieruon redt/sonder auch die sach an jhr selb gar noch eygentlich so es gespilet wirt/allen zuosehenden für die ougen stellet vnd anbildet. Allein wolt ich/dz wir die grosse gnaden so vns der Allmächtig zuo disen letsten zyten bewyset/etwz baß behertzigten. Dann warlich redt yetz Gott mitt vns/vff mancherley wyß/vnd helt vns syn heiligs wort für nit allein mit predigen/sonder auch mit trucken/mit schrifften/mit Psalmen vnd geistlichen liedern/vnd

opinion, reimbursing Apiarius for his foreword with three bushels of spelt.[135]

The Bernese biblical stage continued to employ the *Simultanbühne*, marking specific locations for characters of differing faiths. However, where Protestants earlier stood separate from Catholics, the antithetical division of the stage now distinguishes Israelites from their biblical opponents. In *Goliath*, for example, the stage directions speak of "the Jews' fortifications"; at the play's close, the reader is told of triumphant celebration on "Saul's side."[136] In summarizing the events of the play, the herald speaks of viewing "both hordes."[137] The opposing camps of Israelites and Philistines thus appeared on opposite halves of the stage, with the pastures tended by David likely situated on the Israeli side. The scenes frequently alternate between the two halves, such as when Saul's troops express their early confidence with shouts, drums, and bugles, which the Philistines hear and respond to (vv. 731–56). A comparable division between warring camps occurred in *Gedeon*. Similarly, the stage of *Noe* clearly sets the dwelling of Ham and his offspring apart from the home of Noah, although Seth and Japhet apparently had their own marked locations on stage.[138] It is unclear whether *Joseph* employed contrastive staging, but it is possible that the home of Jacob in Israel stood in opposition to Pharaoh's palace in Egypt.

Moreover, the plays consistently reserved a section of the stage for "pointing" figures, who observed and commented on the action from their privileged vantage point, much like Peter and Paul in Manuel's *Vom Papst und seiner Priesterschaft* or the fool in Solomon's

---

durch zierliche spil/mit wölchen die fürnemern geschichten auß H. Schrifft gezogen eräferet/erfrischet vnd glych lebendig den lütten vor die ougen gestellet werden/dz wir wol sagen mügen die wyßheit Gottes rüff vnd schryge vff der gassen. Vß solchen ansehen/hab ich desto lieber dises gegenwertig Spil für mich genommen zuo trucken/on zwyffel/es werde guothertzigen lüten solichs myn fürhaben zuo keinem argen sonder vil meer mittels der gnaden Gottes zuo jrem nutz vnd frommen dienen. Das gebe der Herr." *Sämtliche Dramen*, 655.

[135] "Appiarius von der [Widmung der] spillen wägen Goliats 3 müt dinckel." Fluri, 139.

[136] "Der Juden Schantz": *Goliath*, before v. 1441; "Vff Sauls syten lärman" (after v. 6792).

[137] "Wenn ich die huffen beyd ansich." *Goliath*, v. 6725.

[138] When Noah summons his sons and their families for the Sukkot feast, they convene from three separate locations: "Hie köment dry huffen/von dryen ortten har." *Noe*, before v. 1199.

Idolatry. The works' heralds, for example, are all deictic figures, introducing and later summarizing each day's performance. *Goliath*'s herald, for example, physically points to the Philistines while explaining how their vices have led to their defeat: "For this reason, this horde has had to suffer."[139] However, dramatic deixis is most apparent in the peasant figures of *Joseph* and *Gedeon*, as well as in *Noe*'s Sabatius and Sabus. The sole function of these three pairs is to comment on the events of their respective plays as they observe them. As seen in Chapter Four, for example, *Joseph*'s Bur Anckenbock and Bur Hirßhut offer misogynistic commentary on the trial of Potiphar's wife immediately following its completion. Anckenbock's "Hast ghört was die frow hat gehandlet?" (Did you hear what the woman did?; v. 2013) indicates that he and Hirßhut have been eavesdropping on courtroom events all along much as the audience has. By recapitulating the results of the trial, they summarize the salient points for the audience and append the author's preferred interpretation.

Gedeon's two *Landman* serve as similar observers. After the priests of Baal have discovered that someone has desecrated their altar, the two peasants appear as travelers and express their bewilderment at the uproar around them. They specifically announce their intent to stay and observe events in order to divine their meaning:

Erst Lantman:
Wie hands ein glöuff yn diser stat?
Der ander Landman:
Jch weiß nit/wer jnen than hat
Sy hand ein sömlich zsamen louffen
Als wöltens all einander rouffen
Schlahen/stechen/würgen zerhouwen
Erst Landman:
Bind an die Roß/wir wend gan schouwen
Vernän vnd gsen/was sy die sach
Die dlüt also vnruwig mach (vv. 1321–8)

The first peasant:
What sort of a commotion is going on in this city?
The second peasant:
I don't know who did something to them. They're running around in such confusion as if they wanted to brawl, strike, stab, strangle, and dismember one another.

---

[139] "Drumb diser huff hat müssen lyden/." *Goliath*, v. 6753.

The first peasant:
Tie up the horses; let's go look, listen, and see what is making the people so restless.

The peasants subsequently watch as Baal's priests incite a crowd to surround Joash's house and demand Gideon's surrender. After Joash has quieted the mob, the first peasant gives his interpretation of events:

> Gsich fründ/wohin es kommen ist/
> Wie zletzt vßschlitzt der pfaffen list/
> Die der abgott Baal muoß spysen
> Wie sy bruchent anschleg vnd wysen
> Wenn jr gschwetz nit mer helffen wil/
> So richtens an ein sömlich spil
> Sy hand vns trogen lange zyt/
> Das heiter an der Sonnen lyt (vv. 1601–8)
>
> Look, friend, at what it's come to, how in the end the trickery of the priests, whom Baal's idol must nourish, is revealed, and how they employ plots and similar methods. When their blather will no longer help them, then they resort to games such as these. They've deceived us for quite some time. That's as plain as day.

The second peasant then responds with a criticism of naive superstition and a defense of Joash's *fromme herschafft* (pious magistracy), as quoted in Chapter Four. These two figures are otherwise not part of the play's plot, so that they become seemingly neutral observers of the riot while passing by. They later observe and comment upon the departure of all "fearful and trembling" Israelites (Judges 7,3), whom Gideon has given leave to return home (vv. 2890–957). As rustics, their interpretation of events is designed to appeal to members of the peasant estate among the audience, the very class whom Rüte and the Bernese council wished to dissuade from religiopolitical disobedience. In essence, the two *Landman* model proper viewing for the audience.

Correspondingly, Sabatius and Sabus provide an internal interpretation of events in *Noe*. Unlike the peasants of *Gedeon*, they do not explicitly thematize their role as observers, but their comments make clear that they, too, have been watching events from a separate vantage point until they feel compelled to speak out against Nimrod's accumulation of power (vv. 3489–558; vv. 4625–74). As indicated by Sabatius's impassioned speech for liberty upon the establishment of Nimrod's dominion, the brothers model audience response much as *Gedeon*'s peasants, speaking for all Swiss against the tyranny of nobility. Indeed, Sabatius's soliloquy replaces the closing interpretation of the play by the herald, who now simply requests the audience's favor and sends it on its way home (vv. 4707–28). Hirßhut and Anckenbock similarly function as modified heralds at the end of *Joseph*'s first day of performance. Lastly, any of these deictic figures might have, through gesture and facial expressions, provided additional visual commentary for the audience.

The contrastive use of space and the appearance of deictic figures were thus common to all Bernese biblical plays. However, the most conspicuous example of the direct influence of contemporary Protestant imagery is *Osterspiel*. The play is essentially a recreation of John's vision of the heavenly throne, the so-called *majestas Domini* image of Revelation 4–5. In founding his stage directly on contemporary illustrations of this biblical book, Rüte drew on a long-standing tradition of Protestant apocalyptic imagery extending back to the woodcuts of Lucas Cranach the Elder for Luther's September Testament of 1522, which were themselves based on Albrecht Dürer's highly influential *Apocalypse* of 1498.[140] The Swiss Protestant tradition of illustrating Revelation was equally strong. For his 1523 Basel edition of *Das gantz New Testament*, one of the earliest reprints of Luther's translation, Thomas Wolff commissioned Hans Holbein the Younger with the creation of 21 new woodcuts; we have already encountered Holbein's image of Revelation 17 as an illustration for *Abgötterei* (fig. 15). Bernese theologians and councilors were also highly interested in interpretations of the Apocalypse, as seen in Chapter Four. Just as Sebastian Meyer's *In Apocalypsim Iohannis Apostoli [. . .] Commentarius*, written in Bern in 1539, inspired some of the Reformation's most extraordinary polemical images,[141] Rüte's *Osterspiel* is one of the sixteenth-century's most unique plays. It joins Manuel's *Von Papsts und Christi*

---

[140] For a discussion of Dürer's Apocalypse, see Panofsky, *The Life and Art of Albrecht Dürer*, 51–9. The complete set of Dürer's Apocalypse woodcuts, as well as woodcuts from two of Dürer's likely sources, the Quentell Bible of ca. 1479 and the Grüninger Bible of 1485, can be found in Kenneth A. Strand, ed., *Woodcuts to the Apocalypse in Dürer's Time. Albrecht Dürer's Woodcuts Plus Five Other Sets from the 15th and 16th Centuries* (Ann Arbor: Ann Arbor Publishers, 1968). For a facsimile edition of the text of Dürer's Apocalypse, unfortunately without all woodcuts, see Kenneth A. Strand, ed., *Dürer's Apocalypse. The 1498 German and 1511 Latin Texts in Facsimile plus Samples of Dürer's Woodcuts and Gräff's Copies* (Ann Arbor: Ann Arbor Publishers, 1969).

[141] Petra Roettig, *Reformation als Apokalypse. Die Holzschnittfolge von Matthias Gerung im Codex germanicus 6592 der Bayerischen Staatsbibliothek in München*, Vestigia Bibliae 11/12 (Bern: Peter Lang, 1991).

Gegensatz and Valten Voith's *Ein schön Lieblich Spiel von dem herlichen vrsprung* (1538) as one of three sixteenth-century Protestant plays based directly upon a visual source.

Textual evidence indicates that the play's performance was essentially a giant *tableau vivant* modeled on contemporary illustrations of the *majestas Domini*. This motif depicts God, the heavenly throne, and the Lamb of God, all surrounded by twenty-four elders as well as by the symbols of the four evangelists: a lion, an ox, an eagle, and an angel. Of the various representations of this theme in sixteenth-century art, the play's frontispiece (fig. 21) corresponds most closely to Holbein's illustration of the passage in Wolff's New Testament edition of 1523, although the vignette need not have been based upon the play's performance. Other aspects of the play can be found only in contemporary illustrations, not in the original biblical text. Phrases such as *der vorderst vff der rechten syten* (the foremost on the right side; before v. 125), *der vorderst ältest vff der linggen syten* (the foremost elder on the left side; before v. 304), and *der hinderst eltest* (the elder farthest back; before v. 385) indicate that Rüte grouped the elders in two clusters on either side of the throne, most likely in two half-circles, as in most illustrations. Above all, the references to the positions of specific elders refute assertions that John's descriptions of his visions in the play are merely "spoken scenery," which was not actually present during the performance.[142] It is reasonable to assume that most elements of John's vision appeared on the stage: the heavenly throne, a surrounding rainbow, seven torches and, of course, the Lamb of God.

Performed just three years prior to the Religious Peace of Augsburg, *Osterspiel* culminates the union of Protestant art and drama begun by Manuel's *Von Papsts und Christi Gegensatz*. The play's astonishing economy of text stands in marked contrast to Rüte's other biblical dramas, suggesting that the audience predominantly engaged the work visually. This is corroborated by John's repeated emphasis on "seeing" the content of the play. Through him, the audience participates in the physical revelation of God's final dealings with humankind. Just as Rüte had earlier stressed in *Goliath* that biblical

---

[142] Cf. Kenneth Fisher, "Hans von Rüte: A Dramatist of the Swiss Reformation" (Ph.D. dissertation, University of Texas at Austin, 1975), 129; Wolfgang F. Michael, *Das deutsche Drama der Reformationszeit* (Bern: Peter Lang, 1984), 145.

drama is *wesenlich*, a real or essential embodiment of Scripture, the *verborgne stimm* (hidden voice) of *Osterspiel* promises John a similarly physical incarnation of divine prophecy:

> Johannes was ich heissen dich
> Das thuo bald vnd biß ghorsam mir
> So wil ich wäßlich zeigen dir
> Was künfftiger zyt sölle bschähen (vv. 60–3)

> Johannes, what I bid of you, do that quickly and obey me. Then I will show you, in physical form, what is to come in the future.

John's frequent reminders that he is simultaneously viewing what he describes repeatedly draws the audience's attention to the stage; often it is difficult to decide whether his enjoinders to "See!" pertain to himself or apostrophize the audience.[143] The *hinderst eltest* also entreats John, and with him the spectators, to look upon his vision (vv. 413–4). Lastly, in interpreting the play at its close, the third herald underscores the significance of the *figura* (tableau) in interpreting the play: "Wies ist in der figur erkennt" (As is apparent in the *figura*; v. 675).

It should be noted that the staging techniques employed by Rüte and Manuel were not unique to Protestant drama. Deictic figures, for example, frequently appeared in the religious drama of the Middle Ages, as seen in the so-called *rector processionis* of Corpus Christi plays, the character of St. Augustine in the Frankfurt passion play, or the church fathers in the Lucerne passion play.[144] Rüte's use of the term *figur*, which denoted living tableaux in medieval plays,[145] similarly

---

[143] "Jch sich des Himmels thür vffgon" (v. 55); "Jch sich yetz vber Sonn vnd Mon" (v. 67); "Sich siben Facklen vor dem Stuol" (v. 93); "Was sich ich mer im Stuol vnd drunder" (v. 97); "Wie ist mir in dem gsicht so wol" (v. 108); "Jetz sich ich/das ich vor nie gsehen// Sich/in dem stuol deß Herren sitz" (vv. 416–7); "Ich muoß baß sehn wz druß wöl werden. / Sich sich/diß Lamm will zuohin gan" (vv. 432–3); "Sich/nieman thuot jm widerstand." (v. 438); "Nun muoß ich wyter sehen zuo// Was Englen sich ich vmb den stuol?" (vv. 501–2).

[144] See *Das Zerbster Prozessionsspiel 1507*, ed. Willm Reupke, Quellen zur deutschen Volkskunde 4 (Berlin/Leipzig: de Gruyter, 1930); *Frankfurter Dirigierrolle—Frankfurter Passionsspiel. Mit den Paralleltexten der "Frankfurter Dirigierrolle", des "Alsfelder Passionsspiels", des "Heidelberger Passionsspiels", des Frankfurter Osterspielfragments" und des "Fritzlaer Passionsspielfragments*, ed. Johannes Janota, vol. 1 of *Die Hessische Passionsspielgruppe. Edition im Paralleldruck* (Tübingen: Niemeyer, 1996); *Das Luzerner Osterspiel*, ed. Heinz Wyss, 3 vols. (Bern: Francke, 1967).

[145] On dramatic *figurae*, see Matthias Schulz, *Die Eigenbezeichnungen des mittelalterlichen deutschsprachigen geistlichen Spiels*, Germanistische Bibliothek 2 (Heidelberg: Winter,

indicates a basic continuity in performance practice. It is even possible that the actors entered the stage in procession at the beginning of a performance, as was customary for passion plays.[146] What nonetheless makes the performance of sixteenth-century Bernese drama quintessentially Protestant is the recombination of traditional elements to create a new viewing experience. The plays now stimulated reflection upon the trials of their protagonists, rather than identification with or pity for them. They also gave physical form to Protestant theology, as is most apparent in the staging of *Abgötterei*. Whereas devils, Christ, and the inhabitants of earth once mingled together on the *Simultanbühne* of passion plays, humanity no longer had direct contact with heaven or hell on the Bernese stage, at least not before death. Bern's Reformation theater thus lost the transcendence of earlier religious drama, as noted for other Protestant plays.[147] But in making the gap between earthly and divine experience tangible, Bernese plays illustrated the necessity of faith, and faith alone, in bridging that gap.

1998), 226–47; Wolfgang F. Michael, "Die Bedeutung des Wortes 'figur' im geistlichen Drama Deutschlands," *Germanic Review* 21 (1946): 3–8.

[146] *Joseph*'s herald states in his introduction to the play that the "group" "proceeds in": "Jch will vch sagen/was das düt// Das jr gsend/wie die schar harfart / Beckleidt vff frömde wyß vnd art/." *Joseph*, vv. 2–4.

[147] Barbara Könneker, "Luthers Bedeutung für das protestantische Drama des 16. Jahrhunderts. Geschichte und Heilsgeschichte in Bartholomäus Krügers *Neuer Action von dem Anfang und Ende der Welt*," *Daphnis* 12 (1983): 545–73.

CHAPTER SIX

MUSIC, PLAY, AND WORSHIP

> The 22nd of January was the Feast of St. Vincent, the patron of the city of Bern since time immemorial. Thus the canons of Bern had planned an extravagant celebration of the feast. On the evening before, they sang Vespers quite solemnly. When it came time for the organist to strike up the Magnificat, he played the song "Oh you poor Judas, what have you done that you've betrayed our Lord in this manner." This was the last song that was played on the organ, for soon afterwards it was dismantled.
>
> —Heinrich Bullinger, *Reformationschronik*

On 22 January 1528, as the local Protestant disputation was drawing to a close, the burghers of Bern received their first direct taste of Zwinglian reform. This date marked the Feast of St. Vincent, the city's patron saint, but its celebration in 1528 stood in stark contrast to the pomp of years past. The sextons rang the minster bell thrice in the course of the day to call the faithful to mass, but no worshippers or priests responded, convinced either of the folly of the office or perhaps of the futility of opposing the council's reformist zeal.[1] Among Bern's "societies," the Butchers alone instructed their chaplains to celebrate mass at their guild's altar. For the service, they had to supply their own positif organ: The minster organ was locked, having sounded a final time during Vespers the evening before.[2] It

---

[1] "Wiewol die sigristen zuo allen ziten und messen hochzitlich zünten und luten, so kam doch nieman, der weder meti, prim, terz, sext, non, vesper noch complet singen, ouch weder früeg-, mitel, noch hochmes halten wölte, dan alein die mezger, als widerwärtige, hiessen ire zwen kaplan uf iren altaren das fest mit gesungner mes und verdingtem posityf—dan die kororgel beschlossen—und morndes jarzit mit selmessen began." Anshelm, 5:244. See also François de Capitani, *Musik in Bern: Musik, Musiker, Musikerinnen und Publikum in der Stadt Bern vom Mittelalter bis heute*, Archiv des Historischen Vereins des Kantons Bern 76 (Bern: Historischer Verein des Kantons Bern, 1993), 36–7; Feller, 2:161.

[2] The original quote for this chapter's epigraph reads as follows: "Den 22 January was der tag S. Vincenty, welchen die Statt Bernn von allter har für iren patronen gehept, Dorumm die Chorherren zuo Bern, gar ein kostlich fest zuo hallten angesähen hattend. Vnd Sungend gar solemnitetisch des abents die Vesper. Vnd alls der

was later dismantled and sold for 130 crowns to Caspar Colmar, organist in Sitten.³

The fate of Bern's minster organ under the city's new Protestant government vividly illustrates the Zwinglian Reformation's initial eschewal of music, in particular singing, as a means of worship. In stark contrast to Luther's Wittenberg or Calvin's Geneva, Zurich forbade the performance of church music during religious services from 1524 until 1598. Indeed, in 1527, Zurich magistrates ordered local organs not sold, but destroyed.⁴ Bern's official resistance to the otherwise popular practice of hymn singing proved slightly less stalwart, but its break with Catholic musical tradition was no less radical. Thirty years passed following the Bernese Disputation before the council, in 1558, instructed young schoolboys to sing one psalm during the Sunday service.⁵ Not until 1574 did the magistrates fully relent and allow the singing of psalms by the congregation, one before and one after the weekly sermon.⁶

The reintroduction of music to religious worship in Bern was the result of a long, complex, and—viewed from the twenty-first century—often imperceptible process. It would likely not have occurred when it did without the arrival in the late 1540s of the moderate Zwinglian theologians Wolfgang Musculus and Johannes Haller, both

---

Organist vff das Magnificat schlachen sollt, macht er das Lied, O du armer Judas, was hast du gethan, daß du unseren Herren also verraten hast. vnd was das das letste lied, das vff der orgelen geschlagen ward. Dann bald hernach ward die orgelen abgebrochen." Heinrich Bullinger, *Reformationschronik*, ed. J.J. Hottinger and H.H. Vögeli (Frauenfeld, 1838; Zurich: Theologische Buchhandlung, 1985), 1:437. See also Capitani, *Musik in Bern*, 37; Arnold Geering, *Die Vokalmusik in der Schweiz zur Zeit der Reformation. Leben und Werke von Bartholomäus Frank, Johannes Wannenmacher und Cosmas Alder*, Schweizerisches Jahrbuch für Musikwissenschaft 6 (Aarau, 1933; Amsterdam: Swets & Zeitlinger N.V., 1969), 38, 179–81.

³ Geering, *Vokalmusik*, 38, note 1.
⁴ See Hannes Reimann, *Die Einführung des Kirchengesangs in der Zürcher Kirche nach der Reformation* (Zürich: Zwingli-Verlag, 1959); Garside, 57–62.
⁵ Gerhard Aeschbacher, "Die Reformation und das kirchenmusikalische Leben im alten Bern," in *450 Jahre*, 234; Capitani, *Musik in Bern*, 38.
⁶ François de Capitani has recently suggested, against earlier consensus, that the year 1574 does not mark the beginning of *Gemeindegesang* in Bern. He argues instead that psalms continued to be sung solely by a choir of schoolboys: Capitani, *Musik in Bern*, 39, 42. Cf. Aeschbacher, 234; Geering, *Vokalmusik*, 41; Marcus Jenny, *Geschichte des deutsch-schweizerischen evangelischen Gesangbuches im 16. Jahrhundert* (Basel: Bärenreiter, 1962), 284; Max Zulauf, *Der Musikunterricht in der Geschichte des bernischen Schulwesens von 1528–1798*, Berner Veröffentlichungen zur Musikforschung 3 (Bern/Leipzig: Haupt, 1934), 5.

of whom actively supported church singing. Nor did the Reformation put an end to the private activities of local composers, who continued to produce secular and religious works throughout the mid-sixteenth century.[7] The equation of factors leading to Bern's official rehabilitation of devotional music is, nonetheless, incomplete without an examination of the choral and instrumental interludes of the local stage. Contemporary plays provided a sanctioned forum, perhaps the only sanctioned forum, for the public performance of religious music in Bern between 1528 and 1558.[8] Hans von Rüte's five biblical dramas preserve the texts of eight hymns, and further references to choral music, such as *Chorus, Gsang*, or *Hie soll etwas gsungen werden*,[9] indicate that singing formed a constitutive component of local Reformation theater. Regrettably, despite Arnold Geering's initial exploration of the ties between Swiss Protestant theater and Renaissance choral music some sixty-five years ago,[10] the music of Rüte's plays has received only passing mention in more recent studies of musical life in post-Reformation Bern.[11]

The composition and performance of music for Bern's Reformation plays took place in two contexts: Protestant hymn singing and the choral interludes of German Renaissance dramaturgy. A corresponding analysis of the city's biblical plays (local carnival plays contain little music) reveals that Bernese musicians cultivated an independent local tradition of Protestant devotional music, distinct not only from Lutheran or Calvinist compositions, but also from the semi-Zwinglian Swiss hymnals emanating from Constance. The plays' rich musical legacy demonstrates that the councilors of Bern had a higher tolerance

---

[7] See most recently Christine Fischer, "Zwei Huldigungskompositionen an die Stadt Bern und ihr musikalisch-gesellschaftliches Umfeld in der ersten Hälfte des 16. Jahrhunderts," in *BGZ*, 567–78.

[8] The council instructed in 1538 that the teacher of the city school teach his pupils to sing psalms, but it is unclear whether the students performed publicly. See Aeschbacher, 234.

[9] *Chorus* appears throughout *Goliath* (for example after v. 2922), *Gsang* throughout *Gedeon* (after v. 1930) and *Noe* (after v. 2914). The direction *Hie soll etwas gsungen werden* (Something should be sung here) occurs in *Joseph* (after v. 646).

[10] Geering, *Vokalmusik*, 66–80.

[11] Cf. Aeschbacher, 225, 232; Capitani, *Musik in Bern*, 50; Fischer, 572, 578. While Capitani notes correctly that Cosmas Alder created two motets for Rüte's *Noe*, he incorrectly gives the date of the drama as 1552, six years after the play was actually performed. A.E. Cherbuliez similarly incorrectly dates *Goliath*: Antoine-Eliseé Cherbuliez, *Die Schweiz in der deutschen Musikgeschichte*, Die Schweiz im deutschen Geistesleben, Illustrierte Reihe 18 (Frauenfeld/Leipzig: Huber, 1932), 32.

for devotional music than earlier assumed. Rüte's *Osterspiel* alone is proof of this: although the play's prominent interludes have earned it the label *oratorium*,[12] the council members in attendance registered no objections to the performance of hymns. Above all, the plays situate their songs in specific social contexts, giving us a clearer picture of the socioreligious position of music within the Bernese community. Not all music is salutary, but devotional songs of praise and commemoration are fully sanctioned, sounding at moments of crisis and thanksgiving. Indeed, *Osterspiel*'s audience apparently joined in the singing of "Christ ist erstanden" ("Christ is risen"), providing at least one variant of *Gemeindegesang* (congregational singing) in Bern prior to 1574, even if these voices were raised in the city's secularized Franciscan monastery and not in the minster during religious services.

Zwingli, Bern, and the Music of Swiss Protestantism

Given Zwingli's opposition to music in worship, one might assume that the reformer lacked an appreciation of the musical arts. In fact, the opposite is true. From his early youth on, Zwingli displayed an astonishing aptitude for all forms of music.[13] As reported by contemporaries, he was adept at several instruments, especially the lute.[14] Indeed, so great was Zwingli's musical proficiency that his adversaries construed it as a sign of decadent worldliness, nearly preventing his appointment as lay priest to Zurich's Great Minster in December of 1518 and leading Catholic opponents such as Johannes Faber and Thomas Murner to deride him as a "piper" and a "fiddler."[15] He was no less skilled at composition, attested by the surviving music for three original songs: the "Pestlied," written after Zwingli's recovery from the plague in 1520; the "Kapplerlied," composed in the aftermath of the First War of Kappel in 1529; and an undated musical setting for the 69th Psalm.[16]

---

[12] Geering, *Vokalmusik*, 72; Emil Ermatinger, *Dichtung und Geistesleben der deutschen Schweiz* (Munich: Beck, 1933), 200.
[13] Garside, 7–26.
[14] Ibid., 8, 13, 22. For a review of other research on Zwingli's musicianship, see Konrad Ameln, "Kirchenlied und Kirchenmusik in der deutschen reformierten Schweiz im Jahrhundert der Reformation," *Jahrbuch für Liturgik und Hymnologie* 6 (1961): 150–1.
[15] Garside, 16, 65–9.
[16] Markus Jenny, "Die Lieder Zwinglis," *Jahrbuch für Liturgik und Hymnologie* 14

Nevertheless, despite his intimate knowledge of and love for music, Zwingli concluded from his scriptural studies that liturgical reform necessitated cleansing church services of instrumental as well as choral music. Intent on restoring the Pauline purity of early Christianity, he had searched Scripture for evidence of the divine institution of music in worship. In his assessment, he found none. Despite the recorded performance of devotional music in the Old Testament, Zwingli determined that this practice derived from humankind, not from God. Referring instead to Moses and Hannah, who prayed silently to the Lord (Exodus 14:15; 1 Samuel 1:13), as well as to Christ's instructions to pray in private (Matthew 6:5–13), Zwingli concluded that Paul's command to "sing psalms and hymns and spiritual songs with thankfulness in your hearts to God" (Colossians 3:16) stipulated that singing be done in the heart alone, i.e. in quiet reflection:[17]

> Hie leert uns Paulus nit das prülen unnd murmlen in den templen, sunder er zeigt das war gsang an, das got gevellig ist, das wir nit mit der stimm, als der Juden senger, sunder mit dem hertzen die lob und bryß gotes singind.[18]

> Here Paul does not teach us to roar and mumble in church, but shows us that true singing which is pleasing to God, so that we sing the praises and glory of God not with our voices, as Jewish singers, but with our hearts.

To Zwingli's mind, then, only silent prayer was true prayer. A congregation unskilled in the reading of music would be incapable of singing God's praises in proper reverence, because its members would focus on the task of singing rather than on worship: "When one prays, mouth and mind are not long on the same track, much less so mind and song."[19] Paul had similarly allowed for singing in 1 Corinthians 14:15, but only when mind and spirit were united. Given Zwingli's conviction of the frailty of human nature, which similarly

---

(1969): 63–102. English translations of the Plague and Kappel songs can be found in Garside, 23–6, 69–70.

[17] Garside, 45. In Strasbourg, Colossians 3 led Martin Bucer to the opposite conclusion, namely that congregational singing was God-ordained. Bartlett R. Butler, "Hymns," in *OER*, 2:292.

[18] "Auslegen und Gründe der Schlußreden," in *ZW*, 2:350.

[19] "Nun ist mund und gmüt, so man bättet, nit lang uff eim weg, vil weniger gemüt und gsang." "Auslegen und Gründe der Schlußreden," 2:352.

led him to reject all devotional images as potentially idolatrous, he believed that the union of mind and spirit called for by Paul was humanly impossible.[20] Music was thus incompatible with true worship and could have no place in religious services. Based on this logic, Zwingli bid farewell to all singing in church:

> Alde, min tempelgmürmel! Bis mir nun nit schade; guot weiß ich wol, das du mir nit bist. Aber bis grüßt, o frommes, innwendigs gebett, das vom gotswort erweckt würdt imm hertzen des gleubigen menschen.[21]

> Adieu, my temple mumblings! I am not sorry for you. I know well that you are not good for me. But welcome, O pious, inner prayer that is awakened in the hearts of believing men through the Word of God.

Zwingli announced his planned liturgical reforms at the Second Zurich Disputation of October 1523, but allowed for their institution at an unspecified later date, prior to which the faithful were to be educated in the necessity of change.[22] Finally, on Maundy Thursday, 13 April 1525, the council put Zwingli's changes into practice, and church singing vanished from Zurich churches for over two generations.[23] While some scholars believe that Zwingli would have eventually allowed the singing of hymns had he lived beyond the initial stages of reform,[24] others argue that the theologian was willing to accept discrepancies between Zurich's liturgy and that of other Swiss Protestant cities in order to preserve what he believed to be the purest form of worship.[25]

Indeed, not all Protestants in Switzerland and Southern Germany adopted Zwingli's views with such stringency. Bern's unquestioning embracement of music-free worship in 1528 contrasted markedly with church affairs in Basel, St. Gall, and Constance. Through their ties to Strasbourg and Augsburg, these cities had come into contact with Lutheran hymns before Zwingli's views on church music had taken root.[26] According to the Basel reformer Johannes Oecolampadius,

---

[20] Garside, 49.
[21] "Auslegen und Gründe der Schlußreden," 2:353.
[22] Reimann, 16.
[23] Garside, 58. See also Ulrich Gäbler, *Huldrych Zwingli. Eine Einführung in sein Leben und sein Werk* (Munich: Beck, 1983), 97, 153.
[24] Jenny, *Geschichte d. dt.-schw. Gesangbuches*, 158; Reimann, 18 ff.
[25] Garside, 64–5, esp. note 21.
[26] Jenny, *Geschichte d. dt.-schw. Gesangbuches*, 7.

congregational singing began spontaneously in his city during the Easter of 1526. Originally an expression of faith alone, the singing of Protestant hymns became also a protest against the suppression of that faith once the Basel council forbade them as seditious.[27] Oecolampadius and his congregation continued to sing in public, and the council, bowing to pressure, eventually allowed adherents of the new faith to sing psalms in designated churches. This represented the first official establishment of congregational singing in Switzerland. St. Gall soon followed, beginning with Luther's "Aus tiefer Not schrei ich zu dir," sung by schoolchildren on 8 September 1527 before and after the children's sermon. Six years later, at the request of local schoolmaster and pastor Dominik Zili, the St. Gall council authorized him to compile a Protestant hymnal, the first in Switzerland.[28]

However, Zili's work had little influence outside St. Gall and was soon eclipsed by the combined efforts of Johannes Zwick and Ambrosius Blarer in Constance. Although not a member of the Helvetian Confederacy, Constance nevertheless had close economic and political ties to its southern neighbors. Like Strasbourg, it was a member of the *Confessio Tetrapolitana*, which adopted a moderate, mediating theology between Lutherans and Zwinglians. These factors allowed the Constance hymnals, with their distinct melding of Lutheran and Zwinglian practice, to find acceptance throughout Switzerland and serve as model for similar works in Basel and Schaffhausen. The first *Konstanzer Gesangbuch*, no longer extant, likely appeared around 1533; the initial surviving edition of 1536/37 was the first of over ten subsequent revisions of the work throughout the remaining sixteenth century.[29]

---

[27] Christoph Johannes Riggenbach, *Der Kirchengesang in Basel seit der Reformation. Mit neuen Aufschlüssen über die Anfänge des französischen Psalmengesangs* (Basel: H. Georg, 1870), 12; Geering, *Vokalmusik*, 38. The singing of hymns as an act of dissent occurred elsewhere as well: see Inge Mager, "Lied und Reformation. Beobachtungen zur reformatorischen Singbewegung in norddeutschen Städten," in *Das protestantische Kirchenlied im 16. und 17. Jahrhundert. Text-, musik- und theologiegeschichtliche Probleme*, ed. Alfred Dürr and Walther Killy, Wolfenbütteler Forschungen 31 (Wiesbaden: Harrassowitz, 1986), 25–38; Robert W. Scribner, "Flugblatt und Analphabetentum. Wie kam der gemeine Mann zu reformatorischen Ideen?" in *Flugschriften als Massenmedium der Reformationszeit. Beiträge zum Tübinger Symposion 1980*, Spätmittelalter und Frühe Neuzeit 13 (Stuttgart: Klett-Cotta, 1981), 70.

[28] Jenny, *Geschichte d. dt.-schw. Gesangbuches*, 159–61; Geering, *Vokalmusik*, 39–40.

[29] Jenny, *Geschichte d. dt.-schw. Gesangbuches*, 7–10, 17–22, 77–139.

Given the broad popularity of the Constance hymnals, they inevitably found their way to Bernese territory. Indeed, circumstances surrounding the Constance hymnal of ca. 1552 have prompted hymnologist Markus Jenny to postulate that it was printed for use in Biel (Bienne) and Western Switzerland, including Bern.[30] In this year, hymn singing officially took root in Biel, where Jacob Funkelin (or Fünklin), a pupil of Blarer's, had been active as pastor since 1550. Blarer himself, like Funkelin a refugee from Constance following its occupation by the emperor in 1548, joined his former pupil in 1551, and together the two reintroduced ecclesiastical music locally according to Constance practice. Their success likely necessitated a reprinting of the Constance hymnal for the Biel congregation, together with a new appendix. From Biel, the hymnal found its way to Bern and other surrounding Protestant regions. Indeed, the surviving exemplar of this edition contains entries placing it in Köniz, just south of Bern, during the eighteenth century, if not sooner.[31] Even if Jenny's postulation of a Biel hymnal remains speculative, the establishment of congregational singing in the nearby town would not have gone unnoticed in Bern.[32]

During the 1530s and -40s, however, musical life in the city on the Aare largely resembled that of Zurich. Although the churches were silent, secular music continued to thrive. Even following his liturgical reforms, Zwingli had continued to practice and support *Hausmusik*, private musicmaking at home with friends and family.[33] Bern also possessed a small circle of music lovers who met in private for practice and recitals.[34] The exact composition of this group is uncertain, but it most certainly included Mathias Apiarius, the first printer in Switzerland to print music with movable type,[35] as well as members of the *Stadtpfeiferei*, musicians in the pay of the city. The

---

[30] Markus Jenny, "Das evangelische Lied der Berner Kirche im 16. Jahrhundert," *Musik und Gottesdienst* 5 (1951): 106–8; Jenny, *Geschichte d. dt.-schw. Gesangbuches*, 121–2.

[31] Ibid., 17–8. The exemplar, Jenny's "Zü 2," is now housed in the Zentralbibliothek Zürich, Zwingli 2003.

[32] Capitani, *Musik in Bern*, 37.

[33] Garside, 67–9.

[34] Fischer, 578; Aeschbacher, 233.

[35] Adolf Thürlings, "Der Musikdruck mit beweglichen Metalltypen im 16. Jahrhundert und die Musikdrucke des Mathias Apiarius in Straßburg und Bern," *Vierteljahrsschrift für Musikwissenschaft* 8 (1892): 389–418. For a collection of songs printed by Apiarius and his sons, see Hans Bloesch, ed., *Dreißig Volkslieder aus den ersten Pressen der Apiarius* (Bern: Schweizer Bibliophilengesellschaft, 1937).

Stadtpfeifer had been in existence since at least 1375, accompanying Bernese troops on military campaigns, playing for receptions of visiting nobility, and later even serenading promenaders on summer evenings from the minster spire.[36] The number and type of instruments played varied; the main group generally consisted of four members, but the council also retained twenty-eight part-time military musicians.[37] These *Feldpfeifer* also took an active interest in the city's musical life, as demonstrated by Mathias Apiarius's dedication of Johannes Wannenmacher's *Bicinia* (1553) to *Feldtrompeter* Michael Kopp and *Feldpfeifer* Wendel Schärer, as well as to his son Sigfrid Apiarius, a city piper at the time.[38] During the fifteenth century, the four core *Stadtpfeifer* performed on the shawm and the flute; following the Reformation, however, the instruments of choice were the *Posaune* (sackbut, or medieval trombone) and the zinck (cornetto).[39] As we shall see, the *Pfeifer* likely also played for performances of Rüte's dramas; "Veni electa mea" by Cosmas Alder, like Wannenmacher a former cantor at St. Vincent's, was performed *vf pusunen* (on sackbuts) in Rüte's *Noe*.[40]

---

[36] Arnold Geering, "Von den Berner Stadtpfeifern," *Schweizer Beiträge zur Musikwissenschaft* 1 (1972): 106; Capitani, *Musik in Bern*, 19–23. An ordinance of 1572 describes the musicians' duties as follows: "Iren gnaden zudienen, fröud und kurtzwil zemachen, es sye in gemeiner versamlung des Regiments uf besundre festtag, als ze Ostern und andern zyten, dessglichen wo und wenn sy wither berüft und gheissen wurden zewarten und zudienen vom Senat gemeinlich oder etlichen uss inen und burgerschaft besunder, es sye ankunft frömder Herren und botschaften uss der Eidtgnoschaft und anderstwohar in gemeinen Ladenschaften und malziten, ouch uf erlichen gselschaftsmalen und by andern, die ouch dessen gewalt und ansehen handt, sy zuberüffen, ir musicspiel zuhören, im selben sich jederzyt willig und gehorsam ane verdruss erzöigen. [. . .] Und ouch in Summers zyt nach dem nachtmal aber uf dem kilchturm mit iren instrumenten gegenwürtig sin, die music celebrieren. m.g.h. [Meinen Gnädigen Herren] und andern, so vilmalen da spacieren, zu recreacion und lust." As quoted in Capitani, *Musik in Bern*, 44.

[37] Capitani, *Musik in Bern*, 45.

[38] Geering, *Vokalmusik*, 151. The dedication is reprinted in Robert Eitner, "Mathias Apiarius Vorrede," *Monatshefte für Musikgeschichte* 8 (1876): 101–4.

[39] Geering, "Von den Berner Stadtpfeifern," 106. On the shawm and the zinck, see Keith Polk, *German Instrumental Music of the Late Middle Ages: Players, Patrons and Performance Practice*, Cambridge Musical Texts and Monographs (Cambridge: Cambridge University Press, 1992), 50–4, 71–3; Andreas Masel, "Doppelrohrblattinstrumente: A. Europäische Instrumente," in *MGG*, Sachteil 2:1349–62; Lorenz Welker, "Zink," in *MGG*, Sachteil 9:2383–90. *Posaune* could refer to a trombone (= double slide) or a slide trumpet (= single slide); I am uncertain which of these two instruments was common in Bern. On the terms sackbut, trombone, and slide trumpet, see Polk, 56–9.

[40] Geering, "Von den Berner Stadtpfeifern," 108; cf. Geering, *Vokalmusik*, 171.

Alder and Wannenmacher were both accomplished composers. Together, they represented the heart of post-Reformation musical life in Bern.[41] Were it not for the protection of the Bernese council, however, Wannenmacher might not have lived to take part in the city's new Protestant culture at all. Following his three years as cantor in Bern from 1510–13, he moved to Fribourg and by 1515 had became cantor of the city's newly founded St. Niklaus Collegiate Convent, created on the model of Bern's St. Vincent convent. Through Peter Falk, Fribourg's mayor (1516–19), he became acquainted with Zwingli and came to support the new faith. The Fribourg council, however, actively opposed Protestantism, and in late 1530 Wannenmacher was arrested and tortured for his faith.[42] Only the intervention of the Bernese council saved him and two compatriots from an uncertain fate. Exiled from Fribourg, he became secretary in Interlaken, where he lived until his death in ca. 1550. Most of his extant compositions date from this period. His duties often brought him to Bern, however, and his gratitude to the city found musical expression in the motet "Encomium urbis Bernae" (1535), also known as "Salve magnificum genus," the opening line of its anonymous Latin text.[43] Cardinal Matthäus Schiner is said to have been an aficionado of Wannenmacher's art,[44] and a number of his compositions gained broader recognition through their publication by Heinrich Glarean in his *Dodecachordon* (1547) and *Musicae epitome* (1557).[45]

Like Wannenmacher, Cosmas Alder earned his living as secretary for the city once the Reformation put an end to his professional musical career. Born ca. 1497 in Baden (Aargau), he became a stu-

---

[41] For a summary of these composers' lives and works, see Hans Joachim Marx, "Wannenmacher," in *Musik in Geschichte und Gegenwart*, 1st ed., ed. Friedrich Blume (Kassel: Bärenreiter, 1968), 14:237–8; Martin Just, "Alder," in *MGG*, Personenteil 1:416–7.

[42] Anshelm records the events as follows: "Witers so haben die von Friburg diss jars etlich der iren umbs gloubens willen mit gfenknus und mit dem henker geschmächt und verjagt, und mit namen irer nüwen stiftkilchen decan, her Hansen Holard von Orben, der stift singer, den künstlichen musicum und componisten, her Hansen Wannenmacher von Nüwenburg und iren artlichen organisten, mgr. Hansen Kottern von Strassburg, getürnt, ufs strekstülle gesezt, dass der henker sprach: was man mit biderben êrenlüten handlen wolte, und getrungen, ire stat und land ehewig und one gnad ze verschweren." Anshelm, 6:24–5. See also Fischer, 571; Geering, *Vokalmusik*, 139–40.

[43] Fischer, 568–9.

[44] Thürlings, 409.

[45] Fischer, 568; Geering, *Vokalmusik*, 135–6; Thürlings, 409.

dent at Bern's St. Vincent convent singing school around 1504. He left in 1511 during Wannenmacher's term as cantor and returned to become cantor himself in April 1525; his whereabouts during the intervening fourteen years are unknown. His time in this office was brief, lasting only until August 1525. Surviving documents offer no reason for his decision to leave the position, but it has been suggested that conditions at the *Kantorei* had become too poor for him to make remarkable improvements.[46] He nonetheless remained a member of the convent until its dissolution, after which, on 15 April 1528, the council appointed him *Bauherrenschreiber* (Secretary for Public Works). He held this office until his death from the plague on 7 November 1550. Like Wannenmacher, he seems to have become an ardent Protestant. Following Zwingli's death in 1531, he composed a lament (*Trauermotette*) for a Latin text by Heinrich Wölflin.[47] He also gained some notoriety in 1539 for his involvement with the composition of "Ein new lied von der uffrur der Landlüten zu Interlappen" (the "Interlaken Song"), which derided Catholic Unterwalden for its less-than-clandestine support of the Oberland uprisings of 1528. Unterwalden obtained a printed copy of the song and brought the matter before the Swiss *Tagsatzung*, so that the Bernese council was forced to punish Alder with a fine and a brief imprisonment to avoid a serious rift within the Swiss Confederacy.[48] It is further assumed that Alder also sang the praises of Bern in an anonymously transmitted motet entitled "Musicorum Bernensium Catalogus et eorundem Encomion" (A Catalogue of Bernese Musicians and their Praise).[49] Even if Alder is not the composer, the surviving incipit aptly exemplifies the period's frequent symbiosis of music and politics: "Floreat ursine gentis canentum sacer ordo" ("May you blossom, holy order of singers of the Bearish [Bernese] populace").[50]

[46] Geering, *Vokalmusik*, 159.
[47] Eduard Bernoulli, "Cosmas Alders Komposition auf Zwinglis Tod," *Zwingliana* 2 (1907): 136–44; Geering, *Vokalmusik*, 172.
[48] Geering convincingly argues that Alder's only guilt consisted of advising the printer on Bern's and Interlaken's coat-of-arms for the broadside's title page: Geering, 162–4.
[49] Fischer, 574–6; Geering, *Vokalmusik*, 172–3.
[50] Musical encomia seem to have been a longstanding tradition in Bern. The sole surviving work by Bartholomäus Frank, Wannenmacher's and Alder's predecessor as cantor at St. Vincent's (1488–1502), is a motet in laudation of Jost von Silenen, Bishop of Sitten (1482–96). Geering, *Vokalmusik*, 100–1, 121–6.

Although psalm singing was not introduced to Bernese worship until 1558, Wannenmacher's *Bicinia* and Alder's *Hymni sacri*, both published posthumously by Apiarius in 1553, offer evidence for a flourishing Protestant musical culture in Bern prior to its official rehabilitation. The melodies of Wannenmacher's eight psalms from the *Bicinia* are based upon Strasbourg hymns: seven from the Wolff Köpfel hymnal of 1526, and one from that of 1530.[51] Despite their publication twenty-five years following the Bernese disputation, Wannenmacher most likely created these songs during his early years in Interlaken in the 1530s.[52] Apiarius's foreword makes apparent that the *Bicinia* circulated among music lovers in Bern and were likely sung as *Hausmusik*.[53] Indeed, Geering suggests that they were taught to local schoolboys after the council arranged in June of 1538 for all pupils to sing psalms: Johannes Kiener, who compiled Wannenmacher's *Bicinia* for Apiarius in 1553, had become local schoolmaster in 1552 and likely gained access to the compositions through his position.[54]

Alder's hymns may also have been performed as *Hausmusik*, although this is probable only for those compositions whose original lyrics did not contravene Zwinglian doctrine. As the hymns originated ca. 1525 during Alder's period as cantor at St. Vincent's,[55] all theologically unacceptable passages underwent a Protestant revision at the hands of Wolfgang Musculus prior to their publication, as exemplified by Musculus's christological redaction of "Ave, maris stella," originally a Vespers hymn for the Feast of the Annunciation:

---

[51] Geering, *Vokalmusik*, 152. See also Thürlings, 410.

[52] Geering further postulates that Wannenmacher's religious motet "Grates Domino jugiter referamus" originated following the Reformation. Geering, *Vokalmusik*, 146, 152.

[53] The relevant passage from Apiarius's foreword is as follows: "Hab ich dise acht Psalmen und andre Lieder zutrucken fürgenommen und das uß sunderlichem antrib und furschub Joannis Kiener, Leermeisters in der Loblichen Statt Bern, welcher im und für sich selb, diewyl er nit der wenigst Musicus ist, vorgenante Psalmen und Lieder zusamen gelesen, welche vorhin der fürträffenliche Musicus und Componist, Johans Vannius, Wannenmacher genant, seliger gedechtnuss hinder im verlassen und mit sunderm flyß für sich selb componiert und zusamen gesetzt, damit so etwan zwen zusamen kämend, sich erlustigen möchtend." As quoted in Eitner, 102.

[54] Geering, *Vokalmusik*, 64, 99.

[55] Andreas Marti, "Gottesdienst und Kirchenlied bei Wolfgang Musculus," in *Wolfgang Musculus (1497–1563) und die oberdeutsche Reformation*, ed. Rudolf Dellsperger, Rudolf Freudenberger, and Wolfgang Weber, Colloquia Augustana 6 (Berlin: Akademie Verlag, 1997), 218; Andreas Traub, "Die Hymnen von Cosmas Alder und Wolfgang Musculus," *Die Musikforschung* 36 (1983): 16; Geering, *Vokalmusik*, 159; Thürlings, 413.

Ave, maris stella,	Ave, maris stella,
Dei mater alma	Dei patris nate
Atque semper virgo,	Atque semper deus,
Felix caeli porta.	Felix coeli porta.[56]

Hail, star of the sea,	Hail, star of the sea,
Nourishing mother of God	Born of God the Father
And yet ever a virgin,	And yet still God,
Blessed gate to heaven.	Blessed gate to heaven.

Together with these hymns, four pieces written by Alder for Rüte's plays survive, and Geering suggests that Wannenmacher's "Invidie Telum" of 1544 was written for the performance of a non-extant Latin play.[57] We will return to these compositions later in the chapter.

Musculus's editorship of Alder's hymns points to the final factor in the Bernese council's endorsement of congregational singing, namely its active support by Zwinglian theologians within and without the city. The publication of the *Bicinia* and *Hymni Sacri* in 1553 would likely not have occurred had Musculus and Johannes Haller not arrived in Bern from Augsburg following the emperor's imposition of the Interim there.[58] Both men were well familiar with Protestant hymn singing from their time in this city. Indeed, Haller is the author of at least one hymn text that survives in the Bernese *Kantorenfolianten* (cantor folios) of 1603.[59] Musculus has similarly long been considered an author of Protestant hymns, although his identity with Wolfgang Mösel, whose name is given as author for six texts in the Constance hymnals, has recently been questioned.[60] Nonetheless, other evidence for Musculus's musical talents remains uncontested, such as his skill at the organ. Most importantly, he vigorously supported devotional music from the beginning of his appointment in Bern.[61] His opening lecture as theology professor at the *Hohe Schule* concerned the psalms, his preface to Alder's hymns explicitly recommended the

---

[56] Geering, *Vokalmusik*, 170; Traub, 17.
[57] Geering, *Vokalmusik*, 150.
[58] See for example Marti, 223–5.
[59] See Jenny, "Das evangelische Lied," 100–2; Jenny, *Geschichte d. dt.-schw. Gesangbuches*, 284–5; Zulauf, 2; Eduard Bähler, "Dekan Johann Haller und die Berner Kirche von 1548 bis 1575," in *NBT 1924*, 7.
[60] Manfred Schuler, "Ist Wolfgang Musculus wirklich der Autor mehrerer Kirchenlieder?" *Jahrbuch für Liturgik und Hymnologie* 17 (1972): 217–221; Marti, 204–18. Cf. Jenny, *Geschichte d. dt.-schw. Gesangbuches*, 85–6.
[61] M. Schuler, 218; Reimann, 48, note 14.

performance of music during worship,[62] and in 1551 he was handsomely rewarded for the dedication of his commentaries on the psalms to the Bernese council.[63] This work, *In Sacrosanctum Davidis Psalterium Commentarii*, went through at least six reprintings following its publication by Johannes Herwagen in Basel in 1551.[64] Guillaume Farel praised it to Haller, and Calvin placed it on a par with Bucer's corresponding interpretation.[65] Its authority even served Zurich clergy in their efforts to introduce hymn singing in their own city, as demonstrated by the following passage from Johann Jakob Wick's *Von dem christlichen Gesang* (On Christian Singing), published anonymously in 1586:

> So schreibt auch der gottselige gelehrte prediger Wolffgangus Musculus [...] in seiner vorred über die außlegung der psalmen, was großen trosts, vermahnung und stärcke er mitten in aller trübsal auß dem psalmensingen empfangen, alß er noch der kirchen zuo Augspurg vorgestanden [... und ...] daß denen kirchen nicht wenig mangle, in welchen die Gesang Davids, so am allerdienstlichsten seien, das gmüht in gottseligkeit zuo bewegen, gar underlassen oder nicht gesungen werden.[66]

> In his foreword on the explication of psalms, [...] the blessed, erudite preacher Wolfgang Musculus also writes of the great comfort, admonition, and strength he received during times of sorrow from the singing of psalms and that those churches lack much in which the songs of David, which are most effective in fostering piety in one's mind, are omitted or not sung.

Psalm singing was finally officially introduced in Bern's churches in 1574. Just as Musculus's writings served Wick's ends, it appears that Zurich theologians had at least indirect influence on the development of affairs in Bern. Ludwig Lavater, archdeacon and later antistes in Zurich, dedicated his *In libros Parlipomenon sive Chronicorum*

---

[62] Marti, 219–20; Traub, 16–7. Musculus's preface, together with a dedicatory poem by the Zurich theologian Rudolf Gwalther, is reprinted as Appendix VII in Geering, *Vokalmusik*, 216–21.

[63] Rudolf Dellsperger, "Wolfgang Musculus (1497–1563). Leben und Werk," *BZGH* 59 (1997): 227; Geering, *Vokalmusik*, 98; M. Schuler, 218.

[64] Craig S. Farmer, *The Gospel of John in the Sixteenth Century: The Johannine Exegesis of Wolfgang Musculus* (New York/Oxford: Clarendon Press, 1997), 3. See also Marc van Wijnkoop Lüthi, "Druckwerkverzeichnis des Wolfgang Musculus (1497–1563)," in *Wolfgang Musculus (1497–1563) und die oberdeutsche Reformation*, 379–85.

[65] Farmer, 4.

[66] As quoted in Reimann, 48.

Ludovici Lavateri Tigurini commentarius, in which the defense of devotional music plays a central role, to the Bernese council in 1573.[67] While Lavater's arguments were intended primarily for the councilors and citizens of Zurich, his dedication of the work to the Bernese council was perhaps meant to convince wavering magistrates of the wisdom of singing God's praises. In 1572, the council had already moved towards a full rehabilitation of church music by commanding the *Stadtpfeifer* to join the children's choir in psalm singing, likely in an effort to improve the quality of song.[68] The council's final step was to poll the local clergy on the matter.[69] The enthusiastic response removed any remaining misgivings, so that, effective Easter 1574, the council decreed "des einem gefallen wölle, das man jedes suntags vor und nach der predig singen sölle" (may it please one to sing every Sunday before and after the sermon).[70] Johannes Kiener, who had been instrumental in the publication of Wannenmacher's *Bicinia*, was appointed cantor to lead the congregation and the children's choir in song. As the minster organ had been sold in 1528, their singing was at first unaccompanied, but the *Stadtpfeifer* were directed in 1581 to support the singers on their instruments.[71]

Looking back across a half-century of musical development, four stages become apparent in the rehabilitation of church music in Bern: 1) between 1528 and 1538, the council apparently discouraged the singing of psalms, believing them incompatible with proper worship;[72] 2) from 1538 to 1558, local boys were taught psalms in school, but church services remained without music; 3) between 1558 and 1574, a choir of schoolboys sang one psalm each Sunday prior to the sermon; 4) beginning in 1574, a cantor led the congregation, together with the boys' choir, in singing two psalms, one before and one after the sermon. The publication of Rüte's five biblical dramas occurred within the second period between 1538 and 1558. Like the singing of psalms in school, the performance of religious music in Rüte's

---

[67] Reimann identifies six main themes in the commentary concerning church music: "1. Die Musik von David eingeführt; 2. Die Anfänge der Musikausübung im Tempel; 3. Zwei Arten sakraler Musik; 4. Der Mißbrauch der Musik; 5. Die Kraft der Musik; 6. Der Kirchengesang ein Adiaphoron." Reimann, 40.
[68] Capitani, 39.
[69] Zulauf, 4.
[70] As quoted in Capitani, 39. See also Zulauf, 4.
[71] Aeschbacher, 234.
[72] Zulauf, 2.

plays constituted a transitional period, an experiment on the compatibility of song and worship conducted, consciously or unconsciously, outside regular church services. Unlike the children's songs, however, the musical portions of Rüte's biblical works were performed before an audience, making local theater the only attested public forum for devotional music prior to its limited reintroduction to Bernese worship in 1558.

The Choral Interludes of Renaissance Theater

The popularity of Protestant hymns was not the only factor that contributed to the musical embellishment of Bernese Reformation plays. As an outgrowth of Catholic liturgy, the religious theater of the Middle Ages had regularly incorporated instrumental and choral music in its performances. Humanist dramaturgy was equally fond of musical interludes, and choruses began to appear in Renaissance plays in the late fifteenth century. The marriage between music and drama may well have been so common that Protestant theater-goers and theologians perceived no apparent contradiction between the hymn singing at Cross Lane, where Rüte's works were likely performed, and its absence in the Bernese minster just a short walk away. A brief discussion of the musical interludes of sixteenth-century German and Swiss drama offers an explanation as to why Rüte was free to incorporate religious music in his plays while it was banned in church.

By the 1530s, choral music had become an integral component of German Renaissance drama. The tradition had begun with the choral interludes of Johannes Reuchlin's *Scaenica Progymnasmata*, or *Henno*, of 1497. *Henno* was not the first humanist drama in Germany to incorporate choruses (that honor belongs to Jakob Locher's *Historia de rege francie* of 1495),[73] but it was *Henno*'s overwhelming success

---

[73] See Bernhard Coppel, "Jakob Locher und seine in Freiburg aufgeführten Dramen," in *Acta Conventus Neo-Latini Amstelodamensis. Proceedings of the Second International Congress of Neo-Latin Studies*, ed. P. Turnman, G.C. Kuiper and E. Keßler (Munich: Wilhelm Fink, 1979), 263. The musical interludes of *Henno* have their roots in the chorus of Reuchlin's first play, *Sergius vel Capitis Caput*. See Glenn Ehrstine, "Scaenica Faceta: The Choral Odes of Johannes Reuchlin's *Scaenica Progymnasmata* (1497)," in *Acta Conventus Neo-Latini Bariensis: Proceedings from the Ninth International Congress at Bari, 29 August–3 September 1994*, ed. Rhoda Schnur et al. (Tempe, Arizona: Medieval and Renaissance Texts and Studies, 1998), 235–41.

among contemporaries that established the practice among humanist playwrights. Vernacular authors quickly followed suit. Of the 220 plays examined by the nineteenth-century musicologist Rochus von Liliencron in what is still the only comprehensive study of the topic, seventy-five contained choral interludes between acts.[74] Even when no distinct interludes were present, singing was often an integral component of stage events, so that the majority of contemporary theatrical works contained some form of choral music. Renaissance dramatists even combined choruses with dance, initiated by Conrad Celtis in his *Ludus Dianae*, performed in 1501 before Emperor Maximilian in Vienna.[75] Most importantly, Reformation playwrights readily adopted musical interludes for the Protestant stage, beginning with two Basel plays of 1532, Johannes Kolroß's *Fünferlei Betrachtnisse* ("Five Types of Contemplation") and Sixtus Birck's German-language *Susanna*.[76] Paul Rebhun's *Susanna* (1535; first edition 1536) displays the classic structure of Protestant choral drama, namely five acts separated by four choruses, but additional choruses occasionally appeared at the opening or close of a play. Catholic playwrights such as Georg Macropedius were also fond of choral interludes, but it was predominantly Protestant authors such as Joachim Greff, Thomas Naogeorgus, Bartholomäus Krüger, and Nicodemus Frischlin who continued the custom on into the seventeenth century.

In addition to introducing danced choruses, Conrad Celtis developed new harmonic settings for Latin odes that exerted a lasting influence on the development of homophonic choral music. Like others of his time, Celtis believed that Horace and fellow classical poets had originally sung their odes accompanied by a kithara.[77] In addition to being Germany's first poet laureate, Celtis was an accomplished musician, so that he set about re-creating this music with

---

[74] Rochus von Liliencron, "Die Chorgesänge des lateinisch-deutschen Schuldramas im XVI. Jahrhundert," *Vierteljahrsschrift für Musikwissenschaft* 6 (1890): 314.

[75] Liliencron, "Chorgesänge," 316–7, 344–5; Conrad Celtis, "Ludus Dianae," in *Ludi Scaenici*, ed. Felicitas Pindter (Budapest: Egyetemi Nyomda, 1945), 1–6.

[76] Johannes Kolroß, "Fünferlei Betrachtnisse, die den Menschen zur Buße reizen," in *Schweizerische Schauspiele des 16. Jahrhunderts*, ed. Theodor Odinga (Zurich: J. Huber, 1890), 1:51–100. Kolroß was also the author of Protestant hymns. See Theodor Odinga, *Das deutsche Kirchenlied der Schweiz im Reformationszeitalter* (Frauenfeld: Huber, 1889), 53–5.

[77] Rochus von Liliencron, "Die Horazischen Metren in deutschen Kompositionen des 16. Jahrhunderts," *Vierteljahrsschrift für Musikwissenschaft* 3 (1887): 35; Garside, 11.

the assistance of his pupil Petrus Tritonius.[78] Celtis's ultimate goal, however, was to employ this music as an aid in the learning of Latin verse. Tritonius's resulting four-voiced compositions, published in 1507 under the title *Melopoiae*,[79] wholly subordinated their melodies to the metrical patterns of each ode. Moreover, they departed from the customary polyphonic arrangements of the period in their harmonic simplification, arranging the lower parts as chords in support of the uppermost voice, which now carried the melody instead of the tenor. Celtis had already employed this homophonic "ode style" of composition for the interludes of *Ludus Dianae*, and it soon became characteristic for play choruses in general.[80] As Wannenmacher's "Invidie Telum" is strongly reminiscent of this manner of composition, Geering postulates its creation for an otherwise unknown Latin play, but his conclusions remain speculative.[81] A much more apt example of humanist choral odes in Switzerland exists in Zwingli's compositions for the Zurich performance of Aristophanes's *Ploutos* ("Wealth") on New Year's Day, 1531. Zwingli had studied in Vienna under Celtis and likely sang the new odes with other students at the end of lectures, as was Celtis's wont.[82] Zwingli's settings for *Ploutos* do not survive, but they were likely four-part homophonic compositions based on the ode style.[83] Above all, Ludwig Senfl's 1534 reworking of Tritonius's settings helped propagate the new manner of composition.[84]

Although Celtis's innovations were intended as a pedagogical device, the subsequent inclusion of homophonic choral odes in religious plays soon influenced church music,[85] as the homophonic treatment of

---

[78] Lewis W. Spitz, *Conrad Celtis. The German Arch-Humanist* (Cambridge: Harvard University Press, 1957), 80–2.
[79] *Melopoiae sive harmoniae tetracenticae super xxii genera carminum heroicorum elegiacorum lyricorum & ecclesiasticorum hymnorum* (Augsburg: Erhard Oeglin, 1507).
[80] Liliencron, "Chorgesänge," 350.
[81] Geering, *Vokalmusik*, 150; repeated in Fischer, 572.
[82] Garside, 12–3; Jenny, "Die Lieder Zwinglis," 74.
[83] Jenny, "Die Lieder Zwinglis," 75.
[84] Ludwig Senfl, "Lateinische Oden: Varia carminum genera," in *Sämtliche Werke*, ed. Arnold Geering and Wilhelm Altwegg (Wolfenbüttel: Möseler Verlag, 1961) 6:71–87. Several of Tritonius's and Senfl's settings are contained in Eduard Stemplinger, *Das Fortleben der horazischen Lyrik seit der Renaissance* (Leipzig: Teubner, 1906), passim. See also Joachim Draheim and Günther Wille, *Horaz-Vertonungen vom Mittelalter bis zur Gegenwart. Eine Anthologie* (Amsterdam: B.R. Grüner, 1985), 16–7, nos. 3–4.
[85] Liliencron, "Chorgesänge," 313; E. Refardt, "Die Musik der Basler Volksschauspiele des 16. Jahrhunderts," *Archiv für Musikwissenschaft* 3 (1921): 199–219.

melody proved ideally suited to congregational singing. Motets usually called for four vocal parts, requiring skilled singers for their performance. By placing the melody in the discant voice, however, the new ode style, when applied to hymns, allowed a congregation untrained in choral music to hear the melody in the upper register and to sing along with the choir. The *Fünfftzig Geistliche Lieder vnd Psalmen* (1586) of Württemberg court preacher Lucas Osiander, son of Nuremberg reformer Andreas Osiander, were the first to fully develop this compositional style for congregational singing (*Kantionalsatz*), but the trend towards homophonic hymn settings is apparent as early as 1546.[86] In Garside's summary of the development, "music which was the direct outgrowth of exclusively classical and philological research, the product of a secular institution and secular ideas, came eventually to exert an extraordinarily pervasive influence on the religious music of the sixteenth century."[87]

Although the Basel plays of Kolroß and Birck were apparently the first Protestant vernacular dramas to incorporate musical interludes, the choral music of Swiss Reformation theater remained distinct from that of Lutheran drama to the north. In the latter, choruses were generally sung between acts, making them *Festchöre*, or interludes with no direct connection to the action of the play.[88] In most Swiss plays, however, choral music is frequently part of the plot itself, so that these are referred to as *Bühnenchöre*, or stage choruses.[89] Liliencron explains the predominance of stage choruses in Switzerland by postulating that the civic actors of Swiss dramas, unlike the schoolboys who performed Lutheran plays, lacked choral training; playwrights were thus obliged to rely on traveling musicians or city musicians (i.e. *Stadtpfeifer*) for the performance of the allegedly simpler *Bühnenchöre*.[90] Even Refardt, who includes Kolroß's *Fünferlei Betrachtnisse* and Birck's *Susanna* in his analysis of sixteenth-century Basel drama, similarly assumes that stage choruses were simpler, usually written for one voice.[91] Yet Kolroß's and Birck's plays of 1532,

---

[86] Liliencron, "Chorgesänge," 310–2.
[87] Garside, 12.
[88] Refardt, 200.
[89] Ibid., 200. Refardt's terminology reflects the generic distinction between *Rahmenmusik* and *Bühnen-* or *Inzidenzmusik*. See Detlef Altenburg and Lorenz Jensen, "Schauspielmusik," in *MGG*, Sachteil 8:1035.
[90] Liliencron, "Chorgesänge," 347.
[91] Refardt draws his conclusions in the absence of printed music. Refardt, 205.

which were performed by townsfolk as opposed to young scholars, contain *Festchöre*. Moreover, Alder's surviving choral compositions for Rüte's plays conform to neither Liliencron's nor Refardt's hypotheses in this regard. The two surviving motets from *Joseph*, although *Bühnenchöre*, tend towards the humanist ode style for four voices.[92] In addition to suggesting that Protestant stage music in Bern developed independently from that in Basel (not at all improbable considering that Basel, unlike Bern, embraced congregational singing), these compositions demonstrate that the putative absence of trained singers is not a factor in the Swiss preference for stage choral music. Given the overall lack of act divisions in sixteenth-century Swiss drama, the cause was likely much more banal. Simply stated, one cannot perform choral interludes between acts (*Zwischenaktmusik*, i.e. *Festchöre*) when a play has no acts, nor breaks between them. Furthermore, the lack of act divisions was typical for late medieval dramaturgy as it continued to be practiced in Swiss Catholic cities such as Lucerne. If the Lucerne Passion Play at times required 156 musicians for a performance,[93] Swiss Protestants were not about to let themselves be outdone in the display of musical skill, provided, of course, that that skill served the praise of God.

The Music of Bernese Reformation Drama

The original editions of Rüte's five biblical dramas preserve no written music. Nonetheless, five songs are contrafacta or traditional compositions such as the "Te Deum," so that their melodies are found in other sources. Moreover, four works created by Alder for the plays *Joseph* and *Noe* survive in manuscript. We can thus reconstruct a total of nine compositions, a mix of original and common melodies comprising somewhat less than a third of all choral music originally performed in the plays. A variety of instrumental pieces appears as well, ranging from refined four-part works for sackbuts to the trumpet blasts of battle scenes. The uncertain dating of *Goliath* makes it difficult to gauge how constitutive music originally was for the local Reformation

---

[92] Geering, 174.
[93] Refardt cites this number for the play's 1583 performance. We know, however, that the play was performed in a similar form in 1545, contemporary with Rüte's activities as playwright. Refardt, 209.

stage: *Joseph*, performed in 1538, calls for music on only four occasions, but *Goliath*, possibly performed in 1535, does so eleven times. For the later plays of *Gedeon*, *Noe*, and *Osterspiel*, however, musical interludes become increasingly intertwined with events portrayed on stage. A *truwer gsang* (*Gedeon*, vv. 1097–122) is sung when the protagonists are troubled, while occasions of celebration call for a *Lobgsang* (*Noe*, after v. 1843). By 1552, the interludes of *Osterspiel* account for at least one-third of the performance and form an integral plot component. Most importantly, the occurrence of song in specific contexts, such as thanksgiving, consolation, and especially prayer, allows for a re-evaluation of the sociocultural status of devotional music in post-Reformation Bern. A review of the plays' surviving compositions and song texts, together with their function within each play, reveals that Bernese Zwinglianism united music and worship in a much closer mutual relationship than suggested by the city's formal prohibition of hymn singing in church. Indeed, congregational singing not only was modelled on stage in *Noe*, but also likely took place among audience members at the close of *Osterspiel*.

Joseph is the first of Rüte's dramas for which music survives. Its motet "Da Jacob nun das Klaidt ansach" ("When Jacob saw the coat"), "one of the monuments of sixteenth-century German music,"[94] is likely Cosmas Alder's best known composition. The work survives together with "Wie Joseph in Egyptenlant" ("Joseph in Egypt"), a second motet composed by Alder for the play, in an instructional partbook compiled ca. 1547 by the Bernese musician Christoph Piperinus for Basilius Amerbach, son of Basel lawyer Bonifacius Amerbach.[95] The motet owes its fame in part to its long-term attribution

---

[94] John Kmetz, "Da Jakob nun das Kleid ansah and Zurich Zentralbibliothek T 410–413: a well-known motet in a little-known 16th-century manuscript," *Schweizer Jahrbuch für Musikwissenschaft* Neue Folge 4/5 (1984/85): 71. See also Gustave Reese, *Music in the Renaissance* (New York: W.W. Norton, 1954), 679; Friedrich Blume, "Das Zeitalter der Reformation," in *Geschichte der Evangelischen Kirchenmusik*, ed. Friedrich Blume, 2nd ed. (Kassel: Bärenreiter, 1965), 53–4.

[95] Universitätsbibliothek Basel MS F.X. 5–9, nos. 32–33. An edition of the motet based on this manuscript can be found in Eduard Bernoulli, *Aus Liederbüchern der Humanistenzeit. Eine bibliographische und notentypographische Studie* (Leipzig: Breitkopf & Härtel, 1910), 104–7, Beilage XV. "Wie Joseph in Egyptenland" is edited in *Psalmen und Geistliche Gesänge von Johannes Wannenmacher (Vannius) und Cosmas Alder (Alderinus)*, ed. Arnold Geering, Musikalische Werke schweizerischer Komponisten des XVI., XVII. und XVIII. Jahrhunderts 3 (Geneva: Edition Henn, 1934), 49–51, no. 6. On the manuscript, see John Kmetz, "The Piperinus-Amerbach partbooks:

to Ludwig Senfl, to whom Georg Rhau erroneously assigned the composition in his *Neue deutsche geistliche Gesänge* of 1544.[96] In 1933, however, Arnold Geering pointed to the authority of the Basel partbook in determining authorship and further noted the works' relationship to Rüte's *Joseph*.[97] Considering that Alder and Rüte were colleagues, both serving the city as secretaries, their collaboration on local performances seems only natural. Although the partbook makes no mention of the play, the two motets correspond exactly to the two passages in *Joseph* that call for choral music: "Hie soll etwas gsungen werden" ("Something should be sung here"; after v. 646) and "Hie soll abermals etwas gsungen werdenn" ("Something should again be sung here"; after v. 1291). In the first case, Joseph's brothers present Jacob with his son's bloodied coat; his subsequent soliloquy ends the scene just before Alder's motet begins. After the first two lines, the song text renders Jacob's lament in the first person, echoing his stage soliloquy in its themes of disconsolation and death (cf. Appendix, Text I). The lines "o wee der grosen noth/mein lieber Son der ist todt" ("alas, the great anguish/my dear son is dead") and "O Joseph Joseph mein lieber Son" are especially emphasized through their homophonic setting. The second motet, "Wie Joseph in Egyptenlant" (Appendix, Text II), contains even more homophonic sections,[98] strongly suggesting that Alder here consciously adopted the humanist ode style of composition. The piece appears just after Joseph has been imprisoned for his alleged molestation of Potiphar's wife. Although *Joseph* is not divided into acts, Alder's two motets

---

six months of music lessons in Renaissance Basle," in *Music in the German Renaissance. Sources, Styles, and Contexts*, ed. John Kmetz (Cambridge: Cambridge University Press, 1994), 215–34.

[96] *Neue deutsche geistliche Gesänge für die gemeinen Schulen*, vol. 11 of *Georg Rhau. Musikdrucke aus den Jahren 1538–1545 in praktischer Neuausgabe*, ed. Joachim Stalmann (Kassel: Bärenreiter, 1992), 414–8, no. 120. See also *Newe deudsche geistlische Gesenge für die gemeinen Schulen*, 2nd ed., ed. Johannes Wolf and Hans Joachim Moser, Denkmäler deutscher Tonkunst 34 (Wiesbaden: Breitkop & Härtel, 1958), 180–1, no. 68; Ludwig Senfl, *Sämtliche Werke*, 6:32–5, no. 20; Noah Greenberg and Paul Maynard, eds., *An Anthology of Early Renaissance Music* (New York: W.W. Norton, 1975), 147, no. 18. The composition has been recorded by New York Pro Musica, directed by Noah Greenberg: Ludwig Senfl, *Composer to the Court and Chapel of Emperor Maximilian I*, Decca DL 79420.

[97] Geering, *Vokalmusik*, 173–5. The manuscript transmits "Wie Joseph in Egyptenlant" anonymously, but its obvious connection to "Da Jacob nun das Klaidt ansach" and *Joseph* leads Geering to assume Alder's authorship for this motet as well.

[98] Ibid., 175.

form a type of act division through their placement between central scenes. This again suggests that Alder and Rüte were familiar with the choral odes of humanist dramaturgy, especially as Rüte's direct source, the *Joseph* of Cornelius Crocus, has no musical interludes despite its five-act structure. The play further calls twice for instrumental music, once when Pharaoh convenes his councilors, and once when Joseph becomes Pharaoh's advisor;[99] it is likely that musicians from Bern's *Stadtpfeiferei* performed these pieces. There is no mention of interludes during the play's second day, which portrays Joseph's dealings with his brothers in Egypt, but it is possible that additional music was performed without being noted.[100]

Gedeon contains both an increase in instrumental music[101] and the first song lyrics to appear within one of Rüte's texts: the *truwer gsang* "Drumm das wir handt die Bott veracht" ("Because we have disregarded the commandments"; Appendix, Text III). The song's three strophes were sung separately, the first two upon the Israelites' recognition of their fall from God's law (after v. 522) at the play's outset, and the third following Gideon's victory over Israel's enemies near the end of the play (after v. 3925; cf. vv. 1123–35). The *truwer gesang* thus accounts for two of the play's five choral interludes. Moreover, its recurrence at the play's close frames Gideon's story, linking the two successive days of performance through the repetition of its melody. Its strophic structure is a 13-line bar form consisting of two two-line *Stollen* and a nine-line *Abgesang*. As it corresponds to no extant melody,[102] it apparently was not a contrafactum. Nonetheless, the first nine lines of each strophe are nearly identical to the metrical structure of Luther's "Ein veste Burg" (A Mighty Fortress is Our God), first printed in Joseph Klug's Wittenberg hymnal of

---

[99] "Man blast in rat" (after v. 1391); "Tryumphisch music/mit pasonen oder veldtrommeten" (after v. 1757).

[100] Liliencron notes that some plays expressly left the performance of choruses to the discretion of their players. Liliencron, "Chorgesänge", 343.

[101] The increase consists mainly of the sounding of trumpets during war councils or battles: "Trummetter bloßt vff" (after v. 2187); "Trummetter blaßt vff" (after v. 2843); "Blasent/brechent die krüg vnd schryent" (after v. 3583); "Hieruff ein hoffblasen/mit posunen/trumeten/vnd heerbaugken" (after v. 3959).

[102] Cf. Phillip Wackernagel, *Das deutsche Kirchenlied von der ältesten Zeit bis zum Anfang des XVII. Jahrhunderts*, 5 vols. (Leipzig, 1864–77; reprint Hildesheim: Olms, 1964); Johannes Zahn, *Die Melodien der deutschen evangelischen Kirchenlieder*, 6 vols. (Gütersloh, 1889–93; reprint Hildesheim: Olms, 1963).

1529.[103] The melody of "Drumm das wir handt die Bott veracht" may thus possibly have followed that of Luther's, with the final lines repeated as a da capo. Lastly, the notes accompanying the song's third strophe, rendered in the past tense, indicate that the text of *Gedeon* (as well as that of Rüte's other plays?) was printed following its performance: "When Gideon was victorious and had struck down his enemies with the help of God, the following strophe *was* sung."[104]

The most interesting aspect of *Gedeon*'s remaining choral music is not what was sung, but when it was sung. In addition to an unspecified *Gsang Gott lobend* (Song praising God, after v. 1722) at the close of the first day's performance, choral music sounds immediately following prayer on two occasions (after v. 1930; v. 2575), as illustrated by Joash's plea for Gideon's success in battle:

> Gnädiger barmhertziger Gott
> Gib Gedeon vnd siner rott/
> Mittel vnd weg/ouch macht vnd krafft/
> Das sy die gottloß heydenschafft/[...]
> Mögent überwinden vnd fellen [...]
> So wil jch Herr dich loben prysen/
> Ouch all gmein/vnd kilchen an wysen/
> Das sy vererint dinen nammen/
> Erhör min pit/min Herr gott/Amen.
> *Gsang.* (vv. 1911–30)

> Merciful, benevolent God, grant Gideon and his company the ways and means and strength and power to overcome and strike down [...] the godless heathens. [...] Then I shall praise and laud you, Lord, and command that every congregation and church honor your name. Hear my plea, Lord God. Amen.—*Chorus*

The occurrence of song in such close proximity to Joash's supplication marks a striking contrast to Zwingli's call for silent prayer. Given the choruses' tendency to amplify preceding dialogue, as we have already seen in *Joseph*, it is likely that the composition contained some type of entreaty to God. This is the earliest indication offered

---

[103] Markus Jenny, ed., *Luthers geistliche Lieder und Kirchengesänge. Vollständige Neuedition in Ergänzung zu Band 35 der Weimarer Ausgabe*, Archiv zur Weimarer Ausgabe der Werke Martin Luthers, Texte und Untersuchungen 4 (Cologne/Vienna: Böhlau, 1985), 100.

[104] "Alß Gedeon den syg behalten vnd sine find mit der hilff Gottes erschlagen/ward das nochuolgent gesetz gesungen" (after v. 1122).

by the plays that song and prayer were by no means mutually exclusive in Bern's still young Reformation.

By 1546, song and prayer are directly linked in *Noe*'s hymn "Ach Herr vernim / min kläglich stim" ("O Lord, hear my plaintive voice"; Appendix, Text VII). "Ach Herr vernim" is also the only song text transmitted by Rüte's plays for which a melody by Alder survives.[105] The composition is situated within Noah's lament following his discovery of Ham's rebellion. Once Japheth and Shem have told their father the news, he asks them to leave so that he may pray in private:

> Ach min sün gand von mir ein klein/
> Biß ich min lieben sun bewein [. . .]
> *Bättet knüwendt.*
> O Herr/verlych mir gnad vnd huld
> Dann es ist gwüßlich nit min schuld
> Das Cham vom glouben tretten ist
> Es kumpt jm har von ß'tüffels list
> Jch han arbeit mit ernst dran kert
> Das er dins willens wurde glert [. . .]
> Din heil laß bliben in mim samen
> Das mengklich hochbryß dinen namen.
> *Das erst Gsatz deß trurigen Gsangs.* (vv. 3371–90)

> Alas, my sons, leave me for a while until I have shed tears for my dear son. [. . .]—*Prays kneeling*—O Lord, grant me your grace and favor, for I am surely not to blame for Ham's fall from faith. It's come upon him from the devil's trickery. I labored in earnest that he be taught your will. [. . .] Let your blessing remain in my seed, so that many will praise your name.—*The first strophe of the lament.*

Although Noah has sent Japheth and Shem away, his prayer is not the silent *innwendigs gebett* called for by Zwingli in his *Auslegen und Gründe der Schlußreden*. Nor is the *trurig Gsang* superficial musical embellishment. Noah intersperses its three strophes individually at distinct moments in his appeal. The second strophe, which deals with Satan, occurs just after Noah has cursed "the devil's suggestions and council";[106] the third, in which Noah asks that his request be granted, concludes the supplication. As with "Drumm das wir handt die Bott

---

[105] The song, preserved in the Universitätsbibliothek Basel (MS F. IX. 32–35, no. 13), has been edited by Geering: *Psalmen und Geistliche Gesänge*, 52–5, no. 7. See also Geering, *Vokalmusik*, 175.

[106] "ß'tüffels ingeben vnd rhat" (v. 3430).

veracht" in *Gedeon*, the hymn's strophes are sung separately to highlight certain passages. In *Gedeon*, the composition framed the overall play and united the two days of performance; here, the intermingling of song with Noah's prayer gives his plea added solemnity. Unlike "Da Jacob nun das Klaidt ansach," however, "Ach Herr vernim" is not topical. At no point does it specifically refer to Noah's conflict with Ham. Rather, the song might serve anyone in time of need.[107]

This suggests that some of the songs from Rüte's plays were sung as devotional hymns in other contexts. At the very least, we know that the second song in bar form from *Noe*, "Das truren ist vergangen" ("The mourning has passed"; Appendix, Text IV), circulated outside of Bern. The song appeared in Marburg in 1552 under the title "Eyne ermanung an die Teudschen, das sie jre alte Freiheit helffen retten" ("An admonition to the Germans to help save their ancient liberty"), in which an otherwise unknown Henrich Engel appended four additional strophes to Rüte's original three.[108] According to this late source, the song is based upon the melody "Frisch auff in Gottes namen, du werte teutsche Nation" ("Arise in God's name, you worthy German nation") from the 1540s.[109] However, Klaus Jaeger has recently drawn attention to a High German version of the first strophe, which appeared in the third edition of Christian Egenolff's *Gassenhawer Vnd Reutterliedlin*, printed in Frankfurt in 1535.[110] Considering that the Egenolff setting is also not original, "Das truren ist vergangen" is in either case the first verifiable contrafactum in

---

[107] Indeed, as noted by Klaus Jaeger, the song's three strophes are contained in "Ein Klagliedt vom Fall Adams vnnd Heua," printed in 1550 by Johann Daubmann in Nuremberg, and advertised with the subtitle "Von Gott hilff vnnd trost zu bitten, Jm streitt Menschliches lebens hie auff erden." This version combines "Ach Herr vernim" with the three strophes of Leo Jud's "Dein, dein sol sein" (1540); Jaeger suggests that it was performed in this form for Jacob Rueff's *Adam und Eva*. See *Sämtliche Dramen*, 3:86–7; Wackernagel, 3:725, no. 835.

[108] Wackernagel, 3:1069, no. 1238. See Klaus Stephan Jaeger, "Hans von Rütes Osterspiel. Edition und Untersuchung" (M.A. Thesis, Freie Universität Berlin, 1993), 262; Odinga, *Kirchenlied*, 80–81. Jenny gives the redactor's name as Hans Engel: Jenny, *Geschichte d. dt.-schw. Gesangbuches*, 288.

[109] Erk lists an *Einzelliederdruck* of 1545 as the earliest source; Liliencron however dates the song to 1540. See Ludwig Erk, ed., *Deutscher Liederhort* (Leipzig: Breitkopf & Härtel, 1893), 2:99, no. 290; Rochus von Liliencron, *Die historischen Volkslieder der Deutschen vom 13. bis 16. Jahrhundert* (Leipzig: Vogel, 1869), 4:156–7, no. 469. The composition is also found in the 1549 edition of Georg Forster's *Der dritte Teyl schöner lieblicher alter vnd newer Teutscher Liedlein*. At least one other contrafactum of the melody exists beyond those by Rüte and Engel: "Ein new lied von dem gefangenen herzog Heinrich von Braunschweig." See Liliencron, *Volkslieder*, 4:279–82, no. 516.

[110] *Sämtliche Dramen*, 3:84–5.

the Bernese plays. The piece, a *Lobgsang*, occurs as Noela and Noegla, the wives of Japheth and Shem, give thanks in the company of their daughters for having escaped the flood. More specifically, the women link the song to the play's theme of bearing witness. Like the staging of the "Small Play" during the Sukkoth feast, "Das truren ist vergangen" is performed so that subsequent generations will not forget God's benevolence:

> *Japhets Eefrouw*
> Das wir von gots straff sind erlößt/
> Vnd durch den tod nit ouch erößt/
> Das ist Gots wunder/macht/vnd krafft/
> Aber die fröud/die vns ist gschafft
> Durch disers werck/ist grösser gsin/
> Dann alle wunder mögent sin/
> Man mags nit sagen/schryben/singen/
> Sy ist ein ding ob allen dingen/
> Sy ist das end der Gottes werck
> Darumb er zeygt sin gwalt vnd sterck/[...]
> *Sems Eefrouw*
> Dem Herren Gott zuo danck vnd pryß
> Sungent wir mit frölicher wyß/
> Das lied das jr von vns hand glert
> (Das truren ist in fröud verkert)
> Das singent yetz von hertzen grund
> Nun schryent lut/thuond vff den mund.
> *Gsang*. (vv. 1068–89)

> *Japheth's Wife*:
> It is God's miraculous work, His power and might, that we were delivered from His punishment and did not suffer death as others. Yet the joy that was given us through this work is greater than all miracles combined. One cannot express it in words, print, or song. It is greater than all things. It is the purpose of all God's works, the reason He displays His power and strength. [...]
> *Shem's Wife*:
> To thank and praise the Lord God, we sang with a joyous melody the song that you have learned from us. (The sorrow has turned to joy.) Let us sing it now from the bottom of our hearts. Shout it out loudly, open your mouths wide.
> *Chorus*

Just as Noela and Noegla model the singing of God's praises for their daughters, the actors do so for the audience. Moreover, the song appears to be a familiar one, not only for the daughters, but perhaps also for those in attendance. The appearance of the first strophe in Egenolff's *Gassenhawer Vnd Reutterliedlin* makes it difficult to say if Rüte was the author, but he may have composed the text as early as 1535 for the first performance of *Goliath*.[111] In all cases, "Das truren ist vergangen" was popular enough to return six years later in *Osterspiel*.

Noe's third song, "Gelobet sy gott vnser herr" ("Praised Be the Lord Our God"; Appendix, Text V), reappears in *Osterspiel* as well. In the present play, it is given as a series of thirteen couplets; no known melody survives. Like "Das truren ist vergangen," it is a song of praise, possibly a paraphrase of Psalm 148, which also calls upon all creation to glorify the Lord.[112] The shared context of thanksgiving links the two compositions, so that the latter song complements the earlier one. However, whereas "Das truren" was sung in private by women, "Gelobet sy gott" is performed publicly by Noah's combined kin while he and his sons make the Lord a burnt offering. The combination of song and sacrifice elicits a direct response from God Himself:

> *Noe*:
> Nun han ich euch drumb b'samlet har [...]
> Das wir danckent vmb die guotthat
> Die vnß rychlich von Gott zuostat
> Mit opffer vnd frölichem gsang
> Das von grund vnsers hertzen gang. [...]
> *Gsang.*
> Gelobet sy gott vnser herr [...]
> *Opffer inn dem als man singt.*
> *Gott*:
> Was liebligkeit ich hie empfind
> Was süssen gschmacks bringt mir der wind?
> Durch den ich ouch ghör vnd vernim
> Ein ton einr einhelligen stim.
> *Noe*:
> Jetz hörent jr on trug vnd list
> Das Gott in mitz vnder vns ist
> Als dick wir ye inn sinem namen
> Versamblet sind vnd kommen zamen. (vv. 1378–421)

> *Noah*:
> I have gathered you together here [...] that we may give thanks with sacrifice and heart-felt song for the benevolence that God has richly bestowed upon us. [...]

---

[111] As postulated by Jaeger, *Sämtliche Dramen*, 3:85.
[112] Ibid., 3:85.

Chorus
Praised be the Lord Our God [...]
Offering as one sings.
God:
What delight I feel here. What sweet taste does the wind bring to me? I also hear upon it the sound of voices raised in unison.
Noah:
You now hear without deceit that God is in our midst as often as we are gathered and come together in His name.

The parts of the patriarch and his descendants in *Noe* required at least 42 actors for speaking roles; others may have assumed smaller parts with no dialogue, such as the children of Shem and Japheth. All come together for the Sukkoth feast of thanksgiving, and the text suggests that all joined together in the singing of "Gelobet sy gott vnser herr." The setting is thus far removed from the private prayer of "Ach Herr vernim." Nonetheless, the singing of the assembled group is explicitly portrayed as pleasing to God. In particular, Noah's paraphrase of Matthew 18:20 ("For where two or three are gathered in my name, there am I in the midst of them") directly links the Sukkoth gathering to Christian worship, making the performance of "Gelobet sy gott vnser herr" congregational singing in Old Testament garb. This does not imply that such singing was commonplace in Bern at the time of *Noe*'s performance in 1546, but it does demonstrate that the unaccompanied performance of song during worship was considered unobjectionable, a far cry from the "temple mumblings" rejected by Zwingli. Johannes Haller and Wolfgang Musculus would have thus found fertile soil for their support of church music upon their arrival in Bern just two years later.

Two occurrences of vocal music in *Noe* remain: Cham's song concerning Noah's nakedness (Appendix, Text VI), and Alder's antiphon "Veni electa mea" ("Come, my chosen one"; Appendix, Text VIII). Cham sings his song after discovering Noah asleep with open robe; as it is derisive, not devotional, its analysis occurs later among the plays' occasionally pejorative musical contexts. Regarding "Veni electa mea," we would not know it was performed during *Noe* were it not for a marginal note in the work's manuscript: "Cosmas Alderinus faciebat (vf pusunen) Berne 1546 in actu Noe" ("Cosmas Alder did this [on sackbuts] in Bern 1546 in the play *Noe*").[113] Unfortunately,

---

[113] Universitätbibliothek Basel F.X. 5–9. See Geering, *Vokalmusik*, 170–1; Geering, "Von den Berner Stadtpfeifern," 108.

the text offers no direct indication of where this composition would have been situated. Geering suggests that it was performed as the *Gsang mit vieren* (Chorus with four voices), called for during the performance of the *klein Spil*; however, as he himself notes, "Veni electa mea" is a five-part composition.[114] There are, however, two other suitable locations. If the piece was indeed performed as choral music, it could have also served as the otherwise unnamed *Lobgsang* found near the end of the play's first day (after v. 1843). Nonetheless, it seems implausible that the manuscript's explicit mention of the composition's performance *vf pusunen* merely indicates that sackbut players provided musical accompaniment for an otherwise vocal piece. This was common practice at the time and would have needed no special remarks. *Vf pusunen* more likely refers to an instrumental arrangement of "Veni electa mea" for sackbuts. There are several occurrences of instrumental music during the play, and the concert given by Jubal in the *klein Spil* specifically calls for *Pausunen* (v. 524).

Although some aspects of *Noe*'s music remain speculative, the relatively detailed information concerning the musical interludes of *Osterspiel* renders speculation largely unnecessary. Unlike Rüte's earlier plays, the Apiarius printing of *Osterspiel* includes the text sung for each of its seven choruses. In three instances—"Johanni dem Apostel das geschach," "Te Deum Laudamus," and "Dignus es Domine"—the incipit alone appears, but in these cases the song texts can be largely reconstructed. The "Te Deum" is furthermore joined by a second song traditionally associated with Catholic Easter plays: "Christ ist erstanden" ("Christ is risen"; Appendix, Text XV). Of the three remaining songs, two—"Das truren ist vergangen" and "Gelobet sy Gott vnser Herr"—reappear from *Noe*. The final composition, "Wie hat es sich doch mit vns verkeert" ("What change has come about"; Appendix, Text XII), is a contrafactum apparently written specifically for the play.

This brief overview alone reveals the singularity of *Osterspiel*'s music in comparison to that of Bern's previous biblical plays. Judging from surviving texts, Latin choruses were rare in *Joseph*, *Gedeon*, and *Noe*. Indeed, if "Veni electa mea" was performed instrumentally, then the choral interludes of earlier plays appear to have been written exclusively in the vernacular. *Osterspiel* has two compositions in Latin, how-

---

[114] Geering, *Vokalmusik*, 171.

ever, both of which were associated with the old church. This points on the one hand to *Osterspiel*'s performance for a more exclusive audience, namely for Hans Franz Nägeli and other newly elected council members. Yet it also reveals a greater tolerance for Catholic musical tradition than might otherwise be expected. *Osterspiel* further demonstrates that Bernese musicians were still productively engaged in the reception of Lutheran music some twenty years following Johannes Wannenmacher's *Bicinia* compositions based upon Strasbourg hymn melodies. More than *Gedeon* or *Noe*, *Osterspiel* hints at the plurality of musical life in Reformation Bern.

Osterspiel's first chorus, "Johanni dem Apostel das geschach" (Appendix, Text IXa), is a contrafactum. This label nonetheless understates the song's dependence on its source. Beyond the first three words of its opening line, Rüte appears to have borrowed the text of Luther's "Jesaia dem propheten das geschach" in its entirety.[115] Luther had created the song in late 1525 as a German-language Sanctus for his *Deutsche Messe*.[116] The original text, derived from Isaiah 6:3, begins: "Sanctus, Sanctus, Sanctus Dominus Deus Sabaoth" (Holy, holy, holy is the Lord of hosts). In adapting the hymn, Luther returned to Isaiah and paraphrased verses 6:1–4 in their entirety (Appendix, Text IXb).[117] The distinct parallels of Isaiah's vision to Revelation 4–5 allowed Rüte to adopt Luther's text for *Osterspiel* by merely replacing the name Isaiah with that of John the Apostle. Given the play's anti-Lutheran polemic, the appearance of a Lutheran hymn is not without a certain irony. Nonetheless, Luther's original authorship may not have been known in Bern: Of the two settings of the song appearing in the 1544 *editio princeps* of Rhau's *Neue deutsche geistliche Gesänge*, for example, the first is anonymous and the second by Balthasar Resinarius. In any case, "Johanni dem Apostel" is a vivid example of the ability of sixteenth-century devotional music to cross confessional boundaries.

The same can be said of "Te Deum Laudamus" and "Dignus es Domine." The "Te Deum" was one of the Middle Ages' most ubiquitous hymns, traditionally sung during Matins as well as at public

---

[115] The text reproduces two verses: "Ein Lied./Johanni dem Apostel das geschach / Das er im geist den Herren sitzen sach etc." The second verse agrees entirely with Luther's text; *etc.* suggests that Rüte undertook no further changes.

[116] Jenny, *Luthers geistliche Lieder*, 97.

[117] Ibid., 243–5, no. 26.

festivities (Appendix, Text Xb). It was, above all, a staple of Easter and passion plays.[118] Like the Sanctus, it was translated into German by Luther ("Herr Gott, dich loben wir"), who also simplified its melody (Appendix, Text Xc).[119] Protestant playwrights adopted it as well. In Riga, it appeared in Burkard Waldis's Prodigal Son play of 1527, and it also formed part of the *Weltspiegel* by Basel playwright Valentin Boltz (1550).[120] Rüte was possibly familiar with Boltz's play, although the traditional ties of the "Te Deum" to Eastertide plays alone may have been sufficient cause for its inclusion in *Osterspiel*. Boltz may have made use of Luther's revision,[121] but the hymn continued to be sung in Latin, even by Protestants, and *Osterspiel*'s transmission of the Latin title suggests that the traditional text was sung.[122] Taking the place of the song sung by the twenty-four elders as indicated in Revelation 4:10, the hymn marks the juncture between chapters 4 and 5 in Rüte's paraphrase of his biblical source. However, Rüte first adapts verse 4:11, the original song text, as a responsory, with the foremost elder on the right-hand side of the stage leading the others in call and response. "Te Deum Laudamus" then follows upon this.[123] Given the participation of all twenty-four actors in the responsory, they likely joined together in singing the "Te Deum" as well.

"Dignus es Domine" similarly fulfills the requirement of song as called for in Revelation 5:9–10. Here, Rüte likely adapted the *canticum novum* sung by the elders in Revelation 5:9–10, 5:12, and 5:13. The play transmits a Latin incipit (Appendix, Text XIa), but the exact text sung is unclear.[124] Moreover, Rüte does not directly equate

---

[118] Ernst August Schuler records the occurrence of the hymn in some forty-five plays: Ernst August Schuler, *Die Musik der Osterfeieren, Osterspiele und Passionen des Mittelalters* (Kassel: Bärenreiter, 1951), 39, 328–30.

[119] Jenny, *Luthers geistliche Lieder*, 277–84, no. 31; Zahn, 5:328–30, no. 8652.

[120] Jaeger, 260.

[121] Refardt, 205.

[122] Cf. Jaeger, 260.

[123] "Die vier vnd zwentzig fallend nider/bättend an/werffend jre Kronen für den Herren/der vorderst vff der rechten syten spricht" (after v. 124); "die andern sagend jm also nach" (after v. 128).

[124] The appendix offers one possible redaction of the biblical text of the *canticum novum* (Text XIb). The actual text sung may have been closer to the responsory "Dignus es, Domine, accipere librum" as edited by René-Jean Hesbert in the *Corpus antiphonalium officii* (Rome: Herder, 1970), vol. 4, no. 6448. A related antiphon from the fourteenth century, to be sung *in tempore Paschae*, exists in Einsiedeln (Klosterbibliothek 611, folio 99ʳ). The first-person pronouns and verb forms of the responsory and its corresponding sources (*nos; regnabimus*) alternate with third-person forms (*eos;*

"Dignus es Domine" with the "New Song" offered by the elders to the Lamb of God. Rather, he situates the hymn at the beginning of John's vision of the Lamb, immediately following his admonishment by *der hinderst eltest* (vv. 385–414; Revelation 5:5). He then heightens the solemnity of the Lamb's entrance through two additional musical interludes. Sackbuts sound at the moment when the Lamb takes the scroll from the right hand of God (*Pausunen mit vier stimmen ein Lied*; after v. 438). John then narrates the glorification of the Lamb in accordance with Revelation 5:8–9:

> Sy fallend vor dem Lämmli nider
> Vnd neigend gegen jm jr glider/
> Jr Harpffen sind schon gstelt gar wol/
> Jr guldin Schalen Rouchwerchs vol/
> Das gwüßlich sind der Heilgen bät
> Darab dann Gott wolgfallen het/
> Jch hör schon yetz der Harpffen klang
> Vnd damit gar ein lieblich gsang
> Ein nüw Lied hören ich sy singen
> Macht mir von fröud min hertz vffspringen. (vv. 445–54)

> They fall down before the Lamb and bow their limbs before him. Their harps are already well-positioned, their golden bowls full of incense. These truly are the saints' prayers that please God. Already I hear the sound of the harps accompanied by delightful voices. I hear them singing a new song, which makes my heart leap with joy.

Only now does Rüte introduce "Wie hat es sich doch mit vns verkeert" as a new *canticum novum*. From all indications, it is indeed the play's new song. With the exception of Rüte's minor alteration to "Johanni dem Apostel das geschach," "Wie hat es sich" offers the play's only original song text. As a contrafactum, it is not entirely new, but it is possible that, following Alder's death in 1550, Rüte could no longer arrange for the composition of new music. It is the only song in all of Rüte's plays, original or otherwise, that gives any indication of its melody: "Ein Lied in der wyß/Da Jsrahel vß Egipten zoch" (A song set to the melody of "When Israel went forth from Egypt," before v. 455). This hymn, a paraphrase of Psalm 114 by

---

regnabunt) in other traditions. The first-person perspective seems more likely given the parallels to "Wie hat es sich doch mit vns verkeert" ("Hast[...]/ *Vns vnserm* Gott zuo Künigen gmacht"). Jaeger suggests that a motet composition for four voices was performed (*Sämtliche Dramen*, 3:88).

Matthäus Greiter, was first printed in 1527 by Wolff Köpfel in Strasbourg.[125] Whereas Greiter's text contains two strophes, Rüte's has three; all exhibit a bar form consisting of two three-line *Stollen* followed by a six-line *Abgesang*. Each strophe ends with "Alleluia."

Like Luther's "Ein newes lied wir heben an," Rüte's "New Song" resonates with unmistakable Reformation overtones. Christ figures as savior in all three strophes. The first of the three emphasizes that no one can sing the new song except for those who are born again in the Lord. The second explains that humanity is unable to cleanse itself of Adam's transgression; only Christ can relieve the "burden of sin." The final strophe then returns to the "New Song" according to Revelation 5:10—"Thou [...] hast made them a kingdom and priests to our God"—to announce the universal priesthood of all believers. The combination of Rüte's text with the original melody, "When Israel went forth from Egypt," further links the "New Song" with the release from bondage and a return to Christian liberty. When one considers that "Wie hat es sich doch mit vns verkeert" and "Dignus es Domine" form the structural center of *Osterspiel*,[126] then it becomes apparent that the Protestant overtones of Rüte's "New Song" give the entire play a distinctly christological interpretation. The appearance of the Lamb transcends the scathing Zwinglian diatribe delivered earlier by the Strong Angel, allowing the play to close in the praise of God.

To that end, three final songs are performed before the audience departs. Two of these had been performed previously in *Noe*: "Das truren ist vergangen" and "Gelobt sy Gott vnser Herr." Although there is no substantial variation in these texts between the two plays, their contexts have changed slightly. The "mourning" of "Das truren" had originally referred to the tribulations of Noah and his kin during the flood; now, it denotes the sadness of the world prior to the Lamb's unbinding of the scroll. It is apparently not sung by the elders, but rather performed in a four-part arrangement (*Gsang mit vier stimmen*, before v. 530). "Gelobet sy Gott" marks the end of the play proper prior to closing comments by the third and fourth heralds, echoing the final acclamation of the Lord by the elders and the four apostolic creatures.

---

[125] Wackernagel, 3:93, no. 124. The melody is found in Gottlieb Freiherr von Tucher, *Melodien des evangelischen Kirchengesangs*, vol. 2 of *Schatz des evangelischen Kirchengesangs im 1. Jahrhundert der Reformation* (Leipzig: Breitkopf & Härtel, 1848; reprint Walluf bei Wiesbaden: Martin Sändig, 1972), 280, no. 447.

[126] Jaeger, 180–3; Jaeger, *Sämtliche Dramen*, 3:274–6.

If the reappearance of "Das truren" and "Gelobet sy Gott" adds little to our understanding of the plays' music beyond the songs' apparent popularity (if only with Rüte), "Christ ist erstanden," the third song performed at the close of *Osterspiel*, offers rich compensation. Like "Te Deum Laudamus," the hymn was a standard component of the medieval Easter plays; indeed, it alternated with the "Te Deum" as the plays' traditional closing song.[127] It was also revised for Protestant audiences by Luther ("Christ lag in Todes Banden"), although he apparently did not wish to replace the original tune, which was already the oldest surviving Easter hymn in German.[128] Given the song's position at the end of *Osterspiel*, audience participation is likely here as well.[129] The play's imprint states simply "Hieruff gsungen/Christ ist erstanden" ("Upon this, 'Christ ist erstanden' was sung"; before v. 805). However, the fourth herald apostrophes the council members in attendance immediately beforehand, suggesting that they were among those who performed the song. Moreover, the text that follows is identical with the hymn's Swiss and Southern German variant as preserved in the Protestant hymnals of Constance. Here, the song text is transmitted without music, indicating that the melody was well-known among Swiss Protestants at the time and did not need to be included.[130] Considering the occasional participation of play spectators in choral interludes in other cities,[131] it would have been a simple matter for those in attendance at *Osterspiel* to strike up this popular Easter tune prior to their departure. The hymn is not a new Protestant melody, nor was it sung in church,

---

[127] E.A. Schuler, 53–105 (passim), 147–8; Walther Lipphardt, "'Christ ist erstanden.' Zur Geschichte des Liedes," *Jahrbuch für Liturgik und Hymnologie* 5 (1960): 96–9, 109–11; Ute Monika Schwob, "*Und singt frölich: 'Christ ist erstanden'!* Zur Rolle der Laien bei mittelalterlichen Osterfeiern und beim Osterspiel," in *Osterspiele: Texte und Musik. Akten des 2. Symposiums der Sterzinger Osterspiele (12.–16. April 1992)*, ed. Max Siller, Schlern-Schriften 293 (Innsbruck: Universitätsverlag Wagner, 1994), 161–73.

[128] Jenny, *Luthers geistliche Gesänge*, 109; 194–7, no. 12; Lipphardt, 102–3; E.A. Schuler, 40.

[129] Jaeger, *Sämtliche Dramen*, 3:89.

[130] These versions all render the last verse of the second strophe as *so helff vns der Herr Jesus Christ* as opposed to the more common reading *so loben wir den Herrn Jesu Christ*; they also replace *Kyrieleis* (Kyrie eleison) with *Alleluia*. Jenny reproduces the melody of the hymn based upon the Strasbourg hymnal of 1545. It is first transmitted by Martin Bucer's folio hymnal of 1541. Jenny, *Geschichte d. dt.-schw. Gesangbuches*, 228–9, 296, 321.

[131] "Vereinzelte Beispiele, daß auch die Zuschauer, fast wie die Gemeinde im Gottesdienst, mit eingreifen, indem sie geistliche Lieder singen, bieten Greff's *Lazarus* (1545) and Narhamer's *Job* (1546)." Liliencron, "Chorgesänge," 344.

but the audience performance of "Christ ist erstanden" is perhaps the most clear cut example of quasi-congregational singing prior to its official introduction in Bern in 1574.

Indeed, Rüte's five biblical plays together offered a variety of venues for local singers. *Osterspiel*'s musical offerings are the most varied, ranging between polyphonic arrangements for an apparently separate choir ("Das truren ist vergangen") to the all-inclusive performance of "Christ ist erstanden." The play's other five choral interludes appear to have been sung by the actors themselves, here members of the Blacksmith Society. This is equally true of the hymns contained in *Gedeon* and *Noe*, meaning that the "young burghers" who performed these plays would have required some choral training. Strikingly, however, there is no indication that actors sang in either *Joseph* or *Goliath*. As discussed earlier, Alder's two motets for *Joseph* clearly required skilled performers accustomed to polyphonic song; their texts, moreover, begin in the third person, indicating that they were not sung by an actor from a first-person perspective. The evidence from *Goliath*, for whose eight choral interludes no text or music survives, seems to correspond to that of *Joseph*. The term *Chorus*, which occurs in none of Rüte's other plays, appears only at junctures between scenes,[132] suggesting that *Goliath*'s interludes were *Festchöre* that remained distinct from the play itself and were thus likely also performed by a separate choir.

In accounting for the performance of choral music by the young actors of Rüte's later plays, one likely explanation stands out: the introduction of psalm singing for schoolboys in June of 1538. Rüte recruited his performers from this same age group, so that for the performances of *Gedeon* in 1540 and *Noe* in 1546, he could draw on a pool of young singers skilled enough to perform the plays' choral interludes themselves.[133] This was apparently not yet possible for the performance of *Joseph* in early 1538. The similar absence of skilled actor-singers in the *Goliath* text of 1555 provides further evidence for its performance in 1535, also before the introduction of psalm singing

---

[132] *Goliath*, after v. 2922, v. 4012, v. 4330, v. 4840, v. 4968, v. 6084, v. 6338; *Triumphisch Lobgsang*, after v. 6625.

[133] Zulauf emphasizes that the council's directive of 1538 did not reestablish music as a separate subject, so that the schoolboys' training may have been limited. Still, there is no reason why their lessons would not have been sufficient for them to assume the performance of choral music in Rüte's plays. Zulauf, 3.

in school. *Goliath* and *Joseph* would have thus both required a separate group of trained singers for their respective choruses. However, this should not have proven too difficult: in the 1530s, Rüte would likely still have been able to call upon at least some of the former singers from the city's St. Vincent convent. Alder, as the composer of *Joseph*'s motets, may even have personally directed such a choir during the play's performance. Even after 1538, however, professional musicians still contributed to Rüte's plays. The *Stadtpfeifer* likely continued to perform all or most occurrences of instrumental music, and the polyphonic compositions of *Noe* (*Gsang mit vieren*, after v. 494) and *Osterspiel* were in all probability also sung by a separate choir. By this time, however, these ensembles could have consisted of the best and brightest singers among local schoolboys.

The integral presence of song in all five biblical dramas should not lead to the conclusion that, outside of worship, music was wholly uncensured in sixteenth-century Bern. The plays also contain a smaller, but nonetheless substantial number of scenes in which music possesses negative connotations. Foremost among these is the performance of music as an indication of corruption and debauchery. This occurs not only among the Philistines of *Goliath* (after v. 4968) or Ham's kin in *Noe* (after v. 2914, v. 3074), but also among the Roman clergy of Bernese carnival plays. Indeed, this is apparently the sole function of music in the early stage works of the local Reformation.[134] In *Von Papsts und Christi Gegensatz*, as Cleywe Pfluog and Rüde Vogelnest look on, the papal entourage announces its arrival with trumpets, sackbuts, drums, and pipes.[135] Similarly, when Emperor Alßmär announces his support for the veneration of saints in *Abgötterei*, the Roman priests celebrate with song and stringed instruments.[136] The dancing of Ham's clan at Nimrod's feast in *Noe*, performed following

---

[134] *Vom Papst und seiner Priesterschaft*, *Der Ablaßkrämer*, and *Elsli Tragdenknaben* contain no explicit mention of music. No other examples exist from *Von Papsts und Christi Gegensatz* and *Abgötterei* other than those given as follows. Manuel and his compatriots of 1523 were however not unaware of the polemic potential of music, as witnessed by the public performance of the "Bean Song" on Ash Wednesday.

[135] "Hie zwischen kam der bapst geritten in großem tryumpf im harnisch mit grossem kriegß züg zuo roß vnd fuoß [...]/trummeten/pausunen/trummen/pfyffen." Niklaus Manuel, "Fasnachtsspiel [i.e. 'Von Papsts und Christi Gegensatz']," in *Werke und Briefe*, before v. 63.

[136] "Hie söllent sy prassen/vnd seitenspil/gsang/etc. hören" (after v. 2166).

their adoption of a false religion, exemplifies the disapproval of all music perceived as lascivious:

> Vor dem essen wend wir spatzieren
> Ein yeder sol ein frouwen fieren
> Wöllent ein sittigs täntzli han
> Vnd nach der pfyffen vmbher gan/
> Die fröwli kheren mit den armen
> So wirt vnß fin die läbern warmen/
> Das bringt zuo spyß vnd tranck ein lust
> Vnd dienet ouch zur gsundtheit sust/
> Jr vier/ein yeder lieblich blaß
> Mit sinr stim ein hüpsche tantzmaß. (vv. 2758–67)

> Let us promenade before the meal. Every man shall lead a woman, and we shall hold a decorous dance. Stepping to the pipe and spinning the girls in our arms, that will warm our livers. That spurs the appetite, stimulates thirst, and otherwise promotes one's health. You four, each of you blow your part to a pleasant dance tune.

Although Nimrod declares that their dance will be "decorous," the line separating decorum and scandal in post-Reformation Bern was thin. Immediately following the local disputation, the council began to issue a series of mandates that increasingly regulated dancing in the territories under its jurisdiction. As early as March of 1528, dancing was prohibited during the weeks prior to Easter.[137] It was later banned at the town hall and in the cloister of the former Franciscan monastery. Even at weddings, dancing was regulated: no more than three "seemly" dances were permitted, and men were not allowed to remove their coats.[138] Some Bernese theologians were in favor of eliminating dancing completely, and Rüte's condemnation of the practice at Nimrod's feast encouraged spectators to shun such activity altogether.

Noe also demonstrates music's power of ridicule. Even after the local Reformation, polemic tunes in the style of Manuel's "Song of Bicocca" continued to fan the fires of religious controversy, as illustrated by the "Interlaken Song" commonly attributed to Alder. Although the genre's satire is more closely connected to carnival and carnival plays (consider the performance of the "Bean Song" on Ash

---

[137] Theodor de Quervain, *Kirchliche und soziale Zustände in Bern unmittelbar nach der Einführung der Reformation (1528–1536)* (Bern: Grunau, 1906), 114.
[138] Ibid., 117.

Wednesday in 1523), Rüte adopts it to epitomize Ham's disrespect for Noah. The Bible itself provides little detail regarding Ham's impudence, only that he "saw the nakedness of his father, and told his two brothers outside" (Genesis 9:22). In *Noe*, Ham treats his father as a drunken fool upon finding him asleep following the Sukkoth feast of the prior evening. He purposefully sets out to "diminish Noah's honor" and tells his brothers that the patriarch "can sin as we can."[139] He then returns to his family and announces his arrival in song, rendered below in prose (see Appendix, Text VI for original text):

> I am pleased from the bottom of my heart; this I make known to all people. For I have just found the old man this very hour: he lies as if drunk. His limbs are stretched out, his privates exposed, and his breath reeks of wine. This is the holy life to which he's devoted himself.

Ham's singing pleases Canaan and others among his household, who have already resolved to break with Noah. For the audience, however, the song reveals the depth of Ham's contempt for his father. The episode may have further served as admonishment for those who regularly indulged in similarly polemic songs, which were officially banned following the Second War of Kappel.

A final scene from *Noe* best illustrates the complex and at times seemingly contradictory attitudes towards music in contemporary Bern. Here, Jubal, "the father of all those who play the lyre and pipe" (Genesis 4:21), arranges a small concert for his father Lamech and other relatives during the "Small Play." On the one hand, the passage is clearly intended to show off the talents of local musicians. Jubal begins by boasting of his creation of harmony based upon mathematics:

> Herr/es weißt schon yetz alle welt
> Das ich d'stimm in ein zal han gstelt
> Vß kunst der Matematica/
> Wie jr bald werdend hören da/
> Als ich g'hört d'lüt on regel singen
> Ouch d'vögel süß vnd lieblich klingen
> Da han ich d'Music bald erdacht
> Vnd d'stimmen in ein ordnung bracht. (vv. 487–94)

---

[139] "Man muoß Noe mindren sin eer" (v. 2405); "Noe der hochg'achtet man / Als wol/als wir/ouch sünden kan" (vv. 2451–2).

> My Lord, the whole world already knows that I've arranged voices at intervals according to the art of mathematics, as you will now hear. When I heard people singing without order and the birds sweetly chirping, I soon invented Music and created a system for voices.

After the performance of a polyphonic choral composition, Jubal then groups instruments according to family and, one by one, commands woodwinds, strings, brass, drums, and pipes to play. The resulting concert covers the whole spectrum of contemporary instruments, demonstrating their range of musical expression as well as the skill of their players. There is obvious pride in this display of art, and in other plays, such as the *Weltspiegel* of Valentin Boltz, Jubal's creation of music is explicitly presented as God-ordained.[140] In *Noe*, however, Jubal is the son of the tyrant Lamech, who will not hear God's word and callously puts Enoch's son and brother to death. Lamech values Jubal's music for its worldly applications alone:

> Was krafft ist doch in denen dingen?
> Wie mögent sy so gwaltig bringen
> Mengerley anfechtung ins blüt?
> Sy b'wegent hertz/b'gird/sinn vnd gmüt/
> Die seyttenspil gend früntlickeyt/
> Das man zur liebe gantz wirt b'reit
> Zuo fröligkeit zücht mich der gsang
> So bringt der Jnstrumenten klang
> Vil manheit vnd ein grossen muot
> Es vbertrifft herrschafft vnd guot. (vv. 528–38)

> What power is in these things? How can they stir up so many temptations in one's blood with such force? They move the heart, desire, sense, and mind. The stringed instruments produce sweetness, putting one in the mood for love. Singing makes me glad, and the sound of brass instruments begets virility and great courage. It is greater than riches or the power to rule.

Lamech's daughter, Naamah, responds similarly, exclaiming "Jch bin schier miner sinnen b'roupt" (I'm robbed wholly of my senses; v. 515). Jubal's creation, in Rüte's portrayal, is thus a two-edged sword, giving beauty, but with the power to lead astray.

Nonetheless, Bern's five biblical plays as a whole demonstrate Rüte's support of music as a means of religious edification and even worship. Moreover, they allow for an approximate reconstruction of

---

[140] Refardt, 215.

Rüte's contribution to local musical life. He was apparently not skilled in composition. The music of his dramas either stemmed from local composers such as Cosmas Alder or borrowed the melodies of well-known contemporary hymns. Concerning the latter, Rüte was clearly not beyond altering or even fully adopting the work of others, such as Luther's "Jesaia dem propheten das geschach" or the traditional "Te Deum Laudamus." In both cases, however, *Osterspiel* transmits only the incipit of their texts, a sure sign that these songs already enjoyed a wide circulation. Of the plays' full song texts—"Drumm das wir handt die Bott veracht," "Das truren ist vergangen," "Gelobet sy Gott vnser Herr," "Ach Herr vernim/min kläglich stim," "Wie hat es sich doch mit vns verkeert," and even Ham's song "Jch bin erfröut vß hertzen grund"—only the first strophe of "Das truren ist vergangen" is found in earlier sources. In searching for the texts' author, we need look no further than Rüte himself. Two of these six are known contrafacta, but one—"Ach Herr venim"—was set to music by Alder, and Rüte may have similarly authored the remaining three for original compositions by Alder or another local musician. Indeed, as the text for "Ach Herr vernim" is transmitted in manuscript together with Alder's arrangement, it is not impossible that the texts of other Alder compositions that survive in manuscript, namely "Da Jacob das Klaidt ansach" and "Wie Joseph in Egyptenlant," are Rüte's products as well.[141] Furthermore, given the appearance of "Das truren ist vergangen" and "Gelobet sy Gott vnser Herr" in both *Noe* and *Osterspiel*, these compositions apparently enjoyed a broader popularity in Bern and beyond, as demonstrated by the modified publication of "Das truren" in Frankfurt and Marburg. Considering that Wolfgang Musculus as hymn writer may not have been identical with the Wolfgang Mösel found in Constance hymnals and that only one musical composition is attributed to Johannes Haller, Hans von Rüte was arguably sixteenth-century Bern's most productive author of Protestant hymns.[142]

---

[141] *Joseph*'s indiscriminate directions regarding its choruses (*Hie soll etwas gsungen werden*) may indicate that the play was intended for wider distribution; Rüte's own song texts would have then been omitted so as to leave the choice of choral music to the discretion of other performers. See Liliencron's comments on the omission of choral music: Liliencron, "Chorgesänge," 343. The imitation of Rüte's *Joseph* by Jacob Rueff and Thiebolt Gart would be evidence of this wider reception. See Wolfgang F. Michael, *Das deutsche Drama der Reformationszeit* (Bern: Lang, 1984), 141, 153–4.

[142] Cf. Jenny, "Das evangelische Lied," 110.

Most importantly, Bern's five biblical plays demonstrate strong local support for devotional music at a time when congregational singing was banned from regular worship. The plays' choral interludes were sung as prayer, such as *Noe*'s "Ach Herr vernim/min kläglich stim," or as thanksgiving, as exemplified by "Das truren ist vergangen." These contexts did not appear accidentally upon stage, but rather reflected the continuing role of religious music in daily life. This in turn helps to flesh out the otherwise dry documentation regarding Bern's post-Reformation musical culture. We know that psalms were sung in Bernese schools following 1538; we also know that Johannes Wannenmacher's *Bicinia*, secular as well as devotional, were performed in private as *Hausmusik*. It is implausible that religious compositions were not sung in other locations and on other occasions as well: by Bernese troops in the field, by parents during the illness of a child, by farmers grateful for a plentiful harvest. Indeed, given the existing evidence, it seems likely that the only location where devotional music was not heard before 1558, or especially 1574, was the local minster. Bernese theologians and councilors remained faithful to Zwingli's original exclusion of music from worship, but only during regular church services.

CHAPTER SEVEN

MEDIATING CHANGE

Ich bin erfröüd in mynem gmüt,	It pleases me to the heart
das vns Gott hatt mit syner güt	that God has bestowed his goodness
so vätterlich fürkommen.	upon us in such a fatherly manner.
syn wort hat er herfür gestelt;	He has set forth his Word
das selb dem Bären wol gefelt	that it pleased even the Bear
vnd hatt es genommen.	to embrace it.

—*Eyn lied von dem Bären vnd annemung des Gots wort* (undated)

Viewing the Protestant Reformation from the outset of a new millennium, with advances in computer technology inexorably altering long-standing paradigms of communication, one is struck for both periods by the significance of innovative media in shaping cultural institutions. As the twenty-first century ensues, the electronic exchange of information has impacted commerce, research, and entertainment. It has also left its mark on politics, where official campaign press releases must compete with anonymous authors who offer up rumor and innuendo for immediate distribution. In their sixteenth-century context, Protestants were similar masters of media manipulation. Pouring out vernacular Bibles, theological treatises, and polemic woodcuts by the thousands, the printing press disseminated Reformation thought among the literate and illiterate alike.[1] Meanwhile, humanist rhetoric transformed homiletics, producing preachers whose eloquence alone bore testimony to the new faith.[2]

---

[1] See among others Elizabeth L. Eisenstein, *The Printing Press as an Agent of Change: Communications and Cultural Transformations in Early-Modern Europe*, 2 vols. (Cambridge: Cambridge University Press, 1979); Hans-Joachim Köhler, ed., *Flugschriften als Massenmedium der Reformationszeit. Beiträge zum Tübinger Symposion 1980*, Spätmittelalter und Frühe Neuzeit 13 (Stuttgart: Klett-Cotta, 1981); Robert Scribner, *For the Sake of Simple Folk. Popular Propaganda for the German Reformation*, 2nd ed. (Oxford: Clarendon Press, 1994); Mark U. Edwards, Jr., *Printing, Propaganda, and Martin Luther* (Berkeley: University of California Press, 1994).

[2] Hans Martin Müller, "Homiletik," in *Theologische Realenzyklopädie* (Berlin/New York: de Gruyter, 1986), 15:526–65.

Yet as has been increasingly recognized, Protestants did not confine themselves to the printed or spoken word. Some 100 years after Luther's appearance before Charles V at the Diet of Worms, the Jesuit Adam Contzius lamented in his *Politicorum libri decem* of 1620 that the reformer's hymns had destroyed more souls than his writings and sermons.[3] Calvin, too, fostered congregational singing,[4] and popular songs such as "Eyn lied von dem Bären vnd annemung des Gots wort" ("A Song about the Bear and the Adoption of God's Word") rallied support for the Reformation outside of worship.[5] In Lutheran territories, even painters played a role in propagating the tenets of the new faith, as witnessed by the popularity of the *Law and Gospel* images created by Lucas Cranach the Elder (fig. 41).[6] Summed up in contemporary terms, the Reformation owed its success in part to a state-of-the-art media campaign that exploited early modern communication channels to their fullest potential.

As the preceding chapters have shown, Protestant theater took a prominent place alongside other media of reform. Indeed, its particular effectiveness lay in its ability to unite disparate means of Reformation discourse, creating a whole greater than the sum of its parts.[7] Local musicians frequently performed choral music during play productions, including well-known Protestant hymns in which

---

[3] "Hymni Lutheri animos plures quam scripta et declamationes occiderunt." As quoted in Inge Mager, "Lied und Reformation. Beobachtungen zur reformatorischen Singbewegung in norddeutschen Städten," in *Das protestantische Kirchenlied im 16. und 17. Jahrhundert*, ed. Alfred Dürr and Walther Killy, Wolfenbütteler Forschungen 31 (Wiesbaden: Harrassowitz, 1986), 25.

[4] See Charles Garside, *The Origins of Calvin's Theology of Music: 1536–1543*, Transactions of the American Philosophical Society 69,4 (Philadelphia: The American Philosophical Society, 1979); Walter Blankenburg, "Die Kirchenmusik in den reformierten Gebieten des europäischen Kontinents," in *Geschichte der evangelischen Kirchenmusik*, ed. Friedrich Blume, 2nd ed. (Kassel: Bärenreiter, 1965), 347–68. Ambrosius Lobwasser's translation of the Geneva psalter, published in the 1570s with the homophonic settings of Claude Goudimel, became especially popular in Germany, going through countless printings well into the nineteenth century: Friedrich Blume, "Das Zeitalter des Konfessionalismus," in *Geschichte der evangelischen Kirchenmusik*, 83–4.

[5] The song is reprinted in Theodor Odinga, *Das deutsche Kirchenlied der Schweiz im Reformationszeitalter* (Frauenfeld: J. Huber, 1889), 128–30, no. 12.

[6] Carl C. Christensen, *Art and the Reformation in Germany* (Athens, Ohio: Ohio University Press; Detroit: Wayne State University Press, 1979), 124–30; Joseph Leo Koerner, *The Moment of Self-Portraiture in German Renaissance Art* (Chicago/London: University of Chicago Press, 1993), 363–410.

[7] Peter Pfrunder, *Pfaffen, Ketzer, Totenfresser: Fastnachtskultur der Reformationszeit—Die Berner Spiele von Niklaus Manuel* (Zurich: Chronos, 1989), 150.

an audience qua congregation might join.[8] The stage design of Reformation theater meanwhile adapted the *Simultanbühne* of late medieval drama to the contrastive use of space found in *Merkbilder* such as Cranach's *Law and Gospel*, which physically distinguished between Old Testament and New Testament theology. After a performance, a play text might circulate as a pamphlet, reaching an even larger audience beyond the hundreds originally in attendance. All told, Protestant plays engaged their spectators through sight, song, and speech. Given the contemporary English assessment that Germans portrayed on stage what preachers otherwise treated in the pulpit,[9] the declamations of actors became in essence dramatic sermons, vivified for better retention.[10] Based on its suitability for visual instruction, continental playwrights such as Paul Rebhun and Sixtus Birck unanimously considered religious theater superior to preaching.

In Bern, whose Zwinglian reforms expunged devotional art and music from church worship in 1528, the multimediality of Reformation theater became all the more crucial for promoting the new faith in the absence of other avenues of reception. As a former painter, Niklaus Manuel brought an especially stark visuality to the stage. Modelled after the *Passional Christi und Antichristi* of Philipp Melanchthon and Lucas Cranach the Elder, Manuel's *Von Papsts und Christi Gegensatz* contrasted Christ's humble entrance to Jerusalem, portrayed on one side of the street, with the pomp of a papal procession, passing on the other. So great was the impression of *Von Papsts und Christi Gegensatz* and its sister play, *Vom Papst und seiner Priesterschaft*, that the Bernese chronicler Valerius Anshelm declared them *wunderliche anschowungen*

---

[8] Rochus von Liliencron, "Die Chorgesänge des lateinisch-deutschen Schuldramas im XVI. Jahrhundert," *Vierteljahrsschrift für Musikwissenschaft* 6 (1890): 344.

[9] Peter Ukena, "Flugschriften und verwandte Medien im Kommunikationsprozeß zwischen Reformation und Frühaufklärung," in *Flugschriften als Massenmedium der Reformationszeit*, 167–8. See also Bryan Crockett on preaching as performance: Bryan Crockett, *The Play of Paradox: Stage and Sermon in Renaissance England* (Philadelphia: University of Pennsylvania Press, 1995), 8 ff.

[10] On the kinship between medieval plays and sermons, see Carla van Dauven-Knippenberg, "Ein Anfang ohne Ende: Einführendes zur Frage nach dem Verhältnis zwischen Predigt und geistlichem Schauspiel des Mittelalters," in *Mittelalterliches Schauspiel: Festschrift für Hansjürgen Linke zum 65. Geburtstag*, ed. Ulrich Mehler and Anton H. Touber, Amsterdamer Beiträge zur älteren Germanistik 38/39 (Amsterdam: Rodopi, 1994), 143–160; idem, "Wege der Christenlehre. Über den Zusammenhang zweier mittelalterlicher Gattungen," *ZfdPh* 113 (1994): 370–84.

(wondrous sights).[11] Following the local Reformation, the dramas of Hans von Rüte became the sole sanctioned outlet for religious visual display. Rüte favored apocalyptic imagery for his dramas, both in his adaptation of the Babylonian Harlot of Revelation 17 for *Abgötterei* (1531) and in his translation of the *majestas Domini* motif of Revelation 4–5 to the stage of his *Osterspiel* (1552). Common to the stage design of both authors was a pronounced sign-like quality, which shunned illusionism and marked figures and locations for ready identification. Two techniques in particular worked towards this end: antithesis and deixis. The contrast between competing faiths, whether Catholics and Protestants or Jews and Gentiles, became reified through their physical juxtaposition before the audience. Meanwhile, select commentators appeared on the stage to explicate the unfolding action for the audience. These deictic figures literally pointed to particular scenes and groups that were significant for the interpretation of a play. Late medieval dramaturgy had also employed similar staging techniques, but not to such exclusivity. Rüte's plays in particular strongly reduced the affective aspects of play performances, which had for example been censured by Luther in his *Sermon von der Betrachtung des heyligen leydens Christi* of 1519.[12] Local Reformation theater instead promoted an intellectual viewing, fostering faith, not pity, among its audience.

Bern's biblical drama provided a similarly sanctioned outlet for the performance of devotional music. The city had followed Zurich in abolishing all choral and instrumental music from church services, and this prohibition remained in effect until 1558, when the local council directed schoolboys to sing one psalm prior to the sermon. Not until 1574 did congregational singing as found in other Protestant communities begin. Yet from at least 1538 on, Rüte's dramas directly linked song to prayer, incorporating original works by local composer Cosmas Alder—foremost *Joseph*'s "Da Jacob nun das Klaidt ansach," often erroneously attributed to Ludwig Senfl—as well as traditional hymns such as the "Te Deum." Several songs were contrafacta set to popular Protestant melodies, and all evidence suggests that Rüte himself wrote their texts. Given Wolfgang Musculus's dis-

---

[11] Anshelm, 4:475.
[12] Martin Luther, "Eyn Sermon von der Betrachtung des heyligen leydens Christi," in WA 2:131–42.

puted authorship of six hymns,[13] written not on the Aare, but in Augsburg for the Protestant hymnals of Constance, these contrafacta make Rüte sixteenth-century Bern's most prolific hymn author. Above all, the singing of "Christ ist erstanden" by audience and actors at the close of *Osterspiel* indicates that local biblical plays offered a venue for congregational singing twenty-two years before its official introduction in St. Vincent minster.

The performance of *Osterspiel* in 1552 and the publication of Rüte's *Goliath* in 1555 closed out the local alliance of theater and theology that had begun with the presentation of Manuel's two carnival plays of 1523. Despite the contrast between the solemnity of the latter plays and the scatology of the former, all pursued a common goal, namely the validation of religious reform as enacted by local government. As the local Reformation progressed, Bern's biblical drama represented the continuation of carnival politics through other, in this case less militant means. However, the transition from one genre to the next was not abrupt, but gradual. Theologians of the new faith rejected the carnival celebration as a relic of Catholic ritual and censured all licentious behavior associated with the occasion, but they could not immediately suppress decades of tradition. Locals thus performed two final carnival plays following the introduction of religious reform, *Elsli Tragdenknaben* (1530) and *Abgötterei* (1531). These works responded to the new political and theological constraints placed on carnival in a post-Reformation context by eliminating all transgression from the portrayal of Protestant figures. Yet even Manuel's peasants, though riotous, had distinguished between religious and secular rule in their call for ecclesiastical reform. *Vom Papst und seiner Priesterschaft*, *Von Papsts und Christi Gegensatz*, and *Der Ablaßkrämer* were thus religiously progressive, but politically conservative, demonstrating the futility of assigning any one political tendency to the carnival play as genre.

Indeed, Rüte's and especially Manuel's plays could state their case for Protestantism only by appealing to the broadest audience possible. In a pre-Reformation context, this meant disguising anti-Catholic

---

[13] On the controversy, see Andreas Marti, "Gottesdienst und Kirchenlied bei Wolfgang Musculus," in *Wolfgang Musculus (1497–1563) und die oberdeutsche Reformation*, ed. Rudolf Dellsperger, Rudolf Freudenberger, and Wolfgang Weber, Colloquia Augustana 6 (Berlin: Akademie Verlag, 1997), 204–18.

polemics as civic patriotism following the death of over fifty prominent Bernese citizens at the Battle of Bicocca in April 1522. In all instances, however, the plays' most potent asset was their ability to integrate a broad spectrum of the community in a common enterprise.[14] On the one hand, all actors were recruited among the young sons of local citizens, suggesting that participation was a privilege of the social elite. Given cast numbers ranging between fifty and one hundred, at least some town councilors would have observed their sons on stage, which would have secured their personal interest in a successful performance, not to mention their political interest in being honored at each play, as was Rüte's wont. On the other hand, players required the logistical assistance of other groups in preparing scenery, costumes, and the like. The grand scale of performances provided carpenters, seamstresses, and bailiffs with additional employment. Innkeepers profited from the influx of out-of-town guests, and the council further rewarded actors and musicians for their efforts. Not only did the plays attract spectators from all or most social strata, but several members of the community also had a vested interest in a successful production.

By uniting a substantial segment of the local population in a common undertaking, the plays fostered a sense of identity and solidarity among participants and spectators.[15] Contrasting papal militancy with the Christian code of honor practiced by the Knight of Rhodes and, implicitly, by the fallen Bernese troops of Bicocca, Manuel vaunted political over religious identity. To be Bernese, *Vom Papst und seiner Priesterschaft* suggests, is to oppose Rome. The audience members were then required to decide which group affiliation was more important for them. Once the majority of citizens had converted, Rüte's plays provided orientation for the reformed community by offering a new religious identity, embodied by protagonists who placed their hope solely in God. Like English Reformation plays, the dramas of Manuel and Rüte helped local residents to negotiate

---

[14] On plays as participatory communication, see Robert W. Scribner, "Flugblatt und Analphabetentum. Wie kam der gemeine Mann zu reformatorischen Ideen?" in *Flugschriften als Massenmedium der Reformationszeit*, 73.

[15] On early modern plays as bourgeois *Identitätsstifter*, see Erich Kleinschmidt, *Stadt und Literatur in der Frühen Neuzeit. Voraussetzungen und Entfaltung im südwestdeutschen, elsässischen und schweizerischen Städteraum*, Literatur und Leben, Neue Folge 22 (Cologne/Vienna: Böhlau, 1982), 190–3.

the fundamental social, religious, and political changes of the Reformation. In uniting the media of reform, Bern's Protestant theater became the mediator of reform.

The participation of a broad cross-section of the population in local play productions should, however, not imply that their political content necessarily reflected a plurality of local opinion. At the time of their performance, Manuel's carnival plays stood in opposition to the religious policies of the Bernese town council and likely represented the views of a minority of citizens, even if that minority might have already been of substantial size. Once Protestants had assumed control of local government, they kept a tight reign on the local stage. Rüte acted as censor for plays produced elsewhere in Bernese territory, and his own works likely had the implicit, if not explicit approval of city councilors, who were guests of honor at each performance. Bern's biblical drama offered orientation in the heady early years of the Reformation, but orientation along council lines. In particular, Rüte's plays offer insights on council policy between 1531 and 1552. *Abgötterei*, for example, reflects the confessional tensions in the Helvetian Confederacy between the Diet of Augsburg and the Second War of Kappel, including the efforts of the Catholic forest cantons to ally themselves with Charles V; *Gedeon* revisits the issue of religious revolution to legitimize Zwinglian reform while repudiating Anabaptists and their radical rejection of secular rule; and *Osterspiel* lauds the Bernese church over that of Geneva and Zurich following the signing of the *Consensus Tigurinus* by John Calvin and Heinrich Bullinger in 1549. In presenting council policy between their actors' lines, the plays invited the audience to view the council as it viewed itself: as the true defender of the Protestant faith.

APPENDIX: SONG TEXTS

When multiple texts appear for a single Roman numeral, "a" denotes the incipit as found in the plays' original editions, while "b" and "c" give full texts of the song as it may have been sung.

Joseph (1538)

Ia. *Hie soll etwas gsungen werden* [before v. 647]

Ib. *Da Jacob nun das Klaidt ansach* [Bernoulli, *Liederbücher der Humanistenzeit*, Beilage XV]
Da Jacob nun das Klaidt ansach
mit grosem schmertzen er da sprach
o wee der grosen noth
mein lieber Son der ist todt
die wilden thier haben In zerrissen
und mit den zeenen zerbissen
O Joseph Joseph mein lieber Son
wer will mich alten trösten nun
dann ich vor laidt mus sterben
und traurig fahren von dieser Erden.

IIa. *Hie soll abermals etwas gsungen werdenn* [before v. 1292]

IIb. *Wie Joseph in Egyptenlant* [Geering, *Psalmen und geistliche Gesänge*, no. 6]
Wie Joseph in Egipten landt
verkauft ward uß siner bruder hend,
hat er sin vatter trüwlich klagt
vnd an got nit verzagt.
Israel, vatter min,
din got der gäb dir freud
für alles leid,
vatter min, Israel,
min lieber vatter Israel.

Gedeon (1540)

III. *Hie volgt der truwer gsang* [before v. 1097–v. 1135]
[1.] Drumm das wir handt die Bott veracht/
   Die vns der herr hat geben/
So sind wir aller welt verlacht/

Die fyendt/merckent eben/
  Die Ziend da har/
   Mit grosser schar/
    Vnd allem gwalt/
     Vil tusent falt/
      Vor jnn mög Wir nit blyben/
       Vß vnserm landt/
        Mit grosser schandt/
         Wend sy vns all vertryben/
          Mit kinden vnd mit wyben/

[2.] So rüffen wir den herren an/
     Das er vns wol behüte/
    Vnd synen zorn von vnß wöl lan/
   Durch sine gnad vnd güette/
      Vnd nit verderb/
       Sin heilig Erb/
        Durch fyndes handt/
         Der jetz das landt/
          Mit füwr vnd schwärdt will gschenden
           O starcker Gott/
            Gott Sabaoth/
             Thuo vnß dyn tröster senden
              Vnd allen kummer wenden/

Alß Gedeon den syg behalten vnd sine find mit der hilff Gottes erschlagen/ward das nochuolgent gesetz gesungen
[3.] Lob ehr vnd pryß sy dir geseit/
     Einiger Gott dryfaltig/
    Der vnser fyndt hast nider gleit
     Jnn dinem Arm so gwaltig
      Vnd all jr pracht/
       Zuo schanden gmacht/
        Wir bitten dich/
         Halt gnediglich/
          Din volck vnd sinen samen/
           O höchster Gott/
            Bhüt vnß vor nodt/
             Durch dinen heilgen nammen/
              Zuo allen zyten/Amen.

Noe (1546)

IV. *Gsang* [before v. 1090–v. 1116]
[1.] Das truren ist vergangen/
      Hat sich in fröud verkert/

Nach fröud that vnß verlangen/
  Die hat sich täglich gmert/
  Vnd wirt sich fürbaß meren/
    Biß in die ewigkeit/
    Das kumpt alles vom herren/
    Dem singen wir zuo ehren/
      Diß lied mit fröligkeit.

[2.] O Herr wer thuot dir glichen/
  Jn dinem höchsten thron:
All Götter müssen wychen/
  Vnd mögent nit bestan/
    Die himmel vnd die erden/
    Die Sonn vnd ouch der Mon/
    Sy müssen all verderben/
    Die lütt vor onmacht sterben/
      Wann du din straff last gan.

[3.] Darumb wend wir dich loben/
    Dir ghört allein die ehr:
  Hie niden vnd dört oben/
    Für alles himmelsch heer/
    Hilff das vnß mög gelingen/
      Jn aller nodt vnd pyn/
    So wend wir frölich springen/
      Mit lust vnd liebe singen/
      Zuo ehr dem namme din.

V. *Gsang* [before v. 1388–v. 1413]

[1.] Gelobet sy gott vnser herr
Dann jm allein ghört alle ehr.

[2.] Gelobet sy sin helger Nam
Kein grösser gwalt vff erd nie kam.

[3.] Sin wonung vff dem Cherubin
Vnd sicht inn alle tieffe hin.

[4.] Jn lobent alle sine werck
Deß himelß vnd der erden sterck.

[5.] Die Sonn vnd Mond am firmament
All stern vnd alle element.

[6.] Rägen vnd thouw vnd alle wind
Vnd alle die im ellend sind.

[7.] Füwr/hitz/vnd hagel tag vnd nacht
Yß/frost/schne/kelte mit jr macht

[8.] Die berg vnd bühel ouch die thal
Vnd alles was wachßt vberal.

[9.] Die brunnen/wasser ouch deß glych
Vnd was imm wasser reget sich.

[10.] Die vögel vnd die wilden thier
Der waldochß vnd der zame stier.

[11.] Die priester vnd deß Herren
knecht
Die seelen vnd der geyster
gschlecht.
[13.] Prysen den Gott imm himmelrych
Dann sine güt werdt ewigklich.

[12.] Vnd alles was den athem
hat
Lobe den Herren frü vnd
spat.

VI. *Cham singt ein Lied* [before v. 2610–v. 2614]
[1.] *Das erst gsatz.*
    Jch bin erfröut vß hertzen grund
    Das thuon ich allen menschen kund
    Dann ich han erst in diser stund
        Den alten man dört funden
        Er lyt als sy jm gschwunden.

[2.] *Cham/ singt aber ein gsatz.* [before v. 2619–v. 2623]
    Sin glider hat er von jm gstreckt
    Sin scham die ist im vffgedeckt
    Von wyn er ouch gar vbel schmeckt
        Das ist sin heiligs läben
        Darin er sich hat gäben.

VII. *Diß ist der trurig gsang/ so hieuor by dem Buochstaben Jv. anzeigt wirt.* [before v. 4729–v. 4764]
[1.] *Das erst gsatz.*
    Ach Herr vernim/
    Min kläglich stim
      Damit ich dich thuon bitten
        Vmb dine gnad/
        Das mir nüt schad/
    Min fleisch vnd böse sitten
        Die mich mitt gwalt/
      So manigfalt/
        Von dinem gsatz wend tryben
          Wie gern ich wett/
          Vnd billich sött
          Biß an min endt belyben.

[2.] *Das ander gsatz.*
    So thuot der fyndt/
    Mich also gschwindt/
      Mit vorteil gantz vmbstellen.
        Dardurch er mich/
      Gantz listenklich/
    Von dinem trost will fellen/
      Vff sin verstandt/
      Vnd menschen tandt/
        Nach fryem willen zläben/

Das wär sin bgär/
Drumb hilff O Herr
Sunst ist es alß vergeben.

[3.] *Das dritt gsatz.*
Zuo dir min Got/
An allen spott/
  Rüff ich in minem läben:
    Din hilff vnd rhat/
    Ouch mit der that/
Wöllest mir allzit geben/
Nach diner güt/
Dann min gemüt/
  Zuo dir allein thuot bgären/
    Drumb bit ich dich/
    Thuo gnädigklich/
Mich miner bitt gewären.

VIII. *Veni electa mea* [Geering, *Psalmen und geistliche Gesänge*, no. 5]
Veni electa mea,
et ponam in te thronum meum,
quia concupivit rex speciem tuam.

Osterspiel (1552)

IXa. *Ein Lied* [before v. 113]
Johanni dem Apostel das geschach
Das er im geist den Herren sitzen sach etc.

IXb. *Martin Luther, Das deudsch Sanctus* [Jenny, *Luthers geistliche Lieder*, no. 26]
Jesaia dem propheten, das geschach,
das er ym geyst den herren sitzen sach
auff eynem hohen thron yun hellem glantz;
seines kleides saum den kor fullet gantz.
Es stunden zween seraph bey yhm daran.
Sechs flugel sach er eynen ydern han;
mit zwen verbargen sie yhr antlitz klar,
mit zwen bedeckten sie die fusse gar,
und mit den andern zwen sie flogen frey,
gen ander ruffen sie mit grossem schrey:
"Heylig ist Gott, der Herre zebaoth.
Heilig ist Gott der herre zebaoth.
Heylig ist Gott, der herre zebaoth,
Sein ehr die gantze welt erfullet hat."
Von dem schrei zittert schwel und balcken gar;
das haus auch gantz vol rauchs und nebel war.

Xa. *Gsang* [before v. 148]
Te Deum Laudamus.

Xb. *Te Deum* [Pahlen, *The World of the Oratorio*, p. 345]
Te Deum laudamus: te Dominum confitemur.
Te aeternum Patrem omnis terra veneratur.
Tibi omnes Angeli, tibi Coeli et universae Potestates:
Tibi Cherubim et Seraphim incessabili voce proclamant:
Sanctus, Sanctus, Sanctus, Dominus Deus Sabaoth.
Pleni sunt coeli et terra majestatis gloriae tuae.
Te gloriosus Apostolorum chorus:
Te Prophetarum laudabilis numerus:
Te Martyrum candidatus laudat exercitus.
Te per orbem terrarum sancta confitetur Ecclesia.
Patrem immensae majestatis:
Venerandum tuum verum et unicum Filium:
Sanctum quoque Paraclitum Spiritum.
Tu Rex gloriae, Christe.
Tu Patris sempiternus es Filius.
Tu ad liberandum suscepturus hominem, non horruisti Virginis uterum.
Tu devicto mortis aculeo, aperuisti credentibus regna coelorum.
Tu ad dexteram Dei sedes, in gloria Patris.
Judex crederis esse venturus.
Te ergo quaesumus, tuis famulis subveni, quos pretioso sanguine redemisti.
Aeterna fac cum Sanctis tuis in gloria numerari.
Salvum fac populum tuum Domine, et benedic haereditati tuae.
Et rege eos, et extolle illos usque in aeternum.
Per singulos dies, benedicimus te.
Et laudamus nomen tuum in saeculum, et in saeculum saeculi.
Dignare Domine die isto sine peccato nos custodire.
Miserere nostri Domine, miserere nostri.
Fiat misericordia tua Domine super nos, quemadmodum speravimus in te.
In te Domine speravi: non confundar in aeternum.

Xc. *Martin Luther, "Herr Gott, dich loben wir"* [Jenny, *Luthers geistliche Lieder*, no. 31]

Der Erste Chor.
Herr Gott, dich loben wir.
Dich, Vater inn ewigkeit,
All Engel und himels heer
Auch Cherubim und Seraphim
Heilig ist unser Gott,

Beide Chör zusammen
Heilig ist unser Gott, der Herre
  Zebaoth

Der Ander Chor.
Herr Gott, wir danken dir.
Ehrt die welt weit und breit.
Und was dienet deiner ehr,
Singen immer mit hoher stim.
Heilig ist unser Gott,

Beide Chör zusammen
Heilig ist unser Gott, der Herre
  Zebaoth

Der Erste Chor.
Dein Göttlich macht und herligkeit
Der heiligen Zwelffpoten zall
Die teuren Martrer allzumal

Die gantze werde Christenheit
Dich Gott Vater im höchsten thron,
Den heiligen Geist und Tröster werd
Du König der ehren Jhesu Christ,
Der Jungfrau leib nicht hast verschmecht,
Du hast dem t[od] zerstört sein macht
Du sitzt zur rechten Gottes gleich
Ein Richter du zukünfftig bist
Nu hilff uns, Herr, den dienern dein,
Las uns im himel haben teil
Hilff deinem volck, Herr Jhesu Christ,
Wart und pfleg ir zu aller zeit
Teglich, Herr Gott, wir loben dich
Behüt uns heut, O treuer Gott,
Sey uns gnedig O Herre Gott,
Sey uns gnedig O Herre Gott,
Zeig uns deine barmherzigkeit,
Auff dich hoffen wir, lieber Herr.

[*Beide Chöre*]
AMEN.

Der Ander Chor.
Ghet uber himel und erden weit.

Vnd die lieben Propheten all,
Loben dich, Herr, mit grossem schal.

Rhümbt dich auf erden allezeit.
Deinen rechten und einigen Son.

Mit rechtem dienst sie lobt und ehrt.
Gott Vater ewiger Son du bist.

Zurlösen das menschlich geschlecht.

Und all Christen zum himel bracht.

Mit aller ehr ins Vaters Reich.

Alles, das tod und lebend ist.
Die mit deim teurn blut erlöset sein.

Mit den heiligen inn ewigem heil.
Und segen, das dein erbteil ist.

Und heb sie hoch inn ewigkeit.
und ehrn dein namen stettiglich.

Für aller sünd und missethat.
Sey uns gnedig inn aller not.
Sey uns gnedig inn aller not.
Wie unser hoffnung zu dir steht.
Inn schanden las uns nimermehr.

[*Beide Chöre*]
AMEN.

XIa. *Gsang* [before v. 415]
   Dignus es domine accipere librum etc.

XIb. Revelation 5:9–10, 5:12b, 5:13b [Nestle/Nestle/Aland, *Novum Testamentum*, p. 623]

   Dignus es Domine accipere librum, et aperire signacula eius: quoniam occisus es, et redemisti nos Deo in sanguine tuo ex omni tribu, et lingua, et populo, et natione: et fecisti nos Deo nostro regnum, et sacerdotes: et regnabimus super terram.

Dignus est Agnus, qui occisus est, accipere virtutem, et divinitatem, et sapientiam, et fortitudinem, et honorem, et gloriam, et benedictionem.

Sedenti in throno, et Agno: benedictio, et honor, et gloria, et potestas in saecula saeculorum.

XII. *Ein Lied in der wyß/ Da Jßrahel vß Egipten zoch.* [before v. 455–v. 493]
[1.] WJe hat es sich doch mit vns verkeert/
Ein nüw Lied/Herr/hand wir erst gelert
    Das nieman sunst kan singen
      Dann die du Herr/darzuo hast erkorn
      Vnd dir selbs heimlich wider geborn
    Mit wunder sältznen dingen.
      Drumb wir O Heiland Jesu Christ
      Bekennend/das du würdig bist
        Das Buoch nämmen vß ß'Vatters hand
        Vnd vffzeryssen syne band
        Die siben Sigel glycher gstalt
        Herr/vff zethuon hast macht vnd gwalt/
                          Alleluia.

[2.] Du bist gsin by Gott von Ewigkeit
Dyn namm ist Gottes Barmhertzigkeyt
    Lieb vnd gnad miltigkliche/
      Das wort dardurch all ding sind gemacht
      Himmel vnd Erden/tag vnde nacht
    Ouch Adam Gott gelyche/
      Der hat Gotts bildnuß bald verlorn
      Deß wurden wir in sünden porn
        Vnd dem Welt Fürsten vnderthan
        Dem mochten wir nit selbs entgan
        Biß du Herr in vns gsiget hast
        Vnd vns abgnon der sünden last.
                          Alleluia.

[3.] Dann du/Herr/hast von anfang der welt
    Dyn läben allweg für vns gestellt
      Den Todt zletst für vns glitten/
      Vnd hast also vns in dynem bluot
      Wie erkoufft vnserm höchsten guot
    Wider dyn Erbfynd gstritten/
      Vß allen völckern/sprach vnd gschlecht
      Hast vns vßzogen dyne knecht/
        Vns vnserm Gott zuo Künigen gmacht
        Zuo hochen Priestern würdig g'acht
        Deß sind wir dich zuo loben b'reit
        Jm Himmel biß in Ewigkeit.
                          Alleluia.

XIII. *Gsang mit vier stimmen.* [before v. 530–v. 556]
 Das truren ist vergangen/... [= *Noe* V]

XIV. *Lobgsang Tryumphs wyß.* [before v. 616–v. 641]
 Gelobet sy Gott vnser Herr/... [= *Noe* VI]

XV. *Hieruff gsungen/Christ ist erstanden.* [before v. 805–v. 813]
[1.] Christ ist erstanden/von der martter allen/
 Deß sollen wir alle fro syn/Christ sol vnser trost syn.
  Alleluia.

[2.] Vnnd wer er nitt erstanden/so wer die welt zergangen/
 So er aber erstanden ist/so helff vns der Herr Jesus Christ.
  Alleluia.

[3.] Erstanden ist der heilig Christ/der aller welt ein tröster ist.
  Alleluia/Alleluia/Alleluia/Alleluia.

BIBLIOGRAPHY

Primary Sources

Aargauer Urkunden. 13 vols. Aarau: H.R. Sauerländer, 1930–55.
Actensammlung zur Geschichte der Zürcher Reformation in den Jahren 1519–1533. Ed. Emil Egli. Zürich: J. Schabelitz, 1879.
Actensammlung zur schweizerischen Reformationsgeschichte in den Jahren 1521–1532 im Anschluss an die gleichzeitigen eidgenössischen Abschiede. Ed. Johannes Strickler. 5 vols. Zürich: Meyer & Zeller, 1878–84.
Aktensammlung zur Geschichte der Basler Reformation in den Jahren 1519 bis Anfang 1534. Ed. Emil Dürr and Paul Roth. 6 vols. Basel: Verlag der historischen und antiquarischen Gesellschaft Universitätsbibliothek Basel, 1921–50.
Aktensammlung zur Geschichte der Berner Reformation 1521–1532. Ed. Rudolf Steck and Gustav Tobler. 2 vols. Bern: K.J. Wyss Erben, 1923.
[Anshelm, Valerius]. *Die Berner Chronik des Valerius Anshelm*. Ed. Historischer Verein des Kantons Bern. 6 vols. Bern: K.J. Wyss, 1884–1901.
"Appius und Virginia: Ein bernisches Schauspiel aus dem 16. Jahrhundert." Ed. Fr. von Fischer-Manuel. In *Berner Taschenbuch auf das Jahr 1886*, ed. Emil Blösch, 73–149. Bern: B.F. Haller, 1885.
[Aretius, Benedict]. *Commentarii in Omenes Epistolas D. Pavli, et Canonicas, itemqve in Apocalypsin D. Ioannis*. Editio altera. N.p.: Ioannes le Preux, 1596.
Der Berner Synodus von 1532. 2 vols. Neukirchen-Vluyn: Neukirchener Verlag, 1988.
Bernoulli, Eduard. *Aus Liederbüchern der Humanistenzeit. Eine bibliographische und notentypographische Studie*. Leipzig: Breitkopf und Härtel, 1910.
de Bèze, Théodore. *Abraham Sacrifiant*. Ed. Keith Cameron, Kathleen M. Hall, and Francis Higman. Geneva: Droz, 1967.
———. *Abraham Sacrifiant*. Ed. C.R. Frankish. New York: Johnson Reprint, 1969.
Binder, Georg. "Acolastus." In *Schweizerische Schauspiele des sechzehnten Jahrhunderts*, ed. Jacob Baechtold. Vol. 1. Zurich: J. Huber, 1890.
Birck, Sixt. *Sämtliche Dramen*. Ed. Manfred Brauneck. 3 vols. Berlin: Walter de Gruyter, 1969–80.
Bloesch, Hans, ed. *Dreißig Volkslieder aus den ersten Pressen der Apiarius*. Bern: Schweizer Bibliophilengesellschaft, 1937.
Bucer, Martin. *De Regno Christi*. Vol. 15, *Martini Buceri Opera Latina*. Ed. François Wendel. Paris: Presses Universitaires de France; Gütersloh: Bertelsmann, 1955.
———. "De Regno Christi." In *Melanchthon and Bucer*, ed. and trans. Wilhelm Pauck, 153–394. Library of Christian Classics 19. Philadelphia: Westminster, 1969.
Bullinger, Heinrich. *Reformationsgeschichte*. Ed. J.J. Hottinger and H.H. Vögeli. 3 vols. 1838–40. Reprint, Zurich: Theologische Buchhandlung, 1985.
———, and Hans Sachs. *Lucretia-Dramen*. Ed. Horst Hartmann. Leipzig: VEB Bibliographisches Institut, 1973.
[Calvin, John]. *Ioannis Calvini opera quae supersunt omnia*. Ed. Johann Wilhelm Baum et al. 59 vols. Corpus Reformatorum 29–87. Braunschweig: C.A. Schwetschke et filius, 1863–1900.
Celtis, Conrad. *Ludi Scaenici*. Ed. Felicitas Pindter. Budapest: Egyetemi Nyomda, 1945.
Christ-Kutter, Friederike, ed. *Frühe Schweizerspiele*. Altdeutsche Übungstexte 19. Bern: Francke, 1963.

Chronik aus den hinterlassenen Handschriften des Joh. Haller und Abraham Müslin von 1550 bis 1580. Ed. Samuel Gränicher. Zofingen: D. Sutermeister, 1829.

Corpus antiphonalium officii. Ed. René-Jean Hesbert. 6 vols. Rome: Herder, 1963–79.

Crocus, Cornelius. "Ioseph, Comoedia ex Geneseos Cap. 39 et sequentibus." In *Dramata Sacra, Comoediae atqve tragoediae aliquot e Veteri Testamento desumptae, quibus praecipuae ipsius historiae ita eleganter in scenam producuntur, ut uix quicquam in hoc argumenti genere, iuventuti Christianae proponi utilius poßit.* Basel: n.p., 1547.

[Diesbach, Ludwig von]. *Die autobiographischen Aufzeichnungen Ludwig von Diesbachs. Studien zur spätmittelalterlichen Selbstdarstellung im oberdeutschen und schweizerischen Raume.* Ed. Urs Martin Zahnd. Schriften der Berner Burgerbibliothek 17. Bern: Berner Burgerbibliothek, 1986.

[Edlibach, Gerold]. "'Da beschachend vil grosser endrungen': Gerold Edlibachs Aufzeichnungen über die Zürcher Reformation 1520–1526." Ed. Peter Jezler. In *Bilderstreit. Kulturwandel in Zwinglis Reformation*, ed. Hans-Dietrich Altendorf and Peter Jezler, 41–74. Zürich: Theologischer Verlag Zürich, 1984.

Erk, Ludwig. *Deutscher Liederhort.* 3 vols. Leipzig: Breitkopf & Härtel, 1893–4.

"Das Fastnachtspiel Henselin oder von der Rechtfertigkeit." Ed. Christoph Walter. *Jahrbuch des Vereins für niederdeutsche Sprachforschung* 3 (1877): 9–36.

Fastnachtspiele des 15. und 16. Jahrhunderts. Ed. Dieter Wuttke. 4th ed. Stuttgart: Reclam, 1989.

[Foxe, John]. *The Acts and Monuments of John Foxe.* Ed. Rev. Josiah Pratt. 4th ed. 8 vols. London: Religious Tract Society, 1877.

[———]. *Two Latin Comedies by John Foxe the Martyrologist. Titus et Gesippus—Christus Triumphans.* Ed. and trans. John Hazel Smith. Ithaca/London: Cornell University Press, 1973.

Frankfurter Dirigierrolle—Frankfurter Passionsspiel. Mit den Paralleltexten der "Frankfurter Dirigierrolle", des "Alsfelder Passionsspiels", des "Heidelberger Passionsspiels", des "Frankfurter Osterspielfragments" und des "Fritzlaer Passionsspielfragments". Ed. Johannes Janota. Vol. 1, *Die Hessische Passionsspielgruppe. Edition im Paralleldruck.* Tübingen: Niemeyer, 1996.

[Funkelin, Jacob]. "A Swiss Resurrection Play of the Sixteenth Century." Ed. Newton Stephen Arnold. Ph.D. diss., Columbia University, 1949.

Gart, Thiebold. "Joseph." In *Die Schaubühne im Dienste der Reformation II*, ed. Arnold E. Berger, 5–134. Deutsche Literatur in Entwicklungsreihen, Reihe Reformation 6. Leipzig: Reclam, 1936.

Geering, Arnold, ed. *Psalmen und Geistliche Gesänge von Johannes Wannenmacher (Vannius) und Cosmas Alder (Alderinus).* Musikalische Werke schweizerischer Komponisten des XVI., XVII. und XVIII. Jahrhunderts, 3. Faszikel. Genève: Edition Henn, 1934.

Gengenbach, Pamphilus. *Die Totenfresser.* Ed. Richard Froning. Deutsche Nationalliteratur 22. Stuttgart: Union, 1894.

"Gespräch der Berner Prädikanten mit den Täufern, gehalten vom 11. bis 17. März 1538 zu Bern." In *Quellen zur Geschichte der Täufer in der Schweiz*, ed. Martin Haas. Vol. 4. Zurich: Theologischer Verlag, 1974.

Gnapheus, Gulielmus. *Acolastus: A Latin Play of the Sixteenth Century.* Ed. and trans. W.E.D. Atkinson. London, Ontario: Hunter Printing, 1964.

Greenberg, Noah and Paul Maynard, eds. *An Anthology of Early Renaissance Music.* New York: W.W. Norton, 1975.

Greff, Joachim. *Ein Geistliches schönes newes spil/auff das heilige Osterfest gestellet/Darinnen werden gehandelt die geschicht von der Aufferstehung Christi zu sampt der historien Thome.* Zwickau: n.p., 1542.

———. *Ein lieblich vnd nützbarlich spiel von dem Patriarchen jacob vnd seinen zwelff Sönen/Aus dem ersten buch Mosi gezogen/vnd zu Magdeburg auff dem Schützenhoff/im 1535. iar gehalten.* Nuremberg: n.p., 1535.

[Gruben, Hans von der]. *Hans von der Grubens Reise- und Pilgerbuch.* Ed. Max von

Diesbach. *Archiv des Historischen Vereins des Kantons Bern* XIV. Bern: Historischer Verein, 1894.

Gundelfingen, Heinrich von. "Topographia urbis Bernensis." Ed. Emil Blösch. *Archiv des Historischen Vereins des Kantons Bern* 10 (1880): 177–90.

[Gwalther, Rudolf]. *Rudolf Gwalthers Nabal: Ein Zürcher Drama aus dem 16. Jahrhundert.* Ed. Sandro Giovanoli. Studien zur Germanistik, Anglistik und Komparatistik 83. Bonn: Bouvier, 1979.

Haller, Berchtold, ed. *Bern in seinen Rathsmanualen 1465–1565.* Bern: K.J. Wyss, 1900.

Haller, Johannes. *Tagebuch aus den Jahren 1548–1561.* Ed. Eduard Bähler. Archiv des Historischen Vereins des Kantons Bern 23. Bern: Historischer Verein, 1917.

[Horace]. *Q. Horati Flacci.* Ed. Edward Wickham and H.W. Garrod. Oxford: Clarendon Press, 1975.

Jenny, Markus, ed. *Luthers Geistliche Lieder und Kirchengesänge. Vollständige Neuedition in Ergänzung zu Band 35 der Weimarer Ausgabe.* Archiv zur Weimarer Ausgabe der Werke Martin Luthers, Texte und Untersuchungen 4. Cologne/Vienna: Böhlau, 1985.

Keller, Adelbert von, ed. *Fastnachtspiele aus dem 15. Jahrhundert.* 4 vols. Bibliothek des literarischen Vereins in Stuttgart 28–30, 46. Stuttgart: Literarischer Verein, 1853–8.

Kolroß, Johannes. "Fünferlei Betrachtnisse, die den Menschen zur Buße reizen." Ed. Theodor Odinga. In *Schweizerische Schauspiele des 16. Jahrhunderts.* Vol. 1. Zurich: J. Huber, 1890.

Krüger, Bartholomäus. "Eine schöne vnd lustige newe Action, Von dem Anfang vnd Ende der Welt." In *Schauspiele aus dem sechzehnten Jahrhundert,* ed. Julius Tittmann, 2:1–120. Leipzig: Brockhaus, 1868.

Liliencron, Rochus von, ed. *Die historischen Volkslieder der Deutschen vom 13. bis 16. Jahrhundert.* 5 vols. Leipzig: F.C.W. Vogel, 1865–9.

Luther, Martin. *D. Martin Luthers Werke.* 89 vols. Weimar: Hermann Böhlau, 1883–1983.

Das Luzerner Osterspiel. Ed. Heinz Wyss. 3 vols. Bern: Francke, 1967.

Manuel, Hans Rudolf. "Das Weinspiel." Ed. Walter Haas. In *Fünf Komödien des sechzehnten Jahrhunderts,* ed. Walter Haas und Martin Stern, 211–421. Schweizer Texte 10. Bern/Stuttgart: Paul Haupt, 1989.

[Manuel, Niklaus]. *Niklaus Manuel. Werke und Briefe.* Ed. Paul Zinsli and Thomas Hengartner. Bern: Stämpfli, 1999.

———. "Vom Papst und seiner Priesterschaft." In *Deutsche Dramen des 15. und 16. Jahrhunderts,* ed. Hellmut Thomke, 139–209. Bibliothek deutscher Klassiker 136. Frankfurt: Deutscher Klassiker Verlag, 1996.

———. *Der Ablaßkrämer.* Ed. Paul Zinsli. Altdeutsche Übungstexte 17. Bern: Francke, 1960.

———. "Ein Fastnachtspiel vom Papst und seiner Priesterschaft." In *Die Schaubühne im Dienste der Reformation I,* ed. Arnold E. Berger, 45–113. Deutsche Literatur in Entwicklungsreihen, Reihe Reformation 5. Leipzig: Reclam, 1935.

———. *Niklaus Manuels Spiel evangelischer Freiheit "Die Totenfresser".* Ed. Ferdinand Vetter. Die Schweiz im deutschen Geistesleben 16. Leipzig: H. Haessel, 1923.

———. "Dichtungen des Niklaus Manuel. Aus einer Handschrift der Hamburger Stadtbibliothek." Ed. Fritz Burg. In *Neues Berner Taschenbuch auf das Jahr 1897,* ed. Heinrich Türler, 1–136. Bern: K.J. Wyss, 1896.

———. *Niklaus Manuel.* Ed. Jakob Baechtold. Bibliothek älterer Schriftwerke der deutschen Schweiz und ihres Grenzgebietes 2. Frauenfeld: J. Huber, 1878.

[Melanchthon, Philipp]. "Enarratio comoedarum Terentii." In *Philippi Melanchthoni Opera quae supersunt omnia,* ed. Carl Gottlieb Bretschneider and Heinrich Ernst Bindseil. Corpus Reformatorum 19. Braunschweig: C.A. Schwetschke et filius, 1853.

[Meyer, Sebastian.] *In Apocalypsim Johannis Apostoli D. Sebastiani Meyer Ecclesiastiae Bernen. Commentarius, nostro huic saeculo accommodus, natus, & æditus.* Zurich: Froschauer, n.d.

[Mülinen, Caspar von]. "Die Pilgerreise des Ritters Caspar von Mülinen ins heilige Land." Ed. R. Röhricht. *Zeitschrift des deutschen Palästinavereins* 9 (1888): 184–97.
Murer, Jos. *Sämtliche Dramen*. Ed. Hans-Joachim Adomatis et al. 2 vols. Berlin: de Gruyter, 1974.
Murner, Thomas. *Von den fier ketzeren*. Ed. Eduard Fuchs. Thomas Murners Deutsche Schriften mit den Holzschnitten der Erstdrucke I,1. Berlin: de Gruyter, 1929.
———. "Des jungen Bären Zahnweh: Eine verschollene Streitschrift Thomas Murners." Ed. Joseph Lefftz. *Archiv für elsässische Kirchengeschichte* I (1926): 141–67.
———. "Des alten Christenlichen beeren Testament 1528." Ed. Max Scherrer. *Anzeiger für schweizerische Geschichte* 50, Neue Folge 17 (1919): 6–38.
Myconius, Oswald. *Vom Leben und Sterben Huldrych Zwinglis*. Ed. and trans. Ernst Gerhard Rüsch. Mitteilungen zur vaterländischen Geschichte 50. St. Gallen: Fehr'sche Buchhandlung, 1979.
Naogeorg, Thomas. *Sämtliche Werke*. Ed. Hans-Gert Roloff. 4 vols. to date. Berlin: de Gruyter, 1975–.
Nestle, Eberhard, Erwin Nestle, and Kurt Aland, eds. *Novum Testamentum. Graece et Latine*. Stuttgart: Württembergische Bibelanstalt, 1969.
Nietzsche, Friedrich. *Werke. Kritische Gesamtausgabe*. Ed. Giorgio Colli, Mazzino Montinari, et al. 29 vols. to date. Berlin/New York: de Gruyter, 1967–.
Rebhun, Paul. *Susanna*. Ed. Hans-Gert Roloff. Stuttgart: Reclam, 1980.
Reuchlin, Johannes. *Henno*. Ed. and trans. Harry C. Schnur. Stuttgart: Reclam, 1970.
[Rhau, Georg.] *Georg Rhau. Musikdrucke aus den Jahren 1538–1545 in praktischer Neuausgabe*. Ed. Hans Albrecht and Joachim Stalmann. 11 vols. Kassel: Bärenreiter, 1955–92.
———. *Newe deudsche geistliche Gesenge für die gemeinen Schulen*. 2nd ed. Ed. Johannes Wolf and Hans Joachim Moser. Denkmäler deutscher Tonkunst 34. Wiesbaden: Breitkopf & Härtel, 1958.
Ringoltingen, Thüring von. *Melusine*. Ed. Karin Schneider. Texte des späten Mittelalters 9. Berlin: Erich Schmidt, 1958.
———. *Melusine*. Ed. Hans-Gert Roloff. Stuttgart: Reclam, 1969.
Rueff, Jacob. *Das Züricher Passionsspiel: Jacob Rueff, Das lyden vnsers Herren Jesu Christi das man nempt den Passion*. Ed. Barbara Thoran. Bochum: Studienverlag Dr. N. Brockmeyer, 1984.
———. "Das neue Tellenspiel von Jakob Ruf." Ed. Jakob Baechtold. In *Schweizerische Schauspiele des sechszehnten Jahrhunderts*. Vol. 3. Zurich: J. Huber, 1893.
———. *Jacob Ruffs Adam und Heva*. Ed. Hermann Marcus Kottinger. Bibliothek der deutschen National-Literatur 26. Quedlinburg/Leipzig: Gottfried Basse, 1848.
———. *Jakob Ruffs Etter Heini uss dem Schwizerland*. Ed. Hermann Marcus Kottinger. Bibliothek der gesamten deutschen Nationalliteratur 14. Quedlinburg: Gottfried Basse, 1847.
———. *Ein hüpsch nüwes Spil von Josephen dem frommen Jüngling/vß etlichen Capitlen deß buochs der Gschöpfften gezogen/in sonders lustig vnd nutzlich zeläsen*. Zürich: Augustin Frieß, 1540.
Rüte, Hans von. *Sämtliche Dramen*. Ed. Friederike Christ-Kutter, Klaus Jaeger, and Hellmut Thomke. Schweizer Texte, Neue Folge 14. 3 vols. Bern/Stuttgart/Vienna: Paul Haupt, 2000.
———. *Ein Fasnachtspil den vrsprung/haltung/vnd das End beyder/Heydnischer/vnd Bäpstlicher Abgötteryen allenklich verglychende/zuo Bern inn öchtland durch die jungen Burger gehallten*. Basel: Thomas Wolff, 1532. [*Abgötterei*]
———. *Goliath. Die Histori/Wie David der Jüngling den Risen Goliath vmbbracht vnd erlegt hat. Jst zuo Bern durch ein gemeyne Burgerschafft gespilt*. Bern: Samuel Apiarius, 1555. [*Goliath*]
———. *Dje Hystoria des gots förchtigen jünglings/Josephs/in dem Ersten Buoch Mosy in den 37. 39. 40. 41. 42. 43. vnnd 44. Capitlen beschriben/Jst zuo Bernn durch junge Burger conterfetisch gespilt*. Bern: Mathias Apiarius, 1538. [*Joseph*]

———. *Die Hystori wie der Herr durch Gedeons hand sin volck von siner finden gwalt wunderbarlich erlößet hab/beschriben in der Rychtern buoch am vj. vnd vij. capiteln/Jst zuo Bern durch die Jungen burger gespilt/vff dem vij. tag Martij Jm 1540. Jar*. Bern: Mathias Apiarius, 1540. [*Gedeon*]

———. *Ein kurtzes Osterspil zuo Bern durch Jung gsellen ghandlet/vff dem Sontag Quasimodo nach Ostern/Jm 1552. Jar*. Bern: Mathias Apiarius, 1552. [*Osterspiel*]

———. *Wie Noe vom win vberwunden durch sin jüngsten Sun Cham geschmächt/aber die eltern beid/Sem vnnd Japhet geehret/den sägen vnd fluoch jnen eroffnet hatt/Jst zuo Bernn in Vchtland/durch junge Burger gspilt vff 4. Aprilis Anno 1546*. Bern: Mathias Apiarius, 1546. [*Noe*]

———. "Die Stadtsatzung von 1539." In *Die Rechtsquellen des Kantons Bern*, ed. Friedrich Emil Welti. Vol. 1. Sammlung Schweizerischer Rechtsquellen, 2. Abteilung. Aarau: Sauerländer, 1971.

Sachs, Hans. "Der gantz Passio." In *Das Admonter Passionsspiel*, ed. Karl Konrad Polheim. Vol. 3. Munich: Schöningh, 1980.

———. *Hans Sachs*. Ed. Adalbert von Keller and Edmund Goetze. 26 vols. Tübingen: H. Laupp, 1870–1908.

[Salat, Hans]. *Hans Salat: Ein schweizerischer Chronist und Dichter aus der ersten Hälfte des XVI. Jahrhunderts. Sein Leben und seine Schriften*. Ed. Jacob Baechtold. Basel: Bahnmaiers Verlag, 1876.

———. *Reformationschronik 1517–1534*. Ed. Ruth Jörg. Quellen zur Schweizer Geschichte, Neue Folge I,8. 3 vols. Bern: Allgemeine Geschichtforschende Gesellschaft der Schweiz, 1986.

[Schilling, Diebold]. *Die Luzerner Chronik des Diebold Schilling 1513*. Facsimile edition. Luzern: Kunstkreis Faksimile-Verlag, 1977.

Schwinkhart, Ludwig. *Chronik 1506–1521*. Ed. Hans von Greyerz. Archiv des historischen Vereins des Kantons Bern 36, 1. Bern: Feuz, 1941.

Sehling, Emil, ed. *Die evangelischen Kirchenordnungen des 16. Jahrhunderts*. 15 vols. Vols. 1–5, Leipzig: O.R. Reisland, 1902–13; vols. 6–15, Tübingen: J.C.B. Mohr, 1955–77.

Senfl, Ludwig. *Sämtliche Werke*. Ed. Edwin Löhrer, Otto Ursprung, et al. 11 vols. Wolfenbüttel: Möseler Verlag, 1937–74.

Strand, Kenneth A., ed. *Dürer's Apocalypse. The 1498 German and 1511 Latin Texts in Facsimile plus Samples of Dürer's Woodcuts and Gräff's Copies*. Ann Arbor: Ann Arbor Publishers, 1969.

———, ed. *Woodcuts to the Apocalypse in Dürer's Time. Albrecht Dürer's Woodcuts Plus Five Other Set from the 15th and 16th Centuries*. Ann Arbor: Ann Arbor Publishers, 1968.

Stürler, Moritz von, ed. "Beschreibung des Waldmannischen Auflaufs zu Zürich von einem Zeitgenossen." *Archiv für schweizerische Geschichte* 9 (1853): 279–329.

[Terence]. *Der Eunuchus des Terenz. Übersetzt von Hans Neidhart 1486*. Ed. Hermann Fischer. Bibliothek des Litterarischen Vereins in Stuttgart 265. Tübingen: Laupp, 1915.

[Tritonius, Petrus.] *Melopoiae sive harmoniae tetracenticae super xxii genera carminum heroicorum elegiacorum lyricorum & ecclesiasticorum hymnorum*. Augsburg: Erhard Oeglin, 1507.

[Tschachtlan, Bendicht]. "Bendicht Tschachtlans Berner Chronik nebst den Zusätzen des Diebold Schillings." In *Quellen zur Schweizer Geschichte* I, ed. Gottlieb Studer, 199–298. Basel: Felix Schneider, 1877.

Tucher, Gottlieb Freiherr von. *Schatz des evangelischen Kirchengesangs im 1. Jahrhundert der Reformation*. 2 vols. Leipzig: Breitkopf & Härtel, 1848; reprint Walluf bei Wiesbaden: Martin Sändig, 1972.

"Eine waarhafftige History vß dem heyligen Euangelio Luce am XVI. Capitel von dem Rychen mann vnnd armen Lazaro." In *Das Zürcher Spiel vom reichen Mann und vom armen Lazarus—Pamphilus Gengenbach, Die Totenfresser*, ed. Josef Schmidt, 7–38. Stuttgart: Reclam, 1969.

Wackernagel, Philipp. *Das deutsche Kirchenlied von der ältesten Zeit bis zum Anfang des XVII. Jahrhunderts*. 5 vols. Leipzig, 1864–77; reprint Hildesheim: Olms, 1964.

Wagner, Johannes. *Solothurner St. Mauritius- und St. Ursenspiel.* Ed. Heinrich Biermann. Schweizer Texte 5. Bern: Paul Haupt, 1980.
Waldis, Burkard. "De parabell vam verlorn Szohn." In *Die Schaubühne im Dienste der Reformation I*, ed. Arnold E. Berger, 143–220. Deutsche Literatur in Entwicklungsreihen, Reihe Reformation 5. Leipzig: Reclam, 1935.
Wappenbuch der burgerlichen Geschlechter der Stadt Bern. Bern: Burgergemeinde, 1932.
[Wölflin, Heinrich]. *Heinrichs Wölflis Reise nach Jerusalem 1520/21.* Ed. Hans Bloesch. Bern: Schweizer Bibliophilengesellschaft, 1929.
Zahn, Johannes. *Die Melodien der deutschen evangelischen Kirchenlieder.* 6 vols. Gütersloh, 1889–93; reprint Hildesheim: Olms, 1963.
Zehnder, Leo, ed. *Volkskundliches in der älteren schweizerischen Chronistik.* Schriften der Schweizerischen Gesellschaft für Volkskunde 60. Basel: G. Krebs, 1976.
Das Zerbster Prozessionsspiel 1507. Ed. Willm Reupke. Quellen zur deutschen Volkskunde 4. Berlin/Leipzig: de Gruyter, 1930.
Die Zürcher Bibel von 1531. Facsimile edition. Zurich: Theologischer Verlag, 1983.
[Zwingli, Ulrich]. *Huldreich Zwinglis sämtliche Werke.* 14 vols. Corpus Reformatorum 88–101. Ed. Emil Egli et al. Leipzig: M. Heinsius, 1905–.

Secondary Sources

Abbé, Derek van. "Change and Tradition in the Work of Niklaus Manuel of Berne." *Modern Language Review* 47 (1952): 181–98.
——. "Niklaus Manuel of Bern and His Interest in the Reformation." *Journal of Modern History* 24 (1952): 287–300.
——. *Drama in Renaissance Germany and Switzerland.* Melbourne: Melbourne University Press, 1961.
Aeschbacher, Gerhard. "Die Reformation und das kirchenmusikalische Leben im alten Bern." In *450 Jahre Berner Reformation. Beiträge zur Geschichte der Berner Reformation und zu Niklaus Manuel*, 225–47. Archiv des Historischen Vereines des Kantons Bern 64–65. Bern: Historischer Verein des Kantons Bern, 1980.
Aichele, Klaus. *Das Antichristdrama des Mittelalters, der Reformation und Gegenreformation.* Den Haag: Martinus Nijhoff, 1974.
Altenburg, Detlef and Lorenz Jensen. "Schauspielmusik." In *Musik in Geschichte und Gegenwart*, ed. Ludwig Finscher. 2nd ed. Sachteil, Vol. 8. Kassel/Stutthart: Bärenreiter/Metzler, 1998.
Altendorf, Hans-Dietrich. "Zwinglis Stellung zum Bild und die Tradition christlicher Bildfeindschaft." In *Bilderstreit. Kulturwandel in Zwinglis Reformation*, ed. Hans-Dietrich Altendorf and Peter Jezler, 11–18. Zürich: Theologischer Verlag, 1984.
Ameln, Konrad. "Kirchenlied und Kirchenmusik in der deutschen reformierten Schweiz im Jahrhundert der Reformation." *Jahrbuch für Liturgik und Hymnologie* 6 (1961): 150–53.
Ashley, Kathleen M. "Cultural Approaches to Medieval Drama." In *Approaches to Teaching Medieval English Drama*, ed. Richard K. Emmerson, 57–66. New York: Modern Language Association of America, 1990.
Bächtiger, Franz. "Zur Revision des Berner Christoffel." *Jahrbuch des Bernischen Historischen Museums* 59/60 (1979/80): 115–278.
——. "Bern zur Zeit von Niklaus Manuel." In *Niklaus Manuel Deutsch: Maler—Dichter—Staatsmann*, ed. Cäsar Menz and Hugo Wagner, 1–16. Bern: Kunstmuseum Bern, 1979.
——. "Scheibenriss mit Berner Pannerträger." In *Niklaus Manuel Deutsch: Maler—Dichter—Staatsmann*, ed. Cäsar Menz and Hugo Wagner, 163–5. Bern: Kunstmuseum Bern, 1979.

Backus, Irena. *The Disputations of Baden, 1526 and Berne, 1528: Neutralizing the Early Church*. Studies in Reformed Theology and History 1. Princeton: Princeton Theological Seminary, 1993.
Bacon, Thomas Ivey. *Martin Luther and the Drama*. Amsterdam: Rodopi, 1976.
Baechtold, Jakob. *Geschichte der deutschen Literatur in der Schweiz*. 2nd ed. Frauenfeld: Huber, 1919.
——. "Zwei Berner Romanschriftsteller des XV. und XVI. Jahrhunderts." In *Berner Taschenbuch auf das Jahr 1878*, ed. Emil Blösch, 43–52. Bern: B.F. Haller, 1877.
Bähler, Eduard. "Dekan Johann Haller und die Berner Kirche von 1548 bis 1575." In *Neues Berner Taschenbuch auf das Jahr 1923*, 1–52. Bern: E.J. Wyss, 1922; *Neues Berner Taschenbuch auf das Jahr 1924*, 1–65; *Neues Berner Taschenbuch auf das Jahr 1925*, 1–58; *Neues Berner Taschenbuch auf das Jahr 1926*, 1–61.
Bakhtin, Mikhail. *Rabelais and His World*. Trans. Helene Iswolsky. Bloomington: Indiana University Press, 1984.
Bausinger, Hermann. "Für eine komplexere Fastnachtstheorie." *Jahrbuch für Volkskunde* Neue Folge 6 (1983): 101–6.
Beck, Hugo. *Das genrehafte Element im deutschen Drama des XVI. Jahrhunderts: Ein Beitrag zu den Wechselbeziehungen zwischen Dichtung und Malerei*. Germanische Studien 66. 1929. Reprint, Nendeln: Kraus, 1967.
Beerli, Conrad-André. *Le peintre poète Nicolas Manuel et l'evolution sociale de son temps*. Geneva: Librairie Droz, 1953.
Belting, Hans. *Bild und Kult. Eine Geschichte des Bildes vor dem Zeitalter der Kunst*. Munich: C.H. Beck, 1991.
Bergmann, Rolf. *Katalog der deutschsprachigen geistlichen Spiele und Marienklagen des Mittelalters*. Munich: Kommission für deutsche Literatur des Mittelalters der Bayerischen Akademie der Wissenschaften, 1986.
Bernoulli, Eduard. "Cosmas Alders Komposition auf Zwinglis Tod." *Zwingliana* 2 (1907): 136–44.
Bernstein, Eckhard. *Hans Sachs: Mit Selbstzeugnissen und Bilddokumenten*. Reinbek: Rowohlt, 1993.
Bierbrauer, Peter. *Freiheit und Gemeinde im Berner Oberland 1300–1700*. Archiv des Historischen Vereins des Kantons Bern 74. Bern: Historischer Verein des Kantons Bern, 1991.
Blankenburg, Walter. "Die Kirchenmusik in den reformierten Gebieten des europäischen Kontinents." In *Geschichte der evangelischen Kirchenmusik*, ed. Friedrich Blume, 341–400. 2nd ed. Kassel: Bärenreiter, 1965.
Blume, Friedrich. "Das Zeitalter der Reformation." In *Geschichte der evangelischen Kirchenmusik*, ed. Friedrich Blume, 1–75. 2nd ed. Kassel: Bärenreiter, 1965.
——. "Das Zeitalter des Konfessionalismus." In *Geschichte der evangelischen Kirchenmusik*, ed. F. Blume, 77–213. 2nd ed. Kassel: Bärenreiter, 1965.
Böckmann, Paul. *Formgeschichte der deutschen Dichtung*. Hamburg: Hoffmann und Campe, 1949.
Boesch, Paul. *Die Schweizer Glasmalerei*. Schweizer Kunst 6. Basel: Birkhäuser, 1955.
——. "Eine antipapistische Zeichnung von 1607." *Zwingliana* 9 (1952): 486–9.
Bonjour, Edgar. *Die Bauernbewegungen des Jahres 1525 im Staate Bern*. Bern: Paul Haupt, 1923.
Borgnet, Guy. "Jeu de Carnaval et Antisémitisme: Pureté Théologique et Pureté Ethnique chez Hans Folz." In *Carnival and the Carnivalesque. The Fool, the Reformer, the Wildman, and Others in Early Modern Theatre*, ed. Konrad Eisenbichler and Wim Hüsken, 129–45. Ludus 4. Amsterdam/Atlanta: Rodopi, 1999.
Brady, Thomas A., Jr. *Turning Swiss: Cities and Empire, 1450–1550*. Cambridge Studies in Early Modern History. Cambridge: Cambridge University Press, 1985.

Brandstetter, Renward. *Die Regenz bei den Luzerner Osterspielen.* Lucerne: Gebrüder Räber, 1886.
Brett-Evans, David. *Von Hrotsvith bis Folz und Gengenbach. Eine Geschichte des mittelalterlichen deutschen Dramas.* 2 vols. Grundlagen der Germanistik 15/18. Berlin: Schmidt, 1975.
Brunken, Otto. "Johannes Reuchlin (1455–1522): Scenica Progymnasmata: Hoc est: Ludicra Preexercitamenta. Basel 1498." In *Handbuch zur Kinder- und Jugendliteratur. Vom Beginn des Buchdrucks bis 1570*, ed. Theodor Brüggeman, 331–44, 1163–7. Stuttgart: Metzler, 1987.
Brunnschweiler, Thomas. *Johann Jakob Breitingers "Bedenken von Comoedien oder Spielen". Die Theaterfeindlichkeit im Alten Zürich. Edition—Kommentar—Monographie.* Zürcher Germanistische Studien 17. Bern: Peter Lang, 1989.
Butler, Bartlett R. "Hymns." In *The Oxford Encyclopedia of the Reformation*, ed. Hans J. Hillerbrand. Vol. 2. New York/Oxford: Oxford University Press, 1996.
Bynum, Caroline Walker. "Women's Stories, Women's Symbols: A Critique of Victor Turner's Theory of Liminality." In *Fragmentation and Redemption. Essays on Gender and the Human Body in Medieval Religion*, 27–51. New York: Zone Books, 1992.
———. "The Body of Christ in the Later Middle Ages: A Reply to Leo Steinberg." In *Fragmentation and Redemption*, 79–117.
Caflisch, Leo. "Zur Ikonographie Berchtold Hallers." *Zwingliana* 4 (1928): 455–70.
Capitani, François de. *Musik in Bern: Musik, Musiker, Musikerinnen und Publikum in der Stadt Bern vom Mittelalter bis heute.* Historischer Verein des Kantons Bern 76. Bern: Historischer Verein, 1993.
———. *Adel, Bürger und Zünfte im Bern des 15. Jahrhunderts.* Schriften der Berner Burgerbibliothek 16. Bern: Berner Burgerbibliothek, 1982.
Casey, Paul F. *The Susanna Theme in German Literature: Variations of the Biblical Drama.* Bonn: Bouvier, 1976.
Catholy, Eckehard. *Fastnachtspiel.* Stuttgart: Metzler, 1966.
———. *Das Fastnachtspiel des Spätmittelalters. Gestalt und Funktion.* Hermaea NF 8. Tübingen: Niemeyer, 1961.
Cherbuliez, A.E. *Die Schweiz in der deutschen Musikgeschichte.* Die Schweiz im deutschen Geistesleben, Illustrierte Reihe 18. Frauenfeld: Huber, 1932.
Christensen, Carl C. *Art and the Reformation in Germany.* Athens, Ohio: Ohio University Press; Detroit: Wayne State University Press, 1979.
Clark, Katerina, and Michael Holquist. *Mikhail Bakhtin.* Cambridge: Harvard University Press, 1984.
Clark, Robert L.A. "Community versus Subject in Late Medieval French Confraternity Drama and Ritual." In *Drama and Community: People and Plays in Medieval Europe*, ed. Alan Hindley, 34–56. Medieval Texts and Cultures in Northern Europe 1. Turnhout: Brepols, 1999.
Collinson, Patrick. *Birthpangs of Protestant England.* London: Macmillan, 1988.
Coolidge, W.A.B. *Josias Simler et les origines de l'alpinisme jusqu'en 1600.* Grenoble: Allier Frères, 1904.
Coppel, Bernhard. "Jakob Locher und seine in Freiburg aufgeführten Dramen." In *Acta Conventus Neo-Latini Amstelodamensis. Proceedings of the Second International Congress of Neo-Latin Studies*, ed. P. Turnman, G.C. Kuiper, and E. Keßler, 258–72. Munich: Wilhelm Fink, 1979.
Cramer, Thomas. *Geschichte der deutschen Literatur im späten Mittelalter.* Munich: Deutscher Taschenbuchverlag, 1990.
Crecelius, W. "Hans Rüte in Bern und sein Spiel von der heidnischen und päbstlichen Abgötterei." *Alemannia: Zeitschrift für Sprache, Litteratur und Volkskunde des Elsasses und Oberrheins* 3 (1875): 120–28.
———. "Die Heiligenverehrung in der Schweiz im 16. Jahrhundert." *Alemannia:*

Zeitschrift für Sprache, Litteratur und Volkskunde des Elsasses und Oberrheins 3 (1875): 56–61.
Creizenach, Wilhelm. *Geschichte des neueren Dramas.* 5 vols. Halle: Niemeyer, 1893–1916; 2nd ed. 3 vols. Halle: Niemeyer, 1911–23.
Crockett, Bryan. *The Play of Paradox: Stage and Sermon in Renaissance England.* Philadelphia: University of Pennsylvania Press, 1995.
Dauven-van Knippenberg, Carla. "Wege der Christenlehre. Über den Zusammenhang zweier mittelalterlicher Gattungen." *Zeitschrift für deutsche Philologie* 113 (1994): 370–84.
———. "Ein Anfang ohne Ende: Einführendes zur Frage nach dem Verhältnis zwischen Predigt und geistlichem Schauspiel des Mittelalters." In *Mittelalterliches Schauspiel: Festschrift für Hansjürgen Linke zum 65. Geburtstag,* ed. Ulrich Mehler and Anton H. Touber, 143–160. Amsterdamer Beiträge zur älteren Germanistik 38/39. Amsterdam: Rodopi, 1994.
Davidson, Clifford. "The Anti-Visual Prejudice." In *Iconoclasm vs. Art and Drama,* ed. Clifford Davidson and Ann Eljenholm Nichols, 33–46. Early Drama, Art, and Music Monograph Series 11. Kalamazoo: Medieval Institute Publications, 1989.
Davis, Natalie Zemon. "Women on Top." In *Society and Culture in Early Modern France.* Stanford: Stanford University Press, 1975.
De Kegel-Schorer, Catherine. "Die Ämterbefragungen—zur Untertanenrepräsentation im bernischen Territorialstaat." In *Berns grosse Zeit. Das 15. Jahrhundert neu entdeckt,* ed. Ellen J. Beer et al., 356–60. Bern: Berner Lehrmittel- und Medienverlag, 1999.
Dellsperger, Rudolf. "Wolfgang Musculus (1497–1563). Leben und Werk." *Berner Zeitschrift für Geschichte und Heimatkunde* 59 (1997): 219–39.
———. "Wolfgang Musculus (1497–1563)." In *Die Augsburger Kirchenordnung von 1537 und ihr Umfeld,* ed. Reinhard Schwarz, 91–110. Gütersloh: Gerd Mohn, 1988.
———. "Zehn Jahre Bernischer Reformationsgeschichte (1522–1532): Eine Einführung." In *450 Jahre Berner Reformation: Beiträge zur Geschichte der Bernischen Reformation und zu Niklaus Manuel,* 25–59. Archiv des Historischen Vereins des Kantons Bern 64–65. Bern: Historischer Verein des Kantons Bern, 1980.
Dellsperger, Rudolf, Rudolf Freudenberger, and Wolfgang Weber, eds. *Wolfgang Musculus (1497–1563) und die oberdeutsche Reformation.* Colloquia Augustana 6. Berlin: Akademie Verlag, 1997.
Diehl, Huston. *Staging Reform—Reforming the Stage: Protestantism and Popular Theater in Early Modern England.* Ithaca: Cornell University Press, 1997.
Draheim, Joachim and Günther Wille. *Horaz-Vertonungen vom Mittelalter bis zur Gegenwart. Eine Anthologie.* Amsterdam: B.R. Grüner, 1985.
DuBruck, Edelgard E. *Aspects of Fifteenth-Century Society in the German Carnival Comedies. 'Speculum Hominis'.* Studies in German Language and Literature 13. Lewiston, Queenston, Lampeter: Edwin Mellen Press, 1993.
Dübi, Heinrich. "Miscellen zur bernischen Geschichte: 1) Ein anonymes Fastnachtspiel vom Jahre 1521." *Blätter für bernische Geschichte, Kunst und Altertumskunde* 23 (1927): 161–6.
Eberle, Oskar. *Theatergeschichte der inneren Schweiz: Das Theater in Luzern, Uri, Schwyz, Unterwalden und Zug im Mittelalter und zur Zeit des Barock 1200–1800.* Königsberger deutsche Forschungen 5. Königsberg: Gräfe und Unzer, 1929.
Edwards, Mark U., Jr. *Printing, Propaganda, and Martin Luther.* Berkeley: University of California Press, 1994.
Ehrstine, Glenn. "Motherhood and Protestant Polemics: Stillbirth in Hans von Rüte's *Abgötterei* (1531)." In *Maternal Measures: Figuring Caregiving in the Early Modern Period,* ed. Naomi J. Miller and Naomi Yavneh, 121–34. Aldershot, Engl./Brookfield, Vt.: Ashgate, 2000.

———. "Seeing is Believing: Valten Voith's *Ein schön Lieblich Spiel von dem herlichen vrsprung* (1538), Protestant 'Law and Gospel' Panels, and German Reformation Dramaturgy." *Daphnis* 27 (1998): 503–37.

———. "Scaenica Faceta: The Choral Odes of Johannes Reuchlin's *Scaenica Progymnasmata* (1497)." In *Acta Conventus Neo-Latini Bariensis: Proceedings from the Ninth International Congress at Bari, 29 August–3 September 1994*, ed. Rhoda Schnur et al., 235–41. Tempe, Arizona: Medieval and Renaissance Texts and Studies, 1998.

———. "Niklaus Manuel (Niklaus Manuel Deutsch)." In *German Writers of the Renaissance and Reformation, 1280–1580*, ed. James Hardin and Max Reinhart, 152–65. Vol. 179, *Dictionary of Literary Biography*. Detroit: Gale Research, 1997.

———. "From Iconoclasm to Iconography: Reformation Drama in Sixteenth-Century Bern." Ph.D. diss., University of Texas at Austin, 1995.

Eire, Carlos M.N. *War Against the Idols. The Reformation of Worship from Erasmus to Calvin*. Cambridge: Cambridge University Press, 1986.

Eisenstein, Elizabeth L. *The Printing Press as an Agent of Change: Communications and Cultural Transformations in Early-Modern Europe*. 2 vols. Cambridge: Cambridge University Press, 1979.

Eitner, Robert. "Mathias Apiarius Vorrede." *Monatshefte für Musikgeschichte* 8 (1876): 101–4.

Enders, Jody. *The Medieval Theater of Cruelty: Rhetoric, Memory, Violence*. Ithaca/London: Cornell University Press, 1999.

Erb, James Robert. "Fictions, Realities and the Fifteenth-Century Nuremberg *Fastnachtspiel*." In *Carnival and the Carnivalesque. The Fool, the Reformer, the Wildman, and Others in Early Modern Theatre*, ed. Konrad Eisenbichler and Wim Hüsken, 89–116. Ludus 4. Amsterdam/Atlanta: Rodopi, 1999.

Ermatinger, Emil. *Dichtung und Geistesleben der deutschen Schweiz*. Munich: Beck, 1933.

Esch, Arnold. *Alltag der Entscheidung: Beiträge zur Geschichte der Schweiz an der Wende vom Mittelalter zur Neuzeit*. Bern: Paul Haupt, 1998.

Evans, M. Blakemore. *The Passion Play of Lucerne. An Historical and Critical Introduction*. MLA Monograph Series 14. New York: Modern Language Association of America, 1943.

Farmer, Craig S. *The Gospel of John in the Sixteenth Century: The Johannine Exegesis of Wolfgang Musculus*. New York/Oxford: Clarendon Press, 1997.

Feller, Richard. *Geschichte Berns*. 4 vols. Bern: Herbert Lang, 1974.

———. "Die bernische Reformation und der Staat." In *Feier zum 400jährigen Gedächtnis der Berner Reformation*, 31–42. Bern: Gustav Grunau, 1928.

Fischer, Christine. "Zwei Huldigungskompositionen an die Stadt Bern und ihr musikalisch-gesellschaftliches Umfeld in der ersten Hälfte des 16. Jahrhunderts." In *Berns grosse Zeit. Das 15. Jahrhundert neu entdeckt*, ed. Ellen J. Beer et al., 567–78. Bern: Berner Lehrmittel- und Medienverlag, 1999.

Fischer-Lichte, Erika. *Semiotik des Theaters: eine Einführung*. Tübingen: Narr, 1983.

Fisher, Kenneth. "Hans von Rüte: A Dramatist of the Swiss Reformation." Ph.D. diss., University of Texas at Austin, 1975.

Flanigan, C. Clifford. "Liminality, Carnival, and Social Structure: The Case of Late Medieval Biblical Drama." In *Victor Turner and the Construction of Cultural Criticism. Between Literature and Anthropology*, ed. Kathleen Ashley, 42–85. Bloomington: Indiana University Press, 1990.

Flood, John L. "Albrecht von Eyb." In *German Writers of the Renaissance and Reformation, 1280–1580*, ed. James Hardin and Max Reinhart, 48–54. Vol. 179, *Dictionary of Literary Biography*. Detroit: Gale Research, 1997.

Fluri, Adolf. "Dramatische Aufführungen in Bern im 16. Jahrhundert." In *Neues Berner Taschenbuch auf das Jahr 1909*, ed. Heinrich Türler, 133–59. Bern: K.J. Wyss, 1908.

———. "Das Interlachnerlied." In *Neues Berner Taschenbuch auf das Jahr 1904*, ed. Heinrich Türler, 259–65. Bern: K.J. Wyss, 1903.

———. "Niklaus Manuels Totentanz in Bild und Wort." In *Neues Berner Taschenbuch auf das Jahr 1901*, ed. Heinrich Türler, 119–266. Bern: K.J. Wyss, 1900.
———. "Die Brüder Samuel und Sigfrid Apiarius, Buchdrucker in Bern (1554–1565)." In *Neues Berner Taschenbuch auf das Jahr 1898*, ed. Heinrich Türler, 168–213. Bern: K.J. Wyss, 1897.
———. "Samuel Apiarius, der erste Buchdrucker Solothurns (1565–1566)." In *Neues Berner Taschenbuch auf das Jahr 1898*, ed. Heinrich Türler, 214–6. Bern: K.J. Wyss, 1897.
———. "Samuel Apiarius, Buchdrucker in Basel (1566–1590)." In *Neues Berner Taschenbuch auf das Jahr 1898*, ed. Heinrich Türler, 217–28. Bern: K.J. Wyss, 1897.
———. "Mathias Apiarius, der erste Buchdrucker Berns." In *Berner Taschenbuch auf das Jahr 1897*, ed. Heinrich Türler, 196–253. Bern: K.J. Wyss, 1896.
Francke, Otto. *Terenz und die lateinische Schulcomoedie in Deutschland*. Weimar: Böhlau, 1877.
Frölicher, Hans. *Thüring von Ringoltingens "Melusine", Wilhelm Zielys "Olivier vnd Artus" und "Valentin vnd Orsus" und das Berner Cleomades-Fragment mit ihren französischen Quellen verglichen*. Solothurn: Vereinsbuchdruckerei, 1889.
Gäbler, Ulrich. *Huldrych Zwingli: Eine Einführung in sein Leben und sein Werk*. Munich: Beck, 1983.
Ganz, Paul Leonhard. *Die Malerei des Mittelalters und des XVI. Jahrhunderts in der Schweiz*. Schweizer Kunst 5. Basel: Birkhäuser, 1950.
Gardiner, Harold C. *Mysteries' End: An Investigation of the Last Days of the Medieval Religious Stage*. New Haven: Yale University Press, 1946.
Garside, Charles. *The Origins of Calvin's Theology of Music: 1536–1543*. Transactions of the American Philosophical Society 69,4. Philadelphia: The American Philosophical Society, 1979.
———. *Zwingli and the Arts*. Yale Historical Publications, Miscellany 83. New Haven/London: Yale University Press, 1966.
Geering, Arnold. *Die Vokalmusik in der Schweiz zur Zeit der Reformation. Leben und Werke von Bartholomäus Frank, Johannes Wannenmacher und Cosmas Alder*. Schweizerisches Jahrbuch für Musikwissenschaft 6. Aarau, 1933; Reprint, Amsterdam: Swets and Zeitlinger N.V., 1969.
———. "Von den Berner Stadtpfeifern." *Schweizer Beiträge zur Musikwissenschaft* 1 (1972): 105–13.
Gerber, Roland. "Zünfte und Gesellschaften." In *Berns grosse Zeit. Das 15. Jahrhundert neu entdeckt*, ed. Ellen J. Beer et al., 227–43. Bern: Berner Lehrmittel- und Medienverlag, 1999.
———. "Die Berufsstruktur." In *Berns grosse Zeit*, 205–9.
Gerber, Ulrich J., Hans Rudolf Lavater, and François de Capitani, eds. *Berner Täufertum und Reformation im Dialog. Eine Ausstellung zum 450-jährigen Jubiläum der Täuferdisputation in Bern 1538–1988*. Bern: Bernisches Historisches Museum, 1988.
Gluckman, Max. *Custom and Conflict in Africa*. Oxford: Blackwell, 1965.
Goedeke, Karl. *Grundriß zur Geschichte der deutschen Dichtung aus den Quellen*. 2nd ed. Dresden: Ls. Ehlermann, 1886.
Gordon, Bruce. "Toleration in the early Swiss Reformation: The Art and Politics of Niklaus Manuel of Berne." In *Tolerance and Intolerance in the European Reformation*, ed. Ole Peter Grell and Bob Scribner, 128–44. Cambridge: Cambridge University Press, 1996.
———. "Switzerland." In *The Early Reformation in Europe*, ed. Andrew Pettegree, 70–93. Cambridge: Cambridge University Press, 1992.
Göttler, Christine and Peter Jezler. "Doktor Thüring Frickers 'Geistermesse': Die Seelgerätskomposition eines spätmittelalterlichen Juristen." In *Materielle Kultur und religiöse Stiftung im Spätmittelalter*, ed. Gerhard Jaritz, 187–231. Veröffentlichungen des Instituts für mittelalterliche Realienkunde Österreichs 12. Vienna: Österreichische Akademie der Wissenschaften, 1990.

Greco-Kaufmann, Heidy. *"Vor rechten lütten ist guot schimpfen": Der Luzerner Marcolfus und das Schweizer Fastnachtspiel des 16. Jahrhunderts*. Deutsche Literatur von den Anfängen bis 1700, vol. 19. Bern: Peter Lang, 1994.

Greyerz, Hans von. *Studien zur Kulturgeschichte der Stadt Bern am Ende des Mittelalters*. Bern: Gustav Grunau, 1940.

Greyerz, Kaspar von. "Switzerland." In *The Reformation in National Context*, ed. Robert Scribner, Roy Porter, and Mikulás Teich, 30–46. Cambridge: Cambridge University Press, 1994.

Grüneisen, Carl von. *Niclaus Manuel. Leben und Werke eines Malers und Dichters, Kriegers, Staatsmannes und Reformators im sechszehnten Jahrhundert*. Stuttgart: J.G. Cotta, 1837.

Grütter, Max. "Der Dolch als Datum, zur Datierung der Werke Niclaus Manuels." *Der kleine Bund* (15) 15 April 1949.

Guggisberg, Kurt. *Bernische Kirchengeschichte*. Bern: Paul Haupt, 1958.

Gut, Katrin. "Johannes Hallers *Glückwunschung* von 1584: Ein vaterländisches Spiel." In *Sondierungen zum Theater—Enquêtes sur le théâtre*, ed. Andreas Kotte, 51–95. Theatrum Helveticum 1. Basel: Editions Theaterkultur Verlag, 1995.

Gutscher, Daniel, Susi Ulrich-Bochsler, and Kathrin Utz Tremp. "'Hie findt man gesundtheit des libes und der sele'—Die Wallfahrt im 15. Jahrhundert am Beispiel der wundertätigen Maria von Oberbüren." In *Berns grosse Zeit. Das fünfzehnte Jahrhundert neu entdeckt*, ed. Ellen J. Beer et al., 380–91. Bern: Berner Lehrmittel- und Medienverlag, 1999.

Gutscher-Schmid, Charlotte. "'Diss alles würd er herlich und erberlich, köstlich und guot machen'. Kirchliche Auftragskunst im Zeichen der Nelke." In *Berns grosse Zeit. Das 15. Jahrhundert neu entdeckt*, ed. Ellen J. Beer et al., 516–23. Bern: Berner Lehrmittel- und Medienverlag, 1999.

———. "Fotografische Wiederentdeckung einer Nelkenmeistertafel im Archiv des Bodemuseums Berlin." *Zeitschrift für Schweizerische Archäologie und Kunstgeschichte* 50 (1993): 179–86.

Gutscher-Schmid, Charlotte and Franz-Josef Sladeczek. "'bi unns und in unnser statt beliben'. Künstler in Bern—Berner Künstler? Zum künstlerischen Austausch im spätmittelalterlichen Bern," in *Berns grosse Zeit. Das fünfzehnte Jahrhundert neu entdeckt*, ed. Ellen J. Beer et al., 410–21. Bern: Berner Lehrmittel- und Medienverlag, 1999.

Haas, Leonhard. "Über geistliche Spiele in der Innerschweiz." *Zeitschrift für schweizerische Kirchengeschichte* 47 (1953): 113–22.

Hahn-Woernle, Birgit. *Christophorus in der Schweiz. Seine Verehrung in bildlichen und kultischen Zeugnissen*. Schriften der Schweizerischen Gesellschaft für Volkskunde 53. Basel: G. Krebs, 1972.

Hammes, Fritz. *Das Zwischenspiel im deutschen Drama von seinen Anfängen bis auf Gottsched, vornehmlich der Jahre 1500–1660*. Literarhistorische Forschungen 45. Berlin: Emil Felber, 1911.

Handelman, Don. "Reflexivity in Festival and Other Cultural Events." In *Essays in the Sociology of Perception*, ed. Mary Douglas, 162–90. London: Routledge, 1982.

Harbison, Craig. *The Last Judgment in Sixteenth Century Northern Europe: A Study of the Relation Between Art and the Reformation*. New York/London: Garland, 1976.

Head, Randolph. "William Tell and His Comrades: Association and Fraternity in the Propaganda of Fifteenth- and Sixteenth-Century Switzerland." *Journal of Modern History* 67 (1995): 527–57.

Heinemann, Margot. *Puritanism and Theatre: Thomas Middleton and Opposition Drama under the Early Stuarts*. Past and Present Publications. Cambridge: Cambridge University Press, 1980.

Herrmann, Max. *Forschungen zur deutschen Theatergeschichte des Mittelalters und der Renaissance*. Berlin: Weidmannsche Buchhandlung, 1914.

Hesse, Christian. *St. Mauritius in Zofingen: Verfassungs- und sozialgeschichtliche Aspekte eines mittelalterlichen Chorherrenstiftes*. Veröffentlichungen zur Zofinger Geschichte 2. Aarau: Sauerländer, 1992.

Hidber, Basilius. "Das Theater der alten Berner. Proben aus den drei letzten Jahrhunderten." *Archiv des Historischen Vereins des Kantons Bern* 5 (1863): 611–23.

——. "Der ehemalige sog. äußere Stand der Stadt und Republik Bern." In *Neujahrsblatt für die bernische Jugend 1858*, 3–34. Bern: Huber und Comp., 1858.

——. "Dr. Thomas Murners Streithandel mit den Eidgenossen von Bern und Zürich, mit Urkunden." *Archiv für schweizerische Geschichte* 10 (1855): 272–304.

Hindley, Alan, ed. *Drama and Community: People and Plays in Medieval Europe*. Medieval Texts and Cultures of Northern Europe 1. Turnhout: Brepols, 1999.

Hofer, Paul. "Die Wallfahrtskapelle zu Oberbüren." In *Neues Berner Taschenbuch auf das Jahr 1904*, ed. Heinrich Türler, 102–22. Bern: K.J. Wyss, 1903.

Hofmann, Werner, ed. *Luther und die Folgen für die Kunst*. Munich: Prestel-Verlag, 1983.

——. "Die Geburt der Moderne aus dem Geist der Religion." In *Luther und die Folgen für die Kunst*, ed. Werner Hofmann, 23–71. Munich: Prestel-Verlag, 1983.

Holborn, Hajo. *A History of Modern Germany. The Reformation*. Princeton: Princeton University Press, 1959.

Holstein, Hugo. *Die Reformation im Spiegelbilde der dramatischen Literatur des sechzehnten Jahrhunderts*. Halle: Verein für Reformationsgeschichte, 1886.

Huber, Eugen. "Die Satzungsbücher der Stadt Bern." *Zeitschrift des Bernischen Juristen-Vereins* 10 (1874): 97–134.

Hugelshofer, Walter. "Überlegungen zu Niklaus Manuel." In *Niklaus Manuel Deutsch: Maler—Dichter—Staatsmann*, ed. Cäsar Menz and Hugo Wagner, 51–66. Bern: Kunstmuseum Bern, 1979.

——. "Nach der Niklaus Manuel-Ausstellung von 1979." *Zeitschrift für Schweizerische Archäologie und Kunstgeschichte* 37 (1980): 301–9.

Huggler, Max. "Niklaus Manuel und die Reformatoren." In *Niklaus Manuel Deutsch: Maler—Dichter—Staatsmann*, ed. Cäsar Menz and Hugo Wagner, 100–13. Bern: Kunstmuseum Bern, 1979.

Hundeshagen, C.B. *Die Conflikte des Zwinglianismus, Lutherthums und Calvinismus in der Bernischen Landeskirche von 1532–1558*. Bern: C.A. Jenni, 1842.

Im Hof, Ulrich. "Niklaus Manuel als Politiker und Förderer der Reformation." In *Niklaus Manuel Deutsch: Maler—Dichter—Staatsmann*, ed. Cäsar Menz and Hugo Wagner, 92–9. Bern: Kunstmuseum Bern, 1979.

——. "Die reformierte Hohe Schule zu Bern." In *450 Jahre Berner Reformation: Beiträge zur Geschichte der bernischen Reformation und zu Niklaus Manuel*, 194–224. Archiv des Historischen Vereins des Kantons Bern 64–65. Bern: Historischer Verein des Kantons Bern, 1980.

——. "Niklaus Manuel und die reformatorische Götzenzerstörung." *Zeitschrift für Schweizerische Archäologie und Kunstgeschichte* 37 (1980): 297–300.

Jaeger, Klaus. "Zur Edition der Spiele Hans von Rütes." In *Editionsdesiderate zur Frühen Neuzeit. Beiträge zur Tagung der Kommission für die Edition von Texten der Frühen Neuzeit*, ed. Hans-Gert Roloff. Vol. 2. Chloe 25. Amsterdam/Atlanta: Rodopi, 1997.

——. "Hans von Rütes Osterspiel. Edition und Untersuchung." M.A. Thesis, Freie Universität Berlin, 1993.

Jellicoe, Ann. *Community Plays: How to Put Them On*. London: Methuen, 1987.

Jenny, Markus. "Die Lieder Zwinglis." *Jahrbuch für Liturgik und Hymnologie* 14 (1969): 63–102.

——. *Geschichte des deutsch-schweizerischen evangelischen Gesangbuches im 16. Jahrhundert*. Basel: Bärenreiter, 1962.

———. "Das evangelische Lied der Berner Kirche im 16. Jahrhundert." *Musik und Gottesdienst* 5 (1951): 98–111.
Jezler, Peter. "Die Desakralisierung der Zürcher Stadtheiligen Felix, Regula und Exuperantius in der Reformation." In *Heiligenverehrung in Geschichte und Gegenwart*, ed. Peter Dinzelbacher and Dieter R. Bauer, 296–319. Ostfildern: Schwabenverlag, 1990.
———. "Tempelreinigung oder Barbarei? Eine Geschichte vom Bild des Bilderstürmers." In *Bilderstreit. Kulturwandel in Zwinglis Reformation*, ed. Hans-Dietrich Altendorf and Peter Jezler, 75–82. Zürich: Theologischer Verlag, 1984.
Jezler, Peter, Elke Jezler, and Christine Göttler. "Warum ein Bilderstreit? Der Kampf gegen die 'Götzen' in Zürich als Beispiel." In *Bilderstreit. Kulturwandel in Zwinglis Reformation*, ed. Hans-Dietrich Altendorf and Peter Jezler, 83–102. Zürich: Theologischer Verlag, 1984.
Joyce, G.H. "Keys, Power of the." In *The Catholic Encyclopedia*. Vol. 8. New York: Robert Appleton, 1910.
Junghans, Helmar. "Hausmann, Nikolaus." In *The Oxford Encyclopedia of the Reformation*, ed. Hans J. Hillerbrand, Vol. 2. New York/Oxford: Oxford University Press, 1996.
Just, Martin. "Alder." In *Die Musik in Geschichte und Gegenwart*, ed. Ludwig Finscher. 2nd ed. Personenteil, Vol. 1. Kassel: Bärenreiter; Stuttgart: Metzler, 1999.
Kaiser, Adolf. *Die Fastnachtspiele von der Actio de sponsu. Ein Beitrag zur Geschichte des deutschen Fastnachtspieles*. Göttingen: Vandenhoeck und Ruprecht, 1899.
Kartschoke, Erika. "Fastnachtspiel." In *Einführung in die deutsche Literatur des 12. bis 16. Jahrhunderts*, ed. Winfried Frey et al. Vol. 3. Opladen: Westdeutscher Verlag, 1985.
Keller, Elisabeth. *Die Darstellung der Frau in Fastnachtspiel und Spruchdichtung von Hans Rosenplüt und Hans Folz*. Frankfurt/Berlin/Bern: Peter Lang, 1992.
Kelterborn-Haemmerli, Anna. *Die Kunst des Hans Fries*. Studien zur deutschen Kunstgeschichte 245. Strasbourg: J.H.Ed. Heitz, 1927.
Kindermann, Heinz. *Das Theaterpublikum des Mittelalters*. Salzburg: Otto Müller, 1980.
Kinser, Samuel. "Presentation and Representation: Carnival at Nuremberg, 1450–1550." *Representations* 13 (1986): 1–41.
Der kleine Pauly. Lexikon der Antike. 5 vols. Munich: Alfred Druckenmüller, 1972.
Kleinschmidt, Erich. *Stadt und Literatur in der frühen Neuzeit. Voraussetzungen und Entfaltung im südwestdeutschen, elsässischen und schweizerischen Städteraum*. Literatur und Leben, Neue Folge 22. Cologne/Vienna: Böhlau, 1982.
Kmetz, John. "The Piperinus-Amerbach partbooks: six months of music lessons in Renaissance Basle." In *Music in the German Renaissance. Sources, Styles, and Contexts*, ed. John Kmetz, 215–34. Cambridge: Cambridge University Press, 1994.
———. "Da Jacob nun das Kleid ansah and Zurich Zentralbibliothek T 410–413: A Well-Known Motet in a Little Known 16th-century Manuscript." *Schweizer Jahrbuch für Musikwissenschaft* Neue Folge 4/5 (1984/85): 63–79.
Koch, Bruno. "Reislauf und Pensionen." In *Berns grosse Zeit. Das 15. Jahrhundert neu entdeckt*, ed. Ellen J. Beer et al., 277–85. Bern: Berner Lehrmittel- und Medienverlag, 1999.
Koch, Ludwig. *Philipp Melanchthons Schola Privata*. Gotha: Perthes, 1859.
Koegler, Hans. "Die Holzschnitte des Niklaus Manuel Deutsch." *Jahresbericht der öffentlichen Kunstsammlung Basel 1924* Neue Folge 21 (1925): 43–75.
———. *Beschreibendes Verzeichnis der Basler Handzeichnungen des Niklaus Manuel Deutsch. Nebst einem Katalog der Basler Niklaus Manuel-Ausstellung im Kupferstichkabinett Mitte Februar bis Ende April 1930*. Basel: B. Schwabe, 1930.
Könneker, Barbara. "'Wold ihrs den nicht schir gleuben do?' Joachim Greffs protestantisches Osterspiel." *Daphnis* 23 (1994): 309–44.
———. *Satire im 16. Jahrhundert: Epoche—Werk—Wirkung*. Munich: C.H. Beck, 1991.

———. "Luthers Bedeutung für das protestantische Drama des 16. Jahrhunderts. Geschichte und Heilsgeschichte in Bartholomäus Krügers *Neuer Action von dem Anfang und Ende der Welt*." *Daphnis* 12 (1983): 545–73.

———. *Die deutsche Literatur der Reformationszeit: Kommentar zu einer Epoche*. Munich: Winkler Verlag, 1975.

Koerner, Joseph Leo. *The Moment of Self-Portraiture in German Renaissance Art*. Chicago/London: University of Chicago Press, 1993.

Kohler, Erika. *Martin Luther und der Festbrauch*. Mitteldeutsche Forschungen 17. Cologne: Böhlau, 1959.

Koischwitz, Otto. *Der Theaterherold im deutschen Schauspiel des Mittelalters und der Reformationszeit. Ein Beitrag zur deutschen Theatergeschichte*. Germanische Studien 46. 1926; Nendeln: Kraus, 1967.

Krohn, Rüdiger. *Der unanständige Bürger. Untersuchungen zum Obszönen in den Nürnberger Fastnachtsspielen des 15. Jahrhunderts*. Kronberg/Taunus: Scriptor, 1974.

Kurmann-Schwarz, Brigitte. "'. . . die Fenster in der kilchen allhier, die meine Herren zu machen und in Ehr zu halten schuldig . . .' Andenken—ewiges Seelenheil—irdische Ziele und Verpflichtungen gezeigt an Beispielen von Glasmalerei-Stiftungen für das Münster." In *Berns grosse Zeit. Das 15. Jahrhundert neu entdeckt*, ed. Ellen J. Beer et al., 457–65. Bern: Berner Lehrmittel- und Medienverlag, 1999.

———. "Das 10.000-Ritter-Fenster im Berner Münster und seine Auftraggeber: Überlegungen zu den Schrift- und Bildquellen sowie zum Kult der Heiligen in Bern." *Zeitschrift für Schweizerische Archäologie und Kunstgeschichte* 49 (1992): 39–54.

Lavater, Hans Rudolf. "Die 'Verbesserung der Reformation' zu Bern." In *Der Berner Synodus von 1532. Edition und Abhandlungen zum Jubiläumsjahr 1982*, ed. Gottfried W. Locher. Vol. 2. Neukirchen-Vluyn: Neukirchener Verlag, 1988.

———. "Der 'Synodus' in der Berner Kirche bis zum Ausgang des 18. Jahrhunderts." In *Der Berner Synodus von 1532. Edition und Abhandlungen zum Jubiläumsjahr 1982*, ed. Gottfried W. Locher. Vol. 2. Neukirchen-Vluyn: Neukirchener Verlag, 1988.

———. "Die Froschauer Bibel 1531—Das Buch der Zürcher Kirche." In *Die Zürcher Bibel von 1531*, 1359–422. Zürich: Theologischer Verlag, 1983.

Le Roy Ladurie, Emmanuel. *Carnival in Romans*. Trans. Mary Feeney. New York: George Braziller, 1979.

Lebeau, Jean. *Salvator Mundi: L'"Exemple" de Joseph dans le Théâtre Allemand au XVIe Siècle*. 2 vols. Bibliotheca Humanistica et Reformatica 20. Nieuwkoop: B. de Graaf, 1977.

Lehmann, Hans. "Die Glasmalerei in Bern am Ende des 15. und Anfang des 16. Jahrhunderts." *Anzeiger für Schweizerische Altertumskunde*, Neue Folge XIV (1912): 287–309; XV (1913): 45–52, 100–16, 205–26, 321–46; XVI (1914): 41–57, 124–50, 207–33, 304–24; XVII (1915): 45–65, 136–59, 217–40, 305–29; XVIII (1916): 54–74, 135–53, 225–43.

Lerer, Seth. "'Representyd now in yower syght': The Culture of Spectatorship in Late-Fifteenth-Century England." In *"Aufführung" und "Schrift" in Mittelalter und Früher Neuzeit*, ed. Jan-Dirk Müller, 356–80. Stuttgart/Weimar: Metzler, 1996.

Leuzinger, Jürg. "Berns Griff nach den Klöstern." In *Berns grosse Zeit. Das 15. Jahrhundert neu entdeckt*, ed. Ellen J. Beer et al., 361–5. Bern: Berner Lehrmittel- und Medienverlag, 1999.

Liebenau, Theodor von. *Der Franziskaner Dr. Thomas Murner*. Erläuterungen und Ergänzungen zu Janssens Geschichte des deutschen Volkes 9:4–5. Freiburg: Herder, 1913.

Liliencron, Rochus von. "Die Chorgesänge des lateinisch-deutschen Schuldramas im XVI. Jahrhundert." *Vierteljahrsschrift für Musikwissenschaft* 6 (1890): 309–87.

———. "Die Horazischen Metren in deutschen Kompositionen des 16. Jahrhunderts." *Vierteljahrsschrift für Musikwissenschaft* 3 (1887): 26–91.

Linder, Gottlieb. *Simon Sulzer und sein Antheil an der Reformation im Lande Baden, sowie an den Unionsbestrebungen.* Heidelberg: Carl Winter, 1890.
Linke, Hansjürgen. "Das volkssprachige Drama und Theater im deutschen und niederländischen Sprachbereich." In *Europäisches Spätmittelalter,* ed. Willi Erzgräber, 733–63. Neues Handbuch der Literaturwissenschaft 8. Wiesbaden: Akademische Verlagsgesellschaft Athenaion, 1978.
Lipphardt, Walther. "'Christ ist erstanden.' Zur Geschichte des Liedes." *Jahrbuch für Liturgik und Hymnologie* 5 (1960): 96–114.
Locher, Gottfried W. "Der Berner Synodus als reformierte Bekenntnisschrift." In *Der Berner Synodus von 1532. Edition und Abhandlungen zum Jubiläumsjahr 1982,* ed. Gottfried W. Locher. Vol. 2. Neukirchen-Vluyn: Neukirchener Verlag, 1988.
———. *Zwingli's Thought. New Perspectives.* Studies in the History of Christian Thought 25. Leiden: E.J. Brill, 1981.
———. "Die Berner Disputation 1528." In *450 Jahre Berner Reformation: Beiträge zur Geschichte der bernischen Reformation und zu Niklaus Manuel,* 138–55. Archiv des Historischen Vereins des Kantons Bern 64–65. Bern: Historischer Verein des Kantons Bern, 1980.
———. *Die Zwinglische Reformation im Rahmen der europäischen Kirchengeschichte.* Göttingen: Vandenhoeck und Ruprecht, 1979.
Lumme, Christoph. *Höllenfleisch und Heiligtum: Der menschliche Körper im Spiegel autobiographischer Texte des 16. Jahrhunderts.* Münchener Studien zur neueren und neuesten Geschichte 13. Frankfurt/Bern: Peter Lang, 1996.
Maassen, Johannes. *Drama und Theater der Humanistenschulen in Deutschland.* Schriften zur deutschen Literatur 13. Augsburg: Benno Filser, 1929.
McGrath, Alister C. *A Life of John Calvin. A Study in the Shaping of Western Culture.* Oxford: Basil Blackwell, 1990.
Mack, Fritz. "Evangelische Stimmen zu Fasnacht." In *Masken zwischen Spiel und Ernst. Beiträge des Tübinger Arbeitskreises für Fasnachtsforschung,* ed. Hermann Bausinger et al., 35–49. Tübingen: Tübinger Vereinigung für Volkskunde, 1967.
Mager, Inge. "Lied und Reformation. Beobachtungen zur reformatorischen Singbewegung in norddeutschen Städten." In *Das protestantische Kirchenlied im 16. und 17. Jahrhundert. Text-, musik- und theologiegeschichtliche Probleme,* ed. Alfred Dürr and Walther Killy, 25–38. Wolfenbütteler Forschungen 31. Wiesbaden: Harrassowitz, 1986.
Mâle, Emile. *L'art religieux de la fin du moyen âge en France.* Paris: Librairie Armand Colin, 1908.
———. *Religious Art in France—The Late Middle Ages: A Study of Medieval Iconography and Its Sources.* Trans. Marthiel Mathews. Bollingen Series XC 3. Princeton: Princeton University Press, 1986.
Mallett, Michael E. "The Art of War." In *Structures and Assertions.* Vol. 1, *Handbook of European History, 1400–1600: Late Middle Ages, Renaissance, and Reformation,* ed. Thomas A. Brady, Jr., Heiko A. Oberman, and James D. Tracy, 535–62. Leiden: E.J. Brill, 1994.
Mandach, C. von and Hans Koegler. *Niklaus Manuel Deutsch.* Leipzig: Johannes Asmus, [1940].
Marti, Andreas. "Gottesdienst und Kirchenlied bei Wolfgang Musculus." In *Wolfgang Musculus (1497–1563) und die oberdeutsche Reformation,* ed. Rudolf Dellsperger, Rudolf Freudenberger, and Wolfgang Weber, 201–25. Colloquia Augustana 6. Berlin: Akademie Verlag, 1997.
Martin, Peter. *Martin Luther und die Bilder zur Apokalypse.* Vestigia Bibliae 5. Hamburg: Wittig, 1983.
Marx, Hans Joachim. "Wannenmacher." In *Musik in Geschichte und Gegenwart,* ed. Friedrich Blume. 1st ed. Vol. 14. Kassel: Bärenreiter, 1968.

Masel, Andreas. "Doppelrohrblattinstrumente: A. Europäische Instrumente." In *Die Musik in Geschichte und Gegenwart. Allgemeine Enzyklopädie der Musik*, ed. Ludwig Finscher. 2nd ed. Sachteil, Vol. 2. Kassel: Bärenreiter; Stuttgart: Metzler, 1995.
Matile, Heinz. "Zum Thema 'Niklaus Manuel und die Glasmalerei.'" In *Niklaus Manuel Deutsch: Maler—Dichter—Staatsmann*, ed. Cäsar Menz and Hugo Wagner, 67–74. Bern: Kunstmuseum Bern, 1979.
Menz, Cäsar. "Niklaus Manuel und das Chorgestühl im Berner Münster." In *Niklaus Manuel Deutsch: Maler—Dichter—Staatsmann*, ed. Cäsar Menz and Hugo Wagner, 488–91. Bern: Kunstmuseum Bern, 1979.
———. "Salomons Götzendienst." In *Niklaus Manuel Deutsch: Maler—Dichter—Staatsmann*, ed. Cäsar Menz and Hugo Wagner, 293–6. Bern: Kunstmuseum Bern, 1979.
Merkel, Johannes. *Form und Funktion der Komik im Nürnberger Fastnachtspiel*. Freiburg/Br.: Schwarz, 1971.
Meyer, Almut Agnes. *Heilsgewißheit und Endzeiterwartung im deutschen Drama des 16. Jahrhunderts. Untersuchungen über die Beziehungen zwischen geistlichem Spiel, bildender Kunst und den Wandlungen des Zeitgeistes im lutherischen Raum*. Heidelberg: Winter, 1976.
Mezger, Werner. "'Quem quaeritis—wen suchen ihr hie?' Zur Dynamik der Volkskultur im Mittelalter am Beispiel des liturgischen Dramas." In *Modernes Mittelalter. Neue Bilder einer populären Epoche*, ed. Joachim Heinzle, 209–43. Frankfurt/Leipzig: Insel, 1994.
Michael, Wolfgang F. *Das deutsche Drama der Reformationszeit*. Bern: Peter Lang, 1984.
———. *Frühformen der deutschen Bühne*. Schriften der Gesellschaft für Theatergeschichte 62. Berlin: Selbstverlag der Gesellschaft für Theatergeschichte, 1963.
———. "Die Bedeutung des Wortes *figur* im geistlichen Drama Deutschlands." *Germanic Review* 21 (1946): 3–8.
Michalski, Sergiusz. *The Reformation and the Visual Arts: The Protestant Image Question in Western and Eastern Europe*. Christianity and Society in the Modern World. London: Routledge, 1993.
Möller, Bernd. "Niklaus Manuel Deutsch—ein Maler als Bilderstürmer." *Zwingliana* 23 (1996): 83–104.
Moser, Dietz-Rüdiger. "Bemerkungen zum gegenwärtigen Stand volkskundlicher und literarhistorischer Fastnachtsforschung." In *Fastnachtspiel—Commedia dell'arte. Gemeinsamkeiten—Gegensätze*. Akten des 1. Symposiums der Sterzinger Osterspiele, ed. Max Siller, 129–46. Innsbruck: Universitätsverlag Wagner, 1992.
———. "Lachkultur des Mittelalters? Michael Bachtin und die Folgen seiner Theorie." *Euphorion* 84 (1990): 89–111.
———. "Die Fastnachtsfeier als konfessionelles Problem." In *Das Reich und die Eidgenossenschaft 1580–1650. Kulturelle Wechselwirkungen im konfessionellen Zeitalter*, ed. Ulrich im Hof and Suzanne Stehelin, 129–78. Fribourg: Universitätsverlag Freiburg Schweiz, 1986.
———. *Fastnacht—Fasching—Karneval. Das Fest der "Verkehrten Welt"*. Graz: Verlag Styria, 1986.
Moser, Hans. "Zu Problematik und Methodik neuester Fastnachtsforschung." *Zeitschrift für Volkskunde* 80 (1984): 2–22.
———. "Kritisches zu neuen Hypothesen der Fastnachtsforschung." *Jahrbuch für Volkskunde* Neue Folge 5 (1982): 9–50.
Muir, Lynette. "European Communities and Medieval Drama." In *Drama and Community: People and Plays in Medieval Europe*, ed. Alan Hindley, 1–17. Medieval Texts and Cultures in Northern Europe 1. Turnhout: Brepols, 1999.
———. *The Biblical Drama of Medieval Europe*. Cambridge: Cambridge University Press, 1995.
Müller, Ernst. *Geschichte der Bernischen Täufer*. Frauenfeld: J. Huber, 1895.

Müller, Eugen. *Schweizer Theatergeschichte: Ein Beitrag zur Schweizer Kulturgeschichte.* Schriftenreihe des Schauspielhauses Zürich 2. Zurich: Oprecht, 1944.
Müller, Jan-Dirk. "Melusine in Bern: Zum Problem der 'Verbürgerlichung' höfischer Epik im 15. Jahrhundert." In *Literatur—Publikum—historischer Kontext,* ed. Gert Kaiser, 29–77. Beiträge zur Älteren Deutschen Literaturgeschichte 1. Bern: Peter Lang, 1977.
Müller, Johannes. *Schwert und Scheide: Der sexuelle und skatologische Wortschatz im Nürnberger Fastnachtspiel des 15. Jahrhunderts.* Deutsche Literatur von den Anfängen bis 1700 2. Bern: Peter Lang, 1988.
Müller, Karl. *Die Geschichte der Zensur im alten Bern.* Bern: K.J. Wyss, 1904.
Muralt, Leo von. "Berns Westpolitik von 1525–1531." *Zwingliana* 4 (1928): 470–76.
Nagler, Alois M. *The Medieval Religious Stage: Shapes and Phantoms.* New Haven: Yale University Press, 1976.
Neumann, Bernd. *Geistliches Schauspiel im Zeugnis der Zeit: Zur Aufführung mittelalterlicher religiöser Dramen im deutschen Sprachgebiet.* Münchener Texte und Untersuchungen zur deutschen Literatur des Mittelalters 84/85. 2 vols. Munich: Artemis Verlag, 1987.
Nicolas, Raoul. *Die Hauptvorhalle des Berner Münsters und ihr bildnerischer Schmuck: Eine kunstgeschichtliche Studie.* Neujahrsblatt der Literarischen Gesellschaft Bern auf das Jahr 1921. Bern: K.J. Wyss Erben, 1921.
Niklaus Manuel Deutsch: Maler—Dichter—Staatsmann. Ed. Cäsar Menz and Hugo Wagner. Bern: Kunstmuseum Bern, 1979.
Noser-Hasler, Anna Dorothea. "Einheimische Volksschauspiele des 16. Jahrhunderts." *Lenzburger Neujahrsblätter* 49 (1978): 3–49.
Nowé, Johan. "Kult oder Drama? Zur Struktur einiger Osterspiele des deutschen Mittelalters." In *The Theatre in the Middle Ages,* ed. Herman Braet, Johan Nowé, and Gilbert Tournoy, 269–313. Mediaevalia Lovaniensia I:13. Leuven: Leuven University Press, 1985.
Oberman, Heiko Augustinus. *"Die Gelehrten die Verkehrten*: Popular Response to Learned Culture in the Renaissance and Reformation." In *Religion and Culture in the Renaissance and Reformation,* ed. Steven E. Ozment, 43–63. Sixteenth Century Essays and Studies 11. Kirksville, Missouri: Sixteenth Century Journal Publishers, 1989.
O'Connell, Michael. *The Idolatrous Eye: Iconoclasm and Theater in Early-Modern England.* New York/Oxford: Oxford University Press, 2000.
Odinga, Theodor. *Das deutsche Kirchenlied der Schweiz im Reformationszeitalter.* Frauenfeld: Huber, 1889.
Ozment, Steven E. *The Age of Reform 1250–1550. An Intellectual and Religious History of Late Medieval and Reformation Europe.* New Haven: Yale University Press, 1980.
———. *The Reformation in the Cities: The Appeal of Protestantism to Sixteenth-Century Germany and Switzerland.* New Haven: Yale University Press, 1975.
Pahlen, Kurt. *The World of the Oratorio. Oratorio, Mass, Requiem, Te Deum, Stabat Mater and Large Cantatas.* Trans. Judith Schaefer. Portland: Amadeus Press, 1985.
Panofsky, Erwin. *The Life and Art of Albrecht Dürer.* Princeton: Princeton University Press, 1955.
Parente, James A., Jr. "Tragoedia Politica: Strasbourg School Drama and the Early Modern State, 1583–1621." *Colloquia Germanica* 29 (1996): 1–11.
———. *Religious Drama and the Humanist Tradition: Christian Theater in Germany and the Netherlands 1500–1680.* Studies in the History of Christian Thought 39. Leiden: E.J. Brill, 1987.
Perregaux, Béatrice. "Théodore de Bèze, *Abraham sacrifiant* 1550: Rupture et innovation." In *Sondierungen zum Theater—Enquêtes sur le théâtre,* ed. Andreas Kotte, 13–49. Theatrum Helveticum 1. Basel: Editions Theaterkultur Verlag, 1995.
Pfister, Rudolf. *Kirchengeschichte der Schweiz.* 3 vols. Zurich: Zwingli Verlag, 1964; Zurich: Theologischer Verlag, 1974–84.

Pfrunder, Peter. *Pfaffen, Ketzer, Totenfresser: Fastnachtskultur der Reformationszeit—Die Berner Spiele von Niklaus Manuel*. Zurich: Chronos, 1989.
Plesch, Véronique. "Killed by Words: Grotesque Verbal Violence and Tragic Atonement in French Passion Plays." *Comparative Drama* 33 (1999): 22–55.
Polk, Keith. *German Instrumental Music of the Late Middle Ages: Players, Patrons and Performance Practice*. Cambridge Musical Texts and Monographs. Cambridge: Cambridge University Press, 1992.
Potter, G.R. *Zwingli*. Cambridge: Cambridge University Press, 1976.
Price, David. "Johannes Reuchlin." In *German Writers of the Renaissance and Reformation, 1280–1580*, ed. James Hardin and Max Reinhart, 231–40. Vol. 179, *Dictionary of Literary Biography*. Detroit: Gale Research, 1997.
——. "Hans Folz's Anti-Jewish Carnival Plays." *Fifteenth Century Studies* 19 (1992): 209–28.
——. "When Women Would Rule: Reversal of Gender Hierarchy in Sixteenth-Century German Drama." *Daphnis* 20 (1991): 147–66.
——. *The Political Dramaturgy of Nicodemus Frischlin. Essays on Humanist Drama in Germany*. University of North Carolina Studies in the Germanic Languages and Literatures 111. Chapel Hill/London: University of North Carolina Press, 1990.
Quervain, Theodor de. *Kirchliche und soziale Zustände in Bern unmittelbar nach der Einführung der Reformation (1528–1536)*. Bern: Gustav Grunau, 1906.
Ragotzky, Hedda. "'Pulschafft und nachthunger': Zur Funktion von Liebe und Ehe im frühen Nürnberger Fastnachtspiel." In *Ordnung und Lust: Bilder von Liebe, Ehe und Sexualität in Spätmittelalter und Früher Neuzeit*, ed. Hans-Jürgen Bachorski, 427–46. Literatur-Imagination-Realität 1. Trier: Wissenschaftlicher Verlag Trier, 1991.
Rahn, Johann Rudolf. "Konfessionell-Polemisches auf Glasgemälden." *Zwingliana* 2 (1903): 355–61.
Reese, Gustave. *Music in the Renaissance*. New York: W.W. Norton, 1954.
Reimann, Hannes. *Die Einführung des Kirchengesangs in der Zürcher Kirche nach der Reformation*. Zürich: Zwingli-Verlag, 1959.
Rettig, G.F. "Über ein Wandgemälde von Niklaus Manuel und seine Krankheit der Messe. Ein Beitrag zur Reformationsgeschichte der Schweiz." In *Programm der Berner Kantonschule 1862*, 7–36. Bern: C. Rätzer, 1862.
Reynolds, Peter. "Community Theatre: Carnival or Camp?" In *The Politics of Theatre and Drama*, ed. Graham Holderness, 84–98. Houndmills/London: Macmillan, 1992.
Rhein, Stefan. "Johannes Reuchlin." In *Deutsche Dichter der Frühen Neuzeit (1450–1600). Ihr Leben und Werk*, ed. Stephan Füssel, 138–55. Berlin: Erich Schmidt, 1993.
Riggenbach, Christoph Johannes. *Der Kirchengesang in Basel seit der Reformation. Mit neuen Aufschlüssen über die Anfänge des französischen Psalmengesangs*. Basel: H. Georg, 1870.
Roettig, Petra. *Reformation als Apokalypse: Die Holzschnitte von Mathias Gerung im Codex germanicus 6592 der Bayerischen Staatsbibliothek in München*. Bern: Peter Lang, 1991.
Roloff, Hans-Gert. "Die Funktion der szenischen Bildlichkeit im deutschen Drama des 16. Jahrhunderts." In *Image et Spectacle. Actes du XXXIIe Colloque International d'Etudes Humanistes du Centre d'Etudes Supérieures de la Renaissance (Tours, 29 juin–8 juillet 1989)*, ed. Pierre Béhar, 285–311. Chloe 15. Amsterdam: Rodopi, 1993.
——. "Heilsgeschichte, Weltgeschichte und aktuelle Polemik: Thomas Naogeorgs *Tragoedia Nova Pammachius*." *Daphnis* 9 (1980): 743–67.
Rudwin, Maximilian. *The Origin of German Carnival Comedy*. New York: G.E. Stechert, 1920.
Saxer, Ernst. "Capito und der Berner Synodus." In *Der Berner Synodus von 1532. Edition und Abhandlungen zum Jubiläumsjahr 1982*, ed. Gottfried W. Locher. Vol. 2. Neukirchen-Vluyn: Neukirchener Verlag, 1988.
Scharfe, Martin. *Evangelische Andachtsbilder: Studien zu Intention und Funktion des Bildes in*

der Frömmigkeitsgeschichte vornehmlich des schwäbischen Raumes. Stuttgart: Müller und Gräff, 1968.

[Scheurer, Samuel]. *Bernisches Mausoleum oder Vorderst GOTT Zur Ehr/Lob/und Danck: demnach Berühmten/und sonderlich um die Kirchen Gottes in diesem Land Hochverdienten Männeren zu ruhmlichem angedencken Aufgerichtetes Ehren-Maal.* Bern: Joh. Bondeli seel. Wittib, 1743.

Schibler, Peter. *Vom Kultspiel zum Kleintheater: Aus der Geschichte des bernischen Theaterwesens.* Berner Jahrbuch 1983. Bern: Verbandsdruckerei/Betadruck, 1982.

Schmidlin, Stephan. *Frumm byderb lüt: Ästhetische Form und politische Perspektive im Schweizer Schauspiel der Reformationszeit.* Europäische Hochschulschriften 747. Bern: Peter Lang, 1983.

Schmidt, P. Expeditius. *Die Bühnenverhältnisse des deutschen Schuldramas und seiner volkstümlichen Ableger im sechzehnten Jahrhundert.* Berlin: Alexander Duncker, 1903.

Schmidt, Heinrich Richard. "Stadtreformation in Bern und Nürnberg—ein Vergleich." In *Nürnberg und Bern. Zwei Reichsstädte und ihre Landgebiete,* ed. Rudolf Endres, 81–119. Erlanger Forschungen A46. Erlangen: Universitätsbund Erlangen-Nürnberg, 1990.

Schmidt, Leopold. "Maler-Regisseure des Mittelalters: Bildende Künstler des Mittelalters und der Renaissance als Mitgestalter des Schauspielwesens ihrer Zeit in West- und Mitteleuropa." *Maske und Kothurn* 4 (1958): 55–87.

Schnyder, André. "Weltliteratur in Bern: die 'Melusine' des Thüring von Ringoltingen." In *Berns grosse Zeit. Das 15. Jahrhundert neu entdeckt,* ed. Ellen J. Beer et al., 534–42. Bern: Berner Lehrmittel- und Medienverlag, 1999.

Schoell, Konrad. "Individual and Social Affiliation in the Nuremberg Shrovetide Plays." In *Drama and Community: People and Plays in Medieval Europe,* ed. Alan Hindley, 161–78. Medieval Texts and Cultures in Northern Europe 1. Turnhout: Brepols, 1999.

Schuler, Manfred. "Ist Wolfgang Musculus wirklich der Autor mehrerer Kirchenlieder?" *Jahrbuch für Liturgik und Hymnologie* 17 (1972): 217–21.

Schulz, Matthias. *Die Eigenbezeichnungen des mittelalterlichen deutschsprachigen geistlichen Spiels.* Germanistische Bibliothek 2. Heidelberg: Winter, 1998.

Schulze, Ursula. "Formen der *Repraesentatio* im Geistlichen Spiel." In *Mittelalter und frühe Neuzeit. Übergänge, Umbrüche und Neuansätze,* ed. Walter Haug, 312–56. Fortuna Vitrea 16. Tübingen: Niemeyer, 1999.

Schuster, Peter-Klaus. "Abstraktion, Agitation und Einfühlung. Formen protestantischer Kunst im 16. Jahrhundert." In *Luther und die Folgen für die Kunst,* ed. Werner Hoffmann, 117–21. Munich: Prestel-Verlag, 1983.

———. "'Fuhrwagen' des Andreas Karlstadt." In *Luther und die Folgen für die Kunst,* ed. Werner Hoffmann, 191–2. Munich: Prestel-Verlag, 1983.

Schwarz, Dietrich. "Innerschweizer Alltag im 15. Jahrhundert." In *500 Jahre Stanser Verkommnis: Beiträge zu einem Zeitbild,* ed. Ferdinand Elsener, 71–100. Stans: Historischer Verein Nidwalden, 1981.

Schweizerisches Idiotikon: Wörterbuch der schweizerdeutschen Sprache. Ed. Friedrich Staub, Ludwig Tobler, et al. 15 vols. to date. Frauenfeld: J. Huber, 1881–.

Schwob, Ute Monika. "*Und singt frölich: 'Christ ist erstanden'!* Zur Rolle der Laien bei mittelalterlichen Osterfeiern und beim Osterspiel." In *Osterspiele: Texte und Musik. Akten des 2. Symposiums der Sterzinger Osterspiele (12.–16. April 1992),* ed. Max Siller, 161–73. Schlern-Schriften 293. Innsbruck: Universitätsverlag Wagner, 1994.

Scribner, Robert W. "Ways of Seeing in the Age of Dürer." In *Dürer and His Culture,* ed. Dagmar Eichberger and Charles Zika, 93–117. Cambridge: Cambridge University Press, 1998.

———. *For the Sake of Simple Folk: Popular Propaganda for the German Reformation.* 2nd ed. Oxford: Clarendon Press, 1994.

———. "Das Visuelle in der Volksfrömmigkeit." In *Bilder und Bildersturm im Spätmittelalter und in der frühen Neuzeit*, ed. Bob Scribner, 9–20. Wolfenbütteler Forschungen 46. Wiesbaden: Otto Harrassowitz, 1990.

———. "Popular Piety and Modes of Visual Perception in Late-Medieval and Reformation Germany." *Journal of Religious History* 15 (1989): 448–69.

———. "Flugblatt und Analphabetentum: Wie kam der gemeine Mann zu reformatorischen Ideen?" In *Flugschriften als Massenmedium der Reformationszeit: Beiträge zum Tübinger Symposion 1980*, ed. Hans-Joachim Köhler, 65–76. Spätmittelalter und Frühe Neuzeit 13. Stuttgart: Klett-Cotta, 1981.

———. "Reformation, Carnival and the World turned Upside-Down." In *Städtische Gesellschaft und Reformation*, ed. Ingrid Bátori, 222–52. Spätmittelalter und Frühe Neuzeit 12. Stuttgart: Klett-Cotta, 1980.

Senger, Matthias Wilhelm. *Leonhard Culmann: A Literary Biography and an Edition of Five Plays. As a Contribution to the Study of Drama in the Age of the Reformation*. Nieuwkoop: B. de Graaf, 1982.

Sheingorn, Pamela. "The Visual Language of Drama. Principles of Composition." In *Contexts for Early English Drama*, ed. Marianne G. Briscoe and John C. Coldewey, 173–91. Bloomington: Indiana University Press, 1989.

Simon, Eckehard. "Das Schauspiel der Lübecker Fastnacht." *Zeitschrift für deutsche Philologie* 116 (1997; Sonderheft): 208–23.

———. "Organizing and Staging Carnival Plays in Late Medieval Lübeck: A New Look at the Archival Record." *Journal of English and Germanic Philology* 92 (1993): 57–72.

———. "Shrovetide Plays in Late-Medieval Switzerland. An Appraisal." *Modern Language Notes* 85 (1970): 323–31.

Simon, Gerd. *Die erste deutsche Fastnachtsspieltradition. Zur Überlieferung, Textkritik und Chronologie der Nürnberger Fastnachtsspiele des 15. Jahrhunderts*. Germanische Studien 240. Lübeck/Hamburg: Matthiesen, 1970.

Skopnik, Günter. *Das Straßburger Schultheater: Sein Spielplan und seine Bühne*. Frankfurt: Selbstverlag des Elsaß-Lothringen-Instituts, 1935.

Sladeczek, Franz-Josef. *Der Berner Skulpturenfund. Die Ergebnisse der kunsthistorischen Auswertung*. Bern: Benteli, 1999.

———. "'Da ligend die altär und götzen im tempel'. Zwingli und der Bildersturm in Bern." In *Berns grosse Zeit. Das 15. Jahrhundert neu entdeckt*, ed. Ellen J. Beer et al., 588–604. Bern: Berner Lehrmittel- und Medienverlag, 1999.

———. "Weltgerichtsthematik im geistlichen Schauspiel und der bildenden Kunst des Mittelalters. Gedanken zur Frage der gegenseitigen Beeinflussung von Drama und Bildkunst." *Unsere Kunstdenkmäler* 44 (1993): 356–72.

———. "Der Skulpturenfund der Münsterplattform in Bern (1986). Werkstattfrische Zeugen des Bildersturms der Berner Reformation." In *Les iconoclasmes*, ed. Sergiusz Michalski, 71–94. Vol. 4, *L'Art et les révolutions. XXVIIe congrés international d'histoire de l'Art. Strasbourg 1–7 septembre 1989*. Strasbourg: Société Alsacienne pour le Développement de l'Historie de l'Art, 1992.

———. *Erhart Küng: Bildhauer und Baumeister am Münster zu Bern (um 1420–1507): Untersuchungen zur Person, zum Werk und zum Wirkungskreis eines westfälischen Künstlers der Spätgotik*. Bern: Paul Haupt, 1990.

———. "'Die götze in miner herren chilchen sind gerumpt!' Von der Bilderfrage der Berner Reformation und ihren Folgen für das Münster und sein Hauptportal. Ein Beitrag zur Berner Reformationsgeschichte." *Theologische Zeitschrift* 44 (1988): 289–311.

Soulié, Marguerite. "Le théâtre et la Bible au XVIe siècle." In *Le temps des Réformes et la Bible*. Vol. 5, *Bible de tous les temps*. Ed. Guy Bedouelle and Bernard Roussel, 635–58. Paris: Éditions Beauchesne, 1989.

Spitz, Lewis W. *Conrad Celtis. The German Arch-Humanist*. Cambridge: Harvard University Press, 1957.

Sponsler, Claire. *Drama and Resistance: Bodies, Goods, and Theatricality in Late Medieval England*. Medieval Cultures 10. Minneapolis: University of Minnesota Press, 1997.

Stadler, Edmund. "Mit Hohn und Spott gegen den Papst und seine Getreuen." *Der kleine Bund. Beilage für Literatur und Kunst* 138, Nr. 49, 28 February 1987, 1–2.

———. "Einmal Duldung und einmal Verbot des Fasnachttreibens." *Der kleine Bund. Beilage für Literatur und Kunst* 138, Nr. 55, 7 March 1987, 1–2.

———. "Das Volksschauspiel Burgdorfs im 16. Jahrhundert." *Burgdorfer Jahrbuch* 39 (1972): 22–42.

Stallybrass, Peter and Allon White. *The Politics and Poetics of Transgression*. Ithaca: Cornell University Press, 1986.

Stammler, Wolfgang. *Von der Mystik zum Barock 1400–1600*. Stuttgart: Metzler, 1950.

Steck, Rudolph. "Berchtold Hallers Reformationsversuch in Solothurn (1530), nach seinen eigenen und Niklaus Manuels Briefen dargestellt." *Blätter für bernische Geschichte, Kunst und Altertumskunde* 3 (1907): 241–63.

Stemplinger, Eduard. *Das Fortleben der horazischen Lyrik seit der Renaissance*. Leipzig: Teubner, 1906.

Stephens, W.P. *The Theology of Huldrych Zwingli*. Oxford: Clarendon Press, 1986.

Stirm, Margarete. *Die Bilderfrage in der Reformation*. Quellen und Forschungen zur Reformationsgeschichte 45. Gütersloh: Verlagshaus Mohn, 1977.

Strasser, Otto Erich. "Der Consensus Tigurinus." *Zwingliana* 9 (1949): 1–16.

Street, J.S. *French Sacred Drama from Bèze to Corneille*. Cambridge: Cambridge University Press, 1983.

Streit, Armand. *Geschichte des bernischen Bühnenwesens vom 15. Jahrhundert bis auf unsere Zeit: Ein Beitrag zur schweizerischern Kultur- und allgemeinen Bühnengeschichte*. Bern: Selbstverlag des Verfassers, 1873.

Stricker, Hans. *Die Selbstdarstellung des Schweizers im Drama des 16. Jahrhunderts*. Sprache und Dichtung, Neue Folge 7. Bern: Paul Haupt, 1961.

Stumm, Lucie. *Niklaus Manuel Deutsch von Bern als bildender Künstler*. Bern: Stämpfli, 1925.

———. "Deutsch, Niklaus Manuel." In *Allgemeines Lexikon der bildenden Künstler*, ed. Ulrich Thieme und Felix Becker. Vol. 9. Leipzig: E.A. Seemann, 1913.

Stumpfl, Robert. *Kultspiele der Germanen als Urpsrung des mittelalterlichen Dramas*. Berlin: Junker und Dünnhaupt, 1936.

Sulser, Mathias. *Der Stadtschreiber Peter Cyro und die bernische Kanzlei zur Zeit der Reformation*. Bern: Carl Fromme, 1922.

Tailby, John. "Drama and Community in South Tyrol." In *Drama and Community: People and Plays in Medieval Europe*, ed. Alan Hindley, 148–60. Medieval Texts and Cultures in Northern Europe 1. Turnhout: Brepols, 1999.

———. "The Origins and Beginning of the Nuremberg Shrovetide Plays." In *Le Théâtre au Moyen Age. Actes du 2e colloque de la Societé Internationale pour l'Etude du Théâtre Mediëval, Alencon, 11–14 juillet 1977*, ed. Gari R. Muller, 187–91. Quebec: Aurore-Université, 1981.

———. "Peasants in Fifteenth-Century 'Fastnachtspiele' of Nuremberg. The Problems of Their Identification and the Significance of Their Presentation." *Daphnis* 4 (1975): 172–8.

Tardent, Jean-Paul. *Niklaus Manuel als Staatsmann*. Archiv des Historischen Vereins des Kantons Bern 51. Bern: Archiv des Historischen Vereins des Kantons Bern, 1967.

Tavel, Hans Christoph von. "Kunstwerke Niklaus Manuels als Wegbereiter der Reformation." In *Von der Macht der Bilder. Beiträge des C.I.H.A.-Kolloquiums "Kunst und Reformation"*, ed. Ernst Ullmann, 223–31. Leipzig: E.A. Seemann, 1983.

———. "Niklaus Manuel Deutsch als Maler und Zeichner." In *450 Jahre Berner Reformation. Beiträge zur Geschichte der Berner Reformation und zu Niklaus Manuel*, 313–49.

Archiv des Historischen Vereins des Kantons Bern 64–65. Bern: Historischer Verein des Kantons Bern, 1980.
——. *Niklaus Manuel: Zur Kunst eines Eidgenossen der Dürerzeit*. Bern: K.J. Wyss Erben, 1979.
——. "Folge von Figuren zu einem Schauspiel." In *Niklaus Manuel Deutsch: Maler—Dichter—Staatsmann*, ed. Cäsar Menz and Hugo Wagner, 372–77. Bern: Kunstmuseum Bern, 1979.
——. "Notizen zu den Zeichnungen und Holzschnitten Manuels." In *Niklaus Manuel Deutsch: Maler—Dichter—Staatsmann*, 42–50. Bern: Kunstmuseum Bern, 1979.
——. "Rychardus Hinderlist." In *Niklaus Manuel Deutsch: Maler—Dichter—Staatsmann*, 505–6. Bern: Kunstmuseum Bern, 1979.
——. "Die Stände der Menschen und Schauspielfiguren." In *Niklaus Manuel Deutsch: Maler—Dichter—Staatsmann*, 412–7. Bern: Kunstmuseum Bern, 1979.
——. "Der Totentanz." In *Niklaus Manuel Deutsch: Maler—Dichter—Staatsmann*, 252–9. Bern: Kunstmuseum Bern, 1979.
Tetzlaff, Otto W. "Neulateinische Dramen der Niederlande in ihrer Einwirkung auf die deutsche Literatur des 16. Jahrhunderts." *Amsterdamer Beiträge zur älteren Germanistik* 1 (1972): 111–92.
Thomke, Hellmut. "Niklaus Manuel und die Anfänge des Theaterspiels in Bern." In *Berns grosse Zeit. Das 15. Jahrhundert neu entdeckt*, ed. Ellen J. Beer et al., 542–52. Bern: Berner Lehrmittel- und Medienverlag, 1999.
Thoran, Barbara. "Frauenrolle und Rolle der Frauen in der Geschichte der deutschsprachigen Passionsspiele." In *"Hört, sehet, weint und liebt." Passionsspiele im alpenländischen Raum*, ed. Michael Henker, Eberhard Dünninger, and Evamaria Brockhoff, 113–9. Veröffentlichungen zur Bayerischen Geschichte und Kultur 20/90. Munich: Süddeutscher Verlag, 1990.
——. "Untersuchungen zu den Dramen Jacob Rueffs, des Züricher Zeitgenossen von Hans Sachs." In *Dialog. Festschrift für Siegfried Grosse*, ed. Gert Rickheit and Sigurd Wichter, 75–89. Tübingen: Niemeyer, 1990.
Thürlings, Adolf. "Der Musikdruck mit beweglichen Metalltypen im 16. Jahrhundert und die Musikdrucke des Mathias Apiarius in Straßburg und Bern." *Vierteljahrsschrift für Musikwissenschaft* 8 (1892): 389–418.
Tinsley, Barbara Sher. "Pope Joan Polemic in Early Modern France: The Use and Disabuse of Myth." *Sixteenth Century Journal* 18 (1987): 381–98.
Traub, Andreas. "Die Hymnen von Cosmas Alder und Wolfgang Musculus." *Die Musikforschung* 36 (1983): 16–8.
Trauden, Dieter. "'... daz man dier die recht nit prech ...': Die Bearbeitungen des Fastnachtspiels von Rumpold und Mareth." In *Mittelalterliches Schauspiel: Festschrift für Hansjürgen Linke zum 65. Geburtstag*, ed. Ulrich Mehler and Anton H. Touber, 349–75. Amsterdamer Beiträge zur älteren Germanistik 38/39. Amsterdam: Rodopi, 1994.
Travis, Peter W. "The Semiotics of Christ's Body in the English Cycles." In *Approaches to Teaching Medieval English Drama*, ed. Richard K. Emmerson, 67–78. New York: Modern Language Association, 1990.
Tremp-Utz, Kathrin. "Gottesdienst, Ablaßwesen und Predigt am Vinzenzstift in Bern (1484/85–1528)." *Zeitschrift für Schweizerische Kirchengeschichte* 80 (1986): 52–8.
——. *Das Kollegiatstift St. Vinzenz in Bern, von der Gründung 1484/5 bis zur Aufhebung 1528*. Archiv des historischen Vereins Bern 69. Bern: Historischer Verein des Kantons Bern, 1985.
Turner, Victor. *The Anthropology of Performance*. New York: Performing Arts Journal, 1986.
——. *From Ritual to Theatre. The Human Seriousness of Play*. New York: Performing Arts Journal, 1982.

———. *Dramas, Fields, and Metaphors. Symbolic Action in Human Society.* Ithaca: Cornell, 1974.
Twycross, Meg. "Beyond the Picture Theory: Image and Activity in Medieval Drama." *Word and Image* 4 (1988): 589–617.
Ukena, Peter. "Flugschriften und verwandte Medien im Kommunikationsprozeß zwischen Reformation und Frühaufklärung." In *Flugschriften als Massenmedium der Reformationszeit: Beiträge zum Tübinger Symposion 1980*, ed. Hans-Joachim Köhler, 163–9. Spätmittelalter und Frühe Neuzeit 13. Stuttgart: Klett-Cotta, 1981.
Vetter, Ferdinand. "Schwert und Feder: Niklaus Manuel als Kriegsmann und Dichter, 1522–1528." *Die Persönlichkeit* 1 (1914): 33–44; 108–16.
———. "Über die zwei angeblich 1522 aufgeführten Fastnachtsspiele Niklaus Manuels." *Beiträge zur Geschichte der deutschen Sprache und Literatur* 29 (1904): 80–117.
450 Jahre Berner Reformation: Beiträge zur Geschichte der Bernischen Reformation und zu Niklaus Manuel. Archiv des Historischen Vereins des Kantons Bern 64–65. Bern: Historischer Verein des Kantons Bern, 1980.
Vincent, John Martin. *Costume and Conduct in the Laws of Basel, Bern, and Zurich 1370–1800.* Baltimore: John Hopkins Press, 1935.
Wagner, Hugo. "Niklaus Manuel—Leben und künstlerisches Werk." In *Niklaus Manuel Deutsch: Maler—Dichter—Staatsmann*, ed. Cäsar Menz and Hugo Wagner, 17–41. Bern: Kunstmuseum Bern, 1979.
———. "Kunst in Bern vor und neben Niklaus Manuel." In *Niklaus Manuel Deutsch: Maler—Dichter—Staatsmann*, 202–9. Bern: Kunstmuseum Bern, 1979.
Wailes, Stephen L. *The Rich Man and Lazarus on the Reformation Stage. A Contribution to the Social History of German Drama.* Selinsgrove: Susquehana University Press; London: Associated University Presses, 1997.
Walder, Ernst. "Reformation und moderner Staat." In *450 Jahre Berner Reformation: Beiträge zur Geschichte der Berner Reformation und zu Niklaus Manuel*, 441–583. Archiv des Historischen Vereins des Kantons Bern 64–65. Bern: Historischer Verein des Kantons Bern, 1980.
Walz, Herbert. *Deutsche Literatur der Reformationszeit: Eine Einführung.* Darmstadt: Wissenschaftliche Buchgesellschaft, 1988.
Wandel, Lee Palmer. *Voracious Idols and Violent Hands: Iconoclasm in Reformation Zurich, Strasbourg, and Basel.* Cambridge: Cambridge University Press, 1995.
———. "Iconoclasts in Zürich." In *Bilder und Bildersturm im Spätmittelalter und in der frühen Neuzeit*, ed. Bob Scribner, 125–41. Wolfenbütteler Forschungen 46. Wiesbaden: Otto Harrassowitz, 1990.
Weilen, Alexander von. *Der ägyptische Joseph im Drama des XVI. Jahrhunderts: Ein Beitrag zur vergleichenden Literaturgeschichte.* Vienna: Alfred Hölder, 1887.
Welker, Lorenz. "Zink." In *Die Musik in Geschichte und Gegenwart*, ed. Ludwig Finscher. 2nd ed. Sachteil, Vol. 9. Kassel: Bärenreiter; Stuttgart: Metzler, 1998.
Weller, Emil. *Das alte Volkstheater der Schweiz.* Frauenfeld: J. Huber, 1863.
White, Paul Whitfield. *Theater and Reformation: Protestantism, Patronage, and Playing in Tudor England.* Cambridge: Cambridge University Press, 1993.
Wickham, Glynne. *Early English Stages 1300–1660.* 3 vols. London: Routledge and Kegan Paul, 1959–80.
Wiesner, Merry E. "Studies of Women, the Family, and Gender." In *Reformation Europe: A Guide to Research II*, ed. William S. Maltby, 159–87. Reformation Guides to Research 3. St. Louis: Center for Reformation Research, 1992.
Wijnkoop Lüthi, Marc van. "Druckwerkverzeichnis des Wolfgang Musculus (1497–1563)." In *Wolfgang Musculus (1497–1563) und die oberdeutsche Reformation*, ed. Rudolf Dellsperger, Rudolf Freudenberger, and Wolfgang Weber, 351–414. Colloquia Augustana 6. Berlin: Akademie Verlag, 1997.
Wildhaber, Robert. *Jakob Ruf. Ein Zürcher Dramatiker des 16. Jahrhunderts.* St. Gall: Gebr. Wildhaber, 1929.

Wolfram, Richard. *Studien zur älteren Schweizer Volkskultur. Mythos, Sozialordnung, Brauchbewußtsein.* Österreichische Akademie der Wissenschaften, Philosophisch-historische Klasse, Sitzungsberichte 362. Vienna: Verlag der österreichischen Akademie der Wissenschaften, 1980.
Wuhrmann, Hans. *Das Luzerner Spiel vom Klugen Knecht. Ein Beitrag zur Erforschung des schweizerischen Dramas im frühen 16. Jahrhundert.* Zurich: Juris, 1975.
Wuttke, Dieter. "Zum Fastnachtspiel des Spätmittelalters. Eine Auseinandersetzung mit Catholys Buch." *Zeitschrift für deutsche Philologie* 84 (1965): 247–67
Wyss, Heinz. *Der Narr im schweizerischen Drama des 16. Jahrhunderts.* Sprache und Dichtung, Neue Folge 4. Bern: Paul Haupt, 1959.
Zahnd, Urs Martin. *Die Bildungsverhältnisse in den bernischen Ratsgeschlechtern im ausgehenden Mittelalter: Verbreitung, Charakter und Funktion der Bildung in der politischen Führungsschicht einer spätmittelalterlichen Stadt.* Schriften der Berner Burgerbibliothek 14. Bern: Berner Burgerbibliothek, 1979.
Zapalac, Kristin E.S. "'Item Perspective ist ein lateinisch Wort, bedeutt ein Durchsehung': A Reformation Re-Vision of the Relationship between Idea and Image." In *Meaning in the Visual Arts: Views from the Outside. A Centennial Commemoration of Erwin Panofsky (1892–1968)*, ed. Irving Lang, 131–49. Princeton: Center for Advanced Study, 1995.
———. *In His Image and Likeness: Political Iconography and Religious Change in Regensburg, 1500–1600.* Ithaca: Cornell University Press, 1990.
Zehnder, Leo. *Volkskundliches in der älteren schweizerischen Chronistik.* Schriften der Schweizerischen Gesellschaft für Volkskunde 60. Basel: G. Krebs, 1976.
Zinsli, Paul. "Manuel und Murner. Die Begegnung zweier doppelt begabter Glaubensstreiter in der Reformationszeit." *Berner Zeitschrift für Geschichte und Heimatkunde* 50 (1988): 165–96.
———. "Der 'Seltsame wunderschöne Traum'—ein Werk Niklaus Manuels?" In *450 Jahre Berner Reformation: Beiträge zur Geschichte der Berner Reformation und zu Niklaus Manuel*, 350–79. Archiv des Historischen Vereins des Kantons Bern 64–65. Bern: Historischer Verein des Kantons Bern, 1980.
———. "Zu den Versen auf der Rückseite der Zeichnung Niklaus Manuels vom 'Krieger, der zum Bettler wird.'" *Zeitschrift für Schweizerische Archäologie und Kunstgeschichte* 37 (1980): 260–3.
———. *Der Berner Totentanz des Niklaus Manuel.* Bern: Paul Haupt, 1979.
———. "Niklaus Manuel, der Schriftsteller." In *Niklaus Manuel Deutsch: Maler—Dichter—Staatsmann*, ed. Cäsar Menz and Hugo Wagner, 75–91. Bern: Kunstmuseum Bern, 1979.
———. "Des Papstes und Christi Gegensatz." In *Niklaus Manuel Deutsch: Maler—Dichter—Staatsmann*, 504–5. Bern: Kunstmuseum Bern, 1979.
Zulauf, Max. *Der Musikunterricht in der Geschichte des bernischen Schulwesens von 1528–1798.* Berner Veröffentlichungen zur Musikforschung 3. Bern/Leipzig: Haupt, 1934.
Zürcher Kunst nach der Reformation: Hans Asper und seine Zeit. Zurich: Schweizerisches Institut für Kunstwissenschaft, 1981.

INDEX OF PERSONS

Aal, Johannes, 141
Adrian VI, pope, 90, 93
Alder, Cosmas, 14, 54, 63–4, 249n, 255–9, 266–9, 271, 275, 279, 282–4, 287, 292
  "Ach Herr vernim min kläglich stim," 259, 271–2, 275, 287–8
  "Ave, maris stella," 258–9
  "Da Jacob nun das Klaidt ansach," 14, 259, 267–9, 272, 282, 287, 292
  Hymni Sacri (1553), 258–9
  "Das Interlachnerlied" ("Interlaken Song"), 54, 176, 257, 284
  "Musicorum Bernensium Catalogus," 257
  "Trauermotette" (1531), 257
  "Veni electa mea," 255, 259, 275–6
  "Wie Joseph in Egyptenlant," 259, 267–9, 282, 287
Alleman, Emanuel, 70
Amerbach, Basilius, 267
Amerbach, Bonifacius, 267
Amman, Jakob, 167
Anne, Saint, 45, 121, 211
Anshelm, Valerius, 58, 61, 65, 79, 88, 91, 92, 106, 198n, 207, 223, 256n, 291
Apiarius, Mathias, 54, 62–3, 149, 176, 254–5, 258
Apiarius, Samuel, 63, 76, 144n, 149, 201, 239
Apiarius, Sigfrid, 63, 255
Aristophanes, 27, 77, 264
Aristotle, 26
Asper, Hans, 207n, 216
Augustine, 245

Bale, John, 13
Beatus, Saint, 125
Beham, Hans Sebald, 222
Bèze, Théodore de, 28, 193
Binder, Georg, 138, 141
Birck, Sixtus, 1n, 6, 30–31, 138–9, 142, 159, 162, 217, 263, 265–6, 291

Beel (1539), 30–31
  Susanna (German; 1532), 1n, 138–9, 162, 263, 265–6
  Susanna (Latin; 1537), 142, 159
Blarer, Ambrosius, 253–4
Bletz, Zacharias, 39, 82, 141
Bockstorfer, Sebald, 215
Boden, Jakob, 64
Bodmer, Margareta, 74
Boltz, Valentin, 144n, 278, 286
Bonstetten, Bat Wilhelm von, 94
Brunner von Zofingen, 216
Brunner, Jörg, 45–6, 47
Bubenberg, Adrian von, 127
Bucer, Martin, 28–31, 49, 56, 63, 117n, 186, 195–7, 251n, 260, 281n
Bullinger, Heinrich, 27–8, 49n, 57, 61, 117, 186, 187–8, 197n, 198–9, 247, 295

Cain, 177, 179
Calvin, John, 14, 28, 44, 55–6, 57, 117, 155, 170n, 186, 193–6, 199–200, 248, 260, 290, 295
Capito, Wolfgang, 49, 52–3, 62, 117
Celtis, Conrad, 263–4
Charlemagne, 204
Charles the Bold, duke of Burgundy, 43, 126
Charles V, Holy Roman Emperor, 48, 57, 90, 96, 127–9, 142, 185, 197, 290, 295
Christopher, Saint (*Christophorus*), 150
Cicero, 217
Colmar, Caspar, 248
Contzius, Adam, 290
Couldrette, 60
Cranach, Lucas, the Elder, 13, 66, 106, 207–8, 214, 218–9, 222, 228–9, 234n, 243, 290–91. *See also Passional Christi und Antichristi*
Crocus, Cornelius, 140, 157–60, 165n, 269
Culmann, Leonhard, 8
Cysat, Renward, 39

Daubmann, Johann, 272n
David, 139, 144–6, 148–9, 150, 153–4, 156, 191n, 237
Dax, Paul, 215
Diesbach, von (family), 100
   Anton von Diesbach, 94
   Ludwig von Diesbach (1452–1527), 48, 59
   Niklaus II von Diesbach (1430–75), 59
   Niklaus von Diesbach (ca. 1556), 187
   Wilhelm von Diesbach, 127
Dürer, Albrecht, 66, 215, 243

Eck, Johannes, 48, 49, 72, 127n
Edlibach, Gerold, 216
Edward VI, king of England, 28
Egenolff, Christian, 272–3
Engel, Henrich, 272
Enoch, 179–80, 184, 286
Erasmus, Desiderius, 28
Erlach, von (family), 100
   Anton von Erlach, 48
   Rudolf von Erlach, 127
Esther, 7n, 77–8, 144
Euripides, 137
Eyb, Albrecht von, 60, 138n

Faber, Johannes, 72, 250
Falk, Peter, 256
Farel, Guillaume, 55, 117, 260
Felix, Saint, 129
Ferdinand I, king of Hungary and Bohemia, 51
Feyerabend, Siegmund, 60
Folz, Hans, 82
Forster, Georg, 272n
Foxe, John, 15–6, 22
Francis I, king of France, 91, 93, 96, 170, 185
Frank, Bartholomäus, 257n
Fricker, Margaretha, 69–70
Fricker, Thüring, 61, 70, 127
Friedrich der Freidige, landgrave of Thuringia, 18
Fries, Hans, 64, 66n
Frisching, Hans, 70, 90n
Frisching, Katharina, 70
Frischlin, Nicodemus, 263
Froben, Johann, 62
Froschauer, Christoph, 49, 62, 187, 216
Fullonius, Jakob (Walker), 61
Funkelin, Jakob, 27, 63, 139, 254

Gardiner, Stephen, bishop of Winchester, 15
Gart, Thiebold, 146, 287n
Gengenbach, Pamphilus, 68–9, 81, 213, 216, 227n
   Die Totenfresser (1521), 69
   Die Zehn Alter der Welt (1515), 68–9
George, prince of Anhalt, 3
Gerung, Matthias, 187
Gideon, 144, 168–70, 171–5, 191n, 242, 269–70
Glarean, Heinrich, 256
Gnapheus, Gulielmus, 135, 136, 138, 141, 159
Goudimel, Claude, 290n
Graf, Urs, 66
Grebel, Conrad, 166–7
Greff, Joachim, 1–6, 9, 13, 20, 26, 135, 137, 142, 146, 205, 217, 219, 263, 281n
   Ein Geistliches schönes newes spil / auff das heilige Osterfest gestellet (1542), 1–6, 9, 13, 20, 26, 205, 217, 219
   Ein lieblich vnd nützbarlich spiel von dem Patriarchen Jacob vnd seinen zwelff Sönen (1534), 1, 4, 142, 146
Greiter, Matthäus, 280
Grien, Hans Baldung, 66
Grübel, Sebastian, 215
Guérin, Antoine, 87
Gundelfingen, Heinrich von, 42, 43n
Günzburg, Johann Eberlin von, 183
Gutenberg, Johannes, 63
Gwalther, Rudolf, 215, 260n

Haller, Bertold, 43–4, 48, 53, 58, 61, 62, 104, 117, 128, 187
Haller, Johannes (1523–1575), 56, 75, 145, 185, 189, 195n, 196–7, 199, 248, 259–60, 275, 287
Haller, Johannes (1546–1596), 78
Ham, 144, 177–9, 182, 240, 271–2, 283, 285, 287
Hannah, 251
Hausmann, Niklaus, 1–3
Hercules, 178n, 191
Hermes, 191
Herwagen, Johannes, 260
Hetzel, Cathrin, 74
Holbein, Ambrosius, 216
Holbein, Hans, the Elder, 65
Holbein, Hans, the Younger, 66, 132, 207–8, 236, 243
Holbein, Sigmund, 64–5
Horace, 217–8, 263

Jabal, 179, 182
Japheth, 177, 179, 271, 273, 275
Jetzer, Hans, 58, 64
Joan, legendary pope, 102
Job, 139, 141, 191n, 281n
Johann, bishop of Meißen, 19n
John the Baptist, 141
John the Evangelist, 188, 191, 244, 277
Joseph, 2, 144, 146, 158–65, 237, 268–9
Jubal, 179, 285–6
Jud, Leo, 272n

Kallenberg, Jakob, 65
Karlstadt, Andreas, 222
Kiener, Johannes, 258, 261
Kirchbauer, Thomas, 138n
Klug, Joseph, 269
Kolb, Franz, 48
Kolroß, Johannes, 263, 265–6
Köpfel, Wolff, 258, 280
Kopp, Michael, 255
Krüger, Bartholomäus, 6, 26, 263
Kunz, Peter, 56, 168

Lamech, 179–80, 184–5, 285–6
Lang, Hieronymus, 215
Lautrec, Odet de Foix de, vicomte, 93
Lavater, Ludwig, 260–61
Leo X, pope, 90–92
Leodegar, Saint, 129
Lobwasser, Ambrosius, 290n
Locher, Jakob, 262
Lucretia, 27–8, 210–11
Luke the Evangelist, 244
Luther, Martin, 1–4, 6, 14, 16, 21–7, 29, 30–31, 44–5, 46, 47, 48, 56, 57, 90, 104, 115–6, 137–8, 179n, 186, 192–6, 199, 203–4, 215–6, 218n, 243, 248, 252–3, 269–70, 277–8, 280–81, 287, 290, 292
    "Aus tiefer Not schrei ich zu dir," 253
    "Christ lag in Todes Banden," 281
    Deutsche Messe, 277
    "Herr Gott, dich loben wir," 278
    "Jesaia dem propheten das geschach," 277, 287
    "Ein newes lied wir heben an," 280
    Sermon von der Betrachtung des heyligen leydens Christi (1519), 21, 23–5, 30, 203, 216, 292
    "Ein veste Burg," 269–70

Macropedius, Georg, 138, 263
Major, Georg, 4–6, 13, 30, 205
Manuel, Hans Rudolf (1525–71), 7–8, 70
Manuel, Hieronymus (1520–79), 70
Manuel, Johann Victor (1717–51), 213
Manuel, Magdalena (born 1524), 70
Manuel, Margaretha (born 1516), 70
Manuel, Niclaus (1528–88), 70
Manuel, Niklaus (ca. 1484–1530), 6, 9, 10–11, 12–3, 33–4, 36, 39–41, 45, 49, 50–51, 54n, 57, 61, 63–4, 65–7, 69–72, 82–4, 89–90, 94–6, 98–103, 105–10, 112–3, 115, 119–20, 123, 124, 126n, 132, 148, 150, 162n, 176, 198, 200, 204, 205–15, 221–7, 229, 231, 233–5, 237, 240, 243–5, 283n, 284, 291, 293–5
    Der Ablaßkrämer (1525), 12, 40, 45, 71, 83, 107–13, 121, 130, 213, 229n, 283n, 293
    Barbeli (1526), 72
    Christ and the Adulteress (1527), 208–9
    Dance of Death (ca. 1516–19), 211–2
    Ecks und Fabers Badenfahrt (1526), 72
    St. Eligius in His Workshop (1515), 211
    The Flute Player (ca. 1514–15), 209
    Girl with Impaled Heart (ca. 1510), 210
    Half-Portrait of a Girl (ca. 1510), 211
    The Judgment of Paris (ca. 1517–18), 211–2
    King Josiah Orders the Idols Destroyed (1527), 208–9
    Die Krankheit der Messe (1528), 72
    Landsknecht (1529), 66, 210
    Lucretia (ca. 1518), 210
    The Martyrdom of St. Ursula (ca. 1513–14), 211
    Pyramus and Thisbe (ca. 1513–14), 211
    Schauspielfiguren (ca. 1519–20), 211–4
    Schreibbüchlein (ca. 1517), 211
    Soldier Become a Beggar (ca. 1514–15), 212
    Solomon's Idolatry (1518), 212–5, 226, 240–41
    "Song of Bicocca" (1522), 67, 71, 94, 99, 207, 284
    Swiss dagger device, 66, 72, 107, 132, 209–10
    Das Testament der Messe (1528), 72
    Two Grave Watchers (ca. 1515), 211
    Vom Papst und seiner Priesterschaft (1523), 9, 10–12, 45, 69, 71, 79, 82–3, 89, 94–106, 107, 109, 112,

114, 121, 130, 205, 222–8, 230, 233–5, 240, 283n, 291, 293–4
Von Papsts und Christi Gegensatz (1523), 9, 11–3, 71, 79, 83, 98, 106–7, 205, 221–3, 228–34, 243–4, 283, 291, 293
Mark the Evangelist, 244
Marti, Benedikt (Aretius), 61, 76, 187–8
Martin, Saint, 129
Master HF, 64
Matthew the Evangelist, 244
Maurice, duke of Saxony, 197
Maximilian I, Holy Roman emperor, 263
May, Bartholomew, 45, 89
Megander, Kaspar, 52, 56
Melanchthon, Philipp, 3–4, 13, 106, 136–7, 291. See also *Passional Christi und Antichristi*
Meni, Justus, 138n
Meyer, Sebastian, 45, 47, 56, 187–8, 243
Mösel, Wolfgang, 259, 287
Moses, 4–6, 191n, 251
Mülinen, von (family), 100
  Beatus Ludwig von Mülinen, 189
  Hans Rudolf Mülinen, 94
  Kaspar von Mülinen, 48, 59, 156–7
Murer, Jos, 7, 27, 215
Murner, Thomas, 48, 49, 53, 58, 250
  Des alten christlichen Bären Testament (1528), 53
  Des jungen Bären Zahnweh (1528), 53
Musculus, Wolfgang, 56, 57, 64, 76, 145, 185, 187, 248, 258–60, 275, 287, 292–3
  In Sacrosanctum Davidis Psalterium Commentarii (1551), 260
Müslin, Abraham (Musculus), 145
Myconius, Oswald, 56, 61

Naamah, 179
Nägeli, Hans Franz, 7n, 77, 168, 189, 199, 277
Nägeli, Hans Rudolf, 93–4, 99
Nägeli, Magdalena, 7n, 78n
Naogeorgus, Thomas, 30, 63, 132, 138, 217, 263
Narziß, Painter, 215
Nelkenmeister (Masters of the Carnation), 64
Neukirch, Melchior, 217
Nimrod, 176, 182, 242, 283–4

Noah, 144, 177, 179–85, 191n, 240, 271–2, 274–5, 280, 285
Noll, Anton, 127, 172, 213
Nopus, Hieronymus, 4–6, 13, 30, 205

Oecolampadius, Johannes, 49, 252–3
Osiander, Andreas, 116, 265
Osiander, Lucas, 265
Oswald, Saint, 129
Ottheinrich, count of Pfalz-Neuburg, 187

Pandora, 178
Paul, Saint, 95, 98, 222–8, 234–5, 240, 251–2
Pauli, Johannes, 63
Pellikan, Konrad, 187
Peraudi, Raimund, 18
Peter, Apostle, 96, 98–9, 103, 222–8, 234–5, 240
Petri, Adam, 213
Philip, landgrave of Hesse, 180n
Pilate, 35, 103
Piperinus, Christoph, 267
Plautus, 135, 137, 138n, 158
Plutarch, 61
Potiphar's wife (Sephirah), 158–66
Prodigal Son, 2, 118, 121, 135, 138, 139, 140, 148n, 278
Pythagoras, 191

Rabelais, François, 84–5
Raber, Vigil, 215
Rasser, Johann, 7n, 78
Rebhun, Paul, 1, 6, 8, 21–2, 30, 263, 291
  Susanna (1535), 1, 8, 21–2, 263
Resinarius, Balthasar, 277
Reuchlin, Johannes, 136, 138, 262
Rhau, Georg, 268, 277
Rhellican, Johannes, 61
Rhenanus, Beatus, 61
Ringoltingen, Thüring von, 60
Ritter, Erasmus, 168
Rizio, Angelo, 39, 141n
Rollinger, Wilhelm, 215
Rubellus, Michael (Röttli), 61
Rueff, Jacob, 7, 27, 35n, 135, 141–2, 143n, 146, 184, 216, 287n
  Adam und Eva (1550), 35n, 141, 272n
  Etter Heini (ca. 1538–39), 7, 184
  Job (1535), 141
  Joseph (1540), 142, 143n, 287n

INDEX OF PERSONS

Das lyden vnsers Herren Jesu Christi (1545), 27
Das neue Tellenspiel (1545), 7
Von des Herrn Weingarten (1539), 216
Ruf, Jacob. *See* Rueff, Jacob
Ruoff, Jacob. *See* Rueff, Jacob
Rüte, Cathrin von (born 1531), 74
Rüte, David von, 74
Rüte, Georg von, 74
Rüte, Hans von (born 1549), 74
Rüte, Hans von (?–1558), 6, 9–11, 12–4, 34, 36–41, 57, 63, 67, 69, 72–7, 84, 115, 118, 124–32, 134, 135, 139–41, 143–6, 148–9, 151–7, 159–71, 173–4, 176–84, 186–9, 191–2, 194–9, 205, 220–23, 226, 234, 237–9, 242–5, 249–50, 255, 259, 261–2, 266–74, 276–87, 292–5
  Abgötterei (1531), 12, 57, 84, 115, 118, 124–34, 148, 149, 155, 157, 164, 171, 179, 187, 192, 205, 220–21, 223, 226, 234–7, 243, 246, 283, 292–3, 295
  Gedeon (1540), 6n, 12, 76, 118, 141, 143–6, 148, 149n, 166–76, 222, 239n, 240–43, 249n, 267, 269–72, 276–7, 282, 295
  Goliath (1555), 6n, 13, 38, 39, 76, 77, 134, 141, 143–6, 148–57, 168, 185, 201, 222, 238–41, 244, 249n, 266–7, 282–3, 293
  Joseph (1538), 6n, 12, 14, 39, 76, 118, 140–41, 143–4, 146, 148, 149n, 157–66, 168, 239–41, 243, 246n, 249n, 266–70, 276, 282–3, 287n, 292
  Noe (1546), 6n, 12, 39, 76, 118, 135, 143, 144, 149n, 176–86, 239n, 240–42, 249n, 255, 266–7, 271–7, 282–8
  Osterspiel (1552), 6n, 13, 36, 37n, 57, 144n, 149, 180n, 186–200, 201–2, 221, 239n, 243–5, 250, 267, 274, 276–83, 287, 292–3, 295
  Stadtsatzung (1539), 76
Rüte, Ursula von (born 1544), 189

Sabatius, 182–3, 185, 241–3
Sabus, 182, 241–2
Sachs, Hans, 6, 26, 35n, 138, 144n, 222
  Der Abt im Wildbad (1551), 35n
  Der gantz Passio (1558), 26

Salat, Hans, 39, 53–4, 140
  Tanngrotz, 53–4
  Verlorener Sohn (1538), 140
Samson, Bernhardin, 45, 101–2, 108, 120–21
Samuel, 154, 156, 191n
Saul, 151–7, 165, 240
Schärer, Wendel, 255
Schiner, Matthäus, cardinal, 69, 90–91, 94, 99–100, 101, 256
Schlatter, Michael, 199
Schoen, Erhard, 207
Schöffer, Peter, 63
Schonaeus, Cornelius, 136, 159
Schwarz, Michael, 215
Schwinkhart, Ludwig, 59
Seneca, 135, 137
Senfl, Ludwig, 14, 264, 268, 292
Serve, Jean, 87
Servetus, Michael, 200
Sforza, Francis, duke of Milan, 92
Shakespeare, William, 30
Shem, 177, 179, 181–3, 271, 273, 275
Sigmund, duke of Austria, 127
Socrates, 191
Stein, Albrecht vom, 93–4, 99, 121
Stein, Brandolf vom, 94
Steinhöwel, Heinrich, 60
Stubbes, Philip, 218
Sturm, Johannes, 137, 139n
Suleiman II, sultan, 95
Sulzer, Simon, 56, 193–4, 196
Susanna, 139, 144

Terence, 4, 116n, 135, 136–8, 158–9, 178n
Tetzel, Johann, 101
Tillmann, Bernhard, 205
Tirolf, Hans, 138, 144n
Tritonius, Petrus, 264
Tschachtlan, Benedict, 59
Tubalcain, 179

Ursus, Saint, 127–9
Uz, 183

Viret, Pierre, 56, 193–5
Vogt, Hans, 70
Voith, Valten, 219, 244
Volmar, Melchior, 61

Wagner, Johannes, 141
Waldis, Burkard, 1n, 63, 118, 138, 278
Waldmann, Hans, 86, 216

Wannenmacher, Johannes, 63, 255–9, 261, 264, 277, 288
  Bicinia (1553), 255, 258–9, 261, 277, 288
  "Encomium urbis Bernae" (1535), 256
  "Invidie Telum" (1544), 259, 264
Wattenwyl, Hans Jakob von, 77, 189
Wattenwyl, Johannes von, 188
Wattenwyl, Niklaus von, 89
Wick, Johann Jakob, 260
Wimpfeling, Jakob, 68
Winkelried, Arnold von, 93
Wolff, Thomas, 77n, 132n, 149, 236, 243
Wölflin, Heinrich (Lupulus), 59, 61–2, 257
Wyle, Niklas von, 60
Wyttenbach, Thomas, 61

Zender, Hans, 201
Ziely, Wilhelm, 59n, 60
Zili, Dominik, 253
Zülli, Andreas, 189
Zurkinden, Nikolaus, 200
Zwick, Johannes, 253
Zwingli, Ulrich, 2, 14, 27, 40n, 44, 46, 48–52, 57, 61, 63, 70, 82, 113, 115, 117, 119, 127, 166, 181, 183, 186, 193, 195–9, 202–4, 207, 236–7, 250–54, 256–7, 264, 270–71, 275, 288
  as musician, 250–52, 264
  Auslegen und Gründe der Schlußreden (1523), 251n, 271
  Fidei ratio (1530), 127
  "Kapplerlied" (1529), 250
  "Pestlied" (1520), 250

INDEX OF PLACES

Aarau, 73
Aargau, 42, 256
Aigle, 55
Augsburg, 30, 57, 66n, 127–8, 140, 142, 148, 185–6, 195, 197, 244, 252, 259, 293, 295
   Augsburg Interim (1548), 185, 195, 259
   Diet of Augsburg (1530), 57, 127–8, 295
   Religious Peace of Augsburg (1555), 148, 244

Baden (Aargau), 48, 51, 72, 198, 256
   Baden Disputation (1526), 48, 72
Basel, 45n, 46, 50, 56–7, 60–63, 68, 73n, 75, 81, 117, 119, 132, 149, 187, 213, 216, 236, 243, 252–3, 260, 263, 265–7, 271n, 278
   Klein-Basel, 30, 142
Beckenried, 46
Bern, 6–15, 18–9, 32, 33–4, 36–41, 42–69, 82–4, 87, 88–94, 99–101, 104–7, 109, 112–5, 117–21, 123–9, 132–4, 141, 143–51, 153, 155–7, 159, 162, 166, 167–8, 170–77, 180–82, 184–9, 191–200, 201–2, 204–7, 211, 213, 220–21, 223, 228, 237, 239–40, 242–3, 246, 247–50, 252, 254–62, 266–7, 269, 271–2, 275–7, 282–8, 291–5
   Ämterbefragung, 47, 153
   Äußerer Stand, 37, 133n
   Bernese Bear (heraldic device), 43–4, 53, 62, 132–3, 170
   Bernese Catechism, 200
   Bernese Disputation (1528), 48–50, 53, 70, 72, 115, 118n, 127, 201, 247–8
   Bernese Oberland, 50, 51, 53, 128, 146, 176, 207n, 257
   Bernese Synod (1532), 52–3, 56, 117n
   Chorgericht (marriage court), 50, 70, 119, 162
   city council, 9–10, 13, 14, 32, 34, 36–9, 42–3, 45–8, 49–51, 52–4, 55–7, 59, 70, 73, 74–7, 83, 88–91, 93–4, 99–100, 104–5, 113–5, 118, 124–5, 127, 133, 143, 153, 156–7, 172–3, 175–6, 184–91, 193, 195, 197, 199–200, 202, 205–6, 239, 242, 247–50, 256–8, 260–2, 282n, 284, 294–5
   Easter elections, 48, 156, 186, 189
   Franciscan monastery, 37n, 58, 186, 189, 250, 284
   Gerber (Tanners' Society), 43
   Gerichtsstuhl (Throne of Judgment), 38, 167
   Hohe Schule (Bernese Academy), 7n, 37n, 52, 61, 77, 187, 259
   Kantorenfolianten (1603), 259
   Kreuzgasse (Cross Lane), 37, 68n, 74–5, 79, 106, 126, 168, 223, 262
   Kronenfresser (recipients of French pensions), 93
   Mandat Viti et Modesti, 47, 48
   Metzger (Butchers' Society), 43, 247
   Pfingstmontagseid (Whitmonday Oath), 48, 89
   Pfister (Bakers' and Millers' Society), 43
   Schlußreden (Ten Reformed Theses), 48, 56
   Schmiede (Blacksmith Society), 36, 43, 189, 201–2, 282
   Seckelmeisterrechnungen (treasury accounts), 38, 89, 143n, 149n
   Stadtpfeifer (city musicians), 254–5, 261, 265, 269, 283
   stained-glass industry, 58, 65–6, 207n, 208–9
   Venner, 43, 51, 70, 188–9, 206
   St. Vincent Collegiate Convent (*Chorherrenstift*), 14, 18–9, 46, 63, 126, 256–7, 283
   St. Vincent Minster, 49, 201–2, 207, 247–8, 250, 255, 262, 288, 293
   Zytglogge (Clock Tower), 126, 146
Bicocca. *See* Bicocca, Battle of
Biel (Bienne), 27, 126, 199, 254
Bozen, 215
Bremgarten, 124

Brugg, 42
Burgdorf, 62, 73, 75, 77n

Calw, 18
Cambridge, 28
Chieri (Italy), 70
Cologne, 46
Constance, 7n, 46, 140, 186, 197, 249, 252–4, 259, 287, 293
Crépy. *See* Crépy, Peace of

Danzig (Gdánsk), 215
Dessau, 1–3
Dornach. *See* Dornach, Battle of

Einsiedeln, 278n
Eisenach, 18
Emme Valley (*Emmental*), 73
Ensisheim, 7n
Erlach, 70, 83
Erlangen, 229–30

Ferrara, 92
Franche-Comté, 93
Frankfurt, 272, 287
Freiburg im Breisgau, 17, 73n
Fribourg (Freiburg im Üchtland), 37n, 39, 48, 54, 64, 256
St. Niklaus Collegiate Convent, 256

Geneva, 10, 44, 54–6, 57, 62, 170, 185, 186, 192–6, 199–200, 204n, 248, 290n, 295
Glarus, 50

Haarlem, 136
Hamburg, 71, 95n, 98, 103n, 224, 226n, 229, 231–3
Herzogenbuchsee, 75
Hungary, 96–7

Innsbruck, 197, 215
Interlaken, 54, 75, 176, 256–8, 284

Kamenz, 19n
Kappel, 10, 51–4, 57, 82–3, 127, 129, 134, 152, 165, 176, 197–8, 200, 250, 285, 295
Kirchberg, 66
Kleinhöchstetten, 45
Köniz, 39, 86–7, 254

Langental, 75
Laupen, 62, 126, 150

Lausanne, 28, 46, 55, 56, 170, 193–4, 198
Lausanne Academy, 28, 193
Lausanne Disputation (1536), 55
Leipzig, 48
Lindau, 140
Lombardy, 90, 93
Lübeck, 35–6, 37n, 79–81
Lucerne, 9, 12, 17–8, 26, 36, 37n, 38n, 39, 46, 53, 75, 82, 113, 129, 140, 141, 245, 266

Magdeburg, 4, 141–2, 219
Mainz, 18
Marburg, 128, 272, 287
Marburg Colloquies (1529), 128
Marignano. *See* Marignano, Battle of
Meilen, 86
Memmingen, 109n, 140
Metz, 197
Milan, 39, 43, 69n, 91, 92, 141n
Montreux, 55
Mühlberg. *See* Mühlberg, Battle of
Münsingen, 46
Murten, 55, 62, 126, 150

Naumburg, 46
Neuchâtel, 55, 70, 170
Novara. *See* Novara, Battle of
Nuremberg, 8, 26, 35n, 37, 66n, 69, 80–82, 116, 142n, 265, 272n

Oberbüren, 126–7, 172, 235
Oberehnheim, 53
Oberwallis, 100

Paris, 62

Regensburg, 142, 190
Diet of Regensburg (1532), 142
Rhodes, 95–8, 227–8, 294
Riga, 1n, 118, 278
Romans (France), 86
Rome, 45, 95, 97, 98, 101, 106, 125, 151, 180, 215, 225–8, 234, 294

Sankt Gallen (St. Gall), 252–3
Savoy, Duchy of, 44, 47, 55, 145, 185, 188, 197, 198n
Schaffhausen, 50, 215, 253
Schwyz, 46, 129
Seftigen, 115, 118
Simme Valley (*Simmental*), 42, 167
Sitten, 46, 69, 248, 257n

INDEX OF PLACES

Solothurn, 37n, 48, 52, 63, 73, 127–9, 141, 170
Sterzing (Tirol), 80, 215
Stockhorn (mountain), 61
Strasbourg, 7n, 18, 28, 32, 48, 52, 53, 56, 62, 137, 139n, 140, 196, 251, 252–3, 258, 277, 281n
  Strasbourg Academy, 32, 137

Thun, 125, 207n
Tirol, 80, 81, 93, 119
Toul, 197
Trent. *See* Trent, Council of

Unterwalden, 46, 50–51, 54, 129, 176, 198, 257
Uri, 129

Vaud, Pays de, 54–5, 77
Venice, 96–7
Verdun, 197

Vienna, 18, 215, 263
Vorderösterreich (Western Austria), 93

Wittenberg, 1, 3, 10, 16, 45, 56, 137, 141, 194, 196, 203, 248, 269
Worms. *See* Worms, Diet of
Württemberg, 265

Zofingen, 74, 76, 167
Zug, 46, 51, 129
Zurich, 1n, 2, 7, 8, 27, 35n, 44, 46, 48–52, 57, 61, 62, 68n, 71, 78, 86, 95n, 98, 99n, 103, 114, 117, 127–9, 132, 138, 140–2, 153, 166–7, 170, 184–5, 186–7, 198–200, 203–4, 206–7, 215–6, 224n, 230n, 232n, 235n, 248, 250, 252, 254, 260–61, 264, 292, 295
  Second Disputation of Zurich (1532), 166, 252
Zwickau, 141

INDEX OF SUBJECTS

abbots, portrayal of, 94
Abgötterei ("Idolatry"; 1531), 12, 57, 84, 115, 118, 124–34, 148, 149, 155, 157, 164, 171, 179, 187, 192, 205, 220–21, 223, 226, 234–7, 243, 246, 283, 292–3, 295
Der Ablaßkrämer ("The Indulgence Peddler"; 1525), 12, 40, 45, 71, 83, 107–13, 121, 130, 213, 229n, 283n, 293
adiaphora, 3, 203
Ämterbefragung, 47, 153
Anabaptists, 75, 148, 166–8, 175–6, 295
  Bern Anabaptist Disputation (*Täufergespräch*; 1538), 75n, 167–8
  Zofingen Anabaptist Disputation (1532), 167
Annunciation, Feast of the, 258
Antichrist, 26, 97, 98, 187, 228, 237
Appius und Virginia (1591), 77n
Äußerer Stand, 37, 133n

Babel, Tower of, 182
Babylonian Harlot, 124, 130–32, 223, 235–7, 292
beguines, portrayal of, 94, 227
benefices, 95–6, 132, 171
Bernese Bear (heraldic device), 43–4, 53, 62, 132–3, 170
Bernese Catechism, 200
Bernese council, 9–10, 13, 14, 32, 34, 36–9, 42–3, 45–8, 49–51, 52–4, 55–7, 59, 70, 73, 74–7, 83, 88–91, 93–4, 99–100, 104–5, 113–5, 118, 124–5, 127, 133, 143, 153, 156–7, 172–3, 175–6, 184–91, 193, 195, 197, 199–200, 202, 205–6, 239, 242, 247–50, 256–8, 260–2, 282n, 284, 294–5
  Easter elections, 48, 156, 186, 189
Bernese Disputation (1528), 48–50, 53, 70, 72, 115, 118n, 127, 201, 247–8
Bernese Franciscan monastery, 37n, 58, 186, 189, 250, 284
Bernese Synod (1532), 52–3, 56, 117n
biblical exegesis, 147. *See also* typology

biblical theater, 1–8, 10, 12–3, 21–31, 77, 136, 138–140, 141–8, 148–9, 151, 180–81, 226, 237–46, 249, 261, 263, 265–6, 276, 282–3, 286–8, 292–3. *See also Gedeon, Goliath, Joseph, Noe, Osterspiel*
Bicocca, Battle of (1522), 67, 71, 89–90, 93–4, 98–9, 105–6, 145, 206–7, 294
bishops, portrayal of, 95, 98, 226, 228, 233
broadsheets, 13, 207, 221–3, 291
Burgundian Wars (1476–77), 38, 43, 47, 54, 126, 146n, 170

canon law, 46, 50, 95, 101, 193–4
cardinals, portrayal of, 94, 99–100, 233
carnival
  reformers' views, 113–7
  theoretical approaches, 84–7
carnival customs
  marksmanship contests, 27n, 145
  mummery, 113–5
  Schembartlauf, 116
  überlouffen, 113
carnival plays (*Fastnachtspiele*), 6–7, 8, 9, 12, 33, 37, 54, 67–9, 71, 79–84, 88–91, 101, 105, 113–8, 125, 133–4, 135, 144, 148, 176, 203, 207, 213–6, 222–37, 249, 283–4, 291, 293, 295. *See also Abgötterei, Der Ablaßkrämer, Elsli Tragdenknaben, Vom Papst und seiner Priesterschaft, Von Papsts und Christi Gegensatz*
childbirth, 124, 127
Chorgericht (marriage court), 50, 70, 119, 162
Christliches Burgrecht, 50, 52
Christliche Vereinigung, 51
clerical concubinage, 101, 132, 171, 227
community theater, 12–3, 31–41, 293–5
Confessio Helvetica posterior (1566), 198
confession, 112, 132
confraternities, 35, 36–7, 127

INDEX OF SUBJECTS

Consensus Tigurinus (1549), 57, 186, 198, 295
Contrast Between the Pope and Christ, 229
Corpus Christi plays, 17–19, 35, 135, 245
Crépy, Peace of (1544), 185

deacons, portrayal of, 94
Dominicans, 18
Dornach, Battle of (1499), 145

Easter plays, 16–7, 135, 276–8, 281
Elsli Tragdenknaben ("Little Liz Buck-the-Boy"; 1530), 6, 12, 37, 72, 77, 115, 118, 119–24, 130, 162n, 283n, 293
Eucharist, 2, 16, 19, 56, 181, 193–4, 199
excommunication, 192–5

figurae, 19, 190, 244–5

Gedeon (1540), 6n, 12, 76, 118, 141, 143–6, 148, 149n, 166–76, 222, 239n, 240–43, 249n, 267, 269–72, 276–7, 282, 295
Gerber (Tanners' Society), 43
Gerichtsstuhl (Throne of Judgment), 38, 167
Goliath (1555), 6n, 13, 36, 37n, 76, 77, 134, 141, 143–6, 148–57, 168, 185, 201, 222, 238–41, 244, 249n, 266–7, 282–3, 293

Hohe Schule (Bernese Academy), 7n, 37n, 52, 61, 77, 187, 259
Huguenots, 87, 150
humanist theater, 8, 9, 77, 116n, 135–40, 262–3

iconoclasm, 14, 49n, 64n, 124, 148, 166, 168, 172–6, 201–5
image debate, 13, 23–5, 202–4, 206–9, 216–22
indulgences, 18–9, 45, 79, 95, 101, 105, 106–7, 111, 125–6, 132
Invention of the Cross, Feast of the, 19n

Jews, 21–2, 82, 144, 151–2, 168–70, 174, 180, 222, 240, 251, 292
Joseph (1538), 6n, 12, 14, 39, 76, 118, 140–41, 143–4, 146, 148, 149n, 157–66, 168, 239–41, 243, 246n, 249n, 266–70, 276, 282–3, 287n, 292
Judith, Book of, 1, 21–2, 139, 144, 180

Kantorenfolianten (1603), 259
Karsthans, 107
Klagred der armen Götzen (1529), 50n, 72
Kreuzgasse (Cross Lane), 37, 68n, 74–5, 79, 106, 126, 168, 223, 262
Kronenfresser (recipients of French pensions), 93

Laetare Sunday, 118, 125–6
Landsknechte (imperial mercenaries), 66, 90, 94, 99, 114, 210
liturgical calendar, 84, 118, 125–6, 149, 157
liturgical objects, 205
liturgy, 16, 203, 251, 262
Lucerne Passion Play, 9, 17–8, 37n, 38n, 39, 245, 266

majestas Domini, 14, 243–5, 292
Mandat Viti et Modesti, 47, 48
Marignano, Battle of (1515), 90n, 145
marriage, 121–2
  of clergy, 208
Mass, 16, 19–20, 24, 48, 72
Matins, 277
Meistersinger, 35
Merkbilder, 218–21, 237, 291
Metzger (Butchers' Society), 43, 247
monks, portrayal of, 94, 120, 132, 227. *See also* Samson, Bernhardin
Mühlberg, Battle of (1547), 185
music, 14, 58, 63–4, 139–40, 159, 179, 186, 247–88
  antiphons, 278n
  bar form (*Stollenbau*), 269, 272, 280
  choral music, 27, 186, 249, 258, 261–88, 290–92
  congregational singing, 14, 248–54, 258–62, 265–7, 275, 282–3, 288, 290, 292–3
  contrafacta, 266, 269, 272, 277, 279, 287, 293
  dancing, 4–5, 29, 283–4
  Hausmusik, 254, 258, 288
  homophony, 263–5, 268, 290n
  hymns, 5, 14, 64, 248–250, 252–4, 258–62, 265, 267, 271–2, 275–9, 281–2, 287–8, 290, 293. *See also* psalms

instruments
  drums, 283, 286
  flute, 209, 214, 255
  organ, 247-8, 261
  pipes, 4-5, 283, 286
  Posaune (sackbut), 255, 266, 275-6, 283
  positif organ, 247
  shawm, 255
  trumpet, 255, 266, 283
  zinck (cornetto), 255
interludes, 14, 139-40, 159, 186, 249, 262-6, 269, 275-6, 279, 282-3, 288
Kantionalsatz, 265
Kantorenfolianten (1603), 259
Lobgsang (song of praise), 267, 273-4, 276, 282n
motets, 14, 256-7, 267-8, 279n
odes, 61, 263-6, 269
polyphony, 264, 282-3, 286
and prayer, 251-2, 267, 270-72, 275, 288
Protestant hymnals, 249, 253-4, 258-9, 269-70, 281, 287, 293
  Konstanzer Gesangbuch, 253-4, 259, 281, 287, 293
responsories, 278n
songs
  "Ach Herr vernim/min kläglich stim" (*Noe*), 271-2, 275, 287
  "Bean Song," 79, 106, 125, 283n, 284
  canticum novum, 278-9
  "Christ ist erstanden" (*Osterspiel*), 250, 276, 281-2, 293
  "Da Jsrahel vß Egipten zoch," 279
  "Da Jacob nun das Klaidt ansach" (*Joseph*), 14, 267-9, 272, 287
  "Dignus es Domine" (*Osterspiel*), 276-9, 280
  "Drumm das wir handt die Bott veracht" (*Gedeon*), 269-72, 287
  "Eyne ermanung an die Teudschen, das sie jre alte Freiheit helffen retten" (1552), 272
  "Frisch auff in Gottes namen, du werte teutsche Nation," 272
  "Gelobet sy gott vnser herr" (*Noe, Osterspiel*), 274-6, 280, 287
  Gsang Gott lobend (*Gedeon*), 270
  "Jch bin erfröut vß hertzen grund," 285, 287
  "Johanni dem Apostel das geschach" (*Osterspiel*), 276-7, 279
  "Eyn lied von dem Bären vnd annemung des Gots wort," 289-90
  "Te Deum Laudamus," 266, 276-8, 281, 287, 292
  "Das truren ist vergangen" (*Noe, Osterspiel*), 272-4, 276, 280, 282, 287-8
  "Veni electa mea" (*Noe*), 255, 275-6
  "Wie hat es sich doch mit vns verkeert" (*Osterspiel*), 276, 279-80, 287
  "Wie Joseph in Egyptenlant" (*Joseph*), 267-9, 287
Stadtpfeifer in Bern, 254-5, 261, 265, 269, 283
St. Vincent *Kantorei* (convent singing school), 14, 63, 256-7, 283
truwer gsang (lament), 267, 269, 271-2

New Comedy, 139, 158
Nicodemites, 155
Noe (1546), 6n, 12, 39, 76, 118, 135, 143, 144, 149n, 176-86, 239n, 240-2, 249n, 255, 266-7, 271-7, 282-8
Novara, Battle of (1513), 145
nuns, portrayal of, 94, 114, 227

opus operantis, 15, 23-4
opus operatum, 23-4
Osterspiel (1552), 6n, 13, 36, 37n, 57, 144n, 149, 180n, 186-200, 201-2, 221, 239n, 243-5, 250, 267, 274, 276-83, 287, 292-3, 295

parish fairs (*Kirchweih*), 87
passion plays, 1-6, 23-7, 31, 135, 216, 245, 277
Passional Christi und Antichristi (1521), 13, 106, 214, 222, 228-9, 234n
Peasant Wars (1525), 47, 83-4, 107, 112
Pfingstmontagseid (Whitmonday Oath), 48, 89
Pfister (Bakers' and Millers' Society), 43
poor relief, 108
pope, portrayal of, 26, 79, 83, 89-90, 94-9, 101, 105, 124, 130-32, 179,

187, 192, 194–5, 221–2, 224–34, 236–7, 283, 294
prayer, 104–5, 123, 172, 228, 250–51, 267, 270–72, 275, 288, 292
processions, 126
Prodigal Son, 2, 118, 121, 135, 138, 139, 140, 148n, 278
psalms, 4–5, 14, 201, 248, 251, 253, 258–61, 274, 279, 282, 288, 292. *See also* music: hymns
purgatory, 95
Puritans, 16

Reislaufen (Swiss mercenary trade), 43, 44–5, 66, 93, 95, 98–9, 145, 227–30
Revelation, Book of, 14, 132, 186–8, 189, 190–91, 235–6, 243, 277–80, 292
Revolt of the Princes (1552), 197
Rich Man and Lazarus, 1n, 139
Rumpolt and Mareth play tradition, 119–20

saints. *See also under individual names*
  relics, 121
  veneration of, 51, 124, 126–9, 130, 144, 150, 171–2, 202, 220, 283
Salomon und Markolf, 82
Schlußreden (Ten Reformed Theses), 48, 56
Schmalkaldic League, 128, 185
Schmalkaldic War, 185, 197
Schmiede (Blacksmith Society), 36, 43, 189, 201–2, 282
Seckelmeisterrechnungen (treasury accounts), 38, 89, 143n, 149n
secularization of monasteries, 205
sermons, 3, 4–6, 15, 22, 30–31, 49, 187, 201, 289–91
sola scriptura, 46, 47, 48, 55, 72, 108, 109, 138, 147, 166, 209, 217, 228, 238, 245, 251
Stadtpfeifer (city musicians), 254–5, 261, 265, 269, 283
stained-glass industry, 58, 65–6, 150, 204, 207–9
Sukkoth, 179, 272, 275, 285
Swiss Confederacy, 9, 39, 44, 46, 47–8, 50, 51–2, 53–4, 57, 71, 86, 82–3, 86, 90, 127–9, 134, 141, 151–2, 169–70, 185, 253, 257, 295
  Assembly (*Tagsatzung*), 185, 257
  Associated Members (*zugewandte Orte*), 152

inner cantons (Uri, Schwyz, Unterwalden, Zug, and Lucerne), 46–8, 49, 51–2, 54, 57, 71, 125, 129, 151, 169–70, 176, 295
Mandated Territories (*Gemeine Herrschaften*), 51

Ten Thousand Martyrs, 62, 126, 150
Tetrapolitan Confession (1530), 140, 253
theater
  allegory, 130–33, 236–7
  antitheatricalism, 16, 31, 203–4
  antithesis, 14, 205, 214–5, 221, 226–8, 230, 236, 240, 243, 292
  as visual medium, 3–6, 13–14, 203–5, 214–46
  Bühnenchöre, 265–6
  conterfetisch gespilt, 239
  deixis, 14, 205, 215, 222, 235, 240–43, 245–6, 292
  Festchöre, 265–6, 282
  gesture, 215, 225–6, 234–6, 243
  painter-playwrights (*Maler-Regisseure*), 215
  play within a play, 177, 179–81
  Protestant stage theory, 2–6, 15–16, 21–31, 216–22
  sacramental gaze, 19, 203, 219
  stage (*brügi*), 38, 125n
  stage illustrations, 216
  staging, 13–14, 205, 223–31, 233–46, 291
  tableaux vivants, 19, 186, 203, 221, 223, 234, 244–5
  theological gaze, 23, 219, 292
  vor die Augen stellen, 6, 201, 217, 233, 239, 240n
tithes, 103–4, 227
Tobit, Book of, 1, 21–2, 139, 180
Der Traum (1522), 71, 98, 206n
Trent, Council of, 185
typology, 140, 146–7

"unruly woman," 130–32, 166, 214, 223, 235–7, 292

Venner, 43, 51, 70, 188–9, 206
Vespers, 247, 258
St. Vincent, Feast of (22 January), 247
St. Vincent Collegiate Convent (*Chorherrenstift*), 14, 18–9, 46, 63, 126, 256–7, 283
St. Vincent Minster, 49, 201–2, 207, 247–8, 250, 255, 262, 288, 293

Vom Papst und seiner Priesterschaft (1523), 9, 10–12, 45, 69, 71, 79, 82–3, 89, 94–106, 107, 109, 112, 114, 121, 130, 205, 222–8, 230, 233–5, 240, 283n, 291, 293–4
Von Papsts und Christi Gegensatz (1523), 9, 11–13, 71, 79, 83, 98, 106–7, 205, 221–3, 228–34, 243–4, 283, 291, 293

Wise and Foolish Virgins, 18, 66, 208
Worms, Diet of, 215, 290

Zytglogge (Clock Tower), 126, 146

INDEX OF BIBLICAL CITATIONS

Genesis
  4:21   285
  4:23–24   179
  5:25–29   179
  8:20   179
  9:20   182
  9:22   285
  10:8   182

Exodus
  14:15   251

Deuteronomy
  6:8–9   5

Judges
  6   168
  7:3   242

1 Samuel
  1:13   251
  6:17   151
  13:13–14   154
  15:17–29   154
  17   154

2 Kings
  23   208

Psalm
  114   279
  148   274
  150   5

Isaiah
  6:1–4   277

Matthew
  6:5–13   251
  16   192
  18:20   275
  20:26   166

Mark
  12:29–30   5

John
  3:4   155
  8   208

1 Corinthians
  14:15   251

Colossians
  3:16   251

Revelation
  4–5   186, 190, 243, 277–8, 280, 292
  4:10   278
  4:11   278
  5:3   191
  5:5   279
  5:8–9   279
  5:9–10   278
  5:10   190, 280
  5:12–13   278
  17   187, 235–6, 243, 292

STUDIES IN MEDIEVAL
AND REFORMATION THOUGHT

EDITED BY HEIKO A. OBERMAN

1. DOUGLASS, E. J. D. *Justification in Late Medieval Preaching.* 2nd ed. 1989
2. WILLIS, E. D. *Calvin's Catholic Christology.* 1966 *out of print*
3. POST, R. R. *The Modern Devotion.* 1968 *out of print*
4. STEINMETZ, D. C. *Misericordia Dei.* The Theology of Johannes von Staupitz. 1968 *out of print*
5. O'MALLEY, J. W. *Giles of Viterbo on Church and Reform.* 1968 *out of print*
6. OZMENT, S. E. *Homo Spiritualis.* The Anthropology of Tauler, Gerson and Luther. 1969
7. PASCOE, L. B. *Jean Gerson: Principles of Church Reform.* 1973 *out of print*
8. HENDRIX, S. H. *Ecclesia in Via.* Medieval Psalms Exegesis and the *Dictata super Psalterium* (1513-1515) of Martin Luther. 1974
9. TREXLER, R. C. *The Spiritual Power.* Republican Florence under Interdict. 1974
10. TRINKAUS, Ch. with OBERMAN, H. A. (eds.). *The Pursuit of Holiness.* 1974 *out of print*
11. SIDER, R. J. *Andreas Bodenstein von Karlstadt.* 1974
12. HAGEN, K. *A Theology of Testament in the Young Luther.* 1974
13. MOORE, Jr., W. L. *Annotatiunculae D. Iohanne Eckio Praelectore.* 1976
14. OBERMAN, H. A. with BRADY, Jr., Th. A. (eds.). *Itinerarium Italicum.* Dedicated to Paul Oskar Kristeller. 1975
15. KEMPFF, D. *A Bibliography of Caliviniana.* 1959-1974. 1975 *out of print*
16. WINDHORST, C. *Täuferisches Taufverständnis.* 1976
17. KITTELSON, J. M. *Wolfgang Capito.* 1975
18. DONNELLY, J. P. *Calvinism and Scholasticism in Vermigli's Doctrine of Man and Grace.* 1976
19. LAMPING, A. J. *Ulrichus Velenus (Oldřich Velenský) and his Treatise against the Papacy.* 1976
20. BAYLOR, M. G. *Action and Person.* Conscience in Late Scholasticism and the Young Luther. 1977
21. COURTENAY, W. J. *Adam Wodeham.* 1978
22. BRADY, Jr., Th. A. *Ruling Class, Regime and Reformation at Strasbourg, 1520-1555.* 1978
23. KLAASSEN, W. *Michael Gaismair.* 1978
24. BERNSTEIN, A. E. *Pierre d'Ailly and the Blanchard Affair.* 1978
25. BUCER, Martin. *Correspondance.* Tome I (Jusqu'en 1524). Publié par J. Rott. 1979
26. POSTHUMUS MEYJES, G. H. M. *Jean Gerson et l'Assemblée de Vincennes (1329).* 1978
27. VIVES, Juan Luis. *In Pseudodialecticos.* Ed. by Ch. Fantazzi. 1979
28. BORNERT, R. *La Réforme Protestante du Culte à Strasbourg au XVIe siècle (1523-1598).* 1981
29. SEBASTIAN CASTELLIO. *De Arte Dubitandi.* Ed. by E. Feist Hirsch. 1981
30. BUCER, Martin. *Opera Latina.* Vol I. Publié par C. Augustijn, P. Fraenkel, M. Lienhard. 1982
31. BÜSSER, F. *Wurzeln der Reformation in Zürich.* 1985 *out of print*
32. FARGE, J. K. *Orthodoxy and Reform in Early Reformation France.* 1985
33. 34. BUCER, Martin. *Etudes sur les relations de Bucer avec les Pays-Bas.* I. Etudes; II. Documents. Par J. V. Pollet. 1985
35. HELLER, H. *The Conquest of Poverty.* The Calvinist Revolt in Sixteenth Century France. 1986

36. MEERHOFF, K. *Rhétorique et poétique au XVIe siècle en France.* 1986
37. GERRITS, G. H. *Inter timorem et spem.* Gerard Zerbolt of Zutphen. 1986
38. ANGELO POLIZIANO. *Lamia.* Ed. by A. Wesseling. 1986
39. BRAW, C. *Bücher im Staube.* Die Theologie Johann Arndts in ihrem Verhältnis zur Mystik. 1986
40. BUCER, Martin. *Opera Latina.* Vol. II. Enarratio in Evangelion Iohannis (1528, 1530, 1536). Publié par I. Backus. 1988
41. BUCER, Martin. *Opera Latina.* Vol. III. Martin Bucer and Matthew Parker: Florilegium Patristicum. Edition critique. Publié par P. Fraenkel. 1988
42. BUCER, Martin. *Opera Latina.* Vol. IV. Consilium Theologicum Privatim Conscriptum. Publié par P. Fraenkel. 1988
43. BUCER, Martin. *Correspondance.* Tome II (1524-1526). Publié par J. Rott. 1989
44. RASMUSSEN, T. *Inimici Ecclesiae.* Das ekklesiologische Feindbild in Luthers "Dictata super Psalterium" (1513-1515) im Horizont der theologischen Tradition. 1989
45. POLLET, J. *Julius Pflug et la crise religieuse dans l'Allemagne du XVIe siècle.* Essai de synthèse biographique et théologique. 1990
46. BUBENHEIMER, U. *Thomas Müntzer.* Herkunft und Bildung. 1989
47. BAUMAN, C. *The Spiritual Legacy of Hans Denck.* Interpretation and Translation of Key Texts. 1991
48. OBERMAN, H. A. and JAMES, F. A., III (eds.). in cooperation with SAAK, E. L. *Via Augustini.* Augustine in the Later Middle Ages, Renaissance and Reformation: Essays in Honor of Damasus Trapp. 1991 *out of print*
49. SEIDEL MENCHI, S. *Erasmus als Ketzer.* Reformation und Inquisition im Italien des 16. Jahrhunderts. 1993
50. SCHILLING, H. *Religion, Political Culture, and the Emergence of Early Modern Society.* Essays in German and Dutch History. 1992
51. DYKEMA, P. A. and OBERMAN, H. A. (eds.). *Anticlericalism in Late Medieval and Early Modern Europe.* 2nd ed. 1994
52. 53. KRIEGER, Chr. and LIENHARD, M. (eds.). *Martin Bucer and Sixteenth Century Europe.* Actes du colloque de Strasbourg (28-31 août 1991). 1993
54. SCREECH, M. A. *Clément Marot: A Renaissance Poet discovers the World.* Lutheranism, Fabrism and Calvinism in the Royal Courts of France and of Navarre and in the Ducal Court of Ferrara. 1994
55. GOW, A. C. *The Red Jews: Antisemitism in an Apocalyptic Age, 1200-1600.* 1995
56. BUCER, Martin. *Correspondance.* Tome III (1527-1529). Publié par Chr. Krieger et J. Rott. 1989
57. SPIJKER, W. VAN 'T. *The Ecclesiastical Offices in the Thought of Martin Bucer.* Translated by J. Vriend (text) and L.D. Bierma (notes). 1996
58. GRAHAM, M.F. *The Uses of Reform.* 'Godly Discipline' and Popular Behavior in Scotland and Beyond, 1560-1610. 1996
59. AUGUSTIJN, C. *Erasmus. Der Humanist als Theologe und Kirchenreformer.* 1996
60. McCOOG SJ, T. M. *The Society of Jesus in Ireland, Scotland, and England 1541-1588.* 'Our Way of Proceeding?' 1996
61. FISCHER, N. und KOBELT-GROCH, M. (Hrsg.). *Außenseiter zwischen Mittelalter und Neuzeit.* Festschrift für Hans-Jürgen Goertz zum 60. Geburtstag. 1997
62. NIEDEN, M. *Organum Deitatis.* Die Christologie des Thomas de Vio Cajetan. 1997
63. BAST, R.J. *Honor Your Fathers.* Catechisms and the Emergence of a Patriarchal Ideology in Germany, 1400-1600. 1997
64. ROBBINS, K.C. *City on the Ocean Sea: La Rochelle, 1530-1650.* Urban Society, Religion, and Politics on the French Atlantic Frontier. 1997
65. BLICKLE, P. *From the Communal Reformation to the Revolution of the Common Man.* 1998
66. FELMBERG, B. A. R. *Die Ablaßtheorie Kardinal Cajetans (1469-1534).* 1998

67. CUNEO, P. F. *Art and Politics in Early Modern Germany*. Jörg Breu the Elder and the Fashioning of Political Identity, ca. 1475-1536. 1998
68. BRADY, Jr., Th. A. *Communities, Politics, and Reformation in Early Modern Europe*. 1998
69. McKEE, E. A. *The Writings of Katharina Schütz Zell*. 1. The Life and Thought of a Sixteenth-Century Reformer. 2. A Critical Edition. 1998
70. BOSTICK, C. V. *The Antichrist and the Lollards*. Apocalyticism in Late Medieval and Reformation England. 1998
71. BOYLE, M. O'ROURKE. *Senses of Touch*. Human Dignity and Deformity from Michelangelo to Calvin. 1998
72. TYLER, J.J. *Lord of the Sacred City*. The *Episcopus Exclusus* in Late Medieval and Early Modern Germany. 1999
74. WITT, R.G. *'In the Footsteps of the Ancients'*. The Origins of Humanism from Lovato to Bruni. 2000
77. TAYLOR, L.J. *Heresy and Orthodoxy in Sixteenth-Century Paris*. François le Picart and the Beginnings of the Catholic Reformation. 1999
78. BUCER, Martin. *Briefwechsel/Correspondance*. Band IV (Januar-September 1530). Herausgegeben und bearbeitet von R. Friedrich, B. Hamm und A. Puchta. 2000
79. MANETSCH, S.M. *Theodore Beza and the Quest for Peace in France, 1572-1598*. 2000
80. GODMAN, P. *The Saint as Censor*. Robert Bellarmine between Inquisition and Index. 2000
81. SCRIBNER, R.W. *Religion and Culture in Germany (1400-1800)*. Ed. L. Roper. 2001
82. KOOI, C. *Liberty and Religion*. Church and State in Leiden's Reformation, 1572-1620. 2000
83. BUCER, Martin. *Opera Latina*. Vol. V. Defensio adversus axioma catholicum id est criminationem R.P. Roberti Episcopi Abrincensis (1534). Ed. W.I.P. Hazlett. 2000
84. BOER, W. de. *The Conquest of the Soul*. Confession, Discipline, and Public Order in Counter-Reformation Milan. 2001
85. EHRSTINE, G. *Theater, culture, and community in Reformation Bern, 1523-1555*. 2001

Prospectus available on request

BRILL — P.O.B. 9000 — 2300 PA LEIDEN — THE NETHERLANDS

OHIO UNIVERSITY LIBRARY

Please return this book as soon as you have finished with it. In order to avoid a fine it must be returned by the latest date stamped below. All books are subject to recall after two weeks or immediately if needed for reserve.

CF